The Grace of Four Moons

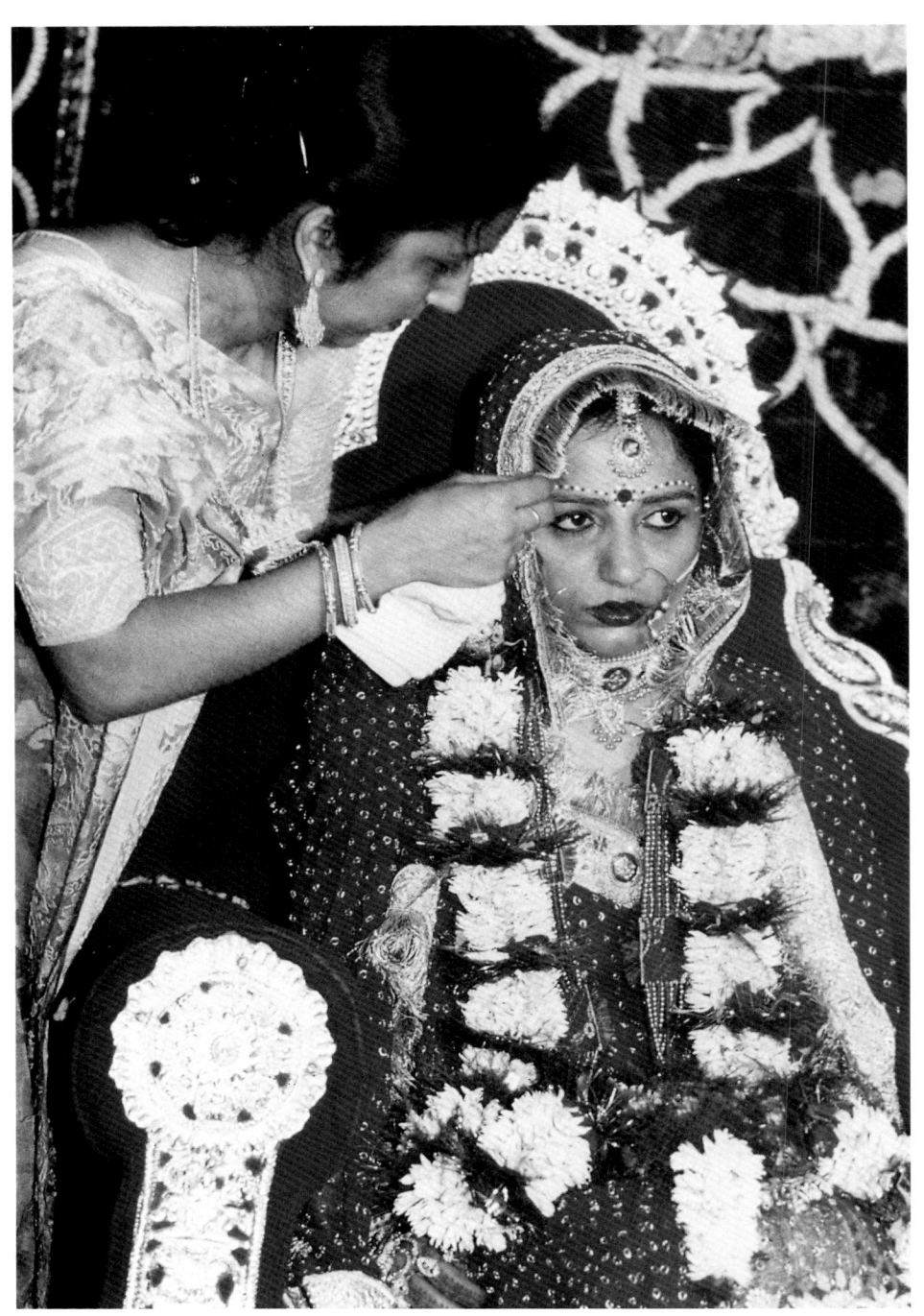

The Grace
of
Four Moons

Dress, Adornment, and the Art of the Body
in Modern India

Pravina Shukla

Photographs by Pravina Shukla and Henry Glassie

Indiana University Press
Bloomington and Indianapolis

Material Culture, Henry Glassie, editor;
editorial committee: John A. Burrison, Marjorie Hunt,
George Jevremović, Charles G. Zug III

This book is a publication of

Indiana University Press
601 North Morton Street
Bloomington, IN 47404-3797 USA

http://iupress.indiana.edu

Telephone orders   800-842-6796
Fax orders   812-855-7931
Orders by e-mail   iuporder@indiana.edu

The paper used in this publication meets the minimum requirements of
American National Standard for Information Sciences—Permanence of
Paper for Printed Library Materials, ANSI Z39.48-1984.

Manufactured in China

Library of Congress Cataloging-in-Publication Data

Shukla, Pravina.
    The grace of four moons : dress, adornment, and the art of the body
in modern India / Pravina Shukla ; photographs by Pravina Shukla and
Henry Glassie.
        p.   cm.
    Includes bibliographical references and index.
    ISBN 978-0-253-34911-8 (cloth)
    1. Clothing and dress—India. 2. Saris—India. 3. Wedding
costume—India. 4. Dress accessories—India. I. Title.
    GT1460.S55 2008
    391.00954—dc22

                                              2007032051

I   2   3   4   5   13   12   11   10   09   08

For my mother,

Neeru Shukla,

*whose beauty and strength of character
have always inspired me*

Contents

Acknowledgments   ix

Part 1. Introduction

1. Body Art in Banaras   3
2. Getting Ready   19
3. Gaze, Sacred and Secular   26

Part 2. Production and Commerce

4. Shopping for Clothes   59
5. Weaving Saris   92
6. Making Jewelry   113
7. Kanhaiya Lal   136
8. Shopping along the Vishvanath Gali   167
9. Assembling Bangle Sets   184

Part 3. Personal Adornment

10. Nina Khanchandani   221
11. Neelam Chaturvedi   239
12. Mukta Tripathi   263

Part 4. Body Art in the Lifecycle

13. After the Wedding   305

14. Before the Wedding   327

15. The Wedding   344

Part 5. Conclusion

16. The Study of Body Art   383

Glossary   431

Notes   433

Bibliography   471

Index   491

Acknowledgments

IN MY CHILDHOOD, when my mother would choose a sari to wear to a dinner party, she would place the sari on her bed, and assign me the task of assembling a matching bangle set for her to wear later that evening. I got an early entry into the creative and satisfying endeavor of bodily adornment, one in which color, texture, sound, and material come together, daily, into a dazzling, portable work of art. I dedicate this book to my mother, Neeru Shukla, who encouraged my personal interest in dress and bodily adornment by creating her own ensembles with care and even designing her own saris. My sisters Divya and Bobby, along with my mother, have all provided me with positive female role models, showing me that loyalty, integrity, and beauty can graciously coexist.

My second debt is to my teachers, who encouraged my scholarly interest in folklore, material culture, dress, and adornment. I thank Alan Dundes, who introduced me to folklore at UC Berkeley, and I thank my teachers and friends at UCLA: Robert Brown, Donald Cosentino, Robert Georges, Fran Krystock, David Mayo, Owen Moore, and Peter Tokofsky. I am especially grateful to my wonderful mentors, Michael Owen Jones and Doran Ross, for teaching me how to study art in culture.

This book could not have been possible without the generosity of the many people in India who valued my fieldwork and provided me with hours of interviews, welcoming me into their homes, shops, ateliers, and into their lives. I am especially grateful to the following friends and family members in India: Hashim Ansari, Neelam Chaturvedi, Vidhu Chaturvedi, Mathuri Chaubey, Anjali Devi, Jitendra Dubey, Kamala Dubey, Nirmala Dubey, Shipra Dubey, Hemant Khanchandani, Nina Khanchandani, Parmanand Khanchandani, Anand Kumar, Chaman Lal, Ashok Kumar Manik, Preetam Kumar Manik, Priya Kumar Manik, Sant Kumar Manik, Gopal Prashad Meenekar, A. P. Mishra, Garima Mishra, Sheela Mishra, Vaibhav Mishra, Vikas Mishra, Priya Misra, Sarala Pandey, Shantibhandra Shah, Shashi Shah, Shalini Shrivastava, B. D. Soni, Mukta Tripathi, and Alok Upadhyay.

For supporting my fieldwork in Banaras and India, and for funding other trips to study body adornment, I acknowledge the following sources: UCLA

Fowler Museum of Cultural History Robert C. Altman Memorial Award, UCLA Fowler Museum of Cultural History Arnold Rubin Memorial Award, Los Angeles Bead Society, Indiana University Summer Faculty Fellowship, The Ford Foundation, and the Silk Road Project.

The following people read versions of this book, providing me with support and helpful suggestions: Donald Brenneis, Henry Drewal, Bill Ferris, Ann Grodzins Gold, Sarah Lamb, Margaret Mills, and Jerry Pocius. I am especially thankful to the members of the editorial board of this series for their help with shaping the final manuscript: John Burrison, Marjorie Hunt, George Jevremović, and Terry Zug.

I thank Zsuzsanna Cselényi, Linda Dégh, Carrie Hertz, Arle Lommel, Fernando Orejuela, Chapla Verma, and Adam Zolkover for help with locating sources and with the style and language of the book. I also acknowledge the help and support of Karen Duffy, Pat Glushko, Sarah Lash, Samantha Matlock, Hilary Virtanen, and Rich Walter. I am also grateful to the useful comments and insights of the students in my graduate seminars on dress and body art. Some of those comments have helped me clarify parts of this book.

I am indebted to the able staff at Indiana University Press for their help throughout the long process of publication, especially to Janet Rabinowitch, Michael Lundell, Rebecca Tolen, Laura MacLeod, Miki Bird, and to Candace McNulty for her copyediting.

My thinking about material culture has been enhanced by the various opportunities I have had of working collegially with bright scholars. I am fortunate to have worked at the American Museum of Natural History with Enid Schildkrout and Heather Nielsen, and I benefited from interactions with the following folklorists in New York City: Robert Baron, Kathy Condon, Kay Turner, and Steve Zeitlen. In 2002, at the Smithsonian Folklife Festival, I was privileged to work with Richard Kurin, Diana Parker, Marjorie Hunt, and Diana Baird N'Diaye.

Many colleagues at Indiana University supported my work. In the Department of Folklore and Ethnomusicology, I thank Dick Bauman, Sandy Dolby, Jason Jackson, Portia Maultsby, John McDowell, David Shorter, and Ruth Stone. I am lucky to have colleagues nearby who share my interest in the study of Indian culture, and for that I thank Purnima Bose, Sumit Ganguly, Radhika Parameswaran, and Rakesh Solomon.

My greatest debt is to my husband, Henry Glassie, for shaping this book and for changing my life. Henry accompanied me twice to Banaras for long periods of fieldwork, and in addition to drawing the maps, he took many of the beautiful photographs in the book. Through his exemplary studies of Ireland, Turkey, and Bangladesh, Henry has taught the world about art and the craft of ethnography. Through his support and affection, he has taught me about love—unconditional and blissful.

Part 1. Introduction

·1·

Body Art in Banaras

EVERY ONE OF US gets dressed in the morning, every day of our lives. Clothing is one of the principal ways by which we express at once our personal identities and our culture. Dress, along with architecture and food, fulfills basic human needs for protection and creativity, while responding to environmental and social conditions. Since all people engage in these shared mediums of expression, one way to understand and compare cultures—and to see regional, local, and personal differences within cultures—is to examine specific modes of clothing, housing, and feeding the body. Schools and museums often utilize this basic triad in introducing children to the diversity of the world's populations.[1] But in contrast to the study of vernacular architecture, and, to a lesser extent, the study of foodways, the examination of everyday clothing is not yet fully developed. Surveys of national dress tend to generalize, homogenize, and anonymize individuals, discounting personal interpretations of social norms. Other books focus on extreme cases—the counter-cultural young with their tattoos, the economic elite with their enthusiasm for high fashion. It is my aim to provide a study of the clothing choices made by ordinary people, in keeping with the theoretical premises of my discipline, folklore, which, to begin, I will define as the study of creativity in everyday life.[2]

I call the realm of my concern "body art," intending to denote all aesthetic modifications and supplementations to the body.[3] My interest in the forms, functions, and meanings of dress and adornment, and especially in the choices individuals make within a web of social constraints, led me to India, an optimal locale for analysis. Decoration abounds; people lavish ornamentation on a wide variety of objects—temples, altars, vehicles, animals, and,

3

especially, themselves. Adornment heightens beauty and wraps the bodies of gods and human beings with auspiciousness. Dress and adornment play a critical role in communication; they are symbolically integral to the lives of Indian people.

The cultural significance of adornment is reflected in language. In Hindi, the word *shringar* denotes self-adornment, but it can also mean beauty, express romantic or erotic love, as well as naming the most important of the nine Sanskrit *rasas,* which are, in the words of the great art historian Ananda Coomaraswamy, "the substance of aesthetic experience."[4] The noun *suhag* is used to name the happy state of a woman whose husband is alive. It means as well the chest that holds her marital ornaments and makeup, and it implies a divine blessing to the one who has not lost the right to ornament herself, as widows have. Vidhu Chaturvedi told me that the word for husband, *sajan,* may have its roots in the word *saj*—embellishment, decoration—because a woman, by acquiring a husband, enters the stage of her life when she is officially encouraged to be ornamented and decorated. Hindi contains almost one hundred different terms for all the varieties of ornaments, defined by shape, size, and location on the body.[5]

Because the majority of the women are so attentively dressed and ornamented, India is a rich territory for mapping the field of choice in the realm of body art. While exploring this conspicuous and visually accessible terrain, I will aim to extract general principles of production, commerce, and adornment that may be applied subsequently in studies of subtler expressions of clothing and jewelry conducted elsewhere, among other populations. One of the advantages of studying body art, especially in a crowded, extravagantly adorned country like India, is the ease with which you can create a visual databank of thousands of examples, since these fill the streets, everywhere you go. Unlike other kinds of artistic expression that are difficult to access, such as furniture or folktales, the spectrum of adornment options—like the varieties of local architecture—are readily available to sight; they can be scrutinized and stored in the mind's eye for retrieval.

The immense diversity of India, owing to the multiplicity of regional and religious cultures, is expressed visually through clothes and ornaments, making instant identification possible. The Hindu concept of *darshan,* of sacred sight, provides a precedent for all nonverbal communication, and helps to shape India's notable orientation to the visual. A religious orientation helps to explain not only the cultural significance of vision, but also the importance of

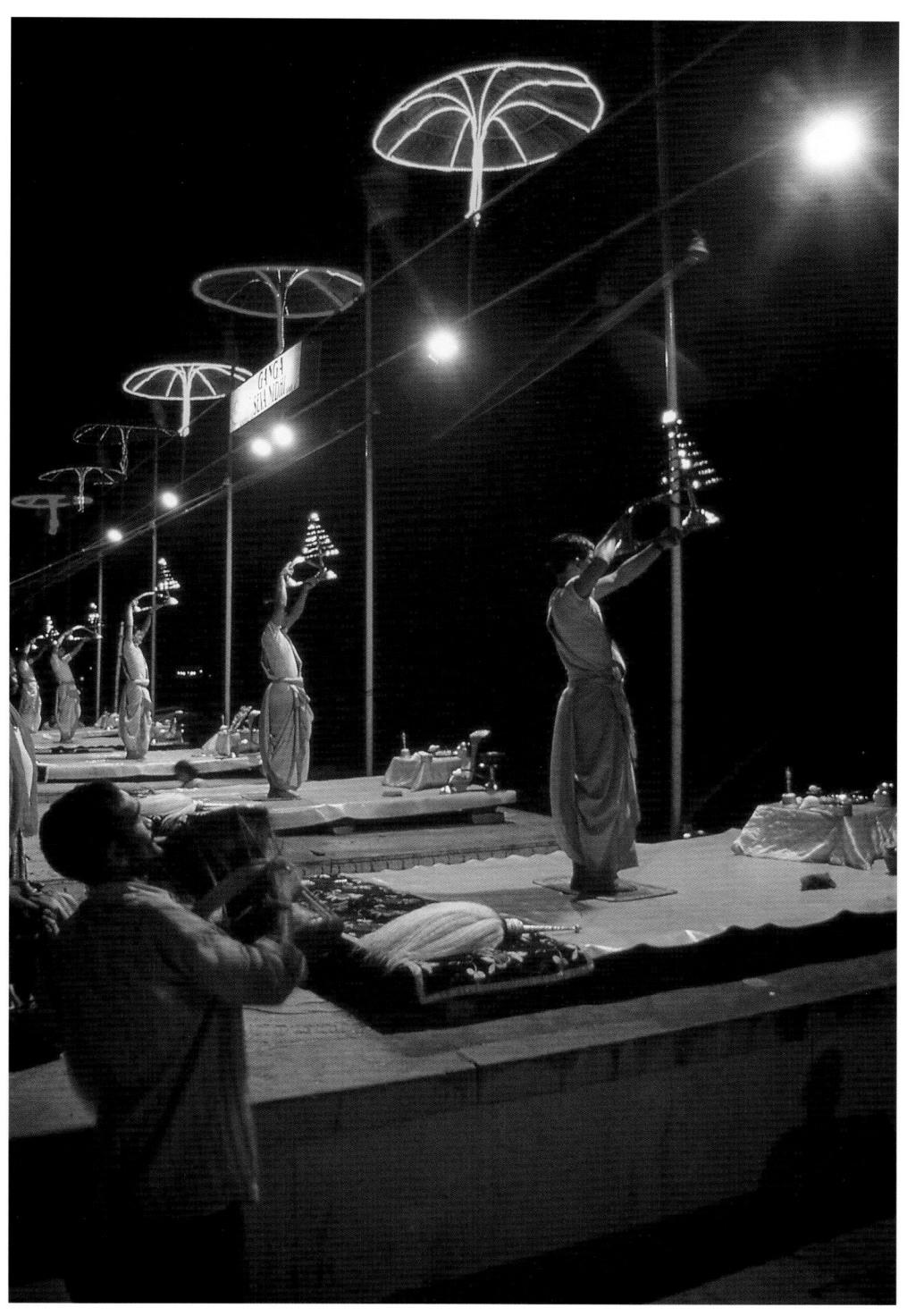

Aarti for Lord Shiva, Dashaswamedh Ghat, Banaras

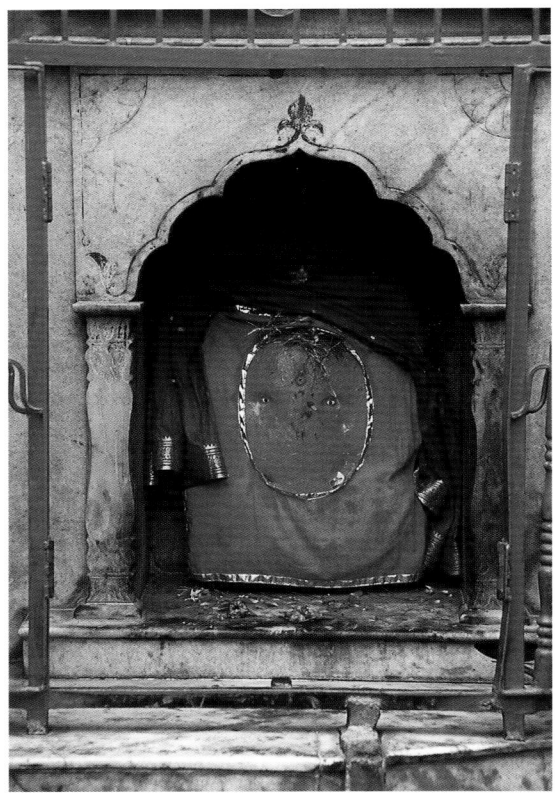

Deities in the streets,
Banaras

Ganesh

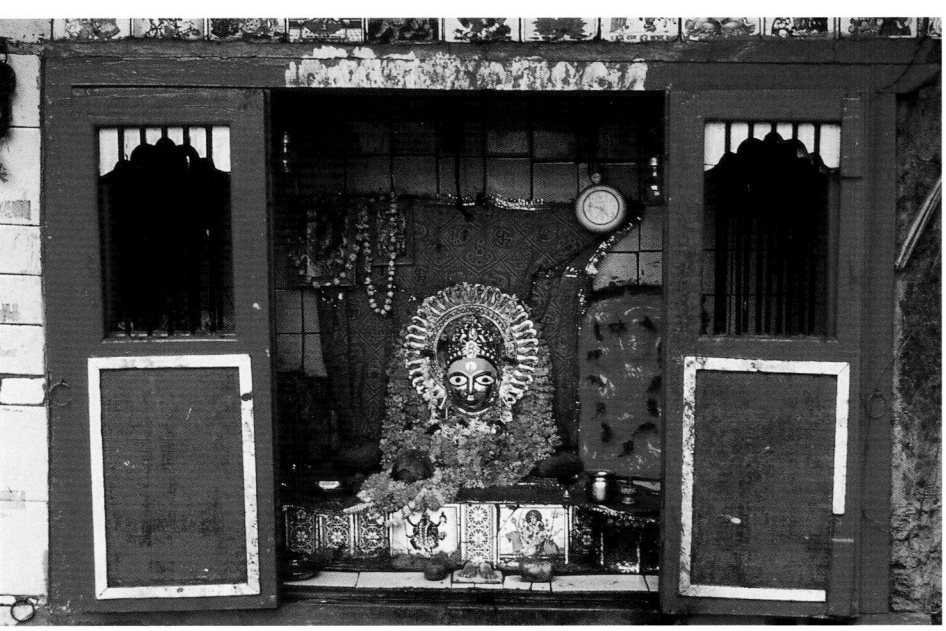

Devi

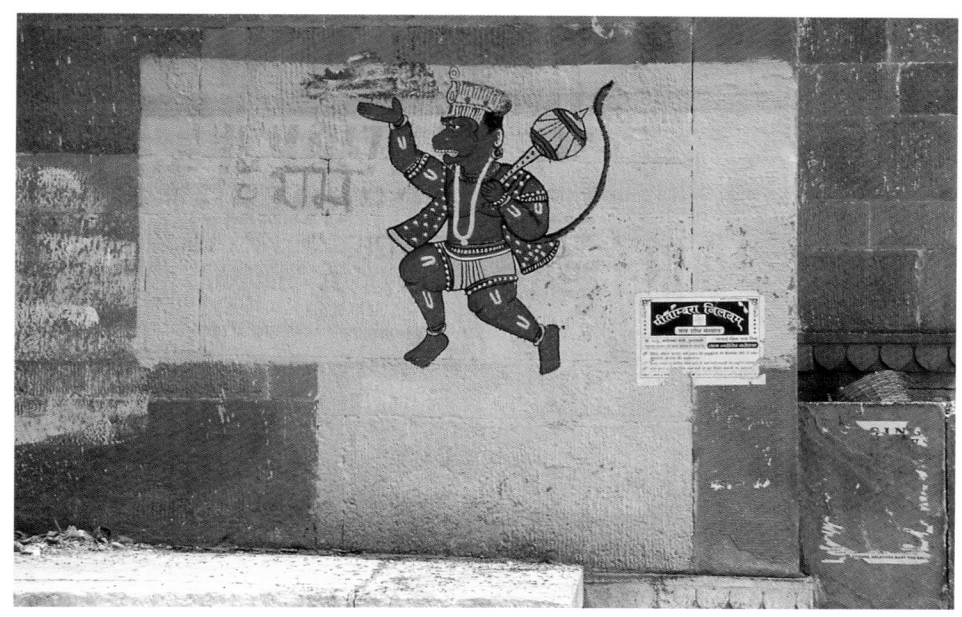

Hanuman

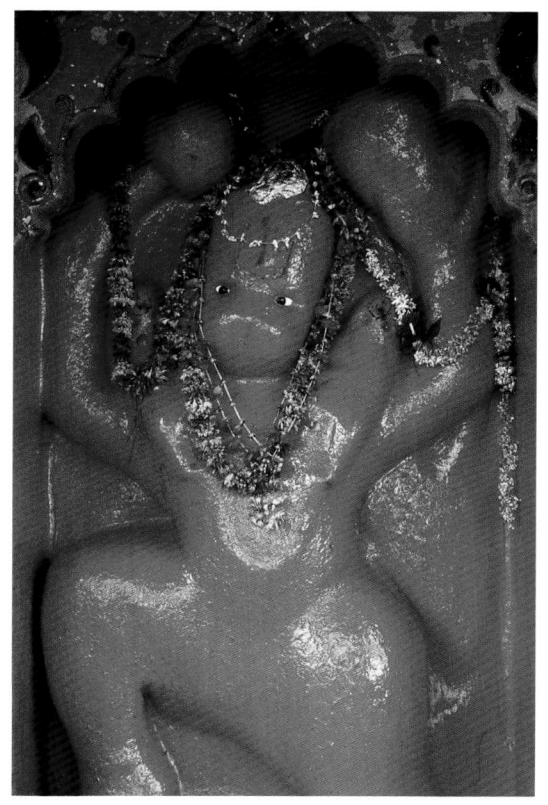

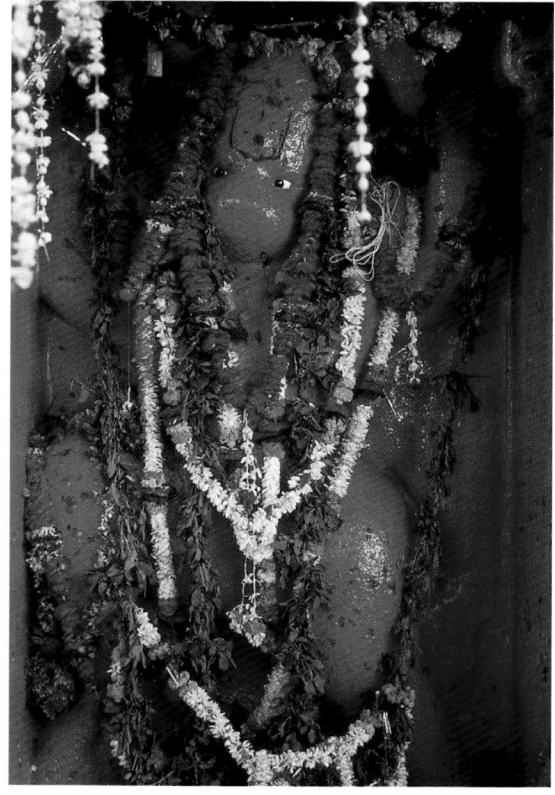

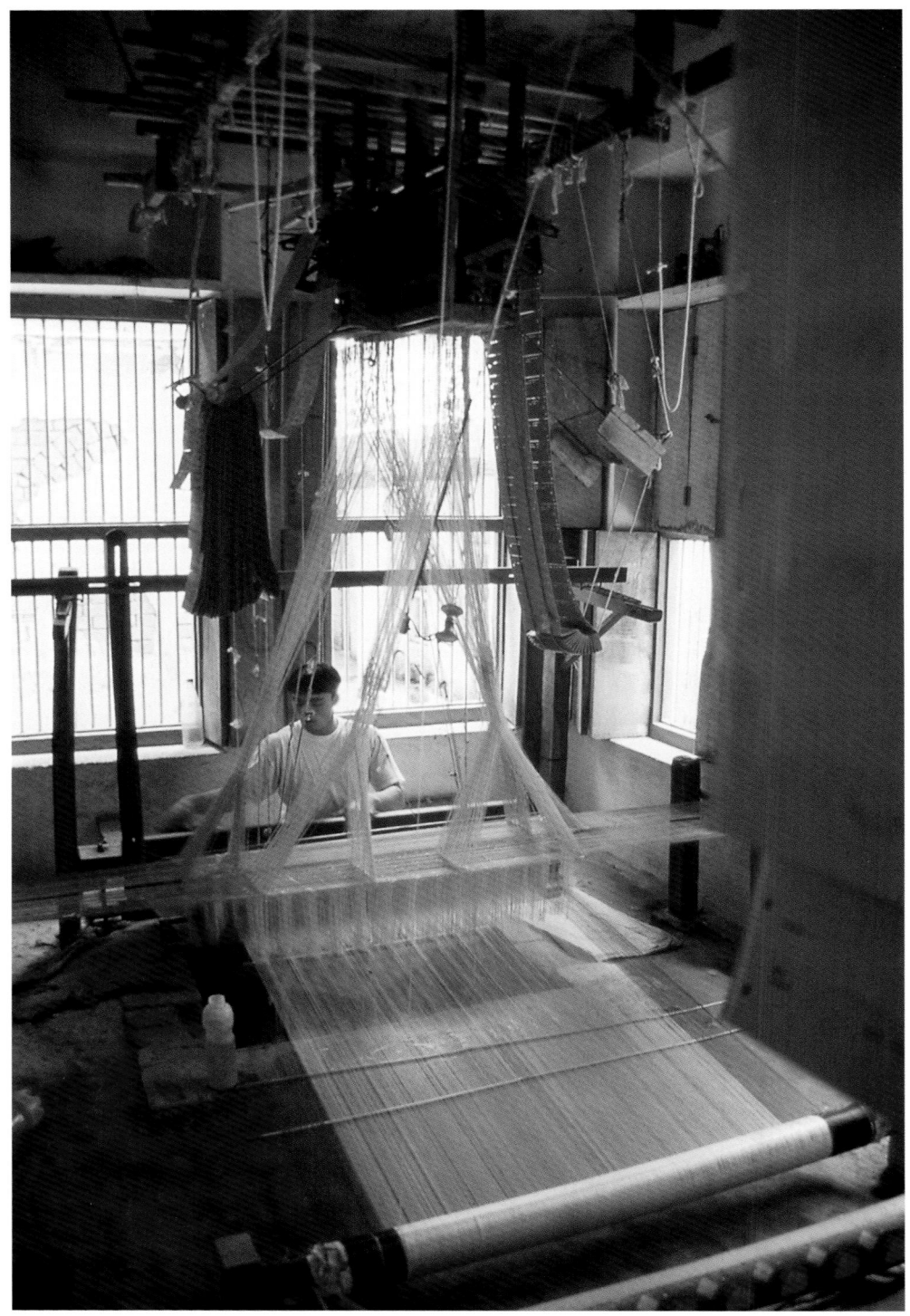

Shahid at the Jacquard loom, Sonarpura, Banaras

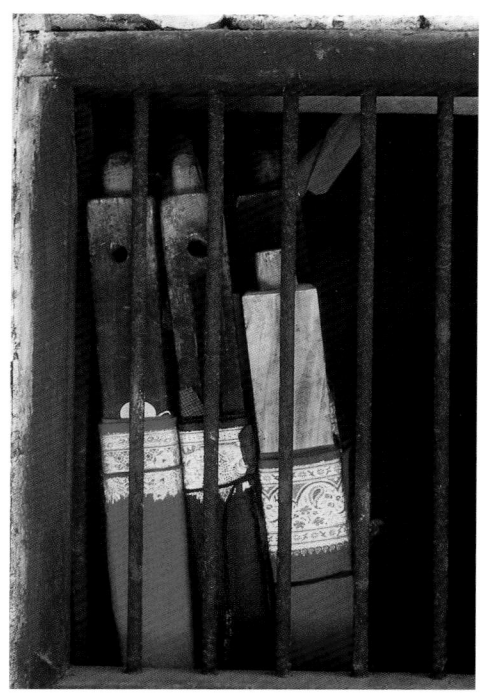

Gold-brocaded Banarasi saris

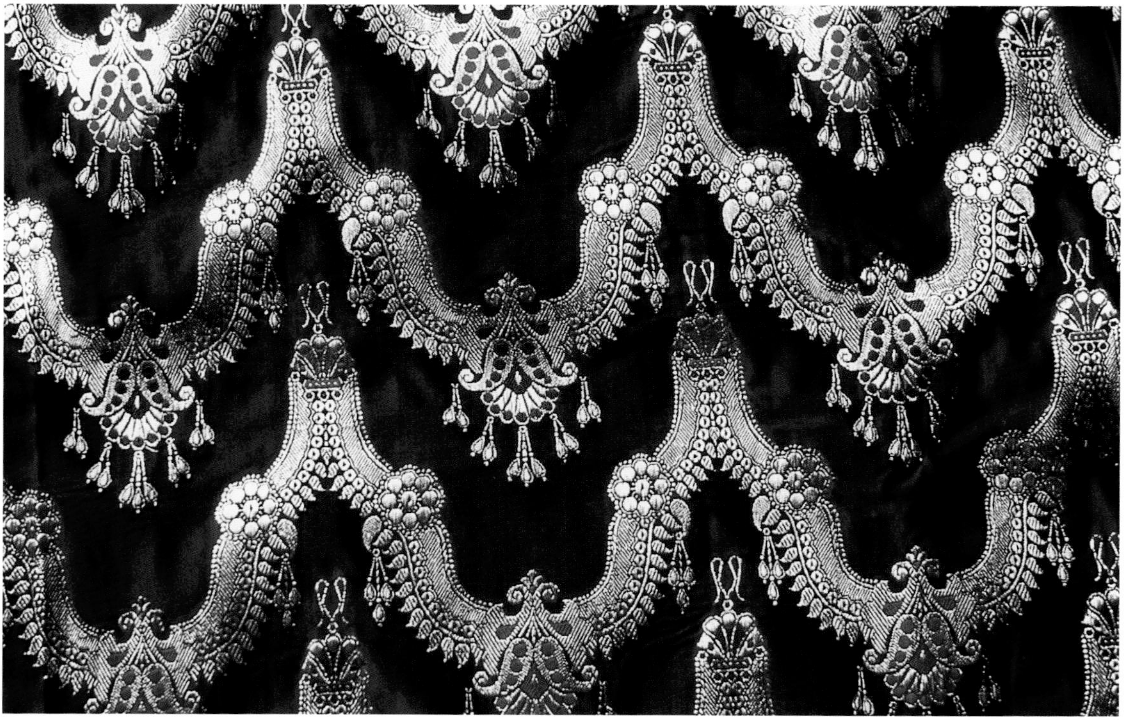

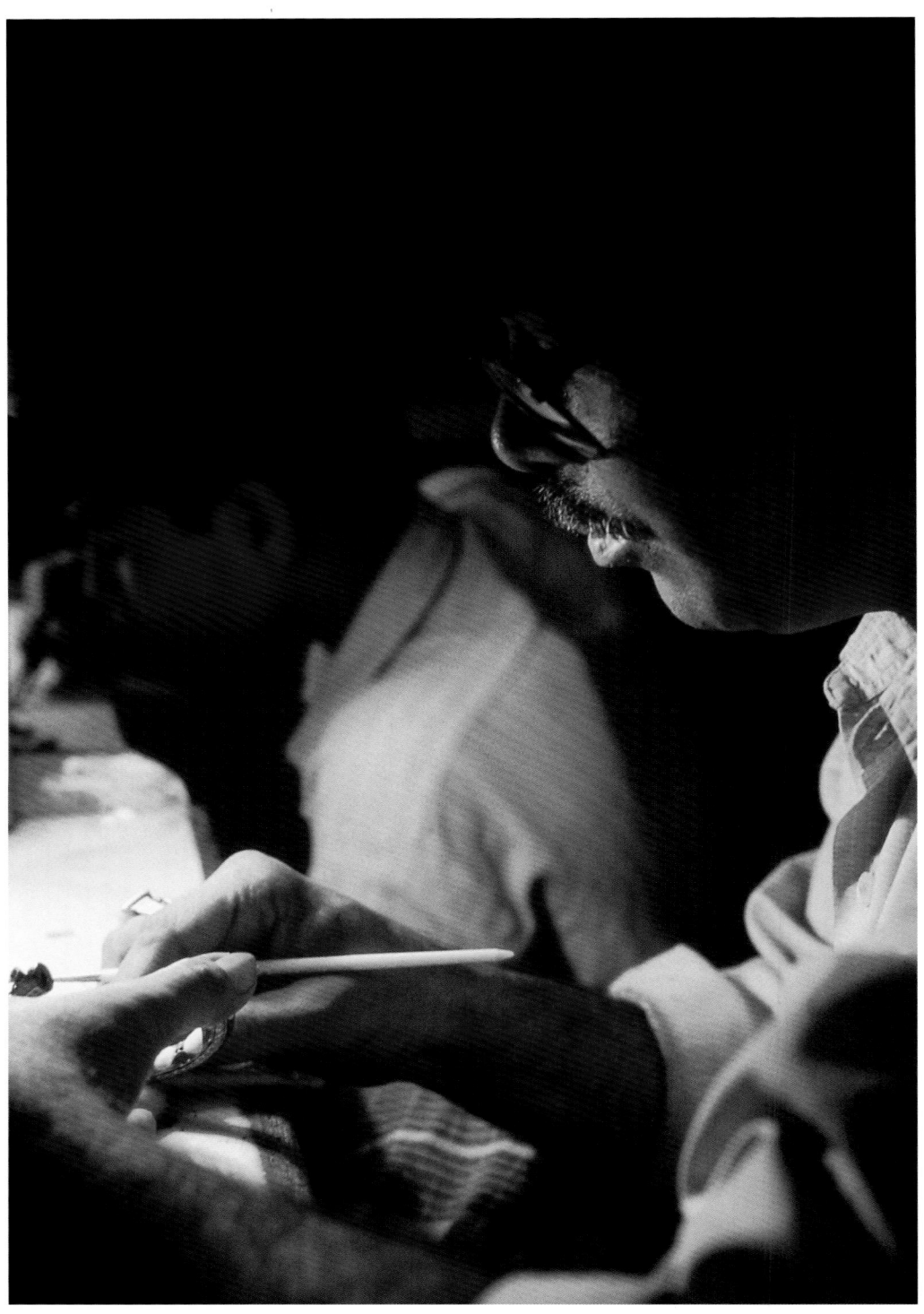

Gopal Prashad Meenekar with his son, Kush Kumar Seth, enameling jewelry

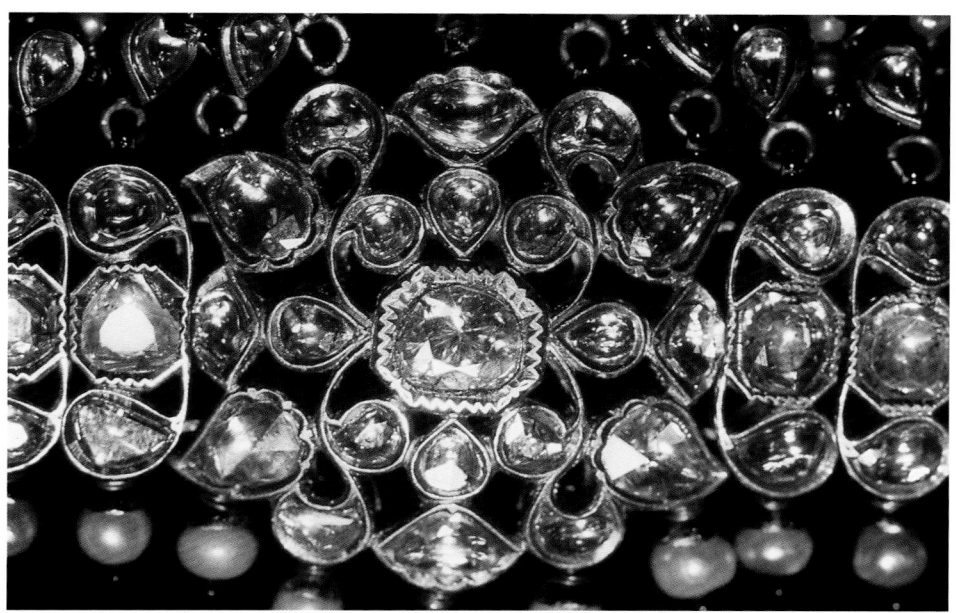

The front of the necklace with diamonds in the kundan setting

Kundan necklace made in Banaras

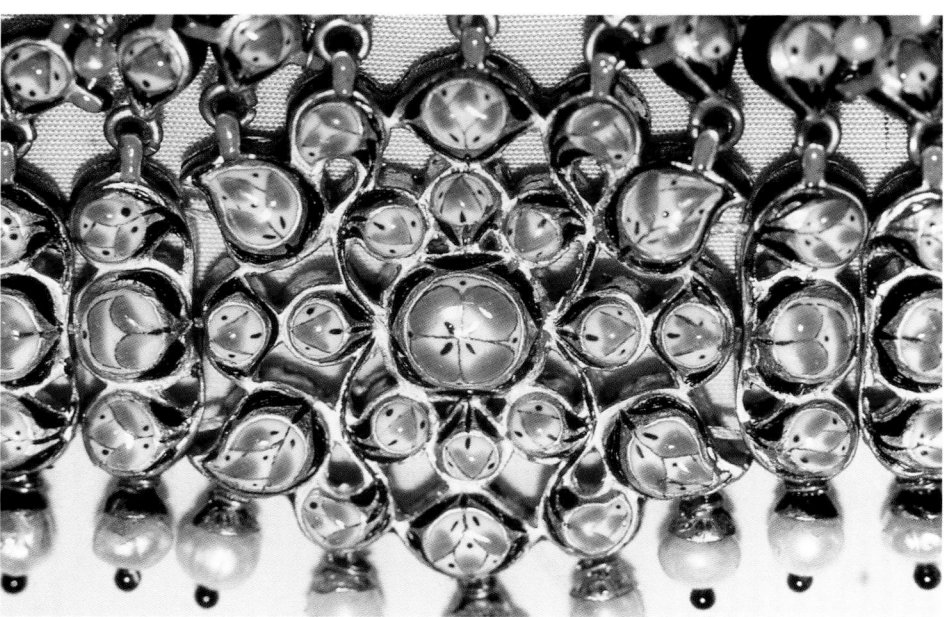

The back of the necklace with pink enameling

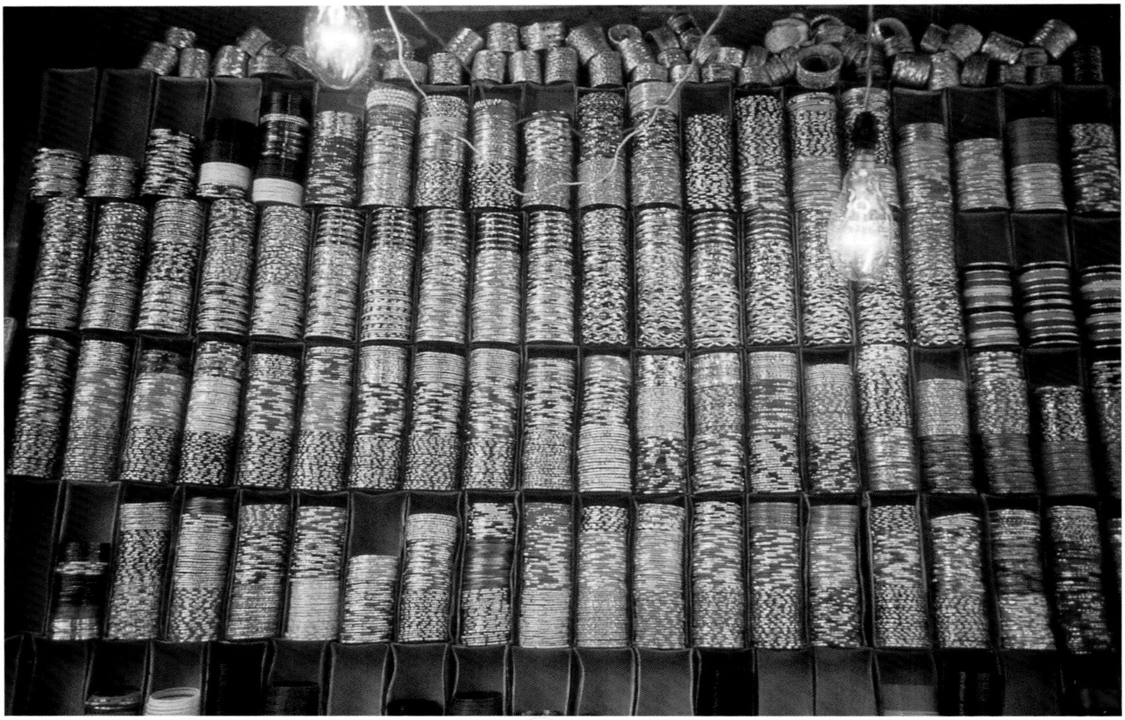

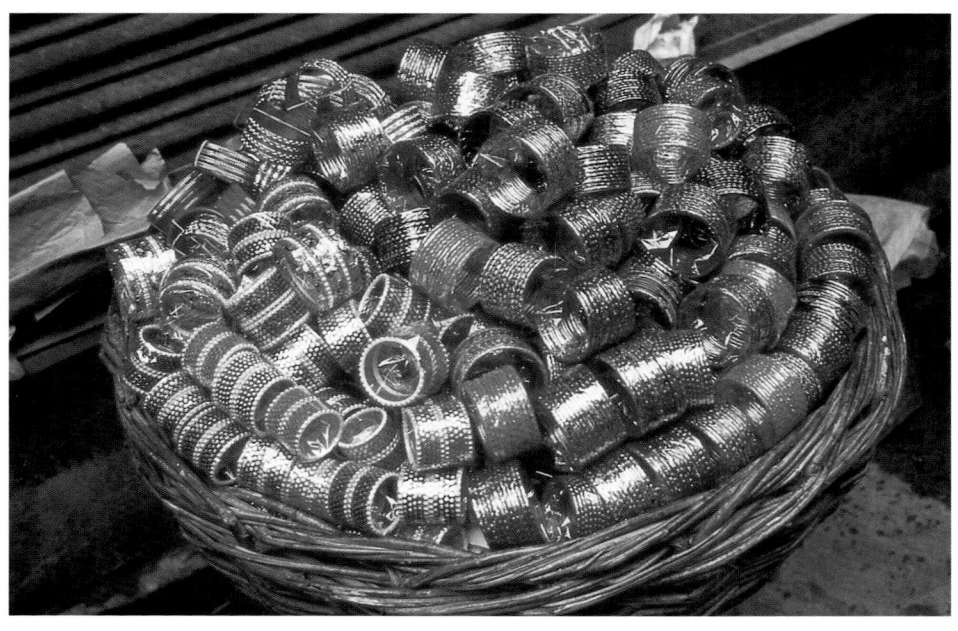

Bangles for sale, Banaras

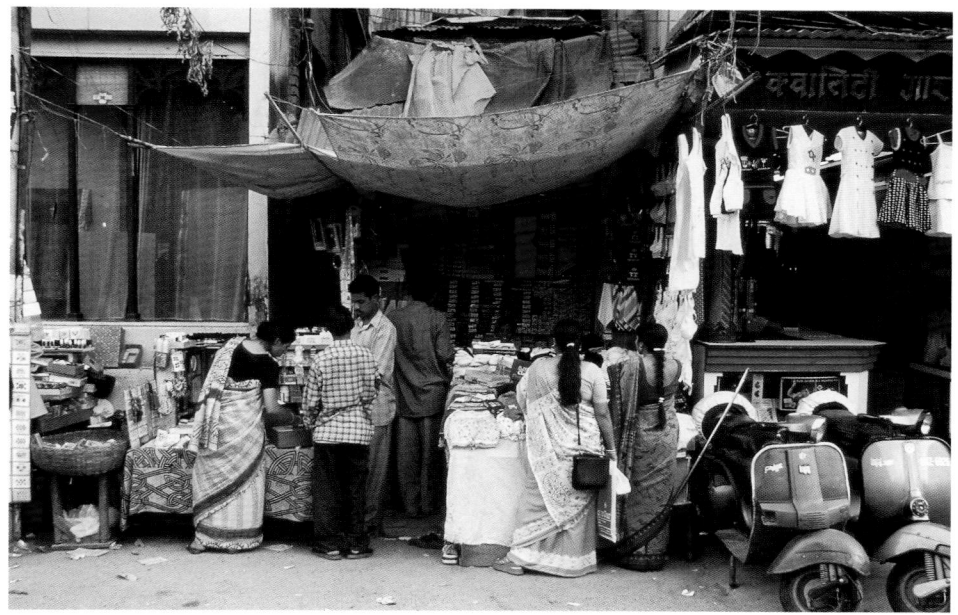

Dashaswamedh Road

Shopping

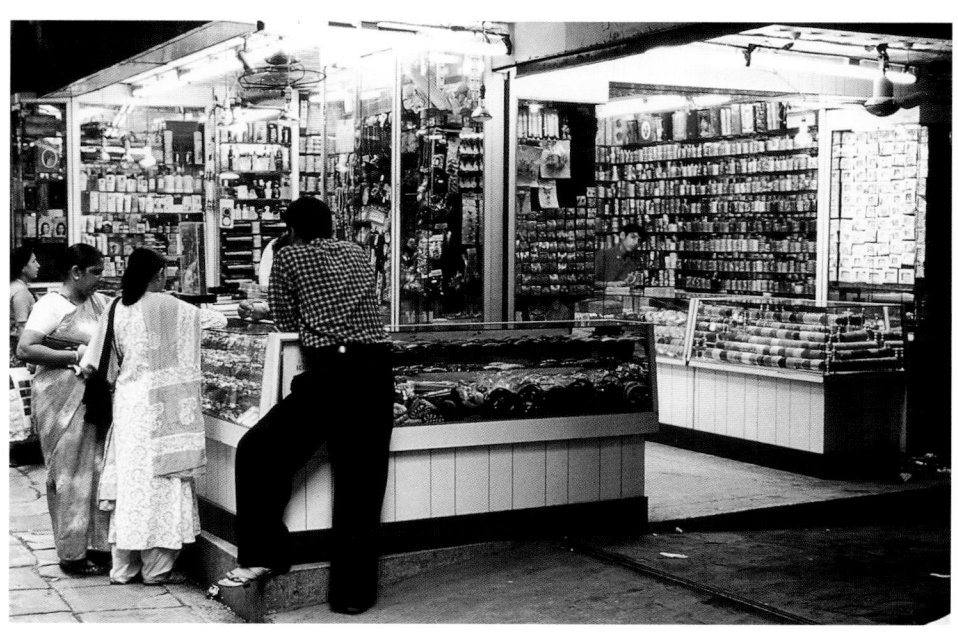

Vishvanath Gali

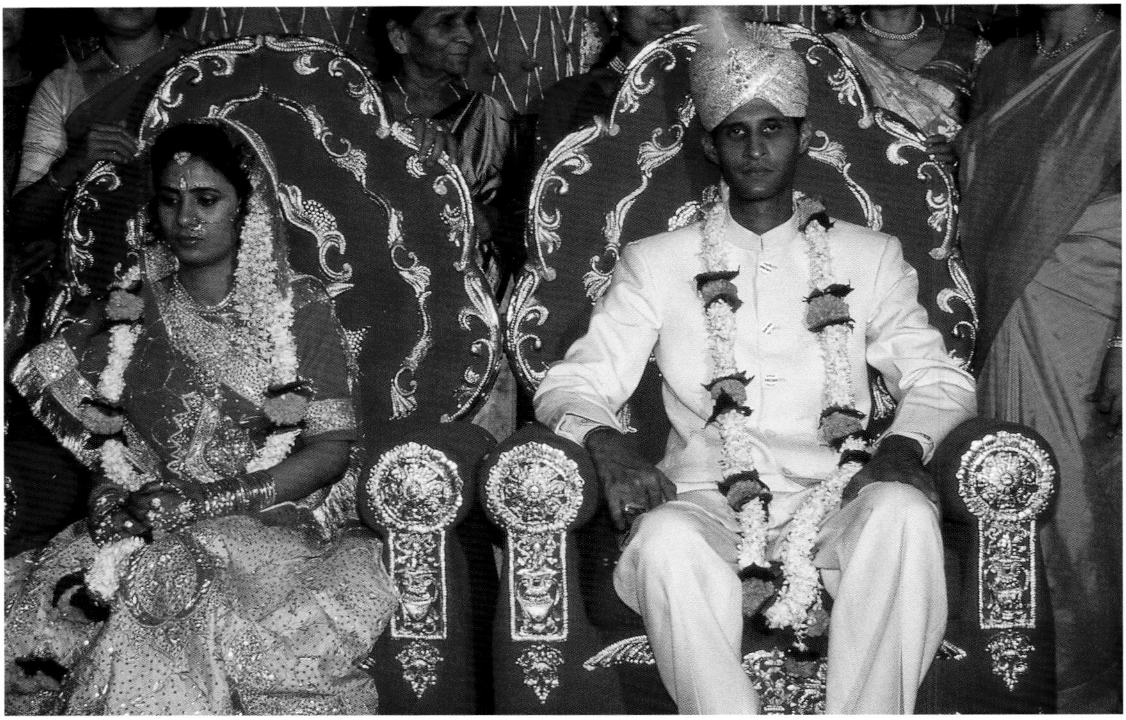

Swati and Shachikant

Hindu Marriage

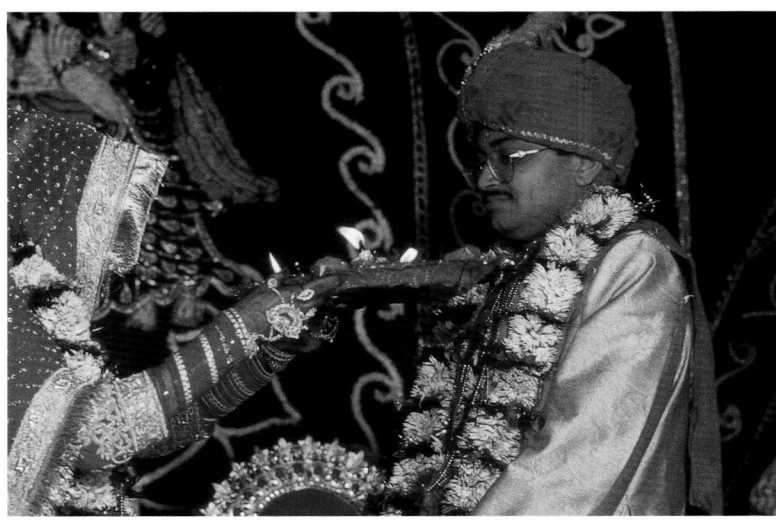

Namita performing *aarti* for her groom

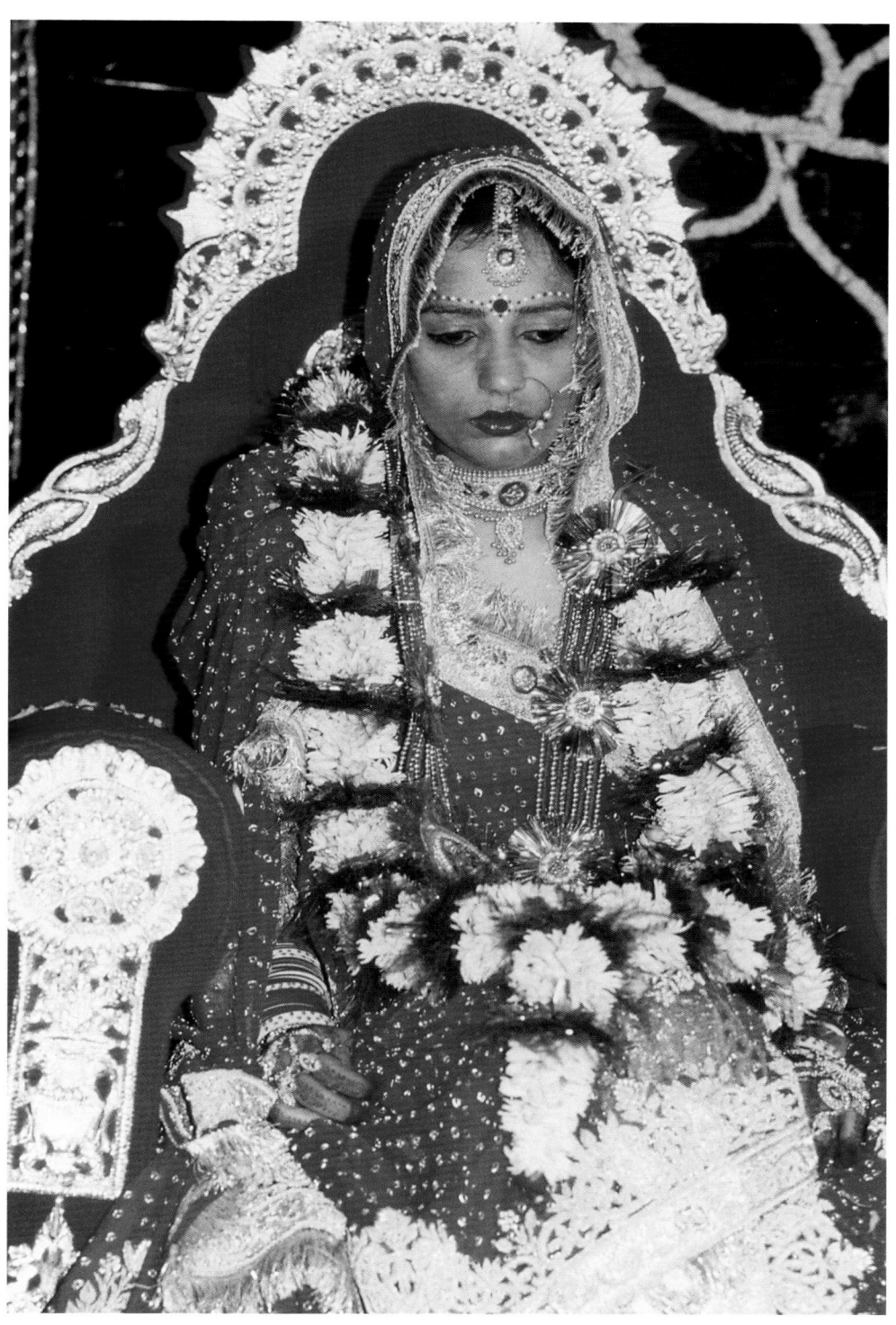

The bride Namita on her wedding day

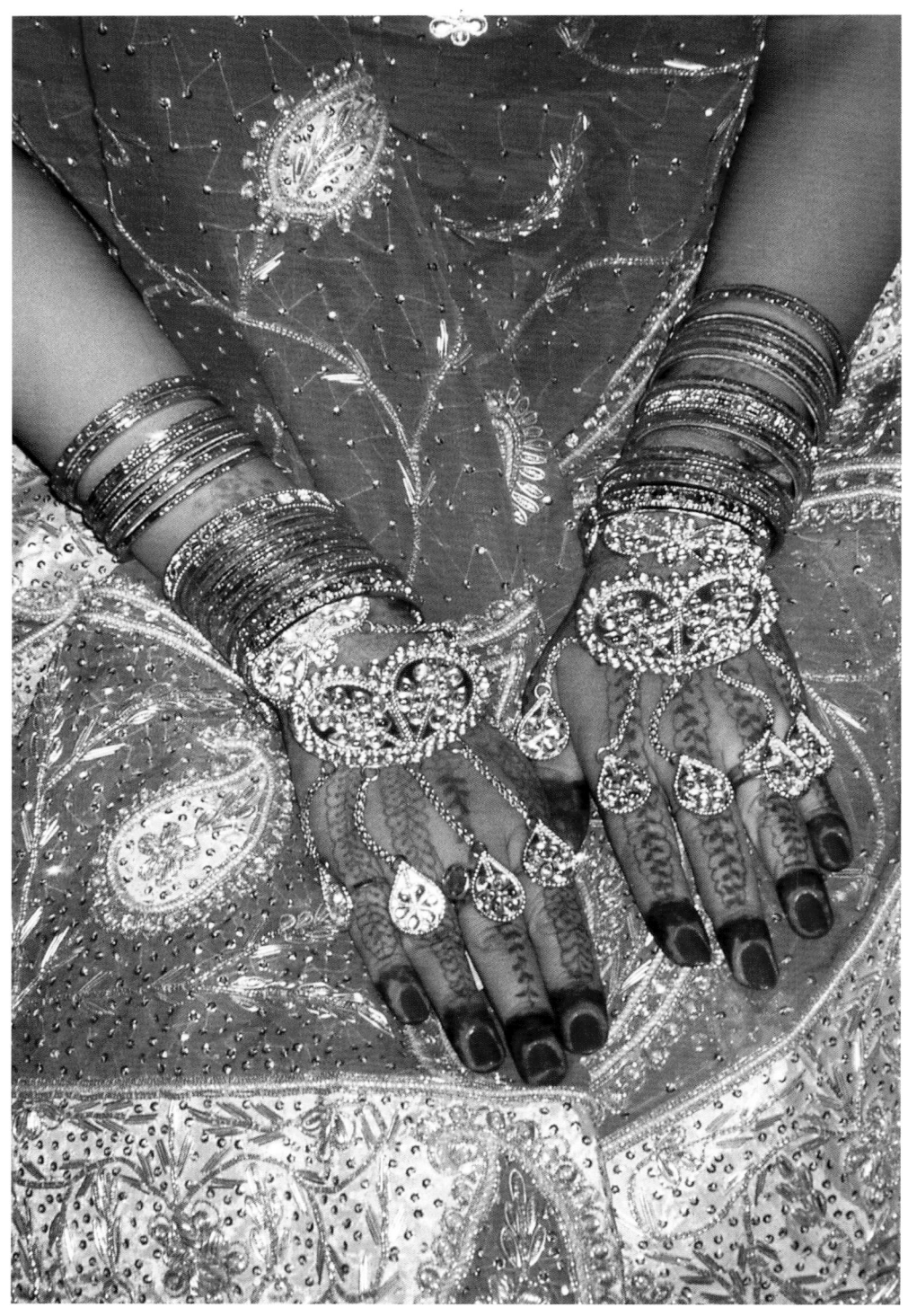

The bride Shalini's hands on her wedding day

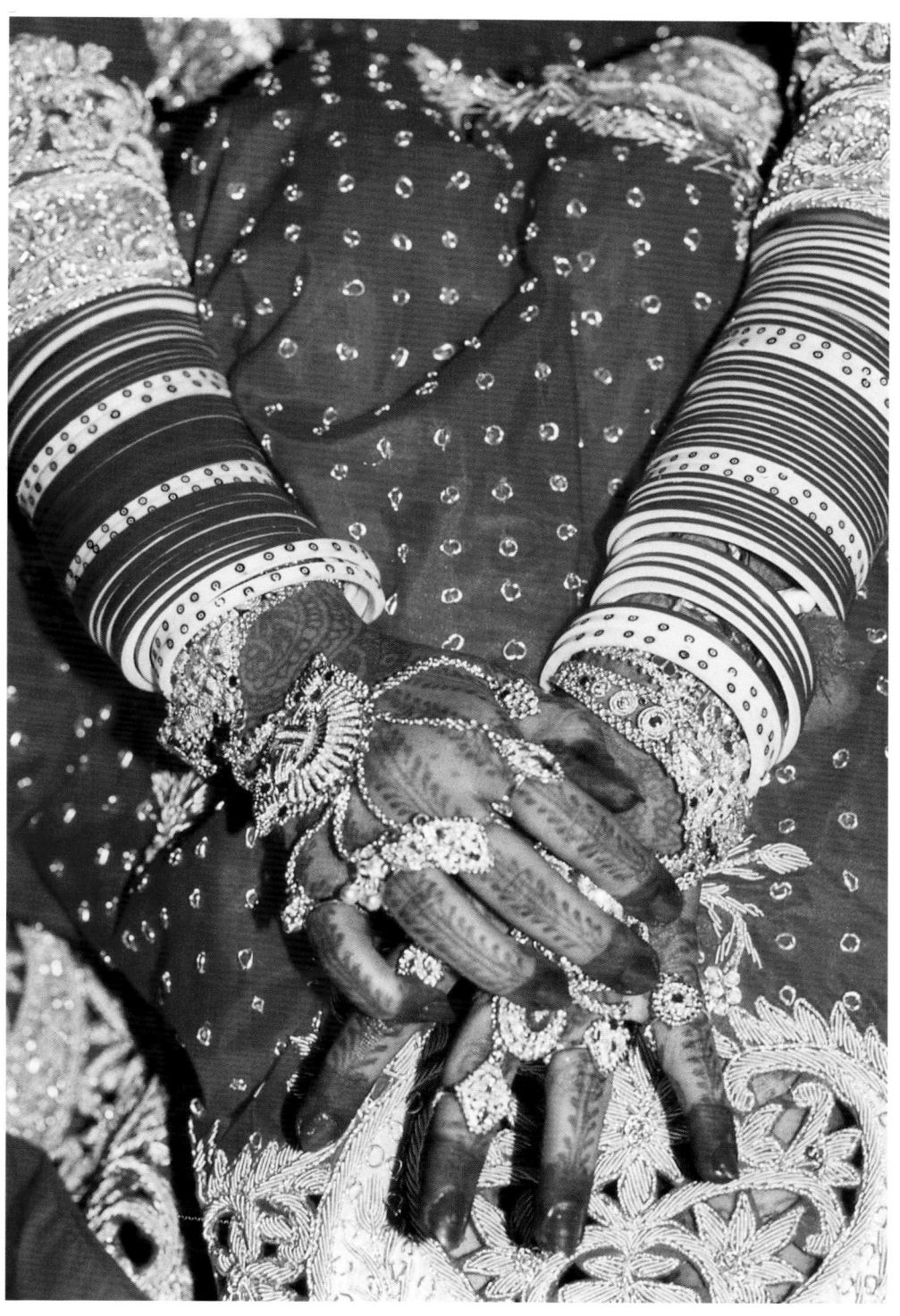

The bride Namita's hands on her wedding day

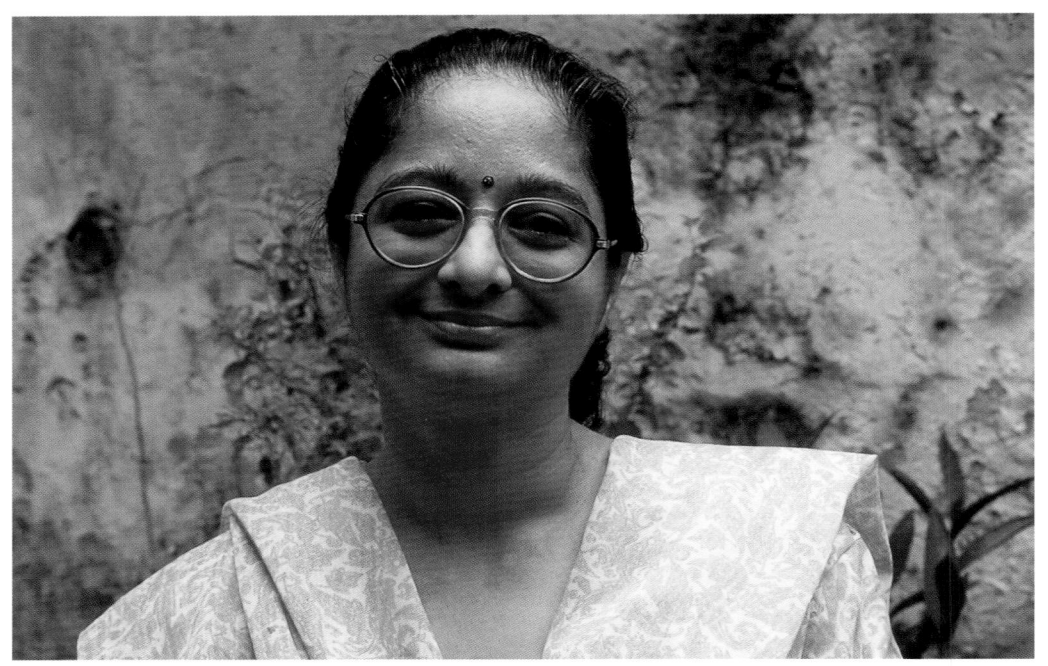

Nina Khanchandani

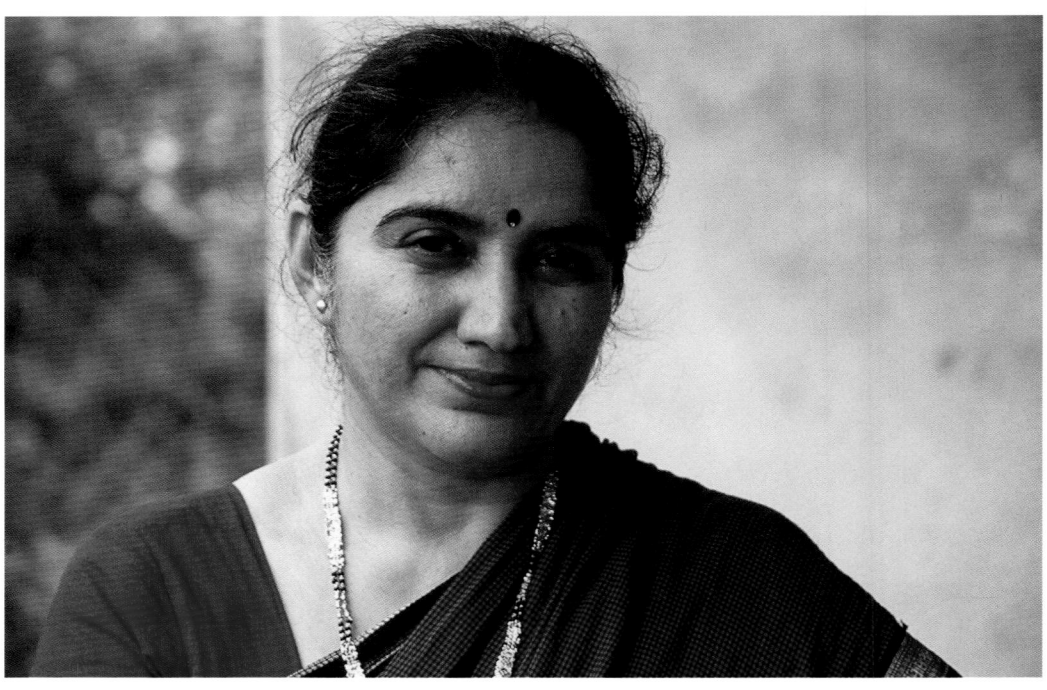

Neelam Chaturvedi

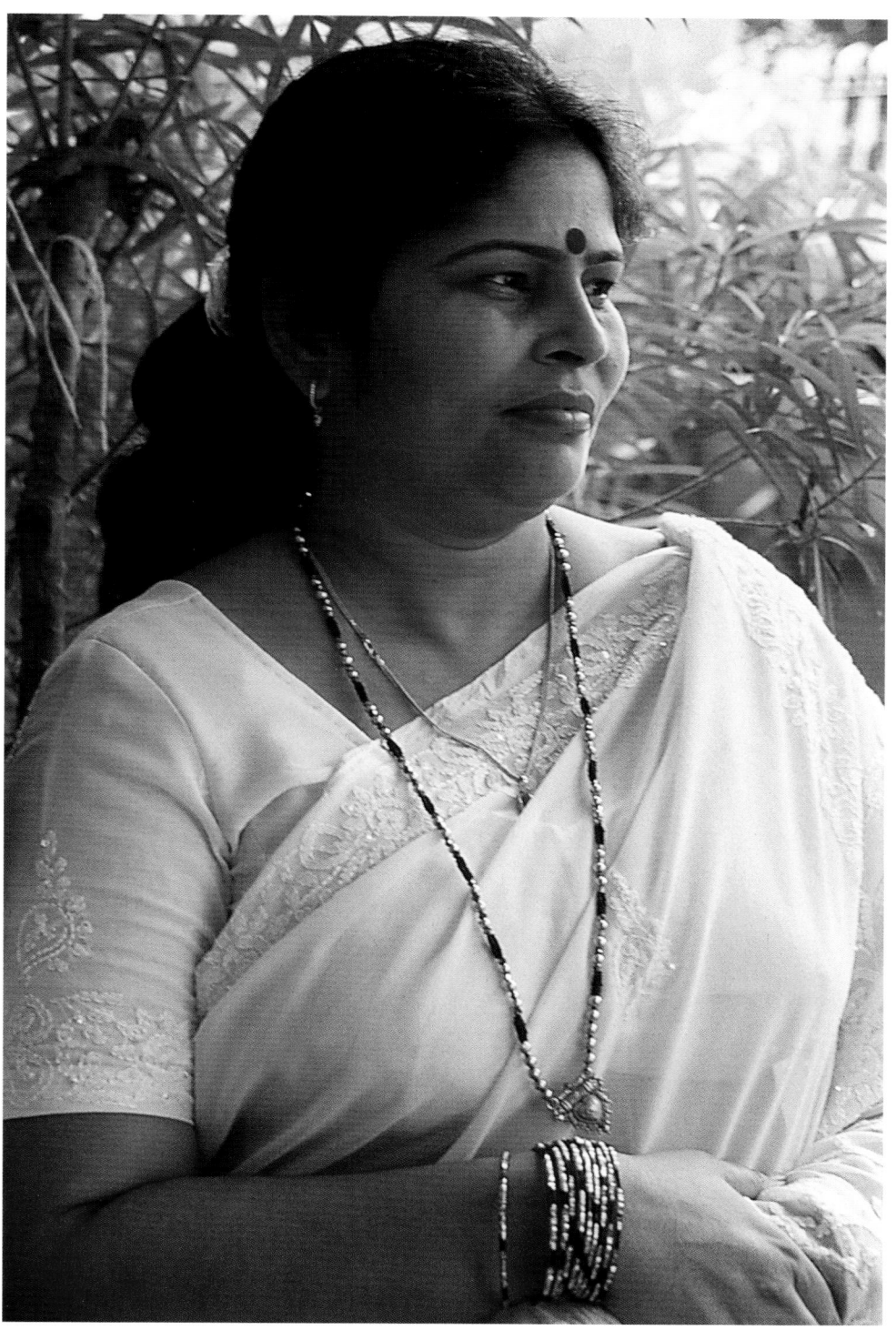

Mukta Tripathi

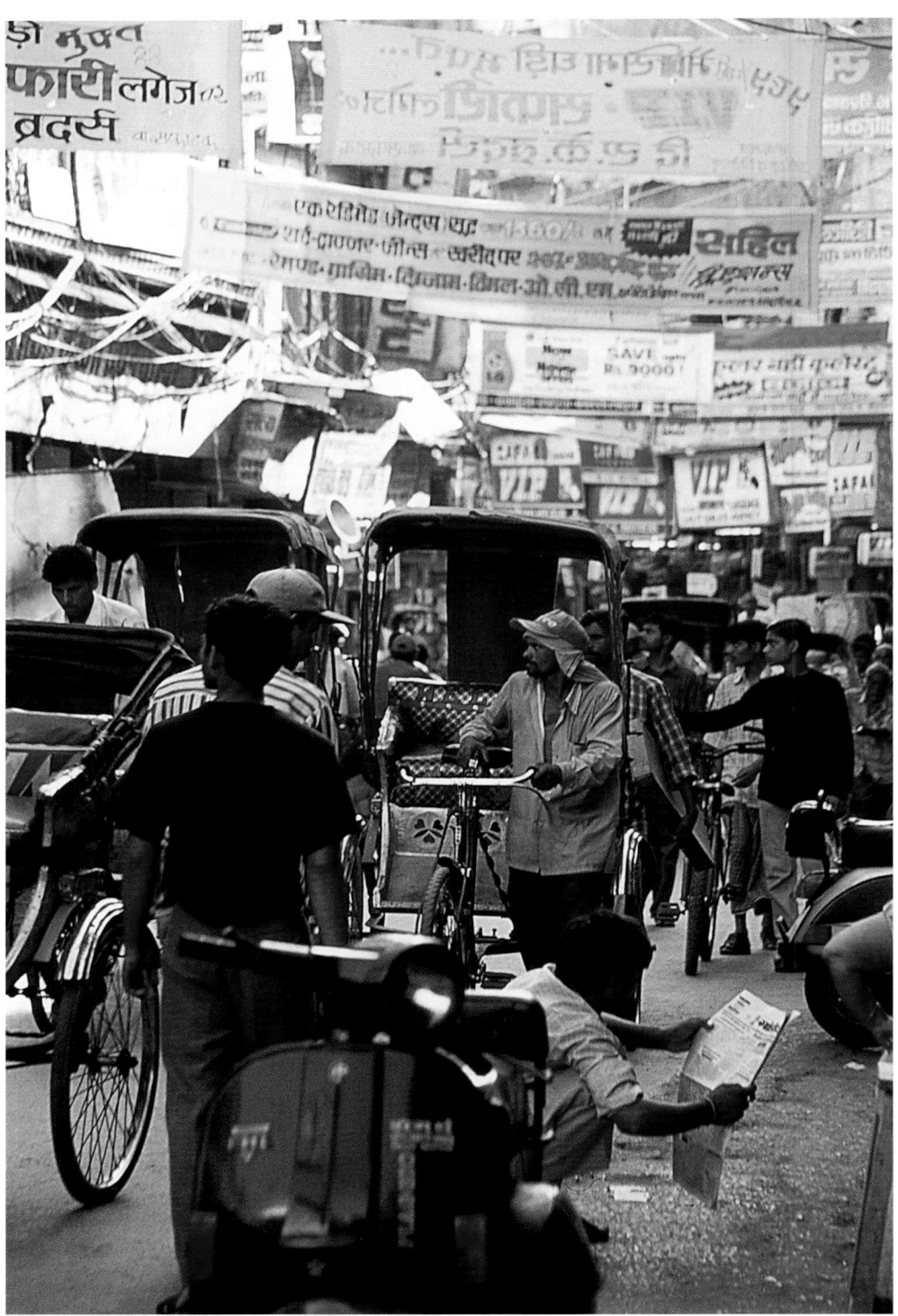

The chaos of Chauk

ornamentation. In many parts of India, shaping the body of the deity out of clay or stone is only the first step in an artistic process that culminates in the painting, dressing, and repetitive ritual adornment of the divine. Religious devotion, whether in temples by *pundits* or in homes by ordinary people, involves bathing, clothing, dressing, and decorating the body of the god—acts that attest to the power of adornment as communication. Since people who are highly religious tend to be more symbolically oriented, a study of signs and symbolic communication through bodily attire becomes particularly relevant in India, allowing, again, for a clear detection of patterns that might be more obscure in other cultural settings.

Just as the specific forms and interpretations of Hinduism vary throughout the country, appearing in slightly modified form within a community and even within a single family, clothing norms likewise unfold within a wide and subtle range. It is this complexity and multiplicity of expression that makes India such an interesting place to study body art and the culture of clothing. Members of different populations dress distinctly—religious affiliation, for example, is readily identified by the clothing of men and especially of women—but a deeper analysis reveals a stunning array of variation within the general tradition of each of the major religious, social, caste, and economic groups found in the country. It is precisely this cultural tendency to divide and separate that Mahatma Gandhi tried to eradicate during his attempt to unite India against the British, when he worked toward liberation through the symbolic and economic significance of cloth and clothing.

A desire to showcase social difference is one of the universal goals of dressing, and this social function is especially obvious in a place of elaborate distinctions like India, where the caste system remains a profound part of daily life. In adorning themselves, people in India communicate religion, caste, and region—and they communicate fashionability and good taste. Some prosperous women told me they abandoned a particular fashion as soon as the maid or "Mrs. Rickshawwallah" started wearing it, erasing the socioeconomic division between servants and those "advanced" people of the higher classes.

The religious importance of seeing and adornment, and the importance of adornment as a marker of identity in a society divided by religious persuasion, caste, and social class—these reasons make India a powerful site for ethnographic investigation of body art. Another reason is found in the richness of opportunities for personal expression. Most items of adornment are still handmade. Every step of jewelry production requires the deft craft of the hand. Textiles are stamped, tie-dyed, and embroidered, while saris are laboriously handwoven. Though many clothes are readymade and bought off the rack, a considerable amount of hand-tailoring allows for creativity on the part of the customers who order clothes that reflect their aesthetic visions, and on the part of the tailors who respond to those visions. Custom-ordered clothes and jewelry allow greater leeway for expression among both producers and consumers than those ground out in a factory; choice in machine-made goods is confined to the act of purchase. Finally, creativity in assemblage is wide and deep for women in India because of the great number of variables in body art—including both the "compulsory" items that must be worn by married women (on the forehead, neck, ears, nose, fingers, wrists, ankles, and toes) and the wide range of options that remain open to free choice.

I chose to situate this study in the ancient city of Banaras, officially known as Varanasi, but still called "Banaras" by its people. My choice involved both personal and intellectual reasons. My parents are both from Banaras, and I have visited the city throughout my life. For me, the experience of India has always been the experience of Banaras. One of my most vivid memories of India involves a beloved item of body art: a pair of denim sandals, embroidered with a red flower, which I was given in Brazil, where we lived at the time. One day, when I was five or six, I was walking through the crowded *galis* of Banaras, distracted by the colorful toys hawked by the street vendors, when I accidentally stepped into a deep pile of dung left by one of the cows that wander the lanes. Horrified, I reached down and daintily unbuckled the clasp, lifting my small foot out, leaving the marvelous sandal behind on the street. Then, stubbornly, I hopped on one foot the whole way home, back to my *Nanaji's* grand old house that was lost inside the maze of narrow alleys. The sacrificed sandal holds many of my feelings toward Banaras: attraction, revulsion, and resilience despite difficulty.

At the end of that visit to India, my older sister and I bought ourselves little aluminum suitcases, which we hoped would impress our classmates back in Brazil. We carried those shiny suitcases proudly to school, and caused so much laughter among the other kids that we came home, put the suitcases away, and never touched them again. Our humiliation taught me a lesson that I would return to as an adult: body art (which includes fashionable accessories) lives in a cultural context, and it rarely transcends local aesthetic norms.

My parents are Indian, yet I was born in Oslo, Norway, and grew up in São Paulo, Brazil, where I lived with my parents and two sisters, Divya and

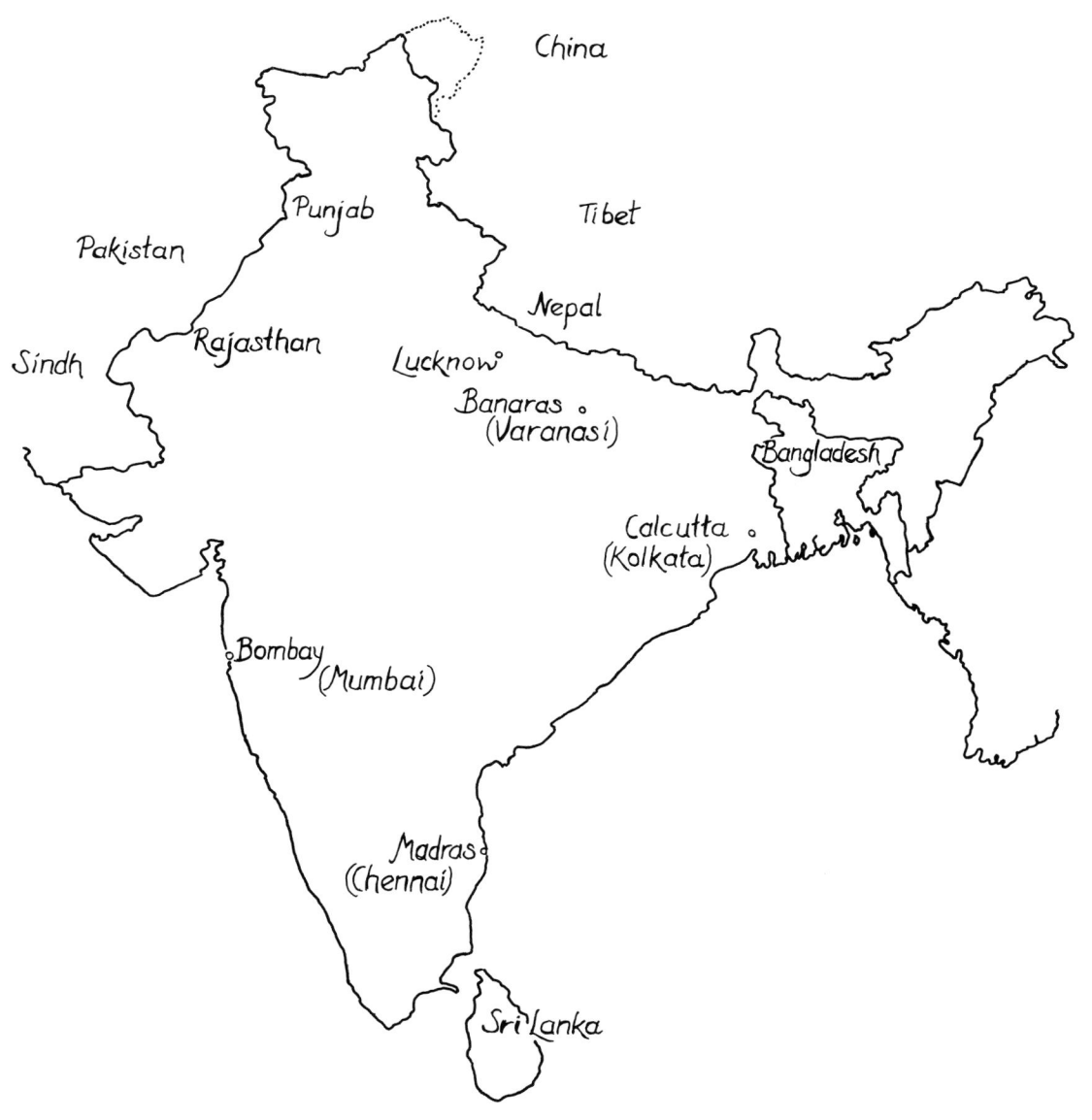

China

Tibet

Punjab

Pakistan

Nepal

Sindh

Rajasthan

Lucknow

Banaras
(Varanasi)

Bangladesh

Calcutta
(Kolkata)

Bombay
(Mumbai)

Madras
(Chennai)

Sri Lanka

India

Bobby, until I was a teenager. We grew up speaking Hindi at home, Portuguese in the streets, and we attempted to master English when we arrived in the United States. In Brazil, our social circle turned within the Indian community; we went to weekly dinner parties where people spoke Hindi and ate Indian food, and where the women, though living in South America, wore colorful saris as an assertion of communal identity and personal pride.

Personal and familial connections to Banaras made it the logical place for me to begin my study of all the aspects of body art: production, marketing, purchase, and personal adornment. This book is by no means an ethnographic portrait of Banaras. I use the city as the backdrop against which to analyze the complex artistic processes of bodily adornment. Banaras is the main pilgrimage site for Hindus—they call it the "Hindu Mecca." This is because Lord Shiva, locally known as Vishvanath—The Lord of the Universe—rules the world from Banaras, from Kashi, the City of Light. Pilgrims add to the city's population of one million as many as two hundred thousand people a day.[6] They come from all over the country and throughout the world of the Indian diaspora to take *darshan* of Vishvanath at the Golden Temple and to bathe in the sacred Ganges. Several times I have been told that if you had a one hundred kilo sack of rice, and put one grain in each of the temples of Banaras, you would run out of rice before you ran out of temples—such is the religious richness of the place.

Banaras is a place for prayer, and it is a place for death. The old, infirm, and widowed come here to die, since the one who dies here escapes the cycles of rebirth, avoiding another lifetime in this miserable world. Processions of relatives carrying wrapped dead bodies can be seen or heard throughout the day, every day, in the old part of the city, where the stores sell clothes and bangles, and the workshops produce saris and jewelry. Advancing aggressively, relentlessly, toward the river where the body will be cremated and the ashes set adrift, the bearers of the corpses chant *"Ram nam satya hei"*: Ram's name is truth; the only truth is Ram, all else is illusion, *maya*.

The throngs of pilgrims, grieving relatives, and tourists—tourists more native than foreign—make for a festival-like atmosphere. The streets are eternally crowded, thick with vendors and pilgrims and cows, loud with constant invitations to visit shops, give alms, or take a boat ride on the Ganga.

Kashi, according to Diana Eck, "condenses the entire universe in its microcosm."[7] In that condensation, the ancient city is a microcosm of Hinduism, and the contemporary city is a microcosm of modern India.[8] Pilgrims visit from all the states of India, and the city contains settled communities of people from many parts of the country. Some run ashrams to house the pilgrims of their own linguistic and cultural group. Others, who came generations ago to live in the city of Shiva, have made this their home. Many of those who came from elsewhere continue to practice the styles of their home state and region, making it possible to see many varieties of clothes and jewelry in Banaras on any given day, and local merchants, wishing to cater to this varied clientele, cleverly stock saris and bangles that represent the aesthetic and regional choices of wider India. A version of India in miniature, Banaras is a fine place to seek general understanding.

Banaras has long been a center for the production of items of adornment. Local craftsmen are famed for pink enameling—*gulabi mina*—which was coveted by the Mughal emperors in the past, and today, while old pieces are displayed reverently in museums, *mina* work is experiencing a revival among a handful of masterful *minawallahs* such as Gopal Prashad Meenekar. Indians associate Banaras with the exquisite gold-brocaded saris known simply as Banarasi saris. Most brides in the country, and in the diaspora, wish to wear and receive for their dowries these lustrous, luxurious lengths of shimmering silk. Banaras's population of Muslim weavers—numbering two hundred thousand according to an estimate by the weaver Shameem Akhtar Ansari—make the saris in one of the city's weaving neighborhoods: Madanpura, Sonarpura, or Alaipura. Increasing national friction between Hindus and Muslims registers tensely in Banaras. The city is, according to many accounts, about 40 percent Muslim and 60 percent Hindu.[9]

Because of the high number of annual visitors and the local production of saris and jewelry, Banaras has a thriving commercial culture, both wholesale and retail, serving the people of the city, the pilgrims from afar, and the thousands of nearby villagers who come to the big city to shop. The steady flow of outsiders brings new ideas to the ancient city, ideas that are evaluated, rejected perhaps, or speedily incorporated, maybe by the local women who are visually inspired by an example on the streets, or maybe by the merchants who wish to appeal to the endlessly fluctuating aesthetic demands of their customers. Conservative Banaras makes a vibrant place to study tradition in exchange with fashion trends and stylistic diversity.

In 1996, I arrived in Banaras to conduct the fieldwork for my dissertation. I lived for seven months in the joint family compound of two of my uncles, in the neighborhood of Lanka, next to Banaras Hindu University. I met

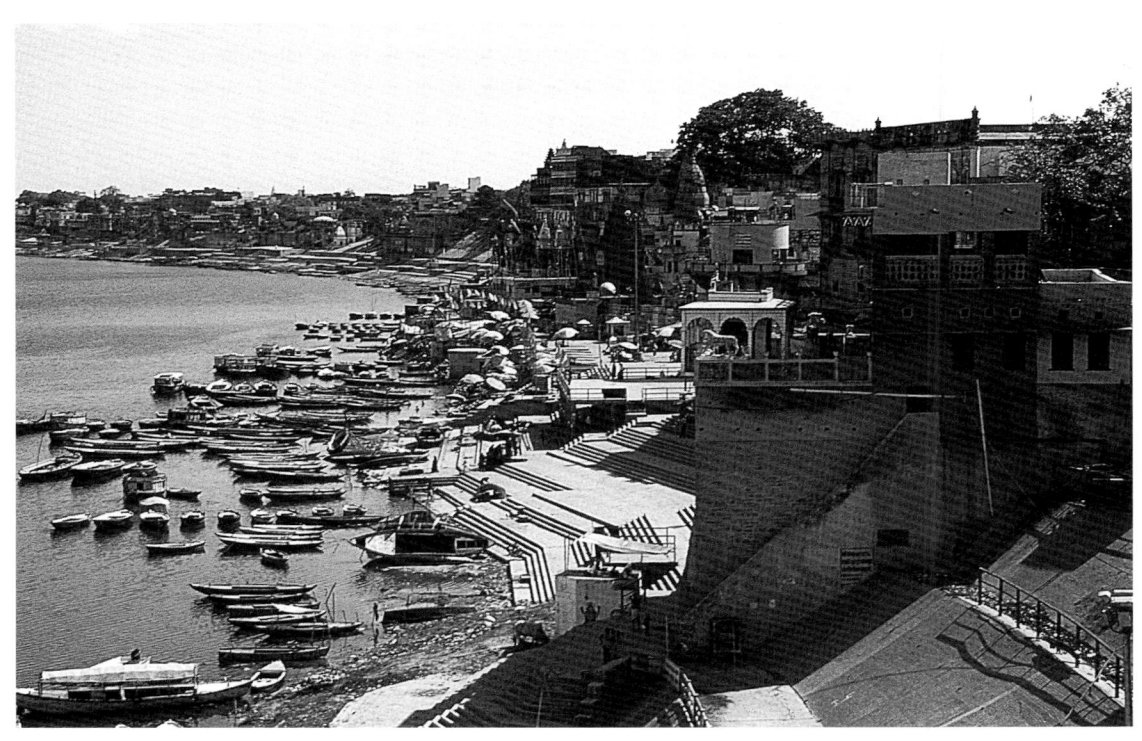

Banaras: The view south, down the Ganga, toward Dashaswamedh Ghat

many of the people I interviewed through connections my family made on my behalf. I was introduced to the owners of the sari and jewelry stores where they shopped, and I was taken to the weddings of my cousins' college friends. Living within a multigenerational, extended-family household helped me understand the dynamics of this common kind of domestic space, and aided me in the formation of questions I would ask the people I interviewed.

Some aspects of my personal presentation during this trip opened routes to understanding. Since I was unmarried then, I wore the *salwar suit* and sparse adornment of young women of my age. A silver and carnelian ring I wore on my left hand, bought in an ethnic boutique in Los Angeles, attracted the attention of the goldsmiths I interviewed who used it as a negative example of what they would *not* want to add to their permanent repertoire; for them, it represented "tourist taste." The nose ring I wore—a stud with a silver flower, a tiny green stone in the middle—was the cause of much negative response; many of my relatives offered to take me to buy a better one. When I switched to the circular gold and cubic zirconia ornament worn by many women, the comments stopped. This incident helped me understand that many unsolicited comments arise from a negative response to an aesthetic choice. Once the nose ring was acceptable, I fit in; nobody complimented me, but neither did they criticize me. Finally, when somebody came to visit my uncles' house, I was often introduced as the relative who is visiting from America, and who washes her hair with shampoo every day. The other women, who wanted thick and glossy hair, oiled it regularly, and washed it only once a week (though they took at least one bath a day). While I was studying body art in India, the people around me defined me by my own practices—some of them pretty strange, apparently—and they reinforced my conception that people are instantly identified by what they do to their bodies.

After accepting a faculty position in the Department of Folklore and Ethnomusicology at Indiana University, I returned for two more trips to Banaras, in the summers of 2001 and 2003. I wished to deepen my knowledge of the city, and to meet a wider array of people, since living with my family had helped but also restricted me during the previous trip. This time, I lived within the *galis,* next to the river, in the heart of the commercial tangle of the city. On these trips I widened the population of people I interviewed, finding them not through my family, but through commercial contacts in public. I also expanded the scope of my study. The dissertation focused almost exclusively on wearing jewelry; this book encompasses the practices of jewelry production and sales, as well as cloth and textile manufacture and retailing. Most important, this book looks at the gendered negotiations that occur within the realm of body art. Men make and sell the items of adornment; women express themselves by creating personal assemblies of meaningful beauty out of the objects that men make and sell. All the merchants and craftsmen I interviewed enjoyed comfortable lives—as defined in Indian terms. The women I spoke with were comparably comfortable, though an unusual proportion of them were Brahmin, since this is my own caste and I found it easy to meet them. These people might be taken to represent everyday, middle-class, urban India.

My methods and theoretical leanings have been shaped by my training in anthropology, folklore, and material culture studies: I gather information through detailed observation and documentation; I seek individuals for long, extended interviews, and favor analyses that result from a collaboration between the patient scholar and the local expert. My orientation stresses the personal in relation to the social. Concentrating on individual creativity within shared aesthetic frames, I position acts and objects in multiple contexts, especially those of creation, consumption, and communication.[10]

One of my goals in writing this book is to contribute to the field of folklore, and particularly to the folkloristic study of material culture, which has yielded outstanding studies of landscape and architecture, of furniture, ceramics, and textiles. Though the folkloristic study of the cultural importance of clothing got an early start in 1937, with Petr Bogatyrev's excellent book on dress in Moravian Slovakia,[11] it has not developed as richly as the study of other aspects of material culture have. Inspired by the anthropologists Andrew and Marilyn Strathern, and James Faris—whose books on Papua New Guinea and Sudan remain masterpieces of body art study[12]—I wish to contribute to the rapidly developing scholarly investigation of clothing by anthropologists, historians of fashion and dress, and museum curators of costume, including Liza Dalby, Andrea Rugh, Verity Wilson, Linda Baumgarten, and Valerie Steele.[13] The serious study of dress and adornment owes much to Joanne Eicher; her decades of dedication have brought to us her energetic new series Dress, Body, Culture.[14] The books in her series offer excellent examples of cultural and historical interpretation, but many are edited volumes, containing fine, brief pieces that are restricted in scope, and it is my desire to connect with the intellectual aims of the authors of this series while providing a more comprehensive case study that integrates the multiplex components of body art in a unified setting.

I was aided in my work by models from material culture, from general studies of dress, and scholarship on other cultural expressions in India helped me come to the conclusions in this book. Of particular importance for me were works on tensions in identity, the dynamics of everyday life, the patterns of male dominance, and the nature of expressive culture in general, and its functions in asserting power and identity in particular.[15] Gloria Raheja and Ann Gold brilliantly examined the use of songs and stories by North Indian women to communicate their sense of oppression and their desire to subvert male dominance.[16] Their conclusions parallel my argument that women's self-adornment functions to express freedom and personal identity.

I join with the students of Indian culture who have demonstrated how people use expressive aspects of their tradition to shape a place for themselves within broad social constraints. My position forms in opposition to some elitist views that take tradition to be a mode of oppression for women. Some have argued that clothing traditions bind Indian women into submissiveness, keeping them literally immobilized in saris and jewelry, while men, they seem to believe, are more liberated because they wear Western clothes.[17] Those who subscribe to such an ideological—maybe colonial—position seem to feel that Indian women would move closer to achieving freedom if they wore jeans and T-shirts like Western girls, because in wearing their traditional clothes, women are submitting to male dominance. In other words, for Indian women to achieve freedom, they must copy foreign women and submit to the domination of men in the West. In one feminist study of post-independence India, the authors celebrate the elite, educated women in New Delhi as a national ideal, even though, rich and working outside of the home, they comprise a miniscule fraction of the total population of the country and remain useless as models to half a billion or so Indian women.[18]

Very few women in India don business suits and enter the male workforce to express their equality. Almost all assert their power and importance by taking control of the world within their grasp, the world around them, coming into mastery of the aspects of the domestic sphere that lie within their command—household maintenance, food preparation, and the rearing of children. For them, for the great majority, self-adornment is a powerful vehicle for self-realization, at once subtle and firm. Though men perceive it to be unimportant and non-threatening, it is an activity filled with a potential for creative satisfaction and social consequence. By means of clothing and adornment, millions of women, including the ones in this book, gain self-esteem, love, happiness, and a psychologically enabling perception of power.

Salik Nishad, a Banarasi artist I met in 1996, cuts intricate shapes out of mass-manufactured *bindis,* transforming them into felt peacocks or cobras. Salik was the first to introduce me to the proverbial saying that when a woman adds a *bindi* to her forehead, she increases her beauty fourfold, adding the grace of four moons to her face. The ability to belong to one's place (India, Banaras), to one's religion (Hinduism), to one's proper developmental stage (married), to express one's aesthetic taste (for there are thousands of varieties of *bindis* available), and to enhance one's own beauty—all this can be achieved by the simple, yet meaningful act of placing a colorful *bindi* on the forehead. Millions and millions of Indian women accomplish this feat every day.

Emma Tarlo, through her superb study of clothing dilemmas, and Sarah Lamb, through her fieldwork on old age, have both excellently investigated the topic of clothing as a means of self-expression in India.[19] And the power of clothing in the subcontinent is a recurrent theme in many recent works of literature by Indian, Pakistani, and Bangladeshi women, both Hindu and Muslim. In her short story "Clothes," Chitra Banerjee Divakaruni shows how dress and jewelry define, in the mind of a young woman named Mita, the transitory stages of her life while providing an anchor to the unconditional permanence of mother love and national identity.[20] Emotions in her story— hope and fear and betrayal—are all outwardly expressed through items of adornment: the pink Banarasi sari she wears to the bride-viewing, the suitcase filled with her trousseau of saris, each containing a sandalwood sachet made of her mother's old saris, the Western jeans and T-shirt she secretly wears once she arrives in her new American home, the violent ceremonial breaking of the marital bangles, and finally, a brave vision of herself in public, wearing a skirt and blouse, dreaming of liberation from the confines of Indian widowhood.

In Monica Ali's novel, *Brick Lane,* the heroine, a young Bangladeshi woman living in London, realizes in a lucid moment "that clothes, not fate, made her life."[21] What you wear, she knows, affects your behavior, your choices, the way others respond to you, and most importantly, how you view yourself. Much of the novel involves subcontinental people trying hard to express themselves, whether in England or in Bangladesh, through dress. One exhibits the patriotism of an immigrant by wearing a sweatshirt with the Union Jack on it. A woman represents the "Bombay Look" with tight white jeans and a lacy blouse, the underwear showing through. A man exhibits ethnic pride by wearing a *punjabi* suit with a skullcap, fleece vest, and work boots.[22] The struggle of these transnational characters for identity through clothes is epitomized by the words spoken by a village laborer back home in Bangladesh: "You think that clothing is just a clothing. But as a matter of fact it is not. In a place like this it is a serious thing."[23]

I have found in my experience that, though most Indian people agree on the practical and symbolic importance of clothes, some of them, especially men, see the serious study of dress as a trivial matter. In 2001, I had the chance to speak of my research first at a conference sponsored by the Ford Foundation in Jaisalmer, Rajasthan, and then at a conference at the National Museum in Dhaka, Bangladesh. At both events, a few women came to me privately and expressed their excitement about my work, but I was dismayed by the responses of the wealthy, educated men and women in the audience. The women who spoke up said that folklore, as they understood it, is the study of "the folk," defined in India as the anonymous, illiterate, impoverished, perhaps tribal person. To analyze the choices made by regular people who live in cities, people much like themselves, rocked their sense of propriety. Although some of these women seemed to see the value of my study in terms of gender politics—the domestic act of personal adornment grants agency to women—they were discomfited by the implication that all women, regardless of socioeconomic position, can consciously deploy tradition in empowering ways.

The men in my audience simply trivialized the whole undertaking, making fun of me for viewing women like their wives as "artists" simply because they did what they do every day. They could not see such a commonplace activity as worthy of documentation and study. It is that attitude I wish to counter in this book. My intention is to show that the common act of dressing and adornment, accomplished by ordinary women in ordinary times, is a worthwhile endeavor, both for the women who are the performers of adornment and for the scholar of cultural creation. I hope this study will reveal the complexity of the art of adornment, and place it in the company of other undertakings in which personal creative energies and general cultural significance blend as art. I rely on many voices, in addition to my own, to support these points—those of the Indian men and women I had the good fortune to know, and also those of the female authors and filmmakers of India who guided me toward a deeper understanding of our shared culture.

I conclude my book by providing a model for the study of body art. It consists of a set of guidelines that I have derived from my study of adornment in India and from my readings in the relevant literature from folklore, anthropology, sociology, history, art history, and the history of fashion and dress. This model begins with the examination of acts of production and commerce, and then moves into the documentation of adornment forms and functions, including the body—the body static and in motion, the body modified in temporary, transitory, and permanent ways, the body dressed, and finally the body seen as an assemblage of many components. Once the items of adornment have been made and sold, and the body has been dressed, it takes on meaning in a series of social contexts. These include the contexts of life history, personal aesthetics, and individual repertoire; the temporal contexts that mark the transition of days, seasons, years, and the cycle of life; the spatial contexts that range from the utterly private to the totally public, from the bedroom through the joint-family home to foreign locales; and the contexts that are culturally constructed, such as gender, class, and religion. The final segment of this model, one particularly relevant for India, is the matter of assessment, both personal and social. In assessment, all the variables unify for judgment: the successful act gains praise or envy; the failed one prompts reprimand or ridicule. In coming to this conclusion, it is clear that I am acting within the paradigm of performance[24] as it has been successfully applied in material culture study for thirty years.

In conclusion, in preparation for the rest of the book, I end with comment on three major matters: language and orthography, the oppression of Indian women, and the goals of this book as a contribution to folklore scholarship.

First, on the topic of language, I allow, as often as possible, the people I interviewed in India to speak for themselves. Their words are presented in the same font size as mine are; they are not diminished and cramped as quotations often are in scholarly writings. I do not privilege my words over theirs.

Many of the interviews happened in a mixture of Hindi and English, which the marvelous flexibility of Hindi allows, and I have tried to retain this mix in my transcripts so the reader can see which words came from which language. I have translated all the statements into English. In the transcripts, I italicize all untranslated words, so the italicized words are either Hindi words I have not translated—*bindi,* for instance—or English words the speaker introduced into the flow of Hindi.

My aim is to render the language accessible to readers who are not familiar with Hindi, so I spell Hindi words without diacritics, sacrificing nuanced linguistic accuracy for ease in reading. I pluralize Hindi words with an "s," again to make them easy to read and to identify the word clearly as a plural. I spell the names of the gods, such as Ram and Ganesh, without the final "a," since that is how they are pronounced in Banaras. The "z" of many Urdu words, such as *nazar,* is pronounced in Banaras as a "j"—*najar*—a colloquial linguistic tendency I have preserved. Even though many place names have changed since the start of this study in 1996, I use the old names, partially because those were the names I learned in childhood but mostly because the people I know continue to use the old names. So, instead of Varanasi, Mumbai, Kolkata, and Chennai, I use the still prevalent old names, Banaras, Bombay, Calcutta, and Madras. Finally, in an attempt to introduce important foreign words, but to control their numbers, I alternate between a Hindi word and its English equivalent, such as *shobha* and grace (the translation that appears in the title of the book), except when there is no proper equivalent, such as, *salwar, sindur,* or *bindi.*

Second, I would like to explain how my book contributes to the topic of women's lives in India. While it is currently fashionable for both foreign and native scholars to fixate on the details of the suffering of women in India—a fact undeniable in its breadth and depth—that is not the only story. What amazes me is how women are able to express themselves, to accomplish their lives *in spite* of the hardships. Instead of seeing all women in India as helpless victims, I focus on those who are not, hoping to reveal the complex reality of India today. While many women suffer from bad marriages and spousal abuse—and these hardships are amply documented in current scholarship, literature, and cinema—many women find themselves in happy marriages, living in the kind of domestic comfort many Westerns enjoy. To show the complexity of the situation, to illustrate the varied reality of women in urban India, I sought out women who were happy, who expressed themselves through the art of self-adornment. In a true feminist spirit, I present the diversity of the female experience in India, describing not only those who are oppressed, but also those who are as free as women are anywhere.

Finally, this book is a work of folklore scholarship. Its aim is to record the life, culture, and art of a particular group of people, in a particular place and time. I seek the articulation of the choices and judgments that ordinary people make regarding the production, marketing, and wearing of clothing and jewelry. I strive to understand how people are able to express themselves as individuals and as members of communal groups defined by family, age, marital status, religion, and region. While the topic of choice in bodily adornment might seem trivial, especially to those in India where such knowledge is commonplace and basic, I document for the future, when change will inevitably come, and much of this detailed data will be lost forever.

A record of the decisions and aesthetic considerations of daily life is important not only for our general understanding of material culture, it is particularly important for our understanding of dress and fashion. Joanne Entwistle ends her magnificent book *The Fashioned Body* by urging scholars to study dress in the everyday, to note how choice becomes manifest in relation to the variables of age, class, race, ethnicity, and occasion. She believes, as do I, that dress should be seen as "situated bodily practice." It should be studied by noting the connections "between fashion and dress and between production and consumption."[25] My study of dress in India answers Entwistle's call for a new direction of study, and it counters the scholars who believe that, while Western people have a complex relationship with their clothes, the "ethnic dress and folk costumes" of others are merely artifacts, better studied as objects disconnected from the human body.[26] Our topic is the body adorned in the contexts of human choice and cultural significance.

·2·

Getting Ready

The most common of artistic acts, getting dressed requires an intricate series of choices. To sample the range of decisions women make on a daily basis, let us follow Rani Mishra, a twenty-seven-year-old Brahmin housewife, as she goes about her routine on a typical September day, in the old joint-family compound in which she lives, in the city of Banaras.

Rani, the mother of two young children, wakes up before her husband, at six in the morning. She rises, still wearing the magenta petticoat and blouse of yesterday's sari ensemble. The sari, a strip of cloth six meters in length, has to be tucked into a frame, provided by the "petticoat," an ankle-length skirt of cotton with a drawstring waist. A "blouse" (called, like the petticoat, by its English name), is a custom-stitched, midriff shirt, which closes snuggly with hooks running down the chest. Women own many blouses and petticoats, which are changed often to match the sari in color and fabric.

At night, Rani, like many women, simply unwraps her sari and sleeps in the underclothes that she has been wearing all day. For sleeping, some women prefer a "maxi," a floor-length cotton dress that some women wear around the house and others wear only in bed. Rani lives with her parents-in-law and her husband's brothers and their families; she feels uncomfortable wearing a maxi in the house, because she considers it an intimate garment. The audience for her daily adornment is large—her extended family, the servants, and the vegetable sellers who come into the house every day with their baskets of produce.

Rani wakes up and reaches for yesterday's magenta sari, which she hurriedly wraps around her. She goes into the bathroom, brushes her teeth, washes her face with water and sandalwood soap, and quickly fixes her hair, fastening it into a bun. She grabs one of the many *bindis* stuck in the corner of the mirror, and places it in the middle of her forehead. Going downstairs, she wakes her sleeping son, gets him ready for school, and sends him off with a snack. By this time, the other daughters-in-law of the household have joined Rani in the kitchen. The three of them start making the breakfast that the family will eat, as well as the lunch to be carried to school by the older children of the family. Rani, being the youngest of the daughters-in-law, is charged with delivering the daily "bed tea,"—a cup of sweet, milky tea—to the old couple, her husband's parents, who remain in bed.

By mid-morning, the men and children are eating their breakfast while the women continue with the preparations for lunch: chopping vegetables, kneading dough for bread, and sorting and cleaning the lentils and rice, removing bugs, pebbles, and other impurities. It is only after the lunch is ready that the women of the house take their baths and change their clothes. They prefer to get clean and dressed after the morning chores are completed, and they will take turns taking baths, since at least one woman must be around the kitchen when some of the children and men return home for lunch. The women serve the food from within the kitchen, carefully rationing out each item, making sure it lasts until the last family member has eaten.

At around noon, Rani goes upstairs to the bathroom adjacent to the bedroom she shares with her husband. Her daily routine, especially in the summer, is to take a bath while simultaneously washing by hand the sari, blouse, petticoat, and undergarments she has been wearing. She emerges from the bathroom in a clean, bright yellow sari, with matching yellow blouse and petticoat. Rani does not like the color yellow, but this sari was given to her, and she wears it around the house. One of the reasons women, including Rani, wear saris made of synthetic fabrics is the ease of "wash and wear." She is able to wash her own daily sari, hang it on the clothesline on the roof of the house, and fold it up at the end of the day, ready to wear again in a few days. Cotton saris need to be washed, starched, and pressed; they are sent out to the *dhobi*. Silk saris are expensive and special, worn only on exclusive occasions, such as wedding receptions. So she chooses synthetics for daily wear.

Rani's saris are bright in color because she is young, the last bride to enter the family. The saris hanging on the clotheslines reveal the age groups of the women who live in the household. The mother-in-law's sari is light blue with pale, tiny yellow flowers, a print fit for an older woman who should wear subtle colors and patterns. As age increases, the sari's color will turn subtler and paler, while the designs will shrink or disappear, until one reaches the pastel sari of the old mother-in-law, who lives in the penultimate stage of life. If she were a widow, her sari would be white, since widows are generally forbidden to wear color. By contrast, the brightest, most boldly patterned sari will belong to the youngest daughter-in-law. In this house, that is Rani.

Before her marriage, Rani wore a *salwar suit,* the usual dress for unmarried women, consisting of a tunic, a matching pair of drawstring pants, with a long scarf. And before that, like other prepubescent girls, she wore frocks, for she was then still young enough to show her knees and legs without shame. Although some married and older women choose to continue wearing *salwar suits,* especially at home, Rani does not. The sari is a sign of the married woman, and Rani prefers not to wear *salwar suits,* partially because such youthful dress embarrasses her now that she lives in a joint-family household, and partially because the sari is still a novelty to her. Saris are also relatively cool; they expose the back and the arms, sheathe the stomach in a thin layer of cloth, and allow air to rise up through the petticoat.

Rani, like most women in India, has long, thick black hair that she wears up in a bun. Hair worn down, "open," is considered sexy; associated with the Bollywood sirens, it too often inspires improper comments from men on the streets. Like many people in India, she washes her hair only on Sundays. During the rest of the week, she allows the natural oil of her hair to blend with the herbal oil she applies once a week, to create the organic luster of hair that is spared the chemical scorch of daily shampoos. On Sundays, after washing her hair, Rani applies *sindur,* the red powder that is a sign of the married woman, into the part in her hair. Throughout the week, she makes sure that the *sindur* is still visible in her part. Its lack is inauspicious, and her mother-in-law would scold her if she did not display this most important of the visual markers of marriage.

Rani returns from her bath in a fresh sari, with her hair fastened into its thick bun and a new *bindi,* a red felt adhesive sticker, applied to the middle of her forehead. After a quick *puja* to the household deities, an act that should not happen before a bath, she is ready to eat her lunch, in the early afternoon, in the company of the other women of the house. After lunch, they pile the dirty dishes in a corner; the woman who comes every afternoon to wash the kitchenware of the household will clean them later. Rani goes upstairs to take a nap in her bedroom. She is a light sleeper, so she removes the half dozen red glass bangles that she wears on each wrist, since their noise will keep waking her up. Rani does not like to wear glass bangles, but she must. Bangles are another sign of marriage for Hindu women, and glass bangles are customary in the state of Uttar Pradesh where she lives. Were she a Bengali, she would wear a set of a white shell and a red plastic bangle on each wrist. If she were Punjabi, she would wear gold bangles instead. Hindu women wear bangles to show not only their marital status, but their ethnic and regional identities as well.

Rani situates herself firmly in her lifecycle, her religion, and her region with her glass bangles. She further locates herself within her stage of life by the number of bangles she wears. The other women of the house wear fewer bangles, for they have been married longer, and it is considered inappropriate for older women to be ornamented with lots of jewelry, though it is perfectly acceptable for a newly married woman like Rani. Her old mother-in-law wears only one glass bangle on each wrist—the minimum number required to show that her husband is still alive. When Rani first arrived in this house, six years ago, she wore anklets with heavy bells on each leg. She wore two dozen glass bangles on each wrist, which she replaced each morning to match her saris. She wore gold hoop earrings, two golden necklaces, a big, teardrop *bindi* on her forehead; and she applied fresh *sindur* daily.

That was when she was the new bride. Her new family expected her to be fully bedecked to celebrate the marital union and the expanded household. She, too, liked the idea of wearing all the fabulous things she dreamed about as a teenager, when, being unmarried, her adornment was prohibited. Now she has been married for six years, and she is a mother. Her responsibilities in the house have increased; she cooks and cleans more than she did as a new wife. She must bathe and care for her children. All of these jobs take time, and they might damage nice jewelry and saris. Her number of ornaments has decreased, and she has temporarily removed the rings that might scratch her infant daughter. The novelty of getting dressed up everyday has worn off. Rani does not change her glass bangles to match her saris anymore; she wears some on each wrist, until they break off, at which point she adds more, not taking care to match them, unless she goes out. She still wears anklets, but now they have tiny bells that make a slight sound. She wears only one toe ring per foot, but these are elegant, with colorful *mina* enamel work on each one. A wife must wear toe rings—along with *bindi, sindur,* and bangles—to signal marriage, but the style of jewelry is left to the individual's discretion. Rani has always liked her feet, and likes to see them decorated with anklets, toe rings, and nail polish. She has in her closet a few pairs of silver toe rings, and she changes them regularly for her personal pleasure.

After the afternoon nap, the household routine continues with snacks prepared for the returning kids and tea for the adults. Many women, including Rani, "get fresh," touching themselves up before the arrival of their husbands. Late in the afternoon on weekdays, before her husband returns from the office, Rani fixes her sari and hair, splashes water on her face, puts on her bangles again, re-attaches her *bindi,* and makes snacks and tea, in anticipation of her husband's return. Sometimes they sit together on the veranda, sipping tea and exchanging the day's news. Many women look forward to this time when they hear about the outside world. Most women do not venture out every day, and when they do run an errand, they leave and return quickly.

Early evening brings the preparation of dinner and helping with homework for the women of the house. The men, who have lived in this house and neighborhood all their lives, usually go out to visit with their male friends from childhood, who are now also married and whose wives have, like Rani, moved into their husbands' parental homes. The men visit each other, drinking tea or chewing *paan,* while the women, once strangers to the new house, rely on the company of their sisters-in-law, forming their community within the household compound.

On special occasions, the women go out to parties, especially wedding receptions and birthday parties, when they wear their best saris and often have their finest jewelry retrieved from the bank locker, where it is stored for safekeeping. A few times a month, Rani will go out with her husband, either to the movies, or to the temple to take *darshan* of the gods. They usually travel on her husband's Bajaj scooter, with her sitting sidesaddle on the back. Today, he told her before he left for work that they would go to the temple in the evening, and that she must be ready when he returns at seven o'clock. After their visit to the Vishvanath Temple, they will enjoy *masala dosas* at a nearby fast food restaurant. After that, they will return to the quiet home, where Rani will lay out her son's school uniform and his knapsack before she goes to sleep.

An hour before her husband's return, Rani starts to get ready. She unlocks the metal *almari* in her bedroom, where her saris are kept, folded and neatly piled. She must decide which one to wear. The choice is a pleasure for Rani, as it is for other women, because while she chooses, she will inventory the items in her possession. Rani takes out a stack of saris, examining each, reminding herself of where she bought this one or who gave her that one. Associations with her family—parents and siblings who are far away—are carried in the saris, which are often given as gifts to women at the end of a visit, when they leave their natal home to return to their conjugal home.

Rani does not take out the heavily brocaded silk Banarasi saris. They are too fancy for a visit to the temple, and they are too hot for this late summer evening. She does not want to wear one of her favorite cotton saris; they have just come back from the cleaners, and must be kept fresh for the upcoming visit to her brother's house. A light pink georgette sari, though pretty, is rejected because it will get dirty on the way to the temple. She will save it for an occasion when they go somewhere in the family car or taxi, comfortably enclosed in a vehicle, protected from dust and smoky exhaust. Rani takes out a parrot-green, tie-dyed cotton sari given to her by a relative who visited from Rajasthan, then remembers that she never got a matching blouse made for it, and finally she selects a dark purple sari, with a thin layer of gold brocading on the edges and tiny diamond-shaped motifs in red sprinkled across the field.

Once she has chosen her sari, Rani must decide on the petticoat and the blouse. She does not have a purple petticoat, but since this sari is not transparent, she can wear a black petticoat that will be indistinguishable at night. She has a purple blouse as well as a red one with gold on the edge. She chooses the latter to bring out the red in the sari's motifs, and to show that she has been keeping up with the latest fashions. Nightly television shows feature actresses wearing saris and blouses in contrasting colors. This is not a wedding reception, where she will be seen by people in her social circle, but she is going to a great public temple, where she might run into people she knows, and, if so, she would like to impress them with her keen, up-to-date aesthetic sense.

After the sari, blouse, and petticoat have been selected and ironed, she turns her attention to the accessories. Rani decides to wear red bangles, rejecting the purple ones, which are not quite the right shade, and the redness, she feels, will match the blouse. Among the red glass bangles, a dozen on each arm, she places in symmetrical perfection four gold ones to bring out the brocaded accents of gold on both the sari and the blouse. This will be a pleasurable outing, she will be alone with her husband, and Rani chooses to dress beautifully to lift her mood and appear attractive to her spouse. She wears more bangles than she does at home because she will not be engaged in housework, because she wants to look good, and because she secretly, certainly wants to look better than the wives of her husband's childhood friends, should they chance to run into each other at the temple.

With half an hour to spare, Rani starts to get dressed. She washes her face, sprinkles lilac powder on her body, puts on her blouse and petticoat, and before wrapping her sari, she steps into her mid-heel sandals that reveal her pretty feet. It is only after she has assessed her new height that she puts on the sari, making sure to adjust it to fall correctly at the ankles. She then puts on the bangles that she has already arranged into sets. After studying herself in the mirror, she removes the bangles, eliminating the golden ones, deciding that they are too dressy for this particular occasion. She must appear beautiful without seeming "gaudy." The exaggerated gaudy look, marked by gold and glitter, is commonly associated with *hijras*—cross-dressed eunuchs—or with village women, who prefer flashy fabrics and prints. Rani avoids the negative and she strives to conform to the look appropriate to her caste and her family's standing. Her mother-in-law frequently reminds her that she now represents her new family everywhere she goes, especially in Banaras, where their family has lived for generations, and she has a certain social reputation to uphold.

Rani continues to wear the short golden chain on her neck which she wears every day, but she decides to add another, a long golden *mangalsutra* with tiny black beads. She owns such a marriage necklace in real gold, but that one is in the bank locker, and she chooses to wear an "artificial" one of gold-plated silver instead. Their visit will take them through densely crowded streets, and rumors of thefts in public have alarmed her. Rani looks in the mirror; she likes the combination of sari, blouse, shoes, and jewelry. She adds a round purple and gold *bindi* to her forehead, leaving her hair in a thick inky bun. The current vogue of "open hair," sported by the heroines of the movies and television, is not for her. After applying face powder, she lines her black eyes with kohl and adds dark pink lipstick to her lips. She has always preferred maroon lipstick, but her husband feels it makes her skin look dark. She squirts some Charlie perfume on her chest, saturating her sari with scent, grabs a little beaded purse and puts in it a handkerchief, a necessity in this sweaty and smoggy city. As soon as she hears her husband honk his scooter's horn, Rani starts for the stairs, then pauses for a last glimpse of herself in the mirror. Lovely, she is satisfied with her choices. She ventures out, ready to be seen.

·3·

Gaze, Sacred and Secular

SEEING AND BEING SEEN are given particular importance in Hindu India by the concept of *darshan,* sacred sight. An understanding of the power of sight in Hinduism—for communication and for blessing—helps contextualize the secular realm of vision, aiding in our appreciation of how individuals make judgments and convey messages based on what people wear. In the moment of worship, eye contact and focused vision establish connection and narrow the gap between the devotee and the deity. In the crowded street, people temporarily join in brief, casual or intense, exchanges of contact through the eyes.

Sacred Gaze

Darshan, auspicious sight, is a visual exchange between a worshiper and a *murti*—a representation of a deity in stone, metal, or clay—during the act of *puja.* Whether or not the statue eternally contains the deity varies in different parts of India. In some places, the statue is a permanent embodiment of the deity that can be worshiped at any time. In others, it is a receptacle into which the deity descends, and through which the god is worshiped. *Darshan* means the gaze of the person looking at a deity and the gaze of the deity looking back at the person. To take *darshan* of a deity—in Hindi, *darshan karna,* to do *darshan*—is proof of proximity, legitimizing the experience of being in the same place as a god. This concept may also apply to seeing an important human being. People used to crowd for a glimpse of Mahatma Gandhi, to take *darshan,* carrying away a bit of him, a fleeting vision of the Great Soul permanently stored in the mind's eye.

When people go to the temple to pray, they often say that they are going for *darshan.* While there, they are engaged in the complete act of *puja,* using their bodies and many of the senses, yet the whole of the experience focuses on sacred vision. During *puja,* devotees enter the temple, feeling the cold floor of marble or tile with their bare feet. They humble themselves, bowing and prostrating their bodies, placing their palms together in the presence of god. They smell the incense and the flowers. They taste the sweet *prashad* given to them by the god—via the priest—as a blessing. They ring the cold brass bell, the sound resonating through the temple, through their ears. With their eyes they appeal to the god, asking for boons, promising to give something in return for the granted request. Thus a contract is made between the worlds, between the worshiper and the god. Although devotion to the gods involves many bodily gestures, and many senses, it is through direct eye contact, through the visual channel, that one asks for a favor or offers thanks to the gods, who in turn bless the faithful by looking back, training their enormous and benevolent eyes upon their devotee.

Diana Eck's excellent book on the topic of *darshan* properly situates this important act within India. She includes in her discussion the importance of *darshan* in the city of Banaras, where sacred sight is of particular significance.[1] Banaras is a pilgrimage site to which people come expressly for *darshan,* to see the city itself, but also to behold the Shiva *linga* in the Vishvanath Temple, and to gaze at Ganga, the goddess embodied in the mystical river. This crowded city, gathering a representative cross section of the population of the country, is not only a place to take sacred sight of the gods; it is also a place of secular sight, where the dense population mingles and mills, where people satisfy their curiosity by looking hard at all who crowd the *galis* and the *ghats.* In this way, Banaras is like the Taj Mahal, where one goes to look at the magnificent mausoleum—and at the other people who have come too, noting what they are wearing, how they walk and talk, and how they look.

In Banaras, as in any Indian city, the streets fill with action; life spills outside into the open. In the narrow alleys, cows rummage through the trash, people cook and chop vegetables, tailors bend over chattering sewing machines, children play, and, with remarkable frequency, men urinate in the gutters. By the river, one sees people washing clothes and bathing, mourners having their heads shaved, and children taking swimming lessons. Ironically,

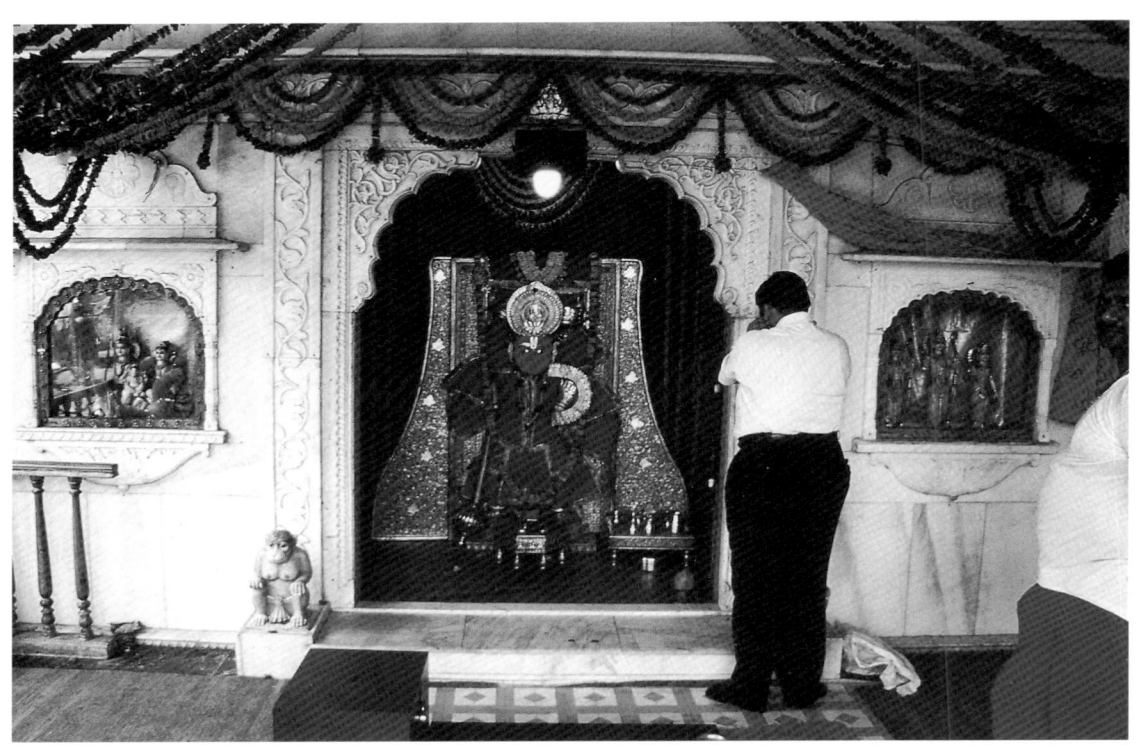

Taking *darshan;* Temple to Hanuman, Jaipur, Rajasthan

although these everyday activities are easily visible, the sacred sights—the reason to come to Banaras—are much harder to see. Contrary to popular, and often romantic, notions of Hinduism as an open and free religion, there are many physical barriers between the people and their gods.

Many of the ancient temples of the city are hidden behind gates and walls and buildings erected between the *mandir* and the street. The walls of the narrow *galis* hide the temples behind them. On almost every street of the old city, especially in the area of the Vishvanath Gali, one may look up, and see an old stone temple that was not noticed in hundreds of previous passings. Many of the temples—including the main Vishvanath *mandir,* the Golden Temple—prohibit entrance to non-Hindus, including the foreigners who had been lured by their guidebooks and their local Indian guides to come to Banaras and see the Golden Temple.[2] Signs posted on this temple and on others, not to mention the gun-toting guards, make it clear that admission is restricted. Once inside the temple, if you arrive at the wrong time, the deity might be asleep, resting behind the closed doors or drawn curtains of the sanctuary. At the appropriate times for *darshan,* particularly during the evening *aarti,* the statues are available for sight, but they are often obscured by bright fabrics and an abundance of shiny ornaments. Part of the satisfaction of *darshan* is that it is an achievement. Despite all the obstacles that stand between you and the god—barred doors, iron grills on windows, armed guards, crowds, mediating priests eager for money, and the statue's veiling clothes and ornaments—at last, with the help of Ganesh, you get through and eventually accomplish sustained eye contact, blissful and calming, soothing and sweet. The struggle has been wholly worthwhile.

Making eye contact with the deity is the most important ritual act, and it is the extent of direct connection made with a god in a temple. In Hinduism, the *pujari* mediates between the god and the faithful. You cannot walk up and touch the main statues in a temple. They are placed in a sanctuary, separated from the people. Relation with them is literally mediated by the priests. Offerings of flowers or sweets are handed to the *pujari,* who places them at the feet of the statue. Divine blessings of sweets, flowers, *aarti,* or *tikka,* are offered to the worshiper by the *pujari,* acting on behalf of the god.

A popular time for *darshan* is in the evenings, during the regular *aarti,* when the *pujari* publicly worships the deity with oil lamps, incense, chants, and finally a distribution of *prashad* to all present. It is a joyous time to be at the temple, when cooling breezes carry incense into the dark, but this crowded event makes it hard to sustain eye contact with the statue. People struggle to see, moving slightly, constantly shifting in the crowd to maintain the god in their line of vision. The gods, in turn, strive to see you as well, to bless you among the crowd gathered before them. For this reason the *murtis* are made with big heads (in proportion to their bodies), and big eyes, and they wear ornaments that extend the frame of their faces and bodies, making them seem even larger, as though they were striving to become visually available to all in the vast assembly, including those far in the back.[3] Images of the gods—the statues in the temples, the pictures at home—are made to sustain your gaze, not only by increasing the size of the head and face, but also by making the gods splendid and beautiful—their beauty inspiring awe, stirring love, and making it impossible to take your eyes off them.

The practical reason to make the god beautiful is to attract the gaze to the deity's face. A sweet and pleasing face fixes your eye on the statue during worship, keeping your concentration on prayer and focused away from the distraction of the noise and crowds at the temple or domestic compound. Asking the deity to help them overcome obstacles, when they pray at the *mandir,* people momentarily escape their flawed lives. They do not think of their hardships; they enjoy the sweet smell of incense, and look upon the beautiful statue, partaking for a brief moment of hope in the magnificence of the god. While beholding the statue in *darshan,* the worshiper is actively engaged in an intense aesthetic experience, forgetting, perhaps, the immediate cares of household violence or poverty or hunger. The temple is a place of distraction, of repose, where the worshiper is engulfed in pleasing sensory experiences: the cool evening air, the shade under a sacred tree, the music and chanting, and the pretty, shiny things that surround the resplendent *murti* of the temple. It can be argued that the grace of the statue is imperative, necessary, basic; it provides worshipers with a temporary refuge from their lives and gives them a glimpse of perfect beauty; it becomes a reminder of the ultimate benevolence of the gods and the blissful eternal life that awaits, if they are granted escape from the incessant cycles of rebirth. The beauty of the Hindu gods is, of course, culturally subjective. What Indians find blissfully attractive has been historically viewed by colonists and ignorant foreigners as portrayals of "infernal creatures and diabolic, multiple-limbed monsters."[4]

Hindu deities are deliberately portrayed by the artists who make *murtis* as incarnations of an abstracted, idealized beauty. Like the *pujaris,* the artists mediate between gods and human beings.[5] Craftsmen derive from scripture or receive as a revelation an image of a god that they in turn materialize for our worship. Makers of Hindu *murtis* in Bangladesh shape the forms and curves of the body of god, they say, by reference to nature, intentionally perfecting nature's inherent patterns and symmetries in their sacred creations.[6] In addition to responding to the beauty of the natural world, Bengali makers of *murtis* in Banaras also deliberately render the faces of the female goddesses, most notably Durga,[7] to look like the latest Bollywood heroines. In 1996, in the Bengali neighborhood of Banaras, I met Phallu Dada, a maker of life-sized clay statues that were modeled on an armature of wood and straw and then painted and ornamented. He told me that the lovely faces of Bollywood actresses Hema Malini, Shridevi, and Mathuri Dixit were the inspiration for his depiction of the face of Durga. Phallu Dada explained that his statues were made on commission to local Bengali private groups, and he was adhering to the wishes of his clients who preferred to worship a statue of Durga that resembled a beautiful screen heroine. (Goddesses and movie stars both represent the pinnacle of a culturally shared notion of beauty. One reason the women became famous actresses in the first place is that they resembled the popularly held images of what Lakshmi, Durga, or Saraswati look like. And then, one reason the deities look so beautiful is that they are modeled on movie stars.)

Rajesh Kumar Gour, co-owner and manager of the Jaipur Murti Bhandar, a factory where statues are carved by hand in the Lallapura neighborhood of Banaras, also noted the influence of Bollywood actresses in the depictions of the faces of Hindu goddesses, especially Durga. He said the "Hema Malini fashion" was at its peak in 1987 or 1988. At that time the actress, known to many as *Sapno ke Rani*—"Queen of Dreams"—was the earthly model for the face of Durga, because it was generally agreed, he said, that she had the face of Durga.[8] Since the actress resembles the image we have in our minds of Durga, artists can use her face to help them shape the perfect face of the goddess. Here again the circle of affect closes, revealing a deep, consistent aesthetic of female beauty.[9] Rajesh told me in 2003 that we are currently in the Aishwarya Rai moment, a time in which the winner of the Miss World Beauty Pageant in 1994 serves as the model for the graceful face of Durga.

Since the Jaipur Murti Bhandar factory provides statues for many parts of India, the owners have had a chance to observe regional variables in taste. Rajesh explained, for example, that Nepalis want their gods to have wider and flatter noses, while Biharis like long faces, and people from Uttar Pradesh and Bengal prefer their gods with round faces. People want their statues to be both beautiful and familiar—fit to a regional concept of beauty. The factory's workers, its *karigars,* also carve stone statues of deceased people, usually commissioned by family members. For this category of work, Rajesh said, his clients want the statue to look like the real person, but his clients look for beauty in the *murti,* because nobody really knows what the gods look like. All we know, he said, is that they are beautiful.

I asked Rajesh if male gods were also commissioned to look like the latest Bollywood heroes. He and his workers laughed at this, explaining that movie influence applies only to the female statues. Men can be like gods in temperament. He said that someone can be "rough-tough" like Shankar Bhagwan—like Shiva—but you would never say that somebody looks like Shiva, only that he acts like the god. But the connection between the beauty of the goddesses and the beauty of ordinary women is a recurrent theme in India. New brides may be likened to Ram's perfect wife, Sita, in behavior, temperament, and appearance. Many women, including the actresses mentioned above, are seen as embodying the kind of beauty associated with Durga, Radha, Sita, or Lakshmi (even though all of these are usually depicted, in essence, with the same face). Men, on the other hand, are seen being as brave as Ram, as "rough-tough" as Shiva, or as strong as Hanuman.[10]

Rajesh told me that the beauty of the statue is concentrated on the face; the worshiper's eye only catches the area from the "*mukut* to *har*"—from the crown to the necklace—because people during *darshan* only really focus on the face. Since the body of the statue is covered with clothes and ornaments anyway, he said, the beauty of the god radiates from the face alone. One of the functions of the ornaments that statues wear is to shift attention to the face, forcing the eye to move up from the necklaces, to move down from the bejeweled crown, and to move in from the elaborate earrings—all of these ornaments serving to bring the devotee's gaze into the auspicious eyes of the god.

About the powerful relationship between ornamentation and the Hindu gods much has been written by art historians, including Stella Kramrisch in her classic study of Hindu temples.[11] It is through their ornaments that we recognize not only the beauty of the gods, but also their identities, attributes, and personalities. Priceless gems adorn the royal couple Ram and Sita, for instance, while animal skins, cobras, and the crescent moon decorate the meditative yogi Shiva. Although the faces and bodies of the gods—whether carved of stone, molded in clay, cast in bronze, or drawn on paper—are similarly idealized, the types and amounts of ornaments differ, according to the mythological character of each deity. Ornaments function to convey messages about the gods in visual representations, as well as in the verbal and written renditions of mythology. The *Ramayana,* in most written, oral, or dramatic versions, contains several key scenes in which jewelry plays a vital role in communication. Ram and Sita, in preparation for their exile, display their generosity by giving away their precious jewelry to their loyal servants. Sita tosses her ornaments from the air when she is abducted by Ravan, in hopes of communicating her whereabouts to her husband. In Lanka, Hanuman proves to Sita his role as Ram's emissary by handing her Ram's ring. And back in Ayodhya, Sita publicly rewards Hanuman's valor by tying a precious string of pearls around his neck.[12]

Ornaments in Hindu mythology, in legends and folktales, signal the power of jewelry to express valor, wealth, generosity, affection, identity, and social relationship. By carefully noting jewelry, clothing, and body art in narratives, we gain insight into the personality and status of the being so adorned. It is this tendency to invest bodily ornament with significance that is carried smoothly from the sacred and ancient realm of religion into the modern realm of common secular life.

Ornaments are not only used by the gods to express their feelings for one another, they are also used by worshipers and by priests to express their love for their gods. Wealthy devotees often give golden ornaments to temple statues as a form of payment for a granted boon, and as a way of courting special favor with the god. Devotees at home and *pujaris* in the temples decorate and dress the gods as a loving act of devotion. Some priests even exhibit their privileged status, and their connection to the gods they serve, by wearing an abundance of golden jewelry themselves. The National Handicrafts and Handlooms Museum in New Delhi contains in its collection an exquisite nineteenth-century necklace made of Shiva's sacred *rukdraksh* beads, gold, silver, and gemstones, that was worn by *pujaris* in Tamil Nadu during ceremonial occasions.[13]

The connection between beauty and *darshan* extends outward from the radiance of the ornamented god, past the gleam of the bejeweled *pujari,* to the jewelry on the body of the devotee. Vendors lined up outside of temples sell offerings to please the gods—cloth, flowers, and sweets—and items to please the *darshan*-seeking worshipers: hair ribbons, rings, bangles, *bindis,* and *sindur.* Gazing upon the lovely face of the god, the devotee is thrilled by beauty itself—the beauty of the deity, of the nature abstracted in the *murti,* of the temple that houses the god and the service in devotion. Taking *darshan*—an act that irrevocably involves the notion of beauty—reinforces the importance of looking good for oneself, for others, and even before the eyes of the god. The deity's grandeur and magnificence extends beyond its body to its throne, its *vahana,* its adulatory priests, and its devout devotees. As Joanna Waghorne has observed for South India, all of these extensions can be seen as further ornaments, glorifying the body and enhancing the status of the god.[14] We, in our role as devotees, not only offer the gods ornaments as gifts of love, but by surrounding the statue with our sincere devotion, we offer ourselves as symbolic ornaments to our gods.

Sacred sight is a way in which Hindu gods are worshiped, and a medium through which knowledge about the divine is acquired visually. The *murtis* in the temples are mediated by the priests who explain and teach about the gods. Images are also commonly brought into the home in the form of calendar art,[15] television serials, such as those of the *Mahabharata* and the *Ramayana,*[16] and comic books.[17] These images are, for the most part, unmediated, carrying little or no text with them, and relying heavily, therefore, on the visual communication of messages through scenery, posture, and body art. In the *Amar Chitra Katha* comic book series, for instance, the personality of each character is depicted by carefully drawn facial features and body types, and by a deliberate choice of clothes and jewelry. The pattern is clear: *rakchas* monsters are fat and ugly, with bulging eyes and wild hair, whereas *deva* gods are slender and beautiful, fair-skinned, with classically symmetrical faces, including elongated deer eyes, sharp noses, and rosebud lips. Goddesses lounge around luxurious palaces; they are always voluptuous, scantily dressed with bare midriffs, heaving, heavy breasts, and broad hips, and they wear thick golden ornaments on many parts of their bodies. Male deities, on the other hand, are rendered as hairless and effeminate, with lovely faces, soft, supple flesh, big eyes, and full lips.

The gods depicted in these popular mediums, unlike the *murtis* in the temples, can be encountered without proper context. When you go to the Durga temple and face the goddess in the main sanctuary, you know that this is Durga. But a calendar art image is devoid of the locational context of the temple, and the accompanying captions of the comic books. Therefore, calendar art images—the most popular representations of the deities—rely more than any other divine portrayal on visual details: facial expression, bodily posture, *vahanas*—the deity's symbolic animal vehicles—and body art. In addition to iconic representations of the gods standing with their palms outstretched in the "fear not" *mudra,* images on calendar art often depict major episodes of mythological narratives, including key scenes from the *Ramayana.*[18]

Valmiki's lyrical epic, *The Ramayana,* was translated from Sanskrit into Hindi by Tulsi Das in Banaras, at Tulsi Ghat, to make it accessible to the masses. Yet many cannot read Hindi or the other languages into which the epic has been translated and published. Though most people have never read the entire *Ramayana,* all Hindus know the general sequence of events, for they have heard stories from the epic told, they have watched the Ram *lila* play, or they have seen performances with painted story boards. The main source of knowledge for the principal events in the epic, though, is the daily visual inundation—calendar art, statues, murals, stickers—all showing the gods engaged in the epic scenes in which they battle with evil and do the right thing.

Hinduism, unlike other major religions, does not have one fundamental sacred book. In India, sacred texts regularly take material form, since in the Hindu religion, "mythic systems are centered by icons, not narratives."[19] People in this place of high illiteracy and multiple, mutually unintelligible vernacular languages, each with its own distinct script, rely on visual imagery of the gods and depictions of their deeds to carry the narratives. These images illustrate the stories, and stories in turn are created to explain the images of the gods.[20] In India, religion is understood through the physical, visual manifestation of its gods and their acts. Images disseminate episodes of the narratives and inspire the construction of narratives. To read an image, you need prior knowledge in order to decipher the coded message, and depending on who you are, and how much you know, you may be able to read deeper and deeper levels of significance.[21] This process of visual deep reading is transferred from the overwhelmingly complex pantheon of Hinduism into the secular realm, enabling people to read subtle communications from visual presentations; especially those created by women, when, getting dressed, they encode messages in their adornment, messages directed simultaneously to different readers who are able to read down to different levels of semantic depth.

In Hinduism, seeing—*darshan*—is a form of direct communication and blessing, and vision is a key mode of acquiring information about the wondrous array of deities. Attending to religious imagery, we gain an appreciation for the concept of sacred vision, and we come directly to an understanding of the shaping ideal of beauty. Cultural notions of beauty have developed out of

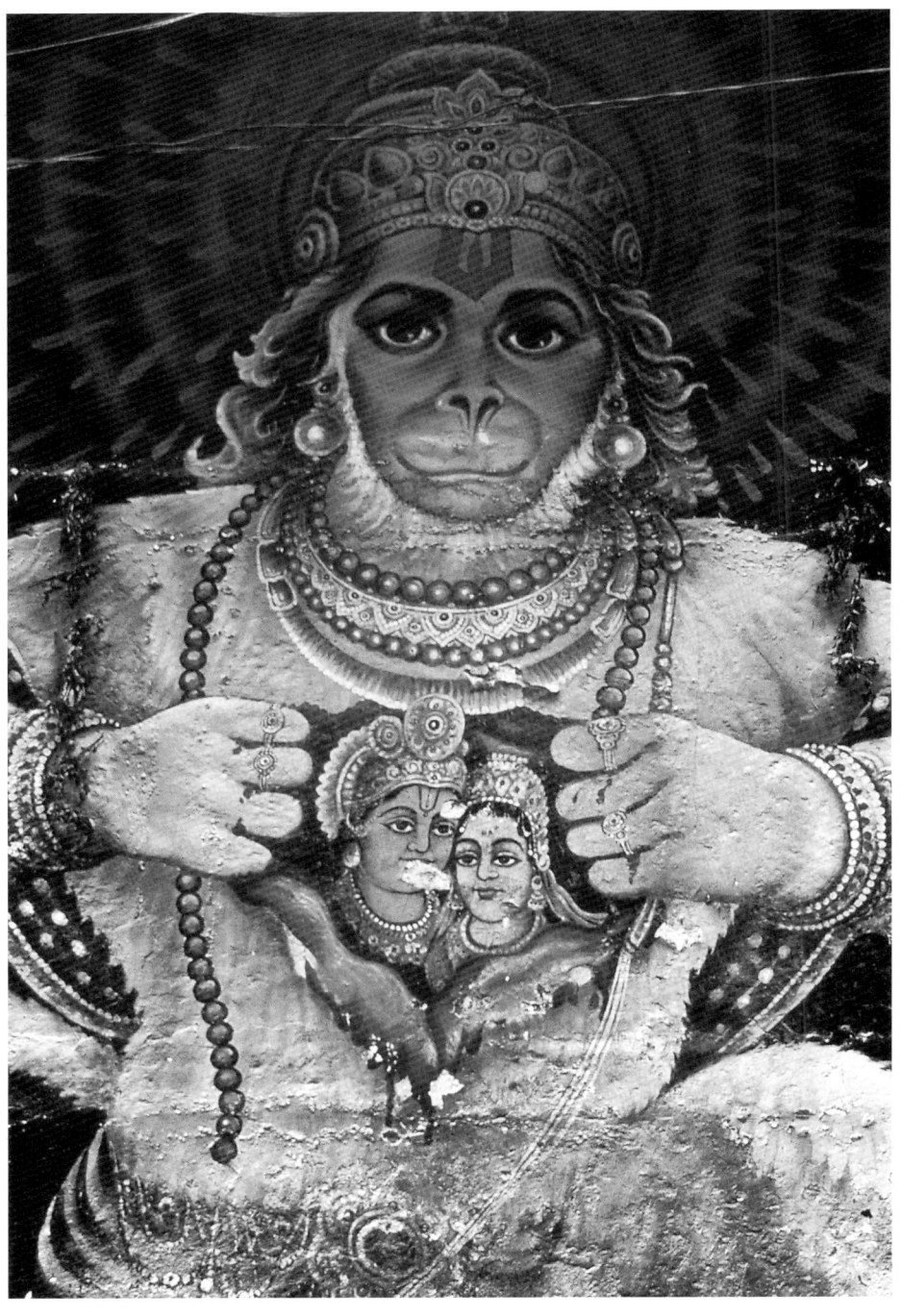

Mural painting of Hanuman ripping his heart open
to reveal Ram and Sita, Vishvanath Gali

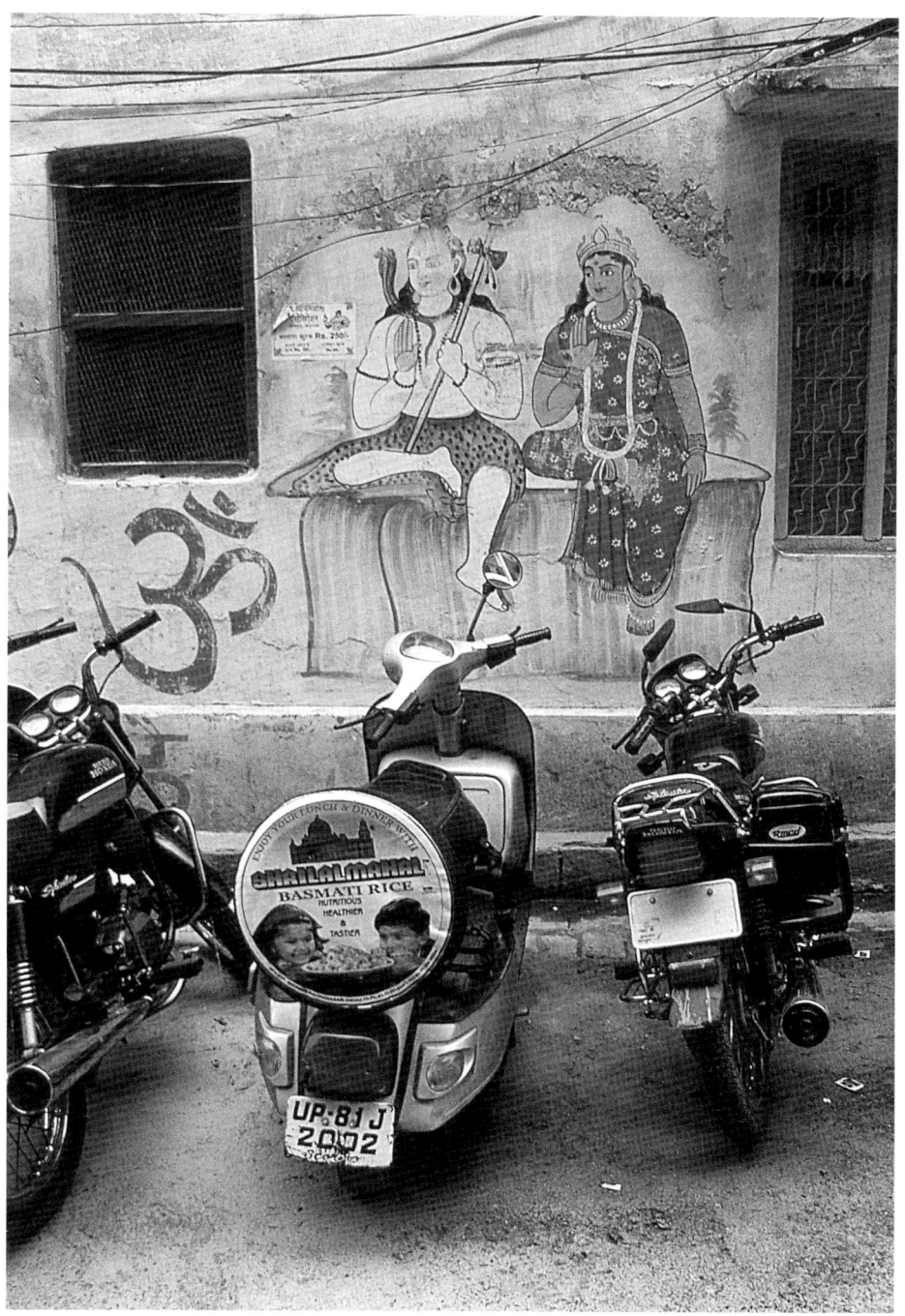

Mural painting of Shiva and Parvati, Luxa Road

Hindu imagery. The beauty of the goddesses, largely inspired by nineteenth-century master artist Ravi Varma's oleographed paintings[22]—are used to assess the most beautiful women of today: movie stars and beauty queens. Then these women become models for the statues of the goddesses. Old ideals of divine beauty are made to fit our current age when pictures of contemporary women are used to shape the look of the statues in the temples.

During *darshan,* what is important is that visual connection has occurred, that you have seen things with your own eyes. It does not matter how long the vision lasts; contact has been made, fleeting though it may have been. Sight can be quick and momentary when the main variables and general parameters of culture lie in the mind. Quick glances are not necessarily meant to gather information; rather, they can be a means of visual acknowledgement. When people—I especially remember my Aunt Nirmala in Banaras—zoom past a shrine in a rickshaw, they quickly make eye contact with the obscured statue within, bowing the head for an instant, while continuing on down the street. Aunt Nirmala took what I call drive-by *darshan.* She knew that at a particular spot just ahead there was a statue of Hanuman, and she paid her respects visually as she sped by, making a point of glimpsing it in symbolic *darshan* despite the crowded street, the closed shrine, and the wobbly, rickety rickshaw.

In an overpopulated country in which vision is an important aspect of worship, people are used to seeing things momentarily, yet deeply. The religious images that are installed in the home and owned by the devotee can be the recipients of prolonged daily vision, while public images may receive only a quick glance, especially during the popular times and places for *darshan.* Rajesh Kumar Gour, of the Jaipur Murti Bhandar, told me a story that perfectly illustrates this point. Early in 2003, Rajesh went to Andra Pradesh for *darshan* of the famous Tirupati Tirumala (Balaji) Vishnu statue. He said that the temple is atop a mountain that requires the pilgrims to climb and climb. In order to see the statue, one needs to purchase a token that enables access.[23] Tokens can be bought for 1, 5, 10, 50, 100, 500, and 1,000 rupees (there are also limited spaces for free *darshan*). Rajesh had requested, four days in advance, a 500-rupee token. On the day of his purchased *darshan,* he woke up at two o'clock in the morning, worked his way through the elaborate security screening, and still waited five hours for his *darshan,* despite his expensive token. When he finally arrived in front of the Lord Balaji *murti,* he could not look for longer than a few seconds, since he was pushed out of the way by a temple attendant in order to make room for the next pilgrim. Rajesh described the beauty of the god by talking about the abundance of diamonds and gold worn by the statue. He said, as many others do, that Lord Balaji is "the richest god in the world."[24]

What is interesting about this particular South Indian representation of Vishnu is that the god is swathed literally from head to toe in jewels—gifts from devotees. His eyes are so powerful that they have to be shielded. So an act of *darshan* of the Tirumala Balaji statue ironically involves limited eye-to-eye contact; the eyes are nearly hidden behind bright blinders. Jyotindra Jain and Aarti Aggarwala, in describing the jewels of the Tirumala *murti*, recommend that pilgrims wear sunglasses during *darshan* in order to protect their eyes from the power of the god.[25] In this case, the contact is between the eyes of the worshiper and the splendid aura of the god. Rajesh did not seem to mind that he was only granted a few seconds for *darshan*. The act of being there was sufficient, and he considered it a blessing to be standing in front of the magnificent god, partaking of his grace, if only for a moment.

Rajesh's personal narrative gives us an interesting perspective on both the concept of *darshan* and the value of pilgrimage. Of importance are the hardships of travel, the cost, the endurance, and the effort to get there, rather than the amount of time engaged in the actual act of *darshan*. The commitment to undertake the pilgrimage is an act of worship, climaxed by the brief yet meaningful visual connection. *Darshan,* in this and many other cases, is not necessarily a matter of careful and sustained sight, but rather of the gathering of an impression, a blur, a glimpse into something that, in combination with preconceived notions, aids in the recreation of an image and a judgment of what was seen. A nuanced understanding of *darshan* helps us understand the quick assessments people make on the streets about others from their appearance, forming opinions by gathering visual information on the fly and later analyzing it in accord with generally understood cultural parameters of appropriate dress.

Secular Gaze

The visual orientation of Indian culture, conditioned by the centrality of vision in the Hindu religion, extends into the secular realm in many ways. Visual communication of status and the importance of symbolic ornamentation, so characteristic of images of the gods, are both historically relevant in relation to Indian *rajas* and emperors. The relationship between a king and his subject is analogous in many respects to that between gods and their devotees. During the courtly display ritual of *durbar,* Indian kings would, like gods, make themselves available for *darshan.* In this self-conscious exhibition, material belongings of all kinds as well as subordinates and servants were proudly displayed as possessions, working together to aggrandize the authority and beauty of the king, as Joanna Waghorne demonstrates in her excellent treatment of *durbar.*[26] Just as the devotees may serve as ornaments to their gods, subjects may serve as ornaments to their kings. By extension, family members—the men well-employed, the women richly dressed, the children well-behaved—can all serve as ornaments to the family patriarch, exemplifying his wealth, grace, and rule. Some scholars have viewed critically the notion that Indian wives can be perceived as ornaments of their husbands and their families. They are not wrong in feeling like that, but the idea does not render women passive, for they work to fill their role and feel that with their grace, personality, and beauty, they reflect positively on their husbands, like a jewel, helping their men and their families, and themselves, look better in the eyes of society. The ultimate modern-day *durbar,* the epitome of something that could be called "secular *darshan,*" is the wedding ceremony, in which the bride and groom sit on thrones, making themselves available to be seen, the new bride dressed literally from head to toe in glittery, beautiful things.

One purpose of this wedding scene in which the bride and groom pose on ornate red and gold chairs is to provide an opportunity for photographs by family members, who take turns standing behind the pair to have a snapshot taken with the newly married couple. The picture proves that one was present at the wedding (much as a snap of oneself in front of the Taj Mahal is preferable to a picture of the marvelous Taj all alone). The visual dimensions of the wedding include the display of the beauty of the bride and the splendor of her clothes and jewelry, which are supplied by her family and therefore reflect their wealth and social position. These messages can be conveyed across space and time, as the transportable, durable photographs capture the moment for posterity.[27] In fact, the power of *darshan,* too, often works through photographic renditions. A photograph of the Vishvanath *linga* at the Golden Temple (where photography is prohibited) is sold everywhere in Banaras, carried in people's wallets and purses, and taken home to be propped on domestic altars.

Just as people function as symbolic ornaments to their gods through devotion and loyalty, so people serve as ornaments to other people, to their kings, husbands, and families. Status is judged by the kinds and amount of ornaments surrounding the deity or person, attesting to the importance of the visual communication of distinctions through things. A man's valor, like a god's power, is intangible and symbolized materially. Military men are "decorated" with ribbons and medals—a style of visual convention that signifies their bravery and heroism. One need not know what each medal denotes; the sheer presence (and accumulation) conveys the message, though, as in religious matters, deeper knowledge brings deeper meanings. Appropriately, India itself was referred to as an ornament of the British Empire, the "Jewel in the Crown," the greatest of its conquests and colonies, the pride of the prettily decorated military men. And India has in fact provided the jewel, the *Koh-i-Nur* diamond, that centrally adorns the British State Crown of the Queen Mother.[28]

While the concept of *darshan* implies a positive vision, there are different kinds of secular sight that expand from the positive and affirmative to the viciously negative. I have argued that Indians understand mythology visually, due to three major factors: the lack of a single authoritative sacred text, the lack of a single written language for the nation, and most important, a theological basis in *darshan* for the power of vision. On the quotidian streets, Indians also use their eyes nimbly, intensely. Foreign visitors are often made extremely uncomfortable by the excessive, relentless staring by the local people, who seem to be able to spend hours soaking in through the eyes every detail of a tourist's appearance: his hair, his clothes, his bag, his shoes, the way he reads, walks, talks, or laughs. The Indian's close and intense staring at others, native and tourists alike, is often remarked by visitors to India, and described in travel novels and guidebooks. Although it is hard to endure in the moment—I always get uncomfortable, then turn and angrily confront my beholders—this act of looking is not malicious in intent. It is just a way that people understand what others, and especially foreign others, are like. And how they choose to clothe their bodies, to stand and move, certainly reveals much about them.

When we went through airport security in the summer of 2003, especially for domestic flights, we found that everything, I mean everything, in our carry-on bags was inspected, piece by piece, ostensibly for security reasons, but actually to satisfy the guards' bottomless curiosity about the things we owned. One security guard at the Indira Gandhi National Airport spent some time looking at the travel toothbrush in the camera bag, opening and closing the tiny plastic container, and flipping through all of our field journals, page by page, not reading anything, just wondering what was inside. These guards were not really looking for forbidden items, but rather taking advantage of their privileged position to sample the kinds of everyday items that people, foreign or local, possess and decide to take along on a trip. It was a perfectly reasonable thing for bright people in dull jobs to do. Curiosity, whether in airports or on the streets, is fulfilled by looking: by taking in details and memorizing visual facts. By satisfying curiosity, through staring sessions, knowledge is accumulated visually, over time.

In contrast to the innocent, curious stares on the streets, there is the malicious gaze motivated by envy, greed, or bad intentions. This harmful vision is commonly referred to as the evil eye, and the wide distribution of the belief—from India through the Mediterranean to Latin America—has long been of interest to folklorists.[29] The concept is known in Hindi as *najar,* a word that simply means sight (the Arabic word *nazar* is pronounced with a "j" in this part of India). Many precautions are taken to avoid becoming a victim of the evil eye, mostly in the form of things that are worn, such as amulets, kohl eyeliner or a kohl *bindi,* and with decreasing frequency, tiny facial tattoos. The danger of flaunting something beautiful—a piece of jewelry or a new baby—is that people will naturally be attracted to this wonderful thing and through a prolonged stare develop a desire to possess it, transferring the evil eye, sometimes unintentionally, to the owner and precipitating a disaster.

Because an unfortunate byproduct of looking good is jealousy and the evil eye, women, especially brides, must present themselves as beautiful while taking care not to look so perfect and proud that others will inflict the evil eye through envy upon their bodies. In *Difficult Daughters,* Manju Kapur's novel set in Punjab, a group of women gather around a new bride, noting her fair skin, her pretty face, and the absence of exquisite jewelry. An elder aunt reassures them that the fact that the bride has a flaw will protect her from receiving a cast of malice from somebody.[30] Fear of the evil eye is one reason why women closely consider the social scenes in which they will appear when they decide whether or not to wear expensive saris and jewelry. If they will be among others who can afford such splendid items, the chances of class and economic resentment, and envious thoughts, are greatly diminished. Many women I spoke with did not display rich possessions in the company of their household servants out of fear of both theft and the jealousy that brings the evil eye.

In contrast, there are ways of looking at something benignly, appreciating its beauty without envy, and participating in its glory while the beauty of the vision influences you in a positive way. This of course relates to *darshan,* but there are other ramifications as well. For example, posters of cute babies are placed in the rooms of expectant mothers, in the hope that the mother's viewing of the image will cause her baby to be born handsome.[31] Most of these posters depict male babies, reflecting the additional desire that the photo will affect not only the appearance of the infant, but the sex as well (even though the sex has already been biologically determined by this time). My mother, like many Indian people, chooses to open her eyes upon a picture of one of her daughters, or an image of one of the Hindu gods, when she awakens in the morning. When she travels, she places a picture of us or an image of a god next to her, so she can reach for it when she wakens and open her eyes upon it. Her reason is to wake up in a positive mood, by looking at something that is loved, so the day will go well. In Bharati Mukherjee's novel *Desirable Daughters,* a young wife keeps her husband's portrait on her night table as a sign of devotion: "Last icon before falling asleep, first worshipful image of the morning."[32] Pictures of the gods, photos of the family or of pretty babies, affect one's mood, orienting the self toward positive, pleasurable, auspicious ends.

Gaze may be neutral, like the long stare in the street, or negative, like the evil eye, or positive, as when one looks upon a beautiful poster of Lord Krishna. To complete this catalog of types of gaze, let us add self-gaze. Any enthusiast of Indian art will be familiar with the many images of goddesses, Parvati especially, or of ladies of the court sitting in front of mirrors or holding hand mirrors, while they are engaged in acts of self-adornment with the aid of attendants. Although gazing in the mirror is often interpreted as a sign of vanity[33] or as a symbolic anticipation of an amorous encounter,[34] it can also indicate an affirmation of self-esteem. Young brides in the homes of their new in-laws may spend much time looking in the mirror, checking their appearance, to diminish the insecurity they feel in a house full of strangers, where people frequently drop by to look at the new bride. Self-assurance is built when you know exactly what you look like, so you do not have to constantly check your reflection in the mirror. Neelam Chaturvedi will expand on this idea in her chapter later in this book. The act of self-gaze then carries connotations, on the one hand, of vanity and pleasure in the image of the self, and, on the other, of insecurity and doubt. This duality is hardly peculiar to the Indian context, but it is one more way in which sight works in the secular realm.

Sight is integral to the study of body art. Although items of clothing and jewelry are felt, smelled, touched, and sometimes tasted (lipstick, for example), they are appreciated by both the wearer and the beholder primarily through the sense of sight. The importance of body art is clear in the act of *darshan.* The devotee identifies the deity and comes to rapture in the god's presence through visual appreciation of the god's formed and adorned body. In the secular realm, body art is also gathered in visually to enable judgments about beauty, and also about wealth, social and marital status, and religious affiliation. In this way, cues given by the type of clothing and the amount, variety, and style of jewelry are all used to recognize somebody as Hindu or Muslim, as married or unmarried, as a member of one of the many groups defined by language or ethnicity in India. Using variables of body art for identification purposes is like using clothes and jewelry in distinguishing Durga from Lakshmi, Sita from Saraswati, or Ram from Krishna.

Seeing through Body Art

Mode of dress has always been a way of making discriminations among the people of India, by both outsiders and insiders. During colonial times, written descriptions and visual representations of the different castes and professions were widely recorded.[35] British colonists were directed to—and inclined to—dress apart from Indians in an attempt to communicate visually differences of culture, religion, values, and ultimately, power.[36]

Today India continues to be a nation divided and subdivided into various groups, most of them recognizable by their distinct body art, which serves to anchor people geographically. Men and especially women in India may instantly communicate their region of origin by their clothes and ornaments. Although the sari is an unstitched cloth, the way in which it is draped, tucked, and wrapped is regionally specific[37] and readily identifiable. Men's *dhotis,* unstitched lower garments, signify the wearer's regional identity by the style of their folds.[38] Turbans[39] and even styles of mustache also express geographic associations. Within the broad frames of regional dress, there are variations associated with specific cities and villages. An outsider, a tourist, will see a group of women as Indian—judged by the national, pan-Indian symbols of sari and *bindi*[40]—but somebody from within the country will most likely be able to decipher coded messages and identify individuals by state and region.[41] If the woman's nose ring is on the right, the woman is from one of the states of South India; a left piercing indicates one of the northern states.

Other variables, such as the gold and black *mangalsutra* marriage necklace, a cluster of ivory bangles, or a garland of white flowers on the hair, all indicate the general part of the country from which a woman comes.[42] More subtle features of adornment, such as the style of embroidery or the colors and details of mirrorwork, send clear messages of specific village affiliation in the states of Gujarat and Rajasthan.[43] A religious communication is implied in these examples, for many of these signs are specific to Hindus.

Most important of the distinctions communicated through body art is that of religion. A recent Indian newspaper article about the nation's population growth charted the differences in the growth rates of each religious community by cartoons of men in religion-specific clothing: the Muslim man in narrow, white *kurta-pyjama,* a vest, cap, and a beard but no mustache; the Hindu in a white *dhoti-kurta,* topknot, barefoot, and clean-shaven; the Sikh in a colorful, baggy *kurta-pyjama,* turban, curly shoes, and full beard and mustache; the Parsi in a stitched gray suit of pants and a jacket along with the characteristic Parsi hat; and finally, the Christian man in a Western-style, navy blue suit, less distinguishable than the others, with no overt "ethnic" hairstyle, facial hair, or head covering of any kind.[44]

Communication of religion through clothing is particularly relevant in Banaras, where the population consists of about 40 percent Muslims to 60 percent Hindus. They live in separate neighborhoods and enclaves, and a walk through any part of town will instantly indicate the religion of the people on the streets, based purely on the clothes the men, women, and children wear. Clothing helps classify people, since all Indian people know the general parameters of what each group should look like. In a recently published interview conducted by the anthropologist Nita Kumar with a ten-year-old Hindu girl in Calcutta, we find that, though the child claims not to know a single Muslim, she knows how to recognize Muslims by their clothes: veils, *kurta-pyjamas,* and caps.[45] Distinct clothing styles function to separate Indians sharply from each other, a fact that Gandhi tried self-consciously to erase in an attempt to unify the nation against the common enemy, the British Raj. While the wearing of *khadi* homespun cloth and the "Gandhi cap" united the Indians against the British, nuanced interpretations of style nonetheless communicated differences in religious, ethnic, and economic identities, as demonstrated by Emma Tarlo in her fine book *Clothing Matters.*[46]

Among Hindus, sectarian marks on the forehead and body stamps may classify the different castes and even denote the followers of Shiva from the devotees of Vishnu.[47] According to Sanskrit law, though it is not followed today, the different castes should wear different colors of clothing: white for Brahmins, red for Kshatryas, yellow for Vaishyas, and dark blue for Shudras.[48] In the previous chapter I sketched some of the variables in women's choices of clothing and adornment. There are similar conventions for men's clothing. Hindu young men wear trousers and shirts, for example, while older men tend to wear white *dhotis* and *kurtas.* Young boys wear shorts or pants and shirts. Little girls are usually seen in dresses and skirts, and women wear saris (if married), *salwar suits* (if young), and jeans if unmarried, urban, and fashionable.

Muslims in Banaras have their own preferred clothing styles. The men wear *kurta-pyjama* sets, made of a polyester blend, with the *kurta* worn long, reaching below the knees. These are considerably looser than the Hindu *kurta* shirts, and have a different cut, collar style, and a distinct central placket with buttons. The ensembles reveal a consistent palette of white, cream, gray, and gray-blue. Many men wear the distinctive *kurta* with a *lungi,* a checkered cotton cloth wrapped around the waist. Muslim men wear prayer caps and sport beards (whereas most Hindu men have only a mustache). Muslim boys of all ages also wear these *kurta-pyjamas* in the same tones as their fathers and grandfathers. The young girls, unlike Hindu girls, do not wear dresses, but rather little *salwar suits*. Grown women wear *salwar suits*, and many are seen, at least in public, in black *burqas,* cape-like coverings that may contain a hood, and may even cover the entire face or the area below the eyes. As Patricia Jeffery's study of veiled women in New Delhi demonstrates, women have mixed feelings about wearing a *burqa* or a veil.[49]

Hindus and Muslims want to express their differences from one another by overt visual communication, achieved by adhering to a mutually understood code of body art. But clothing style often expresses regional, more than religious, identity; Bangladeshi Muslims dress more like Bengali Hindus than they do like Pakistani Muslims. The Punjabi style of dress is worn by both Hindus and Muslims; in the Bollywood film *Pinjar,* a Hindu woman attempting to pass as a Muslim is asked by a group of men to show her tattoo (her name written in Urdu) to prove that she is a Muslim, since they cannot tell her religion by her style of dress, jewelry, or hair.[50]

These general descriptions categorize the types of clothing worn by each of the two main religious groups in Banaras. Within each category and subcategory there are infinite variations, ways in which the wearer asserts his or her personality, individuality, and sense of good taste. In the summer of 2003, we were strolling along the Ganges in Banaras. At the Dashaswamedh Ghat, we saw three young Muslim ladies accompanied by an older Muslim woman, negotiating with a *boatwallah* for a ride on the river. They each wore a black *burqa* covering their bodies and their heads. Even from the back, we could safely guess they were Muslims. In addition, they all had a black cloth mask tied around their faces, exposing only their eyes. Despite these coverings, the young women struck me as wealthy, very beautiful, and sexy. They wore their *burqas* tight, revealing slim, shapely bodies.[51] They each wore high-heeled sandals, making their long legs appear even longer. Their *burqas* were black-black; super saturated, unlike the faded, dingy black of most *burqas* seen on the streets. Each *burqa* had monochromatic metallic sequins, sewn on the back, running down its length, making the women appear taller and outlining the edge of the hood and the bottom edge of the *burqa* itself. The striking decoration, glittering in the sunlight, was flamboyant and attractive, an inherent contradiction to the stereotypical notion of *burqas* as modest, unassuming, and even unattractive.

The young women were all very pale, possessing the coveted light skin tone, and their eyes were rimmed in thick black eyeliner, the dark makeup contrasting with their light complexions. It was to their advantage to be covered up, shielding their beautiful pale skin from the relentless summer sun. By looking at the variables of these women's clothing and bodies—fit, color, and ornament of clothing, shoes, and makeup, in relation to bodily form, height, weight, and age—one can read the messages they are sending. These Muslim, and clearly unmarried women, wanted to appear beautiful, prosperous, and desirable, and in my opinion, they achieved their goals successfully, being by far the most alluring women at the river on that day, despite their black *burqas*.

Knowing that others will be looking at them, people like these young ladies can manipulate their look to emphasize one part of their body, and, thereby de-emphasize another "problem area." The purpose of body art is precisely to draw the eye of the beholder to one section of the body or another, as the clothing and jewelry of the *murti* is meant to emphasize the face and eyes of the deity. Perhaps taking a cue from religion, the face and eyes are also in India generally thought to be the most important features of a woman's beauty. Like the eyes of a *murti,* the eyes of a woman are emphasized by makeup, since big eyes are one of the consistent markers of feminine beauty.

(And now, big yet light-colored eyes, often achieved through contact lenses, are gaining popularity among movie stars and models.) Indian women, like many women from the Middle East, draw heavily around their eyes with black eyeliner, making them appear bigger, and creating a focus on the face that centers on the eyes. The eyes are made bigger to call attention to them, but also to underscore the importance of vision; you are attracted to the big, black eyes of a beautiful woman, and become aware of the fact that she is looking back at you.

Makers of gold and silver jewelry say the function of their art is to beautify the woman—and to call attention to itself. B. D. Soni and Chaman Lal, both goldsmiths, have told me explicitly that when they fashion a piece of jewelry, they are hoping that the beholder's *najar* will fall on it, for their item will be competing for the attention of the beholder with all the other items of adornment worn at the time. When women put together a wearable ensemble, they keep in mind that the independent items need to work together, some taking a supporting role, perhaps shaping the background for an exquisite diamond choker or a fancy brocaded sari. Throughout this book, we will look carefully at considerations of this kind, analyzing the creative decisions people make when they put together things that go together beautifully, matching each other, fitting the occasion, and most importantly, working as one to beautify the wearer.

While the goal of the goldsmiths is to create an eye-catching item of jewelry, the goal of their female customers is to buy an item that is not only beautiful but also catches the eye and diverts the gaze toward the part of the body the women wish to emphasize. I asked many women what they would choose and why if they could wear only one type of jewelry on their bodies. The response from Hindu women of all ages varied from choker necklace, to earrings, to nose ring, to *bindi.* Their answer to the second part of the question, though, was consistent. They chose the item because it was worn on or around the face, highlighting the most important location of beauty: the face. This fits the religious pattern of *darshan* and beautiful *murtis:* in the temple and in the streets, the face is the place where beauty concentrates. The Muslim women I interviewed said that the one item they would choose would be bangles, which bring attention to the wrists, glittering with color. These women also believe that the face is the most important aspect of the body, but they preferred to distract attention from the face by pulling the gaze toward the wrists, where shiny bangles offered vibrant contrast to the dark *burqa* that covered the body. Both Hindu and Muslim women direct the beholder's gaze to a particular place, and their decision to do so orders the selection of the jewelry they choose to buy and wear.

The concentrated vision of secular gaze relies, like *darshan,* on an impression, a quick, meaningful glance that gathers information and stores it for mental retrieval. Rajesh Kumar Gour took a quick glance at the statue of Lord Balaji, but that visual flash was enough to confirm his preconceived notions that the statue was beautiful, powerful, and richly adorned. He took previous knowledge with him when he went to take *darshan,* so he knew what kinds of visual details to take in. The same can be said about people who watch others. Sharing culture to some degree with those they see, they know the rules and variables that enable quick judgments and the storage of relevant details in the mind. People know how young and old women should dress, what types of bangles are worn by Bengalis or Punjabis, what colors the widows from different regions should wear. On the streets, knowing which visual patterns communicate developmental status, wealth, ethnicity, and religion, people need but a quick glance to acquire enough information for evaluation and understanding.

Visual information may not be gathered for any overt, conscious purpose. Say you run into the daughter of a friend. Now a young adult, she is no longer wearing a frock, but a *salwar suit.* This information, stored unconsciously, can be retrieved later to confirm the notion that the girl is grown up, having moved up to the proper clothing of a teenager, and she just might be a potential marriage partner for the handsome nephew who has come to visit from Lucknow. What is perceived, whether in the streets or at parties, are flashes of people that the trained eye disassembles and categorizes. Judgments follow, and judgments, whether positive or negative, rely both on select details and on general impressions. The general impression makes a gestalt of the whole look: clothes, jewelry, body type, hairstyle, and social occasion. By your complete look, you are judged, compared to others around you and to memories of your appearance on other occasions.

Starting with the religious precedent for vision in the Indian context, we have moved outward toward a broad understanding of the ways in which religious precepts condition the secular realm. It is my feeling that the emphasis on vision as a mode of data collection and analysis extends beyond the Hindu population to become a general part of the culture of India. Before ending this examination, let us focus on individual women, noting the variables and options in decisions about body art that are based fundamentally on the knowledge that one is being seen and judged by an audience of beholders. Nina Khanchandani and Mukta Tripathi are both Hindu women we will spend much time getting to know in later chapters that detail their personal repertoires and choices in adornment. Nina cares little about adornment and chooses to spend little time and effort on her clothing and jewelry. But she does not like people staring at her, so when she goes to a party she dresses up more than she would like to. At the party, she appears in appropriate dress, her goal being *not* to be looked at. By dressing carefully for the occasion, in the general style, she blends in and, in her words, "stays with the crowd," avoiding extended looks of disapproval or surprise.

Mukta, on the other hand, wants to be the visual center of attraction, and intentionally dresses a bit differently from everybody else at a party. While, like Nina, she will appropriately dress to fit the social context, she will choose a surprising color, a bold print, or a flamboyant style of jewelry. She wants to capture people's eyes by standing *apart* from the crowd. In both cases, these women, Nina and Mukta, present themselves in public, knowing that they will be judged for fitness to social context and in comparison with everybody else's clothing and jewelry. A woman needs to be aware of her dress in relation to others, to fashion, and to the social event, in order to decide whether to blend with the crowd or stand apart in splendor. Either choice assumes she will be seen by others. Given that, she may decide to fade from attention or to demand a long gaze, thereby attracting admiration or, maybe, jealously and the evil eye.

Anjali Devi, a handsome middle-aged Banarasi housewife, enjoys being looked at in the streets. She regards chance gaze in public as a sign of approval for her choice in clothes and a validation of her beauty. Among strangers, in the streets, you are being judged by people who have no idea who you are, so they cannot base their assessment on any prior knowledge of you as an individual. They see you only in that moment, in relation to their general ideas of beauty and dress. Anjali Devi told me that her reason to get dressed up is to make herself appear beautiful to others: *apne ko sundar dikhane,* literally, "to show yourself as beautiful."[52] Her position assumes she is being seen by others, and that she has successfully achieved her goal of beauty when others respond appropriately. Anjali Devi said she assumes she looks good when she gets ready, but when "somebody says you look beautiful, then there is happiness in me, that, 'Yes, I am beautiful.'" She explained that on the streets, this positive feedback comes in the form of extended vision, not words of approval. Anjali Devi said that if she were walking down the street and somebody kept looking at her, "I will be aware that this person is looking at me, and continues to turn to look, and continues to turn to look, I must be looking beautiful; that is why he is looking."

But people need to distinguish among the kinds of looks they get. Sometimes, Anjali Devi explained, people look at you too much and it becomes a visual "taunt." That look says you appear inappropriately sexy. Another is a look of ridicule that says you are overly made-up and look like "a cartoon." If you are walking down the street, she said, and a man looks at you and says, "Wow, what a beauty!" he could be expressing genuine approval of your beauty, or sarcastically mocking an extravagant effort to look good. Feedback, verbal or usually visual and taking the form of a prolonged gaze, has to be judged by the woman and carefully deciphered, just as the beholder judges and deciphers the appearance in visual terms. If she is dressed elegantly within the generally acceptable parameters for her age, caste, marital status, and for the occasion, the beholder's gaze probably implies admiration, but if she has bent too many of the social and aesthetic norms in her adornment, the look probably implies scorn.

Anjali Devi thinks women exhibit their beauty and also their "capacity" through their appearance by displaying on their bodies the kinds of clothes and jewelry they can afford to buy. Anjali Devi is aware that there are different categories of beholders on the streets—family, friends, and strangers—and she dresses to be seen by people of all these kinds. Anjali Devi admits to feeling free when she is outside of Banaras, where there is "no one there to see you." Her statement further qualifies the act of being seen on the streets, even by strangers. No public place is totally anonymous and safe in one's hometown. Somebody could know somebody who knows you. But "out of station," traveling far from one's city, people become more comfortable and they wear what they want. On the streets of an unknown city, you are totally anonymous, and it does not matter what these new people think of you. There is a parallel here in the practice of not drinking or smoking in front of elders or parents as a sign of respect. The gaze of respected people should not fall upon you when you are engaged in an indecent act. Many believe that actions that are immoral, such as drinking alcohol, or indecent, such as wearing a dress that is inappropriate to one's age, should be avoided only if there are known and respected people who might see this breach of a taboo.[53] It is not a matter of a morality within, but of a look from without.

Nitu Dhar, a Hindu woman who lives in the predominantly Muslim city

51

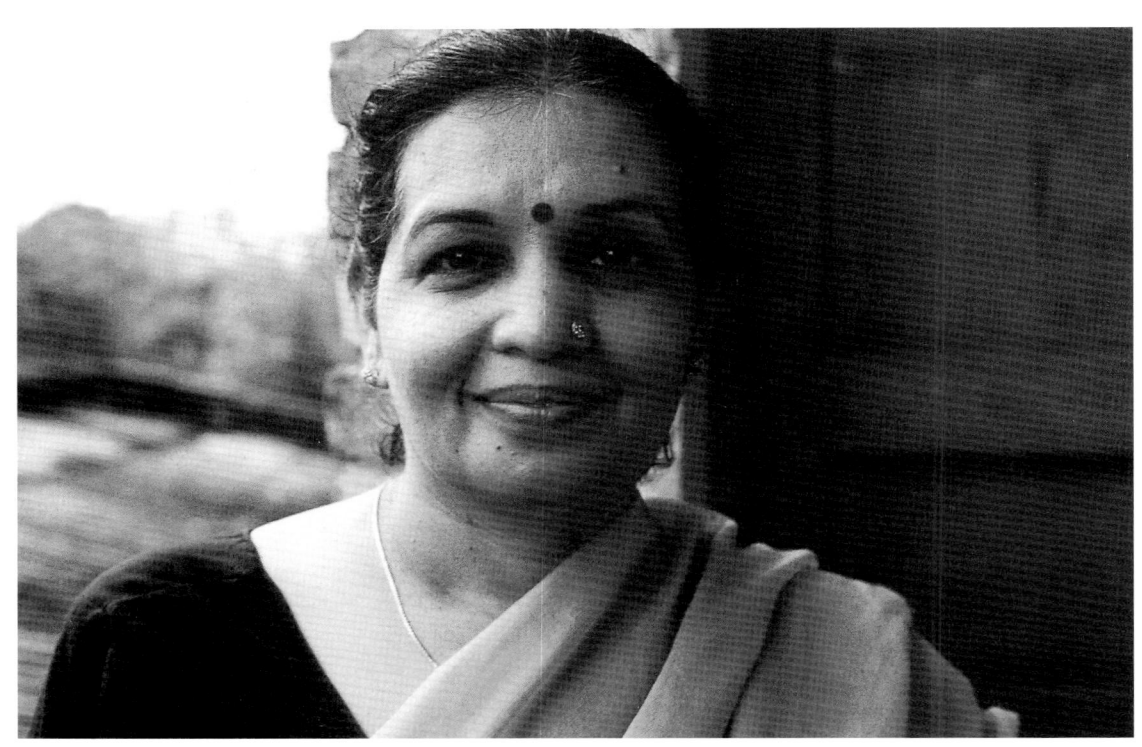

Anjali Devi

of Dhaka, Bangladesh, is part of a tight social network in her city of residence. Since her marriage in 1984 to the sculptor Shankar Dhar, Nitu has stopped wearing *salwar suits,* preferring to wear saris, the more suitable attire for married women. On a recent trip to Calcutta without her husband, she went to see the Victoria Memorial accompanied by her sister. In this touristy outing, Nitu borrowed a *salwar suit* from her niece. Even though this was a public and crowded place, nobody knew her, so she could temporarily break the social rule of dress by wearing a *salwar suit* instead of a sari. When she and her husband traveled together to Sri Lanka, she wore both *salwar suits* and "pant-shirt"—jeans and a T-shirt—because, she said, nobody there knew them. Although she was literally being seen by people, they did not matter, since they were not part of Nitu's network of family, caste, or community. Women, as these examples show, dress one way in their hometown, where they seek visual approval, and then when they travel, many dress as they please, for comfort perhaps, caring little about reaction and sometimes purposefully subverting the social restrictions imposed on them at home.

This relationship among adornment, context of seeing, and explicit communication appears in the works of Indian authors writing about the diaspora. In Anita Nair's novel *Ladies Coupé,* one character, Prabha Devi, is able to persuade her husband to let her wear Western clothes while they are visiting New York because no one will know her there.[54] Her argument is the same as that of Nitu Dhar, the sculptor's wife from Dhaka. For Indian women who are living abroad, native clothes and jewelry function as a sign of ethnicity and a potential magnet for meeting other displaced Indians, as illustrated in a recent short story by Jhumpa Lahiri in which a lonely Bengali man follows a mother and child in Boston after having spotted the characteristic red and white Bengali wedding bangles on the mother's wrists.[55] For second-generation Indian women, born abroad, Indian clothes and ornaments express not temporary displacement but a desire for connection that often yields signs of pan-Indian identity, rather than regional or ethnic identity, as Amita Handa demonstrates in her sociological study of Indian young women in Toronto, Canada.[56]

Nina, Mukta, Anjali Devi, and Nitu, all express an awareness of the fact that women are seen and visually judged. Starting with this basic assumption, each dresses according to how much visual attention she wants, from whom, and how she feels about her beholders. Women are not only the subjects of viewing, they are viewers themselves, making assessments based on visual cues. I will end our examination of gaze in the secular realm by noting the variables upon which assessments are based, starting with the category of self-gaze. Women look carefully at themselves in the mirror when deciding on what to wear. I asked Mathuri Chaubey, a particularly articulate and visually oriented Banarasi woman, to explain her understanding of the importance of self-evaluation during the creative process.[57] She started by stating that one needs to choose the items of body art carefully, noting the social and physical constraints of the body of the wearer, and start with one main item, either a "heavy" Banarasi sari or a "heavy" gold necklace. Although each object is beautiful on its own, worn together they would look ugly. One would have to wear the "heavy" necklace with a "light" sari with a thin border, a "plain" blouse, and small delicate earrings. Mathuri explained that one needs to think about these items in a "combination," that people need to "adjust" accordingly, rearranging the ensemble as they put it together. What this act entails is a degree of critical self-assessment, as a necessary prelude to being seen and judged by others. She continued:

"Often it is said, after you have finished getting completely dressed up—to go to a *party* or a wedding—then you will only look good after you have gotten completely dressed up. You have put on a lot of things, then stand in front of the mirror and *watch* yourself, and eliminate two things from that. Anything. Then only will you really look beautiful.

"That is what people say: that if you are totally dressed up, then eliminate two things and you will look beautiful. This means that people do have some *excess* always. When people get too *conscious*—that I should look very beautiful at the *party* or wedding—then they get *over-conscious*. In that way, people will make *mistakes*."

From Mathuri's comments, we learn the importance of the role of self-assessment, which is achieved through self-gaze—an act that functions as a mirror for the individual and her society. Judgments about what is beautiful, what comprises acceptable attire, and what are considered "excesses" and "mistakes" of adornment are based on a person's reading in herself a reflection of the communal aesthetic standards. This differs from Anjali Devi's assessment of herself, which is based on the reaction of others in the streets to her clothes. She also dresses in accordance with shared norms; then she sees herself through the gaze of others.

I asked Mathuri to comment on how others look at you and judge you by your clothes. She spoke in the hypothetical, but provided examples:

"Say somebody is wearing a lot of *artificial jewelry.* And she is wearing these to look beautiful. But, people will think, 'She has all *artificial jewelry;* she is not from a very good family.' The first thing is this: the family with which you are associated—that is knowable precisely from your jewelry and clothes. People are always trying to *guess,* at least, what kind of family you belong to."

I wondered how exactly these kinds of judgments are made about "family," a word that implies caste as well as social and economic status, and I asked her if she thought that people noticed the materials of the jewelry and reached their conclusions from the fact that this girl wore artificial things instead of real gold. Mathuri said that the cost of the material is only part of it. It is not only what you are wearing, but also how you wear the things; they exhibit your *tarika*—your style—and show how you carry yourself within it:

"Say you are dressed in a really *sober tarika.* It can also be known by the *tarika,* what your taste is. If I look at you, I will know. If a girl were to come here and stand before me, if she is dressed according to her natural *rup*"— form in the sense of embodiment—"not that she has come here dressed to *bluff* me, in which case, I could not tell. But she is dressed according to her true *nature,* then I will certainly be able to tell that this girl is of this *nature.* What is the feeling of this girl? Is she educated or not? Or what is her *taste*? What is her lifestyle? What kind of family does she come from? The way she is *dressed,* I will be able to tell. *Even* her *education* will be revealed to you."

As with religious *darshan,* gaze is often purposeful, an act of seeking out meaningful details, with a specific end in sight. I asked Mathuri to elaborate further. I wanted to know exactly what she looked for in order to discern what she called "education"—which, in India, strongly implies socioeconomic class. She continued:

"If she is wearing a whole lot of jewelry, and she is very dressed up, then that means that she is, *first and foremost,* not educated. If she is wearing too much, she comes here in very much *over-makeup,* then this means that she is not *highly educated.* Because it is often the case that all people hide what they lack, with something. And she—her lack of *education* and *intellect*—that she is trying to *cover* with her jewelry, with her clothes. This intention is revealed, and this does happen. Often this happens. Because, there are some less-educated girls who are always wearing a whole lot of *makeup.*

"Or, some middle, *average-like* boys, they—with nice shoes, nice clothes, dressed nicely—they desire to show that 'I am from a very *rich* family,' that 'I am very *intellectual,*' but they are not. That man who is very *intellectual,* he won't be bothered by what clothes he is wearing, because he knows that 'If I were to talk to anybody, that person would not be *impressed* with my clothes, that person would be *impressed* with my mind.' Some people only with their shoes-clothes wish to *impress* people. They have nothing else anyway; what can they do? This is the case."

As they do when they visit the gods in the temple, when people meet others, they try to connect, learning who they are by studying their appearance, by looking at the things with which they ornament their bodies, making judgments concerning identity, personality, background, and association. Body art is created and read as a matter of visual exchange, of nonverbal communication, through which self-conscious messages are sent and received within a circle of adornment and gaze. Mathuri's keen observations will resonate throughout this book. People are aware of what they wish to convey, and they articulate their wishes when they make, buy, or arrange clothing into the ensemble of the self.

The visual orientation of Indian culture, grounded in Hindu precept, will frame the rest of this study. Keeping in mind the importance of visual communication, and the human desire for creative expression and social approval, the next chapters will focus on how clothes and jewelry are made, sold, and bought. All of these things—*salwar suits* or saris, necklaces of gold or glass bangles—are assessed visually, for customers rarely try things on, and the act of shopping is guided primarily by sight.

Part 2. Production and Commerce

·4·

Shopping for Clothes

THE OLD CITY OF BANARAS runs along the Ganges, the river of the goddess Ganga. Wide steps of stone lead down to the *ghats* at the riverside. Pilgrims and local people descend for prayer, for bathing and washing clothes. *Ghats* in sequence line the riverfront. Two of them are "burning *ghats,*" used for cremation—Harishchandra to the south and Manikarnika to the north[1]—where the continual burning of bodies attracts curious tourists and the local hustlers who offer to take them to see the "dead body fire." Eighty-four *ghats* string along the river, but most of the activity, social and religious, takes place on the steps of the "main ghat." Situated in the middle and numbered forty-one, Dashaswamedh Ghat is the place of the ancient Ten Horse Sacrifice. Here, Lord Brahma came disguised as an ascetic and requested the King of Kashi, Divodasa, to sponsor an extravagant version of the horse sacrifice, the *aswamedh.* The ritual was flawlessly performed, and now all those who bathe here receive the blessings of the horse sacrifice.[2]

During the summer evenings, before the monsoon rains of July and August, the river is low and calm. Once the rains begin the river rises, slowly submerging the steps of the *ghats* and engulfing many of the riverside temples. Early in the summer, pilgrims in great numbers make the ritual journey to Banaras, and they come to Dashaswamedh Ghat to witness the *aarti*—the act of veneration—that honors the goddess Ganga and the god Shiva, whose city this is. A platform on the main *ghat* is rigged with poles that hold loudspeakers and lights. Every night during the summer, young priests swing incense and flames in unison, performing a *puja,* a prayer to the river. At the end of the ritual, sweets are distributed among the people as *prashad,* and the worshipers go down the steps to the river, where they float candles and place a few drops of water on their heads as a symbolic blessing from Ganga.

Ascending the steps of the Dashaswamedh Ghat, you find stalls selling cold drinks, a temple to Ganga, and the Banaras Saree Factory, hinting that this *ghat* is not only the focus of religious activity for the river, but also an entry to the principal commercial center of the city. Away from the river, Dashaswamedh Road runs west to Godaulia, where it intersects the main road that runs north and south, parallel to the river. This main road goes north to Chauk, a center for craft and commerce, and south to Madanpura, where shops for fine saris cluster. Beyond Godaulia, Dashaswamedh Road turns into Luxa Road, a major commercial street lined with large clothing stores, hotels, restaurants, travel agencies, and movie theatres.

At the Godaulia junction, there is a roundabout manned by police officers whose job is to prevent cars from turning east, toward the river. Rickshaws, motor scooters, and pedestrians are permitted through, but this is where rickshaws usually stop to drop their passengers. From this point people walk east, either continuing to the riverbank at the Dashaswamedh Ghat, or turning north at the entrance of the Vishvanath Gali that leads to the Vishvanath Golden Temple, the city's prime destination for pilgrims. Most people visit Banaras for both religious and commercial reasons. The great religious goals—Dashaswamedh Ghat and the Golden Temple—are located east of the Godaulia intersection, and to get to either of them, you have to travel streets and alleys that are thick on both sides with shops selling stone *murtis* and *puja* supplies, shoes, purses, housewares, and especially items of clothing and adornment. Owners of small shops take advantage of the foot traffic, enticing the visitors with dense displays of apparel.

Shopping on Dashaswamedh Road, people stop to look at storefront exhibits of exquisite saris behind glass. They browse through little shops, piled high and spilling over with *salwar suits,* folded or draped on identical mannequins. They stop at makeshift stalls that sell cheap essentials, such as children's underwear and socks, hair clasps, nail polish, lipstick, and packets of *bindis.* On the floor, displayed on printed bedsheets, shoppers find household items: multicolored clothespins, plastic colanders, and cheap duffle bags emblazoned prominently with the Nike logo.

Women wander in little clusters of two or three, haggling with the male merchants, complaining with theatrical animation about both price and qual-

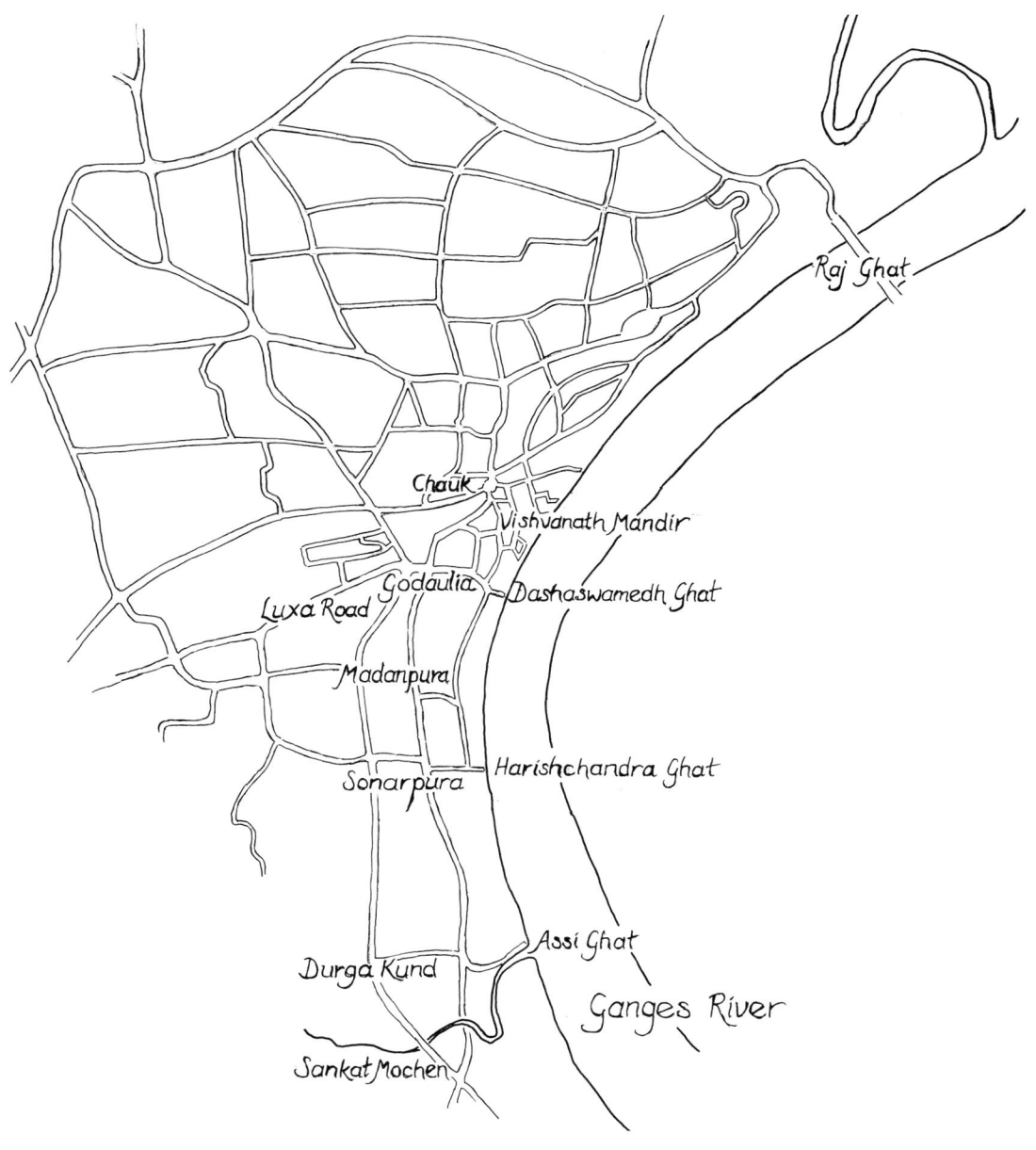

Raj Ghat

Chauk

Vishvanath Mandir

Godaulia

Luxa Road

Dashaswamedh Ghat

Madanpura

Sonarpura

Harishchandra Ghat

Assi Ghat

Durga Kund

Ganges River

Sankat Mochen

Banaras

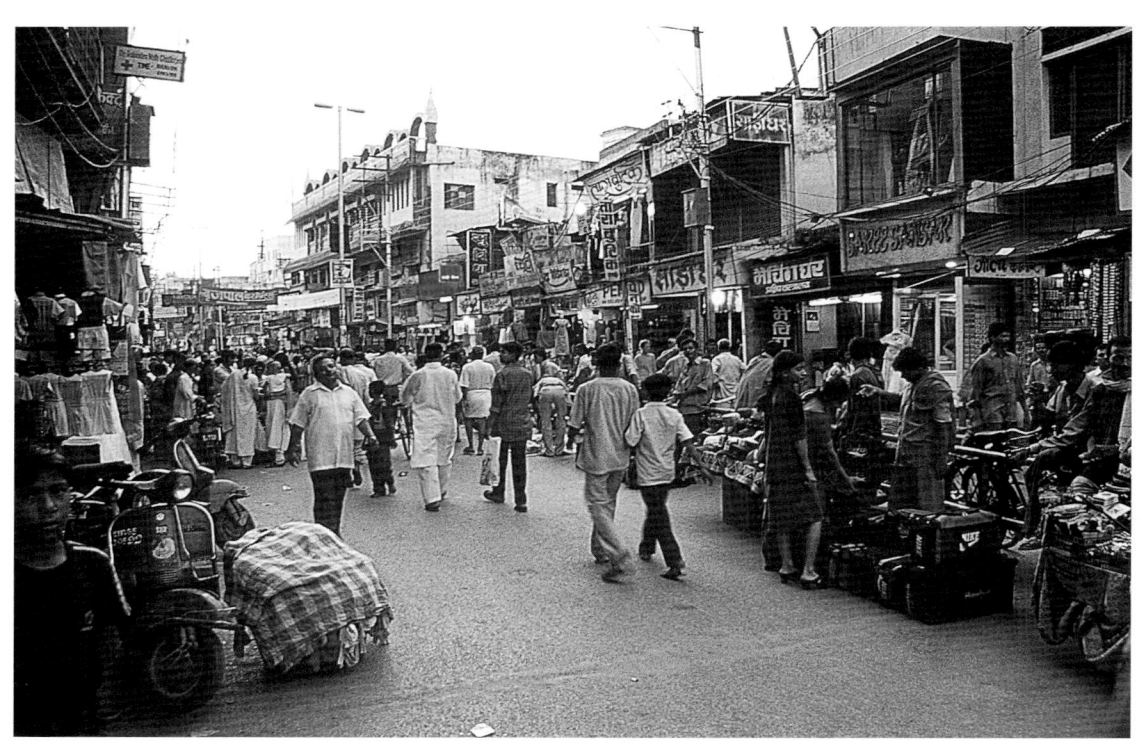

Dashaswamedh Road

ity. They usually prefer to shop in the late afternoon or early evening, after the household chores are done. Avoiding the heat of noonday, they come out in the cool of the evening when they look well groomed and "fresh" in their pressed saris and pretty bangles. Female shoppers make spots of bright color among the tired and sweaty male vendors who have endured the heat and commotion of the city all day.

Shopping on the streets of Banaras is nothing like going to an air-conditioned mall in a big city, Los Angeles, say, or Bombay. The streets are crowded; people constantly bump past, compelling women to clutch their purses. Since the electricity frequently fails, the road is loud with the stuttering putter of generators that bring light to the stores and smoke to the streets. When you choose to venture into the crowds and the dust, it is wise to accomplish as many shopping chores as quickly as possible. That is why there is such a variety of basic items for sale in this short stretch of street. A woman can buy *salwar suits* for her daughter, socks for her son, get a few sari blouses stitched for herself, stock up on *bindis,* and still have time to enjoy a cold lemony Limca Cola and a *samosa* at the Mathur Milan Cafe, a popular fast food eatery on Dashaswamedh Road.

Shops on the street are usually defined by specialty, jewelry, for example, or clothing. They are further subdivided by the gender they serve to. Some stores, clustered toward the river, specialize in men's clothing and shoes, while most of them sell items for women, and the types of things on display indicate clearly that most of the street's shoppers are female. The bigger stores sell saris or readymade *salwar suits.* Small stalls usually carry accessories, such as readymade sari blouses or petticoats. Regardless of their size, the shops specialize in one item—sari or petticoat—making it available in a huge array of colors, fabrics, and styles. By limiting themselves to one category, storeowners are able to offer tremendous variation within type, while cleverly maximizing the severely limited available retail space.

Shops along Dashaswamedh Road sell fabric, and the owners of clothing stores have arrangements with tailors, so a woman need only buy a piece of cloth and give her measurements to the store clerk, who will have the piece stitched by a tailor, for a low commission rate. This convenient arrangement between tailors and merchants makes it easy for the customer who grants the clerk some control in conveying to the tailor what she wants, and also what he thinks she should have. As we shall see, the piece of clothing that is purchased and worn by a woman will have received the aesthetic input of many people, including the merchant and the tailor.

In this chapter, we will explore choice and production in textiles by looking closely at how *salwar suits* and saris are bought and sold. The next chapter will focus on the process of creating the saris that the weavers sell to the merchants and the merchants sell to women. From production to marketing to purchase, all the people involved in these transactions are male except for the customers. The men are both Hindus and Muslims, and the transactions occur both within Banaras and far beyond.

Saris and *Salwar Suits*

Before taking a closer look at commerce, I will prepare us with a survey of the range of textile-related choices women make in their dress for everyday and special occasions. Age and marital status guide a woman's choices of certain items. Readymade clothes, such as dresses ("frocks") and jeans, are usually purchased at the larger department stores on Luxa Road. Saris are usually bought in the grander specialty shops in the Madanpura and Godaulia areas.

Buying a sari requires time and patience; there is an astounding variety to choose from, ranging wildly in color, fabric, print, and price. The Banaras woman also needs many auxiliary pieces in order to wear a sari properly, which extends the number of aesthetic choices she needs to make. In Banaras, women wear saris with blouses and petticoats. In some other parts of India, women do not wear either; instead, they knot the sari in place and conceal their breasts with its end. Whether or not a blouse is worn with a sari depends on regional tradition and occupational need, and it can reflect one's place in the lifecycle, for many elderly women enter a post-sexual stage and dispense with the modest blouse altogether.[3] Like the blouse, the fall and petticoat are variables. If the bottom of the sari touches the ground, it will fray over time. To prevent this, a sari needs a two-yard strip of cotton stitched around the inside of the bottom border. This piece, called a "fall," should be placed on the sari before it is worn. The local woman also needs a "petticoat," a cotton drawstring skirt that is worn under the sari and reaches to the ankles. The petticoat functions as a slip, creating a backdrop for the often-transparent sari, and it provides a frame into which the sari is tucked.

Petticoats can be bought readymade or made to order. A woman must decide what color the petticoat should be, since it might show through the sari, and it will occasionally show beneath the sari when she is walking or sitting. The color of the petticoat will inevitably influence the overall effect of the portion of the sari below the waist. So, the decision can be made to match the sari exactly in hue, or to choose a color that complements the sari in some way.

Once the color has been chosen, the woman will decide on the fit. Younger women prefer tighter petticoats, which create a trimmer fit for the sari, right for a slim figure. Older women prefer the looser petticoats that effect a less revealing sari look, one that does not hug heavy thighs. (It is rumored that Bollywood heroines who wear very tight saris to reveal the contours of their hips and legs do not wear petticoats at all, but rather tuck their saris into tight leggings.) The decisions do not end with color and fit: petticoats can have ruffles attached to the bottom or they can be perforated all over with little eyelet holes.

For the Banarasi woman, the last obligatory component of a sari is a blouse. Fine saris of silk brocade are woven extra long, extended to include a "blouse piece" at one end that is then cut off and tailored. Some of these sari pieces perfectly match the sari in color and fabric, while others reverse the sari's foreground and background motifs, or modify the color scheme slightly. The blouse will be stitched in a style selected by the customer, but its look will be influenced by the way the weaver conceived of that segment of his weaving: did he, for example, add the ornament of the border, or design elements from the sari's field, to the piece he designed for the sari blouse? Many blouse pieces are woven to provide the tailor with enough of the border detail to outline the bottom of the sleeves and the bottom of the blouse with a stream of motifs. The finished product will reflect the woman's choice in the length of its sleeves, in its cut and design, but it will also reflect the weaver's notions in the design and placement of its brocaded decoration. And a sari blouse might also reflect the tailor's interpretation of the weaver's design.

A sari blouse can also be stitched from cloth bought from the fabric shop that sells the materials for petticoats. The fabric, its color and texture, is a choice for the woman, and so is the fit and contour of the blouse that will be cut from the cloth and stitched. Sari blouses are usually tight and midriff in length, but women can choose how tight the fit and how high on the torso to have the blouse rise. Since the blouse, and part of the stomach, will usually show through on at least one side of the sari, decisions will be motivated by aesthetics and modesty. When a sari is worn in the common *nivi* style, as Banerjee and Miller point out in their book *The Sari,* the contour of the left breast is revealed if the sari slips a bit, which adds allure and offers an option

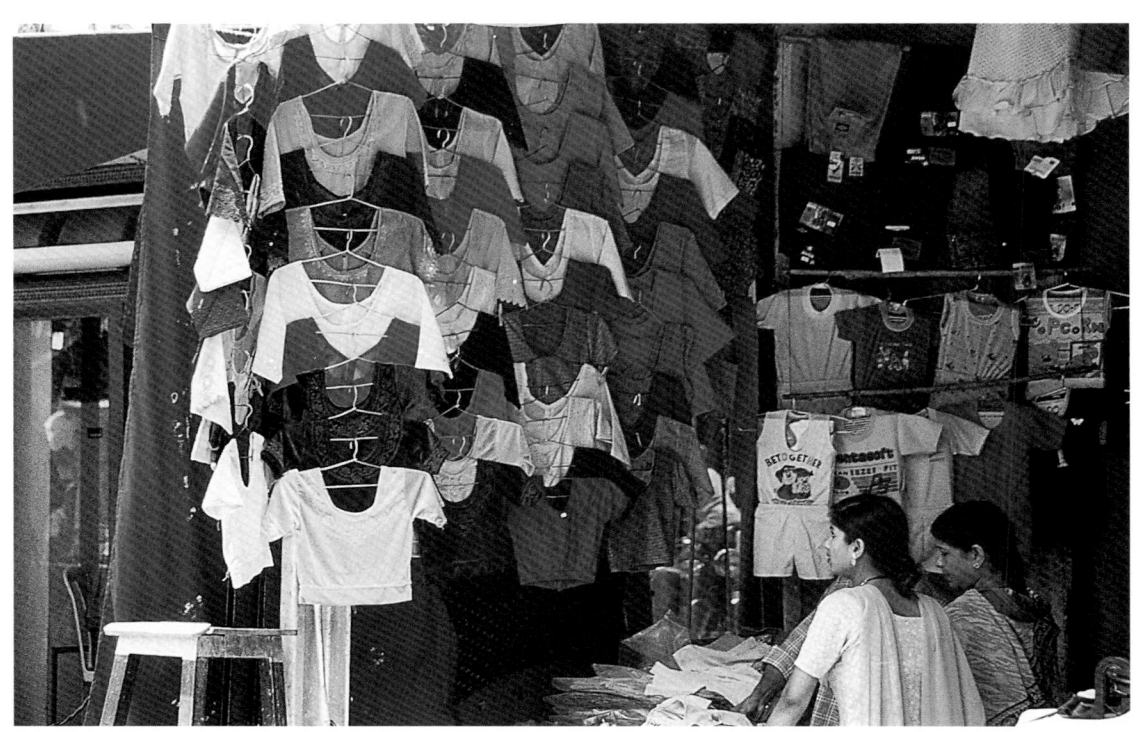

Sari blouses, Dashaswamedh Road

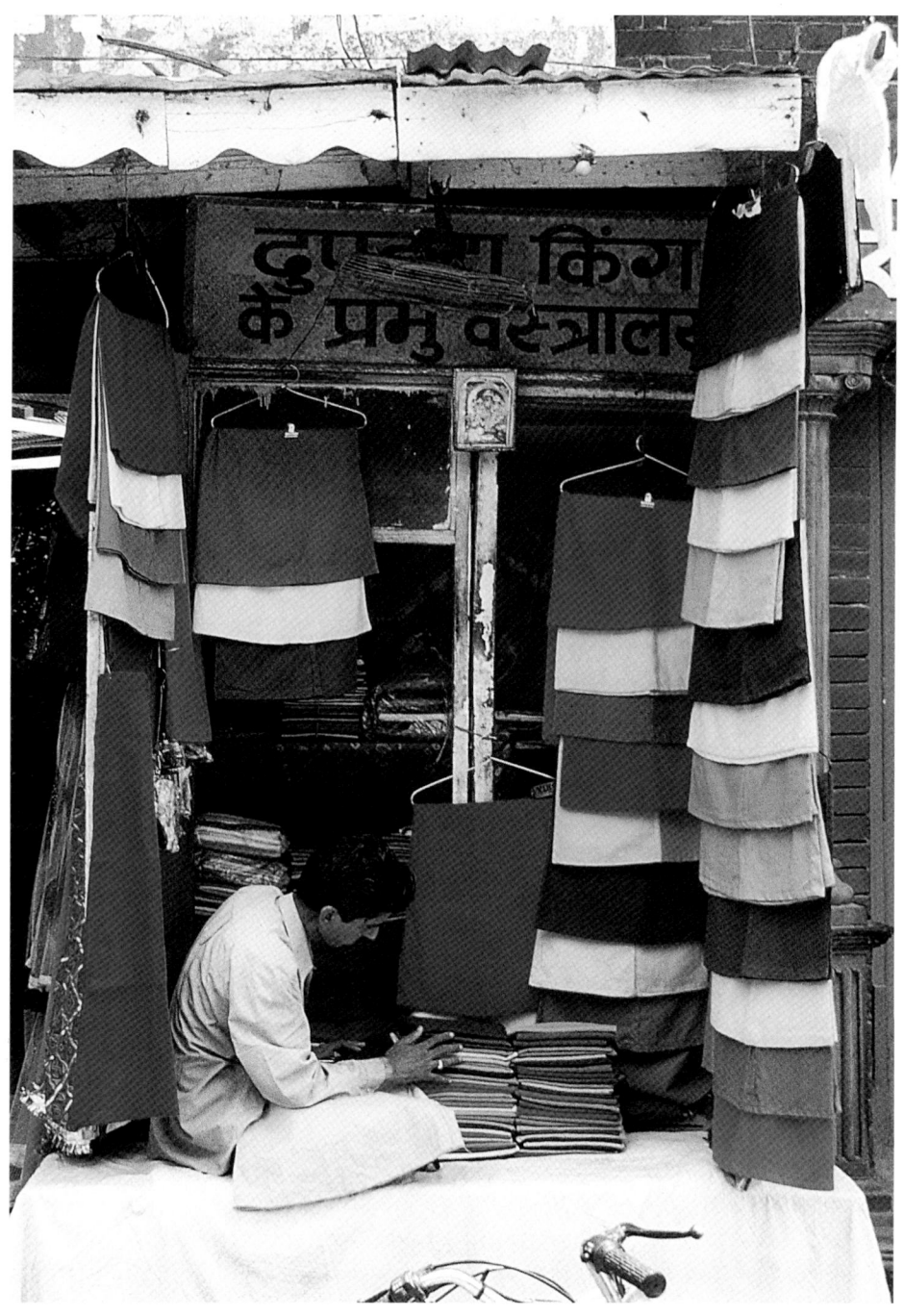

Petticoats, Dashaswamedh Road

for a flirtatious gesture.[4] There is a scene in Gurinder Chadha's movie *Bend It Like Beckham* in which a bride is having her measurements taken for the custom-made *choli* blouse of her wedding *lehanga*. She asks for the measuring tape to be tightened over her breasts, so she will have a form-fitting blouse, because a bosom tightly compressed under a sari or *lehanga* reveals sexy cleavage. Sari blouses may have long sleeves, three-quarter sleeves, short sleeves, or they may even be sleeveless. Blouses with puffy sleeves were stylish in the past, but, as I write, they are avoided by fashionable urbanites who dismiss them as a "village" style, and in fact rural women do like the look of puffy sleeves. Sari blouses may fasten with hooks in the front or the back. Some are backless with ties under the neck and across the lower back. Fashion trends have included little collars, and elaborate embroidery and mirrorwork on the back, for the back is prominently exposed when a sari is worn, especially in the conventional *nivi* style, with the end of the sari trailing over the left shoulder.

The choices made when wearing a sari are forever in flux. Though decisions concerning the petticoat and blouse are made with specific ensembles in mind, one can always mix and match the petticoats and blouses in the *almari* to adjust to some new fashion. The sari itself, a piece of unstitched cloth, can be worn with much variation, in different traditional styles that often index regional identity. Linda Lynton's useful survey, *The Sari*, includes descriptions of numerous draping styles—particular styles for Gujarat, Nepal, Bihar, Orissa, Bengal, and Assam, for the Deccan, Karnatika, Kerala, for Parsis and Tamils, and tribal groups[5]—but increasingly the North Indian *nivi* style is becoming the standard look for the sari. The name, derived from the term "knot" in Sanskrit, is used commonly by textile scholars.[6] In this style, the left end of the sari is tucked into the petticoat, the sari is then wrapped once around to make a skirt, then pleated repeatedly. Tucking this fan of pleats at the waist, the woman drapes the sari behind her, brings it forward, and finally hangs it back over her left shoulder. Fluctuating fashion trends dictate how long the end should hang down, ranging from the level of the shoulder blade to just above the ankle. The *nivi* style is now the common draping pattern in Banaras, although it is locally referred to as *ulta palloo* (opposite *palloo*), in contrast to the *sidha palloo* (straight *palloo*), a style in which the elaborate end piece (the *palloo*) is brought forward over the breasts. The terminology in which the current style is called *ulta*—opposite or wrong—implies that the *nivi* style is new, a contradictory replacement for the old, correct style.[7]

In the summer of 2001, female airline employees and flight attendants in

New Delhi were sporting a "uniform" sari style with long-sleeved sari blouses and a *palloo* that fell nearly to the floor. Sophisticated and suited to tall slender women in high heels, this look signals a vocation in air-conditioned spaces, since the long sleeves would be hot in the summer, and the long *palloo* would make it impossible to engage in housework without tripping over the sari.[8] Women who work in the house usually wear the end piece of the sari short, and bring it forward across the back, tucking the loose end at the waist into the petticoat, thereby creating ease of motion and modesty of appearance while they work.[9] The free end of the sari may also be used during household chores as a handkerchief or a wiping cloth, and it can be tied at the corner to carry keys or money, in the way my grandmother did.[10]

Although both Indians and foreigners consider the sari to be the quintessential garment of the nation's women, the *salwar suit* is gaining popularity, especially for everyday wear, in India and the diaspora. Saris are preferred for Hindu rituals since uncut cloth is thought to be purer than cloth that has been cut and sewn.[11] Saris are preferred for their elegance on formal secular occasions. But there is today an energetic increase in the fashion of "suits," which are also called *punjabis,* after their ostensible region of origin in the Punjab. Recent studies of clothing in India and the Indian diaspora focus on the *salwar suit* as an important medium of expression for women of different ages and ethnicities.[12] A new book titled *The Sari* concludes, in fact, by devoting ten pages to the importance of *salwar suits* in modern India—as a grade school uniform, as college and work attire, and as an increasingly versatile urban option.[13]

Buying a *salwar suit,* like buying a sari, involves many decisions about style, color, and fabric. The ensemble consists of three pieces: the *salwar* pants, the *kurta* tunic, and a long scarf, called a *chunni* or *dupatta,* roughly two and a half feet wide and seven feet long. Many options abide in the relationship between the three pieces. All may be made of the same fabric and print. Or, for example, the *kurta* maybe be made of a white cotton material with red flowers, the *salwar* made of solid red cotton fabric, and the *dupatta* of a red flimsy fabric with white flowers, reversing the pattern of the *kurta.* Or the *kurta* may be black with mirrorwork embroidery in maroon thread, the pants a deep maroon, and the *dupatta* a printed paisley fabric in maroon, beige, and black. As you might imagine, there are endless combinations of fabrics and prints for each of the three pieces, while patterns shift and balance is maintained. Sometimes, dictated by the "latest fashion," *salwar suits* come

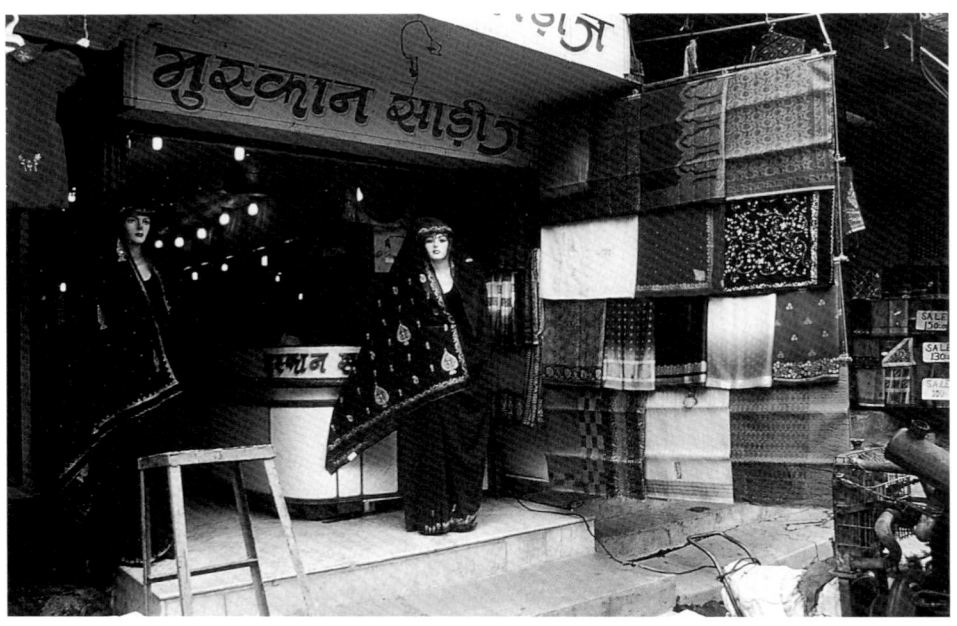

Saris, Dashaswamedh Road

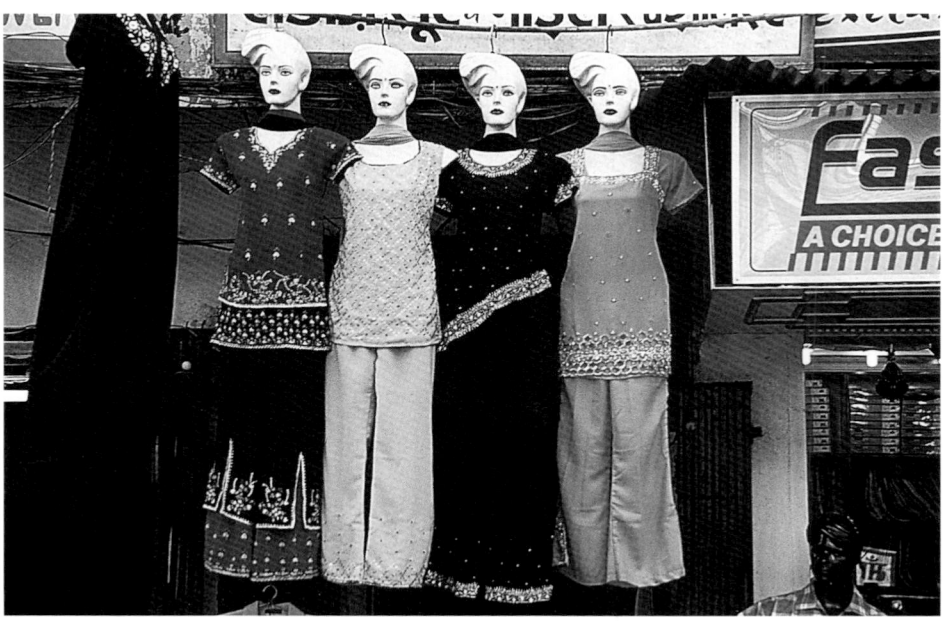

Salwar suits, Dashaswamedh Road

in unalterable sets, but you can always elect to ignore the mode and have things stitched to the color and pattern of your choice. Custom tailoring is not expensive and readymade sets are not mandatory; rather, they are a guide to a fashion that can be exuberantly followed or adamantly rejected. *Salwar suits* change quickly with fashion, and while there are general patterns that are followed by many people, there is always room for personal interpretation of the general trend.

In addition to the selection of the fabric and print, buying a *salwar suit* involves decisions on the fit and cut of the pants and tunic. The pants of the *suit* always have a drawstring top, but they vary in length and in the width and bagginess of the legs. A favorite, timeless style is the *churidar pyjama,* a tight fitting pair of pants with extra fabric below the knee that gathers and stacks, creating a piled series of folds of cloth just above the ankle, where the bottom is fastened with hooks for a snug fit.[14] Pants in this style are associated with the Punjab, and they are worn by both women and men. The handsome Jawarhalal Nehru characteristically wore *churidar* pants, along with the jacket that bears his name, as part of his elegant ensemble.[15]

The *kurta*—the tunic—is likewise variable in its cut. It might be wide or tight, there is variety in the length and width of the sleeves, the height of the slits on either side, and especially the shape of the neck. The length of the tunic varies as well, ranging from upper-thigh to well below the knee. Like most garments of this type, worn by people in many countries in South Asia, the Middle East, and North Africa, the tunic always covers the crotch area of both genders. It is little surprise that people used to such clothing would find blue jeans vulgar, since jeans stretch tight to the thighs and emphasize the forked region of the body.

The 2001 poster for the film *Mujhe Kucch Kehna Hai* ("I Want to Say Something") showed the heroine in a new style of *salwar suit* that had flared bell-bottom pants, and a short, transparent A-line top that came to the top of the thighs (worn with a camisole underneath), and a flimsy, see-through *dupatta.* Most women tend to be less risqué than actresses, so they transformed this movie style into a new trendy look of flared pants and short tunic top. When I was in India in the summer of 2003, I saw *suits* in this style hanging in the cheaper stores on Godaulia. The trend was no longer fresh, the fashion elite had moved on, but the masses were finally being served with readymade *suits* in a style then two years old.

The third piece of the ensemble, the *dupatta,* can vary in style and print, but also, and most importantly, in how it is worn. This floating scarf allows great flexibility in relation to temporary fads. The *dupatta* is most commonly worn draped over the chest, hanging over both shoulders and down the back. It can also be worn draped on one shoulder to fall vertically down on both the front and back. Young university women on bikes and scooters often are seen with the *dupatta* wrapped across the chest and tied on the back, creating a sexy look, since it is tightly bound over the breasts. Women may also tie the *dupatta* over one shoulder and under the opposite arm, striking a diagonal line across the chest. And finally, Muslim and Punjabi women—whether Muslim, Sikh, or Hindu—often wear the *dupatta* over the head to create a modest look while framing the face with color. When entering a temple, Hindu women might comparably use their *dupattas* to cover their heads. Though the *dupatta* is often made of flimsy cloth and does not actually cover the body, its presence implies modesty, like many of the outer garments worn by Muslim women that do not cover much but do provide a symbolic extra layer, as Patricia Jeffery shows in her study of Indian *purdah* practices, and as Andrea Rugh shows in her excellent study of contemporary dress in Egypt.[16]

By the time a woman enters a store to be confronted with the available choices, a series of other decisions have already been made, primarily by the men who have selected the particular pieces available for sale. A study of contemporary dress in India raises many questions, including: how are *salwar suits* bought by the merchants, where do they come from, and how are they selected by customers? In the fine stores of Bombay and New Delhi, women shop for clothes much as they do in the United States. They go into a clean, air-conditioned store and look at the mannequins and through the racks for what they want. In the fancy clothing boutiques of Bombay, I saw exquisite *salwar suits* and *lehanga* outfits made of recycled antique saris that were priced, at that time in 1996, in the thousands of dollars. These expensive clothes were hanging on the racks, and shoppers were free to touch and even try them on. This kind of store is beyond the reach of most people who lack the cash to buy fancy clothes, who would feel uncomfortable entering the haughty stores in the affluent parts of town, and whose wish is to be served attentively. Women not used to being served shop for service as well as merchandise.

In Banaras, as in most parts of India, including the working class sections of Bombay and New Delhi, the style of shopping involves much interaction with the shop owner and workers, who control what the customers see, literally showing each piece of merchandise to every customer, while commenting extravagantly on each and every one. Yet both shopping styles—self-serve and full-service—involve custom-made clothes. Even readymade clothes are altered to fit the body of the customer; one result is a society in which clothes generally fit people far better than they do in places where clothing is mostly bought off the rack as it is in the United States.[17]

Most Indians do not view this common shopping style—in which one sits, to be shown the merchandise, bit by bit—negatively. Americans generally prefer to come into direct contact with the clothes they want to buy, indulging in a semi-erotic pleasure of touch, smell, and sight. Indians, on the other hand, want to be shown the clothes and jewelry, while coming into contact with other (generally talkative) human beings. There is an unspoken attitude among the customers that the merchant should earn his sale by working at showing—without hurry, and with cups of tea—a representative selection of his stock. One might even say that shoppers residing in the United States, a predominantly Protestant country, prefer direct contact with merchandise, just as they prefer direct contact with their God. The Hindu religion is one of mediation, in which priests stand between the people and their deities. The merchant becomes a sort of priest of the commodity, and religious practices help us understand the psyche of consumers as well as worshipers. India is a country of mediation, of servants and hierarchies, of caste and class. When they patronize a store, people want to be served, to be treated with respect and hospitality. People want to sit comfortably, while the salesmen furnish refreshments, and work to make a sale. Unlike Americans, Indians would be offended if they had to paw through the merchandise themselves. In the Indian commercial context, the notion of "self-service" would not be appreciated; it would be taken as an insult.

Hemant Khanchandani

In an attempt to untangle the complicated business of *salwar suits,* I shifted from the general to the specific, and focused on one *salwar suit* shop on Dashaswamedh Road—Dayaram Fashion Centre: Ambassador of Fashion—and its friendly owners, the brothers Hemant and Parmanand Khanchandani.[18] One day at Hemant's shop, I observed a mother and her teenaged daughter enter and sit on the little stools at the counter, the barrier between them and Hemant, who stood up as soon as they came in. The moment these customers arrived, the generator was cranked on, filling the small store with light and starting the rotating fan that moved the hot air around a bit.

The mother spoke for her daughter, telling Hemant that they were looking for "suits" to wear to college. Hemant first asked their price range, then asked about their choice of material—whether they preferred cotton or synthetics. After this initial consultation, Hemant looked behind him at the stacks of neatly folded *salwar suits* stored in cellophane bags, deciding which pieces to show his customers. Turning back to the counter, Hemant opened a few *suits*, spreading the *kurta* on the counter, since the tunic is the most visible and most important of the *suit*'s three pieces; the pants and scarf are seen as auxiliary to the *kurta*. The women asked to see similar *suits* in different colors, purchased a few, and left.

In a department store, including those that sell readymade clothes on nearby Luxa Road, a customer has visual and tactile access to every item for sale. In Hemant's shop, and as we shall see, in most shops selling *salwar suits*, saris, and even jewelry, the customer samples only a limited percentage of the available stock. The only items the customer sees are the ones the merchant has decided the customer will like. The merchant's decision is based on a brief conversation, but even more on visual judgments he makes on the customer's dress and appearance.[19]

Hemant's small shop holds a wide variety of *salwar suits*. Some are plain pastel *kurtas* from the predominantly Muslim city of Lucknow that carry the famous white *chikan* embroidery on the chest, neck, and sleeves.[20] Other *salwar suits* are in the *bandhana* style of the state of Rajasthan, which Rajasthani merchants refer to as "tie and dye." (*Bandhana* means "to tie," in Hindi and Sanskrit, giving us the English word "bandana" for a handkerchief that is knotted.)[21] These tie-dyed *salwar suits* come in many varieties, differing in their combinations of color and the size of the tie-dyed rings. Hemant also showed us a *suit* he described as "Gujarati style" and another he portrayed as "Madhya Pradesh style." Sometimes the most important variable in the *salwar suit* is color, not cut or design. Pastels and other subdued colors, such as gray and beige, are for older women who do not feel comfortable wearing bright colors.

Salwar suits range in color and design, some referencing the different states of India, others attempting to incorporate a wider international sensibility. A black *suit* I saw at Hemant's was reminiscent of a Palestinian textile, with elaborate embroidery in the front and a medallion embroidered on the back, the motifs incorporating an Islamic emphasis on geometry. One *suit* had a West African feel, another carried ancient Egyptian motifs. It is clear that the cloth designers are busy plundering a variety of folkloric traditions, using cheap labor for embroidery and dyeing, while creating an overall look that is Indian but refers to a multitude of other aesthetic traditions. Parminder Bhachu has addressed this fascinating topic of influence, innovation, and tradition by examining the *salwar suit* in England and considering its various modes of social, economic, and aesthetic communication.[22]

Hemant, a man in the business of selling *suits*, must be aware of the ethnic and regional makeup of his customers, and he makes an effort to meet varied tastes. He has modest, subdued *suits* that appeal to older women, and he attracts globally minded college-aged women by carrying *suits* in bright colorful cloth reminiscent of Ghanaian textiles or a fantasy of King Tut's tomb. He caters to women relocated from India's various states by providing the option of wearing an outfit suggestive of the old home state.

Salwar suits are worn by a wider spectrum of the population of Banaras than saris are. *Suits* are worn by Punjabis and by Muslim females of all ages, and they are worn by unmarried Hindu women and increasingly by married Hindu women as well. To succeed in his business, Hemant must be aware of the general categories of merchandise his customers like, and then choose from his wholesale suppliers the best samples of *salwar suits* within each category; his taste then is always imprinted in what the customer takes away from his shop, an outfit generally believed to reflect the woman's unique taste.

Hemant's merchandise represents a spectrum of aesthetic traditions, and it also displays the array of materials and combinations that *salwar suits* come in. You can buy an entire three-piece *salwar suit,* or a two-piece *suit* that consists of either a readymade *kurta* or a *kurta* cloth piece, each with a matching *dupatta.* For these, you must have the *salwar* pants stitched from cloth you buy separately. A third option would be to buy a two-piece ensemble, consisting of the top and pants, leaving you the task of buying an appropriate *dupatta,* or using one you already own, or buying a strip of cloth and having it dyed to your desire. The end result will always be a three-piece ensemble, but a customer may start with one piece (only the *kurta*) or two pieces (*kurta* and pants, or *kurta* and *dupatta*), and exercise her creativity and fashion sense to end up with the complete *salwar kurta* outfit.

While doing fieldwork in India I wore *salwar suits,* something I do not do in the United States. I needed to buy some *suits* in Banaras, and that resulted in my acquaintance and eventually my friendship with Hemant and his family. On one occasion, I chose to buy a *kurta* piece and accompanying *dupatta*. The *kurta* cloth had a sage green background—named *mehendi* after the color of dried henna powder—and was sprayed with tiny gold-colored flowers. The cloth came with a four-inch-wide gold border piece. The *dupatta* was golden beige with the same tiny flowers, this time in *mehendi* green, reversing the color combination of the *kurta*. Each of the ends of the *dupatta* had the same border motif, but printed in a band eight times as thick, making the ends visually heavy, aesthetically reinforcing the way the *dupatta* is worn, with the ends hanging down.

After I had selected the pieces, there were other decisions to be made, namely how to stitch the *kurta* and what kind of pants to have made. Hemant asked me to trust him, to let him choose on my behalf. Such offers are common in stores selling clothing and jewelry. Once a woman has chosen a store she trusts—one that harmonizes with her aesthetic sense—she will trust the judgments of the male professionals there, the merchants and craftspeople who know their merchandise best. I trusted Hemant, and he proceeded to describe to me how he would have the *kurta* stitched. He would make it "Sindhi style"—his style; his family is from Sindh—in the same way he would have made it for his own wife or daughter. The *kurta* was designed as an A-line tunic, reaching below my knees. The neck he chose was modestly cut, well above the cleavage line. Hemant communicated the preferred neck design to his tailor by using a number that was assigned to that particular cut on a battered photocopy of an illustrated chart of necklines that both Hemant and his tailor had. The sleeves were straight and short because it was summertime. The border section of the original cloth piece, instead of being attached to the bottom end of the tunic as intended, Hemant decided to have stitched down the front, forming two parallel vertical bands of gold.

For the pants, Hemant gave me his unsolicited opinion—a thing often received from people in Banaras. He said that based on my height and weight (relatively tall and slender for an Indian female), he would commission a pair of *churidar pyjamas*. At his command, a helper from his shop ran down the street, returning with a few bolts of green fabric, Hemant chose the right color to match, his brother Parmanand took my measurements (length of legs from waist to ankle and circumference of ankles), and the transaction was completed. I was to return within the week to retrieve my *suit*.

When I came back to pick up the outfit, Hemant showed me a picture he had been given by the wholesaler who sold him the fabric for my *suit*. The photograph showed a fair-skinned young model with dyed reddish hair in a *salwar suit* made from the cloth I had purchased, though hers was navy blue instead of *mehendi* green. Her *suit*, however, was stitched in what Hemant called the "old style," the gold border piece attached to the bottom hem of the *kurta* and to the end of the short sleeves. The general cut and height of the *suit* was the same as mine; the only marked difference was in the interpretation of where to attach the border motif. She wore navy blue baggy pants, very unlike the sleek *churidar pyjamas* of my outfit. In the background of the picture appear the words "Karishma," a reference to the company that produces the cloth. To complete the look, the model—young and hip—was wearing ice-blue nail polish on her toes and metallic-silver platform sandals.

Hemant got this photo and others like it when he purchased the cloth at the wholesale market. The photographs are meant to serve as models for the individual merchants, directing the stitching of the cloth. But storeowners may choose, as Hemant did, to reject the styles depicted in the pictures and create improved, improvised individual variations, such as Hemant's Sindhi version. Hemant showed me the picture so that I could appreciate his creativity and see how much better my *suit* was than this woman's. At the end of the visit, Hemant gave me the photo, saying he had no use for it anymore. I glued it in my field journal, not knowing what use I had for it either. That summer, I walked the streets of Banaras in that *suit* chosen from the limited selection of Hemant's stock, made in Hemant's Sindhi style of *kurta,* in pants that Hemant thought would suit my body. I did not have to take his advice, but I did. Were I to receive compliments on that *suit*, who should deserve the credit, Hemant or me? Who did that *suit* reflect, the merchant or the customer?

Hemant told me that most of his customers buy *suits* readymade, yet many alter the *kurta* to make it fit better if they are thin, or have it made completely from scratch if they are too "heavy"—the more commonly used English euphemism is "healthy"—to fit into the standard one-size. Many women get pants custom-made to their liking, disproving the notion that all women follow fashion blindly and want to wear what everybody else is wearing. Hemant stressed that although he helps women select exactly what they want—after all, he must make a sale—his customers ultimately buy and wear the styles that reflect *him,* not them.

Hemant and his older brother Parmanand not only work together at the Dayaram Fashion Centre, they also live together nearby on Luxa Road. The brothers share a joint household with their widowed mother, their wives, their young adult children, and their youngest brother, Sawal. Hemant's wife, Nina, and Parmanand's wife, Jaya, take care of the household and also share the duty of managing the tiny store located in the front of their house, the Pariwar Provisions Store. Each couple has one son and one daughter. The girls, Priya and Rati, both attend Banaras Hindu University, the prestigious local institution of advanced learning, while both boys, Ashish and Ritesh, work in the clothing store alongside their fathers.

All family members are Sindhi, a Hindu ethnic group originally from the Sindh region in present-day Pakistan. Hemant's great grandfather was a landowner in Pakistan, but all four of his sons had an interest in the clothing business. The sons established clothing stores in Pakistan, in France, and in Nainital and Calcutta in India. Hemant's grandfather moved to Banaras for religious reasons—to live by the Ganges in Shiva's city. This is a common reason why pious Hindus from many parts of India end up in the holy city. Once in Banaras, Hemant's father followed the example of his uncles and opened a clothing store on Dashaswamedh Road, the same store that Hemant and Parmanand now run. This store was established in 1947 or 1948, a couple of years before either of the brothers were born.

Hemant recalled his father saying that the rent for the store was then ten rupees a month; it is now five hundred. The rent has escalated tremendously because, Hemant said, the street has taken off as a commercial center in the last decade. Dashaswamedh Road was not always a busy shopping street, he told me. In the past the only people who came to their street were *mahatmas,* great souls, who had come to the Vishvanath Golden Temple seeking *mukti*—religious release from the mundane life. Hemant said that shopping was the last thing these people were interested in. But now, with the influx of more worldly pilgrims who are joined in the evening's throng by the people of Banaras, business has improved drastically for the Khanchandani brothers, and for everybody else who owns a store on Dashaswamedh Road.

It is interesting that Hemant and his brother are third-generation cloth merchants and fourth-generation Sindhi immigrants. Although they were born in Banaras, they adamantly identify themselves as Sindhis, not Banarasis. We were served delicious Sindhi food at their house, a fact emphasized with much pride by Hemant. He spoke authoritatively of the "Sindhi capitals" of the world: Bombay, Dubai, and New Jersey. Although Banaras is not one of these capitals, he told me that the city has forty to fifty thousand Sin-

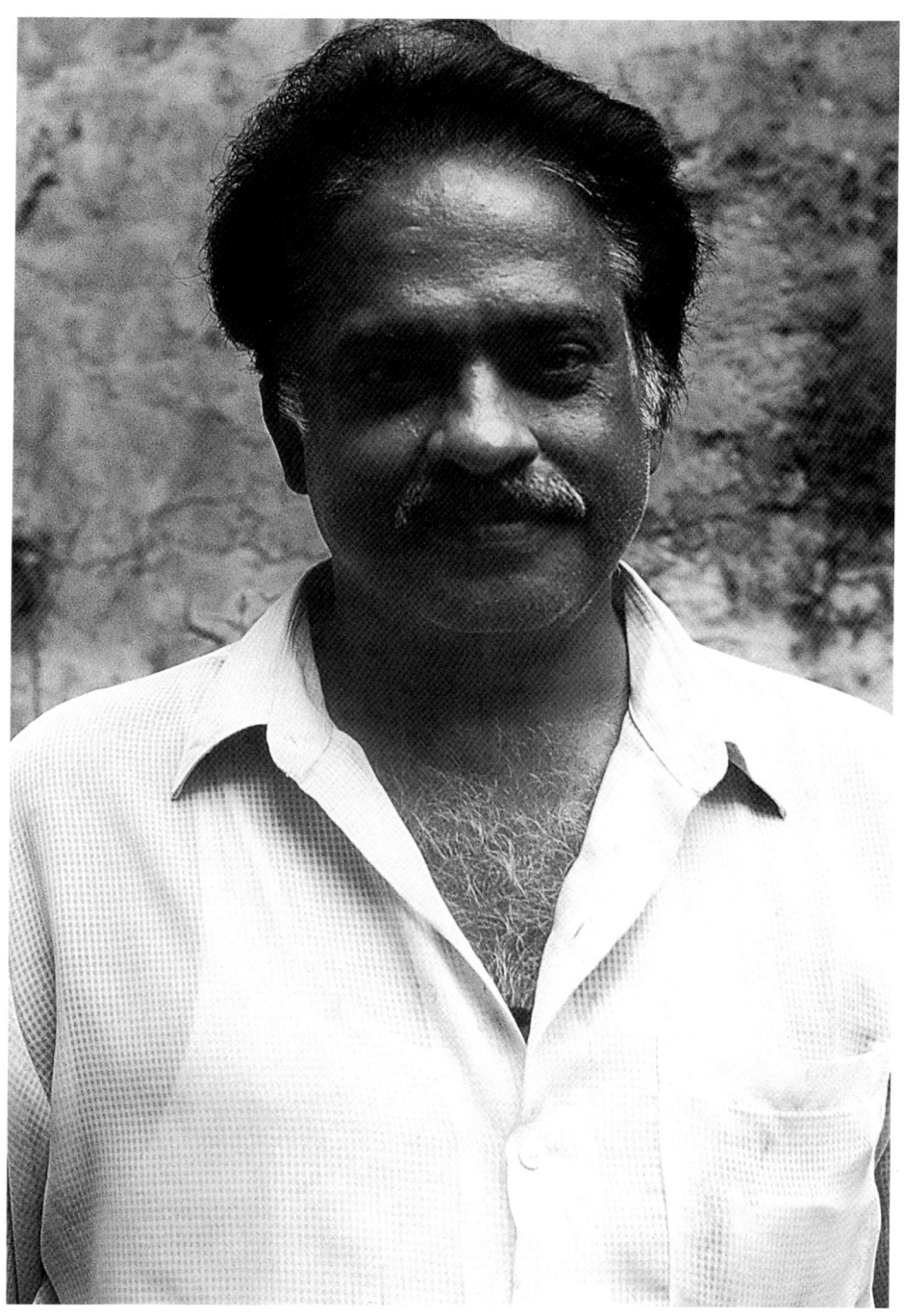

Hemant Khanchandani

dhis. Hemant wanted me to know that Sindhis are a proud people, that if a Sindhi ever needs help or money, he will never be seen begging; A Sindhi will only ask for help from another Sindhi. The members of this displaced ethnic group will always rely on each other for support, he said, and never reveal any weakness to outsiders.

I found their strong ethnic identification fascinating, and particularly relevant to my quest to understand the city of my ancestors. Banaras, deep in history, is an important commercial and religious center that has for centuries attracted a steady stream of outsiders who have settled there. In Banaras, people of many different backgrounds live together, but they are acutely aware of their differences, not only of religion, but also of region and ethnic affiliation. On a few separate occasions during our talks, Parmanand, while speaking in Hindi, used the word "Indian" in telling ways. On one occasion, while he was talking about the shop and its Muslim customers, Parmanand said the "Mohammadies" or "Musulmans" of Banaras start their daughters wearing *salwar suits* at a young age, unlike the "Indians." In this case, it is clear that Parmanand, like many Hindu and even Muslim residents of Banaras, see Muslims as outsiders, not as "Indians," even though they have lived in Banaras for many generations. On another occasion, while making a statement about Sindhis, Parmanand said that they, "unlike Indians," followed a certain custom. In this instance, "Indians" meant not only Hindus (as opposed to Muslims) but also specifically those Hindus whose ancestors lived within the borders of modern, post-partition India.

Although Parmanand and Hemant were born in Banaras, four generations removed from Sindh, they see themselves as outsiders in Banaras and India as well. There are businessmen all over the city who identify with a place and culture beyond Banaras. That fact becomes relevant to our present study when merchants, weavers, and jewelers give advice to the women of Banaras on their dress, because they may be intentionally, or subconsciously, infiltrating the city with the aesthetic sensibilities of their own distant home places. Parmanand and Hemant referred to me as "Hindustani" and "Indian"—presumably because of my Banarasi heritage—but when they were given a chance to suggest a style for my *mehendi* green *salwar suit,* Hemant chose a Sindhi look for me to wear in the city of my ancestors.

Hemant may suggest a style—Sindhi, perhaps—for stitching the *kurta,* but when he buys the cloth, he has to rely on the taste of the multiethnic wholesalers who might very well be trying to influence others to dress like their women. The cycle of influence involves more than Hemant and his customers. It starts with the people who sell the cloth to Hemant in the first place. He explained his business dealings to me in this way. Hemant has local brokers in Bombay and Gujarat. Accompanied by those brokers, he regularly visits the cloth manufacturing centers of these cities. He goes to Surat in the state of Gujarat for synthetic fabrics, and to Bombay for both synthetic and cotton fabrics. At these wholesale centers he buys readymade *suits* and fabric to be made into *salwar suits.*

These purchases are sent back to Banaras, where Hemant has many of the pieces stitched into *salwar suits,* so the readymade *suits* at his shop were either bought as they are in Surat or Bombay, or stitched locally according to Hemant's specifications. Some of the finer *suits* are then shipped out to retail outlets in places as varied as London and Bombay. Choices are made by many people: by the original designer of the cloth in Bombay or Gujarat, by the brokers who identify potential merchandise for Hemant (or buy it on his behalf), and by Hemant himself, who may accept or reject the cloth during his many visits to the wholesalers. Subsequently, tailors in Gujarat, Bombay, and Banaras, men with their own taste, interpret how to stitch the *salwar suit.* And finally, Hemant decides which *suits* to send away and which to keep for his local customers, making educated guesses about the ethnic and regional diversity within Banaras and about the desires of customers as far away as London.

Many of the men in the cloth and jewelry business follow routines like Hemant's. They travel often, visiting wholesale outlets, ordering inventory and becoming exposed to new trends that they introduce to Banaras. Hemant spoke enthusiastically about the life of traveling on business, of sleeping in dormitories with others on the road. Away from their families and daily routines, the businessmen, Hemant said, indulge in vices they avoid at home: they eat meat, drink whiskey, and gamble. In the dormitories they fraternize, eating and drinking together, smoking all night while chatting or playing cards. Hemant himself does not eat meat, drink, or smoke—he is a sincerely religious man—but he still enjoys these moments of wild living.

Hemant's shop is located about a ten-minute walk from both the Vishvanath Golden Temple and the Ganges. Every morning before opening his store, he goes down to the river for *puja.* Every Monday, on Shiva's day, he goes into the *gali* for *darshan* of Baba Vishvanath at the Golden Temple. He enjoys his daily routine in Banaras, its blend of the religious and the commercial, and he enjoys the time he spends on the road. But still, he plans to leave the store one day, move out of Banaras, and settle in Bombay, where his wife was born. His older brother Parmanand would stay in Banaras and mind the provisions store, selling candy, cookies, milk, oil, and other household necessities. Parmanand told me how much easier it is to run a provisions store than a shop for clothing. In the little grocery store, people come in with an idea of what they want. They find it, buy it, and leave happy. In a clothing store you have to show the customers many, many things, trying to appeal to them, trying to figure out what they want, and they still might not buy anything in the end. In the grocery business, Parmanand said, you do not have to sell the merchandise; it sells itself. Although the brothers run a successful business, and though they are good at selling clothing to women, they are both dreaming of retiring, leaving the old family business, and no more hustling *salwar suits* to women.

Pinku Mookerjee

Shopping for a sari tends to involve a more complicated procedure than buying a *salwar suit*. Saris are generally more expensive than *suits,* so they are worn on special occasions before important viewers. Saris are bigger investments in both cost and in time. Women keep saris in their closets for thirty years or more, and may choose to wear one many years after it was bought. For reasons of permanence and investment, saris are chosen more carefully than *salwar suits.* There are many cheap saris, of course, made of polyester or cotton, and worn every day; they are purchased with the casualness of *salwar suits.*

Seeking a fine sari, a woman, usually accompanied by her husband or a few female companions, will enter a shop, perhaps one of the many south of Godaulia, carrying such tantalizing names as Taj Exotica Orient Sarees, Madeena Silk Museum, and Rahman Silk Museum: Saree Paradise. Many of the sari stores in Banaras are air-conditioned; the customer must be comfortable while spending her money on expensive saris. Several women told me that when they were looking for one or two saris, they liked to shop at the Godaulia stores, but when they shopped for many—when they had to buy the saris for the bride's trousseau, for example—they preferred to visit a "wholesaler" store linked to a sari workshop in the Madanpura area. Most of the stores are spacious, with the entire floor covered by mattress pads, encased, unfortunately, in white sheets that show soil and stains. The customers slip their shoes off at the entrance, and find places somewhere on the soft floor. A salesman approaches immediately, sits across from them, and asks what they want. As it is with buying a *salwar suit* or an item of jewelry, the clerk tries to get a general idea of what the customer is looking for—price range, fabric preference, color preference, and the occasion for which the saris are needed. After these factors have been determined, the salesman might bring a stack of saris himself, but more likely he will order a lower-ranked employee to fetch the saris, usually from a back room. The sari stock is often limited, based on the current fashion or the season. All colors and fabrics are not necessarily available year-round.

Saris come in a wide assortment of materials, including cotton—hand or machine-spun and woven—silk, chiffon, crepe, georgette, muslin, organdy, organza, and synthetics, such as nylon, acrylic, and polyester.[23] There are some famous regional sari types that many women try to collect, hoping to own at least one example of each style. Most of these can be purchased in Banaras, and women of Banaras tell me that a desirable collection of wearable saris will contain as many saris from this list as possible: Banarasi silk brocade, Rajasthani *bandhani* tie-dye, Gujarati *patola* double-ikat, Bengali *jamdani,* Bihari *tasar* silk, *chikan* embroidery from Lucknow, ikat silks from Orissa, and the distinctive contrasting border varieties from Kanchipuram, Tamil Nadu. Saris may be factory printed, hand block printed, or batik printed, using the resist-wax dye method.[24] In addition, many women—my mother is one of them—enjoy buying a plain sari in a single color and commissioning embroidery in the color and design of her choice. My mother has also asked the artisans to add sequins, beads, mirrorwork, or appliquéd strips of cloth, particularly along the border, to achieve a beautiful sari, but most importantly, a unique sari that will not be seen on another woman at a social event.

Sari shopping is a leisurely activity, unlike buying cheap accessories on the move along Dashaswamedh Road. Women sit comfortably in the sari shop, away from the gaze of the men in the streets, and they may spend hours inspecting the inventory.[25] During this interaction, shopkeepers order in soft drinks—orange or lemon soda for the women, cola for the men—then tea and snacks, in an effort to keep the customers happy and stationary; the longer they stay, the more likely they are to buy.

Women may buy several saris at once, some for their own use and some to be saved for gift giving in the future. Women frequently give saris to departing female relatives after a formal or long visit. Wedding preparations require the purchase of dozens of saris, since both the groom's and the bride's families are required to give saris to the bride, to other female relatives, to future in-laws, and to servants. Mira Nair's wonderful film *Monsoon Wedding* captures the stress that the bride's mother feels in attempting to match the quantity of saris that had been given by the groom's parents. The movie shows a typical scene of women huddled together at a sari shop, being shown saris by an ef-feminate, friendly seller who tries to please them and cannot resist interject-ing his own opinions. Sometimes the advice (and pressure) comes from the customer's shopping companions, including the husband, as illustrated in the series of interactions recorded by Banerjee and Miller during the fieldwork for their book *The Sari.*[26]

The owner of Ishaq Sarees in Madanpura told me that during the celebra-tion of Eid, Muslim men come to his shop, choose a few saris, and take them home for their wives to select from. He thinks that this is done to minimize the amount of time Muslim women spend outside of the home. Whether his rationale is true or not, the practice offers these particular women the conve-nience of shopping at home, yet it deprives them of choosing their saris from among the entire inventory of the store. Whether or not their husbands have made an initial cut, it is true that women still choose their saris from within the confines shaped by male taste: first by the weavers, then the middlemen, and finally the retail merchants. Yet these men must learn to appeal ultimately to the women who are their customers and whose taste must be taken into account. In this respect, buying saris is analogous to buying *salwar suits.* Both involve a complicated cycle of choices made by members of different genders and of various religious and ethnic backgrounds.

A system that brings people of different castes, classes, religions, and gen-ders together is bound to be abrasive and tense, and I felt some of these ten-sions one afternoon when I visited the Rinku Silk House. I was welcomed by one of its salesmen, the charismatic Pinku Mookerjee. The Rinku Silk House is located in the Bengali *tola* just inside Pandey Ghat, accessible directly from the river or through the *galis* from the center of town. This neighborhood, comprised of people displaced from Bengal for generations, is the center of creation for the *murtis* of Durga, which are modeled of clay upon a straw form that is bound to a wooden armature, just as they are in Calcutta or Dhaka. The neighborhood is adjacent to the Muslim area of Sonarpura, with its numerous sari-weaving workshops, and so a logical commercial connection is made. The large painted advertisement for the sari shop, visible from far out on the river, proudly states that the Silk House is recognized by the government of India, making it a credible business, a safe place to leave one's money.

On the first of many visits, we arrived early in the afternoon when, as in most shops and temples in Banaras, the place was spread with people napping on the floor. The salesman who approached us, Pinku, was by contrast, bright, awake, and energetic.[27] In his mid-twenties, Pinku sported a cool goatee and short hair combed forward, looking much like a hipster in a London underground nightclub. He wore a faded gray T-shirt, dark green cargo pants, and a flamboyant watch on his left wrist; he spoke English well and told us that his dream was to emigrate to Australia.

Pinku's talent, like Hemant's, is to match customers with textiles. He needs to analyze the customer and figure out what in the huge inventory will likely yield a purchase. The price range for saris at his store, Pinku said, varied from 200 to 10,000 rupees (from about $4.00 to $260.00). The saris at the higher end of the price spectrum are mostly packed up and shipped out to Bombay where, Pinku said, people have more money. I would guess that these expensive saris go to the fashion metropolis of Bombay not only because people there are more affluent, but also because the upper class of the city, consisting of people involved in the movie industry or successful businesses, probably have more occasions to wear the opulent, glorious saris of Banaras. Hemant told me that the people of Bombay have better taste than the "backward" residents of Banaras.

One similarity between Hemant's *salwar suit* shop and Pinku's sari shop is that in both places the owner makes an initial selection, on the basis of taste, and a special collection is set aside in the back for shipment to Bombay or other places. Such judgments evidently take place all over the city, being made in the shops for clothing and jewelry, on the basis of some preconceived understanding of preferences linked to caste and regional identity, to urban or rural residence, to economic class and the inclination to follow fashion. Decisions are made by storeowners and clerks with regard to taste and style, and as a result an item that a customer in Banaras might buy is left in the back room or shipped off to Bombay. Another consequence of this practice is that arguably the best things produced in the city of Banaras are automatically taken out of the city, sent away, destined for acquisition elsewhere.

Pinku, like Hemant, sees patterns emerge in what people buy. Like Hemant, whose explanation for the discrepancy in taste between Bombay and Banaras is based on regional aesthetics, Pinku also believes women have differences in taste that are cultural and not necessarily individual. He compared food choice to sari preference, both being matters of consumption. Pinku, a Bengali himself, said that Bengalis like simple, *sada* food and so, logically, prefer simpler saris. Bengali food is less lavish in its spice, and the preferred sari for Bengalis is less extravagant in ornament. There are obviously cultural predispositions toward certain colors or ornaments or overall looks, within which women make their individual choices, asserting personal taste within the framework of their culture. It is useful to know that the sellers of saris and *salwar suits* apply their own understanding of this cultural preference in textiles when they choose what to bring from the back room to show a customer.

Shopkeepers, whether owners like Hemant or employees like Pinku, are not only engaged in the selling of their respective commodities to women, they are actively involved in the purchase of their goods from textile suppliers. Hemant uses local brokers and buys his cloth outside of Banaras, but the Rinku Silk House is located in the city where silk saris are woven, and so its buyer dispenses with middlemen and deals with the weavers directly. Unlike the Muslim sari shops on Madanpura, the Rinku Silk House is owned and staffed by Hindus, which adds a layer of complexity to the dealings between the personnel of the shop and the weavers.

One of the first pieces of information Pinku gave us, during our initial visit, was that the majority of the weavers in Banaras are Hindu. While he offered us this clearly inaccurate fact, he pointed proudly to the mural behind him. The painting, in odd shifting perspective, depicted an unmistakably Hindu man, with a topknot and a delicate black mustache, wearing a white *dhoti*. This Brahmin was shown weaving a gold brocaded Banarasi sari while sitting on a cushion, wearing what looked like a prayer scarf around his neck that fell down over his bare chest. The picture may show a Hindu man dressed for worship at the temple, not work at the loom, but the point is clear: this store wants to create the illusion that its saris are woven by Hindus, thus potentially satisfying a few customers who, due to prejudice, might avoid patronizing the sari stores in the Muslim neighborhoods of Banaras. How could anyone disconnect the art of the sari from the Muslims of Banaras? There are Hindu weavers—maybe 20 percent of the weavers are Hindus—but whatever the religion of the weaver, Banarasi saris are designed by Muslim men, and they evoke the finer qualities of Mughal art and architecture. The weaver of the sari is not the only creator of the textile, as we will see in the next chapter. He works in collaboration with designers, dyers, and other craftsmen.

Most of the weavers in Banaras are, in fact, Muslims. Ten minutes after Pinku had called our attention to the Hindu weaver in the mural, we witnessed an interaction that takes place many times a day, in many shops. Two weavers entered the store and sat down on the floor. They were tall, bearded older men, each wearing a *lungi*, a *kurta*, and a prayer cap. Their clothing and facial hair immediately signaled their religious identity. One of the men held a plastic bag with a folded sari inside. Pinku ignored them while they sat and waited in silence. Eventually he spoke to them, using the informal second person singular verb form—language usually reserved for children and servants. When used in speaking to children it implies informality; when used with adults, it clearly connotes a difference in status. The Muslim men's sari was briefly inspected and contemptuously rejected on the basis of a minor weaving error. They were told to come back later, when the owner of the sari shop would be there.

This short and disturbing exchange, a piece of theater designed to impress us, illustrates the tensions between Hindus and Muslims in the city of Banaras. We witnessed a purposeful breach of social protocol in addressing elders or artists, and a display of the power merchants wield over weavers when they haggle to lower the price of a sari by focusing on minor imperfections. This accomplishes the task of acquiring the sari for a cheap price, simultaneously degrading its craftsmanship and insulting the weaver and the workshop.

Pinku's customers are women, but the sari weavers' customers are men who own and run sari shops. The weavers must please the men who mediate between them and the women who will wear their creations. Owners of weaving workshops must have an idea of what the sellers want in order to shape their products to please them. Before taking a closer look at the process of weaving saris, and the many aesthetic decisions made within the realm of production, it will be useful to understand what makes a sari desirable from the perspective of the merchant to whom the weaver sells. What are the merchant's standards of excellence, and how does he select his store's merchandise from among the tens of thousands of saris available in Banaras—at the weekly market at Golghar or from weavers walking in from the street?

When asked to explain his criteria for excellence in a sari, Pinku said the most important factor is the overall design. The fineness of a woven design is determined by the number of threads that make up the warp, the lengthwise threads that are set in the loom: the higher the count of warp threads, the finer the textile, the better the sari. Through the warp, crosswise threads—the weft—will be woven to create the web. Then, in a Banarasi sari, the shiny, raised design is created by adding an extra weft of *zari,* of gold-wrapped thread. This brocading technique produces an appearance comparable to embroidery, though the procedures are unalike: in brocading the design is woven in, while in embroidery it is added afterward.

The more warp threads a loom has, the greater the delicacy of the pattern, for the gold threads, inserted by hand, go in and out more often, creating finer and finer lines. If the warp count is low, the sari will be woven coarsely and the designs will be simple and blocky. With an increased number of warp threads, the gold *zari* may be woven in to create delicately curvaceous designs—peacocks, curling vines and flowers, the teardrop-shaped motifs familiar from paisley shawls, the heart-shaped motifs based on the *paan* leaf. To Pinku, the fine detail of these intricate designs was the major feature of a sari's beauty. This beauty is the result of the fineness of the weave and the technical virtuosity of the weaver. Assessments of a sari's quality are based not on arbitrary aesthetic reactions but rather on the close examination of the weaver's technical execution.

Pinku's first criterion is one of design: it should be fine and exhibit much meticulous handwork. This second criterion follows: for a sari to display work of the highest quality, it should have thin lines in the design on the front, and lots of waste of the gold thread on the back of the sari. Between appearances on the surface, the *zari* thread floats on the back. When thin lines are created, the *zari* pierces the front briefly, creating much floating. Since the gold threads are expensive, this is symbolically wasteful, since most of the thread is not visible to the eye when the sari is worn; it might be left floating behind, but more often it is cut away to create a light textile. By contrast, women from the countryside prefer the gold threads to show; the saris referred to as "village style" reveal much gold on the front, adding a brilliant shimmer to the surface of the sari and making its expense conspicuous. This village-style sari is visually and physically heavier due to the weight of the *zari* that thickens across the surface with little floating on the rear.

Pinku explained that there are two basic ideas of design. One he called "light design," meaning that the field of the sari textile is sprinkled with dots, spots of gold, or tiny flowers; the motifs separate from one another and spread wide in spacious, symmetrical array, normally in staggered rows. The other type of design he called "heavy," implying a complex design that covers more of the surface of the sari with motifs that are linked together in continuous sequence. Heavy designs are more expensive, since they are far harder to execute. Mistakes in heavy designs are especially noticeable. When motifs are linked—in the floral vines called *jangla,* for instance—every pass of the weft includes extra-weft *zari;* it is time-consuming and it yields an expensive product.

After the design, Pinku said, the quality of the materials was next in importance when evaluating the excellence of a sari. The tissue of a great Banarasi sari must be made of pure, real silk. Pinku said that saris can be woven out of impure silk—threads spun out of a combination of silk and banana fiber, or silk and plastic. Burning is the simple test for purity: silk threads burn like hair, smoothly, as opposed to plastic, which clots as it burns. After demonstrating this technique with the flick of a lighter, Pinku warned us that there are other materials that burn like silk. Buyers must be clever in determining the quality of the silk and not get duped by the workshop owner. Likewise, Pinku said, the *zari* threads should be made of real gold, but they are often faked of plastic.

The quality of the design of a sari can be evaluated visually, but the quality of the materials often escapes detection. Pinku extends his general distrust of the materials to the weavers. They often fool the merchants, he said, by asking a good price for a sari made with counterfeit silk and *zari.* (In reality, an innocent weaver might have been tricked himself by the suppliers of the raw materials.) Interactions between artists and merchants are always mixed with suspicion, but this mood of distrust might be especially exaggerated in Banaras, where the general misgivings between Hindus and Muslims become superimposed on the inherent wariness of business dealings.

A fine sari, Pinku elaborated, is all handwork. Most of the looms in Banaras are handlooms, *hathkarga,* but some are mechanized, the so-called "power looms," whose din can be heard in the narrow streets of the weaving districts of Banaras. Pinku ranked the saris woven in Banaras in this order: on the bottom of the quality scale are saris mechanically woven on power looms, which are simple and cheap. Above these are handwoven saris with no extra weft. And the highest of saris is the handwoven kind made with real silk and brocaded with gold threads. The price of the sari depends on the warp count and execution of the designs. Weaving mistakes bring the overall quality down and might be the basis for the rejection of a sari, as was the case when the Muslim gentlemen brought their work to Pinku's shop.

Pinku's desire was for meticulous, machine-like handwork, but what characterizes handmade things is precisely the variability, the signs of vitality, the marks of the human hand. Slight deviations make each piece unique, adding a dynamic and spontaneous quality that distinguishes handcrafted things from those that are mass-produced. So, there is an interesting paradox in the Banarasi sari: the best ones are totally handmade, but they must be flawless. Excellence is exhibited in the acute, almost machined precision of the hand weaving. The best design—delicate and linked—is best because it is most difficult, because it is the one in which mistakes are most likely to appear, so if it is rendered without a flaw, it seems supernatural in perfection and brings the greatest approval and the greatest price.

The saris Pinku likes best are the ones with supple curving motifs on the front and much floating of the *zari* on the rear; such a design is not forgiving, it allows for no mistakes. The lines of gold thread on the front are so slender and daring that any mistake will be readily noticed, but when the *zari* covers large areas of the front, slight mistakes do not show so much. The *zari* might be expensive but the handcraft is less demanding. The price is lower, and such pieces, which tolerate faulty weaving, are held in low esteem by the sari merchants.

It is interesting to compare the Banarasi sari with the world's most cherished and valued textile, the oriental carpet. In Turkey, small mistakes in the weaving of the rugs are seen by the village women, their creators, to be inevitable, a natural part of their art that enlivens the design. But Turkish buyers, in general, do not care for mistakes and prefer the precision in weaving that Pinku looks for in Indian saris. Foreign buyers of Turkish rugs, however, bored by industrial perfection in the West, look for signs of handcraft and often pay more for rugs with quirky imperfections.[28] Any handwoven textile will contain slight variations that might be considered flaws. These "flaws" may be cherished as spontaneous aspects of the creative process by Turkish carpet weavers, but they are damned as evidence of inattentiveness on the part of the weaver by the buyer of saris in India.

When a woman goes shopping for clothes, the things she finds have been shaped by the standards of the designers and producers, the brokers, middlemen, and merchants who influence her through her choices. What she wears reflects her personal taste. What she owns in her wardrobe, other than the gifts that are never worn, reflect her taste as well. But what she wears or owns or buys from the shops also reflects the personal tastes of the merchants and producers of textiles. In studying a woman's adornment, we naturally appreciate her artful assemblage of sari, jewelry, makeup, and hairstyle. But we need to understand as well the sari seller—Pinku, maybe—who enters into a sort of body art collaboration with his customers. And to understand Pinku, the merchant, we need to travel past him to meet the producers, the men whose aesthetic framework the merchants at once operate within and try to influence. Multiple decisions are made by the team of artists who produce a sari—the men who take spindles of thread and turn them into finely brocaded, luxurious cloth. These artists are the focus of the next chapter.

·5·

Weaving Saris

BANARAS HAS BEEN A CENTER for the production of exquisite brocaded saris for centuries. The colloquial name used throughout India for these saris—the Banarasi sari—implies a continuous association of the beautiful saris with the city where most saris of the type are still made. Saris are woven in the Muslim neighborhoods of Banaras: handwoven in Madanpura and Sonarpura, and manufactured on power looms in Alaipura. Dalmandi, the other main Muslim neighborhood, is the market center for readymade clothes; saris are neither woven nor sold there.

A significant portion of the residents of Banaras are involved in the sari trade in one way or another. Thousands of men (and a smaller number of women) work as weavers, a few of them ranked as masters. Some weaving families have been involved in the trade for generations; others turn to it intermittently to earn extra cash. Kanhaiya Kevat, for example, a charismatic *boatwallah* we met on the Ganges, explained that besides rowing a boat—and working out at the local wrestler's club, which is his favorite activity—he also weaves saris part-time. Many weavers are journeyman workers under the supervision of the families that have owned workshops for generations. These families of Muslim masters, who bear the surname Ansari, occasionally hire a few Hindu workers, such as Kanhaiya Kevat, who is not by caste a weaver.

"Commission boys," males of various ages, roam the streets of Banaras in search of unsuspecting tourists and wealthy pilgrims, and lead them to sari weaving workshops and retail outlets. They apparently act in a spirit of helpfulness, in line with the prevailing tradition of unsolicited advice, but in fact they work for a kickback on the goods inevitably sold. One afternoon, after visiting the South Indian temple, the Kamkotisvar Chikitsalaya Mandir, we were walking back through the *ghats*. At Harishchandra Ghat, a burning *ghat* and thus a tourist attraction, a friendly and rather nerdy young man, Manuj, approached us. He mentioned that his family owned a weaving workshop—a "sari factory" he called it in English, instead of using the Hindi word for workshop, *karkhana*. He offered to take us to see the weavers. Meeting the weavers was high on my research agenda; I would have to make contact somehow, and soon. This was as good a time as any, and so we followed Manuj inland, crossing the main road at the Ashok Hotel and Restaurant, and went into the Sonarpura neighborhood.

Manuj, our guide, would not tell us his full name—a common practice, for the surname immediately reveals one's caste. He worked for the Pooja Handcraft and Generations sari shop, where we were taken first, and introduced to his equally dodgy "uncle" Ashok (who referred to his "nephew" as Sanju, not Manuj). After Ashok piled saris in our laps and we bought nothing, Manuj begrudgingly took us, as he had promised, to a workshop. On the way there, Manuj explained that his uncle owned the looms we were about to see, hired the weavers, and ordered the designs of the saris they wove. Having heard this line before, I was anxious to talk to a weaver directly and hear from him who made the decisions about how a sari was woven.

As soon as we entered the workshop, we could sense the tension that rises when Hindus and Muslims meet in Banaras. Manuj talked to us about the weavers in English, in an attempt to separate him and us from them, and to prevent them from correcting errors in the information he was giving us. But I spoke, in Hindi, directly to Shameem Akhtar Ansari, the man who looked like he was in charge, and arranged to return the next day, without our helpful guide. The episode of the "commission boy" reveals some of the subtle conflicts that are embedded in interactions between Hindus and Muslims, merchants and weavers. The merchants regularly downplay the role and status of the sari weavers—masters of the art of brocading—in an attempt to emphasize their own importance, and possibly as a result of wider and deeper prejudices of economic class and religion.

The next day we made our way back to the workshop, remembering to make a left turn at a modest Hindu street shrine, into a dark alley filled with the unmistakable hum and clatter of Jacquard looms laboring away. The compound of the *karkhana* has four large rooms downstairs, arranged around an open courtyard. Each of the rooms is a workshop containing four looms, and each is under the supervision of a male member of the joint household. Some of the shops have large windows on the outer walls that bring light into the looms and open outward into the maze of narrow alleys. The family owns a total of twenty-two looms; sixteen at this location, and six in a nearby *karkhana.* We entered the first workshop on the right, and met Shameem Ansari again, whom the workers called *bara malik* (the big boss). He smiled a lot and was very friendly. Everybody there was noticeably relaxed, in contrast with the day before, when our "guide" had attempted to control events.

We met Shameem's younger brother, Mohammad Hashim, *chhota malik* (the small or younger boss), who spoke a serviceable, homemade English and who, over time, became my main source of information about the workshop.[1] Since most Muslim men have Mohammad as their first name in India, abbreviated Md. when they write, and since all the weavers have the same surname, Ansari, the middle name is the one that identifies them personally, so our main friend in the shop was named Hashim. Hashim explained that he and his brothers ran this workshop, the room we were in. His cousins, sons of his father's brothers, managed the other three, circled around the courtyard. He said that all of them were Ansaris, which he described as the main "caste" of sari weavers. His statement is interesting, and not inaccurate. The caste system in India extends beyond Hindus. The idea of a caste—an endogamous group traditionally engaged in an occupation—transcends religious identity, and some Muslims, such as the Ansaris, hold a comparable concept.[2] In her book *The Artisans of Banaras,* Nita Kumar describes the Ansari "caste" of weavers as a community with a distinct history and identity.[3]

The rooms in the shop are dark and cool. Eight men normally work in each of them at all times, since saris are usually woven in teams of two. The team is made up of a master and a young apprentice, though for particularly difficult designs, such as the vine-like *jangla,* two masters might weave together. During the summer months, when power outages are frequent, the looms are often brought to a stop when the lights go out and it becomes too dark to weave. The *karigars,* the shop's artisans, sit around, chew *paan* and drink tea, waiting for the electricity to return to the naked bulbs that hang above their looms. Because work is interrupted frequently, the hired weavers are paid by the finished sari, not by the hour. I found it remarkable that every time we visited, most of the workers stopped weaving and sat with us, listening to our chat with Hashim about the looms and the process of weaving. I took it as a sign of friendliness and of their desire to learn that they chose to stop weaving on their work time to participate in our conversations.

The loom that is used to make Banarasi brocaded saris is a complicated apparatus, joining an old Indian pit loom with the intricate Jacquard loom system of perforated cards that control the design of the woven textile. A French invention of the early nineteenth century, once used extensively in North America to weave coverlets, the Jacquard mechanism is now ubiquitous in Banaras.[4] The *karigar* sits at the loom, his legs hanging into a pit that is dug two feet deep. Three pedals control the loom. When a pedal is depressed, it lifts certain warp threads, allowing the supplementary *zari* weft to be woven through to create the design on the surface of the sari. Weavers work barefoot, easing the shifting of the pedals. When the *karigar* tramps on a pedal, a new card is brought into position above him. Metal fingers poke through the holes in the card, causing some warp threads to lift. The weaver inserts the extra weft by hand through this pattern, using separate spindles containing threads in different colors. He follows this by two quick shots of the shuttle through opposed sheds, binding the fabric together.[5] After completing about twelve inches, the *karigar* rolls the sari back around the cloth beam on the loom, covering the woven section with a cloth to protect it from food spills, *biri* burns, or stains from *chai* or sweat. It takes ten days to two weeks for a weaver to complete a sari.

Before the hired *karigar* is brought in to start weaving, the loom has to be set up by Hashim and his brothers. According to Hashim, it takes about fifteen days for a pair of men to set up a loom. This process is tedious and time consuming, since all of the threads of the warp—anywhere from five to eight thousand—have to be individually passed through a series of slots on the loom. The average warp count for the Banarasi saris woven by Hashim's family is six thousand threads.

Each loom is set up with enough length of warp to weave several saris, and a *karigar* will weave between two to six identical saris from one warp. After they are cut from the loom, each sari might be dyed a different color, providing variation in the products of one workshop. The Ansaris told me that saris are woven virtually year-round—more in anticipation of certain holidays, such as their Eid, and for Hindu and Muslim marriages, and less during the rainy season, for the moisture in the air causes the cards to swell and act up in the "machines," the English term Hashim used when talking about the Jacquard apparatus attached to the looms.

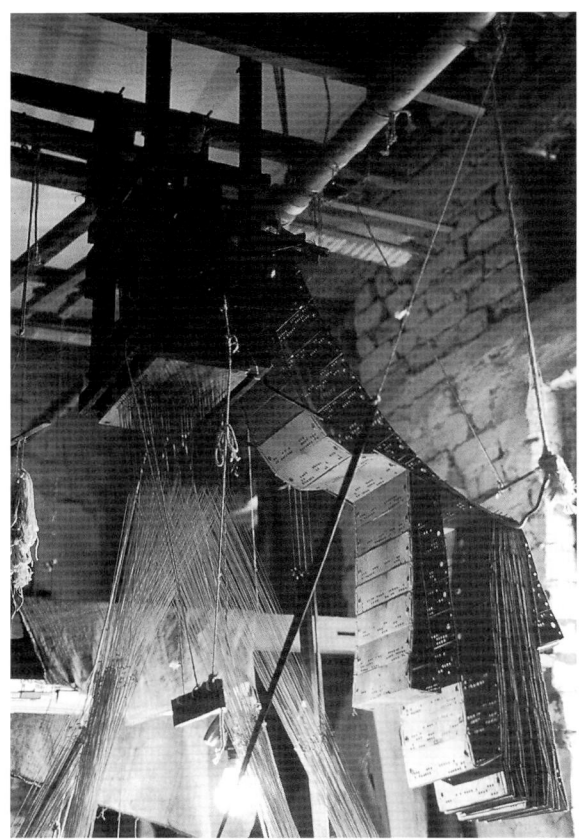

Detail of Jacquard loom. Hashim
Ansari's workshop, Sonarpura.

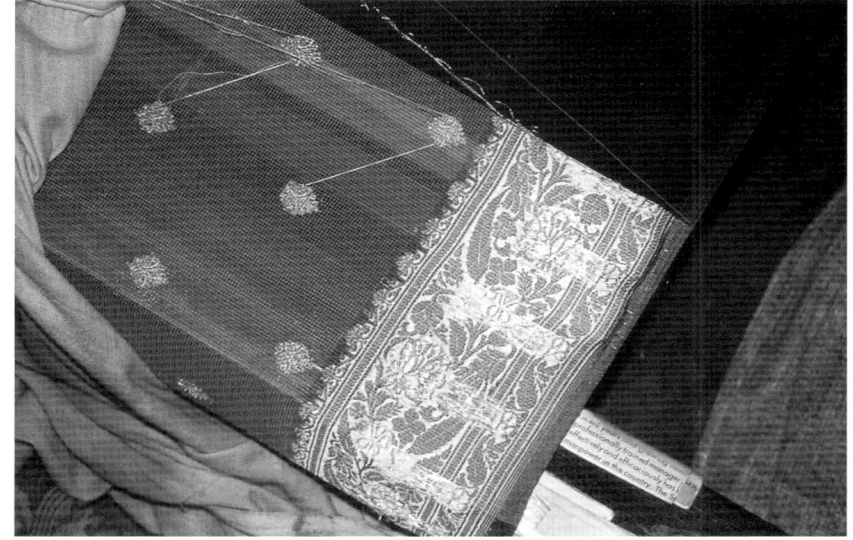

Banarasi sari on
the loom. Sadique
Ansari's workshop,
Sonarpura.

Even though the Jacquard loom seems mechanized, it requires much concentration and skill on the part of the weaver. The master, who sits on the left, controls the pedals, adds the *zari* weft to the left border and to the main field of the sari, and passes the shuttle through. He is accompanied by an apprentice, often a younger brother or cousin. The kid imitates the master while working the right border of the sari. The left border, the one created by the master, is continuous, running the length of the sari; it will become the border on the bottom when the sari is worn. The right border does not need to be as long, since most of the right edge of the sari will be pleated and tucked in when the sari is wrapped for wearing.

The weaver must keep in mind how the sari is meant to be displayed on the body, and make certain adjustments accordingly. If brocaded motifs, for example, are to appear on the upper right side of the sari, then golden cotton threads should replace the metallic ones which are prickly against the sensitive skin of the stomach, where the sari is tucked in. Also, if the sari carries designs across the whole field, the workshop can save costs by omitting brocading in the part of the web that will be hidden in the folds of the pleats. The weaver must retain a mental image of the whole sari, knowing when to switch threads or halt the right border, when to release the motifs of the field. The master *karigar* not only manages his own part, he must keep an eye on the apprentice, for any mistake in the sari will reflect on him.

Much of a sari's beauty depends on the expertise of the weaver. Remembering Pinku Mookerjee's assertion that 90 percent of the *karigars* are Hindus, I asked the Ansari brothers about their estimates of weavers in Banaras. Shameem guessed that Banaras contained about two to three hundred thousand weavers—two to three *lakh karigars*. Hashim speculated that 75 percent of the weavers are Muslims and 25 percent are Hindus whom the Muslims have trained to work for them. He said that Muslim girls do not weave, but that Hindus do push children of both genders into weaving. Hashim added that 90 percent of all Muslims in the state of Uttar Pradesh are in the sari business in some way—as weavers, designers, makers of cards, merchants, or suppliers of materials. Hashim's estimate that a large proportion of Muslims are in the sari trade is quite accurate,[6] making the self-conscious assertion of Hindu domination of the craft—exemplified on the mural at the Rinku Silk House—an interesting index to the cultural importance of the Banarasi sari and a sign of the tensions between merchants and weavers, Hindus and Muslims.

There are a large number of weavers available, and among them the workshop owners notice much difference in artistic skill and work ethic. Hashim said that his family paid the *karigars* by the completed sari, because if they paid them by the hour, the weavers, lacking any economic incentive to weave quickly, would dawdle at work and pause often in reverie. A good *karigar,* he said, is hard to come by, and when one is found, everybody wants to hire and keep him; as Hashim said in his quick, expressive English: "Hard worker is not every time free." One frustration of the workshop owner is finding and retaining industrious weavers among the many independent contractors who come and go at will.

I asked Hashim about his own family's involvement in the sari weaving trade. He responded by reference to the great Mughal emperor who lived from 1555 to 1606, saying that his family has been weaving since before Akbar's time. He continued by tracing the lineage of his craft: "Listen to my words: my father, his father, his father, his father, his father, his father. . . ." Proud of his English and wanting to practice it with me, Hashim declared his family's fated dedication to weaving: "We were born this work, and we will die this work."

We had many opportunities to watch Hashim at the loom, admiring his quick skill in weaving the intricate *jangla* saris. One day I asked him how he learned to weave. He said, at first in English: "Just like you don't have to teach baby fishes how to swim, like that I learned how to weave." Then he elaborated, in Hindi. The truth is a bit less mystical; Hashim sat at the loom with his brothers and learned to weave, serving as an apprentice on the right, until he could move to the master's seat on the left. During his childhood, as I imagine is the case with most of the boys in his neighborhood, Hashim learned from watching as well as from active instruction. He said he would watch, go out and play, watch some more, go play more, come back and watch again. His older brothers—Jamal Akhtar, Mohammad Islam, and Shameem Akhtar Ansari—taught him by giving him hints and gently correcting his mistakes. Eventually, by the time he was thirteen or fourteen, he had ascended to supervising his own young apprentice.

A sari's excellence depends on its weaver's dexterity, but it is also tremendously affected by the cards that feed through the Jacquard apparatus to lift the warp in patterned combinations. A weaver has to trust that the cards will lift up the right warp threads to form intricate, beautiful designs. The cards are punched by hand by *cardwallahs,* another set of independent contractors who work for different weaving workshops. Each sari has three separate sets of designs: one for the border, another for the field of the sari, and most importantly, one for the *palloo,* the elaborate end piece. Designs are first drawn on paper and then transferred onto graph paper, where the tiny squares containing a piece of the design are colored in yellow. To complicate matters, curving motifs must be interpreted as straight lines during this process. The graph paper is subsequently taken to a *cardwallah* such as Manuj Kumar, who works for Hashim in their Sonarpura neighborhood. We watched in wonder while Manuj punched the holes rapidly, translating the design, line by line, onto perforated cards. This tricky craft requires a quick mathematical mind—Manuj, I assume, with better luck in life, would be a millionaire in Silicon Valley—and astonishing hand-eye coordination, as the *cardwallah* interprets whether a piece of the designs needs to be punched in or not. Hashim told me that it takes an impressive five to six days for a *cardwallah* to complete all the cards required to weave one sari.

One advantage of a family-run workshop appears in the deliberate division and distribution of skills and labor among the brothers, ensuring an efficiently run business. While Hashim's workshop, like many others, relies on weavers and *cardwallahs* to work for them, family members accomplish the other important tasks. Assigning titles in English to himself and his brothers, Hashim explained how expertise is divided in the workshop: one brother, Shameem, is the "King of Machines," in charge of fixing the finicky looms; another brother, Hashim, is the "King of Market," buying supplies and selling the saris to shops; the youngest brother, Moshin, is the "King of Dyes," an expert of color combinations and the dyeing of the threads and of finished saris; yet another brother is in charge of the money, paying the workers; and the last and most important is the "King of Design," their old father, Abdul Qayoom, who invents the designs and establishes which designs will be woven on which looms in which seasons.

This system makes much practical sense. Hashim explained that if, for example, he were the one who knew how to fix the machines and the loom happened to break down—and they are always breaking down—while he was away at the market, work would stop until he returned. That is why they divide the tasks in the *karkhana.* The brothers, suspicious of the competitive nature of other weaving families, rely on each other, keeping the secrets of their trade in their house. This is the case with other crafts as well; each of the different skills required to run a successful workshop, whether creating textiles or pottery, depends on experienced masters of particular sub-crafts. In the sari weaving business, Hashim stated, "No man has whole knowledge." In such a complex technology, no individual can master every aspect of the system, so all rely on others who excel in their respective tasks.

The family decided not to teach weaving to the youngest brother, Moshin, an exceptionally handsome man in his early twenties. They knew they needed a color master, a "King of Dyes," in the family and pressed him into this position at an early age.[7] Most saris are woven of threads dyed in the colors that will appear in the finished product, but many saris are dyed, off premises, after they have been woven. This is true for saris woven of chiffon threads, which are treated chemically before weaving. A chiffon brocaded sari will be washed with water, eliminating the chemical and turning the sari white, at which point it can be dyed any color. *Zari* metallic threads in gold, silver, or brass are immune to the dye, so the background color of the sari can be determined after the weaving process has been completed, and the gleaming metallic threads will adjust to whatever color the dyer chooses.

Hashim plays an important role in this system. He is the one who goes to the market to purchase threads and parts for the looms and, most importantly, he is the one who takes the shop's saris to the merchants. He usually goes on this errand one day a week, on Tuesdays, avoiding dealings on Fridays, the day for prayer—*namaz*—for most of the people in the sari trade. Perhaps the most important job that Hashim accomplishes when he is selling at the sari shops is to look at the saris that others are weaving; he learns which ones are currently selling and which ones seem to be out of fashion. These observations, partially derived from the responses of such sari sellers as Pinku Mookerjee, determine what steps the workshop should take to adjust their products to market trends. It is interesting to note that Hashim's observations are not based on what the women on the streets are wearing, but rather on what the sellers are buying. Hashim's target is not the female customer, but the male buyer.

The observations Hashim makes about color, design, and fabric preference are reported back at home, especially to his father, the patriarch, the "King of Design." Mr. Qayoom owns what Hashim calls a "design map," a file containing hundreds of designs. His father consults this "map," lifting designs and mixing the motifs in different combinations to create new saris. Hashim's father invents new design combinations after listening carefully to his son's judgments about successful saris on the market. Once a new design has been conceived, Hashim's family will hire a designer to render it onto the graph paper used by the *cardwallah*. There are about one hundred designers avail-

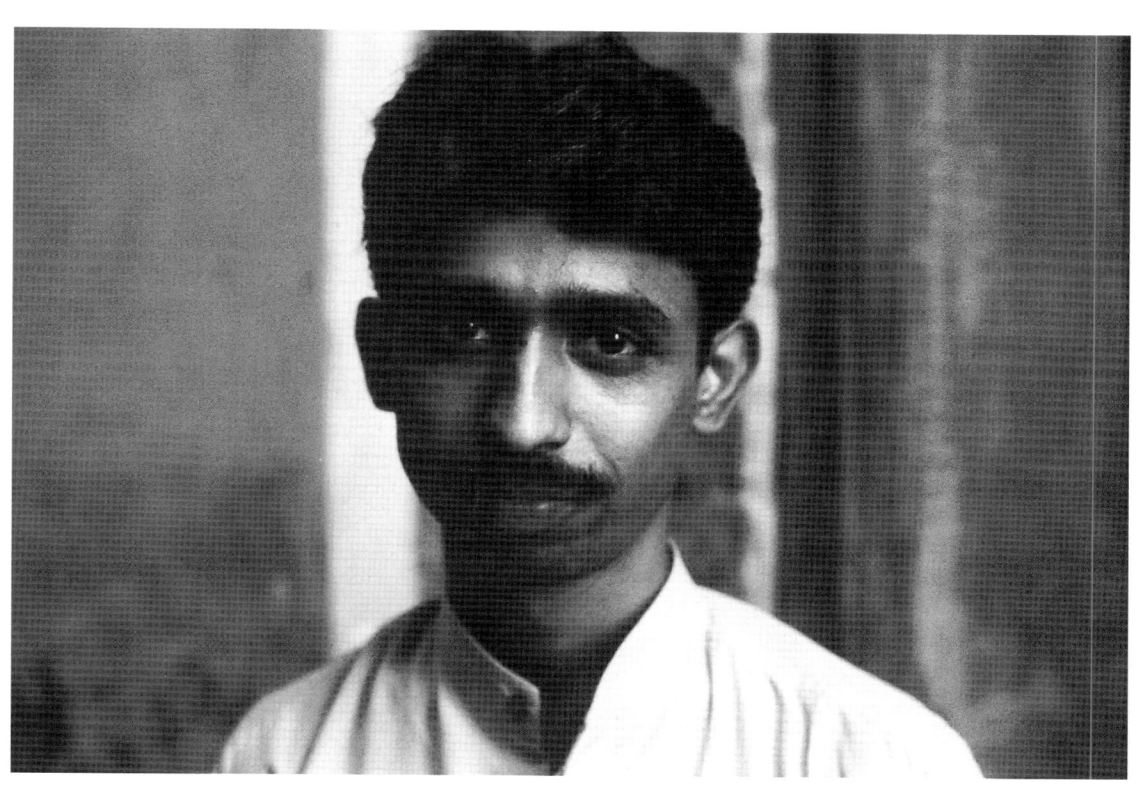

Hashim Ansari

able in Banaras—yet another group of independent contractors. Hashim's *karkhana* knows which designers draw which motifs well, so they choose which one to commission for the work depending on the actual design of the sari. Sometimes different designers are utilized for different parts of the sari; some men are better at borders, others are more adept at drawing the *palloo*.

We see that the variables of a sari are coupled with the skills of the makers of the textile: the designer, the *cardwallah,* the weaver, and the dyer. Among the factors that influence the aesthetics of the sari, one is color. Hashim's workshop weaves saris in light colors in the summer months and dark colors for the winter months. He referred to pastel colors as "English" or "city" colors and rich, bright colors as "village colors." Village women, Hashim said, love color so bright that even a blind person could see it. Differences in the tastes of rural and urban women involve design as well as color. Village people like saris that are "heavy," with much brocade showing on the front, while the city ladies prefer delicate designs. Hashim's assessment of the difference in the preferences of rural and urban women tallies perfectly with Pinku Mooker-jee's judgments. Village style might be visually heavy, overloaded with gold and bright colors, while urban style is subtler in hue and gold brocade, but both kinds of saris require comparable amounts of time and attention, and they can be identical in price.

The masters in the *karkhanas* intelligently weave saris to appeal to certain aesthetic preferences presumed to belong to village and city women, and they also weave to suit the changing seasons. When they weave, the masters must keep the female customers in mind, for the season affects both the color of the sari and its fabric. In the summer months, women prefer the cool of cotton saris in light and pastel colors. In the winter Hashim weaves darker tones in what he calls "silk by silk," saris that are silk in both warp and weft. Finally, in the transitional seasons of autumn and spring, his *karkhana* weaves light and gauzy silk with georgette, or "china" blends, which combine silk and polyester.

Hashim, like other masters, relies on the suppliers to provide him with raw materials of quality. All the supplies he needs he buys in Banaras, "between Raj Ghat and Ramnagar." But these materials are purchased from elsewhere by wholesalers, who go to Surat, Gujarat, for example, to purchase *resham* silk threads and kilos of *zari*. Real *zari* retains its metallic gold color, while counterfeit *zari* turns black, and Hashim proudly proclaimed that he gives a "five years guarantee" that the *zari* on his saris is not defective.

When much *zari* floats on the back of a sari, the workshops usually cut the extra thread away to make the sari lighter in weight. Some claim that the Muslim women of the *karkhanas,* sequestered upstairs in the rooms around the open courtyard, are the ones who do this work. Hashim said the women of their family take care of the children and cook the food,[8] while Hindu women are hired to cut away the *zari.* They are allowed to keep the scraps, as these are now *bekar*—useless for them—and poor Hindus use the *zari* to make *rakhis* for sale. *Rakhis* are shiny ornaments attached to strings and tied on the wrists of men by their sisters on the occasion of the Hindu festival of Rakhi in late summer.[9] I found his statement subversively amusing. Hashim claimed that poor Hindus used the Muslim weavers' waste to celebrate the vital bond between brother and sister. The story I have always heard of the origin of the *rakhi* recounts how Hindu women under siege in Rajasthan, fearing for their chastity and afraid of becoming carried into the harems of Muslim invaders, tied such strings on the wrists of their Muslim captors, morally bonding them as brothers and protectors. (Today many women in Banaras, working in offices mostly populated by men, tie *rakhis* on the wrists of their male co-workers, making them symbolic brothers, and hoping, thus, to prevent sexual tensions in the work place.)

A final variable affecting the types of saris produced in Hashim's workshop—in addition to those of design, color, fabric, and weight—involves the intended use of the cloth. Their *karkhana* weaves "suit pieces" for their own use, since Muslims do not wear saris as frequently as Hindus do. Hashim said that some castes of Muslims, such as the Khans, get married in saris, but the Ansari caste does not. Their brides marry in beautiful *salwar kurta* suits made out of the brocaded silk fabric woven in their workshops. An average sari is about six meters long; a loom can also create pieces of the same length, out of which *salwar suits* are cut and assembled. These have two meters designated for the *kurta,* two for the *salwar* pants, and two for the *dupatta.* The fabric is taken to a seamstress and tailored to fit the woman's body. Unlike Hindu brides, for whom the Ansaris weave fancy saris in shades of red, maroon, and magenta, Muslim brides may marry in any bright color—red, blue, green, or turquoise.

Many factors contribute to a sari's overall quality. The most important, according to Hashim, is the design. The designer of a sari must make a host of aesthetic decisions about the motifs and their artful combinations, about the distribution of these throughout the sari, and about the pattern and connection among the designs on the border, the field, and the *palloo.* Though he puts design first, Hashim believes that the greatest art of a sari lies in achieving the perfect combination of design, color, and material. This skill, or its lack, is the defining factor that separates the master from the worker in a workshop. Hashim stated adamantly that if a *karigar* can design his own saris, he could be the master of a workshop; but those who cannot design are doomed to remain weavers forever.

An excellent sari, according to Hashim, is judged by its design, by the selection of color and fabric, and by the weight of the sari that results from the choice of fabric and the amount of brocading. All of these features lead to immediate sensory reactions. After the overall aesthetic has been taken in viscerally, the eye focuses in on the specific details of the weaving quality and notes flaws in the execution of the motifs and in the web of the fabric. These secondary technical factors, which might never be detected by the ultimate female consumer, are what the store owners, the male buyers of Hashim's saris, notice immediately.

Hashim, and all the owners of *karkhanas,* can control their products only to a certain extent. His family can invent the design, choose the fabrics, dye the cloth, and buy the supplies. But they are at the mercy of the expertise of the other craftsmen and the honesty of wholesalers. The owner of a successful workshop must trust the skill of the *cardwallah,* the dexterity of the hired *karigar,* and the quality of the *zari.*

The Jacquard loom *karigar,* unlike the weaver who works on simpler kinds of looms, has little leeway for spontaneity. He is not allowed to deviate from the design of the sari, nor can he free himself from the mechanical constraints of the loom; his only option is precision. The sari is ultimately judged, at least by the merchants who buy and stock them, on the excellence in execution of the weaving. Merchants narrow their decision down to the only factor in direct control of the weaver. Although the weaver is not at the top of the hierarchy of a sari *karkhana,* often being hired after most of the decisions concerning the sari have already been made, it is ultimately his skill that makes the difference between a good and an outstanding sari.

The path a sari takes from its moment of creation to the body of a woman is long and complicated, involving many people, including producers and suppliers of silk and *zari,* designers, draftsmen, card punchers, loom technicians, weavers, a few merchants and middlemen, and finally, the consumer. In each of these categories, individuals have criteria of excellence, but these do not necessarily correspond or mesh. For example, Hemant Khanchandani of the Dayaram Fashion Centre sees himself as an expert on textiles, not only for *salwar suits* but for saris as well. His main criterion for judging a Banarasi sari is the material: it must be pure silk. Second, he sees the quality of the *zari*. And third, he notices the smoothness of the weaving; the web should not have any shading, any streaks that are revealed when the sari is held up to the light. This defect is caused, according to Hemant, by the uneven seating of the weft, which results from the weaver beating the weft down with inconsistent force. Small mistakes can also be noticeable in the brocaded sections, when the thread of the ground can be detected within the confines of the golden *zari* motif. This problem results, Hemant said, from skips in the smooth running of the cards in the Jacquard apparatus. These are small mistakes that few see. "Nobody knows it," Hemant said, but his expert eye can spot such defects. As a professional textile merchant, he feels it would be his responsibility to detect and reject the saris with such flaws, keeping the overall quality of his merchandise high.

As a point of contrast, let us recall the criteria of another cloth merchant, Pinku Mookerjee of the Rinku Silk House. Pinku judges the excellence of a sari by the warp count and the degree of fine detail in the design that a high warp count allows. He also feels that finer designs, those with delicate lines in the front and excess *zari* floating on the back, yield more attractive saris. Of course, Pinku, like Hemant, acknowledges the need for materials of high quality: pure silk and real *zari*.

Another seller, Nasir Bhai, who owns the Farhan Sarees store on Madanpura Road, judges a sari by the quality of the materials and by the effort exerted by the weaver. He explained to me that the best saris, in his opinion, are what he called *minakari* saris—saris woven with colorful silk threads embedded into the golden *zari* motifs in a way that resembles the *mina* enamelwork on golden jewelry. He said that the price (and quality) of the sari depends on the number of colors in the *mina* motifs. Four different colors on the *mina* border imply a finer sari than one that has only two. Nasir Bhai showed us a sari that had one color embedded in the border motif and four on the *palloo*. This sari was less expensive than one that had four colors on both the *palloo* and the border. The weavers for the second and better sari had to manage many more shuttles while properly negotiating the silk weft of the background, in addition to the *zari* and the four separate *mina* silk threads, for the full length of the sari, because the left border continues from end to end. Nasir Bhai, like many people, believes that if a weaver is executing a fine, complicated design, he will create a higher quality product because of his personal investment of ego, as well as the expense of the work in material and time.

Resuming our survey of the criteria used to judge excellence in saris, we move from Hemant, seller of *salwar suits*, and the sari merchants Pinku and Nasir Bhai, to Hashim, a weaver and the master of a sari workshop, who feels that it is the excellence of design—the ingenuity of mixing and matching traditional motifs—that signals, undeniably, the superior quality of the best of Banarasi saris.

To complete this brief treatment of aesthetic standards, we will need to look at the final key player in our model for study: the female customer who chooses to buy and wear the saris made and sold by these men. Mukta Tripathi answered my question by ranking sari variables in this order of importance: first materials; then color (not abstract colors, but the particular hues that suit her skin tone); and only then did she consider print and design. She said, as some of the men did, that the first thing to consider is the material of the sari, for the wrong fabric instantly renders a sari *bekar*. While the merchants and weavers talked about the quality of materials in terms of an objective assessment of raw products and prices, Mukta, the one who will actually wear the sari, had a slightly different reading of the importance of fabrics. She explained that she prefers cotton, as it is "soothing." It feels cool in the summer and warm in the winter. Her second choice is silk, but she only likes it in the winter, since it is too warm for the other seasons. Finally, in the rainy season, Mukta prefers chiffon saris, since cotton, if wet, will not dry quickly, while wet chiffon dries easily under a ceiling fan. No matter how beautiful the artisans think they are, Mukta rejects Banarasi saris with *zari* for two reasons: they blacken due to the poor quality of the gold threads, and they are now, according to her, "old fashioned."

I asked Neelam Chaturvedi, a self-proclaimed connoisseur of saris, to delineate her criteria of excellence. Without pausing to think, Neelam stated that the sari must be chiffon, and she consistently named the material as the primary criterion. She is in accord with Mukta (and with other women) in emphasizing the importance of the fabric, for its aesthetic qualities in use— once it is draped on the body—and not for its material qualities as a fabric. Neelam said that chiffon is the best fabric because it looks good on the body, hugging and enhancing "the figure." In a light, gauzy chiffon sari, the woman's body is on display. A bulky six meters of thick fabric, folded and draped over

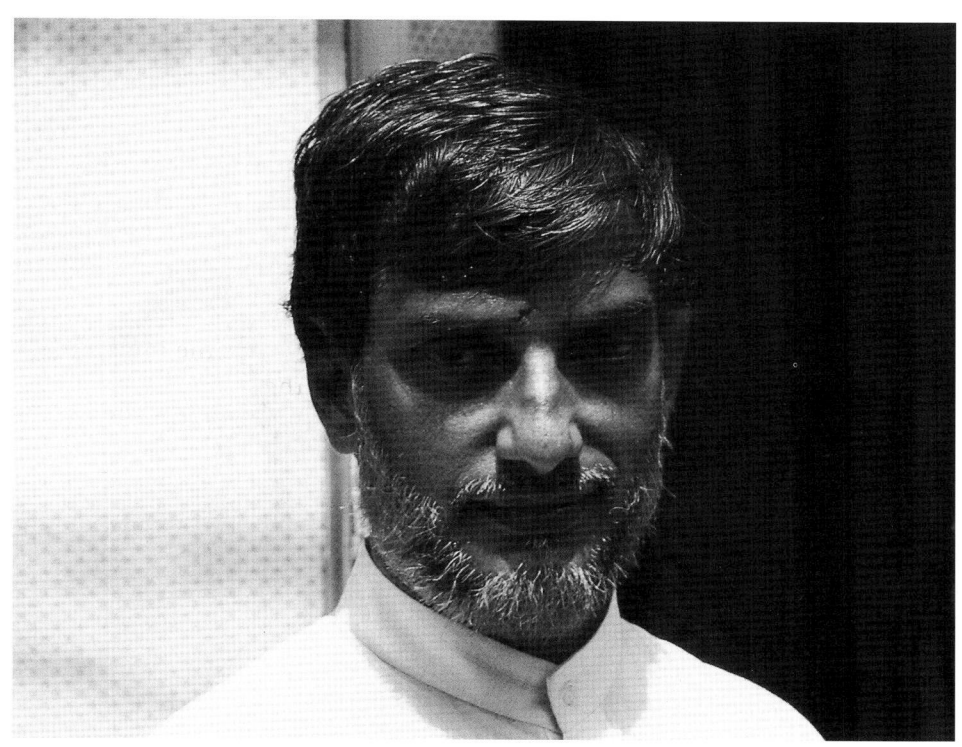

Nasir Bhai

the body, does not flatter a plump figure. Neelam's second choice in fabric is silk, which she judges by touch, testing the sari for smoothness. Like Mukta, Neelam is interested in the feel of the fabric against her skin. She said she likes cotton saris nowadays, for they come in a huge assortment of designs, "parallel" to silk ones in quality. After noting the materials, Neelam looks at the color, attending with interest to the combinations of hue and value. She prefers "matching colors" to "contrasting colors." Finally, Neelam chooses the saris that have much *mehanat*—time-consuming and fine work. In this she agrees with Nasir Bhai's judgments.

Maker, merchant, consumer: their different standards of evaluation reveal the different ways that people can relate to a piece of cloth. Women like the feel of the cloth against their skins, and they like how it looks when draped on their bodies. They evaluate a sari primarily as a thing to use—it should fit the figure and dry quickly in the rainy season—for they use saris in their creative acts of self-adornment. Merchants, by contrast, note the quality of the cloth and the fineness of its weave. These men focus on the implicit material wealth of the textile, which is determined by the complicated design and technical perfection (in which much labor is banked), and by the quality of the silk and *zari* (representing high-cost, high-quality raw materials). The weavers, though, are impressed by an excellent design and the balance among components, for these men are the makers of the saris, and like all artists they are interested in the process and excited by the challenges offered to the mind and hand during the creative act.

Taken together these views form a complementary distribution across the field of possible response to a textile. They intersect, differing more than they conflict. It is currently fashionable in scholarship to stress the conflicts and tensions between patrons and makers of traditional arts.[10] The tensions in the art of the Banarasi saris are very real; they result from differences in the status, caste, ethnicity, and religion of the individuals interlocked in the cycle of negotiation. Sari sellers try to unload their old stock on their customers, who in turn try to push the merchants to a low price during hard bargaining. The owners of sari shops lord it over their salesmen. The merchants bully the weavers. The masters of the workshop push around the journeyman weavers, the hired *cardwallahs* and dyers. And always beyond the differences of economy and status, there are the deep-seated religious prejudices that divide Muslims and Hindus in Banaras.

Yet, while people hold different standards of excellence, it does not follow that they are locked in conflict. All of them, though different in gender, caste, status, or religion, operate together within a coherent cultural system. A general aesthetic sense is shared among them. Everyone develops a distinct awareness of the limitations and possibilities within the tight frame of what constitutes a sari, in particular a Banarasi sari. Within this frame, there is breadth enough for a diversity of reactions and creative options, which are at once enabled and restricted by the particular technological limitations of this tradition. The standard of excellence for any textile, including the Banarasi sari, includes a grand range of choices in design, color, and fabric, set against mastery of the mechanical demands of the weaving process.

In the case of the Banarasi sari, the male weavers and the female customers, both of whom are artists—the one during textile production, the other during the act of self-adornment—are both more forgiving of weaving mistakes than the merchants are. Not being makers of things, the merchants lack compassion for the weaver's difficulties and, perhaps, their need for self-expression. But the merchants have their creative moment, in which many of them are virtuosos—the moment when they sell the creations of other people to the customers who will use them in creative acts of their own. Normally the merchant, viewing the sari as a commodity, judges it with a tough, critical eye. That critical ability serves him, of course, when he buys, but he will also put it on display during a sale, disparaging a piece, even if it lowers his profit, because through his criticism he asserts his superiority to the weaver, the one who can actually make things, but who must work with his hands.

The women are as adept at noting errors in weaving as the men, but they are more tolerant than the merchants. I asked Neelam Chaturvedi if she would still buy a silk sari after she had noticed an uneven weft or some other kind of weaving defect. She said that if she loved the sari—loved the color combination and the design—she would point out the mistake only in the hopes of getting a discount, but if no discount were forthcoming, she would still buy the sari.

An emphasis on technical virtuosity is not peculiar to Banaras. The creation and assessment of the Banarasi sari can be contextualized by looking at two very different traditions of fine weaving: the *jamdani* sari, woven to the east in West Bengal and Bangladesh, and the *patola* sari woven to the west in the state of Gujarat.

In the wide bright windows of the fancy shops on Dashaswamedh Road, next to the locally made Banarasi saris hang delicate *jamdani* saris woven around the centers of Calcutta and Dhaka. *Jamdanis* are regarded through-out India as one of the fine saris women long to own. The ancient home of the *jamdani* is the Dhaka district of Bangladesh, and the modern center of production lies just east of Dhaka in Rupganj, where these intricate saris are woven on bamboo pit looms, comparable to those of Banaras except that there is no machine to set the pattern and the work is done entirely by hand and eye.

In the village of Kazipara, Rupshi, I met and watched the great master Showkat Ali. Working with a helper, he thrusts a slim wooden tool into the warp, follows it with the extra-weft that is placed by hand, and then secures the pattern and the web with two shots of the shuttle. In concept the brocade is exactly like that of the Banarasi sari, but there are no mechanical aids, no Jacquard apparatus, so the *jamdani* fabric flutters with vitalizing variation and the motifs, sketched into the warp by eye, seem angular and geometric when compared with the sinuous intricacy of the Banarasi sari. *Jamdani* saris, like those of Banaras, are woven in two general categories of design: "light," show-ing a repetition of motifs sprinkled regularly over the ground of the cloth, and "heavy," in which interconnected motifs fill the ground. Unlike Banarasi saris, *jamdanis* are woven of exceedingly fine cotton thread, giving them the characteristic transparency of muslin—the look of woven air on which the motifs seem to float. They are coveted precisely for their handcrafted quality, and for the diaphanous web that surrounds the women who wear them with a gauzy haze of light.[11]

Patola saris from Patan, in Northern Gujarat, are woven in a harness loom by two male weavers, both of them masters. These masters are Hindus or Jains, not Muslims as the weavers are in Bangladesh and as they mostly are in Banaras. *Patola* saris are silk double-ikat textiles. Both the warp and the weft threads are tie-dyed separately before weaving commences. In the meticulous weaving process the dyed threads are forced to match up perfectly, revealing intricate designs, such as the popular *kunjar* elephant, as well as flowers, birds, and human figures. When I served as a presenter at the Smithsonian Folklife Festival's celebration of the art of the Silk Road, in 2002, I spent much of my time with three brothers—Vinayak Salvi, Bharat Salvi, and Rohit Salvi—who belong to one of two families of the Salvi weaving caste that still work at this amazing and time-consuming art.[12] The partial sari on display by the Salvis was so remarkable and beautiful that all the visitors, including renowned cel-list Yo-Yo Ma and the former American Secretary of State Colin Powell—experts in the precise arts of music and war—were astounded during their brief visits by the technical virtuosity of the *patola.*

Before Rohit and Bharat can start weaving, Vinayak places the warp and weft threads with great exactitude on a frame, carefully marking the design, and binding the silk threads with cotton cords to prevent certain sections from receiving the dye. These threads are dunked into a dye bath, and then after they dry, some of the old ties are opened while new areas are tied. The process involves tying, untying, retying, and dyeing the thread multiple times, soaking the threads in three separate dye baths to achieve a total of six colors, some as a result of over-dyeing.[13] The art of dyeing requires much patience and dexterity on the part of a master, who must envision bits of the motifs on the individual threads of both the warp and weft.

The second and final step in the preparation of a *patola* sari is the weaving itself, in which two masters work together to combine the warp and weft into the sari's designs. This step requires skill and mathematical precision. The weft is added loosely, and then it is painstakingly adjusted by hand with the help of metal picks, to align the threads to form the patterns. Only then is the weft beaten down into the web. The entire process of making a *patola* sari takes from six months to one year. These saris, highly appreciated and appropriately expensive, are usually woven on commission for affluent people residing in Baroda, Bombay, Calcutta, New Delhi, and cities abroad. Appreciation for this art is not recent; there are a few fine examples of nineteenth century *patola* saris permanently on display in the new Nehru Gallery of Indian Art at the Victoria and Albert Museum in London.

All three of the saris discussed here—Banarasi brocade, Bengali *jamdani,* and Gujarati *patola*—are valued for their beauty, their symbolic communication of high status, and their shocking technical excellence. *Jamdani* saris are appreciated for the skill of the weaver, his hand-eye coordination in creating floating motifs that are evenly spaced and steady in scale, distribution, and design. A slight imperfection, or "mistake," reminds the beholder that this sari was made completely by hand—by a highly skilled human being—which adds to appreciation. *Patola* saris are also completely handmade with a rudimentary loom. And they, too, are marvels of precision, but tiny details—in this case in the dyeing, rather than the weaving—provide, as in the *jamdani,* a subtle wavering from symmetry, such as one finds in nature: both exhibit a vivid ratio of exactitude and variability. The best *jamdani* and *patola* saris, however, are both as machine-like and precise as hand techniques can achieve, and so, in essence, they match the Banarasi sari in aesthetic desire. The difference is that the Jacquard apparatus makes technical perfection possible. The Banarasi process is, in fact, partially mechanized. There is an integral human element to the weaving, but, ideally, the human hand should not be detectable in the final product; a mistake in the weave—a reminder of the person who created it—can cause the sari to be rejected.

All three of these fine saris are valued for the care and virtuosity of the weavers, and all are coveted by the female consumers who display them on their bodies at special events, especially weddings. While the Banarasi sari is the garment of choice for most brides in India, the other two saris might be worn by a guest at the wedding, or generously given as part of the trousseau. Normally commissioned, *patola* saris are sold directly to women by the weavers. *Jamdani* and Banarasi saris are brought by the weavers to the buyers, who inspect for flaws and give the highest prices to the finest and technically most perfect pieces, though of necessity slight variations in the brocading are tolerated more in *jamdani* than in Jacquard-woven Banarasi saris. The artists in all three of these traditions create unbelievably stunning, awe-inspiring textiles that are made by hand and achieve a level of beauty and grace no machine can reach. The weavers in Dhaka, Patan, and Banaras deliver just that: woven splendors in cotton, silk, and gold.

·6·

Making Jewelry

INDIAN WOMEN GENERALLY view their jewelry as the central component of their personal adornment; something to hold, possess, and treasure as well as to wear, it is more important than their clothing. Clothes are used daily to convey multiple messages; they are changed and bought with frequency, but a woman's jewelry is special for many reasons. Its cost is higher, its materials are precious, and its permanence provides a powerful sense of ownership and enables it to be passed down as an heirloom, building connections between the generations. Items of jewelry—like the brocaded saris of Banaras—are carefully chosen by the wearers for their beauty and symbolic value, and, like the saris, jewelry embodies the aesthetic choices made by a series of men—the suppliers of materials, the talented craftsmen, and the wily merchants. The production of jewelry involves complex negotiations of the kind found in the production of cloth. In both cases, the artists, the middlemen, and the sellers are men of different castes, ethnic groups, and religions. In both cases, the products—woven cloth or gold jewelry—can be imported from elsewhere in India or locally produced by *desi* artisans.

Jewelry production involves a team of independent contractors who work together. Each man has his own skill, and most important, his own standard of excellence. The goldsmith, enameller, and stone setter, like the weaver, dyer, and *cardwallah* of the brocaded sari, must each satisfy his own taste, while remaining true to his tradition. These men aim to display their talent and the beauty of their creations without deviating too much from shared aesthetic standards, especially those that appeal to the merchants and their female customers.

In India, goldsmiths might sell their creations through their own shops, but more often, they rely on a *saraf*—an individual who owns a jewelry store and extends to the craftsman the capital needed to buy the costly materials and produce the ornaments, which the *saraf* then sells.[1] In Banaras, many of the finest artisans involved in the production of ornaments sell their creations through Kanhaiya Lal Damordas Saraf & Co., one of the four reputable shops of the Kanhaiya Lal franchise that sell gold and silver in the city. A detailed examination of the store's sales strategies will be the topic of the next chapter, but before analyzing how the finished products are sold, let us look at the creative processes of making jewelry, focusing on a few master *karigars*.

In the chapter on *salwar suits,* we saw how Banarasi merchants—such as Hemant Khanchandani—bring cloth and readymade *suits* from beyond the city. A similar pattern of commerce can be found in jewelry; local craftsmen do not produce all of the jewelry for sale in Banaras. Suppliers like Sandeep Singh,[2] who works closely with the Kanhaiya Lal stores, must be aware of the demands of the customers, decide what kinds of jewelry to acquire, and discover where he can find them. Sandeep, a friendly Punjabi from Banaras, believes that certain types of jewelry cannot be made locally, for example the famous Jaipur *mina,*[3] because Banarasi craftsmen lack the ability to create enameling of such high quality—although this point is adamantly refuted by local *mina* artists. Sandeep said that the kind of *mina* made in Calcutta is imitated in Banaras, but the result is not as fine as the "original" product. In English he said, "Everywhere has its own specialty," and though some items could be made locally, the finest pieces always come from the "original spot," the place where the tradition began and is carried on most energetically.

Sandeep's assertion that imitations are not as good as the jewelry found in the "original spot" seems right, since *karigars* attempting to make a new kind of jewelry are not insiders to the craft tradition of the items they are striving to emulate. They have received no instruction, and they have to figure out how to make such an ornament simply by looking at it carefully; they would not know the techniques, the materials, the tools, the history, and the meanings associated with the process of production. The *karigar* attempting to imitate an item of jewelry—to say it simply—would not have the benefit of the apprenticeship period, which brings a craftsman inside a tradition and leads him toward mastery of the trade—an idea supported by many studies of traditional crafts by folklorists.[4]

Knowing which items Banarasi artists can successfully imitate is part of

Sandeep's talent as a supplier of jewelry. Through experience, for instance, he has learned not to commission local artists to attempt *mina* in the Jaipur style. But Sandeep showed me a photograph of gold necklaces he discovered in Punjab, necklaces he plans to make in Banaras and sell in the local market, hoping to enjoy a temporary monopoly on a new and exciting product. Much of Sandeep's work involves purchasing jewelry elsewhere and selling it in Banaras. He showed me a golden necklace from Gujarat, a type made only there because the technique of filling gold beads with lacquer, Sandeep said, has been mastered nowhere else in India.

Because many items of jewelry are made elsewhere and imported into the city, Banaras does not have an inordinate need for *karigars*. Unlike the sari trade that brings in workers from neighboring villages, Banaras does not need to supply a large national demand for a specialized form of jewelry, as it does with brocaded saris. The city, though, does have special needs, and excellent craftsmen to fill them. Certain famous types of ornaments are associated with Banaras, especially those displaying the exquisite *gulabi mina,* pink enameling, which is prominently featured in museum displays of Indian ornaments and in the major studies of Indian jewelry. These include the books on traditional jewelry by Untracht and by Krishnan and Kumar and the survey of Indian jewelry at the Victoria and Albert Museum by Stronge, Smith, and Harle—and even general books on Indian traditional art, such as Barnard's overview of the artistic traditions of India and Jain and Aggarwala's book on the traditional arts in the museum of New Delhi.[5]

Many of Banaras's artisans in the jewelry trade work within a few blocks of the oldest Kanhaiya Lal store, located at Raja Darvaja, adjacent to the Muslim commercial center in Dalmandi. These *karigars* form a network that spreads away from the store that will ultimately sell their creations. If an item is commissioned by a customer, the procedure might begin in a particular artist's studio, but more likely, the first conversation takes place at Kanhaiya Lal, ensuring the store of their usual 25 percent commission on the jewelry made by local artists. With the help of the owners of Kanhaiya Lal, I was taken to visit many of the artists with whom they have cooperative commercial arrangements. One afternoon, Ramesh Pandey, one of the salesmen at Kanhaiya Lal, took me through the streets and down a narrow corridor that led to an open courtyard, surrounded by tiny one-room shops where the jewelers worked. The first studio, opening right on the street, belonged to Salik Ram Soni, a stone setter. There were jewelers' workspaces across from him, others behind him, and the third studio on the right was Gopal Ram Nagar's space, where he gold-plated silver jewelry. The three additional tenants in this small cluster of craftsmen included Gopal Prashad Meenekar, who occupied the last shop on the right, its front open to the courtyard. Gopal Prashad is a talented enameller, a master of the art of *mina*, as his last name—Meenekar—literally indicates.

As lushly illustrated books of Indian jewelry reveal, one of the most beautiful items of Indian ornament is the pair of golden *karas,* thick gold bracelets with enameling on the inside, precious stones set on the outer periphery, and, at the joint in the circle, a pair of opposed solid gold animal heads—crocodiles, elephants, lions—that add beauty and weight. A few exquisite examples of bracelets of this kind, made in Banaras, are permanently on display in the Bharat Kala Bhavan, the art museum of Banaras Hindu University, and in the special jewelry gallery at the National Museum in New Delhi.[6] The process of commissioning such a pair of *karas* in Banaras might begin with the enameller, Gopal Prashad Meenekar. In 2003, we watched this process when a wealthy customer commissioned a pair of elephant-headed bracelets. After a brief conversation about the desired item, Gopal Prashad assessed the size of the wearer's wrists and calculated how much gold was needed. A boy was deployed to run next door and bring a tablet of yellow gold. The weight of the gold was carefully measured and noted, and the customer paid for the gold ingot. The *minawallah* drew a sketch in his notebook, recording the designs and motifs he intended to place on the bracelets, making a permanent document of his thoughts concerning the commissioned piece.

At this stage the goldsmith Chaman Lal, who regularly works with Gopal Prashad, was called in. In the past, during the production of Mughal courtly jewelry, several different craftsmen were involved: a designer, a goldsmith, an engraver, an enameller, a gem setter, and a stringer. In modern day Banaras, as we will see, the process is streamlined; it can be accomplished by three talented men: the goldsmith Chaman, the enameller Gopal Prashad, and a stone setter, such as Chaman's son Ravish.

Chaman Lal

In the next step of the production of the commissioned bracelets, Gopal Prashad hands Chaman the gold ingot along with a detailed description of the design of the bracelets. Chaman takes the gold home, only to return it once again to Gopal Prashad after he has processed and beaten it into two brace-lets. On the first day of our friendship with him, we accompanied Chaman on his long walk from Gopal Prashad's studio to his own atelier, situated in the living room of his family home, in an apartment house on the outskirts of Banaras.[7] We came unexpectedly, yet found his living room beautifully clean and orderly. His wife, Anjali Devi, although taken by surprise, was delight-fully warm and joined the conversation freely, often interrupting her husband to make things clear. We read her spirited contributions as a positive sign of her comfort with strangers and with her own charming spouse.

Chaman's living room serves a dual function; it is the family workshop in the daytime and a bedroom at night. All the furniture is placed against the walls, leaving a wide open area in the middle, where a plastic green rug, in a Persian carpet design, brightens the space. Around the rug, along three of its sides, stand low wooden tables where Chaman and his three sons work. Goldsmiths work at small tables, sitting before them, cross-legged, and bend-ing close to their delicate task. The process of crafting ornaments does not require much room, since the tools are small and the item under production is intimate in scale. The tidy and easily transportable tools and materials of the trade made it possible for goldsmiths, a few centuries ago, to travel in their work to the palaces of emperors and *maharajas,* where they were often granted special access to the *zenana,* the women's quarters. There they worked on golden ornaments under the watchful eye of the residents, whose goals were to ensure that the gold was not stolen and to give advice on the crafting of their jewelry.[8]

The first step in Chaman's process takes place on the balcony of his apart-ment, where he melts the gold in a crucible, mixing in a little bit of copper and silver to harden it; the addition of these materials leaves the piece 93 per-cent pure. At this time, Chaman hammers the gold into the shape of a vessel, a ring, or a bracelet, and then chisels in the ornamental motifs of the design.[9] It takes Chaman twelve to fifteen days to complete the form of the elephant-headed bracelets. He estimates it will take an additional six to eight days for Gopal Prashad to do the enameling, and another week or so for Ravish to set the stones, requiring a period of one month for the completion of a pair of bracelets by this small team of craftsmen.

To shape and ornament items of jewelry, such as the elephant-headed bracelets, Chaman uses a hammer and slim iron chisels of different sizes to form the design. He calls the chisels *kalams,* and it is interesting to note that this Arabic word, the name for the pen of the calligrapher, is used throughout the Muslim world—from Turkey through Iran and India to Bangladesh—for any pen-like tool used to make a design.[10] Chaman's apprenticeship at the age of nine began with learning how to draw, and then learning how to make the *kalams*, since they are not readily available in the market; goldsmiths make them for themselves. Only after this important skill was mastered was Chaman allowed to learn how to use a chisel.

One of the most pleasant aspects of Chaman's home is the relaxed comfort the family members seem to feel with each other. They work at home, they work for themselves, calmly, without supervision, in pleasant surroundings, the breeze crossing the wide room from one open door to the other. Every time I visited, Anjali Devi was there, handsomely dressed, beautifully ornamented and smiling, generous with her hospitality of tea and snacks. Ravish, the youngest son, who is in his early twenties, sat in the sunlight setting stones, wearing a tank top and a pair of printed Bermuda shorts. Monkeys swung on the trees just beyond their balcony, while the family sat inside, working in silence, chatting, working again.

Chaman told me repeatedly that his immediate family is the most important thing in his life. His feelings have been shaped by personal tragedies. Chaman's father died when he was one and a half years old, and his mother passed away when he was four. An orphan, he was sent to become a goldsmith's apprentice at an early age. Chaman's wife, Anjali Devi, told me that every member of his family—all the aunts, uncles, siblings, nieces, and nephews—have "expired," a common euphemism, borrowed from English. Chaman and his wife feel fortunate to spend as much time as they do with each other and with their three sons: Akhilesh Kumar, the eldest, a master tailor who has turned to goldsmithing; Harashit Kumar, who learned the trade unofficially from the *minawallah* Gopal Prashad; and Ravish Kumar, the youngest, a stone setter, and the only one to be sent to a *guru* for a formal period of apprenticeship.

At first, Chaman refused to bring his sons into his business and worked to help them avoid their eventual fate. Many years ago he sent Akhilesh Kumar to apprentice with Chaman's sister's husband, who is a dressmaker. Chaman describes the craft of the goldsmith as *"jhanjhat ki kaam,"* a finicky, fussy skill that has, after all the hard work, "no refund"—too much work for too little pay. Although negative in words about his profession, Chaman finds much pleasure in the artistic outlet of crafting gold jewelry. He regrets not being able to make the pieces he would most like to make, but goldsmithing requires capital. To make what he wishes, he would have to be able to front the money for jewelry that has not been commissioned.

Even though the individual pieces he makes have all been ordered—the gold for them has all been supplied—Chaman has personal leeway in his interpretation of the broad tradition. Exactly how the golden face of the elephant is rendered, for example, is Chaman's decision ultimately, and it is his contribution to the look of the bracelets. He often consults his nineteenth-century Calcutta design catalogs,[11] searching for new inspiration in old forms. Chaman is able to answer his artistic needs by creating items in gold that modify tradition in ways that bring him pleasure. It is different for his wife, the only woman of the household. She is constantly witness to the crafting of exquisite gold jewelry in her living room, but she is less satisfied in her own creative endeavor. Her art is not jewelry production, but personal adornment. Her desire is not to make but to own and wear glorious gold jewelry. But, Anjali Devi told me, the members of her family cannot afford to wear the things they make. Alienation is stronger for the wife of the weaver or the wife of the goldsmith than it is for the artisan. The men have the right to contribute their skill and taste to the brocaded saris or golden bracelets they make, but their wives cannot afford to wear such things. It is a sadness for Anjali Devi that the masterpieces made in her living room always leave, and when she adorns herself she never has the benefit of such exquisite materials with which to work during her creative act.

Once Chaman and his sons have transformed the block of gold, hammered and chiseled it into an ornament, the piece goes back to the enameller Gopal Prashad for the application of the *mina*. Then Gopal Prashad will return the piece to Chaman so the stones can be set by Ravish, as the gemstones are positioned only after the jewelry has been enameled.

In the process of setting the stones, the piece of jewelry is affixed to a base that has been prepared with lacquer, while the setter exerts pressure, wedging the stone in tightly.[12] The gemstone is either set in a closed, band setting or in an open setting, called the claw setting in the West and *kata* in Hindi. Gopal Ram Nagar, the craftsman who works in electroplating down the corridor from Gopal Prashad, said that the "closed system" is preferred in India, because of the fearful "Indian mentality": people worry that the valuable stone will fall out, and the closed setting that wraps the stone in a band is more secure, though it hides much of the glittery gem. In the West, Gopal Ram continued, they prefer the "*kata* system," which is more beautiful since the entire stone is visible and light is able to enter through the setting and radiate the brilliance of the gem. But, he said, people in "foreign lands engage in chair work." They sit all day in quiet offices, not doing much—so they have no need for the sturdier settings that suit the needs of Indian women, especially housewives, whose chores involve physical labor, even though, since they have money for expensive jewelry, they also have money to hire servants.

The claw system is used rarely in Banaras, though it was introduced to India late in the nineteenth century.[13] In Banaras, the most desirable and elegant style of setting stones remains the Mughal *kundan* style, a beautiful combination of luscious yellow gold with precious gems, and sometimes, in addition, enameling. Since the gem is trapped in a closed setting that blocks the light, a reflective foil made of thinly beaten sheets of gold or silver is placed beneath the stone. After the stone is set in its golden crater, on a bed of sealing wax made of *lac,* narrow ribbons of gold are compressed into place, filling the space around the gem. Instead of placing each gemstone in a bezel especially made for it—a time consuming and exact process—the goldsmith working in the *kundan* style places a stone in a socket that generally fits its size, then wedges it tightly into place by the gold strips that surround each gemstone. The gold used to make these strips is different from that of the ornament; it is 99.97 percent pure, so malleable that it needs no heat to be worked. The ribbons of the outline are lightly cut at angles to create a permanent brilliance without the need for polishing.[14] Chaman's son Ravish makes *kundan* settings on special commission, to the delight and envy of his mother, who thinks of *kundan* jewelry as fit for *rajas* and *maharajas.* It is fit as well for the gods. The glittery encrusted ornaments adorning baby Krishna and his mother on the Tanjore paintings from South India are also appropriately referred to as *kundan* jewelry.[15]

Gopal Prashad Meenekar

Only a small percentage of the locally made jewelry is enameled, even though enameling is associated with the city of Banaras as well as with Jaipur and Banaras can boast great masters today such as Gopal Prashad. The city's religious importance as a pilgrimage site is the main reason for its national renown, but Banaras is important, as well, for the arts of adornment, not only for the brocaded sari, but also for the exquisite *gulabi mina,* literally "pink enameled" jewelry that has been created here for four centuries.[16] In the seventeenth century, the Mughal Emperor Jahangir relocated his administrative headquarters to Banaras, bringing with him craftsmen, manufacturers, and merchants in jewelry, greatly enhancing the city's existing jewelry trade.[17] Later, Banaras supplied jewelry for Lucknow's *nawabs,* who were connoisseurs of fine ornaments. Many people in Banaras believe that the art of pink enameling ended in the city in the year 1923 with the death of the *mina* artist Babbu Singh.[18] But pink enameling has resurfaced recently,[19] and it is experiencing a revival to meet the demands of wealthy customers, of Indian women who are interested in the magnificence and historical significance of the old jewelry.

The process of enameling involves mixing pulverized colored glass with water, and using it to fill the hollowed depressions on a golden surface; this technique is commonly referred to by its French name, *champlevé.* When heated in an oven, the powdered glass hardens to a luminescent finish. Different colors are inlaid, one at a time, since each color sets at a different temperature. The order of application, from hardest to softest, is usually: white, blue, green, yellow, and red. *Gulabi mina* involves a distinct process in which designs such as birds and flowers are painted on the hardened white enamel with pink paint and a tiny brush. The piece is fired one last time, briefly, to set the color.[20]

The enameling that takes place today in Banaras is a combination of the two techniques, as we will learn from Gopal Prashad's description of his work.[21] Gopal Prashad Meenekar, the *minawallah,* comes from a family of Banarasi enamellers. He was apprenticed to his father, whom he regards as his *guru.* Gopal Prashad is currently training his fourteen-year-old son, Kush Kumar Seth, to learn the family art and business. Like Chaman, Gopal Prashad was first charged to master the art of drawing. "You cannot be a *minawallah* if you cannot draw," he says. When we were there, his son often sat by his side while he worked, drawing endless rows of peacocks, parrots, and lotus flowers in a notebook. Gopal Prashad is particularly eager to pass the tradition to his son because, he told me, his own grandfather died with the secret of the ruby-red *mina* that only he was able to achieve, and that knowledge, sadly, has been lost to the family. The red they know how to make now is less saturated than his grandfather's, and it is tinged with pink. His only options are to work with *desi mina,* an expensive Indian stone that yields a dark red, or with *English mina,* an imported product from Switzerland that is considerably cheaper, but much lighter in color. Neither of them gets that perfect red that marked his grandfather's masterworks.

Gopal Prashad's enameling process begins with what he calls *pencil work.*

He plans the design of the jewelry on a piece of paper with a pencil, then once the motifs, scale, and placement have been figured out, he starts carving the design into the gold freehand, without the aid of stencils of the kind that Chaman often uses. Gopal Prashad referred to this second stage as *handwork*. He uses *bulis*—burins—to engrave the design motifs, which will be filled with color. Chaman's workshop creates deep pits to cradle the gems, and the *minawallah* carves the hollower, gentler channels within which the delicate *mina* flora and fauna will appear, once the piece has received its basic form and comes to him from the goldsmith.

It is only after Gopal Prashad has carved the piece with the *bulis* that he chooses the colors for the enamel. An oval Mughal-style ring, which I commissioned from him, for instance, was filled with white in all the background areas, red in all the floral shapes, and green in all the leaf and vine motifs. The two birds were rendered in different colors: the bodies and heads were filled with red, the beaks with green, and the expanded wings with dark blue. Since *mina* work is very delicate in scale, the colors have to be chosen carefully to bring out the motifs of the jewelry, making it so that, by contrast, some colors recede into the background while others step forward into prominence.

Once Gopal Prashad has decided on the colors, he is ready to process the *mina*. He takes out the bits of colored glass he keeps wrapped in a piece of cloth, and stored in a small metal closet in his one-room shop. He pounds the glass with a mortar and pestle, pulverizing it. Impurities have to be separated from the *mina* powder with hydrofluoric acid. Gopal Prashad refers to this chemical as *jahar*—poison—and keeps it locked in a cabinet. He mixes the purified powder with water and a few drops of fruit juice to add a bit of stickiness that will cause the liquid color to adhere to the gold. He buys dehydrated *anar*—pomegranate fruit—which he soaks in water, to extract the tacky essence that he uses as a fixative.

Gopal Prashad's last step involves filling in the tiny channels with liquid color. He uses a paintbrush, applying one color at a time. The jewelry is fired in a small electric kiln in the corner of his studio, at different temperatures depending on the color, for about half an hour per color. If the item is to be painted in the *gulabi mina* style, one final stage remains. Gopal Prashad spends most of his time in the painting process, which is exacting and hard on the eyes. He sits cross-legged at his low wooden table, turns the desk lamp on, and puts on his magnifying eyeglasses. He has oil-based paints from Switzerland which he uses to paint delicate motifs on the *pakka*—literally,

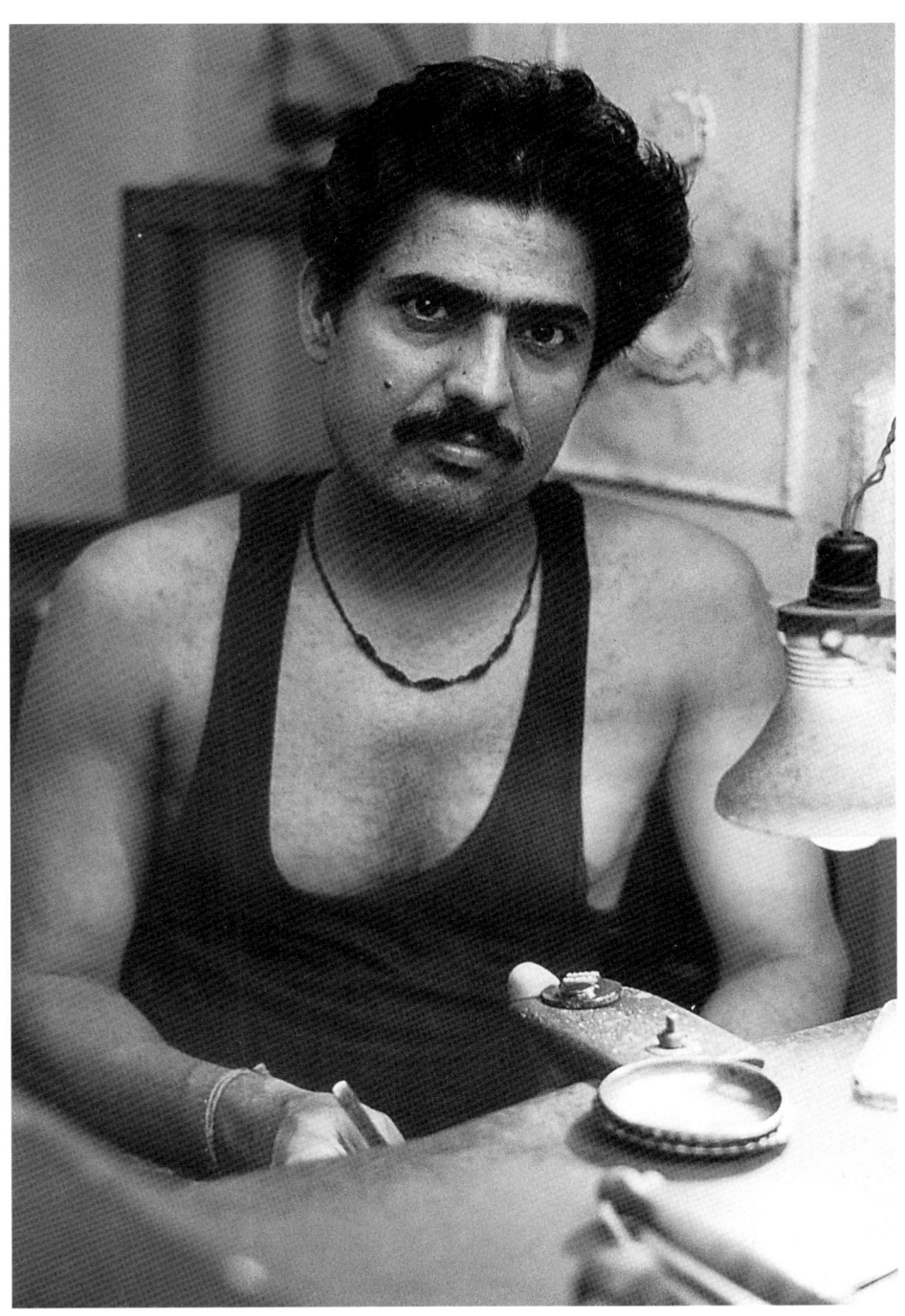

Salik Ram Soni

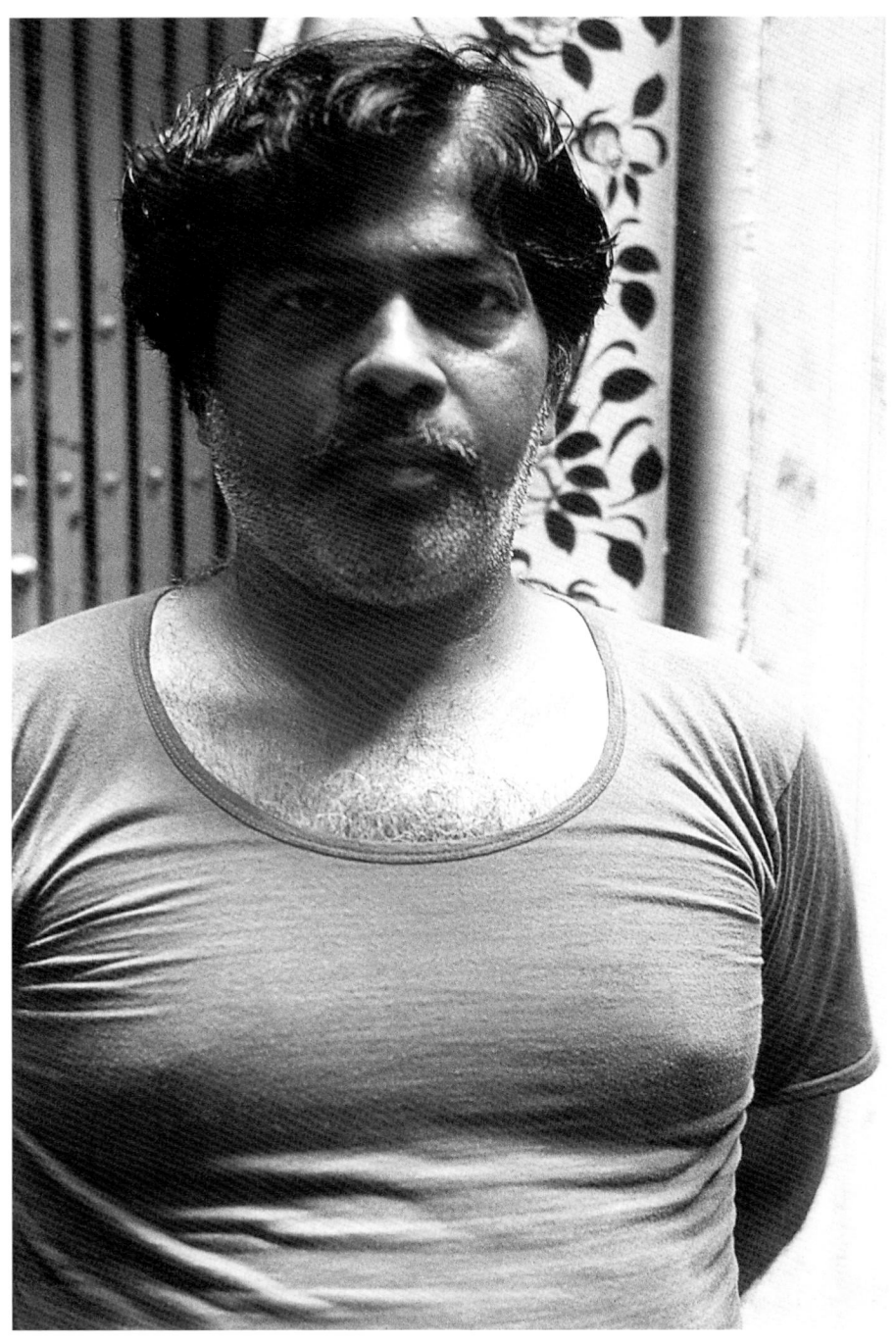

Gopal Prashad Meenekar

cooked—white *mina* background. He dabs a drop of paint with one brush, and then uses another brush to create shading. His art resembles miniature painting: in both cases, precise, beautiful designs are achieved on an unbelievably small scale. Once completed, the *gulabi mina* piece is heated quickly, for about ten minutes, to set the paint so it will not rub off against the skin of the wearer—the *mina* is usually applied to the back or underside of a piece of jewelry, which is placed next to the skin.

Mina appears on the back of gold jewelry that is encrusted on the front with diamonds, rubies, emeralds, and other precious stones. *Mina* is sometimes placed visibly between gems, but usually the exquisite and time-consuming enamel work is done on the back of the ornament; it is never explicitly displayed. The rationale for adding such fine work on the hidden and unseen part of a piece of fine jewelry has often been questioned.[22] Some people have referred to *mina* as a "secret garden," a paradise of birds and flowers intended only for the private enjoyment of the wearer.

When I asked Gopal Prashad why he thought *mina* was added to the hidden side of pieces of jewelry, he laughed and said that many people have asked him that question before. He agreed that the *mina* is there for the pleasure of the wearer, who sees the pretty painting when she is putting the jewelry on, and she knows the jewelry she is wearing is even more beautiful than it appears to the eyes of others, for only a small percentage of *kundan* jewelry has *mina* on it. This fact firmly contradicts the idea that women in India ornament themselves solely for the approval of others. Many women buy a piece of jewelry, for a substantially increased price, just to indulge themselves in the secret pleasure of the *mina* on the back.

The *mina* is mainly for the personal satisfaction of the wearer, but sometimes, Gopal Prashad said, the pendant or earring gets turned accidentally, and if the back is empty and blank, it looks ugly. But if the back has beautiful *mina* on it, the inadvertent gesture, causing the piece to turn, grants the lucky beholder an unexpected pleasure through this fortuitous glimpse of beauty. Anjali Devi, Chaman's wife, argues that *mina* can be detected in passages between the gemstones, and along the sides of the ornament; she does not think that *mina* is truly hidden. As a woman used to inspecting the jewelry on other women's bodies, Anjali Devi knows where to look for *mina* on the ornament, aiding her in the evaluation of the piece and its wearer.

Gopal Prashad gave me another reason for *mina,* and perhaps the most convincing. He said that with *mina* added to the back, the overall value of the ornament increases dramatically. Since the price given for a used ornament is calculated by weight, he said, and the price is set by the current international price of gold, many old pieces are melted down, and the gold is used to craft new jewelry. But if a piece has *mina* on it, then it acquires "antique" value, according to Gopal Prashad, and it is worth much more than its literal weight in gold—and that value reduces its chances of being melted down, and increases the likelihood that the piece will become an heirloom. Fine enamel work, painstakingly applied by a master *minakar,* is valued for its craftsmanship, for the *minawallah's* skilled execution and mastery. Banarasi saris, likewise, are valued for the expertise of the weaver, and the value of the sari surpasses the cost of the silk and the gold threads, just as the value of jewelry with *mina* on its back surpasses its weight in gold.

Although *mina* enhances the beauty and value of a piece of jewelry, Gopal Prashad sees his art as distinct from the ornament's façade of gold and gems. When he plans the design and chooses the colors of the *mina,* he does not care which stones will go on the other side. Decisions concerning the scale and placement of the motifs to be enameled are made without reference to the density and color scheme of the gems. However, when he places the *mina* around a stone, he works for harmony.

On several different days, I watched Gopal Prashad work on the ring I commissioned, with its Mughal-style oval band and its floral motifs in red *mina.* The central figure was a red daisy-like flower, flanked by two blue birds. When it was done, Gopal Prashad was proud of the enameling, but he found the ring *ajeeb,* weird, and *bekar,* useless, because it did not have a diamond in the center, where instead the red flower bloomed. As good as the *mina* was—it is beautiful—the ring, he felt, was too weird without the stone, the beauty and brilliance of which the enamel was intended to enhance.

Gopal Prashad Meenekar's work requires long hours of concentrated patience. While he works, he regularly treats himself to *paan.* All artists, he told me, have their vices; some drink, others smoke, but his vice is *paan.* Banaras is famous throughout India for saris and *mina* and for *paan,* a tasty and habit-forming quid made of a combination of betel leaf, lime paste, shaved areca nuts, and other spices.[23] I asked Gopal Prashad, a *desi* artist with a relish for *paan,* why the local *paan* was so praised. He thought for a minute and said that the quality of the leaves is superior in Banaras, where they are grown; if you go only as far as Allahabad, you will find that the leaves taste different. As Sandeep Singh said of jewelry, the ingredients of *paan* are best in the "original spot."

Gopal Prashad stressed that, while the excellence of *paan* depends on the quality of the raw materials, the artful combination of ingredients is also important. He dabs liquid on the betel leaves when he assembles his *paan.* This liquid, he explained, is prepared with cardamom, cloves, and rosewater to produce the flavor that is special to Banaras. All of these ingredients are shipped from Banaras to Bombay, but the *paan* there is nothing like the superior *paan* of Banaras. Excellence is a result of the quality of the materials and the combination of elements, but ultimately, what matters most is the "hand" that puts it all together. So it is with the Banarasi sari, and so it is with the *mina* of Gopal Prashad. Once the stones are chosen and ground, and the *mina* mixture is prepared with pomegranate juice, it is the expert hand that makes the ornament uniquely luminous, glowing with beauty and the spirit of the artist.

All of the craftsmen we have encountered so far are good at what they do because they understand the tradition they are operating within, and they understand how their work contributes to that larger tradition. They are at once culturally centered and highly individualistic in their attitudes and responses with respect to consumer tastes and trends. The factors that influence their personal visions are the major markers of identity in India: religion, caste, and regional identity. In the previous chapter, we saw how sari dealings in Banaras are charged with tensions between religious groups: the saris are largely woven by Muslim men, bought and sold by both Hindus and Muslims, and worn mostly by Hindu women. The jewelry business in Banaras has few Muslim artisans. Most makers of jewelry are Hindu. Yet they must consider Muslim aesthetics, for Muslim women buy much of the jewelry produced in the city.

Difference between Hindus and Muslims is assumed: a deep wariness divides the population of Banaras. One day Chaman casually told me that Muslims do everything "backward"—in exactly the opposite way of the Hindu. They read backward, from right to left; the men wear *lungis* instead of *dhotis;* they sit and wash their hands differently than Hindus. He said that the writing of "Allah" in Arabic, with its three pronounced vertical peaks, is really the Hindi word "Om" turned on its side. In Banaras, Hindu *karigars* acknowledge that sari weaving lies in the Muslim domain, but the jewelry trade belongs to them (though in their finer achievements, including *mina* and *kundan,* they are emulating models from the height of Mughal art).

Although most of the producers of jewelry in Banaras are Hindus, tensions remain among them as a result of differences of caste and regional identity. India is a country of divisions, and Hindus quickly divide themselves by caste, language, and ethnic group, especially in Banaras, a city of migrants. Interjit Singh Bagga, a Sikh goldsmith from Banaras, believes that many of the pieces of fine jewelry sold in Banaras come from Calcutta, Delhi, Madras, and Bombay because the local *karigars* do not like to work too hard. Banarasi artisans, he thinks, take it easy; his notion exhibits the common stereotype of Banarasis as interested only in *masti*—in pleasure, in the joys of life.[24] Bagga said that the local Hindu customers prefer "safe" jewelry, chunky jewelry that does not break easily, that is "everlasting." The average female customer in Banaras, according to Bagga, does not like "fancy" or "fashionable" jewelry; she stays with tradition. But, in contrast, the Punjabi women of his own caste, he proudly proclaimed, have a more refined taste in jewelry. Punjabis prefer "fancy" jewelry with much *mehanat*—work, effort—in it. Jewelry sold in Amritsar, in the Punjab, he says, is finer; it exhibits beautiful craftsmanship since Punjabi *karigars* are not afraid of work, and, in his opinion, they work harder than all the others.

Even when no Muslims are involved, people locate differences between the skills of jewelers and the tastes of customers. Interjit Singh Bagga genuinely believes that Punjabi goldsmiths are better craftsmen, and that Punjabi women have a more refined taste in jewelry. Similarly, Pinku Mookerjee of the Rinku Silk House, a Bengali, felt that Bengalis, his caste, have a subtler taste in the saris they buy than other customers do. Hemant Khanchandani of the Dayaram Fashion Centre, a Sindhi, if given a choice, will recommend a *salwar suit* to be made in the Sindhi style; it is, for him, superior. The tensions that appear in the commercial realm of Banarasi body art are not restricted to the obvious categories of religion and gender; they extend significantly into ethnic and regional identity.

Tensions exist among different castes of Hindus, and also among the producers and the sellers of jewelry. This chapter's last craftsman—B. D. Soni, a Rajasthani master goldsmith—will expand our understanding of the choices made in jewelry production by describing a different pattern of creation and sale.

B. D. Soni

Bhagwan Das (B.D.) Soni lives and works in Jaisalmer, near the border between India and Pakistan, though he has traveled extensively. Exuding a sophisticated cosmopolitan aura, B.D. carries himself with the Marwari pride of

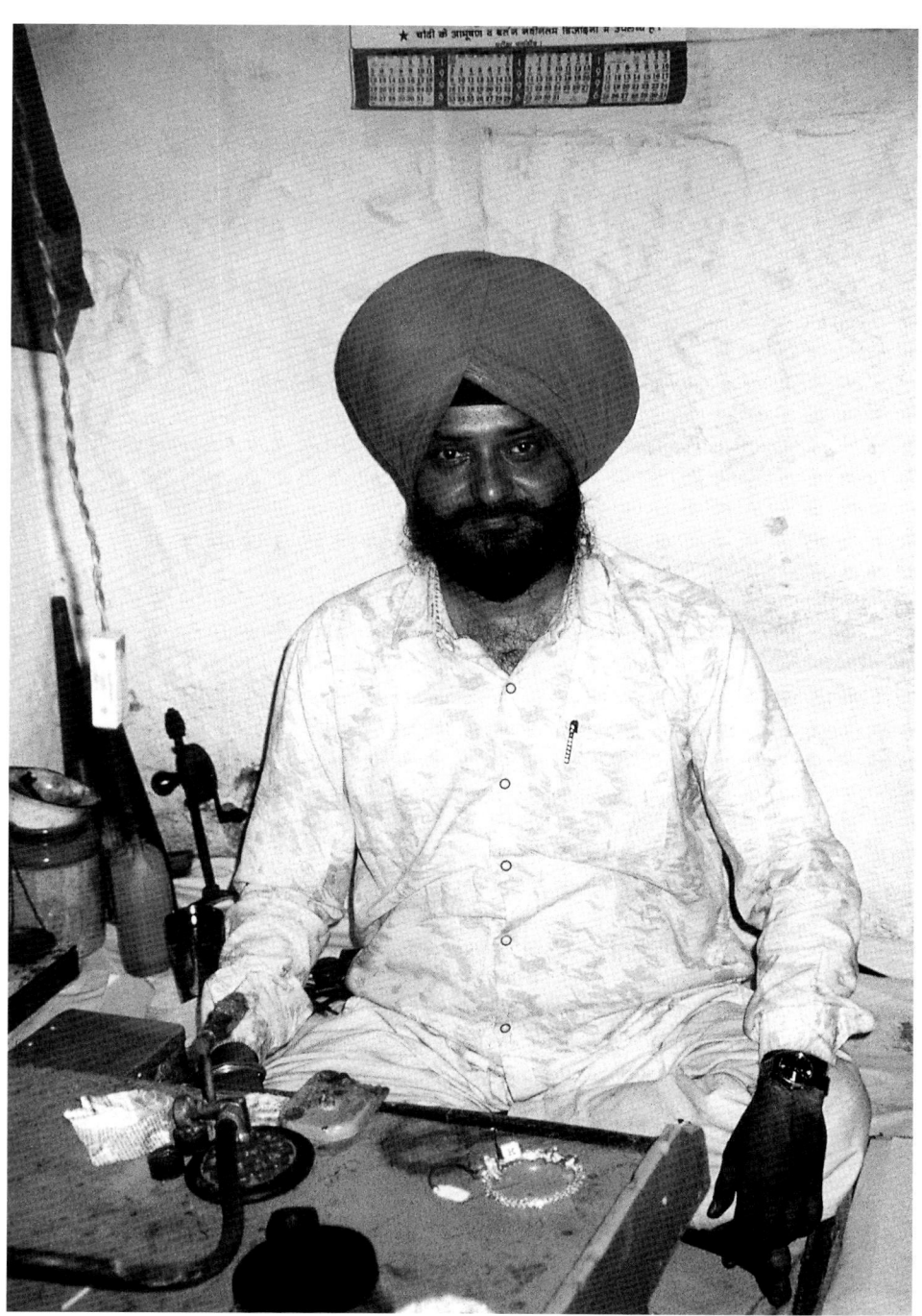

Interjit Singh Bagga

the handsome men of Rajasthan. He wears two flamboyant medallions around his neck, each displaying diamonds in *kundan* settings that signal his trade in fine jewelry. Although B.D. has lived with the art of the goldsmith since his childhood, he served as a superintendent of police for ten years, before returning to the crafting and sale of jewelry in the middle of the 1980s.[25]

As his last name reveals, B.D. comes from a line of *sonars*—goldsmiths. He says he is the eighth continuous generation in his family to work within the goldsmith's caste. B.D. lives in the joint household he shares with his large family, including four other goldsmiths: his father, Govind Lal, and his three brothers, Dean Deyal (D.D.), Prem Kumar, and Ram Chandra (R.C.). The family owns five jewelry shops, including the showroom on the second floor of B.D.'s father's home, which is specially designed to accommodate large groups of tourists. The family not only makes jewelry, but also buys old—"antique"—pieces from local country people, selling these alongside their new gold and silver creations. B.D. has an ingenious system of "replacing" the old pieces brought in by local people with new ones. In the trade, the villager gets a shiny new item of adornment, while B.D. acquires antique jewelry that he sells to tourists or to the dealers in the antiquities market in Bombay.

Being from Jaisalmer, a city roughly half Muslim and half Hindu, B.D. has learned to cater to both facets of the local population. He also wants the business of both villagers and urbanites. This last desire he accomplishes by devoting one of his stores to chunky silver jewelry—the "tribal," village preference—and another store to the finer, golden pieces that are suited to people who reside in the city and affect an urban look. Jaisalmer is a beautiful city. Its architecture, mixing Indian and Persian tastes, recalls its history as a center of long-range trade, and it evokes for tourists fantasies of *The Arabian Nights,* fantasies nearly realized in the intricately carved sandstone of the architectural ornament, the pale desert that surrounds the city, and the "camel safari" excursions taken into the desert as the sand shifts from buff to rose to coral with the sunset. Tourists, having read lush descriptions in guidebooks, make the long trip across the desert, finding their way to Jaisalmer and into the shops of B. D. Soni's family.

B.D. has learned the taste of the tourists, and he has dedicated one of his shops to pleasing them. He sells the "replaced" tribal items—Rajasthani jewelry of the kind that is illustrated in luxurious picture books—to Dutch, German, Italian, and American visitors. He and his brothers craft "tourist items," delicate, silver jewelry with semi-precious stones, to sell to the French, who, he claims, have no appreciation for genuine traditional Indian jewelry, preferring instead a "modern" look. The old tribal jewelry is sold to Indians as well as Europeans, but only, he says, to the "advanced" and "sophisticated" families of Gujarat, New Delhi, and Bombay. And B.D. manages a brisk, lucrative trade with the stars and with studio costume designers and stylists of Bollywood.

B.D. and his brothers work in their collective atelier, pooling their skills, much as family members do in the weaving *karkhanas* like that of Hashim Ansari and his father and brothers. If the Sonis see an item of jewelry they like in a catalog, the family is able to work together to figure out how to make it, each man contributing his special expertise: Govind Lal's lifetime of knowledge that enables estimating the necessary materials; D.D.'s skilled knowledge of soldering; R.C.'s talent for making silver chains for anklets and necklaces; and B.D.'s dexterity in the design and execution of original masterpieces in gold. The Sonis also make new things that are a "mix-up" of old and new items of jewelry, blending old elements into new designs for consumption by high-end tourists and "advanced" Indian customers.

For local customers, B.D. enjoys experimenting to make new jewelry that is traditional in appearance, but uses less material to create a lighter, less expensive version of a conventional piece. He says he is challenged in trying to make a golden necklace that usually costs fifty thousand rupees for half that price, thereby allowing women to own jewelry that they could not otherwise afford. B.D. accomplishes this difficult task by altering techniques, pushing the material, and concentrating on exquisite handwork and lavish finishing. Although such jewelry is labor-intensive, the lower cost of the materials—and especially of the expensive gold—yields a saving in the overall cost of the item, and so it is a worthwhile endeavor for both the customer and the goldsmith.

B.D. recently created a new item, a round medallion pendant, hammered into relief with the image of Ganesh. The god is depicted abstractly in a streamlined, simplified semblance of his chubby, elephant-headed self. B.D. took the inspiration for this particular Ganesh from the abstract renditions on wedding announcements, all of which portray Ganesh, the Lord of New Beginnings. The pendant is a characteristic example of B.D.'s use of a new idea (the abstracted Ganesh) and incorporating it into a conventional form[26] (Ganesh on a silver pendant, worn on a black string around the neck for protection).

Like Hashim Ansari's father, B.D. creates new designs that fit tradition

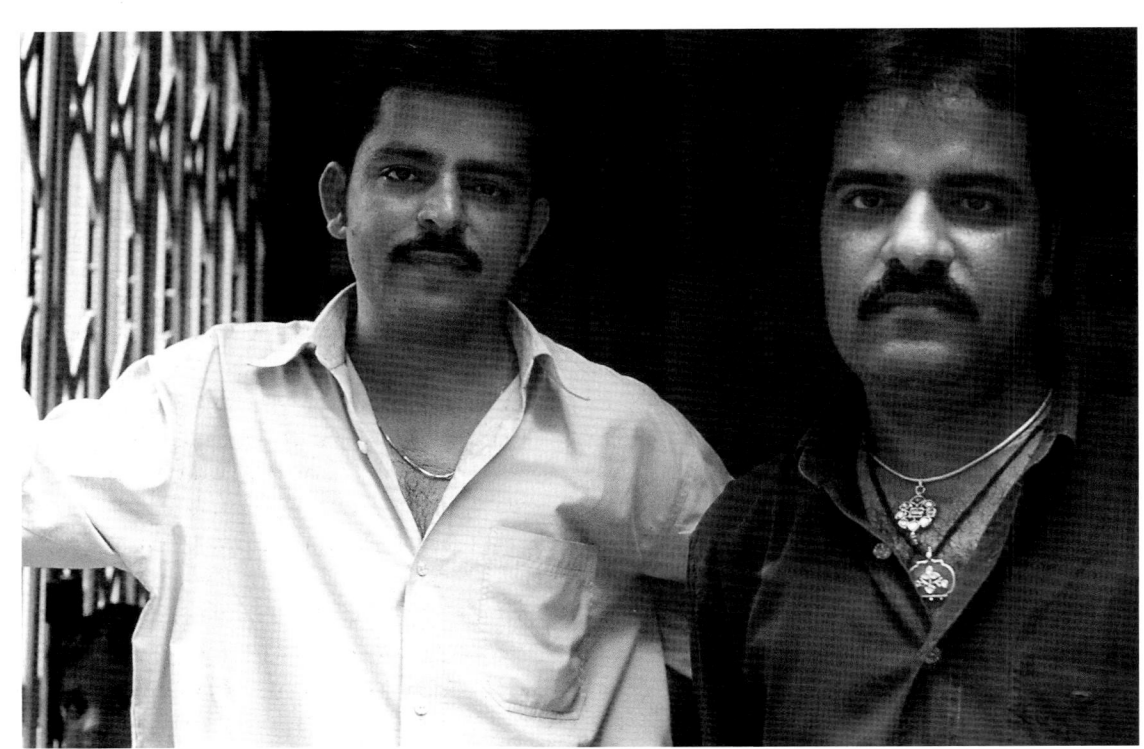

R. C. and B. D. Soni

when he studies old examples, extracts principles, and reapplies them. The designs, he says, belong to him, his family, and his caste. The goldsmiths own the designs, and since they do, since the tradition is theirs, they are free to mix and match in accord with creative impulse. B.D.'s practice resembles that of Abdul Qayoom, Hashim's father, who uses his "design map" to generate a new design for a sari by reorganizing the elements that belong to the Ansari caste of weavers. Both the Ansaris and the Sonis react to the market, and to the current tastes of their female customers, by creating new designs that seem innovative and fresh but deviate little from the culturally shared principles that are inherent in old works.

Despite the similarities, substantial differences divide the crafting of gold by B. D. Soni from the weaving of saris by Hashim Ansari. When Hashim weaves, he uses a system of cards that predetermines the design of the sari, as his father conceived it and as the hired draftsman and the *cardwallah* rendered it. B.D., on the other hand, designs in the act of creation. He eloquently explained that he learned his art by watching his father and imitating his gestures when he picked up the tools and tried to make jewelry. The process of his thinking about jewelry begins with the tools; they are integral to his concept of design. B.D.'s practice contrasts with that of the men from Banaras we met earlier in this chapter: Chaman draws his designs on paper and makes a stencil, which attaches to the piece of gold he works on. Comparably, Gopal Prashad plans the design of his enameled creation on a piece of paper. B.D. does not think with paper and pencil, and then transfer his design from paper to gold. His idea goes directly from his head to the metal; it emerges with the movement of his hands during the act of creation. His art is one of deep concentration, in which design and execution are unified in a virtuosic performance.

B. D. Soni's work in Rajasthan provides us with a distant point for comparison with the system in Banaras. Like Gopal Prashad Meenekar and Hashim Ansari, B.D. works in a family trade. He reaps the benefits of apprenticeship, deep familiarity, and confidence that are the result of generations of accumulated experiences in the trade. Unlike the Ansari family workshop or Chaman's family atelier, both of which must respond to the advice and demands of merchants, B.D. owns the commercial outlet for his creations. There is no middleman to wrangle with, no merchants to give him orders—he sells his own jewelry. This enables direct contact with his customers, which allows him to create and modify his stock swiftly and deftly to meet the specific needs of the men and women who buy his art.

The men who craft jewelry in Banaras, like the weavers of saris, do not need to know exactly what the customers want; that is the concern of the retail merchants who come into direct contact with the female buyers. B.D. has a perspective the artisans of Banaras do not have, precisely because he sells as well as makes jewelry. While Gopal Prashad Meenekar is an expert in the art of *mina,* he does not need to worry about the items of jewelry or clothing that his piece will match; it is not his job to think about the ensemble into which his piece will be placed. His expertise lies in his mastery of his tiny, exquisite craft: the art of enameling.

B. D. Soni, on the other hand, designs, produces, and sells jewelry, and so he must think broadly about the adornment of the female body. B.D. believes that the beauty of a woman is judged primarily by her figure, which must be appropriately highlighted with the right article of clothing. After that, the jewelry should be chosen to accentuate the face—the earrings, nose ring, and necklace will all frame and decorate the face of the wearer. He advises his customers to buy what looks good on them, not what he likes, for he wants them to be satisfied and come back. Having said that, he maintained the common conviction of the merchant, saying that what is bought in his store ultimately reflects his choice, not his customer's.

Women, the consumers in this system of adornment, must at all times focus on the small details, yet keep in mind the big picture. In choosing an item of bodily adornment, women must be able to recognize excellent quality, whether of sari, *mina,* or golden pendant, and they must know how to bring the individual items together into harmonious presence. Women's aesthetic considerations, of necessity, extend beyond those of the artisans who know what is beautiful within their own craft but have no need to consider the ultimate context of use, except as it may filter back to them by chance along the line that runs from the customer through the merchants on the big streets to their tiny workshops in the back alleys. The artisans do not have to visualize their work as part of an artful ensemble on a woman's body. That is her task and art. During a conversation at Chaman's house, I asked him what kinds of clothes *kundan* jewelry looks good with. He answered automatically that everything would match. His wife, Anjali Devi, interrupted, and gave her opinion quickly and firmly: if the *kundan* necklace had emeralds, then it would look good on a red sari, since the contrast would be right. But, she continued, if the *kundan* piece had visible *mina,* and the *mina* was red and green, then it would look nice on a green sari. And, Anjali concluded, if the necklace had pearls, then the white of the pearls would be properly displayed against a blue sari.

Much to her husband's surprise, Anjali Devi's response showed that she had worked these aesthetic considerations through—as the other women we will encounter in this book have also done. It is the sellers, not the makers, of saris, and even less the makers of jewelry, who must be aware of the appropriate relation of adornment and occasion to bodily type, in order to give their advice—and sell their wares—to female customers. In an orientation comparable to that of B. D. Soni, who is at once designer, creator, and merchant, the salesmen at the Kanhaiya Lal jewelry store range widely in their aesthetic considerations, thinking beyond the beauty of the particular piece and trying to envision whole ensembles of jewelry on the specific bodies of their customers. The evaluative criteria of the men of Kanhaiya Lal, and their sales strategies, will be the focus of the next chapter.

·7·

Kanhaiya Lal

MUCH OF THE JEWELRY produced in the city of Banaras is sold at one of the four Kanhaiya Lal stores. The process of selling and buying jewelry has many similarities with the selling and buying of clothing, and some marked differences. The purchase of expensive ornaments for weddings is analogous to the purchase of fine Banarasi saris: both are selected carefully for special occasions. Everyday jewelry—inexpensive toe rings, say, or silver anklets—is bought with the casual ease of the *salwar suit* for daily wear. But, in general, the big difference between clothing and jewelry is that jewelry is more costly and permanent; it provides "economic security" to the owner. It can be sold quickly if a sudden need for money arises, and its expense and permanence naturally add a level of attentiveness to the process of buying it. In this chapter, we will look at the kinds of jewelry people buy, who buys it, and why; we will consider the factors governing a customer's choice and, finally, the persuasive tactics of the salesman. Although Banaras has hundreds of commercial jewelry outlets—most of them tiny one-room shops—we will focus our attention on the largest of them, the Kanhaiya Lal franchise of stores.

There are four Kanhaiya Lal sister stores in Banaras. Kanhaiya Lal, whose family came from nearby Mirzapur but who was born in Banaras, established the stores that bear his name. He had two sons, Makond Lal and Damordas Lal. The oldest of the stores is Kanhaiya Lal Makond Lal Saraf & Co., established in the Rani Khua neighborhood in 1896. The next one, Kanhaiya Lal Damordas Saraf & Co., opened in 1911 at Raja Darvaja, adjacent to the Muslim neighborhood of Dalmandi. Two more stores complete this group: the Kanhaiya Lal Alankar Mandir store, from 1953, and the most popular jewelry

136

store in the city, Kanhaiya Lal Swarna Kala Kendra, established in 1958 and centrally located in Godaulia, in the heart of commercial Banaras.

During my first fieldtrip to Banaras, my aunt Nirmala Dubey took me to the Kanhaiya Lal store at Raja Darvaja—"The King's Door." Most of the interviews and observations presented in this chapter took place in this store between 1996 and 2003.[1] The shop is situated back from the busy intersection of Chauk, close to a mosque. Being located in a *gali* that is inside another *gali,* it is hard to find. Take a left turn at Chauk and you are in a maze of alleys, thick with shops selling things wholesale. After another turn, and a hot walk through a narrow crowded street, a subtle blue sign in Hindi signals the way into the dead-end passage that takes you to the Kanhaiya Lal store. It would be nearly impossible to find if you did not know what you were looking for. The last time we were there, we had to crawl over a rickshaw that was jammed into the alley and piled high with bolts of plastic tarp. Hard though it may be to find, I have never been there when it was not full of customers.

The constant stream of customers, of men and women from the city and the neighboring villages, implies deep loyalty and trust. Most of the people who come are faithful, repeat customers who have been coming for years, and sometimes for generations. The store's hidden location makes it comfortable for female customers to spend time shopping for jewelry, lost and safe within, far from the eyes of unknown people. This is an important detail for people do not wish to be seen buying expensive things, and they can hide their purchases carefully before returning into the streets. The store's location meets the needs of women in other ways as well. It provides a safe haven for Muslim women to sit and shop comfortably among familiar men, letting their black *burqas* open to reveal the colorful clothing underneath. And the shop provides a discreet setting for women who engage in the embarrassing activity of selling their personal ornaments for immediate, emergency cash.

When entering the store, people remove their shoes, leaving them outside where a guard slumps inattentively on a chair. Just inside, to the right and left of the main entrance, there are booths with seats and tables where customers can sit to be shown jewelry. Most prefer to sit on the usual large mattress that covers the floor. Toward the back, a low wooden barrier crosses the shop, behind which the owners and managers of the store sit. Behind them opens the vault where the jewelry is kept. The salesmen shuttle back and forth between the customer and the senior manager, who is charged with fetching and returning the jewelry in the safe.[2]

To eliminate confusion, only one of the owners or one of the managers goes to the vault in the back at any time. He retrieves velvet-lined boxes full of jewelry, flips them open to inspect the contents, and then hands them to the salesman, who will carry the boxes to the customer. When the boxes are returned to the manager, he flips their lids again to be sure that nothing has disappeared. The salesman, not the customer, conveys to the manager a description of the jewelry that is to be brought from the back. The item brought forward by the manager reflects his understanding of the salesman's understanding of the customer's desire. Because there is so much mediation in this process, it will be interesting to spend a little time getting to know the men of Kanhaiya Lal, learning who they are and how they understand the psychology and aesthetics of their customers.

The boss of the operation is Arun Agrawal, the son of Damordas Lal and the grandson of the founder, the original Kanhaiya Lal. Arun is friendly, but shy. When he is in the store, he sits cross-legged at the place of power: a low table in which the money is kept in a locked drawer, and on which a black rotary phone sits. To his left, just inside the wooden barrier, is the place where Arun's maternal uncle, Shantibhadra Shah, usually sits. Customers affectionately refer to him as *Mamaji,* "maternal uncle." Shantibhadra has worked at this store since 1952; his duty now is to chat with customers—joking with the men and teasing the women. He does not handle money, he told me, nor does he go back into the vault. Two additional men regularly occupy the managers' inner space, behind the low counter, in front of the rich vault: Shashi Shah, Shantibhadra's son, and Piyush Agrawal, the great-grandson of Kanhaiya Lal. The store also employs an accountant, several guards, and eleven men who are considered "staff," including the men whose job is fetching refreshments for the customers. There are four sellers, of whom Ramesh Pandey and Rajesh Agrawal are ranked as the "chief salesmen."

Shantibhadra calculates that there are about three hundred jewelry shops in Banaras, one hundred being wholesale operations. In his estimation, Banaras has five hundred *karigars* involved in the production of jewelry, including those who work with gold, silver, *mina,* and precious stones. The store is located within walking distance of many of these jewelry workshops, including that of Gopal Prashad Meenekar. Shantibhandra said that their store has a continuing relationship with approximately twenty major *karkhanas* where jewelry is crafted.

The artisans supply the Kanhaiya Lal shop with standard items of jewelry on a regular basis. Only 3 percent of the merchandise is special-ordered by customers. It is the job of wholesalers, such as Sandeep Singh, to introduce new items into the stock of the store. These wholesalers stimulate change by bringing novel items from elsewhere, usually Calcutta, Bombay, or Madras. If the new things sell well, they may become staple items to be commissioned by Kanhaiya Lal from one of their regular *karigars,* or from another artisan who might prove to be better at the task. Piyush Agrawal said that if an item of jewelry requires "*tar* work"—filigree—they would use a local Bengali *karigar,* since Bengalis are generally adept at this specialty.[3] Comparably, bracelets requiring what Piyush called "dice work"—faceting—are best accomplished by one of the local Punjabi craftsmen. Ornaments made in Banaras often incarnate the acknowledged expertise of regional craftsmen who have settled in the city.

Piyush explained that while the Kanhaiya Lal store is always required to have traditional examples of Indian jewelry in stock, they must also introduce new items—for the store has a limited number of customers, and to keep them happy, they must regularly rotate the stock to reflect "the latest fashion." When I asked what the latest fashion was in 2003, Piyush said that for those of the middle class, it was jewelry made of plain gold with no stones, while for those of the upper-middle class, the fashion was gold ornaments with gemstones, especially diamonds. The upper class, he said, preferred jewelry in the "Western style," and he showed me an example, a platinum necklace with an asymmetrical pendant containing a green stone in what he called an "abstract design." It was, in my opinion, one of the store's least attractive items of jewelry. Piyush's generalizations reflect the common attitude that taste in India is inextricably tangled with social and economic status, a recurrent theme of this chapter.

Although all the men at Kanhaiya Lal share the experience of working in the store, each of them has his own opinions and tastes. One afternoon in the summer of 2003, arriving at the store after visiting the *minawallah* Gopal Prashad, I decided to pose a question to this team of experts: Why is *mina* placed on the back of ornaments? A visiting *karigar* gave two reasons. First, he said, it is the way it has always been; in other words, it is traditional. Everybody seemed to agree with this first response. Encouraged, he continued, saying that *mina* on the back of *kundan* makes the necklace a "two-in-one" piece, allowing the woman to reverse the necklace on occasion and wear it with the *mina* on the front. This second answer made the salesmen laugh and they began to tease the *karigar,* saying that no one would wear the necklace with the precious stones on the back, against the skin, and the *mina* facing out.[4]

Shantibhandra, the old "uncle," interrupted the teasing to give a historical explanation. In the old days, he said, women were soft, delicate, and the gold backing of a necklace would scratch their skins, so *mina* was added on the back to provide a smooth surface for their sensitive necks. Over time, he added, the *mina* would increase the value of the piece, echoing the answer Gopal Prashad had given me earlier. Shashi Shah, Shantibhandra's son, listened, but disagreed. In his opinion, jewelry has two purposes: to look good for others, and to satisfy the self. While the *kundan* side dazzles the eyes of the beholder, the *mina* side provides personal pleasure to the owner; *mina* is for the private satisfaction of the woman who owns the piece.

Piyush offered his opinion by posing a question: if an item of jewelry has the exquisite, decadent *kundan* work on the front, why should the back not be beautiful as well? He said that women always look at the back of things, during purchase, be it a sari or an item of jewelry. The back should display the aesthetic excellence of the front. If somebody were to pick up a *kundan* necklace and turn it over to find a blank, plain back, the piece would disappoint the beholder's expectations. The *mina* aids in the selling of an expensive piece. Piyush said that only those who are *jankari*—knowledgeable and appreciative—have *mina* on the back of their jewelry. Of all the *kundan* items sold in the Kanhaiya Lal store, only 5 percent have *mina* on the back. This conversation among the men of Kanhaiya Lal shows the variation in attitudes and knowledge about jewelry among professionals. The real reason for *mina* on the backside of jewelry, of course, includes all of the above explanations. There is truth in all of them, and they help explain the impulse to add expensive and exquisitely skilled enamel work to the hidden side of opulent ornaments.

Astrological Rings

Enameled ornaments are rare. By contrast, a common category of jewelry bought at Kanhaiya Lal is the astrological ring. The belief in astrology and gemology is old and general in India. The power of the celestial bodies is strengthened if beneficial, or weakened if malignant, by the wearing of certain gemstones. Since the sun literally penetrates the stones worn on the body, its power surges, along with the inherent power of the stone, and drives into the wearer through the skin. Many of the residents of Banaras come to the Kanhaiya Lal stores to buy rings, pendants, and other articles of jewelry that contain a stone that has been prescribed for them by a *pundit.* Cheaper versions of astrological stones and other medicinal ornaments are available at small specialized stores, most of them in the Vishvanath Gali, close to the Golden Temple. Many adults in India—men and women alike—wear an astrological ring of some kind; some even wear several at once. For the stones to work, it is imperative that the back of the gem remain in contact with the skin (through an open setting), and the stone must be located in a visible area of the body, allowing the sun to penetrate through the stone to the body, fully activating the gem's effect. Many parents place powerful stones on their babies for protection. Vijay Bhadu Singh, an expert on stones who works with the Kanhaiya Lal store, told me that when a baby is born, the parents often place a *munga* (coral) or *moti* (pearl) as a pendant on a black string around the infant's neck. This keeps the baby safe from *najar,* the evil eye, and provides the baby with *shanti,* the peace of mind that many stones bestow upon their wearers.

There have always been sympathetic reasons to place stones on a child, Vijay Singh said, and he told me of a practice from the recent past when ornaments of ivory were worn in the belief that they would insure the baby's teeth to come in strong. Nowadays, he said, a pearl pendant brings a calm beauty—"sobriety"—to the child, which aids in making the child as attractive and graceful as the moon, the celestial body associated with the pearl. Children wear these stones around their necks for five, ten, or twelve years, at which point the stone might become a ring to be worn, or it might be abandoned altogether. Adults wear stones for health and sanity, Vijay said; the gems called "kidney stones," for example, are worn to aid in the treatment of real kidney problems.[5]

In this system of astrology, there are nine principal stones. Each one of these is associated with each one of the nine celestial bodies—the sun, the moon, the five planets (Mercury, Venus, Mars, Jupiter, and Saturn), and the two "imaginary planets" (Rahu and Ketu).[6] It works like this: a troubled person visits a *pundit* who is an astrologer. He looks at the person's birth chart to discover which planet is causing the cosmic disturbance that has produced the problem or thwarted the expected success in personal or professional life. Then the *pundit* suggests the stone that will ameliorate the astrological effect. If the planet is Mars, for example, the stone to cure the impediment is coral, and it is worn on the ring finger of the right hand. (Some believe that the hand on which the stone is to be worn depends on the gender of the individual: women should wear healing stones on their left hand, and men on their right.) The finger on which the stone should be placed is determined by another ancient Indian science—palmistry—which connects the mounds on the palm at the base of each finger—and therefore a particular finger—with certain planets. There is a finger and a stone associated with each major celestial body. (The planets Uranus, Neptune, and Pluto do not play any role in this system, since they were discovered after it was devised.)[7] A consultation reveals the planet causing the trouble and determines which stone and the finger on which an astrological ring should be worn. Usually, the size of the stone is also prescribed. A customer need only bring the name of the stone and the approximate size to Kanhaiya Lal, and the manager will have the ring crafted in either silver or gold.

There is much difference from expert to expert, but here is a list of the nine stones, with the most usual variations and astrological associations and the finger on which they should be worn: ruby (Sun) worn on the ring finger; pearl (Moon) worn on the little finger; emerald (Mercury) worn on the little finger; diamond (Venus) worn on the little finger; coral (Mars) worn on the ring finger; topaz or yellow sapphire (Jupiter) worn on the index finger; blue sapphire (Saturn) worn on the ring finger; cat's eye (the imaginary planet Ketu) worn on the little finger; and *gomed* (zircon), "cinnamon stone," or white sapphire (the other imaginary planet, Rahu) worn on the middle finger.

Sometimes, for general well being, people like to cover every contingency by wearing a uniquely *desi* piece of jewelry, a *nauratan*—a "nine stones" piece that auspiciously represents the entire Indian planetary system.[8] The strikingly colorful combination of nine gemstones appears commonly as a pendant or a ring, and members of both genders wear it. As would be expected in a genuine tradition, there is some difference among people as to which stones comprise the set.

Not all people who wear stones have been told by a *pundit* to wear them; some people decide on their own to wear the gems. Three of the set of nine—pearls, rubies, and coral—are thought to be relatively benign; they suit everyone and cause no harm. But not all stones are appropriate for everybody. People are advised to "test" a stone's suitability before purchasing it, since some gems are deemed to be exceptionally powerful. I have grown up hearing horror stories about women who wore diamonds when they should not have, and the results were disastrous for members of their families. In one such story I heard from my mother in childhood, a woman greedily wears a diamond in the morning, without testing it first. In the course of the day, she injures herself in the kitchen, her husband loses his job, and her son is hospitalized with a cracked skull.

Vijay Singh said that diamonds are unsuitable for about 1 percent of the population; those people cannot wear the stone, and must not even have it in the house, so that the other members of the household cannot wear it either. The other dangerous stone is *nilam,* blue sapphire, which, like the diamond, cannot be worn by everyone.[9] I asked Vijay how people could test their immunity to the destructive powers of the blue sapphire or diamond. He said you should put a borrowed stone under the pillow overnight. If you wake having experienced no nightmares, no pains, or fear, and if no accidents happened overnight, then it would be safe to wear the stone.

I asked the Kanhaiya Lal men if people always went to a *pundit* first to get a recommendation for a ring or pendant. They laughed, and said no. In the holy city of Kashi, Shashi said, every man is a *pundit;* there is no need to consult a real priest! He said if you get four men together at any given moment, one of them will certainly know what stone to wear and will freely share his knowledge. Many customers count on the expert knowledge of Vijay Singh, Shashi Shah, and the others at Kanhaiya Lal, to help them find a cosmological cure for their ailments. The men of the store regularly share their opinions; their astrological knowledge as much as their aesthetic sensitivity is part of their job as expert salesmen.

Buying Jewelry

Once a year, in the celebration of Divali in late October to early November, the Hindus of Banaras have a need to buy a new item of jewelry. During the night of Divali, a holiday commonly referred to as the "festival of lights," people place hundreds of candles outside their newly whitewashed houses, ritually illuminating the path to welcome the goddess of wealth, Lakshmi, into their homes. To symbolize prosperity, all residents of the household wear new clothes for the family *puja,* and there must be a new item of metal, ideally of gold, placed on the altar, especially for the Dhan Teras celebration commemorating Ram's victorious return to Ayodhya after fourteen years of exile. This piece of metal can be a coin or an item of jewelry. If the family cannot afford gold, silver or brass can be used. Many people buy a stainless steel kitchen utensil.[10] For families that can afford it, the religious holiday provides a yearly excuse for adding to the personal stock of ornaments. During this time, customers go to Kanhaiya Lal to purchase gold or silver jewelry, coins, or even tiny statues of Lakshmi and Ganesh made of solid silver.

The most important single occasion for which jewelry is purchased in India is the wedding. Certain ornaments are traditionally bestowed on the bride by both her parents and her parents-in-law. What exactly is bought, and in what quantity, depends on numerous variables, including religion, caste, regional identity, village or city residence, economic status, and individual family tradition. Marriage rituals vary tremendously throughout India, and there is much variety in the list of prerequisite gifts of dowry jewelry. Generally speaking, the bride gets married in the jewels and clothing given to her by her family, and she leaves for her new house bedecked from head to toe in ornaments, clothes, and shoes that have been given to her by her new in-laws.

Wedding ornaments are purchased by a small delegation that includes members of both sexes, and may involve the bride herself. Among the people I interviewed there was a general consistency on seasons of marriage. Muslims, I was told, can marry anytime during the year; they buy wedding ornaments all year round. City Hindus marry in either the summer wedding months, March through June, or in the winter, from November to January. Villagers, on the other hand, seem to marry in the summer months. Shashi estimates that these dates fall between March 15, after the Holi celebrations have ended, and June 20. An astrologer who matches the charts of the bride and groom determines the exact date of a Hindu marriage.

Interjit Singh Bagga, the goldsmith, explained that peasants marry in the summer because farming people sell their crops at this time, between March and June, and they have, as a result, an immediate surplus of cash.[11] The fields are cut and not yet replanted, providing an empty space to host the marriage festivities. That space includes a tented area for the ceremony, a place for the reception, and possibly room to sleep out-of-town relatives. Interjit Bagga said that since the price of food, including milk, is higher in the summer months, a wedding feast, which customarily feeds hundreds of people, is more expensive than a wedding held in the winter. This leads the country people into trying to stretch their available financial resources. One result is jewelry that is lighter in weight and cheaper in cost, and the jeweler has to adapt his craft to meet the financial situation of the farmers.

Shashi told me that the people who live in the villages near Banaras still have an unofficial system of early marriages, even though child marriages for Hindus were made illegal by the Native Marriage Act, passed in 1872, which set the bridegroom's minimum age at eighteen and the bride's at fourteen.[12] Shashi explained that many girls are married between the ages of twelve and fourteen, but they continue to live with their parents. On the occasion of this marriage ceremony, which Shashi called a "half marriage," the girl's parents give her a symbolic amount of jewelry, and her in-laws double that amount, as a sort of bride price. Then, four or five years later, when the girl has reached "maturity," a "full marriage" occurs, after which she goes to live with her husband and his family. At this point, the parents give their daughter a much larger amount of jewelry as a dowry, a gift she will take with her, insuring her respect and status in her new home. This system allows the girl's parents to have a few years in which to stockpile the jewelry needed for the *bidai,* the official farewell of the bride.

From their personal experience, the men of Kanhaiya Lal said that city dwellers usually buy gold while villagers prefer silver ornaments, which they leave in their bright silver color. City people often buy silver jewelry but have it gold-plated and pass it off as gold. The wedding ornaments bought by city and village people differ not only in amount and taste, but also in the metal of choice. For the residents of Banaras who can afford it, Shantibhandra said, the ornaments bought are 10 percent silver and 90 percent gold. Some villagers might buy all their items in silver, though others adjust according to "financial capacity." Since there are certain prescribed or "compulsory" pieces, people make decisions beforehand about what needs to be bought. Then they arrive at Kanhaiya Lal armed with a list of the ornaments to be purchased that day.

The list includes as many of the following items as a Hindu family can afford. For the head: a *mantikka* (a gold or silver ornamental *bindi* for the forehead, suspended from a chain worn on the hair); a *jhumar* (an ornament that attaches to the hair on the left side of the head); nose rings, including a large hoop—*nath*—to be worn during the wedding, and small ones for daily use; and a variety of earrings. For the neck, there are chokers and chains, both thin and thick, such as the *haar,* a long heavy necklace. On the arms, there are armbands, and different types of bracelets, including *karas* with decorative animal heads, thick bangles called *kangans,* and thin bangles called *churis.* The bridal *hathphul*—"hand flower"—ornament, composed of five rings attached by a chain to a bracelet, is a necessary item. A variety of rings complete the hand jewelry. For the waist, brides receive a *kardhani,* a silver and *mina* belt of chain that flatters the waist. A silver keychain that hooks on to one side of

145

the sari symbolically denotes the bride as a member of a household, who has responsibilities as well as her own set of keys. Finally, the feet of a married woman should always be decorated with anklets, which have different names depending on the thickness and style, and toe rings, the number worn and design left up to individual discretion.[13]

Various factors influence the choice of ornaments during purchase. Shashi and his father, Shantibhandra, both said many times that villagers prefer silver ornaments that are chunky. That is the village style. Rural people favor weighty jewelry because they wear ornaments while working hard, whether in their own fields or as manual workers in street construction, often carrying rocks or bricks on their heads. The heavy ornaments are sturdy and will not break during daily use, and they might bring a substantial amount of cash if they are sold. Some salesmen in the store believe that poor people would prefer to wear gold, and once their economic position improves, they replace their silver with gold. It could seem that village people wear silver out of economic necessity, but this urban attitude toward rural taste deserves to be questioned, and we will return to this topic shortly.

Another factor that conditions the choice of ornaments relates to one's children, the inheritors of the jewelry. If a woman only has daughters, she might consider weight when buying jewelry for herself. There is a chance that the ornaments might be sold and melted down to buy her daughter a brand new set of jewelry for her dowry. In any case, the daughter will not wear her mother's jewelry and new jewelry will be bought for her wedding. On the other hand, if a woman only has sons, then the jewelry can be purchased not only for weight (and therefore resale value), but for its workmanship as well, because that jewelry will most likely be given to the daughter-in-law, and remain in the family as an heirloom. Jewelry given to a daughter will, in theory, go to another family.[14] Of course these are not rigid rules, and mothers do pass family heirlooms down to their daughters. One woman I talked to said that she intends to pass her jewelry to her daughters because she knows they, for sentimental reasons, will not sell it. She thinks that her daughters-in-law probably would sell the jewelry, for they have less emotional attachment to her than her own daughters do. Many women with whom I talked mentioned their children's upcoming marriages as a consideration in buying jewelry for themselves. Looking into the future helps the consumer discriminate between a purchase that is temporary—a piece of fashionable delight, lasting no more than a lifetime—and a purchase that is permanent, destined to be passed along for generations.

Women buy jewelry for special occasions, and also, of course, for daily wear. Since all married women in India are supposed to wear certain ornaments, the everyday items break frequently, and need to be replaced often. Many of the customers at Kanhaiya Lal come regularly to purchase toe rings, anklets, nose rings, and sometimes earrings and finger rings. The jewelry worn on the feet is made of silver, and so is relatively cheap. When a woman comes to buy anklets, she may buy three or four pairs at a time, keeping a little stock at home, since anklets get caught on clothing or bed sheets and break often. Toe rings and anklets come in a surprising variety of designs and styles, some of them with passages of *mina* in blue, yellow, red, and green. Women say they prefer inexpensive jewelry for daily wear because it might break or get lost or stolen.

Everyday jewelry, though not as fine and sumptuous as that for special occasions, is what women handle and change regularly; their other jewelry is virtually inaccessible, locked away, and worn at most a few times a year. The most expensive jewelry of the most prosperous women is apt to be stored in a safety deposit box in a bank. This often includes the gold and silver given to a woman as part of her dowry at marriage. Many women I talked to have not seen this jewelry for years and do not remember exactly what it looks like. The "locker" box only grants access to the authorized persons listed on the official forms, and it is often, I am told, registered under the names of the husband and his parents, not in the name of the woman whose jewelry is stored in the bank for "safe keeping."[15] (This raises a question: is the jewelry kept safe from thieves and light-fingered servants, or from the woman who owns it and might sell it without the knowledge of her husband and his parents?)

Shashi said that many of his customers view jewelry as "psychological *aram*"—comfort for the mind—and as a "capital investment." Men, in his opinion, do not trust the banks fully, and, referring to their wives as "banks," they would prefer to keep their fortune in the form of jewelry. For this reason, he said, people of two economic classes come to Kanhaiya Lal with frequency to buy ornaments. The "maximum purchasing capacity," Shashi said, is found within the highest and the lowest classes in India. The richest people naturally have much disposable income, allowing them to indulge in fleeting fashions. They can buy expensive jewelry in the latest style. The people of the lowest class have a need to invest their money in jewelry for "economic security." The poorest people buy all year round. They keep a tally of the number of items they own, and try to increase this amount by buying a new thing every month, as a way of investing in the future. These items, Shashi said, are not bought to wear; rather, they are stored away safely for use in the case of a family emergency or the marriage of a child. People of the lowest socioeconomic class, according to Shashi, usually buy solid silver pieces, such as thick *kara* bracelets or heavy necklaces, that can be sold easily. The people of the middle class, Shashi says, do not have much extra money, since their needs escalate with their income, resulting in an amount of surplus cash far smaller than that of the people who make less money than they do. (Urban people usually have less money than those of the same economic class who live in villages, because the basic needs of urban life take a bigger bite out of the family budget.) Aside from the purchase of toe rings and other small things, middle-class customers buy only for special occasions. They are not as interested in stockpiling ornaments for emergencies as poorer people are, nor do they buy with the whimsical abandon of the rich.

After familial decisions concerning financial and social matters have been made, aesthetic considerations are taken into account. Whether buying everyday jewelry or an ornament for a special occasion, people naturally choose ornaments that they think will look good on them. An analysis of the aesthetics of fine jewelry must consider the customer's criteria for appropriate and beautiful jewelry, and also the salesman's, since customers must choose jewelry out of a selection presented to them by the workers at Kanhaiya Lal. The salesmen and managers are the ones who make quick decisions about what should be brought out from the vault, and they are the ones who give advice, solicited or unsolicited, as to what things look good.

Selling Jewelry

I asked Shashi to tell me how he helps customers make aesthetic decisions. What factors are involved in purchasing jewelry? He started by saying that it is his strong belief that not all jewelry is right for all people; only jewelry that suits an individual should be bought, and worn, by her. Shashi listed the personal factors that should influence a customer's decisions. When choosing jewelry, he said, the first thing to bear in mind is age—the "age factor" is the most important consideration. This makes sense, since one of the purposes of jewelry is to communicate age and, consequently, developmental status. Shashi explained that Indian women of a given age wear a certain amount and a certain kind of jewelry. If an old lady, he said, were to deck herself in great quantities of ornaments, she would look ridiculous, "like a cartoon."

From the jeweler's prospect, Shashi said, women fall into two general categories of age: those between the ages of sixteen and forty, and those in the forty-five and above class. Within these broad age groupings, Shashi said that other things need to be considered when selecting jewelry, such as social occasion and social status, for these matters are intertwined and cannot be judged separately from one another. Shashi illustrated his point by bringing up a hypothetical example of a sixteen-year-old girl who wears a demure thin chain around her neck, as befits her status as an unmarried adolescent. If the chain were made of gold, and the girl was the daughter of a maid, then everybody would start talking, gossiping among themselves, wondering where she got the money to afford a golden necklace, and they might come to the conclusion that she stole it from somebody. In that case, the girl must be conscious not only of her age and unmarried status, but she also needs to take into account her "family background," which further conditions the choice—and judgments—of the jewelry she wears.

Shashi explained that this sixteen-year-old girl would need to consider her place of residence as well as her marital status and economic class. An urban young woman would wear little jewelry on a daily basis—perhaps small earrings and one or two finger rings—but it would be normal for a rural girl to wear the following items every day: a golden "nosepin," a "sober" chain with no pendant, silver earrings, a hairclip, anklets, and bangles of silver, glass, or plastic.

But, Shashi emphasized, considerations of the suitability of jewelry go beyond age, family status, marital status, and urban or rural identity: they must take in the occasion, and consequently the fit, of the jewelry with the rest of the outfit the person is wearing. Shashi said that with a sari, one could wear a long or short necklace, a *kardhani* belt and *bazuband* armbands. All of these would look good with a sari, but the last two pieces would not match a *salwar kurta* suit, since the waist is not usually marked and the upper arms are usually covered by the garment. Jewelry should suit the cut of the clothes and the skin it exposes, and also the style of the clothes. Cheap "black metal" ethnic jewelry only looks good with jeans, while "lightweight," "sober" jewelry matches everyday *salwar suits* best. A *salwar kurta* outfit is considered relatively casual attire for non-Punjabi Hindus, so fancy jewelry should not be worn with it. Aesthetic considerations of all kinds, Shashi continued, are about more than the type of outfit, sari or *salwar suit;* they should direct patterns of variation within each category. With a cotton sari, for example, a "lightweight" necklace and demure bracelets would allow the "get up" of the sari to come through. With Banarasi brocaded saris or South Indian fancy silk saris, "heavy" jewelry looks better. These are Shashi's opinions, but they also exemplify the advice he gives to customers who bring to the store the outfits for which they are seeking complementary jewelry.

The other major factor to consider when choosing jewelry is obviously the body of the wearer. Shashi said that one of the purposes of jewelry is to increase the *shobha,* the grace, of a woman. Choosing the wrong ornaments for one's body type can defeat this goal. Shashi gave me specific examples to illustrate his point: If a skinny woman were to wear a choker necklace, she would look graceful. But if a fat woman wore a choker, she would look bad, presumably because the choker called too much attention to her thick neck. A short, fat lady, Shashi said, should choose long necklaces and long earrings. Conversely, a tall woman should choose the short, compact jewelry that looks better on her. But, Shashi said laughing, if a short lady were to wear "short ornaments" then she would look even shorter. In addition to weight and the all-important factor of skin color, hairstyle matters. Shashi believes that if a woman has a "bob cut" or "ponytail," then she should wear "lightweight" jewelry, apparently because when the hair is tied back or cut short, jewelry worn around the face stands out on its own, without the customary framing of thick black hair.

Finally, Shashi explained, ornaments should fit the time of day; "daytime jewelry" is different from "nighttime jewelry." Since the time of the occasion usually determines the nature of the event, his point seems logical: a school function would take place in the afternoon, while a wedding reception would normally take place at night. The occasion will accordingly help determine the tone for the other components of the body art ensemble: clothing, shoes, and makeup. And finally, items of jewelry should not only match the clothes, the person, the occasion, and the time of day, they should also match each other. Shashi declared firmly that nothing ruins a look more than mismatched jewelry. Again, he conjured up hypothetical sets: It would be a mistake to wear a fine *kundan* necklace with cheap silver bracelets. If a woman were to wear *kundan* on her neck, she should wear *kundan* on her ears as well. The same rule applies to gold and silver; the ornaments of an outfit should be one or the other, especially if they will be seen in the same visual frame. These guidelines do not extend to the jewelry worn on the feet, which is always made of silver. A reason to buy different items of jewelry at the same time is to insure a proper match among them, while benefiting from the expert advice of the men of Kanhaiya Lal. Shashi and the others answered all of my questions about aesthetics without hesitation; the men have spent many years working out these general patterns. They gave quick and well-thought-out answers.

The main men at Kanhaiya Lal—Arun, Shashi, Piyush, and Shantibhandra—and the salesmen they have trained, have developed sales tactics based on their own understanding of what jewelry suits which women, and on their understanding of the taste and buying style of their customers. This knowledge helps them ascertain what jewelry to bring from the back room in order to create a successful commercial transaction for all involved. Most of their generalizations about the buyer's philosophy dealt with people from the countryside, whose patterns of purchase contrasted with the urban norms. Village customers, both Hindu and Muslim, make up a large percentage of the clientele of the store. The Kanhaiya Lal store at Godaulia, conversely, has a mostly urban core of customers.

The Kanhaiya Lal men I spoke with, especially Shashi Shah, had an almost anthropological interest in village women. The culture and lifestyle of these customers were different and fascinating for Shashi Bhai, an urban man. While I asked him to generalize on the jewelry buying patterns of all his customers, he chose to answer my questions by talking mainly about village women. The following observations made by Shashi reflect how a seller sees the motives of the buyer, and how urban people understand village taste. Shashi's interest in rural culture also supports the pattern we have seen among others—such as Hemant Khanchandani, Pinku Mookerjee, and Chaman Lal—that people in Banaras focus on the differences among people, differences of caste, ethnicity and region, religion, and in this case urban or rural identity.

The city customers, Shashi explained, select jewelry by "seeing design" and asking for "lightweight" or "fancy" items. But village customers like "traditional designs." They think the fancy new items are "not durable"—they are flimsy and weak, liable to break during the rough daily round. Shashi thinks that as formal education increases, the aesthetic preferences of the village customers will change, for even now about 5 percent of the village people prefer fancy items of the urban kind. According to Shashi, both men and women come from the villages to buy jewelry, but the "maximum purchasing capacity" is definitely in the hands of the women. They are the ones who select the items that get bought. The salesmen at Kanhaiya Lal, in anticipation of the women's thoughts, emphasize the "durable"—tough, heavy—quality of the items being shown.

Shashi believes that village customers want two things from jewelry:

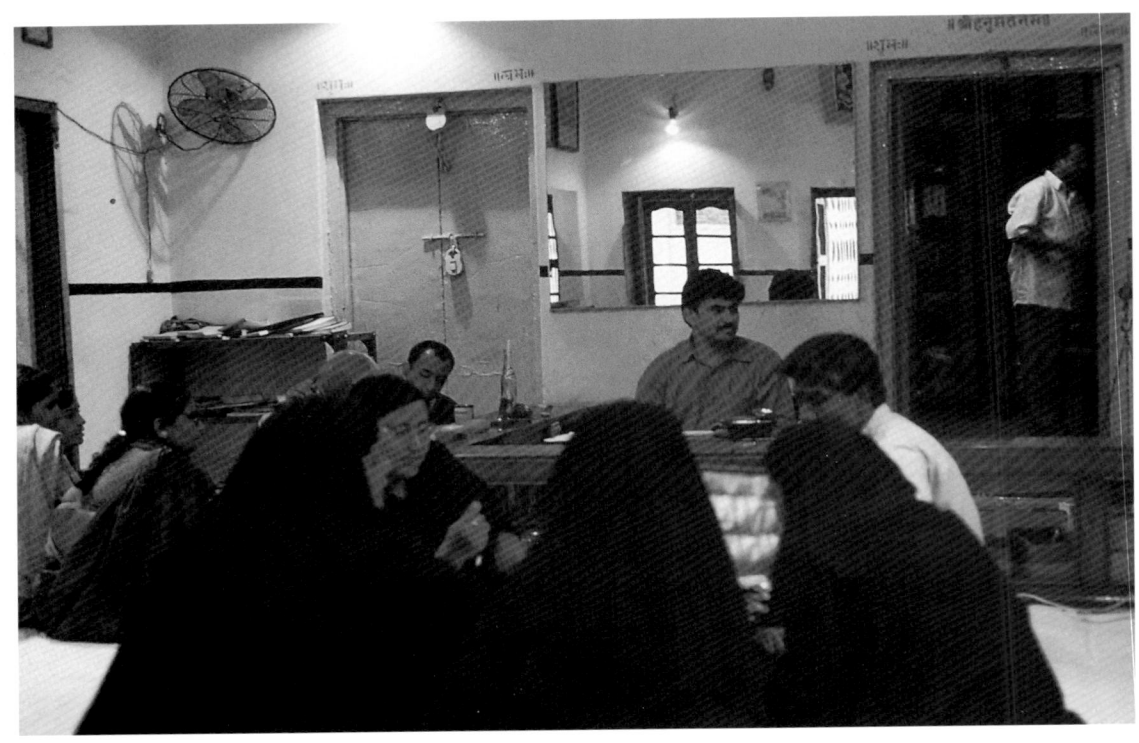

The Kanhaiya Lal store at Raja Darvaja. Female customers sit in the front, while Piyush Agrawal sits behind the counter and Shashi Shah retrieves jewelry from the vault.

items that are durable, and items that can be resold easily. The villagers, he said, "don't purchase from fashion point of view." They invest their money in something that will last and become useful in times of trouble. Since they are buying jewelry from a "deposit point of view," Shashi said, they prefer chunky silver items. These urban men attribute to the rural population a social and economic reason to buy jewelry. Some truth lies in their generalizations, but they tend to undervalue the aesthetic dimension of the choices made by rural buyers. If they purchase ornaments every month as an economic investment, what accounts for how they choose particular items from the thousands of silver ornaments available? If the jewelry were bought for resale only, any shape would do, since it will be sold by weight, but the pieces vary widely in form, and people choose carefully things to wear and things to own that please them; their choices involve aesthetics as surely as durability and investment. If not, they might just purchase and stockpile silver ingots, instead of wearable silver in the form of jewelry.

Village women, no doubt, buy chunky jewelry that does not break during manual labor, but they also like bold ornaments. While urban people invest their money in gold jewelry, rural women prefer to buy silver because they like its look: village women do not have their silver gold-plated, but leave it silver, shiny and reflective. For the same amount of money, when rural women buy the cheaper jewelry of silver, they get many more ornaments to wear, layered upon their bodies, than their urban counterparts do. The urban women I spoke with had comparable preconceptions about the clothing choices of village women. Many women in Banaras told me that village ladies wear saris in bright colors and do not match their saris with their blouses and bangles, in the way city women do, because they cannot afford to buy matching ensembles. If they had the money, urban women argue, they would buy all of their saris in comparable colors, so that their petticoats, blouses, and bangles would fall within a narrow range of hues, and make together a trim match. But we come closer to the truth if we see in the village aesthetic a taste for many ornaments, all aglitter, and for a wide array of clashing and contrasting colors. Their choice to wear clothes that urbanites consider mismatched, and to wear an abundance of jewelry, is more a matter of village aesthetics than a lack of cash.

Another example that illustrates this point is the preference of the *dehati*—village—women for bright orange *sindur* on the parts of their hair. This *sindur* is sold alongside the more common red form which the city women wear. Since both *sindur* colors cost the same and are equally available, the choice of bright orange over the subtler red is purely an aesthetic one.

The rural taste should not be viewed as inferior to the urban, but as different and equally coherent. Village women in chunky silver jewelry and vivid orange *sindur,* in clothes of many colors and saris with lots of the shiny *zari* on the front, operate within their own system and satisfy themselves. They are interested in impressing their neighbors and care little about the reactions of the urbanites. The village taste in India, as in other parts of the world, can be understood as one in which quantity matters, in which more is more.[16] Village women wish to achieve a look of more brightness, more shine, more color, more contrast, and more jewelry in bigger sizes. The rural woman's preference for saris on which the field of the cloth is thick with motifs in gold matches her preference for silver jewelry, since more shine can be displayed for the same amount of money. Throughout India, village fashion also scatters mirrors among the embroidery. Mirrors provide another source of brightness and shine, displayed on clothing as well as textiles hung on the walls. Shiny, mirrored things are also believed to deflect the effects of the evil eye,[17] which is paradoxical, since glitter literally attracts the eye.

Both village and city women buy to suit their taste, and a percentage of each sells their jewelry back for cash. But the rhythm of life is different in the city and countryside. When the crops are sold, late in the summer, village people know a moment of prosperity; but the dead of winter and early spring bring a time when the cash flow slows to a stop. In tune with the swing of the agricultural year, women buy jewelry in flush times, then sell it back in hard times, creating a recurrent pattern in ornamentation that parallels the pattern of the weather and their work. For them, the jewelry store is a form of bank, a place where one goes periodically to get cash and then to get new silver jewelry. Native Americans in the southwestern United States comparably use pawnshops as a form of bank; they deposit their silver and turquoise jewelry there to get cash in hard times, and then buy their jewelry back when agricultural success blesses them with cash.[18] The system in India is different, yet comparable. Village women might sell their jewelry back in a period of need, and when they have money again, instead of buying their own jewelry back (which has probably been sold or melted down), they buy a similar piece, a version of the old that is a new example of a familiar form. And so, logically, village women prefer the "traditional," timeless pieces that can be replaced by similar pieces, again and again, on into the future. City people, on the other hand, do not use the jewelry store so clearly as a bank; when they sell their jewelry to the store, they have fallen on hard times, with no certainty of reversal, and right now what they need is cash. It is surely more traumatic for city women to sell their jewelry than it is for village women who are used to the periodic rotation of their personal stock of ornaments.

At the Kanhaiya Lal store, Shashi said that about 10 percent of his customers sell their jewelry back, but this is still a small percentage of those who buy and wear ornaments. I asked if he thought there were sentimental reasons not to sell jewelry, and he responded that no one wants to part with jewelry, but sometimes they have no choice: "If I were to have a need now, in this *position* what will I do? In that moment, if I were to think *sentimentally* that this is my mother's, I should not sell this. So in this *position* what will I do? If I need now one *lakh* [one hundred thousand] rupees, there has been an *accident*—suppose somebody has gotten sick—I don't have another *source of income*. In this *position* what will I do?"

The price that stores, including Kanhaiya Lal, pay for jewelry bought from customers is determined only by the weight of the piece and the purity of the metal—though there is an exception to this rule if the piece is antique or special in its craftsmanship, as *kundan* and *mina* pieces are. Shashi explained that some fancy items have "less refund" since there is a higher "making charge" associated with them. Gold filigree jewelry, for example, is light in weight but requires much talent and time from the goldsmith, so it is priced higher than its weight in gold, which in 1996, the smiths told me, was forty rupees per ten grams of gold. Solid silver ornaments, on the other hand, insure "full refund," since their monetary worth is determined by the weight of the metal both during the selling and the buying back.

The weight of the jewelry will logically affect its design. Sandeep Singh, the wholesaler who works with the Kanhaiya Lal store, told me that village taste, embodied in jewelry of heavy weight, leads to a particular kind of design, which contrasts with the fine, light, and lacy designs that require little material but much work. The elaborate designs that signal wealth, in which most of the money goes into the craft rather than the materials, renders the piece a bad investment from the point of view of resale. Like the Banarasi saris on which much of the gold *zari* floats on the back, never to be seen, finely worked jewelry suggests wealth in its frivolous waste. Superb in itself, it costs much but will bring little in resale. Fine jewelry is, according to Shantibhandra, the pride of the store. Jewelry that exhibits exquisite "finishing" and much "workmanship" contributes, he believes, to the tremendous "good will" that the store experiences throughout Banaras.

My goal at the Kanhaiya Lal store was to talk to the men, to acquire an understanding of the role gold and silver jewelry plays in the lives of women, and also to come to some understanding of the creative act of selling in order to evaluate the store's impact upon the selection of adornment. The customer buys something she has chosen, but it has been chosen from an assortment selected by the salesmen. While women believe they have bought an item to suit themselves, the salesmen feel that customers buy jewelry and clothing that reflect the tastes of the salesmen. Hemant Khanchandani claims that the *salwar suits* he sells reflect his taste, and B. D. Soni says that his customers buy and wear what he considers to be the most beautiful jewelry. I asked Shantibhandra the same question: whose taste is reflected in an item of jewelry bought in this store? His answer was that it reflected both the customer and the salesman. The major part of the decision—what kind of ornaments to buy—is the customer's choice. The customer may choose to see bangles; yet the bangles brought out from the back room exhibit the salesman's reading of the customer's preferences, and that reading is based on his understanding of her social status, caste, age, and marital status. When selecting which bangles to buy from this grouping, the customer can then ask the salesman's advice. In other words, Shantibhandra believes, as do I, that shopping is a collaborative venture between the seller and the buyer.

I asked Shashi and his father, Shantibhandra, if women actively seek their advice when they are selecting items to buy. Shantibhandra explained that women do not usually come to his shop alone. Female customers, he said, are accompanied by men 50 percent of the time, by other women 45 percent of the time; the remaining 5 percent of customers are lone males. According to Shantibhandra, women will instantly develop a liking for some of the pieces that are shown to them. Shashi added that only young women try on pieces of jewelry; those of "old age" do not put them on, but only inspect them visually, presumably because they lack the *shauk*—the enthusiasm—of the young. After making an initial mental decision, a woman will seek a "second opinion" from each of her female companions. Only after all of these opinions have been collected, Shashi said, will she ask for the "third opinion," that of the salesmen—in this, she seeks the advice not only of a professional but of a male. After all the opinions have been taken into account, a woman is ready to make her decision about which pieces she will take home.

I asked Shantibhandra if he is usually honest when his opinion is sought; it might be dangerous to tell a woman that she does not look good. If the item does not suit her, will he say so? He said he naturally forms an opinion, but conveys it indirectly, gently coaxing the woman to try on another piece that he regards as better suited to her. The act of female adornment encompasses the tastes of the men at Kanhaiya Lal in many ways. Items of jewelry that women buy express the store's choice of talented *karigars,* quite different in background, whose creations, combined with carefully selected items bought from wholesalers, make up the stock of the store. The bosses at Kanhaiya Lal choose and train the salesmen, who in turn choose which ornaments to bring forward, keeping in mind the customer, the occasion, and even the outfit to be matched. And finally, the ultimate act of adornment incorporates the advice and gentle nudging of one of these men, who wants the customer to look good, so that her beauty in public will make an advertisement for the "good will" of the store.

The Salesman's Art

I had watched the interaction between the salesmen and customers at the store many times over several years, when, in 2003, I asked Shantibhandra to describe in detail the art of selling. In a long afternoon interview, I began by asking how specific the customers' notion was of what they wanted to buy. We sat on the floor, both of us leaning on the low counter where the tape recorder ran. He answered in his characteristic animated style, speaking in a Hindi sprinkled with English:

"They ask like this, 'I need marriage things in good *varieties.*' 'I need them.' Then we ask, 'What type of items do you want?' 'What do you want?'"

At this point, the customers will repeat that they are interested in acquiring things in the category of ornaments for the wedding, and they will specify items for the hands, the neck, the ears:

"Then I start showing; for the ears, for the neck, rings. All, I start showing. Then you keep looking, keep looking, keep looking. At least twenty-five, fifty, one hundred, two hundred things you will see. From those you will *select.* If you don't want to *select* from these, then I will call our artisans and say,

'Whatever items, *orders,* you have ready, those items send over.' That stuff, if it's ready, he will send here."

Many of the *karigars* have items in progress, and since their *karkhanas* are conveniently located nearby, they will be able to send a runner with pieces of jewelry that might be suitable. These *karigars* might be men who work exclusively for Kanhaiya Lal, or they might be independent contractors with whom the store often works. Shantibhandra stressed that a *karigar*'s private stash of ornaments is occasionally shown, but the customer usually buys from the store's vast "stock" of jewelry that is shelved in the back room.

"We have a good *stock* that we keep at all times. Now, *near about,* approximately, one hundred, one hundred and fifty *sets* we have kept at all times. Now there is *churi* and *kangan,* these also; there must be one hundred *sets* of these. Rings, if you only want rings, so one thousand, one thousand two hundred rings I will show you. One thousand five hundred rings I will show. If you want to see earrings, then likewise, in that way, one thousand five hundred, two thousand, three thousand *pieces* I will show you. Now among these, you keep *selecting* as many as you want to *select.*"

As Shantibhandra's enumeration shows, at any given time the stock at Kanhaiya Lal far exceeds the number of items in any *karigar*'s private atelier, for the craftsmen lack the capital to have many pieces on hand. Some of the jewelry at the store is grouped into "sets" consisting of a necklace, matching earrings, and a ring. Bangles comprise a different kind of set, as most people will buy two thick *kangans* and two, four, six, or twelve slim *churis* in the same design, to be worn as a set, an equal number on each wrist. I asked Shantibhandra if people actually looked at thousands of pieces of jewelry, and he responded with an exaggerated affirmative nod. Men, he said, do not look at as many items as the women who have more *shauk.* In little groups over many hours at the Kanhaiya Lal store, women not only buy items to fulfill the immediate need of one woman, they also sample the inventory, developing an understanding of what is available and noticing what is fashionable and what is not. During this process, the woman who is buying and her female companions create a mental catalog to help them make intelligent decisions the next time they come to buy. Sitting on the mattress of the floor, drinking tea, and looking at box after box of jewelry, these women are engaging in what

Paco Underhill, in his study of buying patterns, describes as "pre-shopping," a previewing of goods with no immediate intention of purchase.[19]

Next, Shantibhandra described the basic system of selling at Kanhaiya Lal, contrasting it with an alternative system, the one found generally in America, as well as in Bombay, New Delhi, and even Banaras, as we shall soon see:

"A customer will come, with him I will talk; according to his desires I will show. After that, from whatever he selects, I will tell him the price, and take money from him. In your America, they have *showrooms* everywhere. And everything has a *flag* on it, saying this thing costs this much, this thing costs this much. So whatever you like, you tell them you want. That thing they take and give it to you, and you give them the money.

"There, neither the *customers* have that much *time,* to sit and chat, nor do the salesmen—so here you can sit and take my *interview!*"

The common system in India is relaxed, with the customer and the salesman spending much time in the act of commercial exchange, and yet the selling is direct and aggressive, as Shantibhandra says:

"Here, if a *customer* has come, then our *salesmen* will be totally after him, so that he must leave only after having bought something. If we are seeing that nothing is appealing to him, then, 'Hey, order some more things [from a *karigar*], order those particular things.' 'Quick quick, bring *chai.*' Then with *chai,* we sit the *customer* down. The stuff is coming; the stuff has come. Still he didn't like anything, then, 'Order things from somebody else.' We order *paan* and feed it to him. Still he didn't like anything; still we keep him sitting. We are thinking, in one way or another, from him, we will take his money.

"This should never happen that he leaves empty-handed. In his mind this kind of thought should not be born that, 'I went all the way there, hustling, hustling, and I did not find anything. They don't have anything there.' In Banaras, they will say: 'To that big store he went, and found nothing *decent* there.'"

Keeping the customer happy is an obvious goal of Kanhaiya Lal, and it has earned them the loyalty of customers in Banaras. The store wants to sell something—to make money, of course, but also to prove to the customers that the store stocks whatever is desired, and it is only a matter of looking and choosing. Kanhaiya Lal is interested in buying the customer's business for a lifetime, not just making an immediate sale. Shantibhandra understands that if nothing is bought, the customer will not blame himself for being finicky, but rather blame the store for not having what he wanted. He continues:

"The most important thing is to speak to the customers with affection, to listen to their desires, to bring them close to us. So they get *impressed* with us. Then after that, we start to show them the stuff.

"In our store, it is not like the customer has come and immediately: 'What do you want?' 'What will you take?' 'Tell me.' 'Okay, look.' It's not like this. If they have come, sit them down first. 'So-and-so, bring them a drink of water!' Then the water comes, and they have drunk the water. Then the salesman approaches, and he says: 'Sister, what kinds of things do you want?' 'What types of things do you want?' 'In what price range do you want?'

"For half an hour, my salesman will just engage in this kind of chatter. Then he will start showing the stuff; it will be seen, he will show, it will be seen, he will show, it will be seen. And if this is not enough, then, 'Show more.' He will show more. 'Show more.' He will show more. Then, after all this, if the customer's needs are not met, then we will change salesmen!

"Like, here in my store, *senior salesmen* are these two. These two are *senior,* meaning that for any kind of customers, these two have enough of their own *power* that, 'I will conquer these customers somehow.' Sometimes it happens that even they are unsuccessful. Then, 'Shashi, get up, and you go and show.' Then he will go. Sometimes he is not available, then, 'Piyush, you go over and see.' And *by chance,* the car still might not fit into the parking spot!

"After having spent two, three, four hours, and still the car does not fit into the parking spot, and we are noticing that they do have money—they are able to buy—then, I make an effort to bring them to me. I clear this space by me, and bring them to sit by me."

Once the customer sits down near Shantibhandra, he avoids all talk about selling jewelry. He engages the customer in a friendly conversation about the old times, telling anecdotes about the store, and his personal involvement in it over a period of fifty years. His aim is to "impress" upon the customer the long history of the store. What he communicates self-consciously is the fact that the store has been here since the customer's great-grandfather's time, and it is still here, with a new generation now in charge. Shantibhandra believes this kind of historical perspective "impresses" the customer so much that by the end of the conversation, he has surrendered himself 75 percent. The remaining 25 percent is merely a matter of what to buy, since buying, by this time, is inevitable.

Over time, the men at Kanhaiya Lal have worked out their aesthetic preferences and their notions of suitable relations between women and ornaments. And they have devised a system of selling. They have learned how to approach the customer, and how to involve the rest of the staff in their conquest of reluctant customers. The last step employs a psychological strategy by means of which the customer becomes interested in the store and its long history in Banaras. Thus, the individual purchase is located in a grand sweep of tradition and history. The store has been here for years, it will continue to be here for years to come. Today's commercial transaction is part of the tradition of the holy city of Kashi, and the customer is lucky to be allowed to participate in something so grand.

Shantibhandra continued by explaining that if the "customer dealings" take five or six hours, as they sometimes do, the store not only has a rising scale of experienced salesmen, but, as well, the salesmen know how to order refreshments in series, so that the longer the customer stays, the greater the chance for a big sale. They start with water, Shantibhandra said, and then move to *chai*. Then, after an hour, they order in the delicious *lassis* made nearby. Then light snacks, such as *samosas*. Finally, as people start to get hungry, heavier snacks appear and suggest a small meal—as though the customer had come to a friend's house. Shantibhandra remembered that in the old times, about fifty years ago, the Kanhaiya Lal store would offer complete meals of rice, lentils, vegetables, and *roti*, delivered from the upstairs kitchen. In those days, customers from out of town were housed in Kanhaiya Lal's family quarters upstairs, or they were put up in a nearby hotel. He said that the notion of hospitality is of utmost importance in India, and it is expressed—in a home or store—by sincere talk and the generous offering of food and drinks.

Shantibhandra, who is in his seventies, continued to reminisce about the past, saying that marriage receptions were once marked by an extravagant attention to the feeding of guests. Hosts humbly welcomed guests to their homes, for there is a proverb in Hindi, *Mehman Bhagwan hei:* "The guest is God." Now, Shantibhandra said in sadness, the "fashion" is to host wedding receptions at "five-star hotels," in the modern "buffet party" style, where everybody serves himself or herself, as the customers serve themselves in Western-style stores. Being old-fashioned, Shantibhandra believes in acts of devotion and service, whether at home where food is served, or in the store where jewelry is sold. Treating customers with *prem,* affection, bringing them items of jewelry from the back, and helping them make decisions—these acts are more than commercial tactics, they are gestures of respect and service.

Shantibhandra and the other men at Kanhaiya Lal are well aware of the method of selling in America, where a "flag" announces the price, and people choose their own things with little help or interest from the sales staff. Their system is not built out of ignorance of other models of sales, but out of a conscious decision to provide the customer with attention, helping her choose the right ornament, so she can benefit from the accumulated knowledge present in the staff at any given moment.

Kanhaiya Lal's busiest store is the one at Godaulia. It is situated in the heart of the commercial district, where Dashaswamedh Road runs inland from the Ganga. The store has always utilized the same sales system as that used in the Raja Darvaja store where Shantibhandra and Shashi work. In 2003, however, I noticed that the Godaulia store had changed radically. Gone were the booths where a salesman would approach you, as a waiter might in a fine restaurant to take your order, and return to serve you jewelry as though it were a delicious meal. Now, the store has changed to the "showroom system."[20] One enters through wide glass doors that are always closed, since the place is air-conditioned, a rarity in Banaras. Customers sit at the counter on elegant black iron chairs with fluffy beige cushions. The glass counters hold many examples of jewelry, segregated by category, each with a "flag" designating the weight of the piece. There are showcases around the walls, offering more examples for visual sampling. The place is well lit, and light dances and glances from all the twenty-two-carat yellow gold on display. The store feels like the fine jewelry stores in the Little India sections of Artesia in Los Angeles or Jackson Heights in Queens, New York.

The counter closest to the door holds toe rings, anklets, and other inexpensive things. This seems logical from the standpoint of security as well as convenience, since those coming to buy a few minor ornaments can be processed in and out with speedy efficiency. The counter with the necklaces and other substantial and expensive jewelry is set toward the back of the store near the back room, where more jewelry is stored to be brought out in the manner of the old system. On one occasion, I noticed that the customers seated in the back, who were presumably buying more expensive items, were each

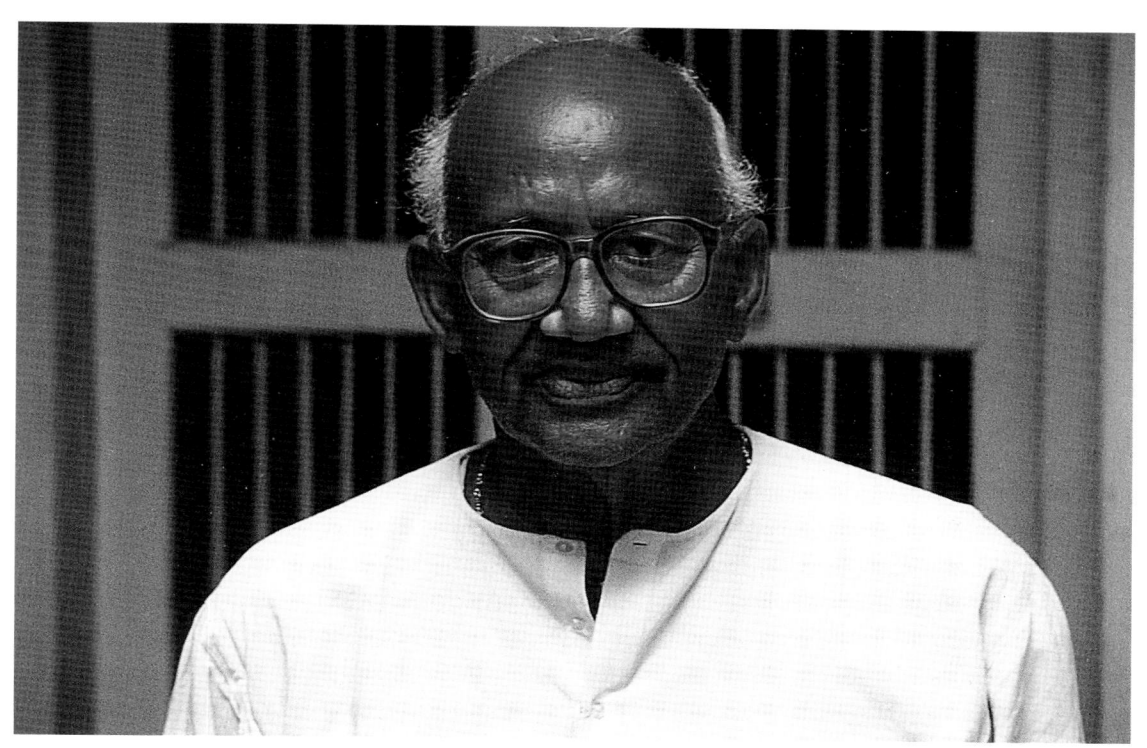

Shantibhandra Shah

offered an icy cold Mirinda orange soda, while the rest of us, who were hot and thirsty but who were buying cheaper jewelry, were left to sit in our heat and thirst.

When I mentioned my surprise at the drastic change of the Godaulia store to Shantibhandra and Piyush, they said the store had to change because an air-conditioned, "showroom-system" jewelry store opened across the street, and to remain competitive they had to modernize as well. Shantibhandra said that the salesmen at Godaulia are told to wear "formal clothes," consisting of trousers and shirts, as opposed to the salesmen in his shop who can wear anything from Western trousers to the old-fashioned white *dhoti* and *kurta* outfit favored by Shantibhandra. Piyush explained that at his store, you need more staff. One man is the salesman, while another brings things from the back. In the Godaulia store, more examples are visible beneath the glass of the counter, and the salesman only needs to lift out a tray and place it on the glass. The ratio of worker to customer is greater at his old-fashioned store, and so service is warmer, more personal.

Piyush and Shantibhandra believe that their customers want the "personal touch." They want to be treated like visiting friends, with a leisurely chat and a cup of tea. At the other store, Piyush thinks, people do not want the salesmen to intervene in their lives; they want to see the merchandise and choose from the stock available in front of their eyes—to serve themselves jewelry in the "buffet style." This new buffet system is direct and unmediated, and it differs from the old style that is usual in the stores of Banaras, whether they sell clothing and jewelry or crackers and cigarettes. The two Kanhaiya Lal stores are about a twenty-minute walk from each other, allowing the customers to choose the style of sale with which they are most comfortable. In this way, the pair of stores meets the needs of all customers, and lets them decide how much involvement the sales staff will have in the jewelry they will ultimately purchase.

The men at Kanhaiya Lal spoke with analytical clarity about the differences in the tastes of urban and rural women. To complete our examination of jewelry selling in Banaras, let us turn briefly to the other major marker of identity—religion—and visit a silver and gold shop that is owned by Muslims and that is only a few minutes' walk from the Kanhaiya Lal store at Raja Darvaja. A sign in Urdu and English announces the Haji Abdul Rauf, Abdul Majeed Saraf and Co. jewelry shop in Dalmandi, the commercial Muslim neighborhood of Banaras, not far from Chauk. Mohammad Sharib, the friendly son of the owner of the shop, says that his store caters mainly to the local Muslim population. I asked him to describe the differences in preference between his Hindu and Muslim customers, and his comments echoed those made by the Kanhaiya Lal men. These shops, one large, one small, one Hindu, one Muslim, were basically quite similar.

Mohammad started by making distinctions of class within each religious category. According to him, "literate Muslim" women and "illiterate Hindus" prefer fashionable, delicate pieces, while "illiterate Muslims" and "literate Hindus" like traditional, ethnic designs. His generalization does not sort neatly with the opinion of the men at Kanhaiya Lal, who grouped people mainly by class, not religion. The statement is telling, nonetheless. In Banaras, a city brutally divided by religious prejudice, Mohammad believes that Hindus and Muslims of the same economic level are at the opposite ends of the aesthetic spectrum.

I asked Mohammad for specific examples of customer preferences, and he gave me the conventional, yet accurate, observations that Hindus prefer jewelry with "mythological" renderings of animals, such as peacocks and elephants, while Muslims like items that depict a crescent moon and a star, as well as geometric designs. He also said that Muslim men, especially the orthodox, do not wear gold, which is a general prohibition in Islam. If they do wear gold, in a watch, for example, they should remove it, as the Mughal emperors did, during *namaz*. Mohammad said that Hindu men, on the other hand, can and do wear gold jewelry because all of their gods do. This is a subtle yet interesting point: the Hindu population, both men and women, find constant visual validation of their jewelry-wearing, since everywhere they look, they will see images of their gods dripping in gold, bejeweled literally from head to toe—except for Lord Shiva who wears a minimum of ornaments when he is depicted as a yogi, and none of them made of precious metals or stones.

Referring to women's jewelry, Mohammad explained that items exclusively associated with Hindus, such as the *mangalsutra* necklace and *sindur*, are increasingly worn by Muslim women for "fashion." This makes sense in a mixed city like Banaras, where Hindus and Muslims are in constant (visual) interaction with one another, and it suggests a casual crossing of strict divides that is certainly common in the relatively more relaxed environment of Dhaka, Bangladesh, where Dr. Parveen Hasan, a Muslim professor of Islamic history at Dhaka University, told me that she does not feel completely dressed unless she wears a *bindi,* which she regards as a basic adornment akin to lipstick. Dr. Hasan also enjoys wearing the sacred Hindu conch shell bangles just "for fashion," as many Muslim women in India and Bangladesh do, along with *sindur* and other religious markings of Hindu married women.

Mohammad made another interesting observation with regard to the sound, or musical quality, of jewelry. It is a belief, he said, that Muslim men should not be able to hear one another's wives, which suggests the titillation men feel for the melody created by women's anklets, bangles, and other jingling jewelry. Mohammad said that there are two categories of women who are known, by Hindus and Muslims alike, to wear loud anklets: witches and courtesans. Men view women who intentionally wear noisy jewelry as prostitute-like, he said, but, he continued, "loose character" is to be judged by many factors—forward behavior, too much talking, the touching of men, and direct eye contact—as well as jewelry and clothing.

Women, Mohammad said, should know the art of moving while wearing jewelry. He made an obvious, yet rare, observation when he said that the body is always in motion, which causes the jewelry and clothing to move and make sounds. He gave the example of dancers who anticipate the motion of their bodies when they put on their costume and jewelry. They pin their saris in strategic places so the cloth will stay beautifully draped while they dance, and they also affix some pieces of jewelry, such as the *mantikka* on the forehead, with a "gum" made of flour and water, to keep it in place as they move. He emphasized that matching jewelry to clothing, body type, and occasion is not enough. Ornaments are judged by how they are worn, how they move, and they are enhanced in their artfulness by the graceful movements of the female body.

Mohammad said that the most important "ornament" of all women, whether Hindu or Muslim, is "shyness." In this opinion, Mohammad was hardly alone. Many people I have spoken with in India—Hindu or Muslim, merchant or customer, man or woman—said the same thing. Personality and behavior, modesty and decorum, enhance the beauty of a woman as much as any glittering item of silver or gold.

·8·

Shopping along the Vishvanath Gali

READYMADE CLOTHING, including *salwar suits,* is sold in the garment district on Dashaswamedh Road, while saris are available in shops south of Godaulia along Madanpura Road. Silver and gold ornaments can be purchased from small shops in Chauk and Godaulia or from one of the big Kanhaiya Lal stores. The last need women have in the creation of their body art consists of daily items such as toiletries, nail polish, henna and hair products, *bindis, sindur,* bangles, and "artificial jewelry."

Women buy these everyday essentials with frequency, for personal pleasure and with little concern for cost, since they are inexpensive and ephemeral; they will be used immediately and not kept for posterity. As women browse through the markets, their choices are spontaneous and casually considered, being inspired by whim or late-breaking fashion. They plan little in advance and do not seek the advice of their husbands or girlfriends, as they do when purchasing expensive jewelry or saris. Shopping for *bindis,* bangles, and imitation jewelry, women are on their own. They engage directly with the salesmen, listening closely as the merchants provide no end of expert guidance.

Inexpensive items of personal adornment are usually bought from the hundreds of small shops along Vishvanath Gali, the lane that leads from Dashaswamedh Road to the Vishvanath Golden Temple. Sankatha Prashad Yadav, a wholesaler of religious beaded necklaces in the Gyanvapi lane, told me that "Vishvanath" means "Master of the Universe,"[1] and it is one name for Lord Shiva who controls the world from his seat in Banaras. Recall that hundreds of thousands of pilgrims come to the city every year to bathe in the Ganges and pray at the Vishvanath Temple, hoping to attain salvation for themselves and their ancestors. Over the past thousand years, the Golden Temple has been destroyed by the invading Mughals, replaced by a mosque, rebuilt as a temple on the site of the mosque, and then destroyed again. The temple standing in Banaras today was erected in 1777 beside the Jnana Vapi Masjid, the mosque built by the Mughal emperor Aurangzeb in the seventeenth century on the site of a previously destroyed Vishvanath Temple.[2]

The temple is located in the middle of a congested maze of allies. The most popular route to the temple goes from Dashaswamedh Road through a gateway shaped like a Hindu temple, and continues along the Vishvanath Gali. The first segment of the *gali* is lined with stores selling women's clothing, ornaments, and household items, while the shops surrounding the temple specialize in religious goods. At the entrance to the temple on Vishvanath Gali, before passing through the security checkpoint, you have an opportunity to buy sweets, flowers, incense, and other offerings for the gods. These will be sanctified by a *pundit* in the temple and the flowers will be given to the deity, but most of the sweets will be taken home as *prashad,* as blessings for those who did not make this visit. Holy gifts from Banaras—*prashad*—come in the form of sweets or red *puja* strings to be tied around the wrist, or as glass bangles for married women.

Along Vishvanath Gali pilgrims mix with the city's residents, who also come to this part of Banaras to buy clothes at one of the stores on Dashaswamedh Road or Godaulia, and to buy a variety of essential commodities inside Vishvanath Gali, many but not all of them with religious connotations—*sindur* powder, turned and painted *sindur* boxes, bangles and "imitation" jewelry, religious amulets, marble and brass *murtis,* musical instruments, pots, pans, and plastic food containers, sweets by the kilo, saris and *salwar suits, kurtas* for men and women with *chikan* embroidery from Lucknow, children's clothes, wooden and plastic toys, hair bands and clips, handkerchiefs, and toiletries including talcum powder, nail polish, lipstick, shampoo, *bindis,* and henna powder.

Many of the goods sold in the tiny shops on Vishvanath Gali reinforce the connection between religion and ornamentation. The proximity of the great temple makes the wifely ornaments sold here particularly auspicious. Beneficial jewelry, such as astrological rings and beaded necklaces, are also considered to be more powerful if they are bought in the shops on the way to the temple. The Hindu act of worship includes the beautification of the gods, and the shops of Vishvanath Gali sell garlands to adorn the statues in the temple and they sell the clothing and jewelry to grace the deities on the domestic altar.

The goods for sale in the Vishvanath Gali meet the needs of creation within the domestic sphere: there are pots and pans, sweets and spices for the kitchen; school supplies and toys for the children; statues and ornaments for the home altar; and objects of adornment for the women of the household. Shopping for the beauty of the gods, the house, and the self combines along Vishvanath Gali. In Hinduism, the domestic worship of the gods is primarily a task for the woman of the house. It is the woman of the house who engages in regular acts of devotion on behalf of the members of the family. This devotion is displayed in *pujas* and fasts, in the decoration of altars and the creation of *rangoli*—designs for the threshold. In addition to their religious duties—buying the materials for *puja*, adorning the gods, and taking *darshan* at the temple for their family members—women have a social responsibility to appear respectable, to display the proper wifely ornaments so as not to bring shame to the family. While shopping along the Vishvanath Gali, women complete many tasks at once: they serve their gods, their families, and themselves.

Adorning the Gods

Pilgrims and local people purchase items for domestic worship from the many shops in Vishvanath Gali that specialize in religious goods. There are stores that sell CDs of *bhajans*—devotional music—and stores filled with *puja* booklets that contain the texts recited during prayers. Statues of the gods abound in a variety of sizes and materials, brass and copper, marble and stone. One of the craft specialties of Banaras is the wooden statue of the deity, carved by one group of craftsmen, brilliantly painted by another, and then used for home decoration, for worship, and especially for assembling domestic dioramas for the celebration of Janmashtami, Krishna's birthday.[3] Stores also sell accessories for domestic altars—seats, thrones, and swings for the gods, bells, incense, and tiny wicks—all to excite the senses of the deities and their devotees.

Ornaments—*shringar*—for the gods are sold in small shops. These include ensembles of clothing and jewelry intended for the domestic *murtis*. A set for Radha and Krishna, for instance, includes a *dhoti*, shirt, and shoulder wrap for Krishna, and a *lehanga* skirt, blouse, and scarf for Radha. These six pieces come in a set, made of the same shiny bright cloth with gold piping around the edges. Jewelry options include various types of crowns, necklaces, armbands, and glue-on earrings. The jewelry for the arm can be purchased separately in pairs to accommodate the multiple arms of some Hindu deities. The jewelry is made of tiny white plastic beads resembling miniature pearls, interspersed with shiny red and green beads to look like rubies and emeralds; the gods wear a version of the fabulous pearl jewelry that is often depicted in miniature paintings from the Mughal period. Domestic statues are dressed for special ritual occasions, such as Divali Puja, but some people change the clothes of their statues more often, even daily, as a sign of devotion. The purpose of these accessories, which are reminiscent of the miniature clothes and jewelry made for dolls, is to honor, to beautify, and to serve the gods on the family's altar.[4]

Brijraj Das Agrawal, the owner of one of these ornament shops, the Kauslendra Shringar, told me that local Muslims make the ornaments that he sells for the Hindu gods. Jewelry and clothing function, he said, to communicate the personality of the various gods, just as it does for human beings. Since Ram is a "dignified god" and Krishna is "playful," the ornaments for these two avatars of Vishnu must be different, Brijraj Das said. The clothes are made to signal the sobriety of the warrior Ram and the liveliness of Krishna, whose ankles cross and whose head tilts when he plays the flute for his lovely Radha. The ornaments, Brijraj Das said, are sold mostly for Divali, and for the birthday celebrations of Ram and Krishna. At these times the beauty of the household and its gods becomes most important.

Clothes, I was often told, express the personality of the wearer, and this is true, too, of the gods. Their clothing and jewelry communicate their character—to children especially who learn to distinguish among the members of the Hindu pantheon by their clothes and ornaments. In Vishvanath Gali, and in Thateri Bazaar by Chauk, stores sell the clothes and ornaments worn by people who impersonate the gods in school plays and *lila* performances. Rajesh Kumar, who owns a shop in the Vishvanath Gali that sells both costumes and ornaments for statues, said that some of his customers are *sanyasis* and *pujaris*—mendicant holy men and priests of the ceremony—who buy jewelry to adorn the statues at ashrams or temples. Women in charge of the household *puja* also buy ornaments for the family altar from him. Schools are the primary consumers of the costumes, since these are used for the Ram and Krishna dramas that are performed by children.[5]

When I asked Rajesh Kumar why statues wear ornaments, he gave a layered answer. The gods should be treated with respect, for some of them, like Ram, are members of royal families. The gods wear jewelry in abundance, Rajesh said, because they are generous, forever giving ornaments to their servants and loyal followers. The glittering display of jewelry on the body of the god is a sign of high status. Rajesh Kumar made an analogy with the turbans worn by Rajasthani men, which through their pattern, color, and folds designate social status. Likewise, the ornaments of the gods express their status as kingly and otherworldly. Their crowns and jewelry, according to Rajesh, add *shobha,* grace, to the gods. And that added grace, he concluded, makes you look at them, and their vision draws you into affection, into devotion, during *pujas.* Ornaments on the gods beautify the statues, but more importantly, they pull the worshiper's eyes to the gods and hold them there—in the passion of *darshan.* People are attracted to ornamented images of the deities, Rajesh said, just as men are to bejeweled and beautiful women.

Rajesh Kumar explained that the color of the costume communicates the personality of the god. Ram wears blue to express peace, since he came to this world to bring peace through his destruction of the demon Ravan. Lakshman, Ram's faithful brother, wears red because he is prone to violence and anger. Sita, Ram's wife, can wear white, pink, or green, which are "ladies' colors" that connote "good character." Hanuman, ever loyal to Ram, wears bright orange—"*sindur* color." Krishna can wear any color, Rajesh said, because he has a "colorful mind." Shiva wears a deerskin, his body rubbed with pale ashes. Villains of all kinds are clad in black. The tone of the god's clothing influences the mood of the beholder, who in the act of *darshan*—or when watching a reenactment of the *Ramayana*—will be brought into the proper emotional state. Ram's and Sita's pastel colors are soothing, attractive; the villains' black is sinister, repulsive.

Rajesh Kumar said that if the costumes and ornaments were to deviate from the expected, then the villagers and children would not be able to recognize the gods. Television serials that depict the deities, such as the popular *Ramayana* and *Mahabharata* adaptations, he said, directly influence the costumes in which the *murtis* are dressed and which the players wear in live dramas. The worshipers in the temples and the shoppers in the streets have a conventional understanding of what the gods look like—an image has been created in the mind's eye by multitudinous experiences, including posters and murals and statues. To recognize the deity, to decode the message of religious body art, people apply their understanding of the relationship between the

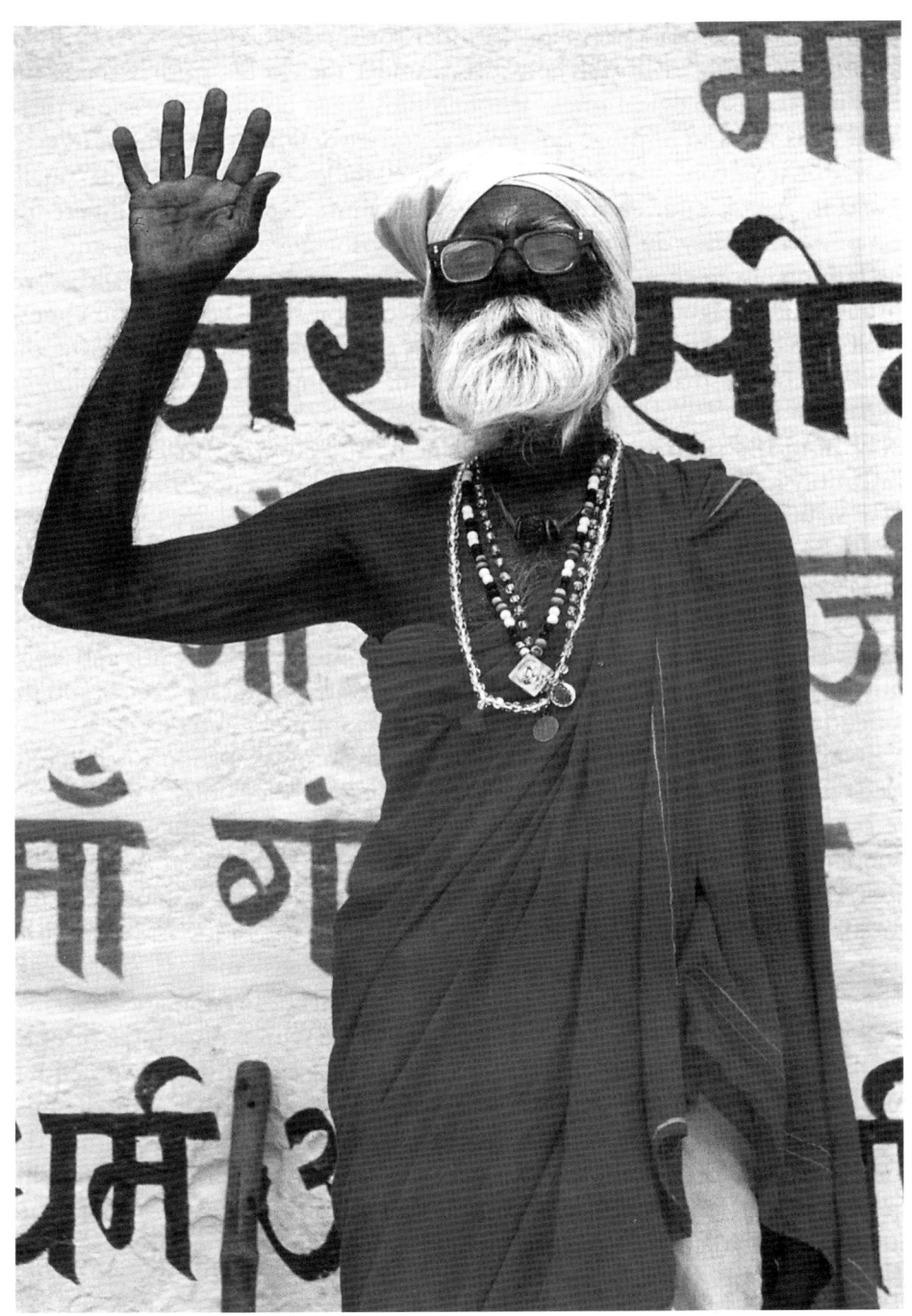

Sadhu on the *ghats,* Banaras

All of the sellers of beneficial ornaments said that a large portion of their customers rely on the merchant's knowledge and advice with regard to the wearing of beads and stones. Vishnu Shankar Chourshia's shop, Beads India, opens onto the street a few steps from the entrance of the Vishvanath Temple. He sells *murtis,* beaded necklaces, and astrological rings. While some people buy astrological rings in precious metals with expensive stones from jewelry shops such as Kanhaiya Lal, many others buy them in Vishvanath Gali where they are substantially less expensive.

Vishnu's shop is a venue for both sales and advice. After consulting a few folded pieces of photocopied paper, he dispenses knowledge about the associations between stones, planets, and the finger on which the ring should be worn. He is a believer in the healing powers of the astrological stones, and readily shares his personal testimony of the benefits that have come to him from wearing the rings he sells. He told me that he used to be tense all the time, so he decided to consult a *pundit.* After reading Vishnu's palm and doing "mathematics" with his date of birth, the *pundit* told him to wear a blue sapphire ring. That was six years ago, and since then Vishnu has been calm and he no longer picks fights on the streets, as he did in the past.

Vishnu holds to the general belief that men should wear astrological rings on their right hands, women on their left, and he has a firm list of associations that has been brought up to date. Uranus and Neptune have replaced the imaginary planets Rahu and Ketu. His list goes like this: Sun/ruby/ring finger; Mercury/emerald/little finger; Venus/diamond or rock crystal/little finger; Moon/pearl/little finger; Mars/coral/ring finger; Jupiter/white sapphire or topaz/index finger; Saturn/blue sapphire/ring finger; Uranus/amethyst or gomed/middle finger; Neptune/tiger's eye or cat's eye/little finger.

Rules govern which finger a ring goes on, and they dictate that rings should be worn on only one hand. That leaves four fingers (for no rings are worn on the thumb), so people often ignore the rules and wear rings mainly to look good. A man might wear rings on all the fingers of his right hand, and, in addition, some rings on his left, wearing the stones that might benefit him, while breaking the rules for appropriate fingers. The healing power of the stone is absorbed through physical contact with the gem, and wearing it on the wrong finger weakens its force; but, as it is with the *rukdraksh* beads, people may choose to emphasize appearance over efficacy.

Cheap rings with plastic stones in the colors of the astrological gems are sold outside the temples. A vendor at the Sankat Mochen Hanuman Temple told me that these are also bought for their healing power. If the real ring cures your problem 100 percent, he said, then maybe the plastic one will cure it 10 percent.

Customers may choose to buy a real gem or a plastic stone in the same color to gain some degree of benefit. This choice is partly influenced by financial capacity, but it is also affected by the sincerity of the wearer's belief in the healing power of astrological rings. If the plastic ring works a bit, then maybe it is time to save up to buy a ring with a semi-precious stone and greatly increase the level of benefit. If the cash builds up and a desire for style rises along with it, then you can choose a diamond at Kanhaiya Lal to replace the rock crystal from Beads India, though both work to control the influences of Venus. The setting may be silver or gold; the choice is made to show one's taste and wealth. People follow the rules, bend them, or ignore them. They consult a *pundit* or accept a merchant's advice. Their choices show where they stand in the confluence of otherworldly power and worldly aesthetics.

Daily Adornment

Many of the stores on Vishvanath Gali sell the essentials of everyday *shringar*—women's ornamentation—and it is believed that the items of wifely adornment worn for the health and life of the husband—the *mangalsutra* necklace, the bangles, *bindis,* and *sindur*—increase in auspiciousness when they are bought near the Vishvanath Temple, the seat of Lord Shiva. Unmarried women keep a fast on Mondays, Shiva's day, hoping to find a good husband. Once married, many women continue the fast as an offering to Shiva, in exchange for the health of their husbands. Daya Manik, a Banarasi woman, explained to me that the goddess Parvati kept a fast in order to win Shiva as a husband. (This episode is described in the version of the *Ramayana* by Tulsi Das.) Because of the success of Parvati's fast—she won Shiva as a husband—Daya said that women keep the fast as a way of "keeping the pattern" started by Parvati herself. Shiva blesses the unmarried women who keep a fast for him by giving them good husbands, since he was the recipient of a woman's love and devotion made manifest in a rigorous fast. Wifely ornaments bought in the stores near Shiva's Golden Temple assure good health for the husband, Daya said, because this is the Indian *parampara,* our tradition.

Certain items of adornment need to be purchased on a regular basis—bangles, *sindur* and *bindis,* toiletries and beauty supplies—and such things of daily use get used up quickly: *bindis* lose their adhesiveness, glass bangles

break. Many women use a monthly trip to the Vishvanath Gali as an opportunity to leave the house and mix in public, partaking of the sensory experiences of this jammed, busy, exciting part of the city. During their outing,
they watch people, gathering ideas about fashion as they scrutinize the other
women on the streets and study the new items in stores. It is a good thing
that a few of the "compulsory" items are ephemeral, since many women live
under the strict control of mothers-in-law who have no choice but to let
them leave the house and spend time shopping for wifely adornments—the
"necessary" items that insure the good health of their husbands, the sons of
their mothers-in-law. Many women I spoke with said they relish the chance
to leave the children behind, get dressed up, and go shopping. They stop at
the Vishvanath Temple for *darshan,* and they look closely at the latest trends
in the streets. Moving at a leisurely pace, jostled by the crowds, they choose
the *bindis* and bangles for the coming month's use. Shopping is often a pleasurable experience, and it is one of the few activities in which women engage
for selfish purposes.[8]

Bindis are sold along Vishvanath Gali in toiletry shops and in tiny stalls
that display hundreds of packets. Salik Nishad comes from a family of boat-
men, but he has been in the *bindi* business for three generations and owns
one such store. Salik's stall sells everyday *bindis*—the round ones—in a variety
of colors and sizes. On most days, women place on their foreheads a circular
bindi in red or maroon, the auspicious colors of marriage. Unmarried wom-
en, especially those attending the university, wear tiny black *bindis.* The black
dot *bindi* suggests fashion and signals a stage in life, for it is worn with *salwar
suits,* and the other markers of marital status, such as bangles or *sindur,* do not
accompany it. Salik said the *bindi* trade has boomed in the last twenty-five
years, with fancy *bindis* now available in every shape, size, and color. In the
past, *bindis* came only in round plastic varieties, accompanied by "gum," a
glue-like substance that had to be applied to the back to make it stick. Craftsmen like Salik cut round *bindis* with fine scissors to make intricate shapes,
such as peacocks, snakes, or scorpions, to adorn the foreheads of fashionable
women. Although *bindis* now come manufactured in these and other delicate
forms, Salik still cuts tiny *bindis* by hand—an exacting task that has cost him
his eyesight.

Salik told me that 90 percent of his customers are Hindu women, but 10
percent are Muslims, confirming the notion that items explicitly associated
with marriage can cross religious divides to be worn for purposes of sheer

fashion. To buy matching *bindis,* his customers often bring clothing with them, so their shopping is part of an efficient campaign. A woman might bring a silk sari to Dashaswamedh Road to have an accompanying blouse and petticoat tailored, then walk that sari over to the stores in Vishvanath Gali to buy complementary bangles and a *bindi,* completing the ensemble she will wear at some upcoming fancy occasion. Over the years, Salik, like the men at Kanhaiya Lal, has developed his own idea of what looks good on whom. He believes the main factor in the selection of a *bindi* is skin color: light-skinned women should wear navy, black, or brown *bindis,* while darker women should stick with reds and maroons. As we shall see later in this book, women believe that *bindis* should be chosen for more than skin tone; they should be selected in relation to the shape of the face.[9] The two geometric forms—face and *bindi*—should be complementary. But Salik's criterion was the shade of the skin.

Although Salik has specific ideas of what looks good, aesthetic advice is not sought from him as often as it is from the men of Kanhaiya Lal. His things are cheap, and, as he said, women already think they know the *bindi* shape that suits their faces; they do not need his opinion. Buying an inappropriate item of jewelry, of course, is a graver error than buying the wrong *bindi,* for *bindis* are used only a few times before they are discarded. Another marked contrast between buying jewelry and *bindis* is the practice of asking the price of the *bindi* only after a selection has been made. Everything is affordable at the *bindi* stall; the typical packet of a dozen *bindis* costs in the neighborhood of ten rupees (about twenty-five cents). Jewelry at Kanhaiya Lal can cost thousands of dollars.

Salik was, nevertheless, very clear about the importance of his commodity, the least expensive of all female ornaments. He said if a woman were to wear jewelry costing one *lakh* (one hundred thousand) rupees and no *bindi,* then that *lakh* would be *bekar*—totally wasted. Without a *bindi,* the face looks *suna,* lifeless and dull. The "beauty spot" of Indian women, Salik said, enhances the *shobha,* the grace, of the face, adding the radiant beauty of four moons.

Imitation Jewelry

"The beauty of the face is most important. With a *bindi,* the beauty is enhanced four-fold," agreed Priya Upahar, the owner of a shop of "imitation jewelry" in Vishvanath Gali.[10] Priya occasionally writes articles about jewelry for the local newspaper, and he is something of an expert on matters of personal adornment. He believes that women should wear *bindis,* and they should carefully choose *bindis* that suit their faces, since the wrong *bindi* can "destroy" a woman's artful presence. If a woman has a round face, Priya believes, then she should wear an oval or *tilak,* tear-shaped, *bindi.* On a small face and low forehead, the *bindi* should be big in order to enlarge the area visually. Consequently, he said, on a big face, the *bindi* should be small, thus diminishing the face slightly. On Vishvanath Gali, many items of body art are available for sale and many words of advice are available at no cost other than time and exasperation.

Priya Upahar sells an increasingly popular variety of jewelry: fake ornaments that are made to look like real silver or gold. He said that his store carries items of jewelry from 100 to 4,000 rupees—a wide range, but affordable when compared to the real thing. A pretty imitation necklace at his store was priced at 300 rupees; the same necklace in gold-plated silver, Priya said, would cost about 1,000 rupees. Cheaper than either gold or silver, the things in his store are made in the same style as real ornaments, and they are made well enough to fool most people. Many women who wear imitation jewelry intend to trick their beholders into thinking it is real gold. A character in Chitra Banerjee Divakaruni's novel *The Vine of Desire,* who sold her gold jewelry to send her son to medical school, told her husband: "I picked up some high-quality costume jewelry on my last trip to India. Our friends will never know the difference."[11]

The main reason to buy imitation ornaments is certainly financial. Still, women who can afford real jewels also purchase imitation jewelry, Priya said, for several reasons. One of them is aesthetic. The quality of his jewelry, he said, has improved drastically in the last decade or so. Imitation jewelry used to look cheap and unattractive, defeating the purpose of getting ornamented in the first place. But now, Priya proudly declared, "imitation jewelry is famous." His store carries the best brand names: Bentex, Lily, and Titan. These products look so much like real gold, according to Priya, that nobody can tell the difference. (Most women I talked to, however, claim to be able to spot imitation jewelry a mile away.) Since imitation jewelry looks good, Priya said, women prefer it to real gold, fearing both theft and loss. Priya assures his customers that his jewelry is beautiful but it does not carry the "risk factor" of real gold.

A major reason to choose imitation jewelry over real jewelry has to do with fashion, which is, by definition, fleeting and fickle. Priya strongly believes that women who choose to follow the trends set by the Bollywood heroines would be smart to buy cheap jewelry in the latest style, and save the bulk of their money for a timeless investment in gold or silver. His merchandise allows women to follow a temporary fad swiftly and completely with no nagging guilt, and his shop has pictures of heroines, cut from movie magazines, glued to the walls and displayed alongside the earrings and necklaces he sells. Some women bring in pictures from *filmi* magazines and show them to him, hoping to buy similar jewelry for themselves. Priya told me that imitation jewelry, made in response to rapidly changing fashions, comes in a greater variety of shapes and styles than gold jewelry, which holds conservatively close to traditional forms. This is yet another argument for imitation jewelry: it is rich in variation, and, being inexpensive, it permits you to wear something new and different with frequency.

Priya Upahar had yet more explanations for why his customers choose to buy certain items from his store instead of Kanhaiya Lal. By his estimate his ornaments will last ten years, at which point, or sooner if finances allow, one can take the item to a jeweler and order a version of it in gold. In this way, the imitation piece of jewelry can serve as a trial, a sample to be experienced in the way that young people in America get a henna design—a "temporary tattoo"—as a trial for a permanent, real tattoo. Priya explained that this system of replacing imitation jewelry with golden ornaments allows a woman to buy and wear certain jewelry—an imitation golden bracelet, let us say—while saving the money that will enable her to exchange the imitation piece for the real thing. As with plastic astrological rings, which are occasionally replaced with real gems after a trial period, imitation jewelry allows for experimentation before making a permanent and expensive commitment. Priya stressed that his jewelry does not hurt the business of the goldsmiths; shops like Kanhaiya Lal will always be full of customers. His jewelry provides another set of choices for women; it makes it possible for them to afford a greater variety of ornaments, and to follow fashions and impulses.

Priya gave me a final, practical rationale for the choice of imitation jewelry. He said that the overall value of gold is depreciating, making it a less wise investment than it once was, and, further, he said that the quality of the gold in Uttar Pradesh is inferior to that from elsewhere, such as Madras. Gold is usually bought on the assumption that it can be converted easily into emergency cash. When a woman sells her gold, it is weighed and tested for purity. The devious people who use second-rate gold, Priya warned me, know that a Hindu woman will never sell her *mangalsutra* necklace, since this is her main symbol of marriage, something that she will never part with, even in a time of duress. For that reason, Priya said, *mangalsutra* necklaces are often made of impure, heavily alloyed gold, but women never find out. Ironically, the most important of all ornaments is the one that is most often tainted, because it is the one that will never be sold and therefore never tested. Such concerns naturally fill the already fearful mind of the customer. Suspicions rise: if the gold is impure and I am being cheated, why should I give my money to the fancy gold shops?

Priya's customers often come alone. There is little need for deliberation and advice; his items are relatively cheap and temporary. Women, he said, prefer to come in the afternoon, while the children are at school, for they need *shanti,* peace, to be able to shop comfortably. When restless children come with them, women are "full of tension." They select haphazardly, and leave quickly.[12] Priya believes that customers need to be in a good mood to shop, especially at his store, where women do not buy things out of necessity, in the way they buy groceries. Here, they buy for pleasure, for fashion. In Priya's shop, as in Salik Nishad's *bindi* stall, customers choose items with little regard for cost; they ask the price only after their selection has been made.

Priya has a professional as well as a personal interest in ornamentation. He strongly believes that the act of personal adornment is an artistic endeavor that depends on skills that are not possessed by everybody. Most women, in his opinion, fail to achieve a successful ensemble of clothes and jewelry. Some women know the kinds of jewelry that suit their bodies, skin color, and face shapes, but most do not. Priya thinks that many women think first of a favorite color, then buy a sari in that color, and then choose ornaments to match the sari; but most do not choose clothing in colors that flatter their complexions or body types, nor do they buy jewelry that harmonizes with their facial features. Priya has a well-thought-out notion of what looks good, but he is not always asked to share his taste with his customers. Occasionally he will say that something looks good on a customer, when, in fact, he thinks it looks bad. A sale is a sale.

Unlike Shantibhandra at Kanhaiya Lal, who tries to dissuade women from buying things he considers inappropriate, Priya may praise the wrong ornament if he feels the woman is inclined to buy it. Most women do not

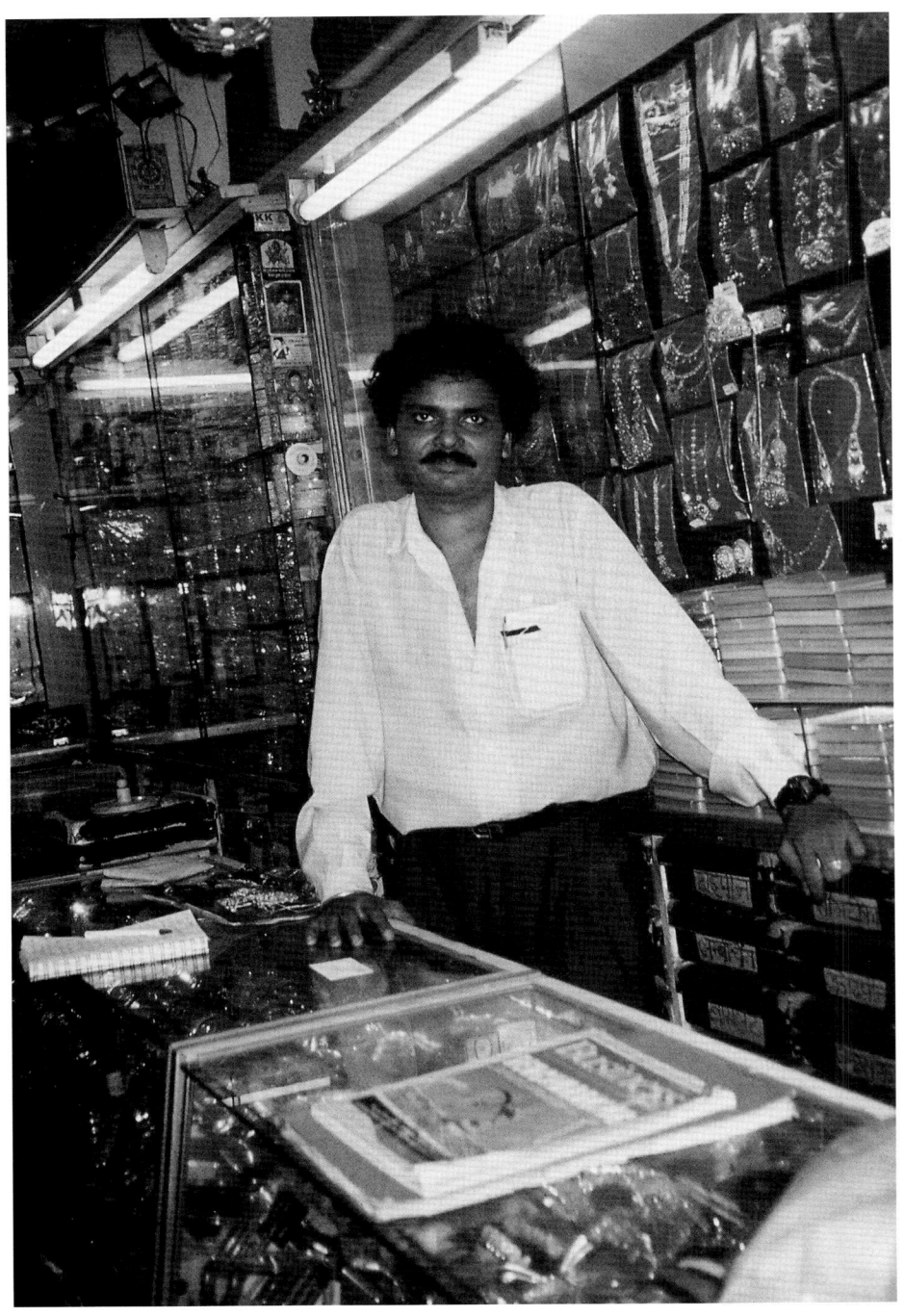

Priya Upahar

possess the fine art of personal adornment anyway, he feels, so: let them buy the wrong jewelry. But, unlike the men at Kanhaiya Lal, who give their honest advice in exchange for a customer's lifetime of loyalty, Priya is interested in making an immediate sale. The customer will probably only wear the ornament a few times, then give it away, and she is unlikely to return to his shop anyway. He does not need to place the right ornament with the right woman, but that is the goal at Kanhaiya Lal; theirs is an eternal union, founded upon the permanence and value of gold. Priya's customers quickly purchase relatively cheap jewelry that quickly comes into fashion and then quickly goes out. Their interest is in looking good right now: up to date, in line with the fad of the moment. Priya, too, is in it for the short term. His interest is in making quick money; long-term customer loyalty is not his concern.

The shops that sell exquisitely crafted ornaments of precious metals and gems aim for long relations with their customers. The shops that sell inexpensive beads, *bindis,* and imitation jewelry aim for quick turnover. Along Vishvanath Gali there is a third pattern in the commerce of adornment. In it the customer and the salesman enter into the prolonged, collaborative creation of an ensemble. This is the business of bangles. Of all the ornaments sold in Vishvanath Gali, the bangle is the most commonly bought. Bangles deserve detailed analysis and they are the focus of the next chapter, the last in our exploration of Indian commerce.

·9·
Assembling Bangle Sets

BANGLES—WORN on the wrists as a sign of the married estate—are the most common item of ornamentation in India. One of the best-known examples of ancient Indian art is a small bronze statue of a "dancing girl" from Mohen-jodaro (2200–1800 BC); she is naked except for a necklace and twenty-nine bangles.[1] Women often cite this metal statue to illustrate the continual importance of bangles among Indian people. Banaras is, along with Jaipur and Calcutta, famous for the wide variety of bangles available for sale, mostly in the Vishvanath Gali. The sellers of bangles are more like the sellers of imitation jewelry than they are like purveyors of expensive silver and gold. Bangles are cheap, ephemeral items frequently bought "for fashion." But as this chapter will demonstrate, there is a special skill to the selling of bangles. Bangles are generally bought in combinations or sets that are assembled by talented salesmen. The art of bangle selling involves combining bangles of different widths, styles, colors, and materials into a coherent and dazzling unit.

Shri Chand & Bros. Bangle Shop

Bangles bought from the stores along the Vishvanath Gali are considered *prashad,* a blessing from Shiva that pilgrims carry home with them for all the married women of the household. I counted forty-nine bangle shops and stalls along Vishvanath Gali, attesting to the importance of this kind of adornment. Right at the entrance of the Vishvanath Gali from Dashaswamedh Road, on the left side of the narrow lane, one of the area's oldest bangle shops stood for over fifty years: Shri Chand & Bros. The store is now gone. The owners, the Gupta brothers, were a great source of information for me in 1996.[2] From their position right at the gate of the teeming *gali,* they had witnessed much in their half-century, and using details I learned from them, I will speak generally about bangles and their purchase in Banaras. Later, I will turn to the creation of bangle sets and the art of their sale.

Many of the usual patterns of shopping for ornaments in the Vishvanath Gali apply to the purchase of bangles. Most of the customers are Hindu women who shop alone. Hindu men and Muslims of either gender make up but a small percentage of the clientele. Since bangles are usually cheaper even than imitation jewelry, and since they are worn daily like *bindis,* women purchase them with little concern for cost. As it is with Hemant Khanchandani's clothing shop a few yards away, the Gupta brothers' store must respond to the diverse population of the country, meeting the needs of the ethnic differences of Banaras and of the visiting pilgrims. Many regions of India have special bangles to denote marital status; the Gupta brothers' store sells most of them, supplying women of different castes with their own bangles, whether they are buying them for fashion or as *prashad,* a souvenir of pilgrimage.

The Gupta brothers explained to me how they decide which bangles to order. Glass bangles, they said, are stocked for the local customers from Uttar Pradesh and for those visiting from the states of Rajasthan and Bihar, since married women from all of these regions must wear glass bangles. For Punjabi, Sindhi, and Rajasthani brides, special bangles, called *chura,* are ordered. To Bengali married women, the store sells the customary pair of bangles, one in red *lac* or plastic and the other of the traditional conch shell or a cheap white imitation in plastic.[3] The wrists of a woman often designate not only marital status, but also her region of origin and possibly her region of residence. I know a woman who wears the red and white pair on each wrist and half a dozen glass bangles as well to communicate that she is a married Bengali woman who currently lives in Uttar Pradesh.[4] The Gupta brothers said that they also carry "gaudy" bangles for the Muslim customers who buy new bangles to celebrate Eid. For college girls, they stock wide *kangan* bangles that fashionable customers wear with jeans and *salwar suits.* While people usually choose bangles to fit their regional identity, their caste, religion, and social and educational positions, some pilgrims, the Guptas said, choose to take home, for their own use, "typical Banarasi" bangles—a souvenir of the pilgrimage for themselves, and an indicator to others of their travel and urban experience. (It is not clear to me what exactly these "typical" bangles are. All the bangle merchants I spoke with had different opinions on the definition of the Banarasi bangles, but there was a general consensus that they must be made of glass and be somehow "fancy" in design.)

Bangles made of different materials, including gold, come in standard sizes, varying by diameter. Bangles for babies and little girls come in these sizes: 4a, 6a, 8a, 10a, 12a, and 14a. Bangles for women are measured differently: 2.2, 2.4 ("average size"), 2.6, and 2.8 ("healthy size," for women with thicker wrists). Because international tourists do make up a small category of customers in the Vishvanath Gali, some stores sell bangles in especially large sizes to accommodate the bigger bones of foreign women. A bangle vendor referred to the bangles in this last category as "elephant size": 2.10, 2.12, 2.14, and 3.[5] Women know their bangle size as they do their shoe size, so they generally do not bother trying bangles on when they buy them. This is preferable for the seller, since glass bangles break easily, and trying to slip them over large hands usually leads to broken glass. Street vendors of glass bangles, who peddle their wares from door to door, are famous for being able to massage and twist a woman's hands, fitting them into relatively small glass bangles, which, because they are snug around the wrist, are less likely to break when they are worn. It seems no problem for the peddlers of bangles, but I was told that merchants at stores are reluctant to touch the hands of their female customers, which is regarded as an unnecessary and often embarrassing intimacy among strangers. Both Hindu and Muslim vendors told me that this taboo is observed with particular strictness when a Hindu merchant deals with his female Muslim customers.

When they buy bangles, women first tell the merchant their size and preference in materials—glass, metal, *lac,* or plastic—and they also tell their choice of color, and the variety they are interested in, fancy or plain. Many bangle stores, including the Shri Chand shop, operate like the Kanhaiya Lal jewelry store, where gold jewelry is kept in a vault in the back. In these stores, the bangles are stored in little paper boxes, kept behind the sellers who sit cross-legged at the customer's eye level. Once a customer asks to see specific bangles, the merchant reaches behind him for several boxes and shows them to her. The customer cannot visually sample the entire inventory of bangles, but must rely on the merchant's assessments of what she should see. Most thick bangles—*kangans* and *karas*—are sold in pairs, while thin *churis*—made of glass, metal, or plastic—are usually sold by the dozen and bought for daily use. Depending on her marital status and personal preference, a woman might wear six or twelve on each arm, or only two or three per wrist. An older woman whose husband is still alive might wear one bangle on each arm as a modest sign of the blessing of marital continuity.

Since bangles are bought for special occasions as well as daily wear, women often bring outfits with them to the shop so as to purchase a perfectly matched set of bangles. Bangle merchants, including the Gupta brothers, assemble for their customers sets of different types of bangles to match these fancy outfits. The set for each hand might include a dozen thin monochrome glass or metal bangles, four thicker metal bangles distributed symmetrically throughout the set, and for the outer edges, two bangles encrusted with imitation pearls or rhinestones. After an initial set has been created by one of the Gupta brothers, the customer might ask for it to be made "lighter" or "heavier"—simpler or more ornate. At her request the set is tweaked, some bangles are added, others removed, and the new set is ready for the customer's reaction. This process continues until a satisfactory combination has been achieved. The sets are assembled with incredible speed; the brothers hold bangles of different types on their outstretched fingers, rhythmically weaving their creation into shiny, glittery, new combinations as sets are formed and formed again.

One's own wedding is the most important special occasion for which a set of bangles is purchased. The Guptas told me that the assembly of a bangle set for the *jaimal* ceremony—when the bride and groom ritually place garlands of flowers around each other's necks—can take as long as forty-five minutes. During the *jaimal,* most of the bride's body is covered with clothing, including her head, which is draped in brocaded silk, but her arms are visible, and her wrists appear prominently in the visual frame shaped by the garland and the head of the groom. This act of exchanging garlands is often the focus of photographs, so wedding bangles are chosen both to look good at the moment of the exchange of flowers and, most importantly, to look good forever in the multitudinous photographs snapped by dozens of cameras. Many of the other choices the bride must make concerning her jewelry, facial makeup, and clothing are also explicitly influenced by how they look through the camera's eye, as we shall see later in this book.

The Gupta brothers told me that red was not arbitrarily chosen as the color of wedding clothing and bangles; rather, it was selected for its power to evoke love, since red is an "active" color. In contrast, they said, green is "fresh"; white denotes "peace"; blue is "cold"; and black is "spiritual." The

187

Gupta brothers said the color of the bangles affects the mood of both the wearer and the beholders. Certain colors are associated with certain seasons. Green and red should be worn during the winter, they said, and pale colors during the summer. This association of a bangle color with a season reminds us of the choices sari weavers make. Hashim Ansari's workshop weaves light, "English" colors in the summer and dark, "village" colors in the winter. Since customers prefer to wear certain colors during certain seasons, sari and bangle shops must shift their stock with the weather. The Gupta brothers stressed that people do not merely react to seasonal factors. They make deliberate choices, since colors express the personality of the wearer. The association of a color with a woman's personality is consistent with the idea, outlined in the previous chapter, that the colors worn by the deities reveal their characteristics: Ram's peaceful authority requires blue, while Krishna's playfulness is shown through a rainbow of colors. Color evokes feelings in the witness, who is moved by the colors on the body in both sacred and secular settings. Color is chosen for its desired affect on others.[6] If a woman wears a bright red sari to an afternoon sober occasion, she is making a deliberate choice, and sending a self-conscious message, which many will feel is too flashy and sexy, unless she is a brand-new bride.

Although the Shri Chand & Bros. shop is now closed, Rama Bangles, run by Rabindranath Gupta, a third Gupta brother, is still very much in operation in the Vishvanath Gali. Rabindranath told me that his family owns four bangle shops, but he prefers to work at this one, in the heart of Vishvanath Gali, because this is an "international lane." There is always much excitement, he said, in this "congested" alley. His shop, like the one formerly managed by his brothers nearby, has few bangles on display. The only bangles visible in the glass showcase on the street are glass ones, arranged in groupings by color. Rabindranath makes bangle sets only upon demand, which is a marked difference between his store and the fabulous Priya Bangles store, where we are headed. Rama Bangles sells only traditional glass bangles, but they are available in a wide variety of colors and styles that appeal both to pilgrims and local women. In 2001, Rabindranath Gupta carried a new style of ornate glass bangles he referred to as "Ganga Wave." While we were visiting with him one day, sitting on the floor of his shop and drinking tea, a family of pilgrims from Andra Pradesh stopped by and bought two dozen Ganga Wave bangles in light blue. The wife chose the bangles, the husband paid for them, and then he promptly handed her the little cardboard box bound shut with a rubber band. With the memory of the *darshan* of Baba Vishvanath in their minds, the Golden Temple's red *tikka* on their foreheads, and a cluster of Ganga Wave bangles in their hands, the family left Vishvanath Gali and Banaras, taking with them Shiva's blessings in various forms.

In addition to stores such as Shri Chand & Bros. and Rama Bangles, there are small bangle stalls in the alley. Their proprietors sit on wooden stools to hassle the passersby, hustling their goods. One such stall on Vishvanath Gali is Raj Jewellers, owned and run by Raj Kumar. Though he snares a small portion of the customers who mill along Vishvanath Gali, Raj Kumar's observations were, for the most part, very like the ones made by the owners of much larger shops. There is considerable consistency, it seems, in the taste of the women in Banaras. Salik Nishad, the *bindi* seller from the previous chapter, believes that *bindis* provide grace to a woman, adding the moon's splendor to her face. Raj Kumar agrees that ornaments worn on the face highlight a woman's beauty. *Bindis* are noticed immediately, Raj Kumar said. As soon as people meet, they look into one another's faces. But, he added, bangles complete the picture, for once the eye moves away from the face, it inevitably falls—the bangle seller believes—on a woman's wrists. They should never be without bangles, he said. Even ugly bangles are better than no bangles at all.

Asif Ali owns a small bangle shop in the Dalmandi Muslim neighborhood by Chauk, which is an alternative place to shop for bangles. Asif agrees that the wrists of a woman should not be "empty." A woman who is otherwise ornamented but wears no bangles presents a worthless—*bekar*—look. Muslim women, I was told, should always wear pretty bangles on their wrists. Many Muslim women in Banaras wear black *burqa* coats, some with hoods over their heads. When *burqa*-clad women appear on the streets or in rickshaws, their wrists still shine and glitter, suggesting a hidden beauty. Once they have come inside and seated themselves comfortably among other Muslim women, the beautiful clothes, hidden under the *burqa* and symbolized by bangles, will be exposed to admiring view.

Asif Ali said that Muslim women come to his bangle stall in Dalmandi instead of going to one of the stores in the Vishvanath Gali because the conservative families of his neighborhood are more relaxed when their women shop close by. He also said that women are more comfortable dealing with a Muslim salesman than they are in buying from one of the Hindu men in Vishvanath Gali, the alley that carries the throngs of pilgrims to the main Hindu temple of Banaras. In describing the differences in taste among the women of the major religions in Banaras, Asif Ali said that Muslim women prefer "sober" and "simple" styles, while Hindus like "gaudy" bangles. Raj Kumar, and all the other Hindu bangle sellers with whom I talked, said the opposite. Muslim women, they said, wear shiny, "gaudy" bangles, while their women showed a more restrained taste. Whether or not there is a decipherable difference in the actual preferences of Muslim and Hindu women, there certainly is a distinct difference in how the vendors of the city conceive of the tastes of the two groups.

Back at the Vishvanath Gali, Raj Kumar made an interesting observation about women's shopping styles. He said that they either come to his store with an idea of what they want to buy—usually from having seen bangles they liked in a movie—or they come with no prior notion, but acquire a liking for certain bangles once they see them in his store. Women, in his view, have "no imagination." They are influenced by movies and the media, or by him and his merchandise. Some women I talked with, such as Mukta Tripathi, agreed with Raj Kumar's opinion, feeling that the level of creativity in bodily adornment was low. This lack of imagination seems nearly fated when women deal with manufactured items like bangles. Choice among hundreds of options does have its creative aspect, but where creativity truly emerges is in the assembly of sets. Someone else, perhaps far away, made the ornaments. This is less the case with the finer items of clothing and jewelry, which can be custom-ordered by a customer who selects from different raw materials—silk or cotton, silver or gold—and commissions innovative objects made to personal specifications. But bangles—along with *bindis,* imitation jewelry, handbags, and shoes—have to be chosen from the mass-produced varieties displayed in the stores. Creativity, then, is most often and clearly expressed by the artful combination of these purchased things with other items of personal adornment. Choice is expressed partly by selecting which store to frequent, and, in the case of bangles, which salesman to draw into collaboration in the assembly of sets. If you are looking for the most beautiful bangles in Banaras, and for talented salesmen to give advice about fashion, the choice is Priya Bangles.

Priya Bangles

The biggest and most extravagant bangle store in Vishvanath Gali, Priya Bangles offers a clean, spacious shop and the largest selection of bangles in Banaras.

The store is owned by the Manik family, whose ancestors came to Banaras five generations ago to live in Shiva's city. Their bangle shop has been in its current location since the 1940s. In the 1990s, the Manik family added another store, a "sister concern" that sells imitation jewelry, called Preetam Jewellers: Heaven of Jewellery. From the outside, on Vishvanath Gali, the store's glass vitrine displays mannequin heads in funny wigs, wearing the necklaces and earrings sold by Preetam Jewellers. The storefront window does not advertise bangles, though bangles comprise the largest percentage of the inventory. Upon entering the store through the narrow door, you encounter a glittering, shiny space, dancing with brightness and color. The long glass display counters to the left exhibit countless readymade bangle sets in an amazing array of colors and types. The mirrored wall behind the counter has shallow glass shelves that rise to the high ceiling carrying metal monochrome bangles in every color, wrapped in cellophane. The customer is able to appraise sets in the counters visually, and ask for them to be modified by choosing the exact color that will match an outfit perfectly.

The right side of the store offers a similar display of glass counters and shelves, but these hold the wares of Preetam Jewellers: imitation jewelry for women, and some accessories for men. The back wall of the store is the place for toiletries and glass bangles. The cheapest of their bangles are the glass ones, so they are given the least attractive display space. In the middle of the store, the acting manager sits in an island booth, cross-legged on a cushion at eye-level with the customers. The manager of Priya Bangles, like the manager of Kanhaiya Lal, is the one who handles the financial transactions, sitting with two calculators and a locked box full of money. The usual occupant of this island of power is Ashok Kumar Manik, the gracious owner of the establishment. He runs the shop with the aid of his friendly and equally handsome sons: Priya Kumar, Preetam Kumar, and Sant Kumar.[7] (Ashok Kumar named his twin stores after his two oldest sons.) In addition to the four men of the family, there are usually six additional young men at work in the Priya Bangles section (three sellers and three helpers), two salesmen in the Preetam Jewellers section, and a *paniwallah* boy whose job it is to fetch water, *chai,* and cold drinks for the customers. The sole female employee in this store of women's adornment stands at the back, at the toiletries station, providing comfort for customers who need to buy embarrassing things, such as the monthly necessity of "feminine gadgetry."

The Manik family lives close to their store in a big, multistory house. After a generous dinner one night, Ashok Kumar and his wife, Dayal Kumari, having put in a long busy day, went to sleep, and the three sons and I chatted for a couple of delightful hours about their shop. I started the conversation by asking them about the stock of their store, what they carry and how they choose what to order. Sant Kumar, the youngest brother, began by explaining that few of the bangles are made in Banaras. The glass ones are made nearby in Firozabad; the others come from Calcutta, Delhi, and Bombay.[8] Their store either sends a buyer to these bangle-manufacturing centers, or a representative—a wholesaler—comes to them with samples. Their methods, that is, are the ones generally used by clothing and jewelry sellers in Banaras. Sant Kumar continued, saying that it is not the individual bangles that matter, but the "collection" amassed by a store. He, like many others, employed the analogy of the famous Banarasi *paan.* Though all the ingredients come from elsewhere, the best *paan* is Banarasi *paan* because of the excellence of its assembly. Priya Bangles, Sant Kumar said, is successful precisely because they specialize in carrying "all varieties" of bangles, assembling an irresistible collection from which to choose. Women have different tastes, and by having a few examples of every type of bangle, Priya Bangles can satisfy all the customers who come into the store. Sant Kumar proudly stated that 99 percent of the people who enter their store buy something, for the "bangles fashion" is always on.

Once a wide array of bangles has been ordered and made available in the store, the brothers watch what sells and what the customers request, learning about current demand. Preetam, the middle brother, explained that they do not watch Bollywood films or look at people on the streets to figure out the latest fashion; they know the fashion by carefully observing their customers' purchases. Here the Manik brothers differ with the members of their sales staff, who passionately watch films, studying what the Bollywood stars wear. Preetam explained that the manufacturers who send their representatives to his store are the same people who place the bangles on the wrists of Bollywood's beautiful heroines. The bangles worn in Bollywood are mass-produced and already available when a movie is released. Bangles, in this way, are unlike the clothing that can be ordered from the local tailor only after it has been admired in a movie. The Manik brothers order, albeit indirectly, the bangles that appear in the latest hit film, because all fancy bangles come from the same source—the clever wholesalers who, through their contacts with film costume designers, get into the movies the same bangles they get simultaneously to fine shops like Priya Bangles.

I next asked the Manik brothers about their customers. They told me that they serve both locals and pilgrims, both Hindus and Muslims, but most of the clientele is female. Preetam said the local women come to shop at around one or two o'clock in the afternoon, after their families have been fed lunch. If they are buying for a special occasion, women will most likely bring an outfit to match the bangles. The salesman looks at the outfit and decides what kinds of bangles to show her. This choice is based on the color of the clothes and, more importantly, on the approximate cost of the garment. If the outfit costs 1,000 rupees, then the bangles shown should be in the 400-rupee range. A 25,000-rupee wedding *lehanga* warrants a 3,000-rupee bridal bangle set. Expensive outfits naturally suggest an affluent customer with refined taste and an important occasion for which such an outfit would be worn, calling for a finer, more expensive set of bangles. The cost of the bangle set is important because the bangles are accessories to the outfit, and, while they should cost less than the clothing, they should be priced proportionally to reflect a coherence of style and expense.

The clothing brought in by a woman provides the salesman with insight into her financial status, and also her taste. These are important clues to go by when creating a matching bangle set. Priya Kumar, the oldest brother, explained that their salesmen also note the clothes and jewelry the customer is wearing as well as her style of talk, her gestures, and the way she carries herself. In addition, the salesmen analyze the bangles the customer asks for, and how she reacts to their prices. All of these visual and behavioral clues signal her social status, marital status, ethnic and regional identity, her personal taste, and the level of her *shauk* for ornaments. Everyone in India reads everybody's body art by these signs; but the salesmen of Priya Bangles are masters of this cultural system. They use the visual evidence everyone uses, but they use it with practiced deftness to make their living.

Priya Kumar continued by explaining that it is hard to articulate exactly what the salesmen use to read the customers, since they act on instinct and experience, but he said that just as I, a professor, would know before giving an exam which student would get a sixty, which one would score an eighty, and which would receive a perfect one hundred on a test, in the same way, when a customer walks into their store they know who will buy how much. They have the "experience" necessary to be able to read the "purchasing power" of each customer.

Because Priya Bangles serves a varied population, they have salesmen who differ in expertise. Some of their salesmen are better at handling village women, others are better with older women, and some are better at selling to "smart ladies." Priya Kumar told me that part of the job the brothers and their father must do is to match the right salesman to the right customer. It is their task, as the supervisors and most experienced men in the shop, to be able to read a female customer quickly and send the right man to her, ensuring, as Shantibhandra does at Kanhaiya Lal, that the sale will be a success. Priya Kumar compared their work with the work of doctors: there are some who specialize in eyes, others in hearts, and others in feet. He asked me if I would send an eye doctor to do the job of a foot doctor. Of course not: the right salesman must be sent in to do the right job.

Local customers shop in the afternoons and evenings. Before noon, Sant Kumar said, the customers are mostly pilgrims returning from the temple. Since the ritual of *darshan* in Banaras includes a bath at dawn in the Ganges, followed by a visit to the Vishvanath Temple,[9] most pilgrims have left the Vishvanath Gali by late morning. Preetam said that the pilgrims buy little, since they are not in the "purchasing mood," not only because they have come with religious, and not commercial, motives, but also because they do not bring much money with them, wary of the high level of *chori*—robbery—that takes place around the Vishvanath Temple. Preetam seemed to be referring both to actual thieves who prey on pilgrims and to the *pundits* who cunningly extract thousands of rupees from innocent devotees by forcing them into rituals at the temple's many altars. Preetam left his statement ambiguous, allowing for both interpretations.

Sitting in the living room next to his wife Daya, Priya Kumar explained that the items of *shringar*—bangles, *sindur,* and *bindis*—purchased on Vishvanath Gali are auspicious. He said it is a *purana parampara*—an old tradition—in India that these wifely ornaments, when bought at a pilgrimage site such as Kashi (Banaras), Haridwar, or Ayodhya, increase the life of the woman's husband. He said, pointing to his widowed grandmother, Prempati, who sat asleep among us, that the life of a woman is over when her husband dies, though Prempati, in fact, experiences both respect and freedom within her loving family. Priya Kumar clarified his reasoning by saying that women do not necessarily want to increase the lives of their husbands out of love for them, but because their husbands ensure a good life for them, since women enjoy a certain "confidence" while their husbands remain alive, and their lives worsen radically when they become inauspicious widows.

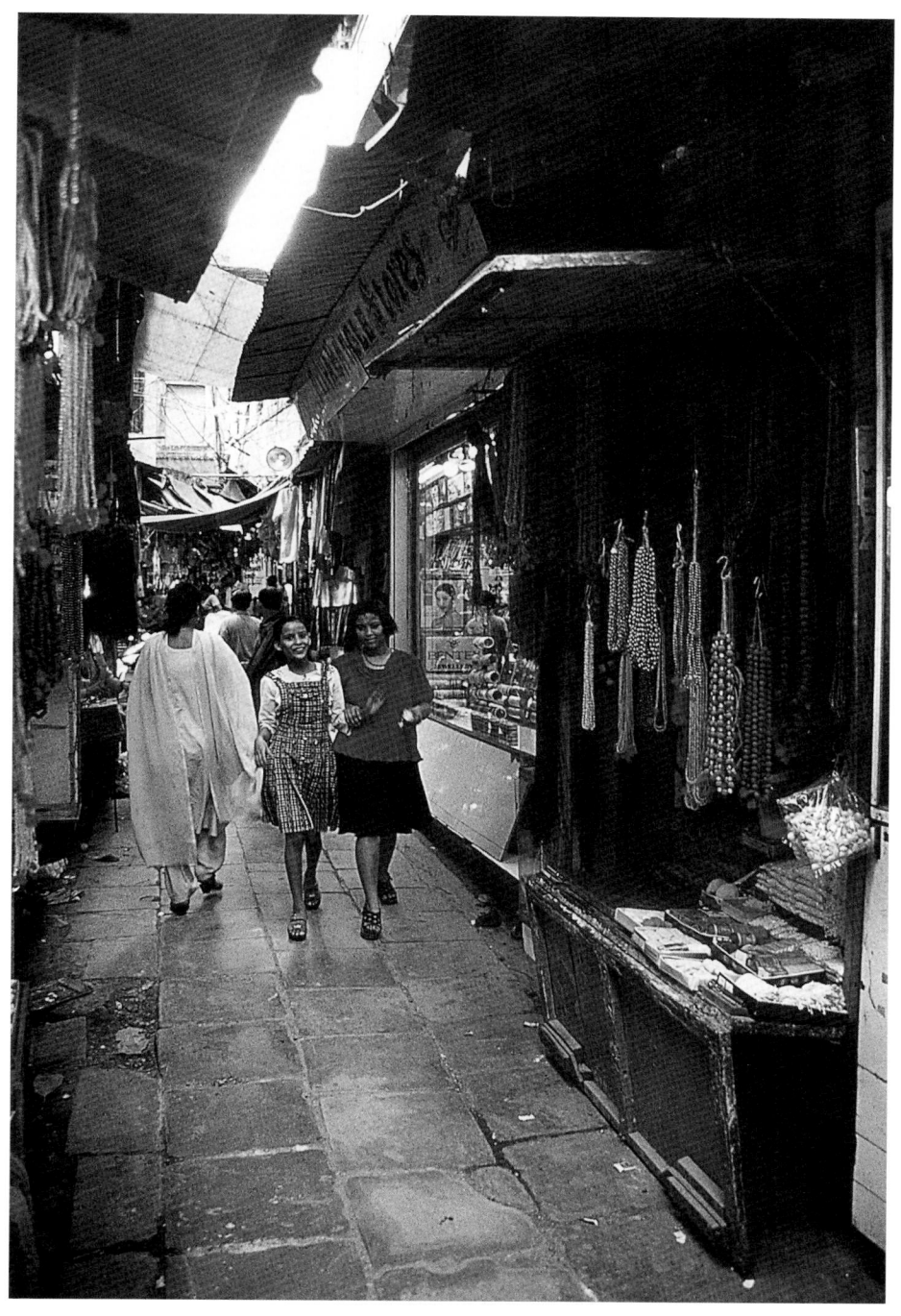

Priya Bangles: the store nestled inside Vishvanath Gali

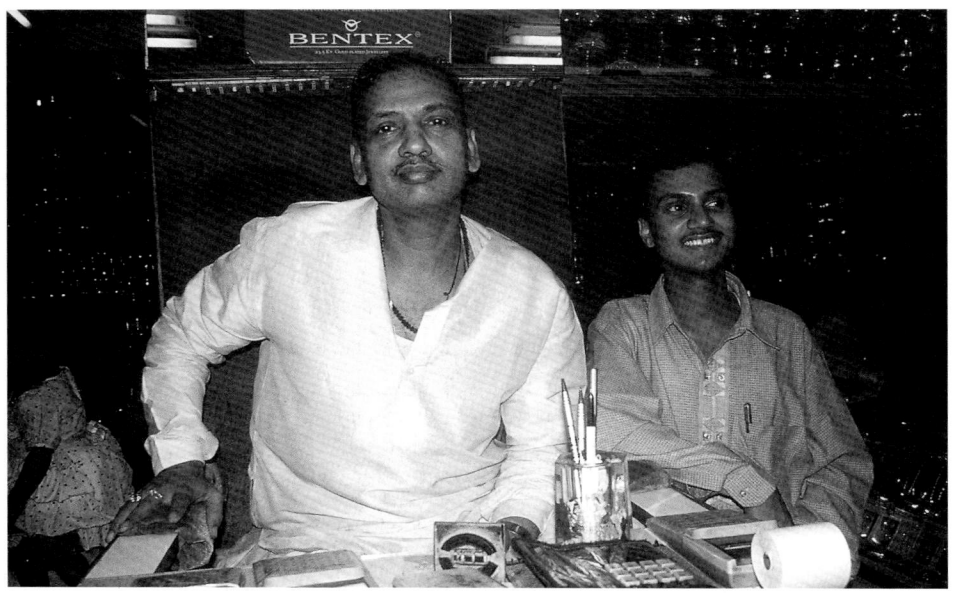

Ashok Kumar Manik, the proprietor, and his son Sant Kumar at Priya Bangles

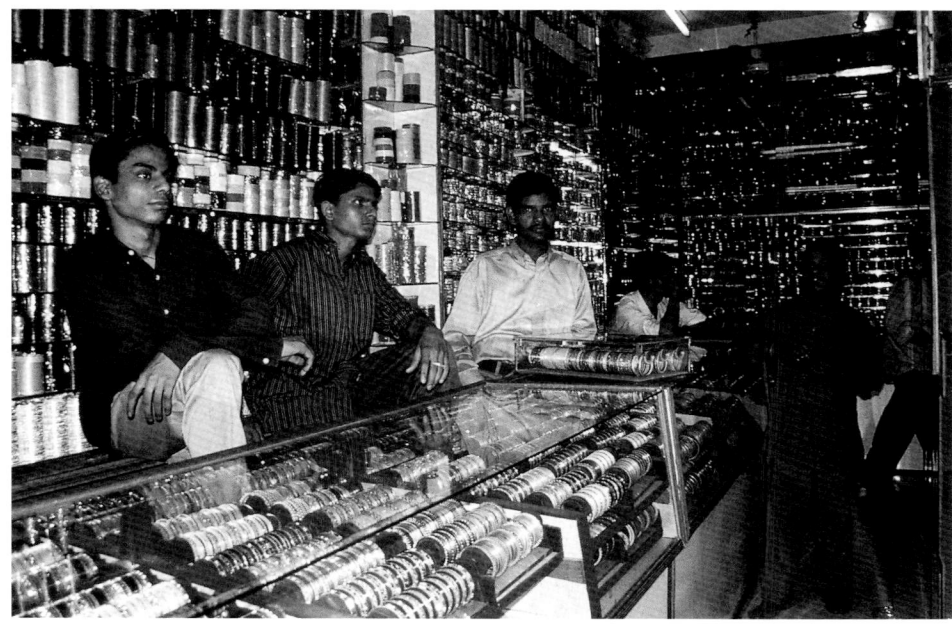

Priya Bangles: salesmen Anand, Pintu, and Mintu

Priya Kumar's wife, Daya Manik, told of the fast she kept for Shiva when she was a young unmarried woman, hoping for a good husband—which she certainly got. She started keeping the fast right after graduation, at the age of sixteen, and stuck to it until her marriage, performing *puja* to Lord Shiva in the morning and eating only fruits on his day. Shiva and marriage connect. Ritual fasts for Lord Shiva, kept prior to one's marriage, on Shiva's day, Monday, and on the special service on Shiva's annual night, Shivaratri, will bring a good husband. Bangles and *sindur* bought in his *gali,* in his city, ensure long life for one's husband. Shiva, the wildest and arguably the most male of the Hindu gods, is represented by the phallic *linga.* Inside the Vishvanath Temple it is Shiva in the form of the *linga* to whom a woman prays on behalf of her husband, either the desired husband of the future or the actual man of the present.[10] Bodily ornaments, many of which mark and celebrate marital status, naturally take on special significance in Banaras, the city of Shiva—Vishvanath, the Lord of the Universe.

Priya Bangles stands out among the stores in Vishvanath Gali for its size and brightness, for its enormous stock, and for the throngs of women who constantly fill it. I first interviewed Sant Kumar in the store in 1996. Five years later, when I returned to Banaras, I came to the store to reestablish the connection, but also to shop for bangles. I went in with a specific need: I wanted to buy some bright yellow plastic bangles I had noticed yet passed up during my previous trip. As soon as I entered the store, a charming young salesman began helping me. He followed me, showing me not only the yellow bangles I wanted, but also many others he thought I would like. I asked to see red glass bangles. He showed me some cheap and rather unappealing ones, and then proceeded to show me a set he quickly made up of twenty-four blood red metal bangles interspersed with thin silver ones. Compared with what I had asked for—plain glass bangles—his metal set was more attractive and far superior in quality and in its saturation of color. Barely listening to what I was saying, he showed me the latest fashions in bangles, and things he thought would look good on me. He noticed that I wore many bangles on each wrist, so he always showed me "full" bangle sets, with lots of bangles for each arm. After seeing some of his creations, I began to weaken and trust his judgment. He did have good taste and an aptitude for making pretty sets.

Though I somewhat politely tried to get rid of him, he stood firm, positioning himself between me and the rows and rows and rows of bangles that lined the back wall. He was nice, he smiled constantly, but he was one of the most aggressive people I had ever encountered and I became increasingly frustrated. He annoyed me, but I left the store an hour later with a big bag of bangles, having spent over two thousand rupees. I was carrying bangles I did not know I liked or wanted, but I had been somehow persuaded that they suited me and that I needed them. Later, once reason had replaced confusion and anger, I realized that although I had been coerced into buying more than I wanted, I was actually happy with the purchases and glad to have received the salesman's advice. Walking through the Vishvanath Gali with my new ornaments, I became aware that I had encountered a master of the bangle business. If he could satisfy me, a reluctant customer who walked in with a simple and specific idea of what she wanted, what could he do with an indecisive, eager customer? I reached our room, unpacked the beautiful bangles, and made a mental note to return to interview the salesman.[11]

Anand Kumar

Anand Kumar, this master, was twenty-two when we talked on my last visit, in 2003. He had been working at Priya Bangles for twelve years, having started as a general helper at the age of ten. He told me that it takes a minimum of five to six months for someone to be able to rise in the hierarchy of the store, starting as a *paniwallah* or a stock boy and eventually making it to salesman. Anand started selling shortly after his arrival because, he told me, his *dimak*—his mind—has always been very *tej*—sharp. Anand grew up in a house populated mostly by girls—he has five sisters—so he is able to do this work; he called it "ladies' work." To master it, he said, you have to be interested in it and you have to start doing it in childhood. Only if you develop a knack for it will you be any good. Both Anand and another salesman there, Mintu Kumar, agreed that only 10 percent of men are able to do this ladies' work. Anand explained that in order to be able to accomplish the task of matching bangles to clothes—one of the requirements of his job—you have to develop an awareness of adornment, coming to a personal interest in such things, what he called *shauk ki cheez*. He told me that he has always wanted to work with bangles, and he is, surely, perfectly suited for the job.

All day long, Anand handles bangles. Many have glitter glued on them, and after a few hours on the job, the glitter has spread everywhere. On many occasions I noticed Anand checking himself in one of the store's many mirrors, running his fingers through his hair. As a result—intentionally or not—

Anand's hair and face, always bright and shiny, are sprinkled with shimmering specks of glitter, giving him a sprightly disco look. He is friendly, and due to his youth and slight stature—he looks even younger than his age—he can engage in innocent flirtation with his female customers. Shantibhandra Shah at Kanhaiya Lal is too old to be a threat, so his flirtations are charming, and Anand seems too young. These men, apparently beyond sexual possibility, are able to tease, flirt, and joke with their customers without insult or intimidation. I asked Anand what kind of customers he preferred. Smiling, he answered that he likes to sell to "smart ladies" whose style he admires, who appreciate the latest fashion, who are young and hip. These women literally embody the style Anand prefers. They wear the clothes and jewelry he finds most attractive, and he makes sets of bangles that appeal to them but also to him. In an interaction of this kind, the aesthetic preferences of the customer and the salesman come together, creating an ideal commercial situation.

I asked Anand if he watched Bollywood films, or if he ignored them like his bosses, the Manik brothers. He responded with an enthusiastic "yes," saying that he not only watches films multiple times in the theatres on Sundays, when the store is closed, but he watches them at home, on the "CD" player (a form of DVD). He told me that he stops the movie with a remote control at the scenes in which a heroine's bangles are prominently displayed and analyzes them carefully, memorizing the assembly of bangles. Back at the store, Anand aims to do more than recreate the look; he aims to perfect it. When Anand watches these films, he carefully deciphers the principles of their bangle sets. He asks questions like these: At which point does the pattern start to repeat itself? Where is the axis of symmetry located? What is the relationship between the thin, monochrome *churi* and the thicker, fancier *kangan*? How many kinds of each are there, and what is their spatial relationship? After Anand has understood the principles of the assembly, he can make it better, so that his sets are reminiscent of the ones in the movies, but even more beautiful. Like a true artist, Anand is not in the habit of imitation, but rather takes inspiration from examples and works toward perfection.

During my last visit, in the summer of 2003, Anand showed me a photograph that was given to the store by a distributor of bangles, to be used as a guide in assembling sets. This picture reminded me of the photograph that Hemant Khanchandani was given that showed how *salwar suits* should be stitched from the cloth manufactured by Karishma Imports. Anand then handed me a photograph of a bangle set made famous by the current hit film,

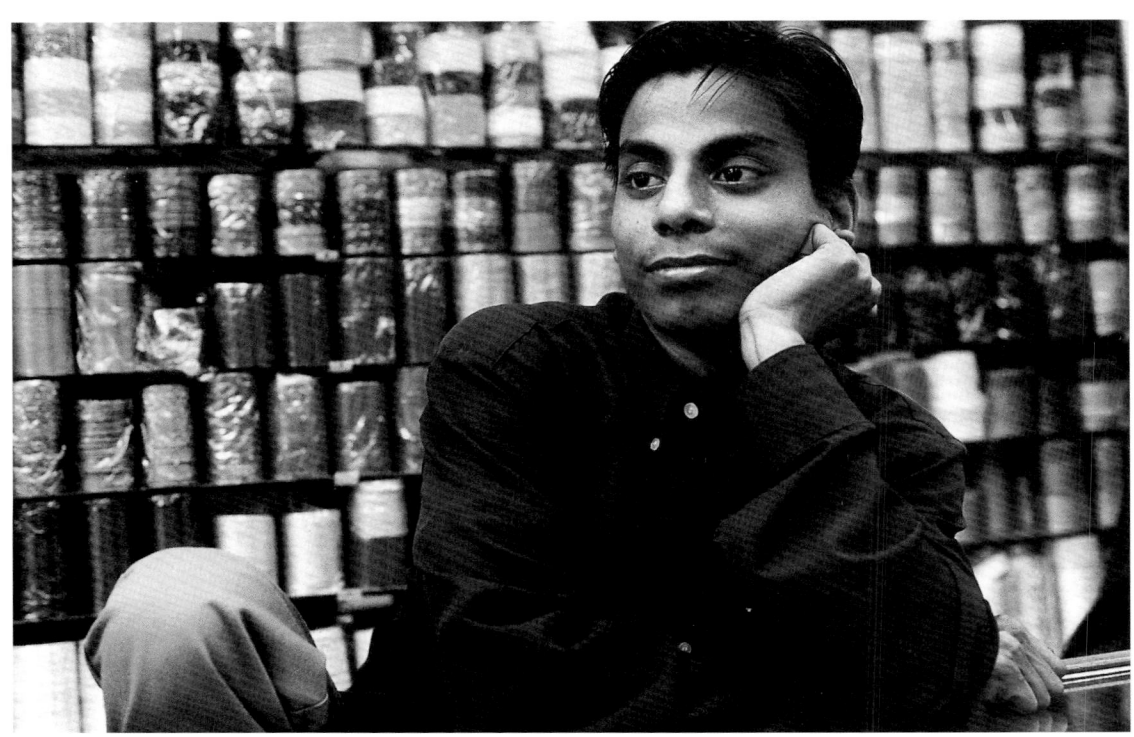

Anand Kumar

Devdas—although the bangles are seen on the screen, on the wrists of the gorgeous Aishwarya Rai, for less than a minute. The photograph showed a set for one hand; it consisted of five clusters of four thin maroon *churis,* each placed between two thin gold bangles. At each end of the set, functioning like a border, there was a wide *kangan* embellished with round rhinestones along the entire circumference. In the field of the bangle set, among the groups of maroon and gold *churis,* were two wider rhinestone *kangans,* each one with a dangling umbrella-like pendant, elegantly encrusted with rhinestones. This last feature—the bangle with a dangling pendant—is what the movie *Devdas* had introduced to the current fashion.

The pattern of the bangle set in Anand's photograph went like this: wide rhinestone *kangan,* then one group of four maroon and two gold *churis,* then the wider *kangan* with the dangling pendant, then three separate units of maroon and gold *churis,* separated by two wide rhinestone *kangans* similar to the one in the beginning of the set, then another dangling *kangan,* and finally the last group of maroon and gold *churis,* concluding with a rhinestone *kangan.* Although the set was symmetrical, the dangling bangles were located toward the outer edges, with the middle section consisting mainly of three separate layers of maroon and rhinestone. The placement of the dangling *kangans* toward the outside of the set gave the assembly a slightly unbalanced feel.

Anand's revision of the set is cleaner; he added more dangling *kangans,* and more color in each segment. He quickly made up a set to show me; it had two thick pink *kangans* with mirrorwork at the beginning and end of the set, and between them there were groups of six thin pink *churis* surrounded by two thin gold bangles, each demurely embellished with a few subtle rhinestones. There were five of these pink and gold *churi* units, on the pattern of the original example, but Anand's set was more delicate in look, and bolder in color, since he used six pink bangles per group instead of the four maroon ones in the photograph. Anand's set had four thick rhinestone *kangans* with dangling pendants, not two. It was like this: one thick pink mirrorwork *kangan* on the outside, followed by one group of six pink and two gold *churis,* then a dangling *kangan,* then a pink and gold unit, another dangling *kangan,* another pink and gold unit, a dangling *kangan,* a pink and gold unit, then the fourth and last of the dangling *kangans,* the last unit of pink and gold, and finally, the second pink mirrorwork *kangan* on the outside, matching the one at the beginning of the set, holding it together in firm, glittery symmetry.

Anand's creation was clearly inspired by the movie version. But he added more of the dangling bangles and distributed them evenly through the center of the set. The pink and gold units appear five times, yet his set has more color and less shine, since he created a thicker layer of color by adding more individual colored bangles, and he used fewer rhinestones. Most notably, his set is more balanced, since the dangling ones—adding visual weight to the set—are in the middle, perfectly placed between equal numbers of the pink and gold *churis*. Anand's set is also well placed temporally, for it makes a clear reference to a current fashion by having more of the key item that makes the set trendy: the *kangans* with the dangling pendants. In comparison, the two sets—the manufacturer's and Anand's—exemplify the mix of conformity and ingenuity in the work of a salesman in a bangle shop, whose aim is to create a set that looks sufficiently like the one in the movie (and the photograph supplied by the bangle manufacturer), and yet is different enough to be unique and eye-catching for the customer who wants to wear a bangle set that is trendy but outstanding.

Anand's ultimate goal is to add to his bangle sets what he constantly referred to, in English, as "get up." The glitter, the shine, the style—the special quality achieved by bangles in perfect blends—is what he means by "get up." Instead of wearing clothes and jewelry that are ill-suited for each other, one should choose things that elegantly complement one another, that each enhance the beauty of the other, bringing out the "get up"—the snap and allure—of each category of bodily adornment. A well-chosen emerald green pure silk sari, for example, will bring out the "get up" of a ruby and pearl *kundan* necklace. I took many pictures of the bangle sets that Anand composed; these photographs, documentary shots taken during fieldwork, were meant to be viewed only by me, to be used later during formal analysis. Although Anand understood the purpose of the photographs, he still insisted on selecting the appropriate backdrop for each of his creations before I could take my shots. For certain bangles—before I was allowed to photograph them—he placed behind them a black cloth. For some, he chose the white of my notebook pages as the setting, and for others, he placed the sets of bangles in front of the red lid of the boxes the bangles are packed in. Anand said that unless the right background was placed behind his bangles, the "get up" would be lost, ruining the beauty of his art.

As this instance shows, Anand is aware that his bangle sets are to be viewed against a backdrop of clothing. Like all vendors and makers of art for a woman's body, Anand understands that his creations—assembled bangle sets—will appear among other men's creations—the weaver's sari, the tailor's *salwar suit*,

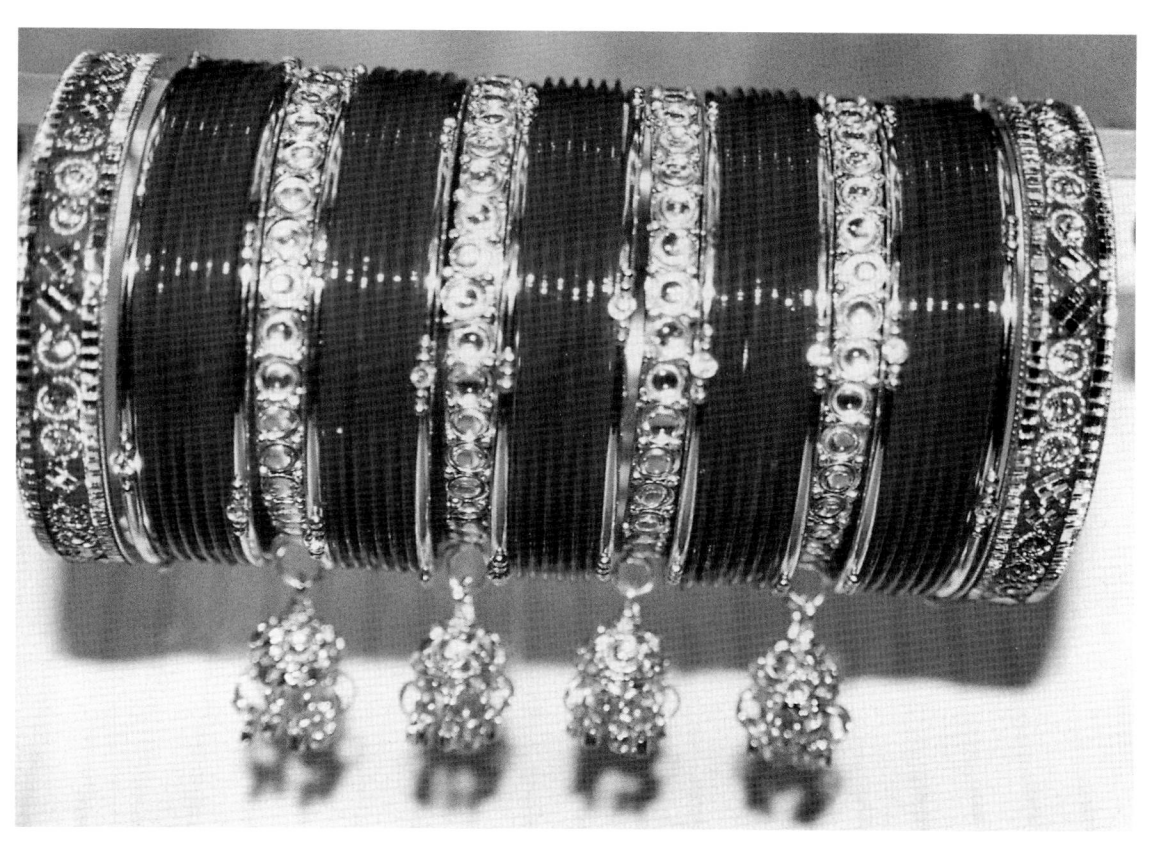

Anand's version of the *Devdas* bangle set

the goldsmith's jewelry—all to be assembled by a woman as part of her presence in the world. But Anand's contribution to a woman's ensemble comes after the creations of the other men. He must be aware of the other pieces already in place, most notably the clothes. At the end of this sequence come the women themselves, who are the final artists in this creative process; they assemble the elements that have been made, sold, and selected.

The sari weaver, like Hashim Ansari, makes the item of adornment that comes first in the series of choices. The other items will be chosen to complement his sari. In this way, he contributes to the overall look by setting a standard of color, of texture, of gloss, of style. Anand comes at the end, after the other decisions have been made, including the sari blouse and the jewelry. Anand's act must be excellent in itself and yet it must fit perfectly with the items already chosen. Hashim's art might be the starting point, but Anand's art has the power to ruin the look, or to provide it with the ideal "get up." A perfect bangle set can elevate the other items, while integrating the entire ensemble.

Selling Bangles

After I had watched Anand at work on several occasions, I asked him to explain to me his sales tactics. He was trained by the Manik brothers and he works in their shop, so he follows their general guidelines, yet he has his own slant on things. Anand said he starts assessing a customer's style as soon as she walks into the store. He notes what she is wearing, and tries to find a pattern in the kinds of things she looks at. Like the other sellers, Anand gets a general idea of the taste and identity of his customer, then shows her items that have previously satisfied the kind of woman he thinks she is. He classifies women by wealth, marital status, religion, region, and urban or rural residence. When a woman asks to see a bangle set of a certain color to match an outfit, Anand and the other sellers at Priya Bangles will make a different set for a Muslim young woman than they would for an older Sindhi lady.

The salesmen at Priya Bangles have a set idea of who likes what. I asked Anand to assemble "typical" bangle sets for different kinds of people so I could photograph them. He worked with quick delight, making set after set. One consisted of only three *lac* bangles. The middle *kangan* was thick, encrusted with fake pearls, rhinestones, and beads, while the outer ones were thinner and plainer. This was the style of Gujarati and Marwari older women.

Anand told me that these women from northwestern India like *lac* bangles, and generally they share the same taste. Next, Anand showed me a set that would appeal to *dehati*—village—women, whose taste, according to Arun Mehta, another Priya Bangles salesman, is all *chamak-matak,* gleaming and glistening. Anand's example of the village style was bright indeed; it had four sets of three glittery gold-colored glass bangles, separated by two layers of imitation gold bangles. I thought the set was beautiful, but it definitely exemplified what urbanites categorize as the "gaudy" look of village women.

Anand also showed many groups of typical wedding bangles—for Sindhis, for Punjabis, for Rajasthanis, for urban young women, and a set of red glass bangles painted with multicolored polka dots for the local village brides. Anand also showed me a pretty set made for "smart ladies" in the city who are in their late twenties to early thirties, and either unmarried or newly married. This set contained only thirteen bangles per wrist, and it had no glass bangles, because Anand said that smart ladies do not like the "tension" generated by the loud clatter of glass bangles.

The smart ladies' set provides a good example of Anand's creations. Though he placed the bangles in sequence from one end to the other, he ordered the overall pattern conceptually by bilateral symmetry. He used three kinds of bangles. Of the first, a thin *kangan* with clear circular stones, he used three, placing one at each end and one in the exact center. Of the second kind, a thick glittery *kangan,* he used two, placing one on each side of the central bangle. Of the third kind, a slim blue metal *churi,* he used eight, placing pairs of them between all the others. If I number these kinds of bangle in reverse, the symmetrical order will be clear: 3112113112113. This set, Anand said, was not too "heavy." It fit, he felt, the taste of modern women.

Day in and day out, many women prefer to wear plain glass or metal bangles in a single color, or thin golden bangles. Elaborate sets of the kind Anand assembles are usually bought for special occasions, and they are bought to match certain outfits, which the women often bring with them to the store. Sant Kumar said that women between the ages of twenty-five and thirty-five are the ones who buy bangle sets. This is the age group that includes the newly married, the category of women who are encouraged to be fashionable and extravagantly bedecked. It is socially acceptable for younger married women to have more *shauk*—more interest—in ornamenting themselves; it is considered appropriate for young married women to wear flamboyant bangles that express care and cost.

Many customers shop at Priya Bangles precisely because the salesmen are experts at combining bangles into sets. The display cases at Priya Bangles hold many readymade sets, which offer a starting point in the process of assembling a custom set. Anand told me that when a customer comes in with a special request, he first shows her an example from the display case. With a real model in front of her she will be able to put her thoughts into words, and Anand can hear what she likes and does not like about that particular set. Then he shifts one bangle or another, or several, quickly transforming the original set into another, altering the colors or the degree of fanciness, or the overall look—heavy or light, subdued or bright—developing swiftly out of the old a brand new set. While she watches, his hands move rapidly and the very set she wanted appears nearly magically before her eyes.

Anand's sets combine thick and fancy *kangans* with thin, monochrome *churis,* as we saw with his smart ladies' set. *Kangans* come in a huge variety of styles and colors; they are often festooned with beads, mirrors, rhinestones, fake pearls, and rubies. Usually more than one style of *kangan* will appear in a fancy set.

Sets framed with fancy *kangans* are filled in with *churis* that add volume and, most important, color, to the bangle set. Colored *churis* come in glass or metal. Bangles of glass are the traditional wifely bangles of the state of Uttar Pradesh, and they make a sound that is familiar and pleasing to women and men. Most bangle sets, however, are assembled out of metal *churis.* The Manik brothers gave various reasons why metal bangles are now used instead of the traditional ones of glass. Metal bangles come in a wider array of colors, enabling a more exacting match of bangle to outfit. Sant Kumar said that metal bangles have a better "finish," for they have a surface coating that adds shine to the overall set. Metal bangles also have no visible joints. Glass bangles, which are made by hand in Firozabad, come in a limited number of colors, and they are made in a continuous spiral, which is cut into a series of open circles that are closed and fused. The joint at the point of fusion not only provides an unattractive interruption to the bangle's perfect circle, but it is also a point of weakness. Glass bangles usually break at this joint, and many come from the manufacturers already broken.[12] If many of the colored *churis* of a set break, the symmetry will be destroyed, the balance lost, and the whole set might become worthless. A bangle set made with metal *churis* assures the long life of a whole family of bangles.

Metal bangles are considered cost efficient; they last longer but they cost little more than glass ones. At Priya Bangles, a dozen glass bangles cost twelve to fifteen rupees, while a dozen metal ones are priced at fifteen to twenty rupees. The two kinds of bangles differ in available sizes. The smallest glass bangles are size 2.2, allowing for a snug fit, ideal for everyday use. The smallest metal bangles are size 2.4. Anand explained that all "fancy" bangles come in larger sizes. The bigger are looser, and the reason, Anand said, is that fancy metal bangles, especially when they are designed for special occasions, are put on and removed more frequently than glass ones, which are worn constantly—they are not taken off, they eventually break off—so, metal bangles are bigger to allow for quick and easy removal and replacement. But large bangles also look different on the wrist; they move around and slide down over the hand. This last feature would make big metal bangles uncomfortable for daily wear by women whose small wrists are better suited for the 2.2 size.

When Anand begins to construct a bangle set, he decides first on the base color. The color of the outfit will determine the color of the thin *churis.* That color established, he chooses a pair of thick *kangans* to be placed at each end of the set, making its border. Then he selects thinner *kangans,* usually four of them, to be distributed evenly throughout the set. Between the *kangans,* at regular intervals, he will place about twenty-four thin monochrome *churis,* in groups of two to four. More thin *churis*—in imitation gold or silver, in a glittery style or a complementary color—might be added to complicate the pattern and produce variety, but the balanced regularity and the dominance of the original color will be maintained. These additional *churis* may create the effect of shading by shifting from dark to light in an ombre pattern. The specific variables of a bangle set, of course, change drastically with each new fashion.

I asked Anand if he thought his customers modified the assembled sets once they took them home. He said that women tend to leave the sets intact, keeping them wrapped in cellophane or passing a string through them to tie them together in a bundle. Since most fancy sets are created to match a particular outfit, and since local special occasions often involve many of the same people—friends, family, or business associates—it is often necessary for the salesmen to help people who will appear before the same audience, and who wish to avoid decorating themselves in the same outfits and accessories, by showing them how to modify their bangle sets. If a set is made using pretty *kangans,* usually in shades of gold, one can easily alter the set slightly, adapting it to another outfit. Most fancy outfits, including saris, *salwar suits,* and *lehangas,* have gold appliquéd trim, embroidery, or brocading. A bangle set that contains gold-colored *kangans* and vibrantly colored *churis* can be adapted for another outfit by simply replacing the colored *churis* with new ones in its color.

While Anand and I were discussing whether or not customers reassemble bangle sets, a well-dressed middle-aged shopper, who was eavesdropping on our conversation, volunteered her opinion. She said that she buys bangles at Priya Bangles for "show," to give her (already flamboyant) attire that "heavy look." She said it would ruin the "show of the set"—Anand's "get up"—to take it apart at home and reconfigure the bangles. Anand said that many women come to buy only the "filling"—the metal *churis* in a different color. They use these to replace the *churis* of an old set, keeping the overall structure and original *kangans,* in this way making a new set to match a different outfit.

In theory one could recycle a set by replacing the color endlessly, but this seems rarely to happen. *Kangans* are impermanent; they lose their glitter, the glued-on gems fall off, and most importantly, fashion changes and they are abandoned in a drawer. A bangle set made to look like one featured in a Bollywood film can only be kept in action for so long. Soon the look becomes too dated for the fashion-conscious person who bought the set in the first place. The woman who does not modify or recycle Anand's sets learns how to make sets from him by watching him create sets to suit her. He provides a model for use at home. Just as Anand's examination of the bangle sets in Bollywood films helps him create a better version of his own, women study the structure of Anand's bangle sets and improvise from their collection at home, trying to recreate Anand's sense of balance and style. I asked Sant Kumar whether he thought the function of his store was to sell bangles by providing a huge selection, or to teach women how to combine bangles into sets. He said his store served both purposes, for those goals entwine. The store could not teach or create without a wide array to choose from.

The system of buying bangle sets in India can be seen as similar to the system of buying expensive makeup in upscale department stores in the United States. An American woman can have her face done by a professional makeup artist at the counter of one of the many costly cosmetic companies. Her makeup is applied using solely the products sold by the company, usually with the understanding that she must purchase a minimum number of the products used on her face. While she has her face done, she learns how to apply makeup—in what order, in what proportion, to what end.[13] Similarly, the women who go to Priya Bangles witness the making of a bangle set by a professional, and then purchase the set. They take home an example of how bangle sets are made—the proportions among the bangles, how many of each kind to use, in what order, and how to achieve the necessary "get up."

Anand's sales tactics are like the unofficial method employed by the salesmen at Kanhaiya Lal. He shows cheap, less attractive things at first, then moves up from there. If the customer does not have much money, then the sale can be completed quickly in an exchange of cash for an inexpensive item, and the salesman becomes free to focus on another customer. But if the customer is inclined to buy something better and more expensive, then the initial item works as a negative example, a background against which the subsequent pieces will look smashing. Often the negative examples are left on the counter to provide visual contrast, helping to convince the customer of the superiority of the other pieces. Another tactic employed by Priya Bangles and Kanhaiya Lal, as well as by sari and clothing sellers, is to leave on casual display the store's most beautiful and expensive piece. The more the customer looks at it, the more she will want to buy it. Beautiful things, if well made, will sell themselves. Prolonged visual contact with a splendid sari or a beautifully assembled set of bangles is enough. Desire to own that piece sets in, and the sales pitch becomes unnecessary. And the customer who cannot afford the masterpiece will turn to buy something associated with it, something from the same store.

A feature of shopping in India is the intense attention a customer receives from the salesman, no matter what kind of product she buys. From the moment you enter a store, the salesman is after you, talking to you, watching what you look at, showing you things he thinks you will like, or showing you anything at all until he figures out your taste. The observant salesman like Anand will show you excellent versions of the kinds of things you are already looking at, in the hopes of gaining your trust, and making a sale. The bad salesman, though, will show you whatever comes to hand, whether it suits you or not. If a customer enters a store that sells textiles and asks to see antique mirrorwork wall hangings, a good salesman will show only old handmade pieces, while the bad salesman will show brand new, machine made, touristy cushion covers.

Knowing the salesman is working hard, customers are often reluctant to waste the time of the merchants unless they are willing to buy. I have been told repeatedly that people rarely enter a store to "window shop." It is considered rude to make someone work hard to show you things if you have no intention of buying (though you might accompany friends who are serious and indulge in the guilt-free pleasure of "pre-shopping"). Since that is the case, when women come into Priya Bangles at least one of them is on an earnest commercial mission. The sellers know the buyers want to buy. How much depends on the talent of the salesman. Sant Kumar told me that not only do most of the people who enter his store buy something, the majority of women buy more than they had anticipated. (That was certainly my personal experience at Priya Bangles.)

One successful sales technique employed by the owners of Priya Bangles is to pair each bangle salesman with a helper. Priya Kumar told me that the role of the helper is to provide "support" and complete the "wind-up" of the sale. I often watched Anand and his helper, Vijay Kumar, at work. A customer walks in and shows Anand an outfit she plans to wear at a party. She might suggest something about the price she is willing to pay: "Show me something really nice." "Show me something in the two-hundred-rupee range." Anand deftly, expertly makes a set (for only one wrist). He shows it to the customer, and keeps modifying it to incorporate her continual reactions and desires. "Make it lighter," she will say, or "Use a different shade of this color." "Add more shine," "I want glass, not metal, *churis*." As soon as the customer is happy with the set, Anand hands it to Vijay, who compiles an identical set for the other hand, and packs the bangles in cellophane wrap. Vijay often has to replicate this set in the correct size, since Anand creates his sets with no regard for size; his example was purely visual.

While Vijay is packing up the set, doing the "wind-up" of this sale, Anand is already asking the customer *"Aur kya dikhayen?"*—"What else may I show you?" Without missing a beat, not having lost focus by doing the work his helper is doing, Anand moves quickly to show her other bangles, riding on the momentum of a successful sale. The customer has not been able to break free of Anand's undivided attention; he does not have to turn away from her to find the bangles in her size or pack them up in a box. He is there in front of her, eye-to-eye, and he is already showing her the next group of bangles. The customer is not given a moment to consider leaving; instantly, she is tempted with another tantalizing set of glittering bangles.

This teamwork in sales is quite effective, leading inevitably to the purchase of more items than expected. Once Anand has figured out exactly what you like, after having gone through the process of building a set to your desire, he can quickly apply his new knowledge and make a long series of sets that, fulfilling those aesthetic criteria, satisfy you. Anand has, as he says, a "sharp mind" for ornamentation, and he remembers a customer's tastes. Many repeat customers, he claims, come into the shop and walk directly to him. They trust his taste, and they know he remembers their preferences and will be able to recommend bangles that please them.

Choice and Collaboration

Our analysis of bangles, the ubiquitous Indian feminine ornament, usefully brings together some of the broader principles of women's body art in India. The way that bangles are marketed, bought, sold, and worn, leads into the systems of aesthetics and fashion, and to the different roles men and women play in them. Actions within the realm of production and commerce reveal the choices made by members of both genders as well as the choices made by manufacturers of ornaments, by merchants, by salesmen, and finally by the women themselves.

Fashion in India is linked to the movie industry in Bombay. Actors and actresses are superstars, idolized and emulated by the masses. The actors of Bollywood do not have to compete with singers, television stars, and fashion models for their fan base. A beginning is made in the understanding of contemporary fashions by looking at what the actors wear in the movies, and tiny changes in what they wear are conspicuous, since they are made against a stable ground of tradition, of saris and bangles. In this chapter, we have seen that Bollywood plays a significant role in setting and sustaining trends in bangles. The influence does not start when the movie is released. By then it has already begun. The Bombay motion picture industry regularly previews images from films on billboards and in magazines, often showcasing the beautiful heroine's clothes and jewelry.

Marketing starts before anybody has had a chance to see the film. Bangle sellers throughout India carry the bangles that will appear in the film, and the film has already given its name to the bangles. In 1996, Raj Kumar, the owner of Raj Jewellers on Vishvanath Gali, had in his tiny store bangles from movies that had not yet been released. He had stocked bangles for the films *Chori Chori, Telephone,* and *Rangeela,* hoping that the films would not "flop" and that the bangles would soon be in demand. Hype for a movie starts early, resulting in a frenzied desire to see the film after you have already sampled the music, the costumes, and the bangles.[14] A woman then has four distinct choices: she can be with the crowd, buying the bangles as soon as the film is released and proved a hit; she can get ahead of the fashion wave by buying and wearing the ornaments that will soon be featured in a new movie; or a woman can lag behind the trend, finally breaking down and buying the bangles once they have flooded the market and become hard to avoid and impossible to resist. The fourth and final option, of course, is to ignore the trend altogether.

Most outlets for ornaments—clothing stores and jewelry shops of all kinds—have a connection to Bollywood, India's fashion source. One way of making this relationship manifest is to have bangle stores, such as Priya Bangles, assemble a set seen in a movie, or even by commissioning a craftsman to make jewelry that resembles something a heroine wore in some movie. B. D. Soni, the goldsmith from Rajasthan, lists with pride the movies in which his family's gold ornaments have appeared, including some of his grandfather's making. Shri Chand & Bros., the bangle shop in Vishvanath Gali run by the Gupta brothers, has provided bangles for fifty or so Bollywood films. The brothers said that film directors come to them and explain the scene and the character of the woman who will be wearing the bangles. It was the Gupta brothers' job to decide and provide bangles appropriate to that character in that scene. Bollywood's practice is surely logical: who knows better than the sellers what kinds of bangles certain types of women wear in certain types of situations?

Preetam Kumar Manik, one of the brothers and owners of Priya Bangles, described another obvious connection between fashion and the Bollywood industry. The people who supply bangles to shops are the same people who provide bangles to the costume designers for the movies. An article in the *Hindustan Times* in July 2003 reported on the deal between Sooraj Barjatya, the director of a film titled *Main Prem Ki Diwani Hoon*—"I Am a Fool for Love"—and the Pantaloon company, to market "accessories" related to the film. The products included "T-shirts, jeans and shirts sported by" the hero, Hrithik, and the "lace tops and jeans" worn by Kareena, the heroine. Also available for those who might lust for such things were "key chains, cuddly toys, and notepads." For years, *bindi* and bangle sellers have carried ornaments that made explicit connections with hit movies; now the fashion has expanded to hip clothing for rich urban teenagers, and even to accessories like key chains.

My attention to fashion in India and the West leads me to believe that fashion owes less to upscale designers than it does to innovations made among regular people. Fashion and costume designers are inspired by what people wear in the streets. They take fashions from the people and put them on the actors, modifying them as they do, and then the trend returns. From the street to the runway and back to the street, fashions shift and become identified with stars like Madonna in the West or the Bollywood actress Rekha, who is credited with boosting the fashion of *bindis* in India during the 1980s.[15]

Bollywood and "official" fashion on the one hand, and the traditional preferences of women on the other hand—both are part of one system; they work in relation to one another. The question arises: who influences whom? A movie costume designer, in order to dress his characters realistically, will watch what women wear out on the streets, and even commission the men at Shri Chand & Bros. to make a bangle set for the character.[16] (The Shri Chand men know what to make for the fictional character because they have observed closely and learned the tastes of real women—their customers.) Having admired it in the movies, women will buy a bangle set from the store, but during the act of purchase they will have it modified by a salesman to better suit their taste. Store owners become aware of the choices women make during the collaborative act of set construction, and the next time a movie designer comes in, he will be sold a version of the altered and improved set, and the cycle starts again. In such a system how is choice to be understood? People operate in a system that seems to be feeding fixed fashion preferences to both male merchants and female customers, and yet it is a system in which the merchants and their customers believe they are making the innovative choices, which, indeed, they are.

Let us say a Bollywood movie has set a trend that limits what the merchants, like the Manik brothers, have in stock. Generally bangles, unlike saris or ornaments in gold, are mass-produced. They must be purchased ready-made in forms that are either solidly traditional or dictated by the Bollywood designers. The Manik brothers cannot commission special items, as Hemant Khanchandani can with *salwar suits* or Shantibhandra Shah at Kanhaiya Lal can with gold jewelry. Anand, their employee, chooses to watch movies. From them he learns, and then he chooses not to replicate the film's set, but to improve it, while holding firmly to the traditional principles of order and symmetry.

Women, for their part, must first decide to follow the trend. Many, including some we will encounter in the next three chapters, choose adamantly *not to* wear what the heroines are currently wearing. (This option is possible in a country like India where excellent handwork is readily available, and one may custom-order clothing or jewelry. Many people, then, have the choice to ignore off-the-rack and mass-produced commodities—a choice that only the fabulously wealthy have in fully industrialized societies.) Women may also choose to stay in the realm of the currently fashionable, but wear a better version of what everybody is wearing—better in terms of material (silk, gold), craftsmanship, design, and economic value. If the decision has been made to follow a trend, then women choose the store where they will shop, a decision based on prior experience and an understanding of the quality of the inventory and expertise of the salesmen. Customers tend to choose a shop that reflects their taste, lifestyle, and socioeconomic status. The store, having met these criteria, should have inventory to suit them. In the United States, a woman might buy an undergarment out of necessity at a discount store for ten dollars, or one for one hundred dollars at a luxurious lingerie store—this one bought not so much for necessity as for self-indulgence, beauty, and elegance. Likewise, in Banaras, bangles bought to meet the customary necessity of wifely auspiciousness can be bought quickly at a corner bangle stall, such as Raj Jewellers, for twenty rupees a dozen. But to go into Priya Bangles and spend thirty minutes fine-tuning a bangle set bought for three hundred fifty rupees reflects a series of deliberate choices. Women express this choice by deciding to patronize one store—Priya Bangles, Kanhaiya Lal, Rinku Silk House, Dayaram Fashion Centre—over hundreds of stores with similar items for sale.

Women who choose to follow a Bollywood fashion will choose Priya Bangles as their source. At the store they have a choice of salesmen, but they will go to Anand, who caters to "smart ladies." Working with Anand, they suggest modifications to an existing bangle set, and they may choose to accept his steady patter of unsolicited advice. Once at home, women have the choice to modify the set again. On second thought, women might eliminate the shiny *kangans,* or add another color to the set if they have changed their minds about which outfit they will wear with the bangles. And finally, women must choose what to wear with the bangles: which sari or *salwar suit,* which pair of shoes and handbag, which *bindi,* which gold jewelry, which hairstyle.

Sant Kumar Manik believes that his store has two "mottos": to provide a vast variety of bangles for his customers to choose from, and to educate women on how to assemble bangle sets. Women learn from Anand. They do not need to keep up with the latest fashion or study the films; that is Anand's job. In turn, women teach the men at Priya Bangles. By buying certain bangles and rejecting others, they teach the Manik brothers about current demand, and they influence what the store decides to reorder from the distributors. Women also teach the salesmen about the preferences of real women as opposed to movie heroines when they ask for the sets to be adjusted. The salesmen, noting the patterns that emerge in these revisions, develop new ideas for their customers.

Choices connect, taste overlaps, and the men and women conspiring in the construction of a set of bangles return us to the key issues of collaboration. In sari weaving, while all the men do not share the same criteria of excellence, all of them—the designer, the *cardwallah,* the dyer, the weaver, the merchant—are so close in their standards that together they form an interlocking system of creation that yields magnificent works, grounded in tradition but adapted subtly to fit the style of the moment. Similarly in the retail jewelry shop—whether it sells glass bangles or *kundan* masterworks—the salesmen and their customers are close enough in taste to combine in the creation of a bangle set or the set of lavish gold ornaments for a bride. In both spheres, beneath both production and commerce, there lies a cultural coherence, a similarity of experience that enables spontaneous collaboration.

Having chosen Priya Bangles, knowing it is the store for her, the customer chooses a salesman. Each one of them creates his own sets and puts them in the case at his station. If you are drawn to Anand's sets, to the display at counter number two, then pausing there for the briefest of moments you will find Anand standing by, like an artist at a crafts fair, and he will be quick to react with a smile. Even before talk has begun, you have chosen the salesman whose taste is most like your own. You have read his personality from his sets, as he read yours through your dress. Collaboration has already started.

You show him the sari that you have chosen to wear for a wedding reception. Your choice rides upon the choices made in collaborations among a long series of manufacturers and merchants. He shows you an assembled set, his creation built out of the bangles at hand. Now you react, and the interaction continues until he has created, by hearing your words and reading your expressions, exactly the set of your desire.

Collaboration in the commercial context contains one more wrinkle of complexity. Pinku Mookerjee of the Rinku Silk House does not show the best Banarasi saris to his local customers; they are packed up in the back room and shipped to Bombay. Hemant Khanchandani of the Dayaram Fashion Centre likewise does not offer the best tailored *salwar suits* to his customers, thinking that they will not appreciate them as women in London or Bombay do. Anand does the same thing at Priya Bangles. He is not a producer of ornaments, but he makes an aesthetic judgment on the stock ordered by the owners of the shop, and, he told me, he does not bother showing "smart" *kangans* to village ladies, since they would not appreciate them, much less buy them. A customer does not have unlimited choice when she enters a store. She is shown what the salesman's reading of her suggests to him that she will buy. A significant influence on what a customer buys has to do with decisions made by the salesman, decisions not to show her something that she, given a chance, might want. At Priya Bangles much of the stock is on display, stored on glass shelves, but the customers only see what the salesmen choose to show them.

The art of self-adornment is explained by the common local analogy of Banarasi *paan*. Body art is achieved by a careful combination of things, joined in an artful display, an assemblage. The previous chapters on stitching *salwar suits,* weaving saris, and making jewelry all described creations that were constructed out of raw materials: bolts of cloth, spools of silk, gold ingots. This chapter has focused on the art of assemblage as practiced by the sellers of bangles who arrange manufactured objects into sets. As a woman does when dressing herself, Anand creates an artful combination from things already made, matching color, texture, shine, and size, to shape a final product that is balanced, logical, and most importantly, beautiful.

As women do, bangle salesmen adapt and refine a fashion trend, adjusting it to suit the body of the wearer, matching bangles with outfits and accepting the financial constraints of their customers. The art of constructing a bangle set—like a woman's body art—is the art of an industrialized world in which people no longer reshape natural materials into handcrafted things. Modern creativity yields assemblage. People purchase readymade commodities and arrange them into new units. The modern creator positions things in relation to each other: furniture, rugs, and pictures in the domestic environment, objects of worship on domestic altars, flowers and trees in gardens, jars of food in kitchen pantries, different dishes in the assembled whole of the meal—and the pieces of adornment that women gather over their bodies. Someone else made the parts by hand or machine, but the whole, the assembled creation, is made by you, and your creation is your expression; it is a constructed emblem of your taste and social affinities, your identity. Anand's identity lies in his sets of bangles. His customer's identity lies in those sets, meshed with other items into a coherent presentation of the adorned self.

The art of self-adornment does not start with the woman getting dressed in her bedroom. The process starts with the decisions and skills of a long series of men who make and sell the objects out of which Indian women construct their identities.

In Sonarpura, Hashim Ansari and his brothers choose available drafts-men, *cardwallahs,* dyers, and weavers. They decide where to buy their raw materials. They decide which designs to weave, and how to weave them. Their decisions are not made in isolation. They learn from the owners of the sari shops, who learn from their female customers. Chaman Lal and B. D. Soni, the goldsmiths, decide as Hashim does, attending to materials, technology, and designs to create works that will please the buyer.

On Dashaswamedh Road, Hemant Khanchandani decides which whole-salers to frequent, which cloth to buy, and how to stitch it into a pleasing *suit.* Then he decides which *salwar suits* to ship out, which to keep in the store, and finally, which ones to show a customer when she comes in. Likewise, Pinku Mookerjee must make choices about pairing saris with women, helping them find the perfect match between the look of the sari and their physical appearance, age, and financial status.

Shantibhandra Shah at Kanhaiya Lal, and the owners of imitation jewelry shops such as Priya Upahar, decide what to keep in stock, what to show to whom, and they teach while they sell, bringing their customers toward their taste and shifting their taste toward their customers' desires. Anand Kumar and the sellers at Priya Bangles work as the salesmen at the jewelry shop do, but they accept the additional task of compiling bangles into saleable sets. Sant Kumar said the specialty of Priya Bangles is to have a great "combina-tion" of bangles. His use of the English word defines the art of his shop. The owner's art is to assemble a great combination of bangles under one roof. The salesmen's art is to pick from this assembly and create coherent bangle sets. A woman's art is to choose the shop, choose a salesman and to choose clothes and jewelry. At home, her solo creation mixes and matches the art of the men of India, who have infused her items with their personalities and aesthetic sensibilities.

Having looked at a sample of the men who labor to create objects of adornment in India, let us turn our attention to the women themselves. We have heard from the men, but what do the women think? What decisions are made once the item has left the atelier, left the store, and come into the home, moving from the sphere of production and commerce into a domestic space? As the next series of chapters demonstrates, women judge their items of adornment in the contexts of use, behavior, and interpersonal relationships—and in the context of the self in relation to personality, life history, and the stages in the cycle of life.

Part 3. Personal Adornment

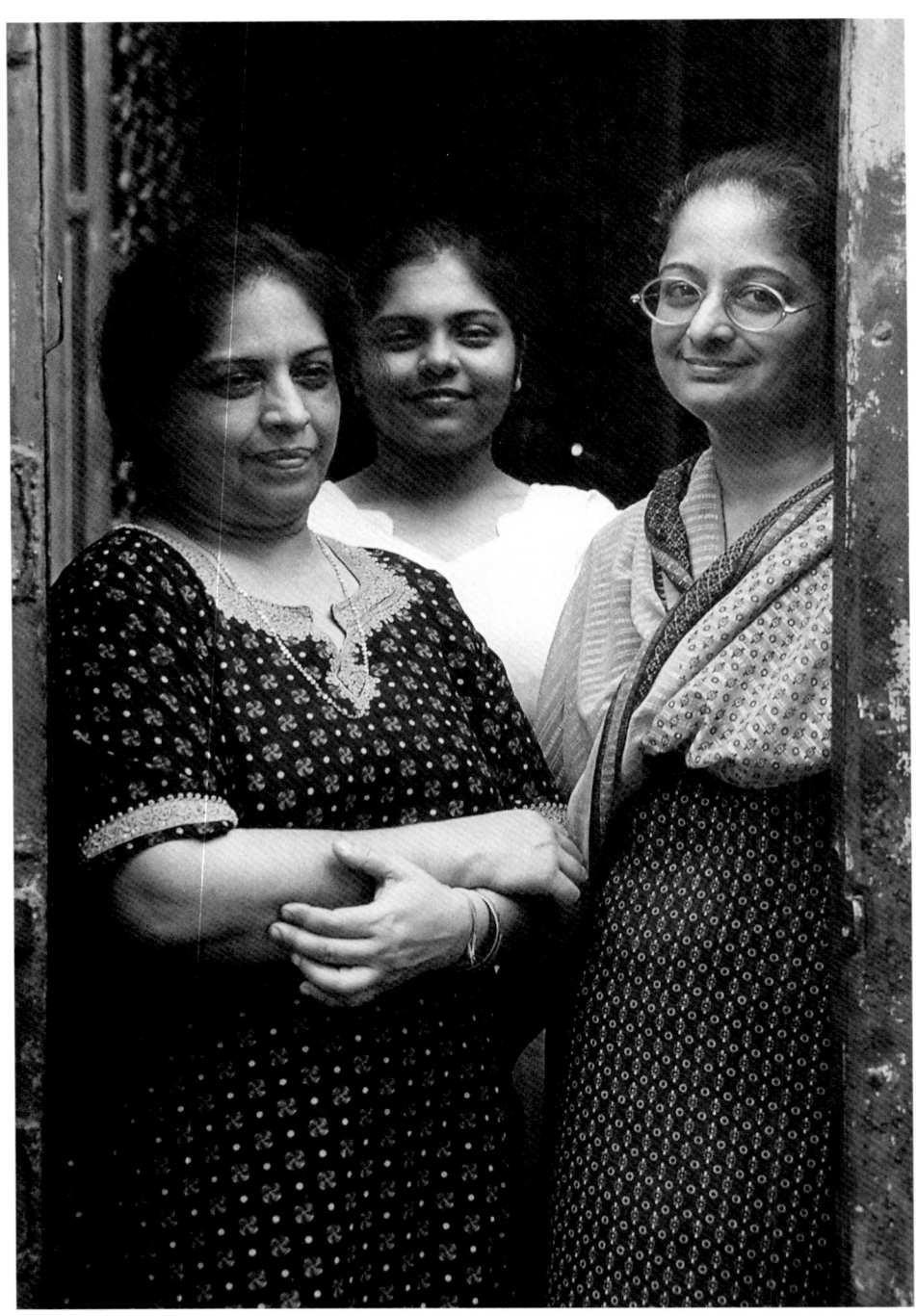

Nina Khanchandani (at right) with her sister-in-law, Jaya, and niece, Rati

·10·

Nina Khanchandani

In India, as in many countries of the world, men are the ones entangled in commerce. They are the merchants, cooks, and waiters, while women work in the domestic sphere. In public, it is easier to meet men, especially the men of commerce who are accustomed to easy exchange, and my quest to meet new women in Banaras began, logically, with a merchant. After several visits to Hemant Khanchandani's Dayaram Fashion Centre, his hospitality of tea and sometimes *samosas* did not seem to him enough. He invited us home for a meal. He lives a short walk from his shop, just off of Luxa Road, which is crowded with hotels, restaurants, and clothing stores. As is usual in Banaras, Hemant shares his home with the members of his extended family: his widowed mother, his older and younger brothers, his wife and sister-in-law, and four young adult children—two his own and two his older brother Parmanand's. Their house is hidden behind a tiny convenience store called Pariwar Provisions, the Family Provisions shop. The name fits, since different members of the family share the duty of running the business. This joint family, in contrast to many others in Banaras, seems to be happy and comfortable, which is one of the reasons I was attracted to Hemant's household.

One Sunday, we had with them a delicious lunch of *pau bhaji*—roasted bread with curried potatoes—savory street food often associated with Bombay. Their version came with diced onions and lemon wedges, and the feast also included ripe mango slices and Sindhi-style fried potatoes prepared with ginger and green chili peppers. After lunch I made plans to come back the next day to talk with the women when the men would be at work and the children would be at work or college. On weekdays, in the early afternoons, lunch is ready and waiting for the arrival of each member of the family, and the women are relaxed and available for long conversations.

The following day I arrived just after lunchtime, expecting to start my interview with the women of the household. I was served lunch nonetheless, and the food was extraordinarily good; a typical North Indian lunch of rice and lentils, but their *dal* was prepared with fresh aromatic curry leaves. The meal was ornamented with three different varieties of pickled curried fruits—known generically as *achar*—as well as *papadam* wafers and *roti* flat bread, and a *lassi* yogurt drink topped with ground roasted cumin seeds. When I complimented the cuisine, they proudly claimed it as Sindhi. Their food, like all meals, reflected the identities of the cooks: in this case, the two daughters-in-law of the household, Sindhi women from Bombay. The food, simple yet delicious, traditional, and most importantly, rich with Sindhi flavor, foreshadowed the themes that would emerge during our hours of conversation about the women's adornment—a form, like food, of material self-expression.

In the usual Indian manner, the main room of the Khanchandani household is furnished with beds. It is a common practice in India to use a bed for sitting in the daytime and for sleeping in the night. Hemant's main room held three beds, two small and one large. This large bed, about queen-size, was covered in a green and yellow Donald Duck bed sheet; it made a comfortable place for the interview. We all sat close together. I started the tape recorder, and began by getting general biographical information on the three women: Hemant's wife, Nina, her sister-in-law, Jaya, and their mother-in-law, Puspa Devi.[1] Out of deference and respect, I began the conversation with questions directed at Puspa Devi. She was friendly, but very shy. Her younger daughter-in-law, Nina, answered the questions for her, revealing her deep knowledge of her mother-in-law's childhood history. This close connection struck me as unusual, since the relationship between a mother-in-law and her daughter-in-law is often tense and antagonistic. Nina not only spoke for her mother-in-law, she was eloquent and outgoing when speaking for herself. She became my main source of information in the household. Her mother-in-law listened carefully while choosing to remain silent, and her sister-in-law, Jaya, laughed along and occasionally chimed in.

I asked Nina to go back in her memory and describe to me what she wore growing up in Bombay. Nina, a sophisticated college graduate, spoke in a mixture of Hindi and English. In an attempt to capture the dynamics of her speech, I use italics for all the words I have not translated from her speech. She began like this: "Whatever was in *fashion,* that is exactly what I wore, such as *belbots* [bell bottom pants], *skirts, maxis* [long dresses], *lungis* [long skirts]. These were all in *fashion* at that time. Whatever was in *fashion,* I wore them all."

Her emphatic assertion of conformity attests to Nina's childhood in the glamorous metropolis, where the fashions set by the movie stars begin to spread outward through the nation. To begin, Nina told of her youthful knowledge of fashion and her desire to follow it exclusively—a practice she has adamantly rejected in maturity. She continued:

"After getting married, I would wear [*salwar*] *suits*. But before marriage too, I wore *suits*. When I went to *college,* I wore *suits*. When there were *parties* or whatever, I would sometimes even wear saris—when I was big enough, that is. Like a *college day* occasion, any other *function,* or a *marriage reception,* during these I would sometimes even wear saris. After marriage, though, *suits* and saris."

Salwar suits are the unofficial uniform of young women, especially those attending university. Nina, a married woman in her early forties, began her young adulthood by wearing *salwar suits* regularly, saris occasionally, and she has since returned to this pattern, as she will explain later.

I asked Nina about her wedding day, which marks the beginning of a woman's life as a decorated being. Ornament is the right and responsibility of a wife while her husband is alive.[2] Nina briefly described her marriage, which took place in 1982 in Bombay. Since Hemant, her groom, would come from Banaras, her parents charged him to bring three Banarasi brocaded saris, including a maroon one for the wedding. The hour-long wedding ceremony took place on the sixth of December. The reception party thrown by her family was on the seventh, and on the eighth she left, moving to Banaras as a new bride. Her marriage, Sindhi style, was simple, without fuss, and it contrasted with what Nina sees as the unnecessary elaboration of the broader Indian tradition, which she generally referred to as "Hindustani."

In the midst of discussing Nina's wedding, her older brother-in-law, Parmanand, arrived from the shop for his lunch. Nina's composure and demeanor did not change, and I noted again the easy interactions of the family, so unlike those that prevail in many parts of Banaras, where women maintain a

223

kind of shy, distanced *purdah,* not only with their fathers-in-law, but also with all of their husbands' older male relations.[3] The *purdah* or *ghunghat* between a woman and her older male relations-in-law can be physical or psychological. Women often leave the room or cover their heads with the ends of their saris, removing themselves from the conversation out of respect and from an imposed feeling of shame. Nina is absolutely comfortable in the presence of both her mother-in-law and her older brother-in-law. This comfort is essential to understanding the personal style she adopts in the arena of the joint family.

After recollections of Nina's wedding, the conversation shifted to a general discussion of Sindhi marriage practices, and Parmanand sat with us and joined in. I asked if they were starting to accumulate jewelry for the dowry of the daughters of the house, young women in their late teens and early twenties. No, they answered, because their children would not marry for many years, and by then, jewelry bought today would be "out of fashion." What women want for their dowry, Parmanand said in English, is the "new fashion." Since his family belongs to the "business class," he said, they can buy items for the dowry at the time of the wedding, something that is impossible for those who belong to the "service class," who must accumulate the dowry over a period of years. But, Nina said, in their particular caste, within the multiple castes of Sindhis, there are no set demands for dowry; you give according to your "financial condition." Since their caste does not emphasize jewelry as much as the others, the women of this household are allowed to be under-ornamented; their relative plainness fits the general Sindhi aesthetic pattern.

In their statements, I left the word "caste" in the ambiguous contexts in which Nina and Parmanand used them. Caste has many different colloquial connotations in modern India. In addition to indexing the rigid hierarchical division of society by occupation—which is the generally accepted scholarly understanding of caste—the term can be used to denote other groups from which preferable partners for marriage can be drawn. Within the caste of Sindhis—people from the Sindh region of present-day Pakistan—there are sub-castes of people who have traditionally intermarried, and regional origin can make for membership in a caste. In vernacular communication among Indians, for example, a marriage between a Gujarati Brahmin and a Bengali Brahmin would be called an "inter-caste" marriage, though both belong to the Brahmin caste.

Everyday Attire

On this, the day of our longest interview, Nina was dressed in a pretty magenta and white printed *kameez* with dark magenta *salwar* pants. Her nose, ears, neck, fingers, ankles, and toes were free of the ornaments that conventionally mark a woman as married. She wore no jewelry except for two gold bangles on her left wrist. Her hair was tightly tied in a ponytail, combed back without allowing for a part in which red *sindur* would be spread auspiciously to assure a long life for her husband. She wore no makeup, no *bindi,* and she put the *chunni* scarf on only when I took her picture. Nina's personal appearance is casual, plain, and somewhat unusual in Banaras. Wearing a *salwar suit* instead of a sari, and wearing none of the "compulsory" wifely ornaments, Nina stood apart. Her sturdy personal confidence and her lack of adornment combine in her attractive presentation of self. I asked her to describe her style, starting with clothing, going on to jewelry, and concluding with an overall philosophy of adornment. She responded to my questions quickly, without dwelling on details in the answers. Nina began by recalling that as a newly married woman in Banaras, she received many new saris, so she wore them; her wardrobe held a large "stock" of saris and nothing else.

Since marriage marks the moment when women start wearing saris regularly, brides receive saris from both sides of the family as customary gifts.[4] The concept of a stock of clothing or jewelry, which Nina raised, is significant. During our attempts to understand people's (body) art, it is tempting to think of them as having unlimited choice or no choice at all, but all choices are constrained and enabled by the availability of the materials out of which creativity develops. Nina wore saris when she was first married because her family gave her saris. Her aesthetic acts were limited by the contents of her wardrobe, and her personal taste became manifest in her choice of which sari to wear on a particular occasion.

She often told me that she has never been comfortable wearing a sari, yet when she was first married, having little choice in the matter, Nina wore saris. During the first two years of her marriage, she used to cover her head at home with the end of the sari or with the *chunni* if she happened to be wearing a *salwar suit.* When I asked her if she remembered the moment when she stopped covering her head, Nina and Jaya looked at each other and started laughing.

Then Nina told me about the time they all went to Gujarat for the wedding of their younger sister-in-law:

"We went to her wedding; the wedding took place in Baroda, so there we got our hair done; the *beautician* had come to do it. So *Daddy* said, 'You have spent all this money, so why are you covering your head? Come on, from now on, stop covering up your head.' From then until now, we have stopped. So, I had covered my head for two years, and she [Jaya] for four years. Since we had abandoned the practice there, when we came back here, we did not continue covering our heads. We would wear a *chunni,* but we would not cover our heads."

It is conventional for a woman's head to be covered at all times in the presence of older male in-laws, and especially the father-in-law, out of respect and deference. If the father-in-law himself gives a woman permission to abandon the practice, then everybody must accept his ruling. On the occasion of his daughter's wedding, their father-in-law declared that Nina and Jaya should not cover their expensive new coiffures, and once the tradition had been broken, they continued to leave their heads uncovered at home in Banaras. They still wore *chunni* around the house; Nina's expression translates literally as "taking the *chunni.*" But even this habit has been abandoned. The third piece of a *salwar suit,* the *chunni* or *dupatta,* is usually worn draped across the chest with each of its ends flowing behind the woman, over the shoulders. Little is concealed, for the material is often flimsy, but wearing the *chunni* is seen as a sign of modesty, appropriate in public or in the presence of men. Nina stopped "taking the *chunni*" regularly at home with the death of her father-in-law.

"But we do not have the *ghunghat system.* If we were to cover our heads, it would be very lightly." By lightly, Nina means that the cloth would rest toward the back of the head, exposing the face prominently. She contrasted the practice of her household with that of many families who follow the "*ghunghat* system," in which the entire face of the woman is covered.

Nina stressed the liberal nature of her caste and her family, whose modern attitudes are a source of pride for her:

"My *family* is *different.* My *mummy* has a *brother-in-law;* in his *family* they still cover their heads. Because their *father-in-law* is still alive, so they do it.

Mummy to this day still does it. If right now her *brother-in-law* were to come here, she would say 'Where is my *chunni*? Quick, give it to me!' Then she will sit here with her head covered, and we will be here just like this!"

Nina laughed heartily at the thought of the brazen young women sitting with their heads uncovered in the presence of elder male relatives.

Nina's family has always been broadminded, and since her father-in-law's death, she has even stopped wearing saris at home. She has switched to wearing *salwar suits* every day, a practice she refers to as a "total change." Nina said: "It has been four years since the death of my *father-in-law.* Before that, I would wear saris more often. Nowadays, I totally don't wear them. Nowadays they are just rotting away!"

I asked Nina when she wears saris now, and she responded promptly: "Only on *party occasions.* Where it looks good. That's it." Her response in Hindi, "*Jaaha per accha lagtahe,*" allows ambiguity. It could mean, "Where it looks good," "Where it feels good (to me)," or even "Where it is appropriate." All possibilities seem right for Nina, because she does what she wants to do, and yet at the same time she is aware of the gaze upon her, and she would like to look passable, if not exactly splendid, for others. She acknowledged that saris look more beautiful than *salwar suits,* but she finds them uncomfortable; they have to be "managed" all the time—the pleats of the sari have to be constantly fixed, and the end piece, the *palloo,* has to be held in place by the left arm and shoulder. Jaya said that the wearing of saris is "full of problems," and Nina claimed to have lost the habit of wearing saris altogether.

Along with clothing style, jewelry defines the marital status and general age of a woman. Whatever clothing a woman is wearing, her jewelry remains the principal marker of her marital identity. Nina explained that her underadornment reflects both her personal choice and the Sindhi tradition. What she considers "compulsory" among Hindustanis—toe rings, anklets, and glass bangles—are not prescribed for Sindhi wives. The Sindhi caste, according to Nina, does not give any "importance" to silver jewelry, so those items that are worn around the feet and made of silver are not mandatory for Sindhis as they are for other castes. On the other hand, precious gems and metals such as gold and diamonds are valued by Sindhis, but these, she feels, are not practical for everyday use.

Nina, like other women, modifies her appearance when she leaves the house for the street. Then, too, she cleverly manipulates the Sindhi aesthetic to suit her own understated sense of style. While responding to questions of adornment, Nina kept her sentences in the plural, deliberately creating a fusion between herself, her sister-in-law, and all Sindhi women:

"We don't wear glass bangles. For *fashion,* if somebody wants to wear them out of *shauk* [interest], *it's different.* But it is not in our Sindhi *tradition. Sindur* is in our *tradition, but we don't put—we don't like it.* If we go outside, then we put a *bindi* on, *otherwise . . . We don't put sindur.* For us there is no *shauk,* understand? *We don't have any interest.* Absolutely nothing is worn by us. No *bindi,* nothing on the ears, nothing on the neck, absolutely nothing is worn."

When it comes to jewelry, she said, she has "no choice," meaning no preferences; "*I don't like anything, I don't wear anything.*" She continued, in English, making a parallel between herself and her sister-in-law, Jaya: "*Actually, in our house, we don't—none of us, even the eldest, my sister-in-law, she also does not have any choice, nothing. It means, we wear it because it is necessary for us to wear, that much only we wear, otherwise no.*"

When we paused for afternoon tea, I was given a chance to think about what she had said. I looked around the room where we were sitting. On the light blue walls of the room hung Hindu religious prints of Hanuman, Ganesh and Lakshmi, Krishna with Arjun. A built-in niche displayed a statue of Shiva as the Nataraj, dancing. These religious images were the only ornaments in the room. Their house is simple; the only decoration—Hindu imagery—is present to insure auspiciousness. The major deities, Shiva, Vishnu (through his avatar Krishna), Hanuman, Ganesh, and Lakshmi, were present without the redundancy characteristic of Hindu domestic displays. The decoration of the house, like the women's body art, was simple, unpretentious, and modest.

Fancy Dress

To understand a person's full repertoire of body art, it is important to look at both special occasion and everyday use, since behavior, scrutiny, and self-consciousness are drastically affected by this shift in the context of display. Nina had very clearly described her plain everyday look, but it developed in the unusual setting of a lenient mother-in-law, a deceased father-in-law, a loving husband, and a close friend in her like-minded sister-in-law. Difficult

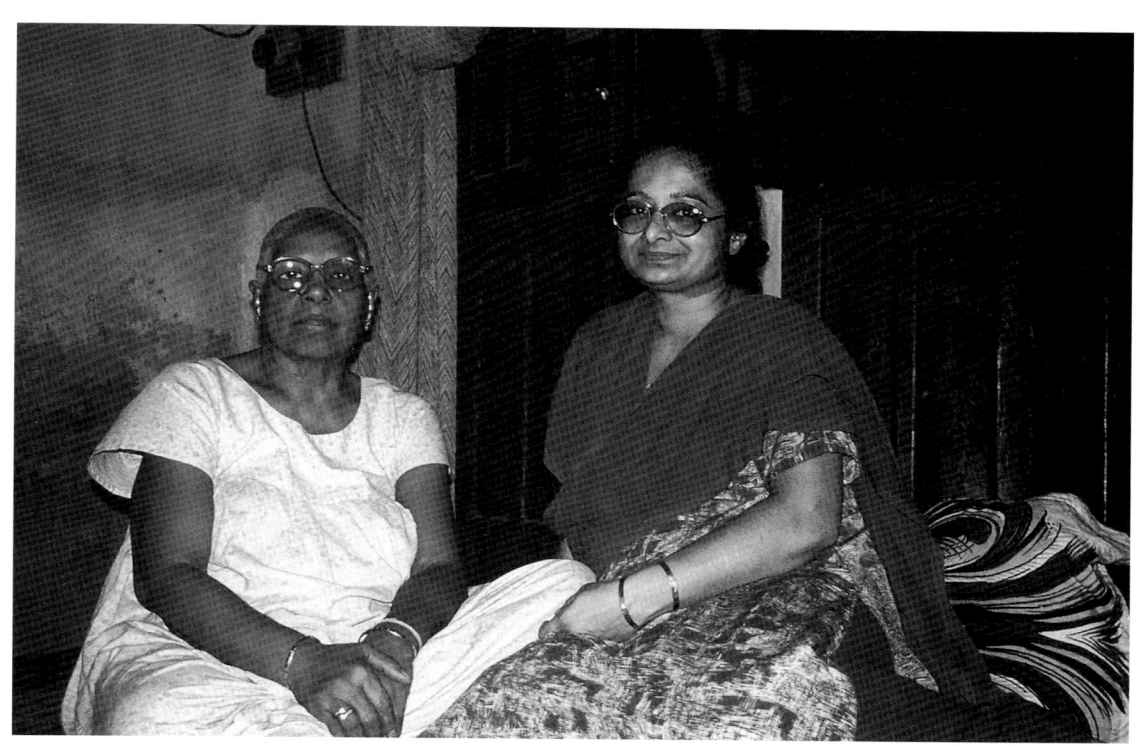

Puspa Devi and Nina Khanchandani

interpersonal relationships often cause other women to become self-conscious in their self-presentations at home, in an effort to satisfy the desires of live-in relations. Nina is lucky not to have this problem.

The most special occasion other than one's own wedding is a marriage reception, where women are encouraged to show off the wealth of the family and their own good taste in extravagant saris and jewelry. I wanted to understand Nina's process of adornment: What choices did she make? How were ensembles created? In what order did she add clothes, jewelry, and other accessories? And for whom did she get dressed?

Nina gets herself ready for a wedding reception—as do most women I talked to—by first choosing a sari. After it has been selected, many women spend some time selecting the jewelry that will highlight the sari and complete the look. There are many strong individual opinions as to the suitability of certain sari fabrics and designs with styles and amount of jewelry. Women will often give specific requests to their husbands, asking them to retrieve certain ornaments from the "bank locker." Nina's dislike of ornaments is not limited to everyday use; it extends to parties as well. When I asked her to describe how she chooses jewelry after she has selected a sari, she said, adamantly, "*We have that same jewelry, that we don't buy everyday: gold. Neither do we wear artificial. So we have to wear that same jewelry. We wear only two bangles and a* [gold] *chain* [necklace] *and that's all, in that way only we go for the reception party.*"

Nina used again the idea of a stock, of a limited set of materials with which to create. If Sindhis do not wear silver, and if they do not buy "artificial gold" or gold-plated silver jewelry, then Nina has no option but to wear her everyday gold jewelry. Women generally own a few sets of expensive jewelry, usually consisting of the ornaments given to them as their dowry. This fancy jewelry can be worn throughout a woman's life during social engagements. Nina used to wear her dowry ornaments when she went to parties, but she has stopped. It is a common occurrence, or so I am told, for gold chains and other items of jewelry to be snatched on the streets, so women rarely wear their expensive jewelry for fear of theft. Nina gave this as the reason why she does not expose her special wedding ornaments at parties: it is dangerous to do so during this bad "time" of crime on the streets:

"I used to wear that jewelry to receptions, but nowadays I don't even wear those anymore, the *time* is so bad that I go to all the parties just like this, wearing two bangles only. Maybe wear a *chain,* or something like that. Go out in a *simple* style. We don't wear—a lot of people wear *artificial* jewelry, thinking that *it should look good. It should look real. They wear it that way. But we don't buy, because, that is also too expensive, and we, I, don't myself have any interest."

Wedding receptions are notorious locations for women to pass judgment on each other's jewelry. One of the factors in this intense analysis is, of course, cost. If the jewelry is artificial, the wearer, through assemblage and attitude, hopes to pass it off as gold. Wedding guests not only try to pass their own artificial jewelry as gold, they try as well to guess which of the other women are wearing fakes, a task requiring a keen eye for detail, a skill many women proudly claim to have. This skill is one Nina does not care to possess, having intentionally abandoned the fashion savvy of her youth:

"I can't tell if somebody is wearing artificial because I don't go to the market, so I don't know what is real and what is artificial. And who cares whether it is real or artificial? It makes no difference to me. And we don't attend too many parties and receptions because we are two of us, so only one goes. Both of us, we don't go; one goes."

Plain on Purpose

Nina feels no pressure from her family, or for that matter, from the fashion industry, to dress in a certain way. I asked her explicitly to elaborate on the notion of audience by asking who she dresses for, whom she wants to please. Her answer, as expected, was: *"First of all, myself. Because I should look good. For my own personal satisfaction. I should look good, I should dress up in such a way that I should not look exceptional. I should be with the crowd."*

Usually when I ask women why they wear their ornaments, they reply with answers that detail cultural prescriptions and pressure from their husbands and mothers-in-law. When I ask again, they admit to wanting to satisfy their own needs as well. The pattern is clear—after giving the obligatory social reason, women then admit to wearing certain ornaments for personal satisfaction. Both answers are correct; the women provide their answers in layers, moving from cultural and public reasons to more personal ones. Free from the social and familial pressures to wear certain kinds and amounts of ornaments, Nina's preference for a simple appearance is an assertion of her own style. Though she chooses an understated look, it remains "with the crowd," still in the general realm of the acceptable. Her look is not necessarily a part of the latest fashion, but neither is it necessarily out of fashion.

While Nina does not search through the market in order to keep up with the latest fashion in clothing and jewelry, her wish to be "with the crowd" requires an understanding of the trend of the moment. Many men and women want to stand out within this frame of acceptability. They push the limits of the fashionable, while carefully remaining within its scope. Their ultimate goal is a beauty that is achieved through nuances of creativity within conformity to shared standards. Nina's personal art is not designed to stand out, but to hold within a range of acceptability, a task no less difficult and challenging. A desire not to look exceptional is atypical and original; Nina elaborated: *"Ah, I should not look extraordinary. I should not be with any—it means, my dress should be according to that occasion, according to the party which I am going to, and my makeup, and my hairstyle."*

Many women in Banaras get dressed to please their husbands, not out of fear of reprimand, but out of love. Nina and Hemant seem to have a warm and comfortable marriage. When I asked to take a picture of them in the open courtyard behind their house, Hemant put his arm around her shoulder, a tender gesture, rare among married couples in India, especially in public. Nina would surely want to please her husband and her family with her outward appearance, as some women do, out of affection. Nina is fortunate that her husband, possibility due to his own Sindhi upbringing, also prefers a plain aesthetic:

"My husband is also very simple. 'You do whatever you want.' No pressure. They don't put any pressure on us—or 'Wear these clothes,' or 'Dress up in such a way.' Nothing like that. Neither does our mother-in-law. She never says 'Wear this dress.' On the contrary, she says, 'Wear jewelry, wear ornaments,' and we don't wear them. We say 'We don't want to.' That's all."

Because personal adornment in India is inextricably linked with caste, religion, and social status, Nina's choices need to be understood not only in the contexts of personal aesthetics and family dynamics, but also in terms of her place. Her style—at the plain end of the conventional—fits her regional tradition, her age, marital status, and loving husband, and it also works in Banaras, a crowded city and a pilgrimage site, where crime on the streets is feared. When Nina compared the city of her childhood, Bombay, with the city of her adulthood, Banaras, she began by remembering Bombay:

> *"There people dress up according to the fashion. And here, people are too conservative—I mean, they dress up in that way, but still over here, it's different, people are a bit backward, in fact, in dressing style . . . Here, if you don't dress properly and go out, all the people, they will look at you, right? Then you become self-conscious, you are aware that people are looking at you."*

The overcrowded and over-curious "local public" on the streets of Banaras spends much time staring at people, and staring becomes leering for many of the men. Nina is tired of being stared at, tired of being the object of excessive gaze on the streets. So, she wants to be "with the crowd," whether on the streets or at wedding parties. It was different, Nina believes, in Bombay, where people are stared at less openly because, in her opinion, the city of her childhood is socially more liberal.

At this point in our interview, Nina's daughter, Priya, returned from school, and she agreed. Priya likes to visit Bombay, but her mother said that Priya feels "patriotic" toward Banaras and always defends the city whenever somebody in her family criticizes it. As it is with immigrant families in the United States, children born and brought up in Banaras feel a special bond with the city that their parents and grandparents, who came from elsewhere, do not share. Despite her fondness for Banaras, Priya agreed that the city is too conservative because it is a holy city "full of *pundits,* full of Brahmins."

Nina is right to be disturbed by "eve-teasing," the practice of young men touching women on the streets—the covert physical harassment perpetrated by local cowards. It is something, Nina feels, that happens particularly in Banaras during crowded public events such as *melas.* Her daughter Priya tried to tell her mother that "eve-teasing" takes place in Bombay as well, but Nina was not willing to listen. She compared the Bombay of her youth, free of hassles, with the Banaras of the present, a disturbing place to bring up young girls. She took the opportunity, at this point, to reiterate her concept of personal appearance. Although she was addressing the tape recorder on the Donald Duck bed sheet, she seemed to be directing her statement toward her daughter: *"You wear any dress, so long as you can look after yourself. If you go out on the streets, roads, nobody should harass you, you can take care of yourself, then you can do anything you want.*"

In the larger context of women's adornment in India, Nina's style exemplifies the alternative of the plain. From her articulate reflections on her simple style, we learn that she makes deliberate choices within a finite range of possibilities. Her desire to appear unornamented, in purposeful contrast to the extravagant adornment of other women, expresses her reaction to the expectations of tradition, caste, locale, and family. A closer look at Nina's style reveals that her seemingly casual appearance is a carefully constructed compromise among pragmatic factors, cultural identifications, and personal desires. Though their styles are different, such a personal coordination of competing influences is also the case with the other women of this book.

The goal of ornamentation is to achieve beauty through an assemblage of clothes and jewelry. The availability of raw materials plays a crucial role in the realization of this artistic endeavor. In order to engage in the creative act of self-adornment, a woman needs first to assess what is available—what she owns—and then decide on how to configure her stock into a personal presence. Nina owns many items of adornment that she does not wear. She has many saris that have been given to her over the years. Her saris are "rotting" in her closet, she said. She does not wear saris often, though she considers them more beautiful, if less comfortable, than *salwar suits.* The absence of saris in her daily repertoire does not signal a lack of a stock, nor does it reveal a lack of an appreciation for saris, but rather her choice of comfort over aesthetics. Similarly, Nina stores her gold jewelry in a bank locker. In this case, Nina chooses the comfort of knowing that the jewelry is safe from thieves, and happily attends parties without displaying the beauty and wealth of the gold jewelry.

Unlike the gifts of saris, which she rejects for daily use, the perfumes she has been given are fully incorporated into Nina's repertoire, reflecting not only her appreciation of fragrances, but also the generosity and taste of the purchaser of the scent, and in turn, the relationship between the donor and the recipient. When I asked Nina if she bought and used perfume, she replied, again using the plural: "*Perfume we use, that we get as gifts. We don't buy it, because we get lots of gifts. My sister-in-law in America, she gives. My parents are there in Spain, they give. Still I have not bought a single one with my money.*"

When I asked Nina if she, like many people, recycled unwanted things through re-gifting, her response was quick and firm: *"Actually, they give me the best. I always like it. They give us the best. So there is no need of giving it to anybody else, and they are so expensive, so we use it."*

The bottles of perfume are used and valued because they reflect the good taste, generosity, and the foreign residence of the givers—her family members. Through perfume, Nina communicates to others and to herself a connection over space; it is a sign of the unity and affection between her and her faraway relatives. An analysis of the stock in use—Nina's perfumes, for instance—reveals, in addition to the aesthetic value of an item, the symbolic value of its interpersonal associations.

People receive gifts—saris and perfumes—but they buy most of the items of body art that they own. Nina wears *salwar suits* because she likes them. When I asked Nina what kinds of *suits* she liked to buy, she answered frankly: *"All those that are available in our shop."* Then I asked whose taste these clothes reflected, and she replied: *"Sometimes our choice, sometimes our husbands' choices. It depends."* Her brother-in-law, Parmanand, who was listening, added that the *salwar suits* that Nina and his wife, Jaya, wore reflected "mutual choice."

The *salwar suits* that Nina prefers to wear happen to be the main items sold in their store, Dayaram Fashion Centre. Daily use of *salwar suits* by a middle-aged married woman is uncommon, and it reflects both her comfort and her family's business. Nina wears *salwar suits* every day because she no longer has a father-in-law to tell her not to, and she has easy access to new *suits* because her family runs a clothing store. The beauty of the design, and the grace of the cut, also exhibit the preferences of her husband, Hemant, and his brother, Parmanand, who often select the prints, colors, and fabrics of the clothing worn by their wives.

In any practical analyses of adornment choices, financial capacity will always play a role. Items that were received as gifts will be worn, even if the recipient does not like them, because they were, in essence, free. On a daily basis, Nina varies her *salwar suits,* choosing from the ones in her closet. Unlike many women, she does not change the jewelry that she wears daily. She rotates *salwar suits* regularly because they can be bought cheaply through the Khanchandani family's business networks. The absence of certain types of adornment in a woman's presentation could reveal her distaste for such items, or her sense that they do not suit her body, or her lack of cash.

The Sindhi Look

In Nina's case, the absence of the jewelry that is worn daily by other Banarasi women is explained partially by her tradition. Sindhi married women do not like plastic and glass bangles or silver ornaments. Sindhi women prefer gold, but, though Nina owns gold, she does not wear it out of personal choice. A lover of fashion in her youth, Nina, in maturity, cares nothing for the whims of fashionable fluctuation. She explains her choice as a negative reaction to the excessive cost of fashionable clothes, especially in Bombay, the vogue capital of India. Nina's reluctance to supplement her wardrobe with expensive clothes is conditioned by the fact that her family members are middle-class merchants in the clothing business. If the women of her household were to buy expensive clothes regularly, their actions could be seen as frivolous and self-indulgent. Many people in India cannot afford to buy new clothes and jewelry on a regular basis. They describe their actions as choices based on caste, family, or social appropriateness.

Arising from the practical matters of acquisition and the incorporation of available materials, an individual's body art is also a self-conscious reference to culture and tradition. It expresses a collective identity, achieved by adhering to in-group norms and rejecting alien practices. Ethnic identification seems particularly important for people like Nina, who are currently displaced in Banaras, away from their home communities. Nina constantly contrasts her Sindhi style to the style of other Hindus in Banaras. When I asked her what kinds of special events she enjoyed, she began by explaining to me the common Banarasi customs, against which she set her Sindhi traditions. Her example was Teej—the day on which married Hindu women fast until the sight of the new moon:[5]

"If you take Hindus, I mean, not Sindhis actually, Hindus—they celebrate Teej. *They fast. They wear new clothes. The women fast for their husbands . . . They wear all that is related to suhag—bindi, churi, payal, sindur, bichiya, they wear. Compulsory it is to wear new dress, new sari on that day. We don't. Sindhis* no. We keep a fast during our Teej, which happens on a different day. But we don't have this—that one should wear new clothes, one should wear a new sari."

236

In describing *suhag*—the auspicious adornment of a married woman—Nina demonstrated an understanding of the cultural mandate for Hindu women to wear specific items of jewelry on a daily basis and on ritual occasions. She correctly listed the "compulsory" items: *bindi, churi* (bangles), *payal* (anklets), *sindur,* and *bichiya* (toe rings). Then Nina moved from general Hindu customs to describe her family's celebrations, including the Sindhi New Year—Cheti Chand. She was particularly animated when she told me about the monthly veneration of Varuna, the Vedic deity of the sky, whose sign is the fish, whose breath is the wind.

A regular ritual in Nina's household is the worship of Varuna on the occasion of every new moon. Nina and Jaya prepare a special meal of rice with sugar, *ghee* (clarified butter), and cardamom, which is placed in a container and sealed over with flour and steamed shut. This modest feast is taken to the Ganga, in lieu of a proper sea, and offered to the god Varuna in gratitude, for he once came to earth in the form of a fish, as Julelal, in a moment of human crisis. This monthly ritual is analogous to the act of giving alms, since the fish of the river are believed to eat the rice dish.

The monthly female act of devotion interested me. I asked Nina if she wore new or special clothes when she took the food to the river. "No, no, no!" she said emphatically. "I go like this, in *ordinary dress,* wearing *salwar kameez,* with the offering in a *bag,* covered up, so that nobody can see what is inside. Like the *dehati* people here, whatever it is they are taking, they place it on their heads like this, and walk like this . . . Like that we don't do!"

When Nina referred to the peasants, the *dehatis,* she pantomimed the way they walk beneath headloads to create a dramatic public gesture that calls too much attention to the effort of transporting ritual gifts. In contrast, Nina, a sophisticated urbanite, discreetly places her offering in a bag, and walks, in "ordinary dress," to the Dashaswamedh main *ghat* to feed Varuna's fish. Once again, the plain Sindhi way has been opposed to the extravagant actions of others. Nina's demure adornment during special religious events conforms to the general Sindhi style, and it stands in direct contrast to both the over-ornamented urban Hindustanis of Banaras and the brightly clad *dehatis,* who come from the country, with their distinctive gait and exaggerated manners.

Nina's outward appearance naturally reflects her Sindhi and Hindu identities while communicating an idiosyncratically personal position. Family and economic factors facilitate her choices, but, at base, they express her perception of herself. She is comfortable in *salwar suits* and wears two gold bangles on her left wrist in a gesture at *suhag,* auspiciously ensuring the long life of her husband. She scents her body with perfumes that recall family members far away. Her regular visits to the beauty parlor for a haircut, a facial, and eyebrow threading she regards as purely "hygienic," acts of necessity, not vanity.

One reason Nina does not spend much effort on adornment is because she finds fulfillment in another daily artistic activity: food preparation. The food she prepares is far from ordinary in appearance, ingredients, and taste. It is, unlike her adornment, hardly plain; it is ornamented with delicious homemade chutneys, diced onions, and hot peppers. My (admiring) assessment of her food could have been derived from extraordinary meals she prepared for a guest. She might have chosen to invest extra time and effort in the meals made to impress a visitor, but we showed up with Hemant unannounced on several occasions and sat down with the family to eat, and the food was always extravagant. Generosity, made concrete in food, it seems, is more important for Nina than shopping and glamorous self-presentation.

Given the limited resources of time, money, and energy, women make many choices, including that of personal adornment. Nina's choice of a crisp, pert, but relatively modest physical display directly reflects her personal philosophy of beauty. Several days before our long interview, when the conversation had turned to female beauty, Nina's daughter, Priya, recited the frequently repeated list of Indian winners of beauty pageants: Aishwarya Rai, Sushmita Sen, Lara Dutta, Priyanka Chopra, and Diya Mizra.[6] Nina agreed that those women were good-looking, but she said, however desirable a shapely figure and a beautiful face are, "*Beauty lies in the nature. Nature and personality.*" Beauty cannot be achieved by owning hundreds of silk brocaded saris, or sets of sumptuous gold jewelry. Beauty lies in generosity and affection, in wit and intelligence—in the gracious personality of a good human being. After she made her statement, I looked hard at Nina, who sat unadorned on the bed, in a simple pale-peach *salwar suit.* She smiled and looked happy, as she always does. At that moment, Nina—in ordinary dress and a minimum amount of jewelry—embodied her own definition of beauty.

·11·

Neelam Chaturvedi

WHEN I FIRST TALKED to Neelam Chaturvedi in the spring of 1996, she was an art teacher in the Sunbeam private school in Banaras. Unlike Nina, a Sindhi living in a Sindhi household, Neelam is a Punjabi married into a Brahmin family from Banaras. Being born in India to Punjabi parents who were displaced from their native Pakistan, Neelam has developed an adaptive personal style. Constant adjustment to different contexts is a main theme of her choices in life and adornment, a pattern evident in our interviews. My main tape-recorded conversations with her, which lasted several hours, took place in Neelam's bedroom, upstairs in her mother-in-law's house a few blocks from the vast red temple dedicated to Durga in Banaras.[1]

When she was growing up in Banaras, Neelam spoke Punjabi at home with her parents, yet she was exposed to Hindi at school and to the local Bhojpuri dialect of the servants. Neelam learned Hindi and Bhojpuri, and, though she was scolded for speaking these ill-regarded languages in the presence of her parents, she grew up speaking what she calls a "mix" of languages. Her shifting between Punjabi and Hindi, choosing one or the other in different contexts, is like the double-coding used by immigrant children who grow up in America, adapting and conforming to two cultures simultaneously.

This blend of Punjabi and Banarasi cultures became official when Neelam and Vidhu chose to marry. Theirs was a "love marriage," a type of union rare in a society where most marriages are still prearranged by parents and other relatives. In describing the clothing and customs of her wedding day, Neelam said the event mingled "some things Punjabi, and some things in the U.P. style." In her Punjabi tradition, the bride wears a sari for the ceremonial ex-

239

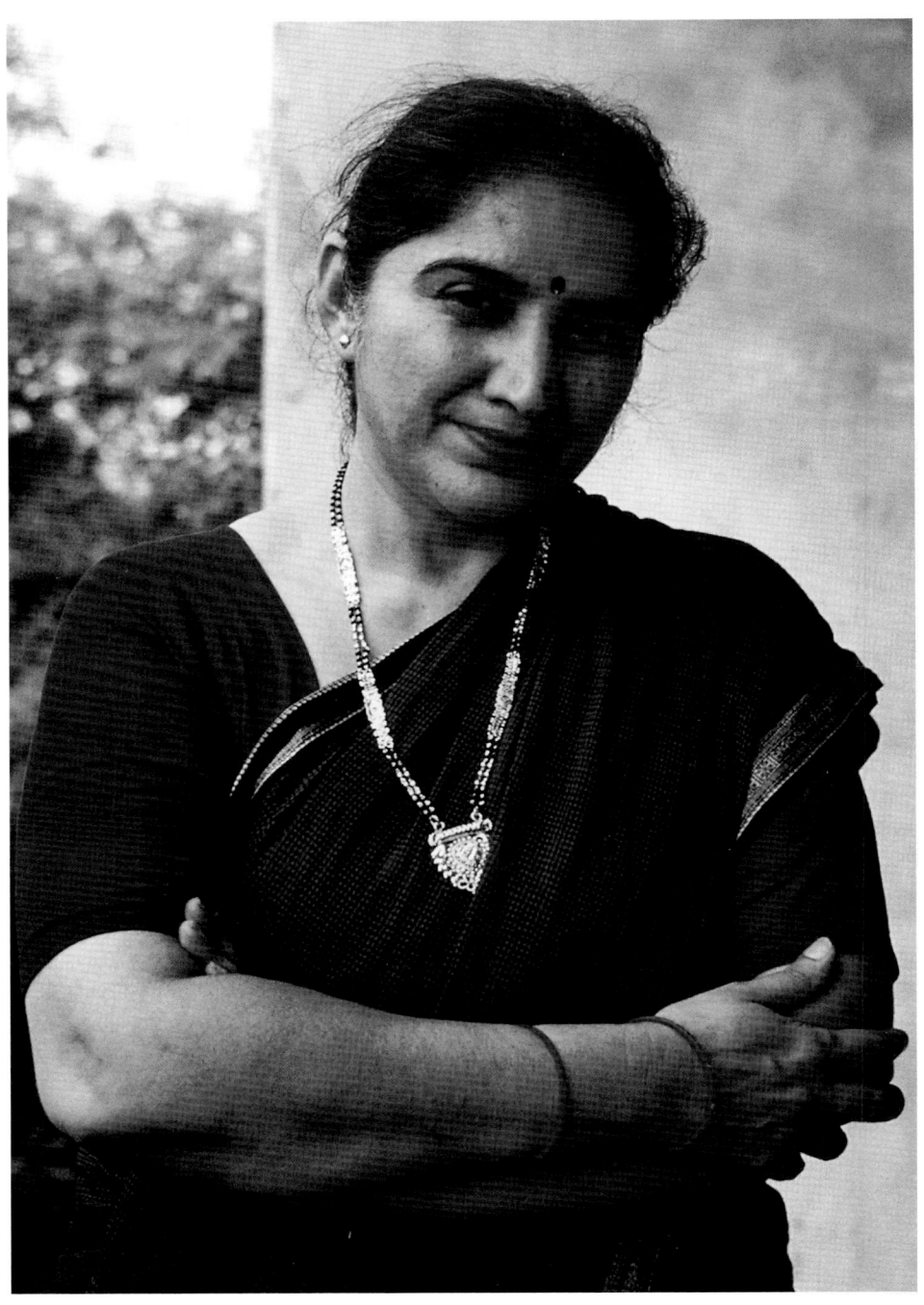

Neelam Chaturvedi

change of flower garlands, then changes into a pink *salwar suit* for the actual wedding ceremony. When the bride arrives at her husband's family home, the pink *suit* is given to an unmarried sister-in-law, a gesture of luck, a passing of marital good fortune. Knowing she would not be entering a Punjabi household after marriage, Neelam chose to alter this custom. For the *jaimal*—the ritual exchange of garlands—she decided to wear the usual Banarasi *lehanga* outfit, an ensemble with a heavily brocaded full skirt, a short shirt, and a long scarf. For the wedding ceremony, Neelam wore a silk Banarasi sari, but instead of the conventional turmeric-yellow sari of most brides from Uttar Pradesh, Neelam wore a *rani* pink sari, a personal choice to retain a connection with the abandoned Punjabi garment and custom.

Preferences from Childhood

Her blending of Punjabi and Uttar Pradesh styles, manifest early in the language she spoke and later in the clothing for her wedding, continued as a way of life for Neelam. To contextualize Neelam's choices in maturity, I felt it necessarily to understand her childhood, the early moment when aesthetic preferences are usually set. I began by asking her to recall her earliest memories of fashion and beauty. We spoke in Hindi, but she occasionally used English words, which I have marked in italics as I have the words left untranslated from Hindi. Remembering back to her first experiences, she said that she was never comfortable with being too "fashionable" in front of her parents, who did not want her to pay too much attention to her looks. They feared that her beauty might attract unwanted attention. She explained: "Maybe my parents would think, 'My daughter is pretty, and nobody should look at her,' and hopefully nothing will happen—as she is a child—that she doesn't get *exploited*. So all people would keep their girls safely. No makeup should be worn, and lots of other *restrictions*."

Even though Neelam grew up in Banaras, her parents remembered the terror of their days in Pakistan at the time of Partition. Their fears were not calmed in Banaras, where antagonism abides between Hindus and Muslims, and they were watchful, wary, and conservative with their daughter. During India's achievement of independence in 1947, the British drew a line through the Punjab separating India from Pakistan and engendering much violence— an episode recounted in graphic detail in history books and novels, notably in Khushwant Singh's *Train to Pakistan,* Bapsi Sidhwa's *Cracking India,* and Salman Rushdie's *Midnight's Children.* In this time of chaos and aggression, ten million people moved across the border, and one million of them were massacred before reaching their destinations.[2] Both rumor and brutal reality, the idea of Muslim men abducting pretty Punjabi girls is a common motif in the tales of Partition, especially those told in Bollywood films. Out of this fear, parents preferred their daughters to seem homely in an effort to keep them safe from imagined harems or a painful future as a courtesan. In India all unmarried women are discouraged from ornamentation. From the parent's point of view, if an unmarried daughter were to appear bejeweled and beautiful, she would possibly attract the attention of dangerous kidnappers, and almost certainly she would attract men from a disagreeable category of local suitor. Intent on arranging the marriages of their children, parents forbid their daughters to have boyfriends, for they might carry them into "love marriages." The wish to prevent an unmarried daughter from appearing provocative in public is hardly restricted to Indian parents; it is a wide instinct.[3]

Within the restrictions imposed by her family, Neelam chose one secret item with which to adorn her young beauty, the Indian "beauty spot"—the *bindi*—widely believed to increase a woman's beauty fourfold:

"I remember that I did not wear a *bindi* until tenth grade. And I would look at others—and they would be wearing *bindis*—so I, I mean, I had some color. I would keep that ready, and just when it was time to go outside, in that moment, I would put it on. So nobody would be able to see, I would grab my bag and go outside, and nobody would be able to see. At home, fully clothed, dressed up, I would walk around, but the *bindi*—just as I was about to go outside—in that moment, I would, standing by the mirror, immediately put on the *bindi,* and go outside. And outside, there is such a crowd that no one is going to come and notice if I am wearing a *bindi* or not, and I would keep going.

"One day, by mistake, the *bindi* was not removed; I forgot. When I was returning from school, I forgot to remove the *bindi.* My maternal grandmother slapped me: 'Why did you wear a *bindi*?' Maybe she was remembering that Pakistan era, because women there were being *slashed,* and girls were being taken [kidnapped]. So in her mind, there was fear. So she did not want, in any way, that 'my girl should look *beautiful.*' That is why one should be totally simple. Don't wear anything on the ear—I mean, I did not wear anything!"

Their fear for Neelam's well-being caused her family to regulate not only her personal appearance but also her behavior. She continues:

"I did not see a *picture* until the tenth grade. Not one *movie* did I see. I had not seen one *picture*. In the eighth grade, they had taken me to a *picture*—a *picture* about the gods. To see that one I was sent. Besides that, I had not seen any *pictures*.

"In a high voice, any song, I could not sing, ever. If I felt like singing a song, and I were to start singing it—it would have been out of the question. If somebody were to hear it: 'Why are you singing?' 'Singing songs is not a good thing.' 'Why are girls singing songs?' Through songs, the *feeling* [of the soul] is revealed—how somebody is, and the ways things are. That is why—'Don't ever sing songs.' 'What, are you a dancing girl, that you sing songs, huh?'

"But, in U.P.—like, I have married into this *family*—here, among all Brahmins, I have noticed that there is a lot of interest in music and art. And it makes a little bit of difference . . . I believe that in my *family*, there must have been fear from that Pakistan era. Because they [in U.P.], they had no Partition, their property has always been *safe*. They don't know all that happened. They of course know that there was so much fighting. My *family* saw it. My *mother* used to tell me that she would sit holding *poison* in her hands. Her *mother* would say that if there is an *attack*, if people come inside the house, then open the container, and all three of you kids, eat the *poison*. There were two brothers and my *mother*. Grandmother had three children: two boys and one girl. In everybody's hand, *poison* was placed. 'If before we are able to escape, if something happens, then just eat the poison.' So that thing, I mean, you can't forget it, can you? For somebody who has experienced so much *loss*, I mean, there is fear still."

Growing up hearing such stories, Neelam learned to respect the prohibitions on her physical appearance.[4] Although she was not allowed to wear makeup or a *bindi* by her traumatized family, Neelam kept herself fashionable by paying close attention to her clothes. Her skirts and *kurtas* were always starched and impeccably ironed, causing her school friends to ask teasingly where she got her clothes washed and pressed. Neelam remembered that her clothes looked so neat, they were so "well maintained," that everybody would say that she probably sent them to Paris to get them laundered and pressed. Today, Neelam channels her personal adornment energies almost exclusively into her clothing. She is passionately interested in all types of clothing—"total," including jeans, *salwar suits*, saris, and skirts—everything "fine and nice." Her interest is directed to clothing partially because she does not take pleasure in jewelry, and in our long interview, she interrupted herself to explain her near-disdain of jewelry—another aesthetic preference she developed early in life.

"For my *mummy*—there is yet another story—for my *mummy*, she likes jewelry very much. And—I mean, very much indeed—and she liked it very much. And she had in her possession a lot of jewelry. One thing is that, in *mummy's* house, she was alone. There were no sisters on my *papa's* side, and there were no sisters on my *mummy's* side. I had neither a paternal aunt nor a maternal aunt. She was alone. My *mummy*, her *family* had in their possession a lot of gold that stayed in Pakistan. When they came here, having fled there, that gold stayed there. My *papa*, he had one hundred *acres* of land, very good land; I mean, people would say that one would have to go around on a horse, that the whole *farmstead*, the whole thing, I mean, could not be seen on foot.

"That all stayed there. They brought from there approximately one *ghara* [large brass pot] of gold, which they were allowed to bring from Pakistan. So one *ghara* of gold my *mummy* had.

"Here in our house there was a servant, Bahadur was his name. And *mummy* and *papa* both went to see a *picture*; at home, he was to watch the house. From the back of the house, a robbery occurred. And all that *jewelry* was gone. It was a big *shock* to my *mummy*, because she had such a *craze* for gold, and she kept remembering that *scene* from the past [from Pakistan]—so much *loss* occurred there.

"My *mummy*, she was so *shocked*, that she thought, 'Now, so much jewelry, with my own eyes, I will never be able to see again.'

"So that *feeling* inside of me does not come. Because I always kept seeing *mummy* so interested in *jewelry*, right: 'How is this made?' 'This is this way.' Whoever she would be sitting next to, she would be talking about jewelry: 'This *ring* of yours, how much was it made for?' 'How is this one?' 'Where was this one bought from?'

"So I thought, 'What is this?' Because it was her interest, that is why she kept asking; whatever someone has interest in. So I could not go over there. Toward jewelry, I could not even glance.

"So I could never even imagine if someone were to say to me, 'Wear a twenty-thousand-rupee necklace,' and I would say, 'Yes, yes, okay.' No. But if someone now were to say, 'There is a five-thousand-rupee sari, it is very nice,' I would certainly say, 'Okay, I'll take it!'"

Neelam's words reflect a lack of interest in jewelry, but she would gladly indulge herself in an expensive and flamboyant sari. Clothing is where her interest lies.

Most girls learn the art of personal adornment from their mothers, as I did. The process entails not only the mother's active instruction on how to apply makeup or keep one's clothes clean, but it also involves hours of quiet observation, and often admiration, on the part of the daughter. But a mother's obsession can affect her daughter adversely, as it happened with Neelam.

Sometimes the impressions and associations developed around adornment are learned more subtly. On my twenty-fifth birthday, my mother gave me the four tiny gold bangles she had worn daily since the time she lived in Banaras as a young wife and mother before I was born. For many days after the gift, my sisters and I would become suddenly aware of our mother's presence, even though she was out of the house at the moment. It took us a while to realize that we were unconsciously listening to the distinct sound her bangles made even though it was now I who was wearing them. Their sound, though, was forever connected with our mother, and the pleasure her presence has always brought to us.

From this personal experience I realized that in India, almost everybody's mother has her own distinctive bangle sound, for most married (Hindu) women wear bangles as a sign of *suhag.* The difference in the sounds mothers create depends on bangles, and bangles depend on caste, region, age, finances, and personal preference. Bangles make sweet sounds when the mother is rocking an infant, caressing a sick child to sleep, or going about her household chores, and especially when she is rhythmically kneading and rolling the varieties of homemade bread. Those sounds are all memories of the joy and comfort of childhood. The pleasant and meaningful domestic sounds associated with her mother directly influence the way a woman wants to sound when she is married herself. And memories of his mother's sounds influence the way a husband wants his wife to move through his own house.

The contrast between the melodic sound of four gold bangles sliding lightly against each other and the loud jangling of a dozen glass bangles lies behind the usually unarticulated difference in jewelry taste of the partners in an inter-caste marriage, like that of Vidhu and Neelam:

"Glass bangles cause *disturbance* in me. They make this noise, then I lift my hand here, then they make this noise, then I lift my hand here, then they make this noise. So I feel, first of all, remove these! The sound is what causes a lot of *disturbance* in me. And for him, it is exactly that sound which he likes so much. But for me, the sound of anklets sounds good, but not the sound of bangles. This is because when I am sleeping, the anklets won't be ringing, but the bangles, if I move a little, then the bangles will clank, and that will cause *disturbance* in my sleep. Some people have the habit, they like it."

Since she is married to a man from Uttar Pradesh, Neelam follows the local custom and wears glass bangles as a symbol of marriage. But since she did not grow up in a household with women who wore them, their distinctive jingly, tinkly sound irritates her, especially in the middle of the night. Her husband, on the other hand, has spent a lifetime sleeping through that noise, and he likes it when he is awake. Punjabi brides wear *chura* during the first year of marriage, a set of red and white plastic bangles. Later, many women opt to wear golden bangles. Both of these ornaments are gentler on the ears than glass ones. Neelam expanded on her dislike for glass bangles:

"Okay, what we wear during weddings—*chura*—with it you cannot hear a sound, with it, there is a lot of *show*—the whole arm will be covered—it will look beautiful, everything is there, but there is no *disturbance* of any kind. There is absolutely no sound. So, that is—having lived in that [Punjabi] neighborhood, in that way, we got used to it.

"Glass bangles, my *mummy* also did not wear. If my *mummy* had worn it, then I would feel good about it. My husband's mother has worn it always. In their household the *symbol* of the bangles has always been there; the wife should wear glass bangles. So, for them it feels right, because they come having heard that sound from the beginning. And I did not hear my mother, so I feel that in the house, nobody's sound should be detected. So for me, it feels a little strange.

"The sound of gold or silver bangles is dim, not loud. These glass ones, they ring too loudly. *Chun-chun, chun-chun, chun-chun.* Like that it rings. Whatever you are doing, the sound is there."

I asked Neelam if her dislike of the sound of glass bangles was limited to her own, or if it included the noisy jewelry of other people as well. Since she lives in a joint household, I was wondering if the sound of her sister-in-law and the other women bothered her too. Neelam thought for a minute before responding to my question: "If the next door people's bangles are sounding over and over, then I will feel bad, like 'What IS it that these people are do-ing, that their bangles are making so much noise?'" Her reference is to the shame associated with intimate activities, such as sexual relations, taking place noisily in private. The house is crowded, and it is embarrassing for noise to carry through walls, which makes an interesting dilemma for a newly married couple since the bride is, by custom, decked, night and day, from head to toe in noisy jewelry.

Neelam's mother never wore glass bangles, and she does not like their sound, but she has very positive feelings about the subtle sound of the tiny bells—the *ghungrus*—that are placed on the clasp of anklets. It is a pleasure she seeks, and she asks for the optional bells to be placed on new anklets when she buys them. The sound of the anklets belongs to her familial and regional tradition, and Neelam loves it, just as people from Banaras love glass bangles.

During Punjabi weddings, Neelam said, the groom must give a *chhalla*—a little ring with three tiny bells on it—to the bride's younger sisters and her friends in payment for the ritual pranks they play on him. Since weddings are gatherings for large numbers of related people, any young girl of the bride's family becomes, de facto, a younger sister-in-law who is entitled to the gift. The new brother-in-law arrives with a bag full of cheap silver rings, prepared to pass them out during the wedding, and any girl growing up in a Punjabi community naturally develops positive feelings toward the ring and the sound its *ghungrus* make. The excitement of wearing jewelry in early girlhood, and the positive associations of family and celebration that are attached to wed-dings,[5] become subconsciously linked to the sound of a small cluster of bells. When a Punjabi girl grows up and starts to look forward to her own wedding, the sound of the silver bells shifts from the relished ring of childhood to the bridal anklets of adulthood, while the positive associations evoked by the tinkling bells continue.

Shopping for Saris

Neelam likes the tinkle of anklets, but what she really likes are saris. When I asked her to describe how she shops for saris, she began by saying, first of all, that she cannot wear saris of another's choosing. She must select her own. She never hurries, but shops for saris "*aram-se*"—with ease and calm. "I never go to buy only one sari," she said. "If I like five saris, I will buy all five."

In a sari shop, Neelam looks at what she calls the "racks" of saris, folded and piled in a way that reminds her of books stacked high in a bookshelf. She asks the salesman to riffle his thumb down the pile, briefly exposing the color and print of each one. She calls her personal procedure the "book style," because the salesman shows her all the "pages"—the sheets of floral and geometric prints on silk and cotton. Neelam has the salesman repeat his performance from rack to rack, until she has visually sampled the entire store. Only then is she ready to start selecting saris to examine closely, perhaps to take home.

As we have seen, a woman will typically enter a sari shop and take her place on the mattress on the floor, while the salesman, sitting across from her, starts dropping saris through the air, opening them with a flamboyant gesture, and letting them flutter down onto her lap, trapping her in mounds of floral and paisley. Once a pile of saris has accumulated, she will choose a few from among the ones the salesman has presented, asking to see them again while the rejects are taken away to be folded by an assistant. Neelam refuses to buy a sari in this way. She insists on seeing the entire stock before making her selections. She interrupts the normal process, and her purchases reflect her taste, not the salesman's understanding of her taste.

After browsing in this library of saris, Neelam is ready to choose. I asked her if she only chooses saris that she thinks will look good on her, given the specific considerations of figure, skin tone, or height. I also wondered if she tries the sari on while she is in the store, by placing one end of it over her shoulder and looking in the mirror. Neelam is confident of her looks, and trusts her eye: "If at first something looks good to me—looks good to the eye—then I feel if I were to wear it, it would look good on me."

Neelam never tries saris on before buying them. She chooses by looking at the printed design—for she prefers printed to brocaded pieces—and then carefully studying the *palloo,* the decorated end that hangs over the shoulder. Once the saris have been bought and taken home, she puts them away in her wardrobe. For the next few days, like an eager child with a new toy, she takes the saris out of the *almari,* looks at them, then puts them back. She does this two or three times, excited by her new purchases, and she lets the excitement build up before she wears them. She will choose to wear a new sari for the first time, she said, only if she feels she looks good at the moment, with freshly shampooed hair. She does not put on *sindur,* lipstick, or bangles while trying on a sari, because if the sari looks good on her while she looks plain, then it will certainly look even better when the other adornments are added, the ones Neelam calls "extra makeup."

I asked Neelam where she got her fashion sense. She said she does not watch TV nor go to Bollywood films and does not regularly consult fashion magazines. She does, however, notice people on the streets who look good: "If, let us say, I think a woman is beautiful, in that way, I see her *personality* and it looks *attractive* and good, then I will certainly look at her, from top to bottom: 'What IS she wearing?' If she looks good, 'What is the *visheshta* in it, what makes it look good?'" When Neelam notices an attractive person on the street, she does not try to memorize the look in order to recreate it later. She looks intensely to understand the *visheshta*—the special attribute—the person radiates. (Like Anand Kumar at Priya Bangles, Neelam tries to extract an essence of aesthetic quality from what she sees, an essence that she can then creatively apply.) If she spots somebody wearing a *khas*—special—sari, she will keep it in mind, and recall it later when she goes shopping.

"Some *khas* saris I even ask for *especially.* If there is a *specialty* in that sari: it is expensive, it is *silk,* and it also looks good. I will certainly need to buy this one, to wear at *khas* occasions, it is the *latest model.* Like, for example, Banarasi saris are becoming *outdated,* with these big-big patterns and *all over* full of designs. Nowadays, *fancy saris* have arrived. So after having seen a few of them, you understand that, 'Yes, there is a market for these.' If they are hanging outside of somebody's showroom, then you understand that, 'Yes, these I need to buy.' In this way, you understand."

Although Neelam does not actively attend to the media that diffuse fashion—television, movies, and magazines—she is exposed to their results indirectly when she watches people on the streets who have been influenced and when she looks at the fashionable saris and jewelry that are featured in the shops of Banaras. One setting for display of the latest fashion is the workplace, where people place their new acquisitions before the eyes of admiring co-workers. So it is at the Sunbeam School.

"In my *school,* there are so many staff members that among them I find so many *models,* people willing to *model.* From them I figure out what is the *latest fashion.* Because every person continues to follow the fashion; those things they probably get from TV, but since I don't watch TV, when they come all *fit,* then I think: 'Hers looks good,' 'Hers I like.' From these, I *select,* 'This one looks good,' and that's the one I wear myself."

In the Joint Family Household

Unlike most women in Banaras, Neelam works outside of the home, and that fact greatly influences her choices of adornment. She has a need for a professional look, and her co-workers create a set of expectations she must meet. All women in India are aware of the different contexts in which they are being judged and in which they will communicate through self-adornment. Besides the contexts of home and social gatherings, professional women must meet the demands of the workplace, as Neelam does six days a week.

Neelam wears a sari to work, but when she comes home, she usually changes into a *salwar suit.* Such *suits* are also called *punjabis,* and Neelam, a Punjabi herself, is most comfortable when wearing one. The self-presentation of men and women at home reflects taste less than it does physical comfort, but living in close quarters, people must appear clean and neat. Neelam describes her daily look in these terms:

"It can be the case that I have *cotton* clothes, nicely washed and kept, or the sari comes back from being *starched,* and I feel fresh, clean, and washed. I have put on a *bindi,* I have put on *sindur.* I have put on bangles, okay. That's it. That is how much I will get ready. If I were to go out, I would get dressed in a better *tarika,* in the *tarika* of a sari of going out."

At home Neelam prefers a simple look, but she is consistent in liking her clothes clean, starched, and pressed. Even at home, she maintains the laundered "Parisian" effect that astounded her classmates when she was a girl. What she wears to be comfortable at home, Neelam knows, would not be appropriate outside. She uses the Hindi word *tarika* to mean a way or a style or a method. (This casual use of the word *tarika* can be contrasted with its formal use in Arabic to mean the discipline of a Sufi order.)

Because Neelam shares her house with her mother-in-law, the simple *tarika* of her home must include the "compulsory" wifely ornaments of *bindi, sindur,* and glass bangles, which she wears without much complaint. She has enjoyed wearing *bindis* since her childhood, and now, in adulthood, she indulges her passion by owning dozens of packets in a wide variety of colors and shapes. Wearing makeup at home, however, she considers extravagant and unnecessary: "Makeup has its own place. If you are going somewhere, then, okay, put on makeup; otherwise, just to sit there . . . Okay, take a shower, change your clothes, and sit inside the home. To have full *shringar* done and to be sitting inside the house—that I don't understand!"

As Neelam's comment implies, even though joint-family households are full of people—residents, servants, and visitors—it seems a waste of time and expensive materials to wear "full makeup" for this domestic audience. There is no need to impress the intimate audience at home; full *shringar* should be reserved for special observers.

At home, though she does not like noisy glass bangles, she wears four on her left wrist, and a watch on her right. She told me that she cannot wear many bangles at the school where she works because the administrators do not want the teachers to wear much jewelry. This proscription happens to suit her, and she uses the school's regulations as a rationale for her relatively understated display of jewelry, just as Nina Khanchandani uses Sindhi tradition as an explanation for her lack of interest in jewelry.

Though Neelam cannot wear many bangles at work, she needs to wear a few to signal her identity as a married Hindu woman in the state of Uttar Pradesh, so she puts four on her left wrist. Neelam writes on the chalkboard with her right hand, and if she wore bangles on that wrist, the noise would distract the students during class. In a later conversation, Neelam remarked that teachers and doctors (and presumably other professionals) should not wear much jewelry, for the sound, distracting in the workplace, would disturb the concentration needed for teaching or surgery.

Glass bangles mark the married Hindu woman from Uttar Pradesh, but with a small number of bangles on one wrist and a watch on the other, the communication is further qualified: this woman is a professional. It is generally understood that only "professional ladies" have a need for a watch and only they wear the minimum amount of "obligatory" jewelry, so Neelam is participating in a new movement in fashion that can be seen throughout India, most prominently in the big cities of Bombay and New Delhi, where more women than in Banaras (but still not many) work outside the home. These urban professional women have set a style—watch and scant jewelry—that is followed now by women who do not work outside the home, but who belong to what Neelam refers as the "higher gentry"—further complicating the visual signals that Neelam sends.

Neelam may complain about glass bangles, but she wears them, and I asked her why. Instead of giving me the usual reason—pressure from her mother-in-law—she answered honestly, using the word *kara* for the ornate bangles others call *kangans:*

"If it were a matter of my choice, then I would, right away, instantly, wear gold bangles; glass ones I would not wear! But, I mean, I don't have gold ones, and I have *karas,* but I don't like the fashion of *karas.* If I were to wear one-one *kara* [one on each wrist], then it would look too simple, and everybody would say that she is too simple. Who knows what they would start thinking. That is why it is better to just put on glass ones."

Having no "stock" of golden ornaments Neelam wears glass bangles, just as Nina's limited stock of clothes caused her to wear saris when she first married. But if Neelam wears glass bangles reluctantly, she also wears them carefully and with style. She chooses color combinations every morning to match her saris. There is no possibility, she said, absolutely no chance that her bangles would not match the colors of her sari on any given day. As soon as she chooses her sari, she chooses matching bangles and quickly puts them on.

The social pressure to wear "compulsory" glass bangles does not force women to change them often and to match them with their clothes. People find it inauspicious for a married woman to have bare wrists, but there are no hard rules about number or color or style of bangles; these are up to the individual. Neelam may dislike glass bangles, but like most human beings, she adapts and tries to find pleasure and creativity within social prescription. Choice and individuality appear in the adornment in which Neelam claims to have "no choice." What emerges is a personal *tarika* that threads through the shifting complexity of traditional values.

At Work at the Sunbeam School

At school, Neelam appears simply adorned to maintain what she calls, in English, "dignity" in front of her students. I was curious about the school's dress code, and Neelam assured me that the Sunbeam School has rules that all teachers, regardless of gender, must follow:

"We are taught how to be dressed at school. It should not be that the end of the sari, in front of the children, is constantly falling. You are constantly fixing your own *dress*. No. It should be *pinned-up,* there should be new *pleats* [on the sari]. You should go in the right way. If your hair is coming out, you are not to go in such a *dirty* way. If the teacher looks so *gandi,* it is not a good thing. Come with *pinned-up* sari, hair in a braid. Come in a proper way."

If the school authorities are unhappy with your appearance, you will hear about it. The adjective *gandi* means both "ugly" and "dirty"—the two concepts being obviously related—and the word intentionally retains ambiguity in Neelam's sentence, and I believe, in the school's regulations about proper attire. Neelam further details some of the suggestions made to the teachers: "To some people, especially, they give *warning* and tell them that: 'You should cut your hair.' 'You should dye your hair.' 'You should come not in those clothes but these clothes.' These types of *instructions* are given."

Many elderly and most middle-aged people in India, both men and women, dye their hair black. When the hair of a careless teacher shows too much gray, the administrators of the school demand that she conform to the common youthful look of black hair. The school officials provide much advice, and Neelam continues:

"'Your hair is coming in front of your eyes, how are you teaching the kids?' 'How are you seeing their *corrections?*' 'Come wearing a *hair band*!' In this way it is said.

"In my place, in the winter, *blazers* have to be worn. Not shawls. Somebody will say, 'I feel cold in my ears.' Somebody will say, 'I feel cold in my hands.' So how will you *teach,* if you are only feeling cold? If everything is *covered,* then how will the children see? That is why: 'Come in a *blazer.*' 'Inside the pockets hands should not be placed. Come properly.' The male members of the staff have to wear *ties.* There are no restrictions on *makeup.*"

A sari exposes the waist, back, and arms, so many Indian women wrap shawls around themselves in the winter. The shawls are beautiful and surprisingly warm, especially when made of pure wool. The advantage of a shawl is that you can arrange the fabric in many ways, choosing to expose an arm if cooking or to cover the entire torso, engulfing both arms, if you are cold. Shawls, like all wrapped clothes, require constant adjustment, and like saris they need to be held in place as the body moves. A wool cardigan, what

Neelam calls a "blazer," stays in place and does not need to be adjusted to cover a suddenly exposed stretch of skin, nor does it shroud the body, muffling the teacher in a mound of wool.

Saris, *dupattas,* and shawls—all draped textiles—add grace to a woman's movements and posture. The look of the fabric is maintained by the ways in which a woman moves and holds herself so that the garment will fall in the desired manner. The little feminine gestures of maintenance and arrangement, subtly sexy, do not fit the workplace, and certainly do not fit a classroom full of easily distracted children. So saris are secured with safety pins at various places, and *dupatta* scarves are pinned to the *kurta* underneath so they will not move. Neelam said that teachers are not allowed to wear sari blouses with deep necks that reveal cleavage when they bend over the desks of their pupils. There are also regulations governing the style and materials of saris: thin borders are encouraged, and saris in cotton or synthetic fabrics are preferred to fancy silk or the diaphanous chiffon. To communicate a professional look, one fit for an educational environment, the teachers are asked to look "dignified"—not elegant or sexy. In Rupa Bajwa's novel, *The Sari Shop,* a seller becomes exasperated as he tries to provide professional-looking saris to his customer, "a literate woman, Head of an English Department," who asks for "something to wear to college, not to a village fair . . . , some dullish colour, you know. Like brown or grey."[6] This is not something found only at the Sunbeam School or in India; there are American universities that post dress codes for their faculty and students, requesting that they appear clean, neat, and professional.[7]

As Neelam said, there are no restrictions placed on the wearing of makeup; it is a woman's own choice whether or not she should come to school wearing lipstick. There are few rules regarding jewelry; the school has no "objections" as long as the jewelry does not make much noise. The teachers, Neelam said, should follow what she called "silent fashion." Neelam said, "If the entire *school,* the entire *staff* were to wear anklets, to wear glass bangles, then why would the children have any need to scream? The teacher's *music* would be everywhere!"

The teachers follow the school's rules without much complaint. Neelam chooses a new *bindi,* a new sari and matching bangles every morning for school. She changes the shade of her lipstick and nail polish often, to look good at work. I asked Neelam if she did so to please the school officials, and she answered: "No, all the kids also think that 'My teacher is nice.' They also feel, 'Yes, this Miss is nice.' 'That Miss is really nice.' 'This one looks pretty.' 'This one teaches really well.' The children also feel *attracted* to the teacher. It makes a difference, it makes a difference on the *personality.*"

The teacher's attractive appearance brings her benefit: the children will pay attention, they will not misbehave, and they will favor her above others. It is natural for a teacher to want the admiration and respect of her students. Neelam proudly said exactly what the anthropologists Banerjee and Miller report in their book about the sari: students admire their favorite teachers so much that they often tell their mothers to look and act more like them.[8]

Teachers, by entering the educational workforce, have to deal with the scrutiny of impressionable schoolchildren, the watchful eye of the school officials, and the competitive gaze of their colleagues. The context of work in public adds a level of complication to one's self-presentation, albeit an exciting one. Neelam meets this challenge six days a week with a freshly starched cotton sari, matching bangles on one wrist, a watch on the other, and an attractive and dignified presence.

At Parties

The special occasion of the party, like the common occasion of work, requires adjustments of adornment that prompt judgments. Neelam, like any Indian woman, is keenly aware of the close "inspection" given her by the other guests at parties—observations that are sometimes mild and passive but sometimes harsh. Neelam, like many women, uses the verb *tokna*—to scold—to characterize the reactions of guests at social events. Though they are less formal than the rules at school, there are rules and standards of appearance that guests are expected to meet, as Neelam explains:

"I am conscious *especially* when I have to go to a wedding, and everybody is going to look at me, and they will say: 'She has come from the Chaturvedi *family,* and is not wearing jewelry, is not wearing that.' So thinking about this, I get ready in front of the mirror. 'That I do have jewelry, and to show you that I do, I am *especially* wearing it!' *Otherwise,* no.

"There is also this *alarm* in the head that I have to go [to the party], and every single person will be scolding and noticing, and will be *pointing it* out there, so: 'Wear, wear, wear!'"

In Private

Body art is built for context, and contexts are diverse. Neelam dresses for the public—for the street, the classroom, the party—and she dresses for distinct private spheres: downstairs, where she sits with the rest of the family, upstairs in her private room when she is with her husband, and finally, upstairs in her private room when her husband is asleep or away and her audience has been reduced to herself alone.

The joint family compound is a semi-private space, through which people, related and not, move constantly. When she is at home, Neelam conforms to the wishes of her mother-in-law and to the norms of local custom, since she is always within view of others. She wears the obligatory wifely ornaments that make up the *nishan*—the sign—of a married woman from Uttar Pradesh. Her appearance is like her appearance at work, except she exchanges the sari she wore at school for a comfortable *salwar suit.*

In India, people normally change into "home clothes" when they arrive in the house. They remove their shoes at the threshold, and change their clothes soon after entering so as to keep dirt outside of the house. Their practice also reduces wear and tear on their clothes. Nice saris, if worn at home, would be stained by spills, ripped, and subjected to frequent hard washings. Most clothes in India are handed over to a *dhobi,* a washer, who removes the dirt by beating the clothes on a rock or slapping them on the floor, and then spreading them to dry in the sun that fades their colors. This method, though effective in cleaning, is harder on fabrics than washing machines are. So, once home, nice clothes are removed and hung up, probably to be worn another day. This habit is practical, economical, and comfortable. At home, people tend to wear light cotton clothing, which is cool and casual, right for housework or lounging around. Since the social spaces of the house—the living room, veranda, and central courtyard—are not totally private, they require appropriate dress. At home, many Indian women wear "housecoats" or "maxis," long cotton dresses usually made from printed floral fabric. Home clothes should not be too revealing or sexy, nor too formal or glamorous. Alluring dress would cause the neighbors to speculate on intentions: why would she look so chic at home when her husband is away? Such judgments are relentless, and a source of irritation.

The only area of the house that is truly private is the bedroom. Couples

256

are given a private room in the joint-family compound soon after marriage for obvious reasons. Their private space becomes a refuge where the couple can be alone and engage in mildly flirtatious behavior—holding hands or sitting close together—affectionate gestures considered too embarrassing for the more public areas of the house.

The private context of the bedroom allows Neelam to communicate personally to her husband through her bodily adornment. Punjabi brides wear *chura,* the red and ivory-colored plastic bangles, for the first year or so of their marriage, after which they switch to golden bangles. Neelam wore *chura* for the first year of her marriage, then replaced them with the glass bangles traditionally worn in Banaras. Many years later, when she was no longer a new bride, Neelam was shopping on Vishvanath Gali and saw beautiful *chura* wedding bangles for sale. They were the "latest fashion," sprinkled with gold and silver "shining dust," and she fell instantly in love with them. She bought two "full sets," about two-dozen bangles, and wore them in her room for her husband, who loves to see her in jewelry.

Neelam took delight in telling me about this nearly scandalous act—her wearing of jewelry reserved "only for the newly married." She bought the bangles because they were Punjabi, and the kind of bangles she has always liked, pretty without the noisy clatter of Banarasi glass. Her husband likes to see her wearing much jewelry, and she wore a bride's pretty bangles for him in their room. No one else would ever see them, and Neelam wore the *chura* because she loves her husband. That is what she told me, expressing a sentiment uncommon among women, especially those who find themselves stuck in arranged marriages. They had a love marriage, and because they have no children, they can focus on each other more than other couples might. Neelam describes her situation well:

"It is like this, that on me there is no *responsibility.* There are no kids. There is nothing. I don't have to worry about anything. I just have to worry about my husband, and he only has to worry about me. The two of us only have to worry about each other: 'Yes, Neelam wants this from the store. I should bring this home.' 'Okay, he wants this thing.'—I mean, we are in tune with each other's needs.

"For those that have kids, they are always so *busy,* so *upset* about the children: 'Today she wants this.' 'Today he wants this.' After that, they are exhausted: 'Okay now so-and-so has come over to meet with the kids.' All day long, their *routine* is kept so *busy*, that in the middle of all this, they can't understand if *attention* should be paid more to the husband, or paid more to the kids, or paid to the guests that have just arrived, or to the family. If there are in-laws, then, 'Should I pay attention to them?'

"So, in this way, they are *irritated*. This *irritation* sometimes is linked to the children, sometimes it is linked to the husband, sometimes it is just part of the house. This is the way it is. In this way, we don't get *irritated*. We also get *irritated*, but not in this way. We get *balanced* because, later, in the *end*, it is the two of us who come together."

In the privacy of their bedroom, Neelam wears some jewelry for her husband that she does not like. Glass bangles, which belong to his tradition, not hers—he is Banarasi, she is Punjabi—are the key example. I asked her what happens if Vidhu falls asleep before she does. She laughed, and admitted that she removes the bangles as soon as he is asleep, since glass bangles cause "disturbance" to her own sleep. Neelam's husband sometimes travels on business, staying out of town for a few months at a time. I wondered how Neelam responded. When she gets upstairs, utterly alone, with no one to please but herself—would she wear any jewelry when he was out of town? "No, then I wouldn't wear," she said. When she is the sole beholder of her adornment, Neelam chooses not to wear much jewelry.

On Vacation, Far from Banaras

There is no single standard of adornment that women adhere to at all times. Personal adornment is created and recreated to fit specific social situations. Neelam's attitudes about what should be worn are contingent upon the public and private contexts she occupies regularly. Decisions about clothing and jewelry depend primarily on the expectations and judgments of the audience at each of her venues—at work, at parties, relaxed in the parlor, bejeweled for the bedroom. Neelam enters her final important context of display when she goes on vacation with her husband. Being away gives Neelam a chance to move among people she does not know. The public streets of an unknown city can, ironically, become nearly a private arena for display, since in walking through them, one is free from the scrutiny of the "local public." One may wear different clothes, and even eat different and forbidden food, when away from home. Arjun Appadurai argues that food consumption during travel, at restaurants, can result in an alteration of ordinary food norms because one is away, protected in anonymity from those who might see and judge.[9]

While in Banaras, Neelam has to conform to the rules of the school and to the social pressure to look good, to dress in accordance with her family and caste standards, but when she is away on vacation, she can ignore those regulations and the rules of age and marital status. When Neelam and her husband are "out of station," she likes to wear jeans and "tops," an outfit usually reserved for younger, unmarried women. On a trip to the hill station of Nainital, in northern Uttar Pradesh, Neelam wore "black metal" ornaments, trendy silver jewelry she bought at one of the tourist shops along Janpath Road in New Delhi. Neelam also took along an "artificial pearl" set to wear while sightseeing with her husband.

Neelam could wear jeans and black metal jewelry in Nainital because nobody was there to scold her, nobody to gossip about her inappropriate attire. She could dress like a college girl. It could be that a romantic getaway with one's husband, when social and professional responsibilities are left behind, allows one to fantasize about youth and love, and so to revert to the clothes worn before marriage. Youthful clothes feel liberating, so does artificial jewelry, and for both there are practical reasons. Jeans are easier to pack and wear on a trip, and expensive jewelry carries with it a fear of crime and loss. Traveling on Indian trains, sleeping in strange hotels, surrounded by unknown, perhaps untrustworthy, people would lead to much anxiety if one were carrying or wearing valuable heirlooms. Wearing artificial jewelry is sensible, and it can be left behind in the hotel room, because stealing cheap things is not worth the risk.

Since my initial interviews, Neelam has relocated with her husband to Rajasthan. She is still a teacher and visits Banaras and the home of her mother-in-law regularly, so the pattern of her life has not changed dramatically, but living in Rajasthan with her husband, away from a joint family, has expanded her private contexts of body art. When she is home, Neelam told me, she feels free to roam the entire house in the clothes she had previously worn only in her bedroom, such as trousers, T-shirts, and shorts. In the scorching hot weather of Rajasthan's desert, shorts and T-shirts, though they expose the legs and arms, make sense.

In each context of display the audience differs, but all ultimately interconnect. How one looks at work, for example, is not confined to the workplace; it will be communicated verbally to others in other social settings. The word

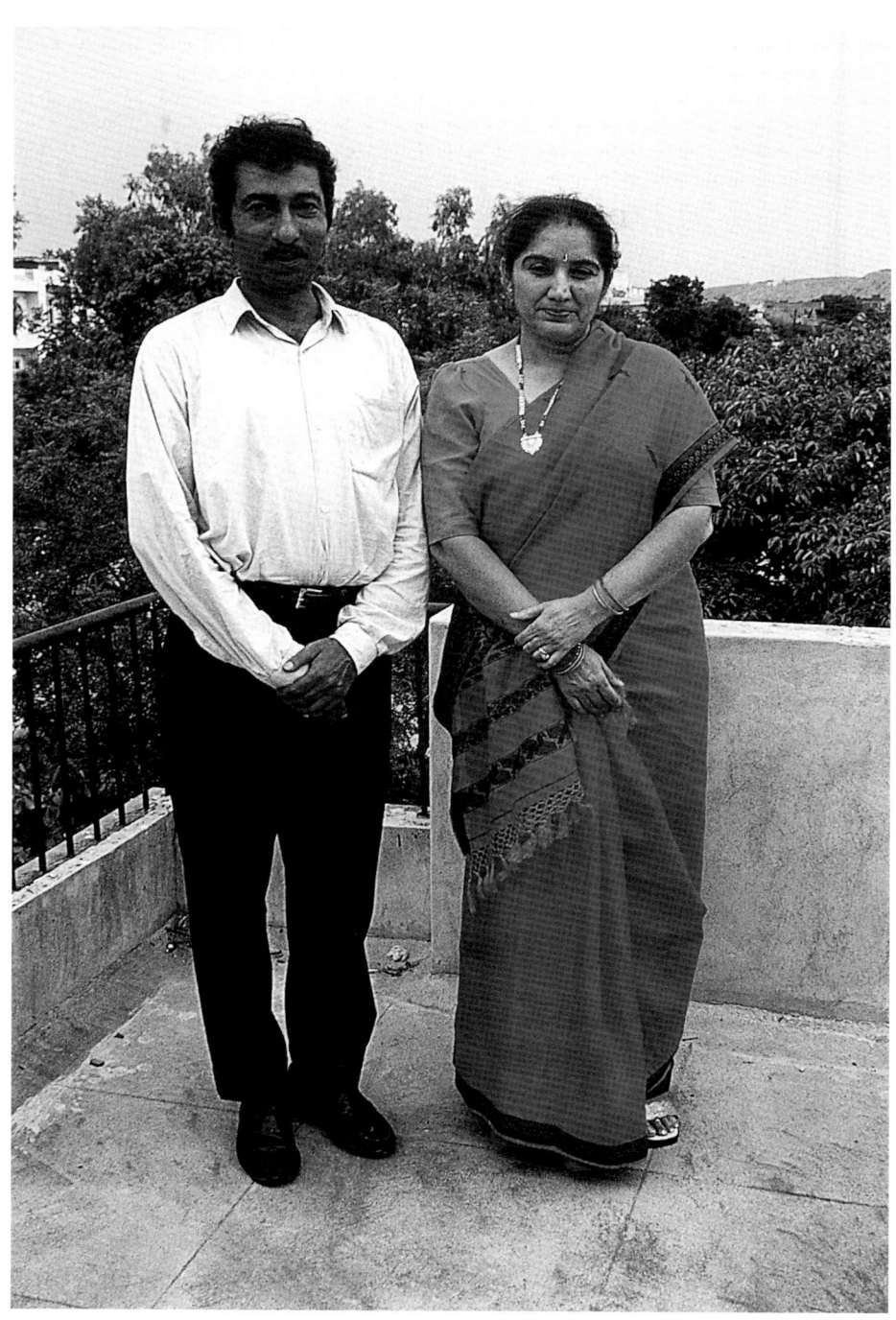

Vidhu and Neelam Chaturvedi

will circulate among the people of a social network that is constantly reconfigured, transforming as it reaches out to connect with other networks, circling back, expanding outward.

When analyzing body art, it is important for us to remember that contexts are not mutually exclusive—they run together in influence. But to arrive at the relation of art to meaning, and context to context, we must situate bodily display in a range of distinct settings. I asked Neelam who she wants to look good for, and she gave me a layered answer. In the bedroom, she wants her husband to like her look. Downstairs, she wants to please her mother-in-law. Outside of the house, in the marketplace, she wants to look good for others, but also for her husband, who will "compare" her to other women on the streets, and think, "My wife is pretty at home, *and* here among other women." At wedding receptions, she wants to look good for the people attending the party, so that they will compliment her in the presence of her husband, reinforcing his positive opinion of his wife's beauty. He will be assured that not only does *he* think his wife is pretty, but others feel the same way too. Neelam's intelligent analysis of her motivations shows that, while the audience differs at each venue, there are two main constants—her husband and herself.

Choosing to look good for the students and teachers, or for the other guests at a party, is really choosing to look good for yourself, since you are conscious of how others react to you in all of the environments you occupy. The question is, who do you want to look good for? The final answer for Neelam—as it is for most women—is herself. I asked her how she knows she looks good.

"I will not be looking at myself, constantly looking at myself, because I have seen that some people walk on the streets and are only looking at their own selves, and that is a really bad habit. This is a really bad habit that they don't even glance at others, but are constantly looking at their own selves: 'How do I look?' 'I look like this.' 'I look like that.' So, no! When I get *dressed up,* I will stand in front of the mirror and inspect myself well. Then all day, I will not look at myself in the mirror.

"If I get dressed up one day, I go downstairs, and as soon as I get downstairs, *mummy* [her mother-in-law] says: 'This sari looks good, you look good.' Then my sister-in-law has said it. Then I go forward, and so-and-so has said it: 'You look nice today.' I go further still, and somebody else says: 'You look nice.' As long as there are compliments, I know that I still look good. I don't have to look in the mirror yet."

Neelam leaves the house in confidence. She wants her husband to appreciate her beauty, and acknowledges the comparisons he makes with other women. She wants to look good for herself, though she is attentive to response, to the compliments by which she checks her appearance.

The Tradition of the Self

Neelam creates her adorned presence to fit some specific context of viewing. Her clothes, makeup, and jewelry are chosen in relation to one of her contexts: the public arenas of work, parties, and travel, or the private arenas of home that range in intimacy. Although Neelam's body art differs in each of these contexts, there is an aesthetic consistency in her appearance; she is always more interested in her clothing than her jewelry. The self develops a tradition; there is an overarching personal style that prevails despite shifts of scene. Neelam Chaturvedi's style is different from Nina Khanchandani's, and both women are consistent within their own sets of preferences.

For Neelam and Nina, tradition is a framework within which they choose to operate, working simultaneously within it and against it to express an individual style. Tradition is not a law, mandating women to be and look a certain way; rather it is a flexible construction, held in the mind and perpetually open to manipulation. Both Neelam and Nina acknowledge the norms of acceptable adornment in India; they recognize the expected standards of caste, marital status, and age. Then, Neelam and Nina, like most women in India, elect to express their unique aesthetic and social preferences by working within the norms, the expectations, while creating their own distinct version of the general tradition of body adornment. They wear the clothing and jewelry that exhibits their traditions of the self, and, doing so, Neelam and Nina literally embody their desire and mediate the demands of religion, caste, society, and family. They adhere to social norms, yet they are unequivocally themselves, complete, and exactly like no other.

·12·

Mukta Tripathi

THOUGH MARRIED WOMEN in India are expected to be ornamented, some prefer to pay little attention to adornment and wear the minimum of jewelry, like Nina Khanchandani. Others, like Neelam Chaturvedi, indulge their affection for one kind of adornment—in her case, the sari—and downplay the others. Mukta Tripathi, a woman in her mid-forties and a mother of two, is, by contrast, passionate about all kinds of adornment.

I was directed to Mukta precisely because she is known to have a grand sense of personal style. Our conversations were lively and easy, because Mukta has carefully considered the variables that most people intuit but few can articulate.[1] Mukta spoke energetically, interrupting herself to illustrate her points. She succinctly verbalized the aesthetic choices women make daily, actively enriching their lives with creativity.

A Standard of Beauty

Mukta began her treatment of the levels of visual decision by focusing on the beauty of the actual piece of adornment. The item of jewelry or clothing, she said, must be good-looking. She likes to change her jewelry often, and, like most married women in Banaras, she buys new glass bangles regularly. But unlike others, Mukta also changes her *nath* (nose ring), *bichiya* (toe rings), and *payal* (anklets) with frequency; she finds it fun to vary her "compulsory" jewelry.

I asked her what criteria she employs when shopping for jewelry, and she

263

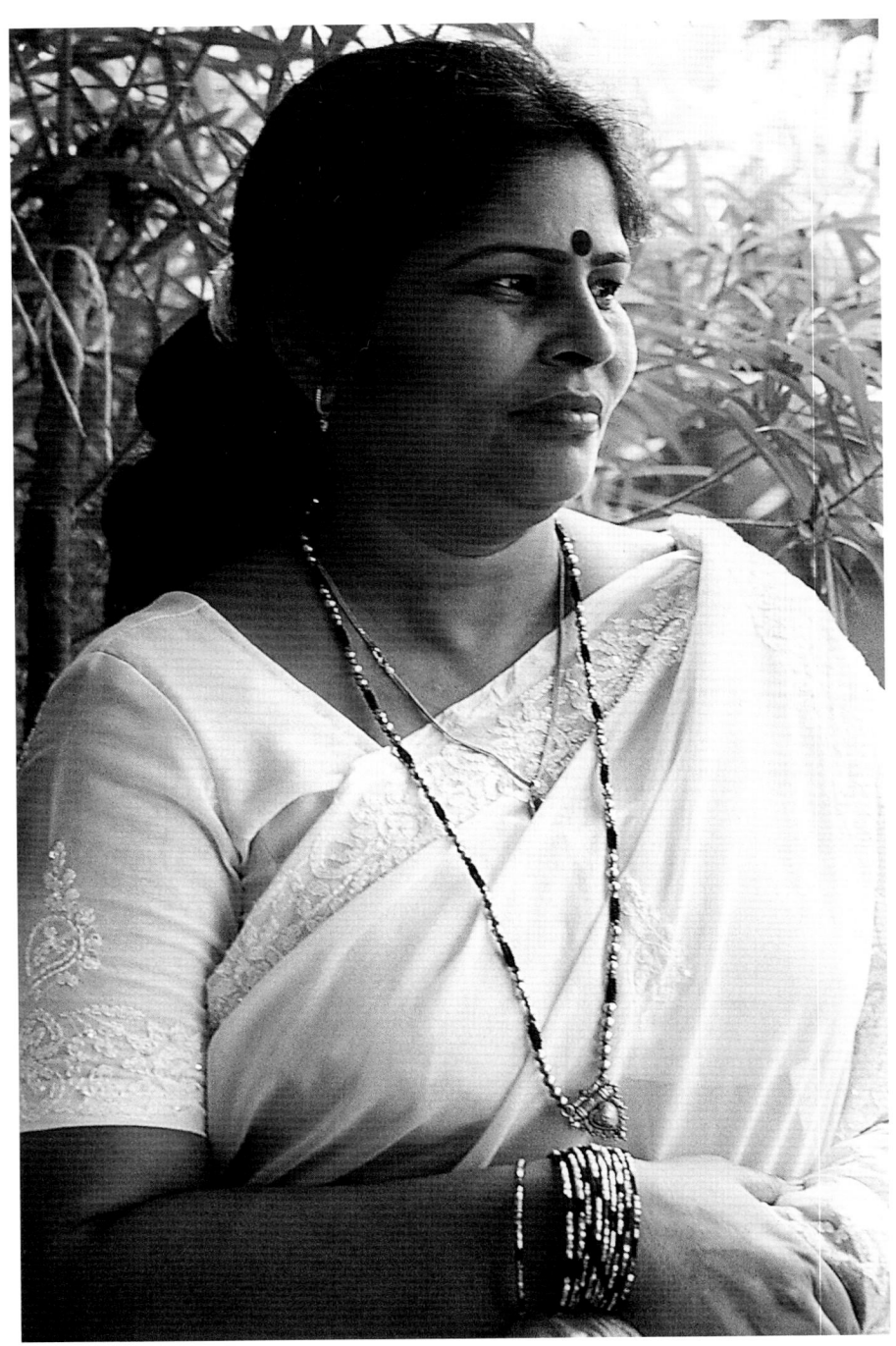

Mukta Tripathi

answered that she likes "delicate" toe rings and anklets that are *nakashi*—intricately worked—yet strong. Glass bangles, or *churis*, she chooses for color: "With *churi*, the *color* I wear, I always wear *bright colors*, not *dull colors*. Because when I wear *bright colors*, my hands look *saf*. And with *dull colors*, the hands look *daba-daba*. When I wear clothes, I wear *bright* clothes. I don't wear *dark* clothes."

Brightly colored *churi* have the ability to make Mukta's hands look *saf*. The term, in its etymological depth and linguistic spread, derives from a word for simply woven, undyed cloth, and carries connotations of simplicity, innocence, and cleanliness. In colloquial Hindi, *saf* means clean, and it implies fair skin. By contrast, dark or dull colors make Mukta's hands seem *daba*, the word repeated for emphasis. *Daba* literally means "crushed," and it implies a muted and lackluster look.

What one wears can influence the perception of skin tone; the right color can make the hands look fair, suggesting membership in a high, non-laboring social class. For this reason, Mukta prefers "delicate" anklets that "add *softness* to the feet," and she carefully avoids the "heavy-heavy" anklets that make her feet "look like the *dehati* people's—look *gavar-type*."

Mukta likes bright jewelry that is delicate in form, and she avoids chunky ornaments that are associated with villagers—the *dehati* and *gavar*. Her consistency in clothes and makeup attests to a strong and consciously developed personal style. When she selects clothing, Mukta's main interest is not in the material or print, but in the color of the fabric: "My preference is always *light*. I always like *sober, light*. *Dark* clothes, and *dark* things, I don't like very much. I wear things of my *liking*, and if somebody gives me something of my *liking*, then I wear it. Because I only wear very *sober-type* clothes, I can't wear very *dark* lipstick. I like all *light-light shades*. These *reds, maroons*, those don't *suit* me."

Mukta sees a reciprocal relationship between an ornament and the body being ornamented. Jewelry, clothing, and makeup make the body beautiful, but one must also maintain the beauty of the body itself; it is the background against which ornaments are judged. Mukta pays particular attention to the body's ends—the hands and feet—for these parts, always on display, are often neglected. To take full advantage of ornaments for the hands and feet, Mukta takes special care of the context on which she arrays her display—her body: "I always wear bangles. I never just let my hands be. I feel like, just like my *face*—how people are always concerned with their *face*—in that way, I am always concerned with my hands and feet. A lot of people think of hands and feet: 'Oh, what is the purpose of these? Leave them alone.' But I give a lot of care to my hands and feet."

She does so, she told me, by avoiding regular nail polish, for its chemicals ruin the natural shine of the nails. She also applies a homemade beauty treatment made of *malai* cream and *besan,* the chickpea flour that is the principal ingredient of *pakoras,* Indian fritters. When mixed with other ingredients, these readily available kitchen substances yield a thick paste that is rubbed on the hands, arms, and face. Once it has been allowed to dry, the paste is washed off, revealing a soft and newly exfoliated skin that glows. Many women make this simple pomade,[2] but it is usually applied to the face and hands, not the feet. Mukta obviously pays careful attention to her feet, and it shows; they are indeed beautiful. For her face, she prefers a simple look: "I don't put *powder* on my face. I wash my face with just a little bit of soap. After having washed my face, I just put on a *bindi* and *sindur,* very *natural.* In this way my face looks good. Not too many *artificial* things. When I wear *sindur* and *bindi,* I feel like *grace* has been added to my face."

Mukta believes that beauty results from an artful assemblage created on the body. Jewelry and the body must match each other; she sees them as interdependent. But individual items of adornment must also suit each other, coming together in an appealing way. While she conforms to the norms of acceptable ensemble, Mukta adds a top layer, rich with personal taste. Most married women in India wear a sari with gold jewelry, especially when they are attending a social function. Mukta is no exception, but instead of simply matching the attire (sari) with the jewelry (gold), she matches the color and material of the sari with the material and style of the jewelry, taking the daily task one step further. I asked Mukta to describe one of these successful combinations. She said, "For example, if there is a *pink color* sari, with that I will wear all pearl jewelry. Like a *pink color* or yellow color sari—with these, I usually tend to wear pearl *sets.* That's what looks good, on *pink.*"

Mukta's instance reveals her taste. The tone of one's skin and the color of the sari are crucial to the judgment of a piece of jewelry. Pearl jewelry, light and delicate, would look best on a translucent background of light pink or light yellow, instead of a visually "heavy" material, with a dense, flashy floral design.

By taking the accepted, and expected, attire to a high level of refinement, Mukta creates a look that is beautiful and, more importantly, unique. Her

266

desire to appear attractive is surpassed by her desire to appear different from everybody else. In her circle of friends, Mukta is known for her taste; she explained: "When I wear a sari—recently I wore a white sari and went somewhere—everybody started saying that 'In the stores there are many saris available, but the ones you bring home, they are very different.'" Encouraged by the positive feedback from her peers, Mukta strives consciously to achieve a look that stands out:

"I think that I should wear things different from other women. Different. Different. For example, if there is a hairstyle going—some *heroine* in a *picture* cut her hair some way—then everybody has also cut her hair that way. At that moment, I will certainly not cut my hair at all.

"Like if there is a sari *fashion,* then all the women—that same sari, that same sari—they will all start buying. That same sari, I will certainly not even touch!

"Or some jewelry fashion—like today this *chain* is in, or this toe ring is in, or this anklet. Then I will not wear those, because it looks so *common.* From lower class to upper class, all people are wearing that same thing. Then those things I will not even touch. I will be totally apart from it, separate."

Mukta not only rejects the fashion trends set by the Bollywood heroines, she rejects what she sees as a conspicuous lack of imagination among the women around her. She wants to look different from the fashion models celebrated by the media, and also different from the women in her immediate circle who display a version of the larger current trend. Mukta, like many women, feels that in wearing what is fashionable one is choosing to look like everybody else, including the maid and "Mrs. Rickshawwallah," thus abandoning all sense of visual discrimination and social class. Here Mukta contrasts with Nina, who wants to "be with the crowd," and with Neelam, who does not pull the trends of fashion directly from the original media sources but, instead, gets ideas for fashionable dress indirectly from her co-workers, the willing "models" at the Sunbeam School. Mukta does not want to look like anybody else, ever. She elaborates:

"I have never—at a *party,* at a wedding—I have never been like every other woman. I have always had my own *personality,* my own look, created to be different. Just like with *spray.* I have chosen one *spray,* so if somebody were to smell my clothes, they would recognize them as Mukta's clothes, because they emit that same scent that I wear.

"Or, there is a soap that is mine. I have kept my preferences separate. It's not like: 'This soap is good, I will use it.' 'This one is also good, I will use it.' It's not like that. All of my things are different."

Since Mukta adamantly wants to be different, since she wishes not to look "common," she has created for herself a "typical" look. From the angle of the common tradition, she stands apart, centered firmly in her distinct, personal tradition. "I like one *typical*—whatever thing I like, I make that thing my own, because that thing looks good on me, and that's it." In order to create, and recreate, her unique look—for a look is unique for only so long as nobody else does it—Mukta must be just as aware of the current trend as the people who are following it closely. How could she know *not* to cut her hair in a certain way unless she knows that a popular Bollywood heroine has just cut her hair in that way? A unique look, by definition, needs to be seen in relation to others. Some knowledge of the current fads is necessary for both Nina, whose desire is to "be with the crowd," and Mukta, whose wish is the opposite. Their goals are opposed, but both create themselves in reaction to others.

For you to be beautiful, Mukta says, your jewelry must be well made and attractive, and its frame of skin or cloth must also be good-looking. But the body, art's walking frame, needs to be suitable—in softness and color, in structure and shape. Jewelry and clothing must go together, and they must go with the body they adorn. In discussing her preferences and look, Mukta spoke openly about the type of her body and the shape of her face, explaining how these factors become crucial when shopping for clothing and jewelry.

One drawback of following a fashion blindly is wearing something that does not quite suit one's body. The result is a clumsy appropriation that ironically thwarts the goal of body art. Even if she wanted to follow a new style, Mukta said, she could not necessarily do so, because her body type is not the body type of the models and heroines who promote new fads. Her rejection of a trend might not result from a lack of appreciation for the style but from deep self-awareness.

My first conversations with Mukta took place in the summer of 1996, when *Dilvale Dulhania Lejaenge*—"The Soulful Shall Carry Away the Bride"—was the most popular movie in India, and the stars, the hero Shah Rukh Khan and the heroine Kajol, were much adored. The soundtrack was omnipresent, spilling continually from shops and restaurants. Posters with scenes from the movie, especially one of Kajol in a lime-green silk *lehanga,* her arms laden with bangles, were posted everywhere in Banaras, and it launched a taste for lime green women's garments. As Kajol was the favorite of the era, I used her as my example when I asked Mukta whether or not she was tempted to imitate the Bollywood stars. Like everyone in India at the time, Mukta knew exactly what Kajol looked like:

"I absolutely am not influenced by *pictures.* Because Kajol, she has a particular *figure,* and certain clothes *suit* her *figure.* I look at my own *figure*—like my *hips,* they are wide. So I don't wear clothes with big-big *prints.* I always buy clothes with small *prints.* I buy very *sober* clothes. I buy clothes with vertical stripes. So that I attempt to look *slim.* I look at my own body in order to buy clothes. If I wear big-big *prints,* then I feel like I am looking fat-fat; wide-wide. Regardless of what *fashion* is current—what is in the *pictures*—in these directions I have never gone. I always pay attention to what I like."

For Mukta, as for any reasonable person, looking good is more important than following a trend. Mukta wears clothes that make her look slim rather than clothes that make her look like Kajol. Their figures are different. Judgments about weight are made in relation with other people, and often in terms of a particular aspect of the body. When she spoke of her preferences in clothing, Mukta said she likes slimming prints, but when I asked her about jewelry, Mukta's answer suggested a contradictory self-view. I asked if jewelry can affect the perception of one's weight, and she responded enthusiastically: "Yes, this is true of jewelry as well. For example, if I were to wear long hoop earrings, then this part of my face looks more sunken," she said, pointing to her cheek, "because this is already hollow, the bone is high here. If I were to wear long jewelry, then this part would look even more sunken." Mukta again touched her high cheekbones, her hollow cheeks, and went on: "In India, in terms of Indian beauty, a *gol-matol* woman is considered beautiful—that her face be full, that she be totally round, that she be *healthy.* That is considered a good thing."

The traditional Indian beauty has a softly rounded "moon face" and a rounded, curvaceous figure, thus the term *gol-matol.* Mukta understands the culturally relative nature of judgments of beauty. She knows that the Indian taste is not universal:

"In *foreign countries,* this sunken thing is considered beautiful. There was a tenant of my *mummy's,* John. He would say that your daughter's *beauty* is a *foreign beauty,* that this part is sunken. But this thing, here in India—Indian people don't like it. Here they see *heroines'* faces, and they see that their faces are full-full, and that is what they like. Because everybody has their own preferences."

Mukta went on to speak of her hairstyle: "Say somebody's face is really full, and they were to wear long earrings, that would also not look good. Hairstyles also depend on the face. If somebody has hollow cheeks, and she were to wear her hair tightly back, then her cheeks would look even hollower. So the face counts, also the jewelry." Mukta solves the problem of hollow cheeks by not wearing long earrings and not pulling her hair back tightly. In recognition of certain "problem areas" the sensitive and attentive masters of body art adjust their creative assemblage to camouflage one feature and bring another to attention.

In India one crucial variable in beauty is skin color. Mukta explained: "Weight counts, and color also counts. If there is a dark-skinned girl, and she wears pearls, then against the dark, the white-white [of the pearls] will really shine, so it won't look good." Pearls make the dark skin look darker, but, in Mukta's opinion, pearls look good against subtle shades of light pink or pale yellow. Jewelry and its backdrop—the neck or the sari—must achieve a gentle balance of contrast.

I asked Mukta if she avoids certain things because she does not like them, or because they do not suit her—the two being distinctly different aspects of aesthetic evaluation. She said she likes some things, such as red lipstick, that she cannot wear, and continued:

"If I were to wear *dark* things, then—like if I were to wear *dark lipstick—* then my face would look *dull-dull.* If I were to wear *makeup* [foundation], then my face would look black-black. And if I were to wear *light makeup,* then my face would look very *saf.* That is why I don't wear *dark makeup.*

"How things look on my *skin,* I know. For example, say there is a new *makeup* introduced—this kind of *cream,* that kind of *cream*—I can't use everything."

I next asked Mukta to reflect on the *bindi.* An important marker of marital status, the *bindi* is placed prominently on a woman's forehead and is often the first piece of adornment to be noticed. This is what she said:

"Okay, somebody's face is egg-shaped, somebody's is long, somebody's is round, somebody's is square. There are faces of all kinds. So, for example, on my face, with the exception of a round *bindi,* if I were to wear a long one, it would not look good. Or if I were to wear an egg-shaped *bindi,* it would not look good. On my face, only a plain round *bindi* looks good. I can't wear other types of *bindi.*

"When I put a long *bindi* and look in the mirror, it looks like no *grace* has been added to my face."

Men and women are accountable for their aesthetic decisions; they should be able to figure out whether an outfit suits them on the basis of weight, age, or the social context of display. Their awareness makes some people look better than others; some are better than others in maximizing their aesthetic potential.

I wondered if Mukta thought that people could make themselves more attractive by choosing appropriate adornment. She felt strongly that people do have the ability, whether they use it or not, to discover what looks good on them, and most of the men and women in this book agree with her. Mukta illustrated her position with general principles. Fat people, she said, should wear vertical stripes, making them look taller and thinner, and they should not wear tight clothing; a loose-fitting *salwar kurta* suit is right for the heavy woman. These unsurprising observations attest to Mukta's commonsensical approach to body art. She also thinks that a thin person should wear clothes with big prints to appear fuller, causing an optical illusion that expands the frame of the body. Although the Indian media follow the global trend in preferring thin models and actresses, for most Indian people, the thin person looks underfed and overworked, and therefore poor. Women like Mukta do not want to appear too wide, but they also do not want to look skinny.

When it comes to assessments of weight, Mukta wants to make one part of her body appear thinner (her hips) and one part seem fuller (her face). Women like Mukta can view different parts of their bodies separately; their bodies are segmentable aesthetic units. The talent in this analytic act is to consider the parts independently, while making sure they all hold together well. Mukta creates her beauty by carefully camouflaging or emphasizing different aspects of herself: body weight, bone structure, skin tone. These, in turn, are handled appropriately with the right fabric, jewelry form, face cream, lipstick shade, and *bindi* shape. She breaks beauty down, but the beholder perceives an aesthetic whole, a harmonized unit.

While beholders are taken by a person's overall appearance, they have, like the creator, the ability to break a person's look into smaller units for closer analysis. Mukta was able to give concrete examples of combinations that do not look good, based on her observations of people and the generally understood conventions of adornment. In India, the most disturbing taboo of adornment is to wear something that is inappropriate to one's developmental stage. The sight of a fat woman wearing tight clothes can be mildly amusing, but if an old woman were dressed as a young bride, it would be considered scandalous and improper—more than an aesthetic blunder, it is a serious social indiscretion.

Personal adornment in India should be age-specific at all times, for it marks life's transitions. In delineating Mukta's aesthetic criteria and choices about self-adornment, we move from purely aesthetic decisions and build toward choices embedded in developmental contexts.

Wifely Adornment

Jewelry is commonly believed to be a "compulsory" marker of marital status; it dominated one part of my conversation with Mukta. Although Mukta is a self-proclaimed connoisseur of adornment, she admits to feeling sometimes that she is forced to wear certain items of jewelry—the nose ring, for example. She got her nose pierced after marriage, *jaberjasti,* against her will, to appease her in-laws. She was introduced to much of the jewelry she now wears with pleasure at the time of her marriage, when the "compulsory" items marking *suhag*—the blissful state of being married—became part of her daily adornment: *sindur* on the part through her hair, *bindi* on her forehead, *nath* on her nose, a gold chain around her neck, *churi* on her wrists, *payal* on her ankles, and *bichiya* on her toes.

Mukta wears this jewelry, she says, because it is *parampara,* the Indian tradition. Having heard this reason often, from both men and women, I asked Mukta exactly why this is the case, why the Indian *parampara* mandates that women be adorned. She alluded, in her answer, to the power of culture:

"Women wear jewelry in India because it has been made that way. After marriage, these have to be worn. Before marriage, you can wear *salwar kurta,* or any clothes. After marriage, it has been made that in a sari you should stay—the *ladies.* After marriage, they only wear saris. In this way, among us, this has been made, that after marriage one should wear jewelry, one should wear a nose ring, one should wear toe rings. On the neck, one should certainly wear a *chain,* a *mangalsutra.*

"That is why I wear these things. In our family, there is a mother-in-law and a father-in-law, and we are scared that if we appear bare-necked, somebody will scold us: 'Why are you this way?' That is why it needs to be worn."

I asked Mukta if she also wore jewelry for beauty, for *sundarta.* Her response was expectedly enthusiastic, and it added a layer above the notion that jewelry symbolizes migration through rites of passage:

"Yes, I wear jewelry also for *sundarta.* Because before marriage, girls remain very *simple.* After marriage, there is some *change.* With the wearing of jewelry, there is some *change.* So, that is the way: also for beauty one wears jewelry.

"After marriage girls wear *mehendi,* they wear saris, they wear *churis.* They look totally different. You can tell that they are married. And that also feels nice. And before marriage, there is also this desire that 'Once I am married, I will wear these things, I will look this way.' That is why they wear jewelry."

Once she has married, a woman must observe the stricter rules of caste and proper attire. Young women often wear silver jewelry, but once they become *suhagin*—decorated, married—they must change, as Mukta explained:

"In our custom, silver is worn on the feet. They say that people of low class, they wear silver on the neck, silver on the ears, after marriage. In maidenhood, we could wear silver on the ears. But once marriage has taken place, then a silver *chain* on the neck—people don't regard that well. They will say: 'Now that your marriage has taken place, don't wear silver, wear gold instead.'"

The prohibition of silver ornaments for people of high caste or class is ostensibly linked to an association of gold with the goddess Lakshmi and an association of silver with lower caste women. People of the lower castes wear silver to signal their difference and to prevent accidental contamination: it is said that a high-caste person should not drink water from the hands of anyone who does not wear gold. Such factors of religion and caste purity are given as reasons for the separation by caste and age of those who are allowed to wear gold and those who are not.

Wishing to gather rationales for jewelry wearing, I asked Mukta if she believed there was a practical reason for young brides, or any married woman, to wear noisy anklets. Did she wear noisy *payal* as a bride in the *sasural,* her new conjugal home?

"Yes. This is why: Over there, I am the daughter-in-law. And in the *sasural,* you are not supposed to be around your father-in-law, you are not supposed to be around your husband's older brothers. So if my father-in-law is coming from there to here, and I am going from here to there, then if my anklets sound, then my father-in-law will realize that 'my daughter-in-law is coming.' So he will remove himself from the path.

"Because in the old days—now people have started talking to their fathers-in-law—but in the old days, in the villages, people would not talk to their fathers-in-law, or their husband's older brothers. Whenever they would come our way, they would [Mukta clears her throat] so that they will know, so that we will know, that they are approaching. And we also—this is why we are to wear *payal*—that if we are descending the staircase, they will know that the daughter-in-law is coming down, by the sound of the *payal.*"

Noisy jewelry—such as the anklet with bells—creates a lovely sound that pleases women like Mukta and Neelam. It also functions to communicate between relatives for whom interaction is taboo. As Susan Wadley explained in her study of joint families in northern India, all members of the household—including the sons, their wives, and their mother—must show respect to the family patriarch by avoiding certain behaviors in his presence, as a way of maintaining the harmony and the hierarchy of the household.[3] All the daughters-in-law of a joint household share the taboo that keeps them away from their father-in-law, but it is the youngest one, the new bride, who wears the most bells on her ankles. Differences in the number of *ghungrus*—silver bells—on the anklet mark a shift of stage in a woman's life, Mukta said. Young brides, who were previously unadorned, are the noisiest at the time of marriage and for a short while after.

"The new-new daughters-in-law, they mostly wear the *payals* with *ghungrus*. Because there is this new-new *shauk*. Unmarried women think, 'Once my marriage takes place, I will wear the *payal* with *ghungrus* on them.' That *shauk* comes from before marriage, but it is only after marriage that—even after marriage, for two to three years women indulge in this *shauk*. After that, when she has children, then toward jewelry and clothes, that much attention does not go. It does not go *daily*. After marriage, for one year, there are no children anyway, then there is nothing to do; changing jewelry, getting dressed up IS what there is to do. And doing the housework."

I asked if Mukta indulged in adornment for the first few years of her marriage, and she responded: "Yes, when I was a new-new daughter-in-law, I lived at my *sasural*. Then ten people would come to see, to see my face. So I would get dressed up. I would wear nice saris. *Daily* I would wear nice saris. I would be in full-full jewelry. And *full makeup*. But my *makeup* has never been *gaudy—light makeup*."

Mukta refers to the traditional practice of *moo-dikhai*—the showing of the bride's face. Since most marriages in India are still arranged, friends and relatives of the groom come to see the bride, to get acquainted with the new addition to the household. This is one of the main reasons the newly arrived bride is dressed up in the first year or so of her marriage. She must be beautiful and presentable to the parade of the curious. A bride, dressed in her finery, cannot be doing the household chores. Expensive saris would get ruined during food preparation, and outside visitors would see that the older members of the household were already beginning to work the new daughter-in-law. The first year of marriage, then, is a time for the new bride to get acquainted with her new city or village, her new family and home, learning the work routines and food preferences of her new residence. I asked Mukta if she did much work during her first year at the *sasural:*

"No, I did not do work; very little work. For example, I would sometimes prepare the snacks, or make the tea. I would never make the entire meal. I was one year at the *sasural*. After that, when, with my husband, we started living in a separate *flat,* then I lessened the amount of jewelry, then I would not cover my head anymore, then I started to live in my own *tarika.*"

Living on your own is a fantasy and a luxury for many of the young brides I spoke to. You are finally away from the watchful eyes of the in-laws, safe from the scrutiny of relatives and acquaintances. Once in your own flat, you can wear the amount of jewelry you want to wear, you can be less modest, you can start to develop your own individual style, your own *tarika.* This is an important step in the developmental sequence of life, the beginning of existence as an independent married couple.

Many women believe it is improper for a seasoned wife, one who has been married for a few years, to indulge in a young bride's *shauk* for jewelry. Once a couple has been married for a few years, the woman, whether in a flat of her own or in a joint-family household, takes over the chores that are considered inappropriate to thrust upon a new bride shortly after her arrival. Children, likewise, demand time and attention from the young mother.

A woman who is still paying much attention to her personal adornment after many years of marriage risks the censure of her peers. Many view the time a woman spends on herself as time stolen from her house, her husband, and her children. On the other hand, it is socially acceptable to break certain adornment rules if the act benefits other members of the household. Mukta did not wear the obligatory cluster of glass bangles on her wrists when her two boys were babies. She wore a gold *kara,* a thick bangle, on each wrist instead. Glass bangles break easily, and they often break when one is handling an infant, exposing the baby to mild physical danger. Like many women in India, Mukta altered her wifely jewelry when her sons were little.

Changes in body art signal stages in life. Right after her marriage, Mukta was fully ornamented, living in the house of her in-laws. A year later, she relaxed into her own *tarika,* living in a flat of her own. Two years later, she signaled motherhood with her personal adornment; *sindur* and *bindi* communicated her marital status, but the absence of glass bangles told of the baby currently in her charge. As we will see in the following chapters, jewelry marks every major social stage of a woman's life, from maidenhood to widowhood.

One dresses at once to exhibit social status and to fit the context of display. Recalling how Neelam expertly adjusted her appearance to different settings, I asked Mukta to discuss her adornment for daily and special occasions, considering how her theories were actualized in performance.

Simple at Home

Unlike Nina and Neelam, Mukta spent a short amount of time living in a joint family household under the watchful, critical eye of a mother-in-law. Unlike Neelam, Mukta does not work outside of the house. At home, Mukta prefers to be clean and simple: no makeup, no fancy jewelry, cool cotton clothing. Simplicity fits the needs of housework, and it meets the social norm of appearing relatively plain at home. An advantage of daily plainness is how exciting it makes the act of getting dressed up to go out. Like the unmarried girls with their enthusiasm for looking different once married, Mukta cites the thrill of *change* as a benefit of going unadorned through most days and then dressing carefully, slowly, beautifully, for grand special occasions.

"If I were to *daily-daily* wear *makeup,* then when I got ready to go out, there would be no *change.* That is why at home I stay in a totally *simple tarika*—I mean, I will wear clean clothes, nice clothes, but always in *full makeup,* with *lipstick*—no. Just *bindi* and *sindur,* because it is a *sign,* it is a *marriage sign.* That is why I wear these all the time. And if I am to go out, then I will wear some *lipstick,* change the *bindi,* then with the addition of these, it will look good. It looks a little different."

Mukta's adornment for special occasions—for a grand wedding reception or a night at the movies—suits the scene and expresses her. Accustomed to seeing herself in a certain way, she is pleased to look different, prettier, out in public. Mukta and her husband both enjoy the change in her, the way she signals with her body that she is getting out of the house, prepared to face a new audience.

Earlier, Mukta said that she does not follow fashion, that she always wants to look different from other people. Now we understand that her desire is to appear different not only in relation to other people, but also in relation to other versions of herself. At a party, she wants to look different from the movie stars, different from the other women, and different from the way she usually looks at home.

Mukta lives with her husband and two children. Theirs is not a joint-family household; there are few people around. I asked if she were self-conscious of visitors, and how she feels about opening the door while dressed in her *simple tarika.* "I just stay *simple,*" she said. "I go to the door *simple.* That person will see me at that time in a *simple rup.* Say I go to his house someday, and he will think: 'Oh, that day when I went to her house, she looked a certain way. Today, she looks—*changed.*' It makes a difference." She chose her words interestingly when she said, "*simple rup.*" The word *rup* is usually used in the context of gods, implying incarnation in a distinct form; Krishna as a *rup* of Lord Vishnu, for example. Mukta's vernacular application of a sacred concept to the act of self-adornment parallels the secular use of the concept of *darshan*—sacred vision—to include the reception of visual information of all kinds, and to acknowledge, by extended gaze, the beauty of a mere mortal in the street.

Shortly before the long interview with Mukta that I am reporting here, I had interviewed a woman named Aarti at a wedding reception in Azam Ghar, just outside of Banaras. Aarti told me that whenever the doorbell rang in her house, she would quickly put on lipstick and check herself in the mirror before opening the door. I asked Mukta if she also got herself together before opening the door. "No, because, at my house, I am not wearing *makeup* or looking really good. But I look *normal.* My hair is combed, I keep myself *decent* so that if somebody were to unexpectedly come over, I would not have to flee. I mean, I would greet the person. Just like I am right now, that is how I am at home."

In fact, I had unexpectedly shown up at Mukta's mother's house for our interview. Mukta did not know I was coming, yet she looked together. She had on a pale yellow housecoat—an ankle length, short sleeve cotton dress. She had no makeup on, but her face was radiant. Deep red *sindur* filled the part in her hair, asymmetrically placed to the left, and a big round *bindi* of the same shade centered her forehead. Her toenails were painted a shade of burgundy. On her toes she wore a pair of toe rings with tiny silver fish on each ring. She had shiny, delicate silver *payals* on her ankles.

I was most impressed with her hands. The backs of both of them were painted, like a bride's, with henna. She wore a henna version of the bridal "hand flower"—*hathphul*—on each hand, consisting of a single flower in the center, from which leafy vines extended to each fingertip. Her fingernails were painted the same shade as her toenails, and she wore a ring on each hand: on the left a magenta-colored stone set in gold, and on the right a pearl encased in silver. This last piece of jewelry was especially appropriate, for *mukta* means "pearl."

On Mukta's wrists she wore beautiful bangles of a kind I had never seen before, which is surprising given the time I have spent in the bangle shops of Banaras. Mukta's friends say that she has a special ability for finding unique things, and her bangles seemed to prove it. She wore a symmetrical array of bangles on each wrist. Each set consisted of ten blood-red glass bangles, festooned with white dots, bordered by a pair of thick white glass bangles scored with a single black horizontal stripe. The ruby-red bangles were the same shade as her *bindi* and *sindur*. The maroon of the henna stain complemented the nail polish on her hands and feet perfectly. This was Mukta in her *simple rup*. She sat across from me and talked while the tape recorder ran, and I could only imagine how good she must look when she expects to be seen. Mukta continued, reflecting on her behavior and appearance at home:

"In my house, if the doorbell rings once, before the second ring, I have gotten to the door to see who is there. I am home, and at home, *mostly* people are *normal*, and that is how I am. I don't know who that *third person* is, for whose sake I am quickly putting on bangles! It is okay, whoever it is, I will talk to him; if it is his [her husband's] friend, then I ask him in for tea. If he were to invite us to his house, then I would change my clothes, and go in a proper way. Because all people know that women have work to do in the house."

Working at home, women dress modestly. If they adorn themselves before opening the door, their act would be read not as an indication of insecurity—which was the case, I believe, with Aarti—but as a sign of promiscuity. Mukta explained: "This is really stupid that if somebody rings the doorbell, I quickly-quickly change my bangles. That I quickly-quickly put on a *bindi*. It looks strange, right? He will think: 'Look, for me she is coming all dressed up.'"

Body art is always judged in a particular social context. A woman dressed up to receive a male visitor in her home could be misread as flirtatious. As Julia Leslie has made clear, Sanskrit religious law explicitly prohibits a woman from being adorned, and therefore sexually attractive, while her husband is

279

away.[4] At home, Mukta wishes to communicate a sense of normalcy and decency to every visitor: "I don't have to flee: 'Let me quickly brush my hair.' 'Let me quickly straighten the house.' It is not like that. Just like I keep my body, I keep my house that same way. I keep my children that same way."

Mukta's family and home communicate, like her dress, admirable aspects of her personality. All are parts of a single aesthetic-moral system, a single continuum of commitment and conduct. In the acts of *darshan* and *durbar,* worshipers and servants can be read as accessories of the god and king, and, comparably, a loving husband, well-behaved children, and a fastidious, beautiful home can be read as ornaments of a worthy woman.

Ornamented for a Party

I asked Mukta to describe how she dresses for special occasions, how her *rup* for the grand night contrasts with her *rup* for the working day. In describing how she likes to present herself for formal events, Mukta made a few preliminary declarations. Most of her expensive jewelry, she explained, is stored in a bank locker, and it rarely comes out, even for special occasions, so she constructs her look by paying more attention to clothing than jewelry. Mukta maintains consistent categories of jewelry but changes the style within these categories. She always wears jewelry on her toes, ankles, neck, ears, and wrists. The difference between ordinary and fancy adornment is not amount or type; it is, rather, the replacement of the light, *halka* jewelry of daily life with the heavier, *bhara* versions for parties.

All of her jewelry must be made of gold or silver, for she is allergic to "artificial" jewelry. She cannot wear jewelry unless it is gold, or silver that is left plain (which Mukta calls "original *chandi*") or plated with gold. Many women in India trend with fashion by wearing inexpensive, artificial versions of what the movie stars are wearing. Mukta does not, partially because she wants to look unique, and also because her body recoils physically from the artificial.

Keeping these jewelry-related considerations in mind, I asked Mukta to describe the process of getting ready. The first step in her creative act is, of course, buying the materials. Mukta said she has a regular store for each item of adornment: a store in Godaulia for saris, a bangle store in the Vishvanath Gali, a store for gold jewelry in the Lanka neighborhood. She has chosen these stores for the variety of their stock, and she has cultivated a relationship

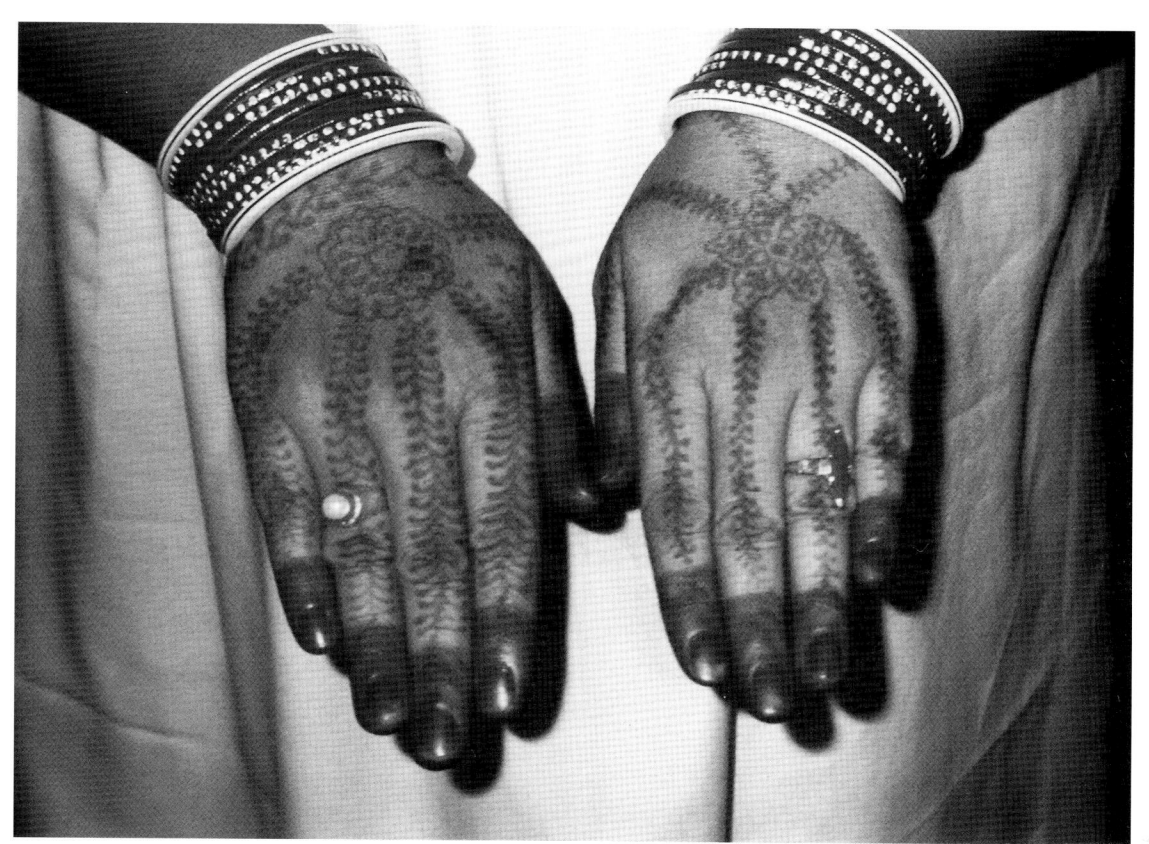

Mukta Tripathi's hands

with the salesmen. Instead of browsing in different places, she goes to her habitual shops and buys what she needs. I asked Mukta to describe the next stage, choosing and then placing items of adornment on her body:

"Before looking in the mirror, when I am choosing my clothes, I am already thinking: 'Will this thing *suit* me or not?' When I am ready—whatever it was that I was thinking about—that 'I will look this way after I am ready.' I had already *made up* in my mind that I will look this way—and after going in front of the mirror, if I, indeed, look that way, then I keep everything on! And if I don't look how I imagined I would look, and if I feel like this thing does not look good, or it is not good, then I remove that thing."

Mukta articulates what many of us experience. An item of clothing looks good in a shop. We imagine how good it will look on us with something we already own. Then often we come, sadly, to discover that what we imagined is not what the mirror brutally reveals. We visualize combinations before trying them on. Then we begin to tinker, making substitutions in the effort to realize the ideal we had conjured up in the mind's optimistic eye.

Next, I asked Mukta to describe the order in which she puts on her sari, jewelry, and makeup. Did she choose the sari first and then decide on jewelry to match? She thought for a moment, then replied: "No, first I make a *set* of sari and jewelry. Then after this, I wear the *chappal—sandal;* after that I put on the sari, after that I put on the jewelry. Then I look in the mirror."

She does not look in the mirror until the ensemble is complete. Each item was selected for its own beauty, so at this stage the question is how the things go together, how they make an aesthetic unit. Mukta continues: "Then, according to the jewelry, then I construct my *hairstyle.*" The process of adornment proceeds step by step. Clothing and jewelry are most important, basic to the whole. Shoes make a difference in height, perhaps causing the sari to be re-tucked for length. Hairstyle comes next, and it matches the jewelry in beautifying the face. At this point, I asked Mukta for clarification, wondering if hair and makeup follow the jewelry, since other women told me that jewelry came last. "Yes," she answered. "This is why: Say the jewelry is round, then accordingly, I will style my hair loose-loose. If I styled my hair first and then took out the jewelry, and it was round, and I had styled my hair tight, then the jewelry would look bad. If I were to wear jewelry first, then if the hair needs to be loose, or styled to one *side,* then I style my hair then."

Each item of adornment—sari, jewelry, hair, and makeup—functions on many levels. Each should display its own beauty—the beauty of the silk brocaded sari or ruby necklace. But each should highlight and complement the beauty of the others, for only then does the entire assembly beautify the woman.

The vision of a beautiful woman can be broken down through layers of perception: a well-made necklace rests atop a well-woven sari, which in turn harmonizes with the sandals and handbag, the bangles glittering on each arm. And ideally this ensemble matches the height, weight, and skin color of the woman, her age and social status. And finally, this vision appears among others at an elegant wedding reception, where women are seen, evaluated, compared. The beauty she has so painstakingly constructed, layer by layer, could be absurd, a sign of derangement, in another setting—down on her knees, say, scrubbing the kitchen floor. Leave the adornment unchanged, but shift the context, and all of her admirable craft might be sabotaged.

With some understanding of the process, I asked Mukta to describe some of her aesthetic preferences for special occasions.

"If I go to a *party,* and everybody is wearing *bright-bright* clothes, then I will wear very *sober-type* clothes, very *sober-type* jewelry. So that within the *party*—among everybody's Banarasi saris—within that, I will wear total *organdy,* or an *organza* sari, completely different type of sari, so that I look different. It's not like I will wear a heavy sari, heavy jewelry, and go to the party wearing the same *lipstick* everybody has on. It's not like that. Then I will wear very *light makeup,* or I will wear flowers—nowadays, at parties, I wear a *bela* flower *gajra,* or earrings of flowers, or a flower necklace—these I will wear so that I will look totally different."

Clothes and jewelry are thought of as "heavy" or "full." Jewelry is heavy when it is chunky and encrusted with gems. Saris are heavy when they are elaborately brocaded, heavy in weight and in design. Mukta's jewelry is light—"sober"—and she wears a light sari made of a delicate fabric—organdy or organza—that is buoyant in color and print, not heavy with saturated color or thick with glittery *zari.*

Her ornament, though still signaling an extraordinary occasion, is made of fragrant flowers,[5] such as the *bela* flower, which surround her with the intoxicating perfume of tuberoses. Mukta often wears jewelry made of flowers:

a *gajra*—a string of flowers—wrapped around the braid of her hair, a *haar* around her neck, and flower earrings. She recalled with pleasure the unusual times when she wore flowers instead of gold or silver because the flowers were beautiful, yet so different from what the other women were wearing.

Mukta places her order with a local vendor of flowers early in the morning of a party, so that it will be delivered to her in the afternoon. By the time she places an order, she has decided on the sari she will wear that evening, and she specifies the color of the flowers she wants interspersed among the white flowers of the garlands. Most of the flowers are white—jasmine, gardenia, tuberose—varieties that, being pollinated at night, attract the agents of pollination by brilliance of perfume rather than brilliance of color.

Mukta often asks for pink or yellow flowers to be sprinkled among the white so her garlands will match her saris. She could ask the florist to make a garland of colored flowers, omitting the white ones, but this would defeat one purpose of her adornment. As Mukta says, replacing gold and silver with flowers is visually original, and it adds another dimension to her assemblage of beauty: the very scent of the flowers. When she enters a party, those who do not see her soon notice the fragrance that follows her as she glides through the crowd. Let the other ladies compete visually; Mukta has added the sense of smell to her splendid presence. Mukta clearly enjoys the positive response her jewelry of flowers brings her. I asked her how she feels when she wears nice things to a party.

"When I feel that I look different, then there is some *vishwas* in the self. And other people see, and they think: 'Why shouldn't I wear things like that; she looks so different, and everybody else looks *common*.' I never have this feeling, that I look *common*. Because I have already thought this out beforehand in my head: That today I have to go to a *party,* I have to wear these things. If the clothes are *light,* then I choose that type of jewelry also. On heavy clothes, if I were to wear *light* jewelry, that would not look good. So I wear jewelry that matches the clothes. Like if I were to go to a wedding, that's what I am talking about."

One of the main reasons people spend time and money on their appearance, as Mukta says, is the psychological lift that comes from being appreciated by one's peers. She began by saying that there is a *vishwas,* a trust in the self, a self-confidence gained from looking good. With this confidence, a woman radiates positive energy. Other women at the party will envy Mukta's look, her ability to choose and match the clothing and jewelry that fit her and adorn her confident presence. Mukta told me about an event that took place a few years ago. She had gone to a wedding reception with a friend, who had applied thick eyeliner to Mukta's eyes. Throughout the evening, Mukta felt *ajeeb*—strange—and self-conscious. She could feel the eyeliner on her eyelids, it made her blink repeatedly, and, not wanting to talk to anyone, she avoided entering into conversations. As soon as she went to the bathroom and washed the eyeliner off, she felt like herself again, regaining her usual "confidence."

Mukta gains *vishwas,* trust in herself, from the visual appreciation she receives at parties, and she builds confidence from knowing her household is in control—her boys are doing well in school, her husband is happy enough with his home life.

Order and Ornamentation in the Home

Ethnographic study centers on everyday life, and I was happy to hear about Mukta's daily routine, which she began to describe when I asked if her desire for uniqueness was confined to self-adornment. She turned to an assessment of her house and children, saying both are clean and presentable. She used the Hindi expression "*saf-suthra*," a common idiom like the English "spic and span" or "neat and clean." The qualities of house and children reflect on the mother and homemaker, the person ultimately responsible for the maintenance of the home and its inhabitants. Mukta told me: "My house is *saf-suthra.* My kids are also *saf-suthre,* and in my *colony,* where I live, everybody says Mrs. Tripathi—everyday I do not make *dal,* rice, *roti, sabjee,* the typical food I don't serve. I'll make *saag paneer* today, *kofta* tomorrow, *besan ki sabjee* the other day. I keep changing the food."

In making food or dressing for a party, Mukta acts with flair.[6] The common food of her place consists of *chaval* (rice) and *dal* (lentils), *roti* (whole wheat flat bread), and some kind of *sabjee* (curried vegetables). That is what most people in Mukta's circle eat every day. In India, as elsewhere, common food varies ethnically and regionally. To be unlike everybody else, Mukta shifts the menu, altering one of the basic dishes. Instead of an ordinary *sabjee* made of potatoes, her family has *saag paneer,* spinach and homemade cheese curry, or *kofta,* vegetable balls fried and steeped in curry gravy, or even *besan ki sabjee,* a curry dish made of fried pieces of chickpea flour dough. All of these variations on the standard *sabjee* are delicious, and they consume more time than frying potatoes and onions in hot oil yet once again. As is the case with her bodily adornment, this special food takes time and energy, and it requires planning in advance. I asked her why she made such elaborate dishes. Mukta answered, "Because, for my husband, when he eats food, he receives happiness from eating the good food that I have made for him. And when he eats at other people's houses, he says: 'The food we ate at their house was not as good as your food.' And then I feel: 'I must make good food; that is why he compliments it.'"

Any host of a dinner party knows the pleasure that comes when people enjoy the food that was prepared especially for them. The hours of shopping and cooking have not been wasted; the guest's appreciation brings feelings of contentment, and even greater is the pleasure of having one's spouse prefer the cooking at home to the cooking that comes from other kitchens. When Mukta's husband comes home and says he likes her cooking best it is heartening, just as it is when Neelam's husband compares her to the other women at a party and pronounces her the most beautiful. It is one thing for your husband to think you are a good cook or beautiful, but it is better if, having eaten a meal out or noticed the other women at a party, he comes home and still prefers you. Mukta's children give her another reason to cook fine meals:

"My kids, whenever they eat food out, they say: '*Mummy,* you make good food. You make it really well.' I want to, for my kids, for my husband—because I don't have to go out for *service,* I am home *full-time* anyway, so if I can't satisfy my man and children in this way, with food and drink—everyday to make *dal-chaval, khichari*—this type of things I don't do."

Mukta's logic is admirable; when you are given a job, you might as well do it the best you can. Preserving high standards and performing with dedication, infusing an action with commitment, whatever the action is—that is the way of the artist. The yield of personal commitment is art.[7] As a housewife, Mukta takes pride in doing a good job. She stretches beyond the minimum. She does not prepare the same basic food every day, rice and lentils, lentils and rice, or *khichari,* which is even easier, being rice, lentils, and vegetables cooked together, consolidating the three basic dishes into one.

She is proud of the quality of the food she prepares, and she is happy with the calm and balanced schedule she has built for herself and her family:

"All my work is done in a *routine,* done in a *timely* manner. If the kids have to go to school in the morning at seven, then at night I *polish* my kids' shoes, arrange their uniforms, then only do I go to sleep.

"In the morning, I don't like to hustle and bustle. 'This needs to be done.' 'That needs to be done.' Everything is done. When I wake up in the morning, I slowly-slowly *brush* my teeth, put the *dal* to boil, make the rice. The work will be done slowly-slowly, with *shanti* [peace].

"The kids know where to find their clothes, their shoes, their school packs. I have put their *tiffins* on the *dining table.* They grab them and leave. There is no chance for panic—like: 'Where are my socks?' 'Where is my tie?' 'Where is my belt?' No."

Indian children wear uniforms to school. They make a lovely sight walking through the street or crammed into a rickshaw clad in matching outfits. Getting children ready for school is harder on the parent if the child has to wear a mandatory set of clothes. Mukta's morning routine involves making sure her two sons have clean and ironed shorts or pants and shirts, a belt and a tie, socks and polished shoes. The standard outfit takes a little planning. A mother cannot grab any clothes that happen to be clean and send her kid out the door.

Mukta lays out the uniforms and prepares food for the boys. Lunch leaves home in *tiffin* carriers. Her husband will take a stack of round stainless steel containers with lids, fastened by a handle. In this handy canister, one compartment can hold rice, another *sabjee,* another folded up *rotis,* another mango pickles. Students carry plastic *tiffins,* like tupperware, filled with a savory meal for noontime. Mukta rises early to prepare the lentils and rice for the breakfast and lunch of her husband and sons.

After Mukta's sons have left for school, she focuses on her husband's daily departure:

"At nine o'clock, my husband eats his food. I unlock his *scooter,* and place his *files* there. I know what time he returns in the afternoon. One hour before that, I enter the kitchen, make the snacks, start the preparations for dinner. Sometimes I even prepare dinner early, and we go out. When we return, I just have to heat the food.

"I mean, all the work is *fit.* My husband never sees me doing housework. Before his return, all the work is done, so that when he comes, I am not stuck in the kitchen. All the work is done, so that after he comes, I make tea, and we eat snacks, and sit for one hour and talk. He says: 'All other women are constantly doing housework. But your housework is all *fit,* and you are all *fit.* It is not like I have just come home, and you are stuck in the kitchen.'

"When the man is made a little happy, then the woman's desire to be different is increased."

Mukta does her housework while her husband is at work, so that she can spend time with him when he arrives.[8] She chooses not to reveal the effort involved in her finished product, whether it is a clean and organized house or a perfectly matched ensemble of clothing. Her pleasure lies in having her creation viewed in the moment of final perfection, when everything is exactly as it should be.

Ultimately, Mukta pleases herself by creating an environment that is clean and organized, but she is also pleased when the members of her family are happy and appreciative. When Arun Kumar, her husband, is happy with her work, her desire to please him increases, and the home is free from tension.

Mukta sees a clear connection in creation and consequence between a well-adorned self and a well-ordered house. She adorns her body and maintains herself for her pleasure, for her family, and for the happiness of the household.

"For me, *churi, payal,* jewelry, sari—in these things there is *shauk,* and I buy these things. Most of my money is *invested* in these things.

"I believe that one should wear nice clothes, eat well, and keep the house well *maintained.* I keep myself, my house, and my kids well *maintained.* If the kids were to have only four sets of clothes, I would still keep them all *maintained.* If I just washed the clothes, I wouldn't just place them somewhere. I would *press* them, fold them, keep them well in the closet.

"I give much care to clothes, to jewelry and things. If these things were to get stolen, that is a different matter. But you should take care of the things you have. Not like: Leave this here, leave that there. Everything should be kept well."

Mukta's desire to keep her house well *maintained* can be understood on two additional levels: she respects the things she owns and feels she should take care of them, and she feels a need to control her house and its workings. Everything is done in a timely manner, everything is placed where Mukta can find it easily. There are no surprises or unexpected delays in doing the daily household chores, as she explains:

"For example, if you open the closet, it is not like: 'Where is the blouse?' 'Where is the petticoat?' Everything is in its place. All petticoats underneath, the blouses separate. Saris separate. If I were to select a sari, then instantly I could find the matching blouse; instantly I am able to grab the petticoat from below. Then when I return, I immediately put the clothes on the hanger. Clothes here and there, that I don't like."

Easily accessible and visually compelling arrangements add to the pleasure of adornment for a woman who claims to have much *shauk* in jewelry and clothes. Mukta's jewelry is also stored neatly. Her bangles are kept in bangle boxes. Anklets and toe rings are grouped in separate categories. Silver jewelry is not mixed with gold, but stored separately. Mukta keeps her *bindis* in what she calls a *"bindi album."* She has taken a regular photo album and placed on its adhesive sheets the packets of *bindis* she owns. When she is getting ready, all she has to do is flip through the album, finding the appropriate size and color of the round *bindi* she will wear.

Mukta's jewelry is kept in accessible clusters by type and material. She classifies them in this way so they will not get snagged and tangled. If one were to analyze the cleanliness of Mukta's house as reflecting only a desire to please her family and others, it would be difficult to explain the elegantly ordered interior of her own closet and the ranked and arranged jewelry that is hidden from all eyes but her own. These secret places are arranged and trimly maintained for her pleasure, not for public scrutiny. Her care of the items of adornment is a loving gesture toward things that she likes to see and handle and own as part of her *shauk,* her enthusiasm for saris and jewelry, as things in themselves, as things to put into order in storage, as well as things to array on her body. Mukta's aesthetic sense expands from the single object to the ensemble of the household:

"[My house] is clean and arranged. I arrange the outside but also the inside of the closet—if I were to open my closet—inside the closet things are also arranged. Even those clothes inside boxes, they are folded; its not like I have stuffed the clothes in there because you can't see them. It is not like that.

"Inside the *fridge* also. Every week I clean the inside of the *fridge*. Inside the *fridge* even, I have lots of *shauk*—that all the wonderful-wonderful things to eat and drink, that if somebody were to open the *fridge,* they would see them there. It's not like the only things in the *fridge* are water and milk. Like, I order a tray of Thumbs-Up / Coca-Cola; it is not like you have to run to the store to get soft drinks.

"I have *shauk.* There is *mineral water,* there is this and that, from top to bottom, these things are stocked in my *fridge.* Whether the children consume those things or not, I have *shauk* that my *fridge* be full, that if I were to go into my kitchen, that the food—I don't eat *achar* [hot pickles], neither does my husband, but still, I have made all *varieties* of *achar,* kept in glass bottles, all arranged on the top shelf, because I like it. If a *guest* comes, then I can offer it to him. I don't eat it, but that doesn't matter."

Mukta keeps a neat, hospitable home. She manages it as well as it can be managed, and having revealed her interest in order, she returns, enthusiastically, to her daily routine:

"In the morning, with ease, I make tea and read the paper. Everybody says: 'Hey, your children go to school at seven in the morning, your husband at nine in the morning, and you are reading the paper?' So I say: 'I cut the vegetables already at night and put them in the *fridge.*' In the morning, in the *cooker,* I start the rice. I fry the vegetables. I make the *raita* [yogurt sauce]. I cut the *salad.* Half of my work I have completed at night, or in the afternoon if I have free time. I do all my work during the times my *husband* is not home. After my *husband* has returned home, I don't do much work."

The precision with which she works adds ease and order to Mukta's mornings. Her husband and children start the day in a good mood, stress free. People who happen to drop by witness the order with which Mukta runs her home. The house is *maintained* with a heightened quality that surpasses necessity. Mukta elaborates:

"If somebody were to arrive at my house unexpectedly, then within ten minutes, I would serve a splendid meal with lots of *decoration* to this person. For example, if I have made *paneer,* then I transfer the food to a dish, and then I cut fresh cilantro on top. If I make *dahi bara,* then on top of that I sprinkle cumin, cayenne pepper, and some herbs.

"I put all these *decorations* on the food, and place the food in a *casserole* dish. After that, *plates,* spoon, fork, *napkin,* I place all these there. *Glass,* I place upside down. I place a little bit of flowers in the middle of the table, for beauty. Then we eat. All arranged.

"If the food is well prepared, then somebody can tell by looking at it that the food is *tasty.* If I am making *sabjee* in a frying pan, then without tasting it, I can tell if it is good or not."

Her last comments make clear Mukta's belief in the power of seeing. A meal tastes better if it is eaten at a well-decorated, beautifully set table. Good food does not need to be tasted; its appearance reveals its quality. Similarly, the appearance of a household communicates the human relations it contains; the home exhibits the feelings the wife has about her family and her duties as a homemaker.

Such visual communication, conscious and unconscious, is directed toward all who can see—both the people of the home and those who visit. Mukta's family moves often, as a result of her husband's frequent new "postings." In 1996, at the time of our long interview, they were living in Dehradun, north of Banaras. By 2002 they had returned. By running the house in an orderly routine, Mukta preserves consistency from location to location. Her proud accounts of her home do not include architectural details or the demographics of the neighborhood, for these variables are not maintained from one place to another. She focuses instead on the workings of the household, and the orderly way in which things are kept. Saris, petticoats, and blouses are stored in the same relationship to each other in the metal *almari* she takes with her to each new house. The routines of food storage, preparation, and consumption can continue despite differences in the layout of the house. Mukta cannot control the fact that her family moves often, but she can control the order of the household, its routines and arrangements, to provide a steady stage for family life.

The Art of Self-Adornment

The orderly house communicates love within the family. Clean and welcoming to the guest, the home also expresses much about the family to each new set of neighbors and co-workers. With each move, Mukta and her family face the curiosity of a new set of people who gather visual clues about the family from their home and possessions and the behavior of the children. A well-maintained home communicates family stability.

Mukta is attuned to the power of looking, to the critical gaze that gathers information and leads toward evaluation. She applies her understanding of visual judgment when making aesthetic decisions about her home and its order, her body and its adornment. She judges food first by its look, not its taste, and she assesses her body art by looking in the mirror long and hard after she has wrapped the sari, slipped into her sandals, and put on all of her jewelry. Only then does she decide on makeup and hairstyle. But before all this, she has visualized everything in her mind's eye in order to make preliminary decisions, whether about the jewelry for her body or the ornaments for her home. When I asked her to talk about the process she uses to choose what ornaments and clothes to buy, this is what she said:

"In these matters, I don't take the advice of other people. I think: 'What will look good on me?' I don't look at others, and notice what bangles they are wearing, and think that I should wear them also—no. First, I will think in my head: 'If I were to wear this, how would I look?' 'Will this thing suit me or not?' I think inside myself these things—like if I were to buy clothes, while in the store, I will think: 'In this sari, I will look this way.' 'In this jewelry, I will look this way.'

"I don't try on the things. I will take the bangles in my hand, and because I know my *color*, right there I think, I prepare my mind to think that: 'If I were to wear these bangles, how would my hands look?' 'If I wore these clothes, then how would I look?'"

Mukta is very clear about the importance of having a realistic mental picture of what the thing will look like once it is on her body so she can make a judgment about buying and wearing. She uses the same tactic on her house. When she moves, she sits and thinks about how the furniture will look in different locations in her new home; she does not try the furniture here, then there, experimenting with different configurations. Her practice yields a trim final product, since she has considered all the options, and she is not forced into hasty decisions while sweaty impatient men lift the heavy furniture and move it again. Able to visualize beautiful arrangements, Mukta easily articulates the principles that govern her choices. Sitting on a bed in Banaras, far from her home in Dehradun, she was able to describe the garnish on her *sabjee,* the flowers on her dinning table.

The ability to visualize artful combinations entails the many tasks that contribute to Mukta's multi-layered understanding of aesthetics. First of all, you should be able to detect the beauty of a piece of clothing or jewelry, selecting it from among a multitude of comparable things in a store. You should be able to imagine that item on your body, and then imagine how it could look in relation to other things you own, keeping in mind the limitations and strengths of your physical frame, your financial situation, and the social events when you would be likely to wear the piece under consideration.

This critical weighing of things in relation to things is the core talent of self-adornment. But how is it developed? For Mukta, this ability has been achieved by observing the world carefully and having a clear sense of who she is in relation to others. The key is seeing sharply and thinking broadly.

Most creative acts, including that of adornment, come as personal responses to stimuli. Earlier in our interview, Mukta was critical of women who unthinkingly copied models from Bollywood heroines. She said, "To do *nakal*, you need *akal*. If you don't have any *akal*, how will you do *nakal*?" In Hindi, *nakal* means to copy, to mimic, and *akal* can be translated loosely as creativity or imagination. In order to copy something, you need to be creative enough to manage the imitation successfully. Mukta exemplified with the beautiful actress Shridevi: "If you love Shridevi but don't look like her, that is stupid. You should choose a heroine you look like!"

Mukta has recommended the trick employed by the transgendered *hijras* I spoke with at the Assi Ghat *hijra* colony. They said that the way to cross-dress is to choose a heroine who roughly resembles you in build, skin color, facial features, and style. Then, all you have to do is watch that heroine in her movies to learn how you should dress. Their tactic was reasonable, for the heroine's look is created by Bollywood stylists, professionals whose talent is to match clothes, jewelry, and makeup to a particular woman's look, highlighting the beauty and downplaying the flaws. Clothing and jewelry only look good when they match the height, weight, and skin color of the person they adorn. Mukta is not against imitation; she is against copying without intelligent forethought and self-critical consideration of suitability.

Visual skill, Mukta believes, enables people to note fashion errors, and, more importantly, to use bodily appearances as a way to understand a person's inner nature. When I asked her if adornment is a talent, she said it was, but pushed on to aspects of communication that she considered more important than the aesthetic:

"Yes, it is a *talent*. And from this, others understand—like if somebody were to stand here, from that person's clothes and look, somebody would understand how this person is *mentally*. I mean, how he is, his *nature;* has he *maintained* himself well? People will know this is how this person is. This must be how his house is, how his children are."

A person, to Mukta, is a walking manifestation of the taste and psychology of his home and family life. Men and women are more than linked to their families and households, Mukta said, they are judged in their context:

"The most impressive thing is that, after keeping the children and house well-decorated, a woman also keeps herself *well-maintained*. That is regarded well. That she is able to pay attention to herself, her children—and not that a woman is wearing lots of *makeup,* paying lots of attention to herself, and her children are dirty-filthy, the children's *school results* are low, the husband is unhappy. This is also not good."

Women, both those who work outside of the house and those who do not, have culturally sanctioned responsibilities. A handsomely dressed woman whose house is dirty, whose husband is neglected and whose kids do poorly in school, is reviled as a selfish person, whose self-absorption has led to familial distress. Mukta's daily life is busy with housework; she views spending too many hours in front of the mirror as *bekar,* a wasteful activity. Yet she believes that there is a practical, social benefit for a woman to care for herself as well as her family. One's husband should be satisfied at home so that he does not disrupt other marriages:

"Everybody should be *santosh* [satisfied]. And even after that, if a woman is able to keep herself *maintained*, then that is a good thing. That is a very good thing, I think. And women should do this.

"Those women who don't *maintain* themselves, it is their *husbands* who, here and there, look at other men's wives.

"If I keep myself *maintained,* looking pretty good, then my *husband* has no need to look here and there. Then when he comes home, the house is clean, he will sleep in his bed. But when the house is dirty-filthy, there is noise and confusion, then he will think: 'Let me leave the house for a while.' When he can receive all kinds of *santoshi* in his own house, then he won't want to go outside of the house."

Mukta implies that some women are in essence communicating to their husbands, through messy houses, that they should go elsewhere to find satisfaction. By making the house a place of chaos where the husband feels unwelcome, the wife is suggesting that he should spend his time somewhere else. Her act might be read as a move to empowerment, because many women in India are married to men they did not choose, and whom they do not love. It might be preferable for them if their husbands satisfied their needs elsewhere. Arranging an inhospitable home for the husband could be an unconscious, or even self-conscious, act of defiance, a materially encoded message of rejection.

Folklorists Joan Radner and Susan Lanser have written that women send coded, feminist messages to gain power, to rebel against and subvert social or familial expectations. Such messages can be transmitted "under the very eyes of a dominant community for whom these same messages are either inaccessible or inadmissible."[9] Women communicate through the variable details of the domestic setting to each other, and sometimes to men. Mukta's example shows how a woman can indirectly send her husband away to seek the company of other women. Other examples I have heard about in India include burning the food, seasoning it badly, intentionally "forgetting" to buy the food the husband wants, or even putting food of a brand the poor devil does not like into a carton with the label of his favorite brand. In Manju Kapur's novel *Difficult Daughters,* a first wife communicates to the newly arrived second wife through domestic messages intended solely for her, which their shared husband does not understand. In a series of subtle "accidents," the old wife, Ganga, makes sure the new wife's food is always "too sweet, too salty, too fried, too soggy, too stale, and if possible, too dirty." That way the original wife asserts her control over the kitchen and exhibits her reluctance to relinquish the household and share her husband.[10]

Sometimes the message is not directed at specific individuals and may not even be intentional. Still, people take appearances as coded messages; women in India will persist in reading personalities and intentions through the art of others. In *Ladies Coupé,* a novel by Anita Nair, a mother teaches her daughter how to read the *kolam,* a religious design made daily on the threshold by the woman of the house. The mother declares, "A true wife is she whose virtues match her home," and then she shows her daughter how to decipher the execution of the rice flour motifs on the doorstep: too sloppy signals carelessness and indifference; too elaborate indicates self-indulgence. The perfect drawing is one that is elegant yet restrained, beautiful within reason.[11] The realization that other women are judging one's domestic art—be it food, *kolam,* or self-adornment—motivates the self-conscious desire to look presentable, to avoid reprimand, to gain approval.

Domestic messages sometimes invert the state of affairs—as Radner and Lanser argue in their book on feminist coding—the goal being to hide the reality of the household from others.[12] One woman I met in India kept her house and herself immaculately clean in order to conceal the chaos of the domestic situation in which she was regularly battered by an abusive husband. In her case, the outward appearance of order allowed her to save face, and it was possibly motivated by fear, by a desire to appease her husband in hopes that a harmonious home would stifle his violence.

Not all messages are subtly coded; some are intended as general nonverbal communications. At a love-marriage I attended in Banaras, the aunt of the groom came to the reception wearing a black sari, publicly signaling her disapproval of the union through her choice of color. Keeping your house in a certain way, as a physical manifestation of your feelings, can become a mode of visual communication to your husband, ultimately affecting his behavior toward the family. Self-adornment, the outward communication of one's personality, carries inner feelings to the beholders, and it can affect the behavior of the adorned. Mukta says: "What is inside of me, this *bhau,* I express by ornamentation. I look this way wearing these things." When one wears white or pink, she says, one is more pious, both in look and behavior. The humble behavior of the widow could be affected by the white sari she is pressured to wear. On the other hand, if a woman were to show up at a party in red, she would feel that she looked provocative, and might act that way. The *bhau,* a person's sentiment or emotion, is reinforced for the self and communicated to others through her choice of ornament.

Following this train of thought, we might question how much we can interpret from the visual information presented by a household or a decorated woman. Cultural norms differ with regard to how well maintained a house should be, how much attention a woman should pay to her adornment when she is caring for small, demanding children and a busy, demanding husband.

Every member of a community, in theory, has knowledge of such norms. Choosing to break with tradition can be seen as an act of defiance, easily decipherable by the others in one's cultural unit.

The way a house is kept, the way food is prepared and presented, the way the children are trained in proper manners, and the way a woman looks at a party—all are physical manifestations of personal choice. One woman chooses to neglect her household and lavish attention on herself. Another chooses to look sexy at a party, knowing very well that judgments will be made on her provocative, scandalous attire. A member of a community, one who shares the values of the group, feels comfortable in passing judgment, as these kinds of choices are manifest in the tangible physical realms of the household, the family, and body art.

Mukta's intelligent reflections of the choices she makes in her life help us understand the important role context plays in the creation, and the appreciation, of body art. An item of jewelry or clothing is initially selected on the basis of its own beauty and excellence. From then on, it is viewed and understood in a series of interlocked contexts. A piece of jewelry will be seen against one's body and will be affected by the properties of that physical backdrop. This same item of jewelry must also fit the bodily assemblage, connecting with the clothing, the other items of jewelry, the sandals, hairstyle, and makeup. But this assembly will seem beautiful only if it is situated properly in context—the social context, the context of current fashion, the context of the developmental stage of the wearer.

In addition to those contexts, Mukta understands that body art is also appreciated—by its beholders and its creators—in the context of an individual's personality and personal tradition. An occasion for adornment is embedded in one woman's repertory and style. How you look today increases in significance if the beholder knows what you usually look like, how you looked yesterday, or earlier this morning, in a different context of display.

Finally, Mukta understands that a woman's body art is also judged in the context of one's own family and in the other occasions of creativity: housework, child rearing, and food preparation. After having carefully selected the items of adornment, matched them perfectly to her body, age, and status, Mukta then controls the outward appearance of her house and family, creating the tidy social context within which she is on display. Having managed all the decisions of adornment, Mukta actively constructs a context in which her domestic world seems harmonious, and she makes the setting in which her graceful beauty is witnessed and judged by her ever-changing circle of neighbors, her "local public."

Choice in the Domestic Sphere

In earlier chapters, we came to cultural generalizations about bodily adornment in the public spheres of production and commerce by looking at men who make and sell; their experiences led us toward an understanding of men's involvement in women's body art. Now, through consideration of the self-ornamentation practices of three women—Nina, Neelam, and Mukta—we have derived the key principles by which Indian women make choices about their personal adornment. We have learned that individualized decisions are based on culturally meaningful variables, such as identities of caste, region, and religion; membership in a joint family, the love of spouse and children; the responsibilities and desires of the home and workplace; and the fulfillment of the self's aesthetic and creative needs. In order to understand their breadth of options, we have looked at three women who are similar in socioeconomic standing, educational level, and age. All speak Hindi, live in cities, and have connections to Banaras. By focusing on diversity within a tight segment of the population, we have been able to note nuances of choice, coming to a subtlety of analysis that could not be possible if we had compared poor, lower-caste village women, say, with rich, high-caste urban ladies. Were I to have framed a wide comparison, differences in attire would have become symbolic of cultural differences, of differences between regions, religions, and castes, but holding to a tight comparison, I have revealed the personal differences that obtain within all culturally distinct spheres.

Nina, Neelam, and Mukta exemplify different points along a continuum of adornment preferences that range from plain to fancy. Although they are very different from one another, all three of these women exhibit a strong understanding of themselves in relation to the various social and cultural forces among which their body art mediates. Like most women in India, they are constantly aware of the restrictions and tensions of caste relations, ethnic identity, and the particular customs of their places of residence. Nina lives in a Sindhi household, in a neighborhood that is mixed in its castes, in the city of Banaras where she was not born. Her house is safe and calm, free of caste tensions, and Nina's notions of self-adornment are suitably relaxed and plain. The issue of caste intrudes upon Neelam's household, for she chose an inter-caste marriage. Though Punjabi, Neelam grew up in Banaras, learning to live comfortably among people who were not Punjabis, becoming accustomed to constant adjustments. She is able to satisfy herself, her husband, and her mother-in-law by subtly manipulating her appearance in different areas of the house. Mukta, a Brahmin from Banaras, married into her caste, but her family, moving every few years, exists in a constant state of displacement. Unlike Nina, who has the steadiness of her Sindhi joint family around her, Mukta creates stability through the organization of her household and the routines by which she wraps her family in a cocoon of comfort and order, wherever they happen to be.

The ways in which familial factors influence adornment are complicated, as Neelam makes clear. Though she was born in Banaras, Neelam identifies with Punjabi culture, and she uses the history of the partition of the Punjab to explain her choices. She does not like jewelry because her mother spent too much time worrying about it during the time of their escape from Pakistan and settlement in India. Her mother's obsession led Neelam to care little about jewelry. Yet she explains her dislike of glass bangles by saying that her mother did not wear them. She combines the presence of jewelry in her mother's life and the absence of jewelry in her mother's life to explain her own lack of interest. Whether decisions and associations are conscious reminders of one's childhood or unconscious links to one's culture, caste, and family, they are integral factors in a woman's choice of adornment.

Indian adornment is inextricably linked to the idea of marriage, and by extension, to love. Appearing beautiful and well-ornamented can be a reflection of happiness and comfort in marriage. Nina's comfort in being under-adorned by most standards is a direct consequence of her husband's love and tolerance. Neelam's "love marriage" yielded an inter-caste family environment, but it also provided her with a loving union. A danger of the arranged marriage—one in which the partners did not choose each other—is that the couple might not come to love each other, and that this lack of love might drive one or both of them to seek the companionship of others. Mukta's love for her husband, and especially for her children, inspires her to create a stable home, one in which the food is excellent, where order prevails, where the husband feels welcome. Her work keeps the family intact, a benefit for all members of the household, including herself. Her household, like the *bindi* on her forehead, the *sindur* in her hair, the *mangalsutra* around her neck, is a sign of an honorable marriage.

The body art of Nina, Neelam, and Mukta can be partially understood by external factors—region, caste, family—but of equal, if not greater importance, is their need for creative expression as individuals. Not all women choose to express their creativity through body art, and some have a greater desire to engage in creative acts than others, so the creativity of bodily adornment must be viewed in relation to other possibilities and outlets: child rearing, cooking, gardening, worship, singing, writing. Systemic relations among categories of creation help us understand differences among Nina, Neelam, and Mukta.

Nina does not choose to assert her creativity primarily in adornment. Her main domestic outlet of creativity lies in food preparation, a realm in which she excels. She gains satisfaction as well from regular Sindhi acts of worship, from her bright, successful children, from her close and harmonious joint family. Nina moves toward excellence in feeding and caring for her family, while she chooses to look "ordinary" and "with the crowd" in the realm of body art.

Neelam, on the other hand, works outside of the house as a teacher. When she lived in Banaras, the housework, including the cooking, was left to her sister-in-law, and Neelam met her creative urge in the realm of the sari. Every aspect of her passion brings her pleasure: noticing the saris other women wear on the streets, selecting a sari "book style" in a shop, bringing it home, imagining it on herself, and finally, wearing it to a big social event. Neelam fills her appetite for creativity in adornment through the sari, leaving little room for other items, most notably the jewelry others love, but for which she cares little.

Mukta has a great need for beauty in her daily life. She takes advantage of many outlets for creativity and achieves real excellence in most of them. Her taste is refined in all forms of adornment, ranging from glass bangles, through gold jewelry, to the fabrics and prints of fine saris. Housework for Mukta is not a mere duty, but another opportunity for creativity. She cooks with panache, arranges the items in her pantry and refrigerator with exquisite care, and sets the table beautifully for her guests. Forever adjusting to new cities, Mukta invests special pride in the principal roles she occupies in life: mother and wife. Her children are polite and educated. Her husband is pampered. She does all that and still manages to look smashing at a social event, where she will appear in a "sober" style, exhibiting her tastefully adorned and fragrant self for all to appreciate.

Day in, day out, these three women—like millions of others in India—make personal choices within the inevitable constraints of normal life, enacting the core hope of the feminist paradigm: that a woman should have the right to live as she desires. Some choose professions that take them away from home. Many more choose to excel in the domestic arts of home decoration, food preparation, and their children's education. All of them choose a style when dressing—plain or extravagant, conventional or original—some emphasizing one aspect of appearance, some another. Choice is not restricted to the privileged few who work for big salaries in big cities. Everyone is to some extent free, to some extent unfree, and women find, with courage and delight, ways to express their creative energies and feel the working of their individual will every day when they get up and get dressed.

Part 4. Body Art in the Lifecycle

·13·

After the Wedding

WHEN SHE TALKED about adornment, Mukta Tripathi made clear that a woman's choices are influenced by her personal taste—and by the factors of age and social development. Mukta easily describes the clothes she wore during different phases of her life. As a little girl, until the sixth grade, she wore frocks, skirts and blouses, shorts or pants. From the seventh to the twelve grades, she wore *salwar suits* and jeans, but never skirts or dresses, since it was improper for a young lady to show her legs. As a young bride, she dressed in bright saris and wore makeup and jewelry in abundance. Now Mukta has switched to saris in "sober colors," because, as she explained to me, in India a mother-in-law and her daughter-in-law "should not match." Although Mukta is not yet a mother-in-law, she feels she has reached the age when it is inappropriate for her to show herself as a flashy, young wife.

Mukta, in her forties, prefers saris in tones of beige, cream, and other "light colors," but they shift with the current fashion. In 2003, the trend was to wear saris with a thin strip of monochrome embroidery along the border that matched the field of the sari exactly in color, and to wear it with a blouse in the same color, with the same monochrome embroidery on the edges of the sleeves. Mukta continues to wear "natural, decent makeup." The subtle shift in clothing, marked mostly by its palette, reflects her view of herself as a mother of grown-up boys—the oldest one is in high school—who is still attuned to style. She told me that wearing a lot of makeup ruins the skin, making women look old, which is another reason to decrease the amount of makeup as one ages. Mukta is fully aware of the social and developmental categories women pass through, categories that are publicly communicated by clothing and jewelry. Her decision to abandon certain styles or colors is partially influenced by other people's opinions, for middle-aged and older women are often criticized for being too ornamented.[1] Mukta told me that she would like to wear *salwar suits* occasionally, but her kids made fun of her when she did in the past, calling her "Mukta *didi*"—big sister Mukta—implying that when she wears a *salwar suit* she does not look like a mother, but rather, like somebody's sister (children often hold a rigid and conservative vision of what their parents should look like). On a few recent occasions, Mukta's two sons pointed to older women on the streets whom they deemed to be dressed inappropriately in a style too youthful, and begged Mukta not to dress that way when she becomes "aged."

Rites of passage, which are defined physically and socially, are major celebratory events for individuals and societies; they often inspire art in multiple mediums.[2] One of the critical factors affecting adornment choices in India, especially for women, is the developmental stage of a person's lifecycle. For the male population, Hindu tradition has four set life stages: student, married householder, hermit, and finally religious mendicant.[3] These are the ideal, but rarely realized, stages in a man's life. There is not much specialized clothing to designate the stages of a man's life, other than the school uniforms and short pants for young boys, and trousers, *lungis,* or *dhotis* for adult men, and should men enter the final stage of mendicant, their position is marked clearly by hair and beard, beads, and sparse ritual dress. A change in the marital status of Indian men is not generally signaled by jewelry, though a small percentage of men do wear a gold wedding band.

According to the social critic Vrinda Nabar, the lifecycle of the Indian woman consists of eight roles: girl, adolescent, wife, daughter-in-law, mother, mother-in-law, married yet un-widowed, and finally widow.[4] Although these transitions involve major physiological changes (menstruation, pregnancy, and menopause) they are dramatically marked by a change in bodily decoration. As time is not limited to the linear in India, some aspects of these stages recur, with similar adornment appearing at different phases, most notably during marriage and death. The funeral of an elderly person is called a "second marriage," and the procession to the cremation grounds is referred to as a *barat*—the groom's marriage procession.[5] Certain items of adornment carry auspicious meaning, and they are worn at important religious ceremonies throughout one's life.

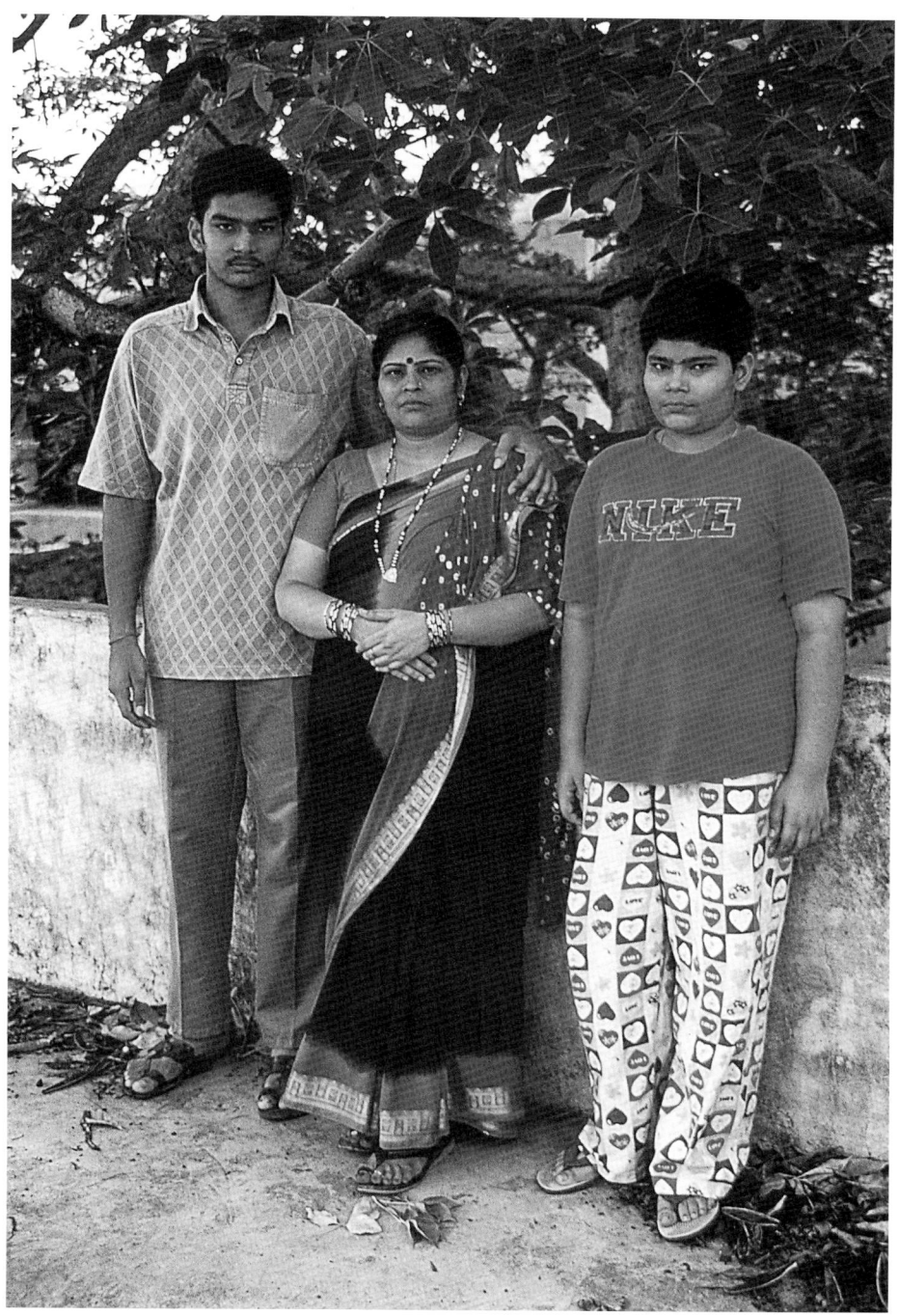

Mukta Tripathi with her sons, Tushar and Vaibhav

In her book on Bengali marriage traditions, anthropologist Lina Fruzzetti argues that lifecycle rituals provide an effective way to study women in India, gaining for scholars valuable insight into the female cultural realm.[6] In accord with Fruzzetti, I believe that studying the dress and adornment of different life stages carries us into the women's view of themselves. So, this and the next two chapters will focus on female adornment as visual markers of the lifecycle, starting with married women and widows, then leading through childhood and betrothal to end at the high point of ritual, the apogee of ornamentation: the bride at her wedding.

Married Women

As we have learned from Nina Khanchandani, Neelam Chaturvedi, and Mukta Tripathi, certain dress and ornamentation signals marital status, yet individual women wear different amounts and types of clothes and jewelry, depending on their preferences. Adornment is a material marker of the changes in one's life, and it affects one's attitudes—by giving social "confidence," for example, to women who are visually marked by all the signs of *suhag*. Ornaments can also affect the behavior of others: women wear *sindur* and other signs of marriage to discourage "eve teasing" on the crowded streets, since men engaged in harassing women are reluctant to touch someone's wife for fear of retaliation by her husband.

Many women don the symbols of marriage—*sindur, bindi,* glass bangles, toe rings, anklets, and *mangalsutra*—with pride. Wearing these ornaments every day is not an oppressive cultural mandate, as a hard feminist interpretation could suggest.[7] Rather, it reveals that the woman has passed through an important rite of passage and achieved maturity. Women in the United States may flash diamond engagement rings among their friends, happy to be (finally) getting married, but for the Indian woman the significance is far greater. An Indian woman who is not married—and does not wear the marital items of body art—may be viewed as coming from a family too poor to afford her dowry and marriage, or as a person who is unable to find a groom. In either case, she will be prevented from achieving maturity and with it a position of significance and power within society. Divorce is not common among the mainstream population of India,[8] and separated women are unwilling to give up the ornaments of marriage, since they would be socially marked as unlucky, as powerless failures. Divorced Indian women may also be stigmatized as loose or promiscuous, and this remains the case in the diaspora, as Bharati Mukherjee suggests in her short story "The Tenant," when an Indian-American professor, while unzipping his pants, declares, "Divorced women can date, they can go to bars and discos. They can see mens, many mens."[9]

An older woman who still wears *bindi* and *sindur,* and is not in a white sari, happily communicates the fact that her husband is still alive; she has not become a widow, for according to one orthodox Sanskrit text, "Of all inauspicious things, the widow is the most inauspicious."[10] Many women wish to die before their husbands, hoping never to experience the lack of respect and loss of ornamentation that characterizes widowhood. Some loving husbands also wish for their wives to pass away before them, knowing the hardships they will have to suffer as widows.[11]

Of the many reasons to wear age-appropriate clothing and jewelry, one is a desire not to seem silly, vulnerable to ridicule as the embodiment of bad taste. Remember how Shashi Shah, of the Kanhaiya Lal jewelry store, said that old women who wear the jewelry suitable for the young look like "a cartoon." Similarly, Mukta's sons mock her when she wears *salwar suits.* Other reasons to switch clothing preferences have to do with the body as it changes and settles into a different shape with childbirth and age. Sugyan Kandpaal, for example, an attractive mother of two young children in Banaras, does not wear jeans any more because she feels that after motherhood "the figure is gone." One of the reasons that jeans remain in the domain of the young in India is that jeans are revealing, and so should be worn only at the time of life when the figure is trim.[12] Many married women, like Sugyan, reject jeans because they feel they no longer look good in tight-fitting garments. Nitu Dhar, in Dhaka, has stopped wearing *salwar suits* because she trusts her husband's opinion that she does not look good in them any more. She prefers to wear saris now, feeling they flatter her figure. Loose *salwar suits* and generously draped saris are right for women who have gained weight and lost the slender body of youth. The decision to exchange one clothing style for another is based less on social pressure than it is on a personal objective assessment of a suitable relation between garment type and body type.

In addition to acting as a visual marker of marriage, ornamentation plays another important role in the lives of married women. Self-adornment and *shauk*—interest—in matters of ornamentation are socially acceptable artistic outlets, encouraged in the first years of marriage. For some women, the creative processes of shopping and selecting items of self-adornment and, consequently, the pride of ownership of saris and jewelry, become key sources of self-esteem.

Many women I have spoken with refer to "problems" experienced by women in India, problems resulting from neglect by their husbands and isolation from their extended family units. Reminiscent of Betty Friedan's "the problem that has no name"[13]—the helplessness and despair experienced by housewives—many married women in India are depressed, taking pills to lift their moods in the daytime and pills to help them sleep at night. Middle-class women who live in cities throughout India, including Banaras, do not engage in much housework, depriving themselves of the physical exertion and sense of accomplishment that comes from cooking a wonderful meal or keeping the house clean. They have cooks, maids, and other servants who engage in the creative acts of the domestic sphere: cooking, gardening, and shopping. Women who have wealth enough feel they must hire servants; it would not look good for them to do their own housework. Consequently, these women are stuck in a double bind. They belong to a socioeconomic class that makes it improper for them to work both outside and inside the house, and they are left with much free time to dwell on the disappointing and unfulfilling aspects of their lives.

One intelligent and very attractive woman I met in New Delhi lives in a nice apartment, where servants perform all the household tasks. Her husband, a busy executive, spends much time at work, and her children are preoccupied by their college education. She stays home all day, deprived of the means to achieve self-esteem. Her sole creative act is to change her attire, up to four times a day, coming up with beautiful combinations of clothes and jewelry, passing the time while pleasing the sole member of the audience for her beautiful display: herself. (Well, technically, there are servants around, but they are usually ignored as if they did not exist.)

This New Delhi woman exercises her freedom of choice and adorns herself as she pleases, changing outfits throughout the day. She is privileged economically and socially, living in her own flat in the nation's capital, away from her meddlesome in-laws. These conditions allow her to assert herself as she wishes, but most women in India, certainly most of those in Banaras, live out their lives in the homes of their in-laws, often under the domination of their mothers-in-law.[14] Along with food preparation and child rearing, personal adornment is a realm within which the mother-in-law imposes her desires and opinions in an attempt to educate—and control—her daughter-in-law.

In the chapters on Nina, Neelam, and Mukta, we saw that all three were affected in their adornment choices by the presence or absence of their parents-in-law. Whether positive or negative, the relationship with the mother-in-law is an important force in how young married women present themselves, both in the house and beyond it.

The Mother-in-Law

In life, a woman progresses from being a young bride and daughter-in-law, to being a mother, and then to being a mother-in-law, thus gaining the long-awaited opportunity to subjugate a new daughter-in-law, teaching her the rules of the house and the proper behaviors that the mother-in-law herself was once made to accept. And so the cycles roll on: after three decades of marriage, the woman lands again at the vexed nexus of the mother-in-law/daughter-in-law relationship, this time playing the opposite role, the one with authority.

Mathuri Chaubey is a highly intelligent, independent woman in her early sixties. She has spent most of her life in Banaras, and in this chapter she gives us the mother-in-law's perspective.[15] The mother of two sons and three daughters, Mathuri has experienced being a mother to five children, and a mother-in-law to two women. When her daughters-in-law first came to live with her she was strict with them, making sure they wore toe rings, anklets, *bindi*, and *sindur*—"twenty-four hours a day," as she was taught. When she was a young daughter-in-law, Mathuri would remove her *bindi* before going to bed and sometimes forget to put it on in the morning; when she arrived at her mother-in-law's room bearing the "bed tea" without a *bindi*, she would get an angry scolding.

When I ask why they wear jewelry, most women mention the dictates of their mothers-in-law, so I asked Mathuri why she wanted her daughters-in-law to wear ornaments. She explained that since these "compulsory" items are a sign of marriage, they auspiciously protect the marriage, and more importantly, the jewelry is believed to protect the husband's life. She said that some believe a careless wife can inadvertently harm her husband's health. Mathuri explained that since widows are plain and unornamented, seeing your daughter-in-law without *sindur* or *bindi*—in the manner of a widow—provides you with an uncomfortable premonition of a mother's worst nightmare: the death of her son. Likewise, Mathuri said that mothers discourage their sons from shaving their heads and mustaches, since this is done only once—when mourning the death of one's father.[16] The contemporary fashion of shaved heads on males—exported from American basketball courts to Indian discos—disturbs many Indian women who expect to see their sons' heads shaved only upon the dreadful event of the death of their husbands. Mathuri recited a rhyme for me that offered the reasonable opinion that a man without a mustache is like an animal without a tail; both are strange to look at.

Mathuri explained that a mother-in-law wants her daughters-in-law to be ornamented, partially to discourage people from talking, from spreading the word that in her household the daughters-in-law are not disciplined enough to comply by the social rules of *suhagin* ornamentation. But, Mathuri said, there is another reason to have one's daughter-in-law wear the wifely ornaments, revealing something about the psychology of the mother-in-law: "A mother-in-law," she said, "will feel bad that she [the daughter-in-law] does not wish my son well. She has come from another house, and does not *love* my son properly. She is not a good woman." This epitomizes the general distrust the members of the household might have toward the daughter-in-law—the only person living in the family home who has not spent much of her life there, having come from "another house." I asked Mathuri if these rules applied only to the new *bahu*—the new daughter-in-law—or to older ones as well, and she replied:

"For new *bahus,* there are *hard and fast rules.* You must wear for one and a half months, regardless. You must wear. Then after that, people get *liberal.* Like when the children are small, and if you are wearing a lot of bangles, then they press against the child. If you are wearing lots of rings, then during massage, they are scratching the baby. So in this way, we make a few allowances."

Mathuri said that the mother-in-law's heart softens with the arrival of grandchildren, causing her to relax the rules of adornment for the safety of the babies. Jewelry, as explained earlier by Mukta, can cause minor damage to infants. Noisy jewelry—anklets and bangles—can wake a sleeping child. Rings can abrade the sensitive skin of tiny babies, potentially causing infections, as Mathuri said, because rings often trap dirt beneath them. Adding to the already complex psychological relationship between these two women—the mother and the wife of one man—is the notion of the mother-in-law's desire for the personal pleasure and social admiration that comes from having acquired a beautiful wife for her son. Mathuri elaborates:

"Everybody wants the *bahu* to appear pretty. Because with the daughter, what happens often is that I can't keep my daughter all dressed up in my house. When she is with me, she is *kumari* [unmarried] and you don't keep a *kumari* girl dressed up. And when the *bahu* comes, if she is also not dressed up, then how will my desire be fulfilled?

"There is this desire always. Say, from childhood, I have a really nice *ornament*, a really beautiful piece. Then I will set that aside, thinking, 'When my *bahu* comes, I will give this to her.' All mothers have this. If there is a really nice thing, if there is only one of them, then buy another one, if there are two sons. If there are two similar things, I will give them to both *bahus*."

Women feel the social pressure to wear less and less jewelry as they get older. Their old interest in fashion is partially filled vicariously by having beautiful young women around the house, dressed up appealingly. Since daughters must remain plain until they are married, at which point they immediately go to live with their in-laws, this desire is logically relocated to the body of the daughter-in-law, the *bahu,* who becomes the recipient of the family heirlooms, insuring that the jewelry stays in the family. Giving jewelry to a daughter, many believe, will lead to a transfer of wealth to her new family.

Echoing Mukta's comment about the inappropriateness of a mother-in-law and daughter-in-law "matching," Mathuri makes it clear that the elevation of status from mother to mother-in-law is marked, in part, by a diminishing of fashion:

"This is the case. Say my *bahu* has come. Now, properly, she should be the one who is nicely dressed up. When the *bahus* have not yet come, or the daughters are still around, and they are young, until then it looks nice for me to be dressed up, to wear nice clothes. But, *above forty,* now my kids are grown, my *bahus* are coming, and if I were to be here that dressed up, then that looks *odd.* I should minimize myself, and they should wear more. This is necessary."

This change in status, this shift in the hierarchy of roles, must be expressed. The mother-in-law is now officially the matriarch, having endured a life of caring for the household and raising children. The duties of cooking, cleaning, and producing the offspring are now the tasks of the younger women. Many women are relieved by this well-earned retirement of sorts, but there is also sadness in the loss of youth and beauty. And in many households a hostile jealously arises between the mother-in-law and the daughter-in-law, since both compete for the love and loyalty of the son/husband. The tense, abrasive relation of a mother-in-law and her son's wife is well documented in anthropological writing and in literature.[17]

For many families, the inclusion of daughters-in-law in the future is a happily anticipated event. It will mark a point in future time when the boys will be grown up, healthy, and successful. The marriage of one's children and the arrival of grandchildren (and grandsons in particular) symbolize prosperity and the continuation of the family line. Interestingly, the fantasy of the incorporation of the daughter-in-law into the household is always talked about with reference to the noisy jewelry a new bride wears. Mathuri remembered the daydreams her late husband had about his future daughters-in-law, whose arrival registered in his imagination as the *chum chum* sound of their anklet bells:

"It is the *kalpana* [imagination] of people that when the *bahu* comes, she will walk *chum chum, chum chum* around the house. This anticipation is around for a long time. Chaubeyji [her late husband] would often say, 'When my *bahu* comes, she will go *chum chum* here, *chum chum* there.' It is with the sound of *chum chum* that he would *recognize* [the idea of] the *bahu*. When the *bahu* comes, 'She will walk like this. She will talk like this. She will make these kinds of food.'"

At this point in the conversation, Mathuri's young granddaughters appeared in the room briefly. Keeping her focus on the talk about ornamentation, Mathuri recalled a shopping trip in which the young girls went with her to Godaulia to buy saris for the wedding of Mathuri's youngest daughter. The children were visibly excited, surrounded by silk and brocade, and they verbally expressed their yearning to get married one day. Mathuri told me that girls of that age see marriage only in its "*pleasure rup*"—in its incarnation as delight, a time of exquisite ornamentation, of luxurious clothing and jewelry. She said that young girls do not see the hardship and suffering that is the reality of marriage. This cannot be anticipated beforehand, she said; it can only be understood with experience.

The Widow

In the cycle of a woman's life, the stage after becoming a mother-in-law inevitably involves death, either the woman's or her husband's. The hardship Mathuri alludes to is a consequence of her widowhood. Being alone for the last two decades, Mathuri has raised all five children and arranged most of their marriages by herself.

The social rules that govern the appearance of widows vary within the different regional, ethnic, and religious communities of India, but general prescriptions call for widows to wear undyed (white) clothing, no ornaments, and no perfume. They should sleep on the floor, stop eating "hot" non-vegetarian foods such as fish, onions, garlic, and some varieties of lentils,[18] and they should eat only once a day. If the widow is a Brahmin, religious law even prescribes her to shave her head, though compliance with that law is rare in the extreme.[19] Mathuri explained that in Banaras widows are not allowed to wear glass bangles, *sindur, bindi,* toe rings, anklets, and red and yellow clothing. She told me of an old local custom that few people follow today. When a woman's husband died, and the wrapped body was about to go on its procession to the river for cremation, the widow was made to dress as a bride again, complete with a red sari, *sindur,* and glass bangles. Before the body was taken away, a hired female servant, while holding the lifeless hand of the dead husband, would smudge the *sindur* off the widow's head, and break the glass bangles off of her wrists. This marked the symbolic end of the marriage, a reversal of the climax of the wedding rites, in which the groom applies *sindur* for the first time to the part in his wife's hair. In the old custom, the men would take the corpse away, and the women would remain in the house with the widow,[20] who had just experienced a traumatic, violent removal of the ornaments she would never wear again. This psychologically horrific event, in which a woman is stripped of her identity and femininity, is described in the anthropological literature, and it is a recurrent theme in the works of Indian female authors, including Chitra Banerjee Divakaruni, Jhumpa Lahiri, Bharati Mukherjee, Manju Kapur, Anita Nair, Rama Mehta, and Mira Kamdar.[21]

Another ritual, also now largely abandoned, followed the death of a woman whose husband remained alive. Many people in Banaras would dress the dead woman in her bridal finery. The widower would place *sindur* on her hair part and glass bangles on her wrists. Her body would be wrapped in a shiny cloth, and she would be burned while wearing all the marriage ornaments. The dead woman would leave the earth in a celebration of her intact marital status. Finally, Mathuri spoke of the funerary rite for an unmarried woman whose parents had expected to see her as a bride someday. Her father would buy for her an expensive Banarasi sari and gold ornaments, the things he always assumed he would give her as her dowry. She would be dressed up as a bride, with the marked absence of *sindur,* and burned in that state, as a sad visual reminder to her parents of the unrealized celebration of her wedding.

All three of these old customs—marking the death of a woman's husband, a married woman's death, and an unmarried woman's early death—are not widely practiced today. All employed the auspicious clothing and ornamentation of a bride at the time of death—to complete the unfulfilled desire of parents to see their daughter as a bride, to celebrate the lucky woman who has died while still married, and to mark the end of an era for the woman who, as a widow, has irrevocably left her life's most important stage.

Nowadays, Mathuri said, many widows only wear a pure white sari for the official days of mourning after the husband's death. Once this period is over, many wear colored saris again, being careful to choose muted hues— what novelist Anita Nair calls "drab moth tones,"[22] such as gray, dull blue, and black. Widows should avoid the celebratory marriage colors of red, pink, orange, yellow, and maroon for the rest of their lives. Today many widows wear a few glass or gold bangles, or a small black *bindi,* but the red *bindi* is avoided since it is too closely associated with marriage. Mathuri herself wears a pair of thin gold bangles on each wrist, along with three brown glass bangles. She wears nothing around her neck, nothing on her forehead, and only one demure astrological pearl ring on her hand. The simple, understated way in which she is ornamented signals her status as a widow. I asked her if she would ever consider wearing a dozen bright *churis* on her wrists again, and she replied:

"No, I won't. *Widows,* they will never wear that many *churis,* you understand? It is necessary to be very *simple.* It is thought that now that they have become *widows,* to be running after *fashion*—there is a reason for this. If *widows* were to be dressed with lots of *chamak-damak* [glitter and shine], then upon going out, people will say something or other. They will *taunt.* Or they will think that in her mind there still is a desire to appear attractive. She is flaunting herself, and therefore, she has a need for a *husband.* Isn't that right?

So in this way, toward her, people develop a wrong *attitude*—people can read somebody's *attitude* through their *dress,* no? Like, 'What does this woman want?' By looking you can figure this out—if I am appearing in front of you, very *fashionably* dressed, what are you going to think? Are you going to think that I am in mourning?"

Social pressures urge younger and older women to banish ornamentation and appear simple. It is believed that widows, like single young women, have no need to sexually attract men. They should not dress tantalizingly. In her study of gender and aging in a village in Bengal, Sarah Lamb concludes that white clothing and the other restrictions on ornamentation do not necessarily function to constrain the sexuality of older and widowed women, but rather, they signal asexuality, a post-reproductive, and in some ways freer, stage of women's lives.[23] The modest look of a widow communicates her adherence to these social rules, and it visually conveys her commitment to a state of mourning for her husband. It is improper to dress up, to display a visual celebration of beauty and life, on the occasion of somebody's death, as Mathuri explains:

"If somebody's *death* has occurred, so, will you be wearing lots of *churi,* jewelry, *bindi* and *kajal,* and go somewhere like that? You won't go. Even if you just got married. On that day, you will wear a very *simple sari* and very *ordinary ornaments,* a thin *chain.*

"A big huge *haar* [thick necklace], even if you are wearing a white sari, with dangly-dangly chunky earrings, if a *death* has occurred in the family, will you go like that? You won't. Never. Among us, it is considered very bad. They will say: 'There has been a *death,* and in this way, in that sari and jewelry, she has come!'"

I asked Mathuri if such judgments are made only of newly widowed women, or also of those whose husbands died many years ago. She said that once the husband is gone, there really is no reason to be ornamented anymore; people will read ornamentation as a sign of promiscuity.[24] Others will think, "To whom is she showing herself," and the woman's inner desire to seem attractive is gone. Mathuri said sadly: "My *life* has now ended with my *husband.* This *fashion life,* it has ended with my *husband.*" I asked Mathuri to elaborate: "Are ornaments worn for the husband?" and she replied:

"Some are. They are worn explicitly for the *husband,* after marriage. Like glass bangles in red and yellow, and red and yellow clothes—red and yellow clothes have a very strong *effect.* If you were to wear really *gaudy-gaudy* clothes, and sit by your *husband,* then in the *husband's* mind a different feeling is born. If you were to wear *chamak-damak* things and go toward your *husband,* what would happen? There is certainly an *excitement* caused by clothes, caused by jewelry, caused by the person's *fashion.*

"So, that *excitement* in a man is caused by another. Some jewelry of mine, or clothes, can *excite* somebody else. So, that thing—what need do I have for that after I have become a *widow*? Why should I wear those things that cause *excitement* in other people, now that my *husband* is no longer here?"

A woman ornaments herself to provoke sexual excitement in her husband, but also to please herself, as we have seen throughout this book. Would the innate desire to please the self through ornamentation also subside with the death of one's spouse? I wondered: if nobody were to pass judgment on Mathuri's appearance, would she still wear the things she wore as a wife? She responded frankly:

"I really liked ornaments; when I used to wear them, I really like them. When I used to wear ornaments in the presence of my *husband,* I really liked it. But now, the problem is, I know that I used to wear them because I was *suhagin*—I had to wear them—and I really liked it. Both *combinations* were present, so I really liked it.

"But now, in my soul that *joy* is not there; that happiness is not there, since the loss of my *husband.* So now, when I see those things, the desire to wear is not there. Now there is sadness inside. If I were to see those things, pick them up, then I don't feel that I want to try them on, try them on and see how I look. I don't feel like that. What I feel is that once I used to wear these things—it was really nice—but now seeing those things causes me *taklif* [suffering], not happiness. Before—because it was my *liking,* and I had to wear, I got an opportunity to wear—so I used to wear with much happiness. But now, looking at those things, I don't feel happiness—instead the opposite, very much sadness I feel; that is why I push those things farther away. I don't like to wear them anymore."

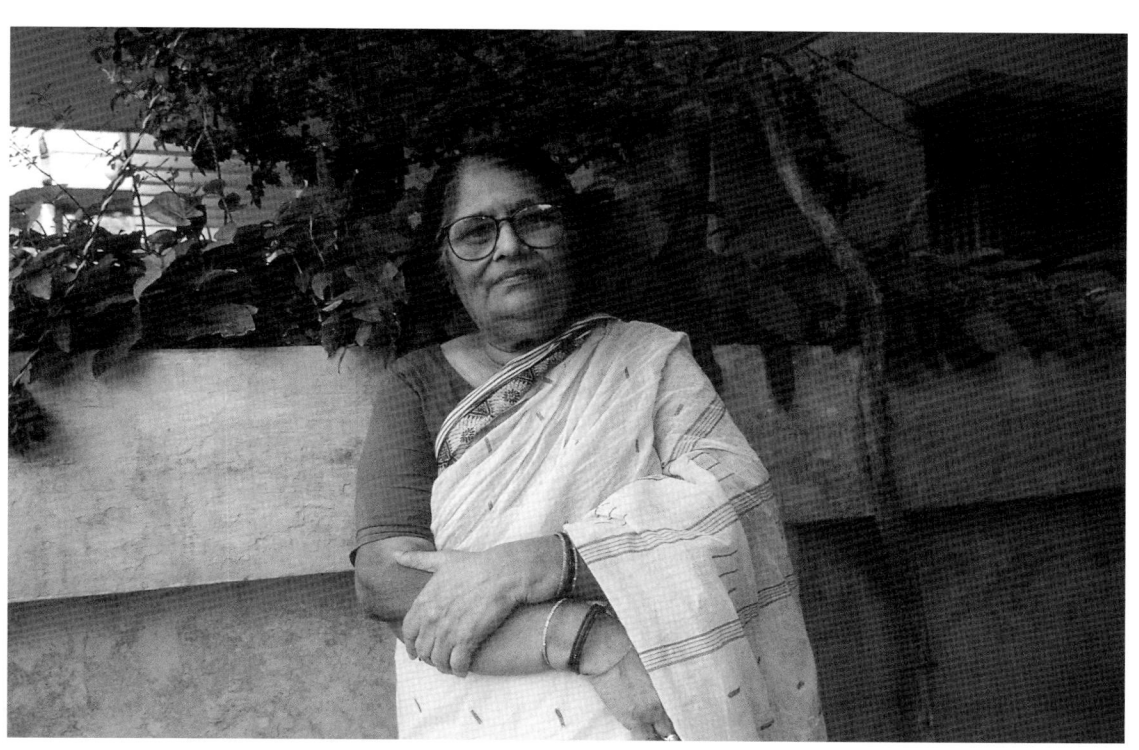

Mathuri Chaubey

Young girls look forward to their marriages, excited by the prospect of being decorated from that day forward. Young brides revel in the pleasure of the new trousseau, which includes luxurious and glittery items meant to launch the couple on their sexual life together. The fantasy of jewelry and fancy clothing is associated with marriage in the minds of single women; then once they have married, acts of self-adornment are linked inextricably with the husband. For many women, including Mathuri, it becomes impossible to separate the desire to be ornamented from the desire to please one's spouse. Mathuri feels pain at the memory of her youthful self getting adorned in celebration of her marriage to her husband, who was once healthy and vital and young, but who is now gone.

If nobody were around, in the privacy of her bedroom, would she consider donning some of her old items of adornment? Mathuri answered that even if the thought crossed her mind, her "*conscience* would not allow it." Some women, she said, cannot control themselves, probably because they never really loved their husbands. If a woman were really "attached" to her husband, then she would "naturally detach" from ornamentation as a gesture of loyalty. When I asked Mathuri if she were to see a woman whom she knew to be a widow with much jewelry on, would she feel that the woman did not really love her deceased husband, she replied: "Yes, I would feel that. And I would feel that she is not a very good woman either. I would feel that she is not a *devotee lady*. She is not *devoted* to her husband anymore."

Sarah Lamb's fieldwork among older women in Bengal shows that women follow the social prescriptions on dress and behavior for several reasons: to control their sexuality, to protect their honor and that of their families, and to atone for their power of destruction,[25] since it is widely believed that a woman is fated to become a widow, and so she has caused her husband's death. Another reason for a widow to dress and behave in the expected manner, according to Lamb, is to continue her life of devotion toward her husband. From Lina Fruzzetti's fieldwork among Hindus in Bengal, we learn that there are two kinds of *prem*—love—that a wife develops for her husband: a conjugal love, and a devotional love.[26] Mathuri's understanding of a social expectation of devotion on the part of the widow is consistent with Lamb's and Fruzzetti's findings.

Many men and women in India object to the notion of women having to be completely devoted to their husbands throughout their lives, including the period after the death of their spouses. This opinion relates to the vehement rejection of *sati*. In *sati,* the newly widowed ended her life by joining her husband on the funeral pyre. B. D. Soni told me that the practice began in Mewar, Rajasthan, as an act of suicide designed to escape the capture and brutal fate of women whose husbands were killed. It has since become associated with the pious and virtuous devotion of a wife toward her dead husband. Although legally banned in 1829, *sati* has resurfaced, at least as an ideal of wifely conduct, since 1987, with the famous case of Roop Kanwar. Willingly or not, she joined her husband in death by mounting the burning pyre with him.[27] A religious reason to die with one's husband is to prevent the soiling of his position in heaven with unvirtuous behavior after his death.[28] A social reason is to avoid the miserable experience of widowhood, recorded in literary passages and oral narratives of the kind collected in Uma Chakravarti and Preeti Gill's anthology.[29]

In the introduction to his volume on the burning of wives, John Stratton Hawley investigates the historical meaning of the word *sati*—widely used to name both the practice and the woman who sacrifices herself. He concludes that, in one interpretation, the word could even imply a woman who is devoted to her husband.[30] Catherine Weinberger-Thomas's excellent book on *sati* also supports this interpretation.[31] It might be said in our day that *sati* is symbolically enacted when the woman, instead of ending her life in the flames, ends her life as an ornamented being when she puts aside her bangles and *sindur.* In fact, many believe that when a husband dies, a woman becomes "half dead," that her social life has ended, and that she should "willingly mortify her body."[32] A plain woman in a white sari has left the celebratory aspect of her life behind, resigning herself to the marginal role that widows tragically occupy in India.

If a woman abandons wifely ornamentation, should she stop paying attention to herself, stifling her desire to appear attractive? Mathuri, respecting her husband's memory, has not engaged in body art of the kind that pleased her as a young wife. She has made appropriate adjustments, remaining true in her devotion to him yet acknowledging the fact that she is still alive and part of the social world. Mathuri has a parallel in the famous example of India's former prime minister Indira Gandhi who, though a widow, was widely regarded for her fashion sense.[33] Mathuri explained her changes in this way:

"I should now be in a *sober tarika.* For example, I have cut my hair. The reason is that if I were to plait my hair in a single braid—with a braid it is necessary—if your braid is long, if you have hair that is long—then it is necessary to add *sindur,* to add *bindi;* then only will *grace* come to your face. But if the hair is cut, then you don't notice the absence of *bindi* and *sindur.* I also cut my hair because I had to work outside, in the *field.* I had to appear presentable. And I had to appear in a *sober tarika.* So what could I do? I had to change myself in some way, to look another way. That is why I had to do this.

"Like, I could *brush* my hair or not, it doesn't make that big a difference, really. Just put on a sari, and if I don't do anything to my *face,* the *grace* is already there, right? If I were to wear my hair in a tight braid, then my face would look *suna-suna.* Like these women [her daughters-in-law], they have that tight braid; if they did not have *sindur* or *bindi,* their faces would look *suna.* It would look bad."

Mathuri went to work "in the field" by working at a radio station. She needed to look professional, presentable, yet plain, like a widow. She achieved this by cutting her hair, causing thick wavy locks to frame her face and eliminate the prominent part that a wife fills with red powder. Young women signal marriage by a change in appearance—the addition of *sindur, bindi,* and other ornaments. Mathuri signaled the change in her status not only by the elimination of red and yellow saris[34] and by a lack of ornaments, but also by the addition of a new hairstyle, which communicated her status as a widow and her regard for her dead husband, and which communicated, too, her independence and healthy self-esteem. Mathuri explained that widows find another way, a new *tarika,* for looking good:

"In all people, there is a habit to make the self *good-looking;* that is there. But now that *tarika* has changed. If I—I want to look beautiful, I don't want to look ugly—so, say, in the era of my husband, *bindi, sindur, kajal*—with these things I looked beautiful. So after becoming a *widow,* I can still look good in a different way. It's not like I will gather my hair up, sloppy, and start looking ugly. This will never be the sentiment.

"Now whatever *atmosphere* has come into my life, within that I will also try to look beautiful. Wear a *matching blouse,* a *sober sari.* So that people don't *criticize,* but that I also look beautiful. Stand apart from others. It's not like this; that now that my *husband* has died, I have smeared mud on my face and arms, and am walking around like that. It's not like that at all.

"No matter how old a woman is, this she will want: That people look at me and be *impressed.* Now there is a different *tarika* of *impressing* the *husband,* right? You are understanding this, no? For the *husband,* there is a *tarika* that creates *excitement* in him. Be totally dressed up, be in a totally *gaudy tarika,* so the husband is totally *excited."*

As Mathuri teaches, different stages in life have different *tarikas*—styles—in each of which a woman finds room for self-expression. The *tarika* includes the appropriate jewelry and clothing and the messages they carry. Unmarried women should showcase innocence and youth, avoiding the provocative. Married women must excite their husbands, at least in the first years of marriage, with babies the goal. Widows can still look good, but they should not look sexy, for the sexual aspect of their lives died with their husbands. Though the Widow Remarriage Act of 1856 made it legal, few widows consider remarriage. Widows are like young unmarried women in their lack of adornment and their lack of a need to excite a man sexually. Although the look is similar, the clothing is different: widows wear saris, not *salwar suits* or jeans. Mathuri concludes: "Everybody desires to be beautiful. *But it should be according to atmosphere, according to place, according to circumstance."*

Each stage has its *tarika,* each *tarika* varies. Differences in a widow's appearance have to do with ethnicity and caste, but also with family circumstances. Hemant Khanchandani, the Sindhi owner of the Dayaram Fashion Centre, has a widowed mother who lives with him. His mother, Puspa Devi, has worn only white clothing since the death of her husband. She wears no *bindi, sindur,* or *mangalsutra*—the items most closely associated with marriage for Sindhis. But Puspa Devi does wear gold earrings, a golden necklace, and gold bracelets. Her daughter-in-law, Nina, explained that Sindhi widows may wear clothing in any color, but Puspa Devi feels most comfortable in white, possibly because she lives in Banaras where white clothing traditionally designates widowhood. The choice to wear white could be partly influenced by Puspa Devi's quiet character, the consequence, perhaps, of her continual mourning for her late husband.

By contrast, Prempati Manik, the widowed mother of Ashok Kumar Manik, the owner of the Priya Bangles store, is flamboyant in her appearance and energetic in her personality. She lives with her son and grandsons—Priya Kumar, Preetam Kumar, and Sant Kumar—in a lofty, multistory house. The family is prosperous and happy, and they treat Prempati with respect and deference. Enjoying an honored position in the home of her son, Prempati wears a white sari with as much ornamentation as she can get away with. On one occasion she wore a crisp, starched white sari with a mint green border, decorated with tiny black flowers. She wore heavy gold earrings and a pair of thick gold bangles on each wrist with light blue glass ones in between. Prempati, a former Hindi teacher who moved to Banaras before India's independence, displays through her body art a confident personality, an economically secure position, and a comfortable familial environment in which she is praised and privileged.

Prempati is lucky to have the unconditional support of her family. Many widows in India, both Muslim and Hindu, are treated horribly; they are viewed as a social and economic burden on their families. This predicament is heartbreakingly depicted in the great Bengali novel *Pather Panchali,* when the old woman is begrudgingly given food and shelter by her distant relatives, who later show only relief at the news of her death.[35] That is why most old women declare a desire to die before their husbands, to avoid the experience of widowhood. Not only are widows considered inauspicious; many women feel compromised in the household, having spent years tyrannizing over their daughters-in-law while they enjoyed the privilege of being married to the head of the family. Once the father is dead, the oldest son assumes the position of patriarch (if there is no resident uncle to outrank the sons) and his wife seizes power over the domestic affairs of the house, displacing the old mother-in-law.

The ideal situation is to be a *sowbhagyavati,* a blessed woman, married and un-widowed.[36] This is the case with Sati Devi, the mother of B. D. Soni, the Rajasthani jeweler. Though elderly, Sati Devi still wears bright clothes in shades of red and pink; in Rajasthan red, pink, and orange are the colors for married women, while blue and green are the colors for widows. Being Rajasthani, Sati Devi does not wear saris, but rather the *choli* and skirt outfit of the local women. After her marriage, she wore the ivory *chura* bangles that go from the wrist up the forearm, but she discontinued wearing them about twenty years ago because, after she had lost weight, the rigid bangles started to poke her arms, chafing her skin. Sati Devi stopped wearing the *chura* for reasons of personal comfort, yet she told me, in English, that since they are now "out of fashion" anyway, it was all for the best. At home, surrounded by her daughters-in-law, Sati Devi is the reigning matriarch. She continues to wear the low-cut, sexy *cholis* that Rajasthani women wear, partly because it is her habit, and partly because she told me she would not look good in Western clothes. Her choices are still aesthetically governed, made with beauty and comfort in mind. Her freedom of choice is enabled by the position she enjoys in her family: her husband, Govind Lal, is still alive, her household is prosperous, and her sons and daughters-in-law treat her with respect.

In Banaras, a widow mourns in a white sari with a marked absence of ornaments. In Rajasthan, Marwari widows wear green *choli* and skirt outfits, but married women may mourn a death in the family by donning a green shawl for two months, becoming symbolic widows in green while still wearing red or pink clothing underneath. Death and color connect as well in the turbans of the men. Govind Lal, B. D. Soni's father, has worn a light pink turban for the last three years. Before that he wore the characteristic turban of his native Jaisalmer, tie-dyed in five bright colors. The pink turban signifies that Govind Lal is the oldest living son, a status he reached when his older brother died.[37] Only local people would understand this code.

Codes of visual communication, like all messages, function to define group membership. Nina and Hemant Khanchandani know how Sindhis mourn, they know what a widow can and cannot wear. Nina told me that Gujarati and Marwari widows may wear *bindis* in either white or black, but not red. Whether true or not, people know what defines the life stages within their own caste, and that it differs from the traditions of other castes. B. D. Soni, a Rajasthani, believes that Sindhi widows living in Jodpur must wear white saris, though Nina, a Sindhi, says that widows can wear saris in every color. B.D. said that these widows may also wear ornaments, so long as they are *mamuli*—ordinary, modest, and unexceptional. B.D.'s wife, Kausalya, and his sisters-in-law, Pushpa, Anju, and Santosh, all disagreed with him, saying widows may not wear toe rings, a nose ring, or a *bindi,* no matter how small these ornaments are. The point to note is that there are discrepancies in individual understandings of these rules, variation that occurs not only between castes, but among people of different genders within a single family.

Here is the question: who are these rules of self-adornment in life stages meant to please? People beyond one's group do not always have an accurate notion of what is being communicated by choices of color, amount, and size of the ornaments. The people I talked to in Banaras said it does not really matter if a Gujarati or Bengali can read the messages encoded in one's attire; the communication is not meant for outsiders but for the people of one's own group. The opinion that matters is not that of the "local public," but that of the members of your own family and caste, and especially the female faction—the people who are completely on the inside, fluent in the language of body art, and able to judge every nuanced choice.

Women adhere to the rules of adornment to please themselves and the members of the in-group, mostly other women of their own caste. This point becomes poignant in the *suhagin* tradition of the wife. Many women have admitted to me, after some time, that one of the reasons they comply with the wishes of their mother-in-law to wear the "compulsory" wifely items is to ensure that no harm will befall the husband. While the mother-in-law's desire is to keep her son healthy (so he will take care of her in her old age),[38] the wife's desire is to keep her husband alive, so she will not suffer the humiliating loss of power that comes to the widow, alone in a house into which she was not born. It is in the woman's best interest to keep her husband alive and well. Why not put on *sindur* and *bindi* if they insure a better life for yourself? Both women—the mother-in-law and the wife—want the same man to live, ultimately to benefit their own position in the household and in society. We return to one theme of this book: women follow societal norms not out of a mindless assent to convention, but as a willful, traditional act that benefits them as individuals on many levels.

·14·

Before the Wedding

THE STREETS OF INDIA are dizzy with color: colors crackle and clash in the temples and shrines, in the marketplace, in the clothes women wear. Colorful ornament enhances beauty and signals desire, whether the goal of desire is worship, commerce, or the communication of one's place in the cycle of life. At the beginning of that cycle, babies are peculiarly vulnerable, susceptible to disease, carried quickly into deaths that many believe are caused by supernatural powers. The tiny bodies of living babies are decorated to attract the benevolence of the gods while fending off malignant spirits. Many adorn the infant with amulets tied with thread around the neck, waist, or arm. Black kohl is used to line their eyes, for protective and medicinal purposes, giving babies a chic and sultry look. A round mark of black kohl, like a displaced *bindi,* is located on the face of the baby, often to one side of the head, to ward off evil spirits or deflect the evil eye cast by envious humans, especially if the baby is notably beautiful.

Once the child has skirted the dangers of infancy and survived the first few years, the family relaxes. Parents let the hair of both boys and girls grow long until about the age of two, when a ritual shaving of the head takes place, ensuring that the new growth will be thick and healthy. Small boys might be ornamented with tiny anklets and other jewelry, looking like beloved renditions of Baby Krishna. Little girls are enveloped in bright colors and decorated with tiny anklets, necklaces, bracelets, and even earrings. Until the age of twelve, girls wear party dresses—frilly, lacy dresses that tie at the back with a big bow—even when they are playing roughly in the dusty streets. During ritual moments when the adult females of the household have henna or *alta* applied to their hands and feet, little girls often join in, innocently accepting the auspicious markings of married women. Too young to be sexually arousing, little girls are resplendent in party clothes and tinkling jewelry.

But around the age of twelve, at the onset of puberty, the danger of pregnancy looms, and parents forbid (arousing) ornament to their daughters until they are safely married. Conservative Muslim families throughout India bring their daughters into *purdah* at the age of twelve, at which point many girls stop attending school and come to spend most of their time inside the house, away from public view. It varies greatly from family to family, but the girl may also be clad in a *burqa* that covers her body, head, and perhaps even her face. Some Hindu and Jain families, conscious of the fact that their girls are the ones being seen on the streets, adopt a form of *purdah* as well. Author Mira Kamdar, in her affectionate remembrance, describes her Jain grandmother's upbringing in Gujarat, where the non-Muslim girls were also subjected to *purdah.* They were made to stay inside the house, invisible to people beyond the family, until they were married.[1] Most Hindu families enforce a sort of *purdah,* not by veiling their daughters, but by disallowing provocative dress and restricting and monitoring the girl's movements beyond the house.[2] Girls at the age of twelve, as we have seen, stop wearing dresses and shorts, and only wear pants or *salwar suits,* garments that cover their legs completely. (It could be argued that a tight pair of jeans becomes sexier than a dress once the girl has matured into the curves that jeans reveal.)

These prescriptions make sense, for people believe it is dangerous for adolescent girls to dress in a way that might excite the burgeoning sexuality of the boys of their age—or, worse, that might even arouse their older male relatives within the household. Young women are taught not only to follow a sort of *purdah* for the body, but also to observe what Monica Ali, in her novel *Brick Lane,* calls "purdah in the mind": keeping the self pure, free of indecent thoughts.[3] Adhering to such norms signals membership in society, for the rules the girls follow apply only to insiders. Outsiders—foreigners or members of other castes and religions—follow other rules, or no rules. In Jhumpa Lahiri's short story "The Treatment of Bibi Haldar," the principal character, a mature woman, is able to wear clothes that reveal her knees and legs—something the women of her age have not done since they were girls—because Bibi, being mentally unstable, stands outside the confines and judgment of normal society, and she is allowed to disregard the taboos respectable women must observe.[4]

328

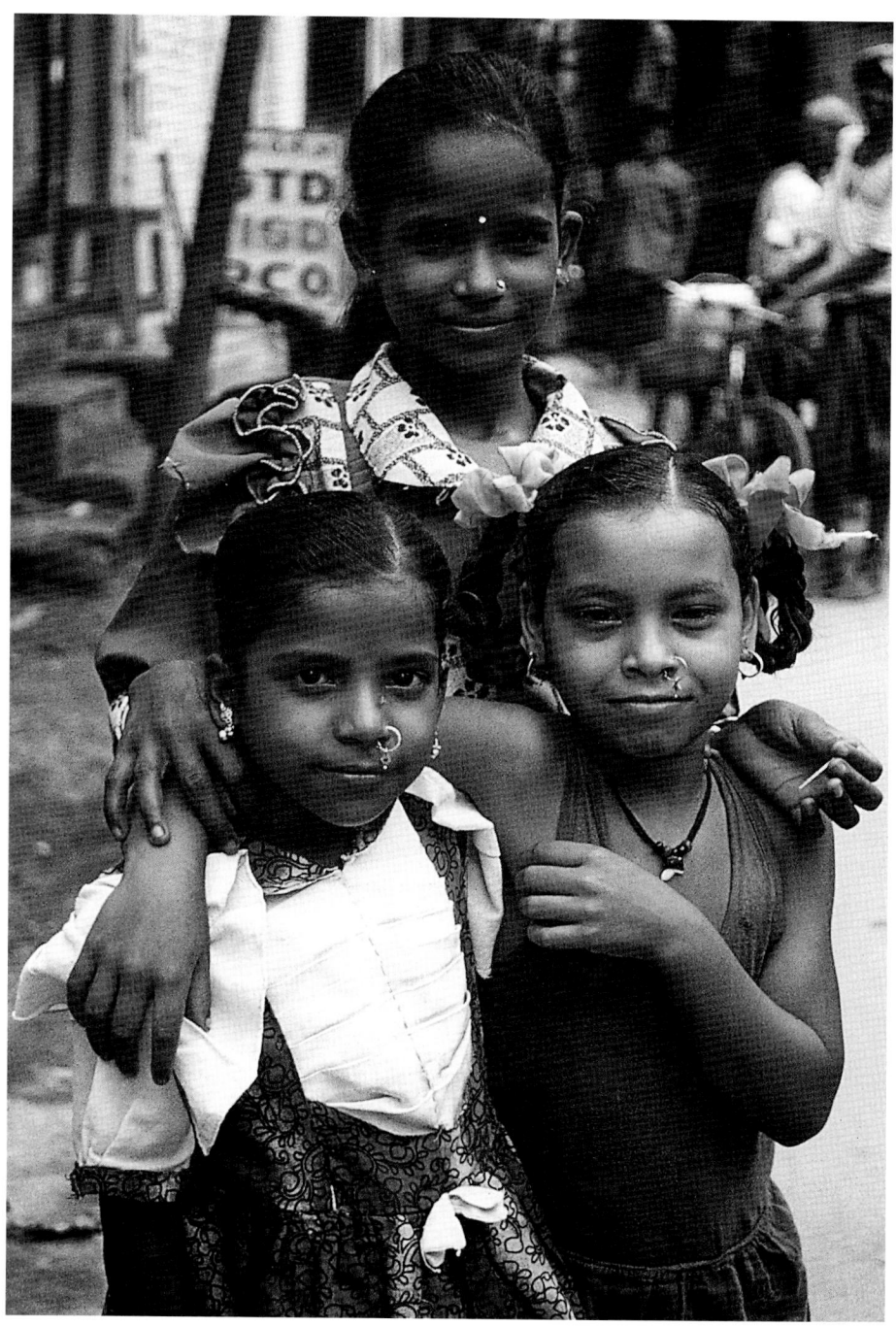

Ornamented young girls: Anu, Rekha, and Manju

Mathuri Chaubey speculated on the reasons why Muslim girls in Banaras are so lavishly adorned just before they enter *purdah*, and her observations apply to conservative Hindu families as well. When girls are young, she said, they can be viewed without harm, so parents highlight the innocent beauty of their daughters in order to create a lasting impression, one that might be retrieved from the mind's eye at the time of matchmaking. Even in *purdah*, Mathuri said, people will remember how beautiful so-and-so's daughter was in childhood, and wonder: "If she was so pretty as a little girl, imagine how she must look now!" Young girls are encouraged to be decorated when it is appropriate—before puberty—to exhibit their potential for mature beauty, for a good match. After puberty, girls must look plain, but the memory of their childish beauty lingers, especially in the minds of those who do not live nearby but who may play a vital role in the arrangement of marriage. The reason to replace the girl's frilly dress with a *salwar suit* is to signal maturity. This signal is sent to the girl; she will start behaving like a woman. And it is sent to others; they will start thinking of her as mature, a potential marriage partner. The transformation from dresses to *salwar suits* visually marks a rite of passage, a change in status that encourages a shift in attitude and behavior—much as shifts in clothing and jewelry later in her life will mark changes to wife, to mother-in-law, to widow.

Maidens

The reasons for a change in body art at puberty seem to make sense from a social and psychological point of view. The main variables that account for the difference in interpretation of how a *kumari*—an unmarried woman—should look are religion, caste, region, and family. Another crucial factor is the social context within which the young lady operates, as the following examples illustrate.

Ram Pyari (Ram's beloved) is the only daughter of the Rajasthani jeweler B. D. Soni. I interviewed her in the summer of 2001,[5] just before her marriage to a Gujarati jeweler's son. Ram Pyari, who was nineteen at the time, spent her days in the joint family compound in Jaisalmer, surrounded by married women—her mother, grandmother, and aunts. Although she wore the usual clothing of *kumari* women—*salwar suits*—Ram Pyari wore much jewelry around the house, surprising given her unmarried status: a gold nose ring, three pairs of earrings, half a dozen plastic bangles on each wrist, three rings on her fingers, and anklets decorated with colorful *mina*. Ram Pyari did not work outside of the house or attend college, the two main public venues of display for a *kumari* woman's body art. Her audience consisted of members of her family instead of judgmental strangers. In the comfort of a jeweler's household, she indulged her interest in jewelry without embarrassment or social stigma.

Many young women in Banaras, and other parts of India, take classes on makeup and henna application, learning a way to make money. Both Laxmi Mishra and Rupali Gupta were learning the craft of beauty at the Aas Art Centre in Banaras in 1996. Unlike Ram Pyari, whose situation reflects a pampered lifestyle of family support and economic security, these young women had to consider their public appearance since they often moved through the public sphere, entering the homes of strangers to adorn the bride and her relatives for wedding occasions. While Laxmi and Rupali spoke expertly about how to match jewelry with clothing, how to apply makeup and create hairstyles, they did not apply their knowledge to themselves since they lacked the cash and remained unmarried.

Laxmi Mishra explained to me why she thought girls at the onset of puberty should become plain and resume personal decoration only after marriage. It does not look attractive, she said, for girls of a certain age to be adorned; you do not want to attract men on the streets, and young girls who adorn themselves provocatively take on an aura of *pap*—of sinfulness. Sin and shame are integral to many people's understandings of why an unmarried woman should not be bedecked on a daily basis. Women of all ages say that a girl should feel *sharam*—shame—if she looks sexy in front of her father, brothers, uncles, and male cousins. In general, both Hindu and Muslim women would feel embarrassed to appear in alluring dress in the presence of the male members of their families, and appearing provocative, or even attractive, outside of the house—in other words, lacking shame in public—is believed to increase "eve teasing," the harassment of women, on the streets.[6] Whether it is to avoid arousing male relatives or strangers with a lack of *sharam,* or inviting social or supernatural retribution by inducing *pap,* young ladies dress with extreme restraint in most social contexts.

Although Rupali Gupta has never attended college, she, like many others in India, has an interesting view of college as a social context. She believes female students should not be too dressed up at the university because, she said, everybody will wonder: "Have you come here to study or for a *fashion pa-*

rade?" As women in increasing numbers attend college in India, this context has come to characterize a new generation's attitudes about personal adornment. In college, Indian men and women go to school for the first time without a uniform, so college provides the first opportunity for a public expression of personality and taste through the choice of clothes and shoes, accessories, makeup, and ornaments. One result is an intensification of competition in personal display among both male and female students, who naturally vie with each other to look good and attract the attention of other students. As we will see shortly, falling in love with another student is one of the ways to escape an arranged marriage, making it imperative to look good in college.

The college years constitute a distinct stage in a woman's life cycle, separating adolescence from marriage, though the privilege of gaining a university education and experiencing the college lifestyle is available to a small percentage of the population of India.

In 1996, I met Somnia Shreebarshira, who, at twenty-five years old, was completing a master's degree in chemistry at Banaras Hindu University. During a long summer afternoon,[7] Somnia allowed me to interview her, in English, about her *kumari* adornment choices, her dreams for marriage, and the way she hopes to look as a young wife. On a daily basis, Somnia, like her girlfriends, wears either jeans or *salwar suits* to attend class, and only a few items of jewelry: a thin gold chain around her neck, two astrological finger rings, and a black *bindi* on her forehead. Although she maintains the demure and understated look that is right for *kumari* college students, Somnia admits that she "secretly likes attention," relishing the special occasions on which unmarried women get dressed up.

Somnia sees wedding receptions as the "biggest occasion in India" to exhibit beauty in the hope of acquiring a good match in a husband. For receptions, *kumari* young women like Somnia wear "heavy *salwar suits*" (silk *suits* with brocading, beads, or sequined embroidery), *lehangas* (fancy ensembles of skirt, shirt, and scarf), or saris. They borrow the saris and gold jewelry from a married sister or sister-in-law, Somnia said, because you will not own your own until after marriage. To complement the clothes and jewelry, young women wear makeup, including eyeliner, lipstick, and a colored *bindi* that matches the outfit. Since everybody dresses up for the wedding party, it becomes a great place to observe the latest fashions and pass judgment on people's marvelous or distasteful attire. If you are dressed particularly well, Somnia said, the other women will react either in front of you, complimenting your outfit, or behind your back with scorn if they are jealous of your look.

Young women, caught between post-puberty and pre-marriage, are in an anticipatory state that affects their behavior and appearance. Daily clothing and jewelry must be defined in opposition to the dress of a new wife, and yet the outfits for special occasions, for wedding receptions especially, are selected to attract a potential husband by displaying the young woman in fine attire as a sort of bride. *Kumari* women are meant to appeal to the parents or relatives of a suitable groom, and so they should appear demurely beautiful, not sexy. This pattern contrasts with Andrea Rugh's observations of Egyptian unmarried women, who, while modestly covering their bodies, wear tight clothes to show off the "goods" to prospective grooms.[8]

In India, marriage is a constant thought in the minds of young women, especially college-aged women in the cities. Just as a man might eagerly await the arrival of his daughter-in-law, signaled by the *chum chum* sound she will make around the house, women eagerly anticipate their life as a wife, the time when they will wear certain clothes and certain jewelry while enjoying a new social status. I was told repeatedly that the new wife's adornment signals the change in her status, and Indians often used the English words "for change" to explain why a new wife wears bright clothes and jewelry.[9] Many people said that if girls keep wearing jewelry and nice clothes throughout their adolescence, to the day of the wedding, then what will "change" once they marry? If adornment is permitted before marriage, then what is there to look forward to after marriage?

Kumari women like Somnia see their college-era attire as temporary. They will not take with them the clothes (jeans and *salwar suits*) or jewelry (black metal ornaments) that they wore to the university. At marriage, these things will be given to a younger sister or cousin, to be replaced with new items in the woman's trousseau. During this transitory stage of pre-marriage, Somnia and her friends, though not betrothed, have an idea of what they will wear once they marry. Somnia plans to wear even more jewelry than she would like to wear, especially at the beginning of her marriage, because she told me it is a "must" to wear certain things, which are "traditional" and "enhance your looks." Somnia will forgo the temporary discomfort of wearing too much jewelry in order to look especially splendid, since she has been waiting for that moment for years, and it will be a thrill, at last, to be bejeweled from head to toe.

In order to plan for the future while they abide in this temporary state of singleness, young women acquire both positive and negative examples, learning what to copy, what to avoid. In speaking of Indian beauty in general, Somnia explained that, for her, the beautiful woman has an oval face, a "proportioned" body on the "heavy side," and long black hair. Not all would say the same thing; for many, the perfect Indian woman has a round "moon face." But it is interesting that everyone holds an ideal of beauty that does not necessarily conform with the one described by art historians or fashion experts. Somnia also said that an Indian beauty must wear ornaments, and she cited the famous ancient bronze statue of the dancing girl for support. She evoked this image, I believe, to suggest that the girl, though naked, is beautiful because of the twenty-nine bangles she wears.

Somnia plans to wear jewelry after her marriage because it is "traditional." She has more than an abstract idea of tradition; she understands how married women adapt general rules to their specific circumstances. She has gained this understanding from carefully observing her mother and married sisters. Somnia's mother is a lecturer in philosophy at B.H.U., a "serious" woman who does not wear much jewelry. Somnia believes lavish ornamentation would not suit her mother's professional status, and her mother wears the obligatory minimum: tiny toe rings, small earrings, a golden chain without a pendant around the neck, and one bangle on each wrist—all to designate her marital status. Somnia's oldest sister reduces the marital adornment even more, wearing no *bindi,* no bangles, and a small—almost "invisible"—amount of *sindur.* Another of Somnia's sisters, a professional like their mother, lives in New Delhi. She is, as Somnia put it, a "career-minded girl," and therefore "of course" wears little jewelry and chooses jeans and *salwar suits,* even after marriage. Somnia wants to work after she is married, and so she hopes to follow the lead of her sisters and mother in their subdued appearance and minimum of wifely ornaments. For Somnia, and other young professionals in urban India, the woman who is dressed in a sari with ornaments on the ears, nose, neck, wrists, toes, and ankles is exhibiting not only a more traditional, perhaps even rural look, but also the status of a house-bound housewife.

Career-minded women who work in offices, especially in New Delhi and Bombay, tend to wear little jewelry, self-consciously evoking urbanity and upward mobility. In her book *The Beauty Game,* Anita Anand recounts an interview with a flight attendant for Air India, who explained that the company's policy mandated that flight attendants embody a "conservative look" with "minimum and basic lipstick and jewellery." In the past few years, however, female flight attendants have been granted the right to wear nose rings, longer

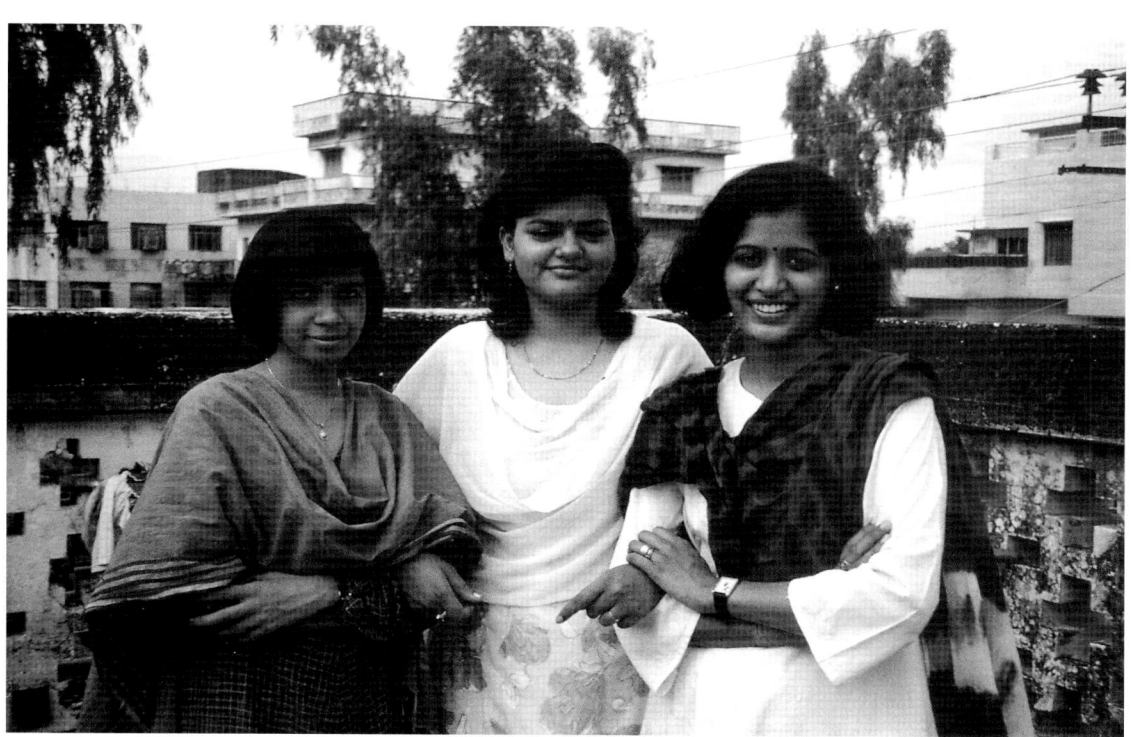

Banaras Hindu University students: Kavita, Somnia, and Priya

earrings, more than one finger ring; and, ironically, they are now allowed to wear the obligatory marriage ornaments of their culture—the *mangalsutra* necklace and toe rings.[10]

Every day *kumari* girls wear simple clothes and jewelry, but this does not prevent them from appearing beautiful in a sober, understated *tarika*. Beauty can be achieved by paying attention to hair, skin, and weight; young unmarried women take care of their bodies instead of focusing on clothes and ornaments. They naturally want to look good at this prime stage of their lives, and their parents support them, since a daughter with a good complexion, a nice body, and thick healthy hair will make the right partner for the ideal arranged marriage.

A Standard of Beauty

Ideal women crowd the Indian streets on murals, billboards, advertisements, calendars, posters, and in shadowy shrines. The Hindu goddess and the Bollywood actress embody standards of beauty.[11] Most men and women, when asked, can enumerate the criteria for beauty in a woman. Her hair is black, thick, and long, worn plaited in a braid; "open" hair is regarded as too sexy.[12] Her hair is parted in the middle, allowing for the *sindur* to be centered perfectly, affirming the symmetry of her face. Women rarely wear bangs; the forehead is open and broad, providing a setting for the *bindi.* An ideal beauty has enormous, deer-like eyes, their size emphasized by a lining of black kohl[13] and sometimes fake lashes. "Sharp" noses are coveted, a sign of Aryan inheritance. Full lips are beautiful, and more beautiful when enhanced with red or pink lipstick (in the past, this was also achieved by chewing betel nut, *paan,* which stains the lips red). A woman's body should be shapely, in the form hyperbolically rendered in ancient stone sculptures.

Most important of the physical traits is light skin. Anita Anand's interview with Mona Irani, an agent for Bombay models, contains a typical reading of female beauty. In addition to having "big black eyes and long black hair," young women who wish to become models should also be "fair, very fair, the fairer the better."[14] Her opinion is general, among men and women, Hindus and Muslims. Light skin is such a valued feature for a woman that in dowry negotiations, the groom's side may lower the amount of expected money if the girl is fair. A pale woman will have more marriage offers since her light tone can counteract the darkness of a groom to yield fair-skinned children—the ultimate hope. Dark skin, in the eyes of many, seems to have the power of canceling otherwise pleasing features. Unattractive yet light-skinned women are desirable in India, much as unattractive blondes are in the West. One will often hear people say of a woman that she is pretty *despite* being dark. Of dark skin, they say in Hindi, *rung saf nahein heh*—"the [skin] color is not clean." Many fair women sincerely view their skin as their best feature, buying clothes and jewelry to highlight its color. Women who are not born light sometimes attempt to attain the coveted color by applying home remedies such as *besan* (chickpea powder) treatments, or commercially bought products like the ever-popular Fair and Lovely skin cream. Although not proved effective by science, this and some thirty other fairness creams, talcs, and soaps enjoy immense consumer popularity in India.[15]

With the recent availability of American and European beauty products, Indian women have new choices. Western cosmetics and the increased presence of Western beauties on television are changing the standards. Light skin is still desired, but women have found new ways to achieve a "light" look. In the past, they used creams and so carefully avoided the sun that wealthy elderly ladies, growing old, untouched by the sun, often become papery white. Now, by highlighting their hair with shades of auburn and wearing contact lenses in grays, greens, and blues, women make their faces, they hope, seem lighter. It is true, too, that super-thin Western models and actresses have influenced Indian female superstars to shed pounds and tone up.[16] This new look, drawn from American celebrities, changes the ideal woman's eyes from black to green, her hair from coal black to reddish brown, and her body from voluptuous to bony.[17] But it must be said that these new standards have been embraced by only a tiny minority in the big cities. For most people, rural or urban, male or female, beauty is that of the goddess and the star: black hair, black eyes, pale skin, and curves.

For many years, the only role models for young men and women in India were the actors and actresses of Bollywood movies.[18] They set the standards; they introduced the new pop songs by lip-synching them on the Bollywood screen. When India only had one channel, Doordarshan, people watched the official news hour in the evening and old Hindi films. Now there are many cable channels, broadcasting not only American and European television shows but also the Indian "serials" that have inaugurated a new category of celebrity: the television star. Film and television actors emulate the look of the Western celebrity, and in copying their Indian role models young Indian women are one step removed from the personalities of the West. Sugyan Kandpaal, a young professional woman from Banaras, said that in the past, you would watch a Bollywood film once a month or even once a week and be exposed to fashion through the film or by making a trip to one of the big cities. Now, in the last eight to ten years, Sugyan said, there are more than fifty channels on television that broadcast the latest look into your home. With cable channels such as MTV and Fashion TV now available, you do not have to seek fashion by going to a movie; it seeks you, rushing at you through the television that babbles now in many urban homes.

The importance of Bollywood stars has been somewhat diminished by the rising celebrity of television actresses, and more by the Indian women who have won international pageants. As we have seen, young girls can recite the names of these queens and the pageants in which they reigned, and Indian men and women of all ages take pride in the fact that the beauty of their own women is finally being recognized internationally. Within the country, local beauty pageants are held frequently at colleges and in neighborhoods, sponsored by magazines and corporations. In order to understand the beauty and cosmetics industry in India, one must note the immense influence of pageant winners in shaping current notions of glamour.[19] The role model has shifted from one who is beautiful, and an actress and a dancer, to one who is just beautiful, and beauty alone might be achieved with the aid of beauty products, contact lenses, and a strict diet.

The challenge is not merely to copy the look of a model or beauty queen, but to be able to get away with following the celebrity style while remaining in the Indian reality. Sugyan Kandpaal shared an incident with me that had happened in her hometown of Banaras two or three years before. A beauty contest was held in a hall for which tickets were sold to prosperous local families. The families gave the passes to their menfolk so they could attend the spectacle. She said that the contestants—girls with a "craze" of becoming the next Miss Universe or Miss World—were well received during the rounds in formal attire, but once they came out in bathing suits—a sight rarely seen in India—the crowd went wild. Men started to shout and whistle, and a few got up on stage and proceeded to molest the women. The show was shut down, the police were called, and the whole episode was spread across the newspapers on the following day. Sugyan told me about the event to support her contention that such activities cannot be handled in a "backward" place like Banaras, where the mentality of the people is not ready to accept calmly a parade of half-naked women. Many in India, in fact, feel that beauty pageants encourage the immoral behavior and sexist attitudes of the youth—as evidenced by the protests at the 1996 Miss Universe event held in Bangalore.[20] Middle-class women, Sugyan said, do not have many options: they can either be traditional or they can be modern, but a confused mix—prancing in a swimsuit in a conservative religious city like Banaras—just does not work. The urban upper class has many more options in this regard, as they do in everything else, Sugyan remarked.

Hindu goddesses provide role models for behavior as well as beauty. The same can be said about secular beauties, whose titillating exploits and fast lives are chronicled in the popular *filmi* magazines, such as *Stardust* and *Cine Blitz*.[21] The attire and style of celebrities set a standard for "advanced" people in India who haunt trendy spots in the metropolis, such as the posh McDonald's in New Delhi's Connaught Place, wearing little jewelry and displaying "fusion" body art, such as a *salwar suit* top with faded, fashionable American jeans.[22] Ethnic silver or black metal jewelry and exotic clothing with embroidery and mirrorwork, sold primarily to foreign tourists, can now be seen on the East-meets-West bodies of *desi* hipsters in the big cities and on actresses in television serials. Other fashion departures I spotted in the summer of 2003 included a thin red line applied with lip liner pencil to the top of the forehead as a gesture toward the thick and powdery *sindur,* which is customarily displayed on the hair part, not the forehead. Evening television stars also consistently wore a big, tear-shaped *tilak bindi* of glued-on rhinestones. Some TV heroines broke with the normal symmetrical look by wearing dozens of bangles, but only on one arm. Shiny, shellac-like lip-gloss, a thick coat of eyeliner on the top eyelid, and dyed brown hair completed the look. I also noted versions of this look on many women on the streets of New Delhi, attesting to the fact that the trends set in the media were quickly followed. This look includes the old combination of *bindi, sindur,* and bangles, but altered enough to seem modern. Holding to unaltered old norms has become, for urbanites, a sign of backwardness: old-fashioned, maybe rural, and certainly not "advanced."

Interviews with celebrities are regular features of movie magazines and the fashion pages of newspapers. In them the stars share their beauty secrets. Every one I read during the summers of 2001 and 2003 mentioned a strict regimen of diet and workout. These celebrities claimed to avoid fatty foods and reject many of the traditional Indian staples, opting instead to munch on salads and fresh fruits. Actresses often referred to themselves as "fitness freaks" who rise early to run around the block for an hour before shooting scenes for their latest Bollywood flick.

If the goal is to look thin, how is an average Indian youth to achieve the workout regimen in the absence of gyms? As is the case in much of India, most of the streets in Banaras are not smoothly paved, and they are jammed with traffic of all sorts—rickshaws, motorcycles, and automobiles, vegetable carts, cows and water buffalo, not to mention the pedestrian throng. Jogging through these streets in little spandex outfits would be ludicrous, if not impossible. There are posh colonies in Bombay and New Delhi where young people could conceivably exercise, and where they could gain access to centers for fitness and weight loss,[23] but despite such opportunities available to a miniscule portion of the population, let us say that the incorporation of American ideas of fitness seems silly in the Indian scene. There is, of course, an ancient Indian tradition of fitness and bodybuilding for men, but it does not seem to be part of the chat in the movie magazines.[24] The reasonable course for women would be to revert to tradition, adapting it to the new emphasis on being slim and trim.

Many adolescents, especially females I knew in Banaras, kept a religious fast once a week, a socially acceptable and respected way of eating less. Each day of the week is associated with a deity, and carries particular prohibitions about food and drink. The association of specific days with certain deities varies by region and caste in India.[25] Within my family in Banaras, Monday is for Shiva, Tuesday and Saturday for Hanuman, Wednesday for Ganesh, Thursday for Vishnu, and Friday for the Goddess. On Wednesdays, for example, one cannot eat grains, tomatoes, onions, or garlic; fruits and yogurt are the norm when fasting for Lord Ganesh. *Kumari* women usually keep the Monday fast, since Shiva is the god to approach for a good husband.[26] Young women I know creatively fulfill many goals at once. They eat little on one day in the week, preserving their trim figures. They please their parents and the gods with their devotion and weekly sacrifice. And their fast supports their prayers for good husbands in the future.

At the same time, many men in Banaras keep trim by wrestling and weightlifting at the *akhara* workout clubs.[27] Regular attendance at these social clubs, or lifting weights alone at home, serves the fashion needs of young men, whose role models—hunky Bollywood actors like Hritik Roshan and Amir Khan—display huge biceps in tight, clingy shirts.[28] The tradition of the *akhara* clubs raises again the connection between Hinduism and bodily beauty. Whether they gather in the *akharas* or sweat alone with the weights in their bedrooms, young bodybuilders admire and worship Hanuman, who epitomizes strength and is often depicted carrying a mountain in the palm of his hand or wielding a heavy mace.

Some cultural commentators have implied that the young people of India, suddenly under the benign influence of the West, have only recently developed an interest in personal beauty.[29] That is surely not the case. Perhaps all people in all times—and certainly Indian people for as far back in time as renditions of the human body in art will carry us—have exhibited a healthy pride in their physical appearance and a need to appear attractive, as demonstrated by the numerous indigenous Ayurvedic recipes for skin, body, and hair care.[30] Religious fasts and *akhara* workouts have been practiced as a means to meditation and prayer, but also as a way to keep the body healthy. Young people have always wanted to look good, and they have tried to look better by following some discipline in imitation of an admirable model. This has not changed. What has changed, and perhaps is always changing, is what exactly is thought to be most attractive. And recently, of course, change has accelerated with the absorption of India into the multinational cosmetic industries' consumer base. The goal is still beauty, though the ideal is changing swiftly at the moment among wealthy urbanites. Parents still indulge their children's—particularly their daughters'—desire for beauty products and fashion, hoping for good arranged marriages. Increasingly, though, the sons and daughters secretly hope to fall in love and escape the fate that their parents have in store for them.

Falling in Love

Personal ads in the newspapers and fashion magazines are full of longing. In them, young people express their love for special others, yearning to talk with them and speak their devotion aloud. Their ads are the result of love-at-first-sight encounters. There has been no interaction, no words passed. The sight of another has set love aflame in the heart. Desire is accompanied by worry. In the New Delhi *Hindustan Times,* for example, youths flood the "Astro Query" column with questions such as this one from Dinesh: "When will I get married? Is it going to be an arranged or love match?"[31] Young people with such concerns are forever on the lookout for the mate of their dreams, and many sightings of the beloved seem to take place in college, or in the "coaching" sessions where an instructor meets with a few students in college entrance exam classes. In such situations, in order for somebody to fall in love with you—and to propose marriage—your task is simple: look good. There is no need to be a good conversationalist, to be witty, funny, or well read—appearance is everything in these scenes where all communication between the sexes is visual.

Once two people have expressed their love to one another, they may sneak away on secret dates, maybe a lunch at a Chinese restaurant—a dark place, run by foreigners who do not pass judgment on the indecency of premarital encounters. Another popular option, I am told, is to hire a bicycle rickshaw for a ride and pay the *rickshawwallah* extra money to put down the canvas cover that is designed for rainstorms but can serve to provide a little privacy. After they have acknowledged a mutual love, couples chat on the phone and go on dates. In the West, going out on a date might lead to love, but in India, it is after love has been established that people go out on dates. Love starts and reaches its height before words have been spoken. Commitment is built on looks; dating follows, then marriage. One had better look good, and look carefully.

This visual fantasy of love is fueled by the plots of Bollywood films,[32] epitomized by the popular movie *Dil Se* ("With All My Heart") in which the hero, played by Shah Rukh Khan, falls in love with the heroine, the actress Manisha Koralia, without ever talking to her. He follows her and eventually dies for/with her, happily sacrificing his life for the beauty of a woman who captured his eyes (and subsequently his heart) in a train station at night. One young man told me of an exceptional experience that unfolded like a dream. He saw a beautiful woman walking home from college. It was raining and she did not have an umbrella. He stepped beside her and shielded her from the rain with his own umbrella, escorting her home. This moment created such a strong emotion in the two of them that they started meeting and eventually went to the courthouse and secretly married, telling their furious parents after the fact that they had entered into an inter-caste love marriage.

This romantic episode, reminiscent of a Bollywood fantasy, shows how important it is to look good, and it returns us to the importance of sight—to *darshan* in the context of Hindu India. Beauty is not only a source of self-esteem and personal pride. It can be the means of escape into the freedom of a love marriage. By following the latest fashion, using the right shampoo, and working out, it seems, one can gain the power to alter the course of one's life. Young people in India will learn the proper manners, attend school, and, if they are fortunate, go on to college as well—all the while preparing for the next and most important stage in their lives: marriage. The wedding is the most glorious rite of passage, and it is the pinnacle of body art.

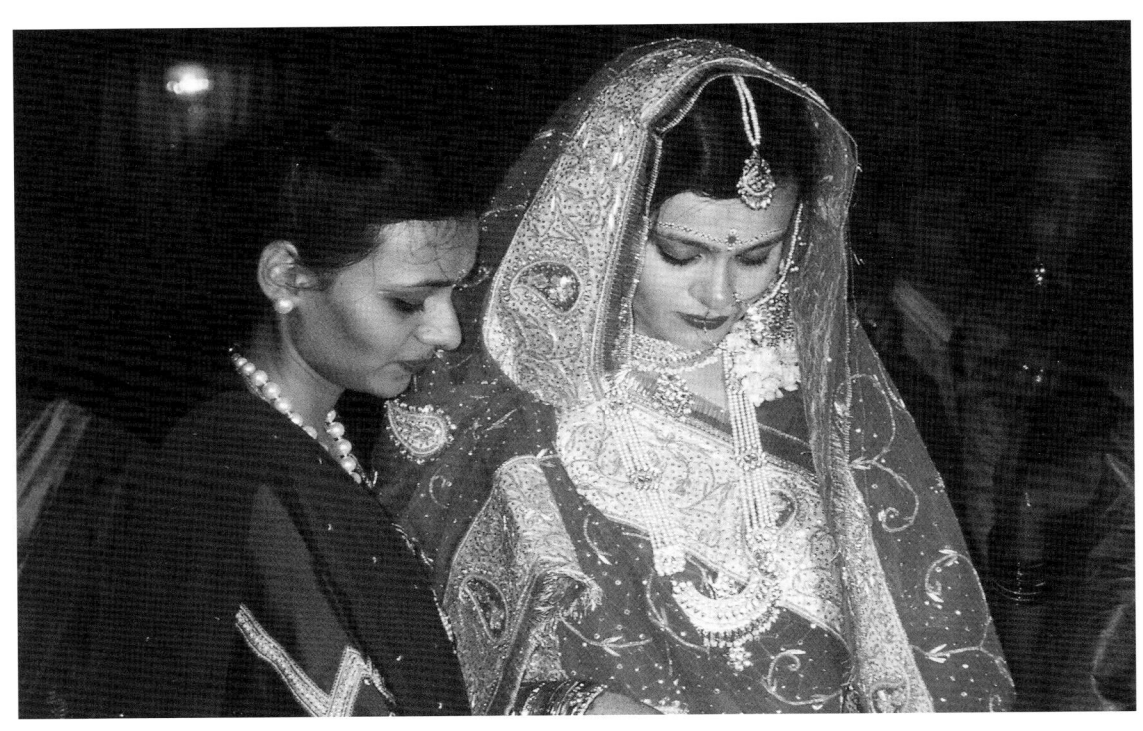

Shalini, the bride, arrives with her sister Nidhi at the wedding ceremony

·15·

The Wedding

On a steamy July evening in 1996, a small gathering of people sat in plastic chairs on the lawn of a five-star hotel in the Mughal city of Lucknow, waiting for the ceremony to begin. The bride, Shalini Shrivastava, looked beautiful as she emerged, accompanied by her younger sister, Nidhi. Shalini wore a magenta silk *lehanga* and covered her head modestly with the *dupatta,* surrounding her pretty face in bright, soft fabric. She wore the customary gold jewelry; the golden *hathphul* on her hands glittered in the flash of the cameras. Shalini approached the platform where her groom, Rohit, waited, dressed in a turban and an off-white suit with a long Nehru jacket, called a *shervani.*[1] The couple exchanged flower garlands to the applause of their family and friends. A rich meal followed, after which most of the guests went home. Only the immediate family and a few close friends remained for the Hindu ceremony that continued into the night, during which the *pundit,* with Vedic chants in Sanskrit, united the young couple in eternal matrimony.

Shalini Shrivastava

Shalini's wedding marked the culmination of three months of preparation, starting in mid-March, after the engagement party. I had the good fortune to attend Shalini's various celebratory events and to spend time with her in Banaras, her hometown.[2] I interviewed her about the upcoming marriage, asking about her expectations concerning the new life that awaited her. At the time she was finishing her studies at Banaras Hindu University, where she had met and fallen in love with her future husband, Rohit. While she embarked on a brave and rebellious love-marriage, Shalini showed an appreciation of her tradition and of the wishes of her elders—her mother and her groom's mother. She sees herself as an independent young woman, one in the "new generation" of Indians. Shalini represents many urban brides today—women who are forging a new way of life for themselves while remaining mindful of the wishes of those of an earlier generation.

I started our conversation by asking Shalini how she currently presented herself as a *kumari,* or unmarried, woman. She said in English that she wore only a "simple chain," a "band ring" and two sets of earrings on each ear. When going out to birthday parties or marriage receptions, Shalini wore two golden bangles in addition. She wore "this only, nothing gaudy or heavy." I asked her to visualize herself after her upcoming marriage; how would she look different? She instantly declared this to be a "good question," then thought for a moment. She said she would wear a "*bindi,* of course," and *sindur,* but not "full *sindur,*" just enough to show through the part in her hair. She looks forward to wearing "lots of *churi,*" at least for a month or two, and matching the glass bangles to the color of her saris. She plans to wear anklets and toe rings for only a month or so, since her mother told her that she must and had already purchased many sets of anklets and toe rings for her daughter's wedding trousseau. As soon as Shalini marries she will live at her mother-in-law's house in Lucknow for a month, and then move to Calcutta, where Rohit has a job waiting for him. Shalini plans to wear the traditional items of jewelry in the first month after the wedding, because the period right after the marriage is especially auspicious and because she will be living with her parents-in-law, who will expect her to look a certain way.

Shalini said that while she stays at the house of her parents-in-law in Lucknow, she will "prefer" to wear only saris, not *salwar suits.* But as soon as she moves into her own flat in Calcutta, she plans to wear *suits,* jeans, and skirts—her usual pre-marriage attire—as well as saris. In Calcutta, she said, she will wear "anything I feel like."

Once in Calcutta, Shalini said, she plans to remove her toe rings and anklets, but she will continue to wear lots of bangles, something she has always liked. She admitted that on the occasion of a visit by her mother-in-law she would once again don the compulsory items of wifely adornment. Then why not wear them always? I asked. Shalini responded, casually: "It is not all that necessary." Like many other women, Shalini understands the necessity of wifely adornment for the first month, and she is aware of how ornaments show obedience to the mother-in-law, but she also recognizes that in her daily life she need not follow these rules. She can switch codes comfortably, to please both her in-laws and herself, alternating between asserting her will and meeting the expectations of her mother-in-law.

If Shalini has always had such a *shauk* for bangles, I asked, then why did she never assert her independent spirit by wearing them before her marriage? Her response shows that no person, regardless of how independent, can act in complete isolation from cultural norms: "In our society we are born and brought up in such an atmosphere, right? Simple living, and wearing *suits,* and going to college, without any makeup, without any *bindi,* just natural." But then, I asked, how could she attract somebody at college if she were never allowed to dress up? Shalini explained that, in her view, "Attracting anybody is not [about] dressing properly, wearing nail polish, putting lipstick and wearing jewelry. You can attract anyone naturally."

Shalini embodies her attitude. She attended college in a demure, simple style, yet attracted her future husband with her personality and sense of humor—"naturally"—without the aid of makeup and fancy clothes. She fell in love, had a love-marriage, and in fact wore gold-plated anklets for her wedding in Lucknow, breaking the Hindu taboo against wearing gold below the waist. She has gotten what many young women in India wish for: a love-marriage, a residence away from one's hometown, and a life away from the watchful eyes of the in-laws and "the local public." Shalini knows when to conform and when to rebel; she asserts her individuality by saying, "I wear all this for my satisfaction. I don't do anything for others, just to show off."

Getting Married in India

Marriage is integral to the study of body art in India; it sets the standard for a woman's appearance in all the stages of her life—as a single young woman, as a bride and married woman, and as a widow (at the end of her marriage). And it is at the moment of marriage that an Indian woman will wear the most ornaments. She will look more splendid, more beautiful, than she will ever look again. This chapter on the wedding will serve as a summary of the ethnography of body art in India, since many of the key principles—making, buying, selling, wearing, looking, and being seen—climax at the wedding event.

Marriages in India are traditionally viewed as alliances between two families, not as manifestations of eternal love between two individuals. Although love-marriages are increasing, arranged marriages remain dominant, especially in the rural areas where approximately three quarters of the country's people live. The bride's father informs his friends that he is seeking a potential groom, and he may even resort to a professional matchmaker. Once the bride's father finds a suitable match—a man who is attractive and well-employed, and who comes from a respected family and a compatible caste, the two fathers arrange to meet each other to discuss the marriage possibilities and the dowry expectations. In many cases, the bride and groom do not meet before the wedding, though they may see photos of their future spouse.

Arranged marriages remain the norm, but some modern couples arrange their own, seeking the help of relatives, friends, or even matchmakers. The main criteria for a union usually involve religion, caste, regional identity, and socioeconomic background. Generally speaking men are chosen for their education and jobs, while women are chosen for beauty and a humble personality, although this is changing, especially within the Indian diaspora. The reasons for these considerations are obvious: a well-educated groom will get a high-paying job and support the family well. Women rarely work outside of the home, and a modest, good-natured bride will not prove obstinate to her mother-in-law.

But things are changing, and recent personal ads in *India Abroad* emphasize the jobs of both genders—physicians, engineers, computer programmers—and the good looks of both the men and women (all men seem to be "handsome," all women seem to be "slim").[3] A groom who is good-looking, tall, and well-built will outrank another potential candidate, just as an educated bride will rise above those who did not attend college. Good-looking parents will produce attractive children, passing on the coveted traits of fair skin, good height, trim bodies, and sharp facial features. Although few women will utilize their education by working outside of the home, people tell me that a wife with a university degree is well suited for raising children and helping them with their homework.

In addition to placing matrimonial ads in newspapers, many families now utilize internet sites such as the popular shaadi.com.[4] Unlike the American ads that focus on hobbies and interests, Indian personal advertisements stress caste and region, the details of education and employment, and the professions of the father and brothers—all these facts convey the social and economic standing of the family. As a character in Kamila Shamsie's novel *Salt and Saffron* says, "Family reputation is the most precious jewel in the bride's *jahez*"—her dowry.[5]

A recent documentary film simply titled *Arranged Marriage,* focuses on people searching for mates through a marriage bureau, a matchmaking agency in Calcutta.[6] The film shows men filling out forms that ask them to specify their height and profession. In the form to be filled by a woman, there is a category for "beauty of face," as well as questions that ask whether she is "well-built or slim," if she is "good-looking, charming or beautiful." The potential bride has to choose, under the subheading of "complexion," one of the following: fair, medium, or dark. The film shows men and women both having to say whether they prefer a "fresh" candidate or a "not fresh" one—someone who is divorced or widowed.

Whether they follow the tradition of arranged marriage or use a marriage agency, newspaper matrimonial column, or family friend, the next stage for the young people usually involves an exchange of photographs. Then the photograph is analyzed for appearance and clues to personality[7]—another testament to the importance of visual communication in Indian culture—and it is only after the photos have been judged, by the individuals and their families, that a meeting is arranged.[8]

For the photographs that will precede the meeting, young men and women often go to a studio to have their pictures taken, and they submit a few photographs for consideration. Preetam Kumar Manik told me that women, such as his future wife, Sunita Seth, submit two photos of themselves, one in a *salwar suit* and the other one in a sari. Preetam said that as far as he knows, there are no rules for men, but he sent over two photos, both showing him in a Western style men's suit.

The next step usually involves a visit by the boy's family to the girl's house (or a neutral public place such as a restaurant). At some point the couple is left alone for half an hour or so, during which shy conversation takes place. This scene is poignantly portrayed in Manil Suri's fine novel *The Death of Vishnu,* in which the young heroine, Kavita, is taken, all dressed up, to meet her potential mate, Pran. Her family takes along a box of *gulab jamuns* that was purchased at a sweet shop but is represented as the *kumari* girl's own culinary achievement, earning her much praise from the boy's parents.[9]

After this mutual viewing—an occasion of simultaneous secular *darshan*—the parents decide on the appropriateness of the match. In the past the decision was theirs alone, but today they normally consult with the boy and the girl, who are granted the right to say no. It is considered improper to disagree with the judgment of the parents or matchmaker, but I have met many people who stopped things cold at this point with a firm no. Still, few people are willing to reject a mate they have seen but once, so most agree to the marriage. Once commitment has been reached, the young couple may go on a few chaperoned dates for dinner or ice cream and talk on the phone, accumulating details about each other. An astrologer is hired to examine the birth charts of both the groom and the bride to determine cosmic suitability, and to establish the propitious time and date for the ceremony.

The Engagement

Rich urban families usually have an "engagement party," a catered event in a fancy hotel, such as the Hotel India or Hotel de Paris in the Cantonment area of Banaras. On this occasion the immediate family and close friends view and meet the future mate and his or her family members—all of whom will soon be relatives. The event climaxes with the "ring ceremony," in which the bride and groom each receive a ring, chosen by the mothers and often placed on the hand by the future mother-in-law, not by the future spouse. This gathering is, in many ways, a precursor to the wedding itself. There is an emphasis on the beauty of the bride, who chooses her outfit carefully and hires, as Shalini did, a beautician to do her hair and makeup.

At the engagement, just as at the wedding, Preetam Kumar told me, you should be able to tell visually—by the clothes and jewelry—the roles the different participants are playing. It should be obvious who the future bride and groom are and who the immediate relatives are. For his own party, Preetam said, his brothers, parents, grandmother, and sister-in-law all wore fancier outfits than the rest of their friends to indicate that the marriage would involve somebody from their family—*ghar ka,* literally, "of the house." Lavish clothes and jewelry, hairstyle and makeup, vary by degree from the inner circle—the bride and groom—to the outer circles: the immediate family, close friends, the extended family, and, finally, business and social acquaintances. Preetam clarified his description by saying that in India outfits are chosen by considering the occasion, then the age group, and then the aesthetics of material, color, and fabric—the last three being chosen to match the general pattern set by the first two factors. Following Preetam's argument, it seems that a wedding or engagement occasion is most significant for the members of the immediate family, so they will select more elaborate outfits to wear.

The Bride's Trousseau

After the engagement has happened and a date for the marriage has been obtained from the astrologer, the bride-to-be starts shopping for her trousseau. It is considered bad luck to buy such things before the union has been made *pakka,* firm. As marriage marks the beginning of a woman's life as a decorated being, the young bride goes shopping with her mother, sisters, or female friends to buy all of her future needs as a wife. Obligatory items include saris, as well as matching blouses and petticoats that have to be tailored. The new wife will also need shawls, sandals and slippers, nightgowns, handkerchiefs, and undergarments. She must purchase a sizable collection of glass bangles (if she is from the state of Uttar Pradesh where wives must wear them) in a variety of colors to match the different outfits of the future. Many pairs of toe rings and anklets are also included, as well as packets of *bindis* and *sindur.* As the *kumari* woman will soon be able to wear makeup regularly, these shopping trips gather nail polish, lipstick, eyeliner, face cream, shampoo, and other indulgent beauty products.

A woman's trousseau contains the new items for everyday use, as well as the jewelry for the wedding day. The bride will wear a jewelry set given by her parents, consisting of these items: at least one necklace, earrings, nose ring, *mantikka* (a bejeweled *bindi,* worn on the forehead, suspended from a chain), rings, bracelets, anklets, and toe rings.[10] The first wedding outfit, a red, pink, or maroon *lehanga,* may be given to her by her mother or mother-in-law, varying with family tradition. Her mother usually gives the second outfit. Among Brahmins in the state of Uttar Pradesh this should be a turmeric-yellow silk sari, but this tradition also varies with each caste and state; for example, among Hindu and Jain merchants in Gujarat, the bride receives a *panetar* tie-dyed sari from her natal home and a brocaded *gharcholu* from the conjugal family.[11]

These items of clothing and jewelry come as gifts, but the bride, accompanied by her parents and friends, selects them. Shalini went with her mother to buy the bridal jewelry. "Mummy was planning on giving me all heavy things because of the money and the weight," she said, but she chose instead to buy the light, "delicate" items she would prefer to wear. Parents like to give their daughters "heavy" jewelry as a way of providing them with economic security; recall that the woman's jewelry is legally hers, and weighty items, when sold, bring more money than delicate ones.

The trousseau may also include old ornaments and family heirlooms. The wedding jewelry and outfit, though, are always bought right before the wedding because women do not want to get married in "old-fashioned" things, even if they are priceless antiques. When Parmanand Khanchandani and his sister-in-law, Nina, spoke about buying the jewelry for the dowries of their respective daughters, they said they would wait until the marriage was about to happen so they could give them ornaments in the "latest fashion." Some mothers collect saris and jewelry for the wedding, beginning in their daughters' childhoods. The custom of accumulating a trousseau over many years is common in many parts of Asia, Europe, and Latin America. What is distinctive of India is that the bride's dowry consists not only of household necessities, such as pots and pans, dinnerware, and linens, but also of the items she will wear on her wedding day.

The new wife will receive clothing and jewelry from her in-laws as well as from her own family. Shalini's mother-in-law went shopping with her and asked Shalini to select the style, color, fabric, and design of her wedding *lehanga.* The groom's family will customarily present the bride with a set number of saris and pieces of jewelry; type and amount vary with family tradition. In May of 1996, I attended the wedding of Swati and Shachi Kant in the city of Azam Ghar, in Uttar Pradesh, a few hours from Banaras. When I interviewed the groom's sisters and mother, I learned that they had purchased two "sets" of jewelry for the bride, each ensemble consisting of a necklace, a ring, and earrings. One was a "heavy set" to be worn on special occasions, while the other was a "light set" for daily use. The bride's gift baskets also included many pairs of toe rings and anklets, silver chain belts, and nose rings. In addition, Swati, the bride, would receive eleven saris, each with matching petticoats and blouse pieces (to be tailored later to her bodily specifications). The women said they shopped for these items of clothing and jewelry in the absence of the bride, which is normally the case for the groom's family. When I asked how they chose, they said they tried to match the bride's attributes—her height, weight, and personality—to the objects they saw, and they also sought things that were "comfortable, showy and beautiful." Although heavily brocaded saris are traditionally given, these women said they preferred garments that could actually be worn. Beautiful, ornate Banarasi saris would remain folded and "useless" in the *almari*.

The Dowry

A dowry consists of the things a woman takes with her to her husband's house after marriage. These goods usually include jewelry, money, and household items. In her book about marriage rituals in Bengal, Lina Fruzzetti explains that two principal gifts go from the bride's family to the groom's: the sacred gift of a virgin—their daughter—and the secular gift of a negotiated dowry in return for the acceptance of the daughter as a bride. Fruzzetti further clarifies that the *dan*—the trousseau—is a personal present of clothes and jewelry for the daughter; it is not technically part of the dowry gift.[12] When a union is being negotiated among the parents in an arranged marriage situation, one of the key questions to be settled is the amount the groom's family expects to receive. Many people, especially those living in villages, will state a sum of cash, and they may add other items, such as livestock or appliances. The assumption is that the boy will be providing the girl with food and shelter for the rest of her life, through his own earnings and his family's assistance. Since the girl will not work outside of the house (though she will surely work hard *inside* of it), her monetary contribution to the household arrives with her, in the form of the dowry provided by her parents.[13] The parents will send their daughter over with a small stash of jewelry for personal use, but the money and other goods are for the entire family. As we have seen, though, the wife's own jewelry may be kept "for safe keeping" by the mother-in-law, in a bank locker or elsewhere, never again to be seen by the woman who is, in theory, its owner.

When the parents arrange a marriage, they agree upon the details of the dowry. In many parts of India, poor people once arranged the marriage of their daughters at infancy, buying fifteen or so years in which they could slowly pay off the dowry debt to the family of the child groom. By the time the girl had reached puberty and was ready for marriage, the dowry had been paid, and a second ceremony was held to send the bride to her new home. In Indian child marriages, which are now generally a thing of the past, the parents did not marry their five-year-old daughters to grown men, as it seems titillating for many to assume;[14] rather, they married a little girl to a little boy, to be united in the future when both came of age.[15] If the girl went to live with her in-laws at an early age, she did not sleep with her husband but rather with her mother-in-law, from whom she learned the domestic craft of home keeping, until she was old enough to consummate her marriage. It is sad to note that if a girl were betrothed and married at a very young age and her young husband died before she ever lived with him, she was still considered a widow, albeit a virgin, and made to wear white saris and no jewelry for the rest of her life.[16]

One rationale for giving one's daughter a dowry that consists of "heavy" items of jewelry, as Shalini's mother wanted to do, is to pass to the daughters their share of the family wealth, since the ancestral home, the furnishings, and other property will generally be given to the sons.[17] Many believe that girls receive their share at their weddings—in the form of gold jewelry—while boys inherit the family's fortune on the occasion of the retirement and death of the parents. It is common for families to marry off their daughters before arranging the marriages of their sons, as my maternal grandfather did in Banaras. The reason for this is to show that the family is prosperous enough to accumulate and give away multiple dowries—one for each daughter—before receiving any dowry from the families of their sons' brides. Less affluent families will recycle bits of the dowry, marrying a son first to be able to marry a daughter next. While foreign observers and the local press are fascinated by the horrible occurrences of bride burning—when a mother-in-law and her son conspire to kill the new bride after taking her dowry—this is thankfully a rare event, hardly the normal state of affairs in Indian households.[18]

Parents send their daughter off to her marriage with gold jewelry for her to wear on her wedding and then on special occasions throughout her life, but also as "economic security," as capital to be liquidated in case of an emergency. In the chapter on the Kanhaiya Lal jewelry shop, we have seen that women occasionally must sell their jewelry, and in Chitra Banerjee Divakaruni's *Arranged Marriage,* three separate short stories tell of women who are able to escape bad marriages, both in India and in the diaspora, by selling their jewelry and buying themselves the freedom that the dowry promised to provide.[19]

The other items included in the dowry are also meant to serve the bride, though indirectly. Parents hope to buy a respected social position for the daughter in her new home by sending with her many wonderful things for the family to enjoy (which may generate resentment among the other daughters-in-law who brought less with them). These items often include appliances like refrigerators, stoves, and color television sets. The groom's family commonly requests a motor scooter—it used to be a bicycle—or, rarely, a car. Now, the husband might occasionally give his wife a lift (she will ride side-saddle on the scooter), but he will mostly use the vehicle to commute to work. Some parents resist giving these extravagant gifts; in Bharati Mukherjee's novel, *Wife,* Mr. Dasgupta "was prepared to give the usual gold ornaments, saris, watch and fountain pen, some furniture, perhaps, but absolutely not a scooter or a refrigerator. . . ."[20]

Expensive dowry items will please the new in-laws and provide a secure position for the new wife, but they tax the financial capacity of the bride's family: the more the household items cost, the less money there is to buy jewelry for her. Although the bride may receive immediate gratification by arriving with many coveted gadgets, these are not hers exclusively, as is her jewelry, and, most importantly, they may not be sold for immediate cash. Appliances and vehicles, unlike gold jewelry, devalue with time, and cannot be secretly sold; everybody would instantly notice the refrigerator missing from the dining room.

My examples carry a general understanding, but the specifics vary greatly throughout India, depending on family traditions, religion, and educational and economic status, and some sampling of the variety can be found in both anthropological studies and works of fiction.[21]

For one example, let me return to Rajasthan. In the last chapter, I introduced B. D. Soni's daughter, Ram Pyari, who was preparing for her upcoming marriage, at once anticipating a happy new life and feeling anxious about leaving the comfort of her extended family. While the women of the household made plans to shop for the trousseau, B.D. and his father, Govind Lal, both expert jewelers, were busy making her wedding ornaments. I was shown a magnificent work in progress: a heavy diamond choker from which dangled multiple strands, each containing several additional diamonds. B.D. told me that this piece was similar to the one worn by his wife, Kausalya, at their wedding, although hers had rubies, emeralds, and diamonds, while Ram Pyari's contains only diamonds, since he prefers the clean look of one type of gem spread throughout the necklace.

In addition to the choker, B.D. was planning to give his daughter a pair of embossed silver-sheathed stools that the couple could use to hold their dinner plates; the stools took him two months to make. Her dowry would also include what B.D. called a "complete set" of jewelry: *mantikka* for the forehead, a *muter mala* (a type of necklace made by stringing together tiny golden spheres), a fancy nose ring, a pair of armbands, a pair of earrings, sixteen gold-en bangles, a pair of *hathphul* (hand-flower ornaments), a silver chain belt, a pair of anklets, and three pairs of toe rings. B.D., as the father of the bride, gives the major items of jewelry—ornaments that are both fancy and pricey. The other relatives, neighbors, and friends, B.D. told me, will give his daughter small everyday items, such as silver toe rings and anklets, finger rings, and modest golden earrings. The customary gift to the bride by a wedding guest, in most parts of India, is an item of jewelry. Most people understand that it is the responsibility of the parents to provide the bride with the heavy items for special occasions, so others contribute light, everyday essentials.

B. D. Soni is the father of three sons and one daughter. All of his children, he explained, should get an equal share of the family's fortune. His daughter, Ram Pyari, is receiving hers now in the form of her dowry. To her new home in Gujarat, B.D. will send with her not only the marvels of the goldsmith's art, but also a sofa set, a refrigerator, kitchen utensils, and a television. When his boys get married (they are all very young), their wives will wear the family heirloom jewels, the priceless ornaments that have been in this family of jewelers for generations. The old jewelry is worn by the new bride who comes into their home; then it is taken back and kept safely in the family's joint possession. Ram Pyari, who will move to another jeweler's family, will take new pieces, some of them replicas of old family ornaments.

B.D. showed me photographs of his younger brother, R.C., on his wedding day. The pictures showed a plainly dressed bride, Santosh, in garments of orange silk, wearing the auspicious red tie-dyed *chundari* on her head that covered her face. Her only noticeable ornaments were the typical *chura,* the set of white plastic bangles running the length of the arm from the shoulder to the wrist, that is traditional in Rajasthan. The bridegroom, R.C., by contrast, wore a flamboyant deep-purple silk suit and an orange turban decorated with two bejeweled *sarpech* ornaments. He wore golden earrings and the family's heirloom rings on many of his fingers, and a beautiful *kundan* emerald and diamond necklace worn over his suit, on prominent display.[22] The men of this family of supremely talented jewelers showcase their wealth, their caste, and their profession ostentatiously on the important occasion of their own weddings.

One of the primary functions of weddings is to display wealth, beauty, hospitality, and of course jewelry. The wedding of B.D.'s daughter, following tradition, will take place at his house in Jaisalmer. They plan to clear the front room to display her dowry items: the TV, the sofa, and the kitchen appliances. In the customary way, they will detail these items in an inventory that Ram Pyari will take to her new home, a kind of a receipt for all the things she brought with her. The exhibition of his daughter's dowry[23] at his home will also include, B.D. told me, a family member whose job will be to explain the items, giving additional information, answering any questions, and acting as a museum docent of sorts. At this event the wedding guests will get an opportunity to see the gifts (and make mental notes for later comparison) and, receiving a guided tour of the goods, they will be able to appreciate the remarkable generosity of the bride's family.

B.D. plans to include Ram Pyari's jewelry in his domestic exhibition of the dowry goods. Unlike Shalini and most other brides throughout the country, Ram Pyari will not get married wearing the heavy ornaments given to her by her parents. If these were placed on the shy body of the bride, B.D. said, the guests would not be able to get a close look at them. By having his masterworks displayed rather than worn, B.D. will put his artistry in gold and gems before the scrutiny of the visitors who, he hopes, will be able to understand the splendor of the materials and the excellence of his skills as a designer and craftsman. His decision, he said, is not a general Rajasthani custom; it is the tradition of the Sonis—the caste of goldsmiths—whose daughters' jewelry communicates not only the economic standing of the family, but also the artistic excellence of its male smiths.

Making the Bride Beautiful

We have briefly followed the general sequence of events and decisions leading up to a marriage ceremony, starting with the choosing of the bride and groom, then going on to astrology charts, trousseau shopping, and dowry negotiations. The final decisions to be made by the girl's parents will involve the details of the wedding invitation cards, the selection of a ceremony venue and its decoration, and choice of the menu for the dinner reception. These decisions are made by her parents and rarely involve the bride herself. There are, however, final preparations that the bride must engage in: determining the last details of her bridal appearance, most notably her hair, makeup, and henna application. Ideally she will consult with several beauticians beforehand, selecting the one who will come to the wedding location to do the bride's makeup.[24] The beautician, always a female, is hired to work at several events connected to the wedding, including the *ladies' sangeet* (a gathering of women for song), the ceremony itself, the *bidai* on the next morning, and even the dinner reception hosted by the groom's family at their house.

The beautician is in charge of the bride's hair, makeup, and henna. In the recent past all of these duties were relegated to a sister or friend, but most women now prefer the services of a professional, specially trained in such matters. When I asked Shalini why she would choose to have an unknown person instead of her sister Nidhi, she answered frankly that she had "no confidence" in the abilities of her sister, and would rather not risk looking unattractive on this most important day of her life.

Selecting a competent beautician is like choosing the right bangle store: you have to find someone with whose taste you agree. At the Aas Art Centre, where the young beauticians from the last chapter, Laxmi Mishra and Rupali Gupta, took classes, I interviewed their teacher, a charming middle-aged man named Ashok Kumar.[25] He runs the tiny school on the second floor of a building off Vishvanath Gali, and he is, like the other professionals in this book, a man who has developed expertise in the body art of women.

Ashok Kumar sees the primary role of the beautician as being, simply, to beautify the bride. If the bride is slightly unattractive, then the beautician can make her look pretty with the addition of deftly applied makeup. If the bride is attractive, the beautician's job is to make her look even more stunning by choosing the right makeup and arrangement for her hair. Most brides, Ashok Kumar said, take the advice of the beauticians, for they are professionals in the business of making women look lovely. As they are apt to when shopping, when they accept the advice of the seller of saris or bangles, women willingly follow the beautician, relaxing into the hands of experts they have learned to trust.

The beautician's role is hardly trivial: Ashok Kumar understands his position as the master of the last step in the beautification of the bride. His decisions will be the culmination, the capstone of the aesthetics of the wedding. The initial decision by the groom's family to accept the woman as a bride had partially to do with her beauty, and that is exactly what the beautician is hired to do: to highlight, for all to admire, the beauty of the bride.[26] Marriages are occasions for the display of both wealth and beauty, but Ashok Kumar believes that what is on display at the high point of the wedding is not the wealth of the family but the beauty of the bride. Many women get married in rented or borrowed ornaments (which are often provided by the photography studio), but as long as the bride looks beautiful in the present and in the photographs, it does not matter that she does not own the jewelry. Ashok Kumar feels that the audience will be dazzled by the magnificence of the woman, and the ornaments, real or fake, owned or rented, will be beside the point.

Ashok Kumar, like most of the people in this book, believes strongly in the power of the entire ensemble to create a unified vision of glamour. If a woman wears wonderful jewelry but a cheap sari and bad makeup, the whole look will be ruined, Ashok said. So he trains his girls to view the wedding outfit and jewelry first, and then make decisions about hairstyle and makeup. On the wedding day, a bride will put on her outfit, next have her hair styled, then she will put on her jewelry, and last of all comes her makeup, the beautician's crowning touch.

Much of the bridal jewelry is placed on the face: the large nose ring, the earrings, and most centrally, the *mantikka* ornament which suspends a gem on the forehead. Then delicate designs will be drawn around these jewels, emphasizing the arch of the eyebrows, to further emphasize the eyes. The bride's hair has to be done first, to clear her forehead, and her jewelry has to be positioned before the beautician can start applying the makeup. Ashok Kumar said that if the gem suspended from the *mantikka* is made of *kundan*, then the tiny dots painted on the bride's forehead should be in green, white, and red, to match the emerald, diamond, and ruby gems of the ornament. If the suspended *tikka* is a rectangular golden frame containing a gemstone, then the motifs could be in the shape of tiny squares, complementing the jewel. The forehead dots that follow the curve of the eyebrows of Hindu brides (and some Muslim ones as well)[27] may be painted on with liquid color or applied adhesively, using *bindis* sold for this purpose. The execution of these dots takes into account the shape and nature of the bride's face and her jewelry, and they must harmonize with the color and fabric of the outfit, matching the hue and luminosity of the bridal garments.

In addition to drawing the delicate forehead designs, the beautician must arrange the woman's hair in a fashionable style that will allow for the *sindur* to be placed on the part by her groom—a crucial moment in the religious ceremony. Other makeup includes eyeliner, eye shadow and mascara, lipstick and blush, and nail polish on both the hands and feet. (Brides in India, like brides in the United States, must look great in photographs, though in person they often look overdone, as though they were made up for the stage.) Affixed to the back of her hair the Hindu bride characteristically has a white garland

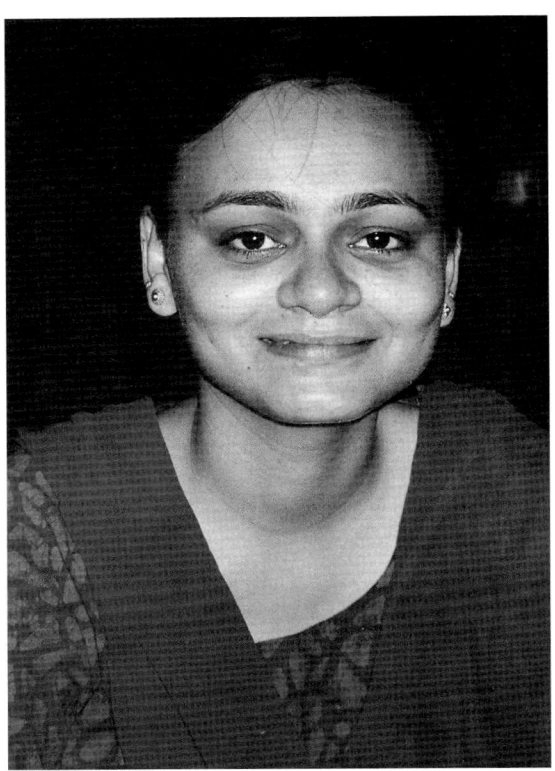

As a maiden

Shalini Shrivastava

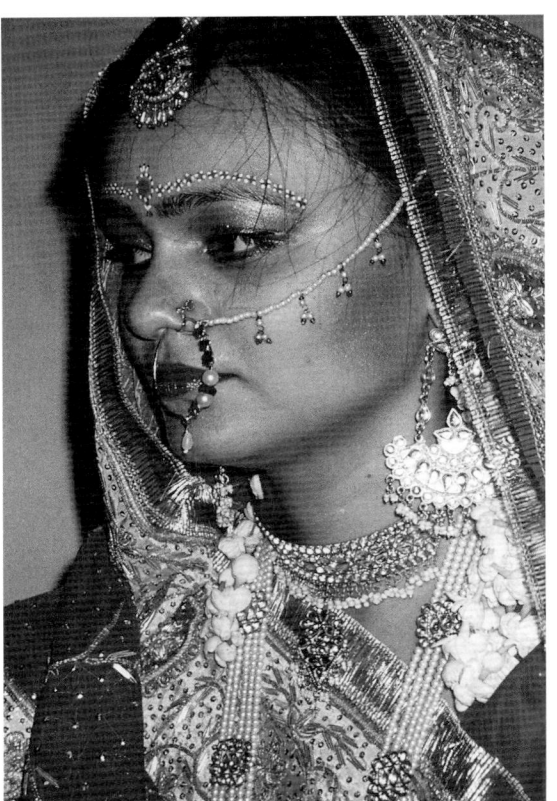

On her wedding day

made of tuberoses or jasmine flowers, hidden beneath the scarf draped on her head but emitting a sweet fragrance, especially for her own pleasure. Henna is applied to the hands and feet of the bride, but this process, as we shall see shortly, happens beforehand, not on the evening of the wedding.

The criteria employed by beauticians yield an agreement among jewelry, makeup, and clothing. An urban wedding has, in essence, two parts, each requiring a separate outfit for the bride. Makeup is applied specifically to match the first outfit, worn during the *jaimal,* in which the bride and groom exchange flower garlands. Makeup is not chosen to match the clothing for the Hindu ceremony, for this event generally takes place in the middle of the night when most people have left, and the ritual is not much photographed. Ashok Kumar told me that the *jaimal* is the event that is witnessed by all and captured by dozens of cameras; it is the focus of the official wedding photographs. The presence of the camera, then, governs makeup choices. Ashok said that in the past tiny glass *bindis* were placed on the forehead of the bride to add glitter and shine to her face, but it soon became apparent that these accessories caught the camera's flash in a rather unattractive way, so they fell quickly out of use. The little *bindis* were attractive in person, on the flesh of the bride, but they ruined the photos so they were abandoned, providing a clear testament to the importance of photography and revealing that visual documentation has become almost more important than experience.[28]

Beauticians, like other professionals of body art, pay attention to the entire ensemble, and knowing the standard of feminine beauty, they work toward the ideal by nuanced manipulations within their realm of expertise. If the bride is dark-skinned, the beautician must avoid shades of dark maroon and brown for the lipstick and nail polish, since these colors are believed to make the skin look dull and dark. If a woman has a high forehead, then the beautician paints long *bindi* designs arching high above the eyes, narrowing the gap between eyebrow and hairline. If the forehead is broad, then Ashok directs the beautician to apply a series of small, round dots. The color of these dots should match the *lehanga* outfit, and also signal the regional identity of the bride. Ashok Kumar said that most Bengali and Punjabi brides prefer a series of alternating red and white dots that match the colors of the bridal bangles for both of these regions. Regional identity governs the general configuration of a bride's clothes, jewelry, hair, and makeup, and the wide regional spectrum has been documented photographically in a volume by the Indian National Institute of Fashion Technology.[29]

Like the decisions involved in purchasing a sari or a set of bangles, the decisions concerning the makeup of the bride are made collaboratively. Some of the choices are made beforehand, in the period of the initial consultation between the bride and the beautician. Other decisions are made when the beautician arrives, burdened with a bag of beauty products, to the chamber where the bride sits, surrounded by her female relatives and *sahelis*—her girl-friends. Beauticians bring an album filled with pictures snipped from maga-zines that show models and Bollywood actresses dressed as brides. (There are also books, such as *The Asian Bridal Look Book,* that show different makeup and hairstyles that match outfits categorized as "contemporary" or "classic.")[30] The professional makeup artist and the bride consult this album together, gathering ideas about beauty and, most importantly, clues as to what makeup and hairstyles are most fashionable. In the hours before the wedding, the bride may be too nervous to make decisions and may resist the beautician's advice, so Ashok Kumar trains his pupils how to persuade the bride to come into compliance with their professional assessments. At this moment of ne-gotiation, persuasion, and confusion, the presence of the close *sahelis* is useful because, as Shalini said, a bride would trust the advice of her girlfriends above the beautician's arguments or her own opinions in this time of stress.

The *Ladies' Sangeet*

With the exception of a few "advanced" types in the big cities, young people in India do not date and have no sexual experience before marriage. Brides-to-be rely on their girlfriends to help with decisions concerning beauty and to help them relax before the exciting yet frightening experience of the wed-ding night. Married sisters, cousins, and *sahelis* will share advice about what to expect and what to do during the first sexual encounter with the husband. In the absence of sexual education classes, which are not offered in school, women rely on these unofficial yet effective channels of sexual information (the only alternative being Bollywood films).[31] The last ritual celebration a woman experiences before her marriage is hosting a *ladies' sangeet,* a gathering of women who sing, dance, eat, and often apply henna. The event can occur as much as a month before the wedding, as Shalini's did, or it can happen the day before, as Sunita Seth's did.

The *ladies' sangeet* takes place at the bride's house. It may be the last time all the girlfriends are together, since women go to live with their husbands, often moving away from their hometowns. A *ladies' sangeet* celebrates the upcoming rite of passage, usually with exuberant singing and dancing. Relaxed and happy in the company of other women, the participants are not as self-conscious as they will be during the wedding itself. Women will play the *dholak*—a drum beaten with the hands—and sing about the upcoming marriage. Many of these are traditional songs that warn the bride about the evil eye, about disasters caused by jealous women who will gaze greedily upon her new ornaments. Other songs will portray her new life metaphorically through references to the ornaments of the wife: the bangles, the anklets, the *sindur*. In Mira Nair's marvelous film *Monsoon Wedding,* a hired female musician sings a song in which bangles take the bride away from her father's house. The anxieties, the fears, as well as the excitement of marriage are attached to the bridal ornaments, symbols of her new life.

Henna, whether applied by a female friend or a hired beautician, often features at the *ladies' sangeet,* especially if the event takes place the day before the wedding, for henna painting is at its decorative peak of saturation on the day after its application. Henna—that is the Arabic word; it is *mehendi* in Hindi—is applied directly to the skin as a paste to create beautiful designs that can last for as long as two weeks. The process begins when the leaves of the henna plant, which are dried and ground to a fine powder, are mixed with boiling water and other additives, such as lemon juice, tea, or coffee, and allowed to sit for several hours. Once sufficiently set, the paste is applied to the skin of the hands and feet with a cone or painted on with a toothpick. A mixture of lemon juice and sugar keeps the henna from drying, increasing the potency of the dye. The henna paste is dark green on the skin, but once it dries completely and is scraped off, it leaves a reddish-maroon stain that deepens overnight.

In India, as in many countries,[32] the hands and feet of a bride are painted in henna designs to mark this vital transition in her life, and to enhance the beauty of her hands and feet so that they complement the gold and silver jewelry. The hands and feet are the only parts of the body, other than the face, that will be visible during the ceremony. They are decorated with red stain in the shapes of flowers, paisleys, and peacocks—the special bird of lovers. Ashok Kumar teaches his students to draw a big peacock in the middle of the back of the hand, so it will show in the pictures of the *jaimal,* when the bride raises her hands to place the flower garland around the neck of the groom. The female relatives of the bride and groom, as well as the groom himself in certain parts of India, may also be decorated with henna, though less elaborately than the bride.

In the recent past henna has become popular in the United States, where it is usually called "henna tattoo."[33] Americans use henna as an ornamental cosmetic or as a trial tattoo—a temporary version of a design they might have inked permanently on their skins. In the United States, designs on the hands often take the form of asymmetrical floral vines that flow down from the index finger and across the back or palm of the hand.[34] This popular American diagonal motif[35] has returned to India, now to be found on the hands of urban brides and movie stars such as Karishma Kapoor. Welcomed into the Indian repertoire, this asymmetrical vine for the hand was common in the chapbooks of henna designs sold on the streets in 2001.[36] Asymmetry, breaking with the old rules of Indian body art, characterizes more than henna designs. In 2003, I saw *salwar suits* at Hemant Khanchandani's shop that were made with an asymmetrical, diagonal cut on the neck or on the bottom hem of the *kurta*. The "Western style" platinum necklaces at Kanhaiya Lal that same year had diagonal, asymmetrical looks as well.

Beauty-school teacher Ashok Kumar, being in his own view old-fashioned, believes that henna designs "must be full" on the hands, covering the palms with motifs in the conventional manner; still, many brides reject this "traditional" look, opting for the sparse trailing vine motif that they associate with the "advanced" taste of America and Bollywood. In April 2004, among the wedding announcements in the *New York Times* "Sunday Styles" section, novelist Salman Rushdie's new bride, Padma Lakshmi, prominently displayed her hand, on which flowers trailed diagonally across her palm in the very latest style of the Indian bride.[37]

The Wedding

As Shashi Shah of the Kanhaiya Lal store explained, there are "marriage seasons" in India, specific times of the year when people get married. Wedding occasions vary greatly by location, caste, and class, but I will sketch, out of my experience, the sequence for a wedding between prosperous Hindus in Banaras, believing it to parallel in form and function, if not in detail, Indian weddings generally. In outline it will resemble, for example, the description provided of village weddings by the great anthropologist Oscar Lewis.[38]

The wedding ceremony is hosted by the parents of the bride and takes

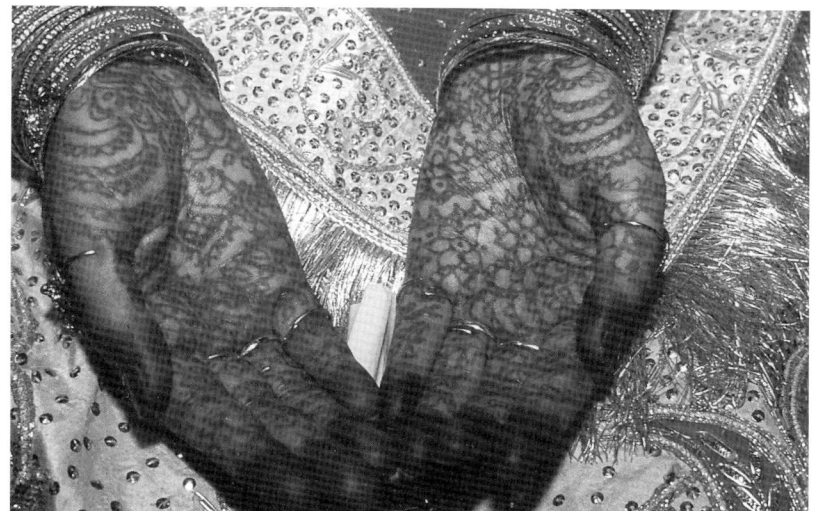

The hands of a bride

Henna

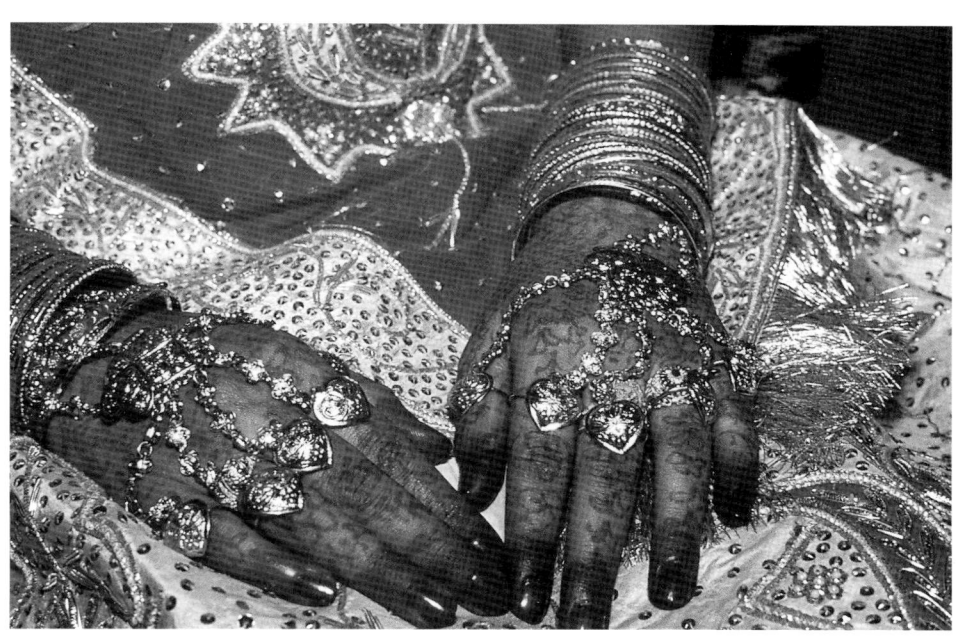

The *hathphul* ornament

place in their home, an upscale hotel, or a rented hall. Whatever the location, the place has to be decorated and arranged specifically for the event, with two structures, one for each of the main components of the marriage ceremony. The *jaimal* will occur on a stage where two ornate red and gold chairs have been placed. The other structure is a tent, the *mandap,* in which the actual Hindu ceremony will occur. Both structures are decorated with garlands of jasmine, marigold, and roses, which add auspicious color and sweet fragrance. For a fee, local companies set up these small pavilions, which are usually made of red canvas, the special color of marriage. In the movie *Monsoon Wedding,* the hired wedding planner, Dubey, initially set up a fashionable white tent that he proudly called the "Y2K dot" model, much to the chagrin of the bride's father, who was horrified by the prominent use of this inauspicious color—the color of the widow—for the marriage of his only daughter.[39] During the argument with the poor but high-caste organizer, the wealthy but lower-caste father demands a colorful tent, in red or yellow—colors that are characterized as "old fashioned" in the film.

Marriage ceremonies tend to occur in the evening. The guests assemble while the bride and her *sahelis* remain in a room apart, getting her ready for the big event. The family's hired *pundit* begins the chanting, feeding the small fire, while the guests snack and await the arrival of the groom. Meanwhile the groom's family and friends gather at his house, or at a hotel if he is from out of town, and after a *puja* in which the groom is circled by flame, they set out for the bride's house in a procession called the *barat*. At the end of the procession, the groom rides an elephant (rented and painted), a horse, or a shiny car garlanded with flowers. Along with the groom comes a young nephew or brother, whose presence symbolically represents the hope for a male offspring from the union. The *barat* is led by music, preferably a small truck carrying loudspeakers and a hired band whose lead singer, a prepubescent boy, belts the latest Bollywood hits into his hand-held microphone. Between the band at the head of the procession and the groom at the rear, his relatives and friends walk in a throng. The young, usually unmarried male relatives and friends gather behind the band, dancing flamboyantly,[40] nowadays in the trendy Punjabi *bhangra* style,[41] hopping rhythmically with their arms raised. The women and older relatives walk behind, between the dancing boys and the seated groom.

The *barat* can take up to two hours in its leisurely, festive crawl from one place to another, pausing periodically to let the people dance and playfully, aggressively block the traffic in the street. Since this parade of singers and dancers takes place in public, it must be contained in some way, and professionals are hired to do just that. They bear pinwheels of fluorescent lights on their heads, surrounded with blinking multicolored bulbs. These tired old men and women demarcate the parade, containing it within the outline of their lights while illuminating the path from the groom's place to the bride's. Representatives from the bride's family are stationed at different posts along the route to offer cold sodas or ice cream to the groom's friends, welcoming them onward.

When the *barat* arrives at the place of the wedding, the bride's parents greet the groom's party with sprinkles of rosewater, garlands of fresh flowers, and *tilak* marks placed on the forehead as a gesture of welcome. To the groom's family, the bride's parents offer baskets of gifts that typically include clothing (saris and shawls for the women, *kurtas* and *dhotis* for the men), cash, gold coins, gold and silver jewelry, five silver *paan* leaves and silver fishes, as well as platters of nuts, dried fruits, and sweets. Shortly after the arrival of the *barat,* the bride emerges from her room. Gloriously attired, shy in manner, she is led to the stage where the groom awaits her to exchange the ceremonial garlands. At this moving and picturesque moment, the guests sit on rows of chairs to view the enchanting profiles of the couple who place thick, matching garlands of flowers around one another's necks. Against the plain white clothing of the groom,[42] the bride's outfit glitters with gold; light flashes from her ornaments and shimmers on the brocade.

Once they have traded garlands, the couple settles on their thrones, majestic chairs upholstered in red velvet and trimmed in gold. Friends and relatives take turns standing behind the couple, posing for photographs. Countless pictures of this scene appear in photo albums, showing smiling members of the family standing behind the seated couple, who usually hold serious, formal expressions, though the groom might relax into a smile for a close friend's camera. The brides, though, are taught to look down timidly, looking pretty but chaste and demure. In this self-conscious display of public modesty, the bride observes what Patricia Jeffery calls "eye *purdah.*"[43] As she looks down, her head is bent slightly, she emphasizes for the camera the *mantikka* on her forehead and the heavy brocade of the scarf draped over her head. Held calmly in her lap, the bride's hands display the golden hand-flower ornaments, with the lacy red henna peeking through the glittery chains.

This is the central vision of a Hindu wedding: a groom in white and a bride who is a "scented red bundle."[44] In this moment of extravagant display, the viewers analyze the variables, judging the beauty and wealth of the bride and her family. The original purpose of the bridal jewelry was to send the daughter away with "economic security," but now that the prime objective is to look good at this moment of display, it makes sense to borrow or rent fabulous jewelry that, transient in the bride's life, will be permanent in the photographs of the wedding. Some of the essential items of the bridal "complete set," such as the hand-flower ornaments, will never be worn again, and if they were purchased, they were purchased for this exhibition alone.

As it was with the king's *durbar* or the god's *darshan,* the primary motive of the *jaimal* is display. This moment when the bride and groom sit in splendor has been added recently to the wedding to provide an opportunity for photographic *darshan.* Since the bride customarily wears clothing and ornaments given to her by her own family, the richness of her ensemble, combined with the extravagance of the whole event, reflects her family's taste and economic capacity. The wealth and taste of the groom's family will also be judged through the bride's body art—in the gifts of clothing and jewelry which they gave her and which she will wear during the *bidai* ceremony on the next morning.

Immediately after the *jaimal,* dinner is served, its menu usually consisting of rich Indian food of a kind not consumed on a daily basis. Lush, fancy, Mughal dishes, such as *paneer* curries, *biriyani* rice with meats, nuts, and raisins, *naan,* and Punjabi *rajma,* are often served, and sometimes the buffet may include stations of Chinese and Italian food, adding cosmopolitan spice to the meal.[45] The bride's family pays for the food, so its quality and variety are other ways they show their wealth, taste, and sophistication.

The menu tends to remain consistent from wedding to wedding, so it is the excellence of the items—the innovativeness of the recipes, the freshness of the ingredients, the combinations of subtle flavors, the visual presentations—that will be judged, just as the bridal outfit and jewelry, consistent as to the components, are judged by their quality. What people evaluate are innovations and qualitative variations within the expected norms. Brides will wear *lehangas* in a shade of red, maroon, or pink, and the required bridal ornaments, but the style, fashionability, materials, and skills of the craftsmen will be noted and admired or not. A stable core of elements—whether in the realm of food, clothing, or jewelry—makes it easy to compare and contrast, enabling a close focus on the details, since the general outlines will hold true for all instances.

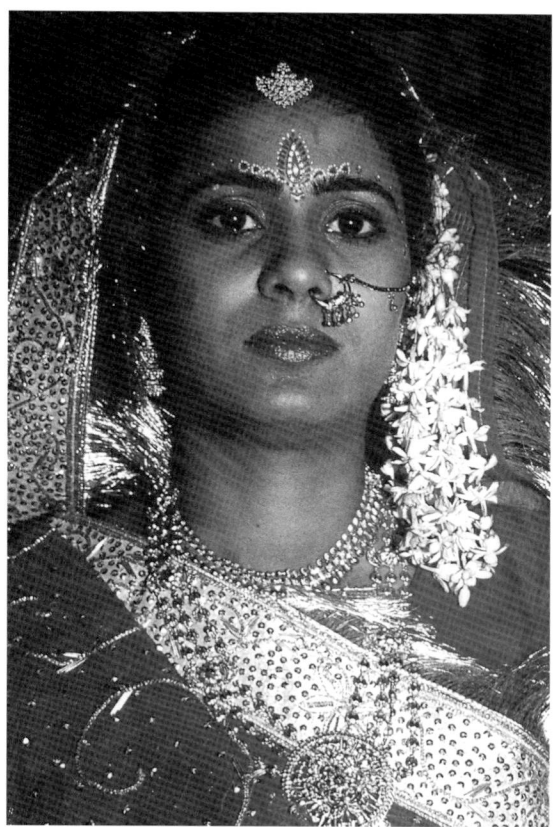

Swati as a bride

On her wedding day, dressed in the gifts of her family

The day after the wedding, dressed in the gifts of her in-laws

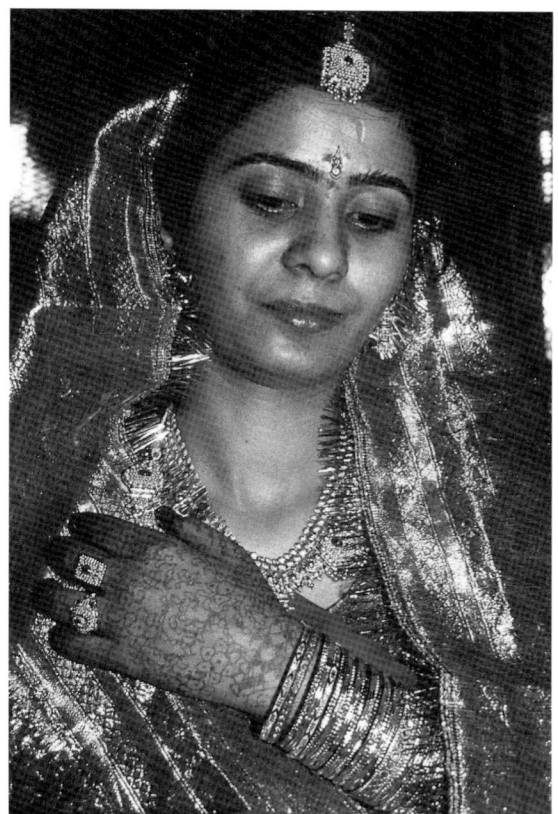

Wedding parties give all women a chance to dress up and express at its best their sense of style. *Kumari* girls aim to look good at weddings, perchance to snag a suitable match, and you will recall from the examples of Nina Khanchandani, Neelam Chaturvedi, and Mukta Tripathi that married women maintain a desire to appeal to their peers by paying special attention to the clothing and jewelry they wear at wedding receptions. Many women I spoke with told me that, throughout the evening, unofficial comparisons are made and silent "competitions" occur among the female guests. Their conversations invariably center on the adornment of the others, drifting into speculations about how much this or that costs and whether the jewelry is real, plated, or fake. Such evaluations happen at every social level, where people are happy to judge viciously among those of their own economic class. Geeta, a poor working woman from Banaras, told me this about the receptions she has attended:

"During weddings, to show themselves that 'I am very *rich*,' to show themselves that 'I am very pretty,' they put on *makeup*—they wear lots and lots, as much as they can—and jewelry, they wear. And heavy-heavy ornaments they wear—at that time they don't seem to be worried about theft!

"*Comparisons* take place. Toward those that are wearing more than me, there is a bit of *jealous* feeling that, 'Oh, she has all of these things.' Then you feel, 'I don't have these things.' Or you see someone and think, 'Hers is really nice. Mine is not that nice.' This *feeling* does happen. It is a bad *feeling*, but then, there is *santosh*—'Look at that person, she doesn't have enough.' Then there is *santosh*, 'I am okay. I am better than that person.'"

Visual scrutiny and comparison can lead to negative, jealous feelings, as well as to an affirmation of personal taste, for we invariably question and challenge the self-presentation of others and learn to refine and confirm our own likes and dislikes. Passing judgment on the creations of others, we build up a storehouse of examples, positive and negative, to use in our own creations, while a style evolves and we bring it into appreciative self-consciousness.

Competitions in this intensely comparative environment can become extreme. At a wedding in Azam Ghar, I stayed at the groom's house along with his friends and relatives. There I befriended a female guest from out of town, Manju, who took pains to be ornamented at all times, not only at the official wedding event but at the groom's house on the days before and after the ceremony. At the reception women want to look good for everybody, including the half of the guests they have not known before. When she was at the groom's house, she told me, Manju had little interest in appealing to strangers; she wanted to impress the people she already knew. Judgments made by known people, as we have seen throughout this book, are more meaningful in India than assessments by unknown others. Manju told me that she does not like to wear heavy jewelry, especially in the summer, when this wedding took place; it makes her feel hot and it gives her skin rashes. Nevertheless, she proceeded to change her ornate saris and heavy gold jewelry a few times every day, though she inconvenienced the groom's family, who had to open and close the small safe where Manju stored her expensive jewelry.

Families display their wealth and status through the clothing of their women, since men's clothes are relatively generic, consisting of either a *kurta-pyjama* set or slacks and a jacket. But saris and jewelry, wondrous in their variety, provide creative outlets through which women express their taste and the financial standing of the household. Costly ornaments and clothing reflect the husband's salary, but the wife's self-presentation is her creation, and she gets full credit for her choices. As Neelam Chaturvedi succinctly explained, women want to look good for themselves, to heighten their confidence; they want to look good for other women, to have an appreciative audience; and they want to look good for other men, whose admiration may cause their own husbands to appreciate them more.

The display at the wedding is triple. First and foremost, the bride is on display, literally up on a stage and shining from head to toe. Second, the married female relatives and guests from both sides exhibit their most splendid adornment, showing themselves in age-appropriate attire that attests to their good taste and the financial power of their husbands. And third, the unmarried women, modestly dressed and demure in their behavior, aim to attract the parents of handsome young men.

In Christian weddings, the formal religious aspect of the wedding usually precedes the dinner and reception. In Hindu India, the order is reversed. The dancing of the *barat,* the spectacle of the *jaimal,* and the delicious meal complete the experience for most of the guests. The Hindu ceremony begins after most of the guests have left, satisfied. The Sanskrit ritual is long and complex. For it, the bride and groom reappear, usually in outfits different from the ones they wore for the *jaimal.* Now the bride wears an auspicious sari, rather than a *lehanga;* over the sari, and over her shoulders and head, she wears a gauzy red shawl, sewn along the edges with *gota,* tinselly fringe of gold.[46] The bride may wear the same jewelry she wore earlier, unless it was artificial or rented, for it is considered unlucky to get married in fake gold. Fake gold is fine for photos; real gold is necessary for the religious ceremony.

During the Sanskrit service, the Brahmin *pundit* sits cross-legged in front of the bride and groom. Members of the bride's family sing and joke, taunting the in-laws, mocking the masculinity of the groom or the meanness of his mother.[47] Humor lightens the mood, entertaining the crowd that sits through the long ritual. At one point in the rite, the gifts that the groom's family gives to the bride are presented in baskets. The groom's mother, at the Azam Ghar wedding, opened each box, one by one, and laid the jewelry out to be seen. The hired photographer took close-up photos of each item.

The jewelry given to the bride by her parents is displayed on her body during the first part of the event, and the jewelry given her by the groom's family will also be displayed. It will be spread out while the marriage occurs in the second part of the evening, and she will wear it on the next day. Subtly, the two sides are in competition, and the guests can compare the generosity of the two families by noting the amount and quality of the gold.

Toward the end of the ritual, when the woman has become a wife with the blessing of the gods, thick silver anklets, *pahjebs,* and toe rings will be placed on her feet by a female relative or a maid. Finally, her new husband ceremoniously places *sindur*[48] into the part in her hair, visually marking their completed union. She will wear this *sindur* every day of her life until she dies or becomes a widow. The *sindur* placed at this time is bright orange; considered pure, it is used for marriages and *pujas.* New wives customarily wear orange *sindur* for one to three months after the marriage, at which point most women, especially those in the cities, switch to deep red *sindur.* Mathuri Chaubey said that in the city, career women wear a touch of red *sindur* to show that they are married, but, to show that they work and in the fashion of the urban professional woman, wear only minimal *sindur.* In the village, according to her, the only real status women can show is that they are married, and so village women wear lots of brighter orange *sindur.* But village women prefer orange—Gayatri, a female *bindi* vendor at the Hanuman Sanchat Mochen temple told me—because it is the "original" color for marriage, while the red *sindur* is merely fashionable. She told me that some *devis*—unmarried goddesses—are depicted with red *sindur,* attesting to the fact that *kumari* women may wear red powder—and so, orange *sindur* is the one that truly communicates marriage.

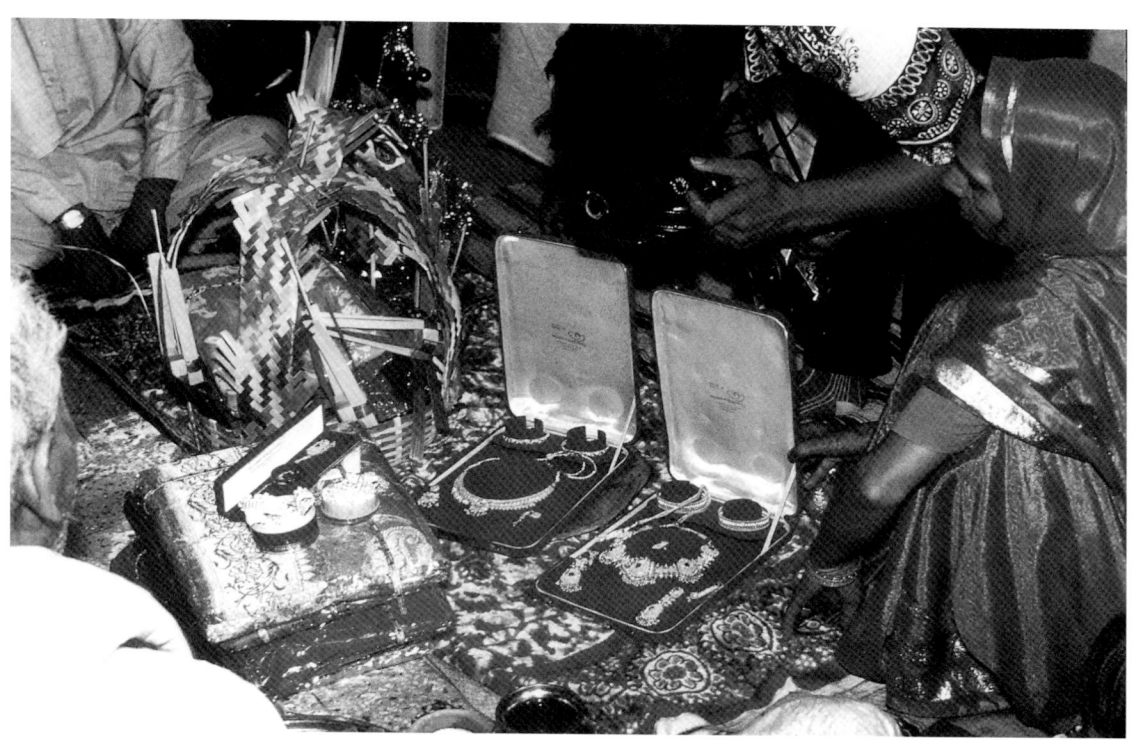

Dowry gifts on display during the wedding ceremony of
Swati and Shachi, Azam Ghar

Sindur is the only adornment strictly restricted to married women (other than, in some regions of India, the *mangalsutra* necklace).[49] *Kumari* girls, when dressed up, occasionally wear *bindis,* bangles, anklets, and toe rings, but no unmarried woman puts *sindur* on for fashion. I asked many people, both men and women, about the significance of *sindur.* Ashok Kumar, the teacher of beauticians, gave me a practical and scientific reason for *sindur.* He said that the powder contains mercury oxide, which chemically enhances a "sex sensation" in the new bride. Newlywed couples are encouraged to consummate their marriage and conceive a child; the *sindur* worn heavily in the first few months is thought to arouse the timid wife[50] as her gaudy clothes and tinkling jewelry arouse the husband. Incidentally, many women who wear sparse amounts of *sindur* after the early phase of their marriages mention another chemical result of *sindur:* it prematurely turns one's hair white.

Sindur, too, carries religious meanings. Women who prefer orange *sindur* associate it with Hanuman. In Banaras, Hanuman is almost always depicted as bright orange in color, and the story I have often heard goes like this: One day Hanuman observed Sita putting a bit of *sindur* on the part in her hair, and he asked what she was doing. Sita answered that she did this every day as a way of displaying her love for Ram, her husband. Hanuman—Ram's devoted servant—feeling that he too should show the depth of his love for Ram, took the little container from Sita's hands and poured the entire contents over himself, covering his body in orange *sindur.* And that is why Hanuman is orange.

The story teaches us to understand that *sindur* symbolizes the eternal love of Sita, and the eternal devotion of Hanuman, for Ram; it connects the two kinds of love a woman should have for her husband: conjugal and devotional. The orange color is so strongly associated with Hanuman that at his great temple in Banaras, Sanchat Mochen, worshipers are offered a bright orange liquid paste to make on their foreheads a *bindi* of *darshan.* Since Hanuman is a bachelor, many believe that *kumari* women should not place his orange *bindi* on their foreheads; it is inappropriate for an unmarried woman to place a *bindi* on her forehead after worshiping an unmarried god, so they put the dab of orange on their necks. *Sindur,* in orange but also in red, takes on a Vaishnavite aura through its association with Ram (Vishnu), Sita (Lakshmi), and Hanuman.

I heard another explanation for *sindur* that connects to Shiva, not Ram, and offers a competing Shaivite story; I recorded it, after all, in Banaras, Shiva's own city. Gajagand Pandey is a retired tailor who works part-time at a corner silk shop a block off the Vishvanath Gali. A Brahmin, he is a man deeply interested in religion and knowledgeable about the folklore and mythology of his city. He told me that the split image that depicts Shiva (on the right) and his wife Parvati (on the left) as two halves of the same person—the sacred form called Ardhanarisvana in the books but which he, like most Hindus, calls Haragori—explains the importance of *sindur*. Pandey said that men are born with their left sides female and their right sides male, while women are female on both sides. During the marriage ritual, the husband places *sindur*, with his right index finger and thumb, on the central part of his wife's hair. This gesture symbolically requests that his wife give him her left side, and he in return will give her his right side.[51] In the past, Pandey said, this dramatic act of cutting, dividing, and unifying—when one becomes two and two become one—was symbolically performed with a dull sword.

The red *sindur*, he said, is the emblematic blood[52] that flows from the splitting of a woman into two parts, after which she is made whole again by accepting a male half at the same time that her husband receives the real female half that replaces his abstract female essence with the particular essence of his wife. The red *sindur*, always visible on the hair part of the wife, commemorates this cutting and rejoining of two individuals, each of whom now contains the same paired essences that embody forever the eternal bond that is marriage. (Interestingly, this bifurcation of the body—male, right; female, left—seems general in India: when palms are read, the right hand is used for men and the left hand for women, and astrological rings are worn on the right hand by men and on the left by women.)

The *sindur* has been applied; the marriage ritual is completed. In many regional traditions, the groom and his relatives return to their house, while the bride spends her last night in her father's home. On the next morning comes the time of the *bidai*, the ritual farewell of the bride. For this occasion the bride is dressed "from head to toe," as I was often told, in the gifts from her in-laws. She wears the things presented to her during the marriage ceremony—a fancy Banarasi sari and heavy gold jewelry. During the night before she wore her family's clothes and jewelry. Then she was still part of her parents' family; now, the official marriage has taken place, and she appears in the ornaments and clothing bought by the groom's side, since she now belongs to a new family—his.

In a sad and moving farewell, after the *puja*, the bride hugs her relatives and, usually sobbing, leaves her father's house. This is especially traumatic for women who move far away, where they will be cut off from family and friends. In Banaras, the bride customarily leaves in a car, carrying on her lap an ornate little domed box, painted red and full of *sindur* powder.[53] While her belongings, packed in suitcases, ride in the trunk of the car, she carries into her new home the prime symbol of her newly acquired status as a wife: *sindur.* When the car arrives, the children of the house pretend to block the door of the car, moving away only when the groom's mother bribes them with money. The new wife steps from the car, and on one of the occasions I witnessed, she steps into flat baskets of rice and lentils, symbolic of prosperity and fertility, of children in numbers. The new couple shyly feed each other with sweetened yogurt, and the bride starts to survey the new house and household in which she will likely spend the rest of her life.

During the next evening, the groom's family usually hosts a dinner reception of their own, officially welcoming the new addition to their family. There are many reasons to celebrate: the son is happily married, the union brings a new alliance with the bride's family, and there is the prospect of grandchildren. The women of the household will enjoy the companionship of the new wife, and they are pleased by the increase in the workforce that will ease their labor, especially because the younger wives are eventually assigned the less desirable housework.

The party at the bride's new home will introduce her to all the people who were not at the wedding (which might have taken place in another city), or who saw her there briefly but did not get to know her. This event is often called the *moo-dikhai,* literally, "the showing of the face,"[54] an act strikingly portrayed in Satyajit Ray's famous film *The World of Apu* when a crowd gathers to admire the grace of the unexpected new bride (played by the beautiful Sharmila Tagore). The new wife is dressed up for the occasion in fancy clothes and jewelry, things provided to her by her in-laws, and a beautician is usually hired to apply her makeup. In some family traditions, the wife will sit down with a scarf covering her head, while the female guests come, one by one, to lift the scarf, see her face, and leave a gift of jewelry on her lap as a blessing and a gesture of welcome. Here, again, the explicit link between beauty, ornaments, and acceptance appears.

This act of seeing and giving is reminiscent of *darshan:* the visitors arrive, receive sight, offer gifts, make connections. Since the new wife is most likely a stranger to all who come, seeing her face establishes acquaintance, beginning the associations among people who are now related and need to become familiar with each other. Although the purpose is to get to know the new member of the family and especially to introduce the women to each other—they will occupy the same social network—showing the bride's beauty is the overt motivation of the event. Her radiance on this night reflects her in-laws' good taste in selecting such a beautiful woman, but it also exhibits their generosity in choosing the clothes, the ornaments, and even the beautician that enhanced her grace. The new wife will eventually acquire her own clothing and jewelry and wear them as she pleases, deciding to match certain clothes with certain ornaments for certain occasions. But on this night, she does not assert her own style. She lets the display reflect the wealth and generosity of her in-laws, arranged on her lovely frame.

For the next three months, or for as much as a year, the new wife will not do much housework. She will slowly come to comfort in her new home, becoming familiar with the others of the household and the chores it requires, and she will slowly take on more and more responsibility.

The bride is bedecked beautifully to be seen by her relatives—and by her new husband. In the West, couples fall in love and decide to get married. It is like that with love-marriages in India, but not with arranged marriages. In an arranged marriage it is after you are married that the process of falling in love begins.[55] This early romantic period in a couple's life is often depicted in Bollywood films, and it is lovingly described in Manil Suri's novel *The Death of Vishnu,* in the moving segments he devotes to Sheetal and Vinod. The new wife wins her husband's love with noisy jewelry and gaudy saris. Then again, if a woman marries a man she does not care much about, she can dress in a way that will *not* excite him, subtly nudging him toward old girlfriends or prostitutes.

Newly married women are encouraged to indulge in their *shauk*—their interest—in body art. The new wife is visually marked by jewelry in abundance, brightly colored clothes, and the effort she puts into creating the whole ensemble. Growing up in India where an ostentatious aesthetic dominates, most women have the *shauk* for ornaments. It runs free in childhood, then it is suppressed in adolescence when, at the age of twelve, girls cease being decorated. Then their *shauk* is allowed to burst forth at marriage. The new bride indulges her fascination, releasing the pent-up desires for fashion and adornment. I am told that young married women should kindle this passion, letting it blaze to burn out in a few years, and then, when they are ready to

Part 5. Conclusion

·16·

The Study of Body Art

AT THE HEART OF THIS BOOK is the belief that individuals shape their lives in relation to both the material environment and the social world, finding a place where personal desires are made manifest by the careful negotiation of resources and responsibilities. Individuals exist simultaneously in a state of self-expression and social connection, communicating personal artistry in ways that are constrained, encouraged, and appreciated by the people they live among. The individuals in this book—the weaver Hashim Ansari, the merchant Hemant Khanchandani, the housewife Mukta Tripathi—locate themselves in conflicting social and physical contexts in which they interact with others, some of whom help them express themselves artistically while others hinder their wishes. All acts of creation in the realm of adornment—the crafting of jewelry, the tailoring of clothes, the selling and buying of bangles—are governed by desire and situated socially. The outcome of action—the sari woven, the sari worn—is like all art a merger of will and circumstance. The women in this book make decisions. They express themselves by working within the rules of tradition that are influenced by history and geography, by religious and social norms.

Human beings everywhere find themselves operating between freedom and constraint. The challenge in body art, as in other creative acts, is to achieve a balance between the aesthetic and the practical, the personal and the social, fashion and tradition. In achieving balance, people fix on certain choices while ignoring other options. The woman in India will express herself through jewelry and clothing, through materials, texture, color, and design, while remaining within the broad limitations of family, caste, religion, region, and taste. Scholars who employ the rhetoric of negotiation may assume that everything is negotiable, but it is not. Financial resources provide conspicuous limits, and social rules of adornment for gender, age, caste, and religion must be acknowledged, even while they are subtly subverted.

In our brief examination of the sari, we saw how the owners of retail shops say they tell their weavers what to make, and the textiles embody the aesthetics and commercial sense of the bosses. The weavers, however, claim they assert their own choices at the loom, making the saris they want to make. Merchants believe that they also tell their customers what to buy. But the women, their customers, say they buy what they want to buy, pushing the salesmen to show them what they want to see, forcing the shop owners to carry the items they want to buy, compelling the merchant to order the workshop to make the saris that will meet the aesthetic demands of the women, completing the cycle of influence. In truth, everyone is correct. All of these individuals find ways of making choices within the streaming conditions of production, sales, and purchase. They influence each other, collaborating indirectly over time and space in the tradition of the sari. Such negotiations, as we have seen, involve exchanges between people who are different in gender, age, class, caste, and religion, in a succession of contexts in which competing agendas of power, finance, and taste collide.

Once the thing is made and sold, once the interactions between producers and sellers are done, the woman's string of choices and compromises continues. The choice to wear a sari requires consideration of age, body, and occasion, of color, design, and fabric. Since the sari is an unstitched length of cloth, whenever a woman puts one on she acts as her own tailor, deciding exactly how to drape it, remaking the garment every time it is worn.

Choice rises in every act of adornment. Only a small number of women—less than 5 percent, I was told by the merchants—commission a piece of jewelry or order a sari to be made to their exact specifications, but all women choose how to dress themselves, some with flair, some plainly. To choose to look like everybody else—to remain as inconspicuous, as conventional as possible—is a decision no less willed than the decision to be a star of the fashion avant-garde. Women can choose to stand out or stand back. Nina Khanchandani wishes to blend in at a party. Neelam Chaturvedi wants her jewelry to blend in while she is noticed for her saris. Mukta Tripathi wants to stand out in every aspect of her body art—her hair, makeup, jewelry, sari, and

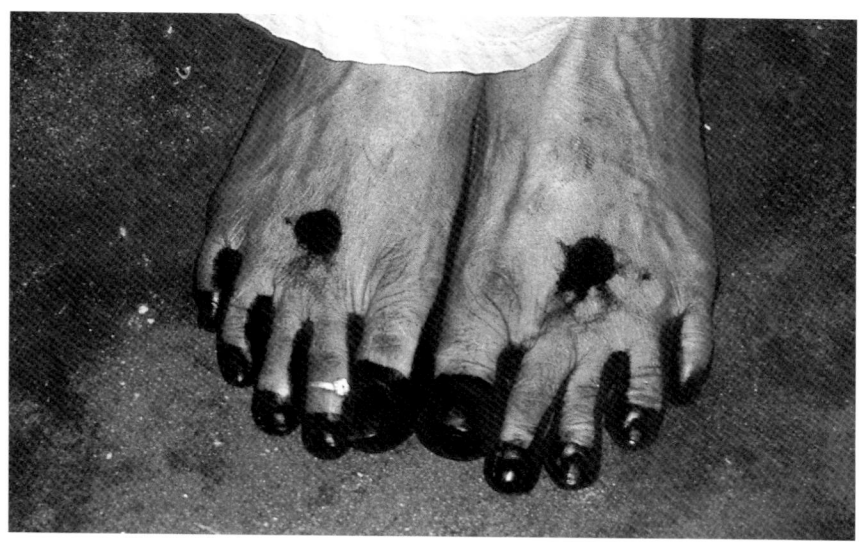

Nirmala's feet

Personal choice: on one day two sisters-in-law in Banaras applied *alta* to their feet as part of a seasonal ritual. Both met the requirements of tradition, but differences in their personal taste are clear in the painted result.

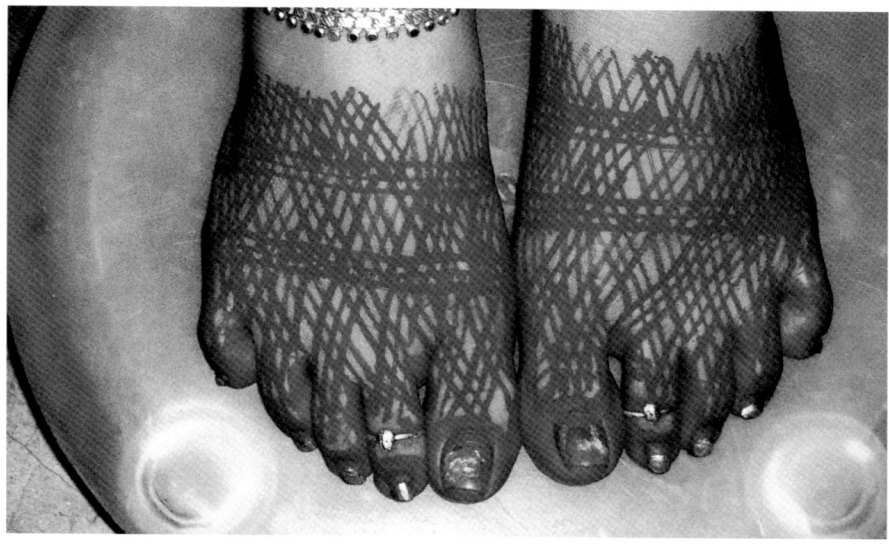

Manju's feet

perfume. These women adorn themselves to please themselves—and to fit into the social scene as they wish to fit into it. Nina's self-presentation could seem passive, but taken in the context of Indian body art, her crisp, plain style is a rebellious act; it runs against the social grain. She says she wants to be "with the crowd," but, in fact, she stands boldly forth in her own spirit.

Folklore and Material Culture Studies

The methods of fieldwork and principles of interpretation I used in this book were derived from the tradition of my discipline, folklore. My discipline's tradition is interdisciplinary, sharing conventions of analysis with anthropology, archeology, cultural geography, history, and art history. Within folklore, my orientation has been shaped by folkloristic studies of material culture that have developed over the last thirty-five years in exchange with performance theory, a paradigm that emphasizes the individual in the social moment of creativity. Creation is understood by attending at once to individuals and their circumstances, looping standards and acts of desire with the forces of consumption and social response. The contrast is with studies that focus on a lone genius floating free of the world, and with studies that see everything as the result of superorganic powers at play. Our commitment is to a believable dialectic of people and the world.

My study is indebted to scholars of material culture who provide models of inquiry that enable considerations of form and function, creation and consumption, and the historical and social forces that bring beauty, meaning, and the power of communication to the things people make.

If material culture is defined as "culture made material,"[1] if objects can be read as representations of culture and culture is a pattern in consciousness, then objects require creators, and study must recognize individuals and individual interpretations of art and tradition, standards and goals. In focusing on the individual in the creative act, material culture studies combine attention to the object—its form, technology, and aesthetics—with attention to contexts of production, where influences, processes, and procedures of evaluation come together. Folklore studies customarily acknowledge the centrality of contexts, those that are visible and tangible, as well as those that lie hidden in the mind yet imbue the act and product with meaning. For the study of material culture, these contexts can be divided into three broad categories: those of creation, communication, and consumption.[2] Attention to the sequential contexts that make up these categories will reveal the life history of the object, and in the course of this revelation we will come toward understanding of the people who make and sell, buy and use, building meaning into their lives through interactions with the materials of their environments.

In the case of body art, a private creation—the body dressed in isolation—is followed by a series of recreations during communicative acts that blend creation and communication in functional simultaneity. The motions of the body—the sly shifting of a falling piece of cloth, the extra pulse of tinkling jewelry—yield little creative acts that are made after the body is dressed but while it is being performed before an audience of beholders.

The process of creation can be subdivided into two procedures: creation out of nature and creation out of culture. Studies of the first kind pay special attention to the gathering and altering of raw substances, making it imperative to examine environmental factors, natural resources, tools, and technological innovations, while analyzing both the cognitive and material processes of creation. Writings on pottery by Burrison, Glassie, and Zug provide fine instances of such work.[3] By contrast, scholars of the second process—the creation out of culture—study how people acquire objects made by others and juxtapose them in artful assemblage, making "things out of things."[4] In this act, the creator works in long-distance collaboration with all the others who have shaped and reshaped those artifacts. The assemblage, as a result, becomes a palimpsest, a layering of the aesthetic visions of many individuals. Public display is often the goal of assembled creations, as Amy Kitchener shows in her documentation of the yard art for holidays.[5] Other assemblages are created for private, not public, appreciation, and Kay Turner's book on home altars skillfully reveals how a layering of things brings about a locus for personal worship.[6]

Contexts of creation yield objects, and the student of material culture would have no reason to study the context were it not for the thing created within it. Though some avoid it, formal analysis of works of art is essential, for it provides insight into the creator's culture and the culture of consumption that he or she imagines. In harmony with their colleagues in art history, students of material culture analyze and assess the formal qualities of things, whether they are paintings, pots, or plain old barns. Close inquiry will demonstrate the relationship of form to form that at once defines and subverts categories, while revealing the limits of environmental and technological constraints. Formal study is basic to the discovery of geographical and historical patterns, as folklorists who are scholars of vernacular architecture have made clear.[7]

Whether or not the analyst acknowledges the fact, the object owes its existence to people at work in particular situations, and one of the most useful moves in material culture research has involved close study of individual creators—not anonymous members of homogenous masses, but real people, with real names and biographies, creators who are allowed to speak, interpreting their art and history in their own words. Notable portraits of individual artists include Michael Owen Jones's of the chair maker Chester Cornett, John Vlach's of the blacksmith Phillip Simmons, and Henry Glassie's of the sculptor Haripada Pal.[8] Such books have taught us that long interviews, long friendships, and attention to oral history are necessary if we are to understand the artist's psychology and worldview—if we are to understand how the productive tensions of tradition and innovation are mediated by the creative act embodied in the object that stands before us and beckons to us through its presence.

Once we have come into engagement with an artist and learned about the artist's life and creations, our inquiry will expand, radiating outward into the contexts in which the artist is defined by gender, age, religion, ethnicity, community, region, nation, civilization . . . These larger contexts, as brought into the creative act and implicated in the work, amplify its meanings. Simon Bronner has explained how the factor of age is critical in understanding the wooden chains carved by retired men.[9] Barbara Babcock and Gladys-Marie Fry have discussed the significant variable of gender and its influence on creativity.[10] The topic of religion and the works it inspires has been documented well by many scholars, including Donald Cosentino in his study of the assembled art of Pierrot Barra, a Vodou priest working in the Iron Market of Port-au-Prince.[11]

Just as artifacts capture spiritual concepts difficult to verbalize, making material culture crucial to the study of religion, artifacts also conspicuously exhibit aspects of social identity.[12] Performance theory orients us to the realization that art can serve to draw people together into groups and to drive them apart, so that groups at once cohere and separate. Through artistic expression, some isolate themselves, becoming outsiders,[13] while others—the Hmong immigrants to America providing a rich case—use art to overcome the past, imagine the future, and confirm a collective identity in the present.[14]

Studying Body Art

The model I offer for the study of body art combines my training in folklore and my ethnographic experience in India. It stretches from the creation out of nature to the creation out of culture, integrating the contexts of creation, communication, and consumption. It begins with the fashioning of raw materials into an object that is sold to a merchant, who sells it to a woman who places it in the assemblage of her adornment. Her assemblage varies in relation to her stage in the cycle of life and the contexts of her presence in the world that range from the isolation of perfect privacy, when she is alone with her understanding of history and culture and taste, through increasingly less private scenes that shift through realms of interaction at home, at parties, in the streets of the neighborhood, until they end in the near anonymity of a distant public place.

That is the pattern implicit throughout this book, and I now make it explicit in segments by delineating categories of investigation, contextualization, and interpretation. Centered by current folklore methods of inquiry, the model expands to incorporate and recognize many of the excellent works on the topics of body art, dress, and fashion history. My hope is to provide a bibliographic foundation for future work,[15] and to suggest directions for study that my training in folklore and my work in India lead me to believe will prove generally fruitful for my colleagues in this important and as yet underexplored realm of human enterprise. I have come to be convinced that any good study should be accountable for four broad categories of information: Production, Commercial Exchange, Forms and Acts of Adornment, Social Contexts of Meaning and Function.

Basic Orientations

To study a piece of body art in the world—a tattoo on the shoulder, a silk evening gown—certain assumptions need to be made. Body art is simultaneously a reflection of the norms of society and an interpretation of such norms by an individual. Then noting the patterns that emerge from a cluster of examples, we are drawn, through a separation of the variable from the invariant, toward aesthetics, meanings, and functions. An individual's body art exemplifies the mediation between the self and the society, reconciling the apparently opposed forces of tradition and fashion.

It is basic, too, to recognize that acts of bodily adornment are always intended, always meaningful, always communicative. The communication is directly conditioned by the acts of seeing and being seen. Acts of adornment are interactive, a part of social exchange, just as they are creative arrangements and a part of personal expression. The tattoo on the body, set in relation to other ornaments and pieces of apparel, at once integrates the body with itself and puts the body in relation to other bodies in a particular social occasion in both time and space. People exist historically, geographically, and socially, and, though continuous to themselves as they shift from context to context, they will be perceived as different to others who evaluate them, now in one frame, now in another. So the same piece of body art might look and function differently in different settings, in different conceptual contexts, in different frames of relevance, and so one piece of body art will simultaneously serve many functions—social, economic, religious, aesthetic.

Furthermore, ornament is an integral part of the daily routine for most of the people of the world all the time. Some people engage in bodily adornment with excitement, and some care little about it. Personality, economic security, gender, social status, familial and social restrictions, cultural heritage—all these condition differences of interest, but interested or not, all people get dressed. In getting dressed, they express themselves, for, within their delimiting conditions, all people make choices. How choices are made within the field of opportunity, how choices are made manifest—these are key questions, and in our analysis we must consider both what is selected and what is rejected, what is worn and what is not.

The model I present has been tested in the study of contemporary body art, and it will be most easily applicable to other such studies, but I believe it may hold hints as well for students at work on historical problems. Full understanding of the dynamic of body art can only come when you can talk directly with the living, but I am certain that historical study is imperative, for it gives background to contemporary action and provides invaluable data concerning practices that have vanished from our experience. Research in archives, libraries, and museums will continue to yield important aesthetic, social, economic, and political data, sometimes supporting the information collected from observations and from conversations with people, and sometimes productively conflicting with the yield from the field. Information gathered

390

from conventional historical sources is often insufficient, since the official record excludes most of the population, especially those marginalized in the record by race or class, gender or occupation. A full understanding of the human complexity can come only from direct fieldwork, from observation of people and things, from interviews designed to elicit oral history and emic interpretation. In studying body art, in observing and listening and seeking pattern, we will find that history and culture and the inviolable reality of the individual are visibly inscribed in the ways that people get dressed every day.

Production

The study of any item of art requires attention to materials, technology, the process of production, and the form of the created object. For body art, we will need to know where the raw materials come from, how they are chosen, how they are processed. Technological study directs us to understand the tools and how they enable the shaping of form. Creation is social, so we will need to know how the craft is taught and learned, how it is developed, practiced and evaluated by the artist.

In this book, we have seen that the production of jewelry and textiles involves a series of men who collaborate directly or indirectly in the creation of the most beautiful things they can manage, given the quality of the materials—gold, *zari,* or silk—and given the fact they must rely on others to do things they cannot do, to melt or shape or enamel the gold, to design or produce the cards for the Jacquard loom. All these people are simultaneously supported, limited, and challenged by tradition. Chaman Lal makes the best elephant-headed bracelets he can. His works are uniquely his, yet they take form within the confines of the famous bracelet type brought to him from Mughal times in palpable examples and in pictures in old sales catalogs. The objects of body art described in this book were all made by men—by smiths, weavers, and tailors, by cobblers and makers of flower garlands. Though women around the world make their own clothes, the Indian women in this book do not; they receive them as gifts, they buy them on pleasant afternoons of shopping. They were made by men.

The men in this book, the producers, worked in teams, whether they were making gold jewelry, silk saris, or cotton *salwar suits.* The men in teams channeled their creativity in accord with the range of possibility in their craft and their reading of market trends. The producers shaped their works for consumption by other men, the merchants who sold them to women. B. D. Soni was unlike the other producers in that he experienced direct contact with his customers, which enabled him to adapt designs quickly and precisely for consumption.

The production phase has not been featured in books on body art, and that lack has worked against integrating body art with the general trends of study in material culture and art history where production is deemed, correctly, to be crucial. Some consideration of technology and its influences on the final product has been given to bodily adornment by the authors of lushly illustrated works that emphasize the beauty of individual objects, while providing important visual documentation of varieties of form and ornament. Typical of these are the regional and national surveys of folk art that feature costumes.[16] The particularly excellent publications on Hungarian traditions stress the delicately embroidered aprons worn by the women and expand to include the embroidered and appliquéd overcoats of frieze, felt, or leather worn by rural men.[17] Techniques of production are regularly sketched in such books on folk art, and they are often amply developed in works on the textile arts that describe looms and methods of weaving, such as the books on the Indian sari by Lynton and Chisti.[18]

Traditionally, in the American southwest men weave in the Pueblos, women weave among the Navajos: generally textiles are produced by members of one gender to be worn by both genders; cloth is not usually produced by the wearer. There are many examples of people, both men and women, who make the objects of their adornment, such as the Kuna women so well studied by Mari Lyn Salvador, who craft their own *molas* and their jewelry.[19] Studies of people who paint their bodies or faces—which number among the most excellent studies yet produced of body art—such as James Faris's study of the Nuba of Sudan, Marilyn and Andrew Strathern's initial study and Michael O'Hanlon's subsequent study of self-decoration in Papua New Guinea, have noted the raw materials available for colors and shine, the techniques of application, and evaluations made by the painters themselves or by others in the community during collective acts of self-adornment or formal display events.[20]

Tattoo artists, too, directly ornament the skin. In Alan Govenar's fine study of the tattoo artist Stoney St. Clair, Stoney speaks about the tools he uses and the process of learning and apprenticeship, and he articulates his criteria for a good tattoo.[21] In observing the interaction between the artist and his clients, by noticing the variables that control decisions of design, and through attending to the potential for conflict that lies within the very permanence of this art form, the scholar of tattooing gets to the heart of the matter.[22]

If a customer for a tattoo chooses a design from a flash on the wall, the artist's task is to render it as accurately as possible—and now, with the aid of computer scans and stencils, the job is not terribly difficult. But when a tattoo is custom-ordered, the artist is challenged not only by the unusual design, but also in reaction to the customer, who has presumably spent some time thinking about the design, who is committed to the tattoo, and who is likely to be critical of the result. The artist, then, is apt to put more concentrated energy into the work, making it worthy of the name art, in response to the challenge and expectations of the customer.[23] The same can be said about jewelry or clothing in India—the artisans are most likely to bring their skills to successful focus in filling a commission from a known and knowledgeable patron. A commissioned piece carries, by definition, limitations set by the customer, yet it allows the artist to experiment and break out of the routine, often, paradoxically, allowing for more freedom of expression. Insight into the artist's intentions, interpretations, and evaluations can only be gained by remaining patient, and spending time, watching, listening, and asking the right questions in the context that is made by acts of production.

Commercial Exchange

I was not following the scholarly tradition of folklore (in which commerce has not been richly studied) when I spent much time in Banaras watching commerce, and as I did I noted two distinct stages in the trade in clothing and jewelry: first, the interaction between male producers and male buyers, and then the interactions between these buyers—sellers now—and their female customers. When she buys a *salwar suit* at the Dayaram Fashion Centre, a customer is asked about the occasion, the price range, and the material, and then she is presented with a small selection to choose from. When she buys gold at Kanhaiya Lal, these factors, in this order, are taken into account: age, social status (including caste, economy, and rural or urban residence), and finally the wearer's body type. By following the questions that merchants ask their customers, we are led into the nature of their interaction, of course, but we are also drawn toward understanding of the way that choices made during

buying and selling invest items of adornment with particular cultural significance. Sales in every case are mediated. Store owners choose their stock from
what is produced and offered to them by the makers. Customers, in turn,
choose what they want from the things that are shown to them by salesmen
such as the bangle master Anand Kumar.

While we watch, learning whose advice the women accept, how the salesmen size up their customers, and how they push their wares, we gain some
purchase on the psychology of sales, the standards of beauty, shared or not,
and what makes acceptable adornment for people of different classes, religions, and stages in life.

In India, salesmen cannot completely control the quality of their merchandise; they buy carefully and wisely things they do not make, and then
they turn to the realm of their control: the counter where they manage the
viewing and selling of things. The salesman inspects his customer, makes a
match, and orders from the back room the thing that he will then puff with
unsolicited advice and sell to her. In the United States, the person who acts
like the Indian salesman is the personal shopper, an expert on style who is
hired by fancy department stores and who walks around with the customer
putting ensembles together that suit the buyer and reflect the latest fashion.
Affluent shoppers seem to trust these style consultants, these experts on taste,
and in India, merchants, salesmen, and "commission boys" create a moment
in which everyone is, de facto, a personal shopper—you may not want the
expert advice, but you will get it.

Commerce has been slighted in books concerned with body art, and in
books on material culture in general. The anthropological literature contains
a few studies that consider trade and barter in the process of exchange for
the tools and materials used in self-decoration.[24] Some historical works have
focused on the vicious eradication of handcraft during colonial expansion,
the great case being the British destruction of the native textile industry of
Bengal, as a result of which Bengalis ceased being profitable producers of their
own wearable cloth and were reduced to being suppliers of raw materials and
consumers of British manufactured goods.[25] Cloth and commerce were integral to the development of Indian and British identities during colonial times.
The rejection of British commercial cloth by the *swadeshi* movement, in the
early twentieth century, acted as a catalyst for Gandhi's independence movement that was symbolized by the spinning wheel and *khadi*.[26] *Khadi,* plain
handspun and handwoven cloth, has been an emblem of political righteous-
ness in India and Bangladesh from Gandhi's days to the present.

394

In her book on the London-based industry of designer *salwar suits,* Parminder Bhachu handles commerce at a large scale, considering the economy of the global diaspora in which female entrepreneurs manage cross-cultural businesses.[27] And Christopher Steiner's study of middlemen in the Ivory Coast—art traders who work between the African producers of wooden statues and the trans-Atlantic buyers of the art—is a model anthropological investigation into the dynamics of commerce.[28]

Forms and Acts of Adornment

An analysis of the art of adornment, of both the objects of ornamentation and the act of getting ready, requires close attention to the created form. The adorned body is a composition of parts: the body itself (whether still or moving), the body modified by things done to it, and finally the body elaborated by things placed on it. A classification system for documenting dress and its properties devised by Mary Ellen Roach-Higgins and Joanne Eicher includes transformations to different parts of the body, supplements and enclosures, and also a category for hand-held things, expanding body art to include purses, canes, umbrellas, fly whisks, and other accessories.[29] A study, then, should account for the role that the body plays in the aesthetic considerations that relate to adornment, and how acts of adornment result in permanent and temporary forms. Every act of adornment embraces multiple effects that cluster, leading to the creative layering of assemblage.

The Static Body

In India, as we have seen, women, and even the men who sell to them, always take into account the body of the wearer before selecting appropriate items of adornment. A woman's height, weight, skin color, and facial and bodily features are integral to judgments concerning what to buy and what to wear. Choices of fabric, color, and print depend on the woman's figure, just as the choices of necklaces and earrings that frame her face depend on the height of her forehead, the curve of her cheeks. Salik Nishad, the *bindi* seller on Vishvanath Gali, felt, just as Mukta Tripathi and Neelam Chaturvedi did, that *bindis* should harmonize with the shape of a woman's face, lest its grace be lost.

In the aesthetics of the body, the surface of the skin is a serious variable. Manipulating the color of the skin is not limited to India, where Fair and Lovely cream sells well. A study of bleaching and tanning practices around the world would reveal much about cultural anxieties about race, class, and social status. Among affluent Caucasians, a suntan implies leisure and expensive vacations that require trips to the beach or ski slopes. The prosperity inherent in a deep tan may account for the recent and rapid spread of tanning parlors to strip malls across the United States. The orange tan of the tanning salon is evenly spread, symbolically rich, and the opposite of the ruddy "farmer's tan" on the neck and forearms that contrasts with the lily white of the shoulders and indicates labor, not leisure. The tan that deepens to mahogany or coffee in the Middle East or India means labor and nothing more; it is associated with servants and peasants who must remain in the sun during the hottest period of the day. By contrast, pale skin on women has historically implied wealth, class, and privilege. It is a rich lady who spends her days in the seclusion of *purdah,* in the shade of the *zenana,* the women's quarters.

The skin covers the form, and only a few studies, such as Bernard Rudofsky's famous *Unfashionable Human Body,*[30] have explicitly focused on the relation of the human body to fashion. Sylvia Boone's comprehensive exploration of the concept of feminine beauty in Sierra Leone provides a good model from Africa of how to analyze different aspects of the face and body, including the body as it stands and as it moves and how ideals of appearance connect with processes of beautification and factors such as age and personality.[31]

The Body in Motion

The body is more than the frame upon which an item of adornment will be featured: it is, as Mohammad Sharib, a seller of gold and silver, pointed out, a thing that moves, that causes jewelry to shift and jingle, that forces women to readjust their clothing and ornaments constantly. Anklets, belts, rings, and earrings—all are often ornamented with bells and chosen for the sound they make, so the fullness of their beauty can only be appreciated when the body is in motion. Likewise, glass bangles, beautiful though they might be, irritate women like Neelam Chaturvedi because of the clatter they make when the hands are busy at housework. Light, glittering from a woman's nose ring or glowing in the folds of a translucent sari, adds an aesthetic dimension to these static objects of adornment when the body and the sun move. The body's motions are of particular importance for Indian women who wear draped clothing—the sari, the *dupatta,* the shawl—all of which add beauty to the woman who is able to manage the constant adjusting and straightening of these unfixed pieces of cloth in a way that, through elegant gestures, enhances her grace and allure.

Some clothing and ornaments are chosen explicitly for the way they behave when the body is in motion. In their outstanding study of self-decoration in the Highlands of Papua New Guinea, the Stratherns noted that paper labels from tin cans were popular in Mount Hagen because of the pleasant sound they made when the wearer swished his head.[32] Dance and performance costumes provide an obvious example of the way in which the weight of the fabric, the method of closure, and the color of the outfit have to be taken into account. Elaborated with glitter, embroidery, and fringe, notably by the vaudeville costume designer Nudie, cowboy costumes, for a brief shining moment, were shared by film stars and country-and-western musicians.[33] Many theatre and dance troupes prefer white costumes, leaving color to the stage lights, so that the same costumes can be used for different productions. Costumes for ballet must be lightweight—the tutus are made of tulle—so as not to hinder the dancer's movements. During Japanese dramas in the *Noh* tradition, the stately movements of the dancers are designed to make a series of displays of the rich fabrics that are essential to the art's spectacle and power.[34] The clothing of the Mevlevi dervishes of Turkey must be constructed to open—like a flower blossoming—and to swirl while they spin, turning as the world turns, rotating in calm elegance, in love of God.

The Body Modified

The frame of this body can be altered temporarily (by adding makeup), transitorily (by losing weight or shaving), or permanently (through plastic surgery or the addition of a tattoo). These sub-categories of bodily modification interrelate. Mukta Tripathi, for example, was aware of the natural beauty of her hands and feet, and she rubbed them with homemade lotion before adorning them with finger rings, anklets, and toe rings. Mukta took particular care of her skin by not wearing too much makeup and by washing her face with a special soap. These would seem like temporary acts, but she is fighting wrinkles and working toward a permanent state of youth, while keeping her skin supple and making it a beautiful background for the ornaments that will temporarily adorn it.

From the standpoint of classificatory clarity, we could say that Mukta puts (transitory) cream on her feet before adding (temporary) toe rings. That may seem an overly fastidious bit of analysis, but it will help us in our consideration of the writings on body art, and I know from much fieldwork that such discriminations ensure that recording in the moment is complete.

In New Delhi and Bombay, fashion-conscious young people are working out: unmarried women are dieting and unmarried men are pumping iron to improve the frame on which tight jeans, tight shirts, and eventually, the beautiful wedding attire will be displayed. More drastic measures—permanent, not transitory—such as plastic surgery to fix the nose, to augment the breasts, or to extract excess fat are rumored to be part of the routine of Bollywood stars. Such procedures are hardly part of the lives of most people, but they are options for the affluent in India as they are in America. The more conventional examples of permanent body art, tattoos and multiple piercings, particularly on various parts of the ear, have been practiced historically by women, and sometimes men, in various regions of India.[35]

Some important works deal with the three classes of body modification—temporary, transitory, and permanent—but they are usually handled without relation to each other. Works on permanent body art focus on irreversible phenomena that carry notions of commitment, fixed identity, and often excruciating pain. Investigations of body molding include historical accounts of head shaping by the Mangbetu of Northeastern Congo, as well as contemporary body shaping, such as Sander Gilman's examination of the cultural history of plastic surgery.[36] Permanent body art includes scarification, once common in Africa. Many scholars have analyzed the patterns of scarification represented on magnificent masks and statues, and others, such as Paul Bohannan, Henry Drewal, Marla Berns, Allen Roberts, and Susan Vogel, have studied scarification on the living body.[37] Tattooing traditions of Polynesia, Japan, and the United States have benefited from historical investigations based on both oral and documentary sources such as drawings and reports by explorers and missionaries.[38] Given the fashion of our times, it is no surprise that there is a growing list of books on contemporary piercing, tattooing, neo-tribal scarification, and even branding practices in the West.[39] While many such books cannot be called scholarly, since they contain little analysis or interpretation, they do provide a visual record of the variety within these practices in our day.[40]

Transitory body art includes things that require maintenance and time, but which can be reversed or eliminated. (It is true that "permanent" modifications, such as tattoos, can be removed surgically, but they leave a permanent mark, and even if no mark is left, as when a small piercing closes up, it is heu-ristically reasonable to maintain a permanent/transitory distinction.) In the transitory class belong acts that change the body—through weight loss, say, or bodybuilding. Studies of weight loss, in particular, tend to the psychological, focusing on extreme cases of anorexia or bulimia, both classified as illnesses rather than as aesthetic choices.[41] The aesthetics of body shaping through exercise and diet, and the purposeful shaping of the body by its clothing, are topics deserving serious study, so it is good that we have the catalog of the Metropolitan Museum of Art's exhibition "Extreme Beauty: The Body Transformed" and Valerie Steele's outstanding book *The Corset,* and it is good that bodybuilding by both men and women has begun to attract the serious writing it unquestionably deserves.[42]

While less extreme than bodybuilding, the growing and training of the hair of the head or face often requires patience and becomes allied to identity. One aspect of male body art comes in the multiple forms of mustaches and beards, which are easily documented in portraits that reveal subtle cultural connections between the East and West—consider the mustache of the Raj-put warrior on the Victorian gentleman—but facial hair has received little scholarly scrutiny.[43] Historical studies of the hairstyles fashionable among men[44]—short, now long, now short again—and of the ways that men have tried to overcome baldness would make useful additions to the scholarship on hair, which now includes such fine studies as the history of African Ameri-can hairstyles and hair products by Noliwe Rooks; the volume on hair and its communicative patterns in Asian cultures by Alf Hiltebeiel and Barbara Miller; and Gananath Obeyesekere's psychological study of the symbolism of matted hair among ecstatics in Sri Lanka who have combined Hinduism and Buddhism.[45]

Permanent, then transitory, and the last of the classes of bodily modifi-cation is temporary. It includes applications that can be easily and instantly eliminated, such as makeup, henna, and paint for the body and face. As the relevant literature shows, these fleeting forms of adornment are usually used to express a temporary status. Brides in South Asia, the Middle East, and North Africa—and among the diasporic populations in the United States—are painted with henna, which lasts long enough to mark the women as brides for wedding occasions, then disappears as the day fades into memory.[46] Among the Hageners and Wahgi of Papua New Guinea, the Nuba of Sudan, and the Wodaabe males of Niger, face paint was applied in celebratory moments to express beauty, health, wealth, and status—fleeting states of being, symbolized in temporary paint.[47]

The meaning of body art can be even more temporary than the form. Aborigines of the Western Australian Desert, for example, painted their bodies with symbols of episodes from their mythic Dreamings. These marks remained significant only during the rituals that were attended by initiated males, and once the men removed themselves from the arena of ritual, they could be seen by women and non-initiates because the marks on their bodies were no longer "secret/sacred." The painting lost its meaning once it was removed from the ritual scene.[48] Such an extreme instance, in which temporary art is less temporary than its meaning, shows how important it is to ask people what their body art represents in differing contexts, for the communication will change, if only subtly, as the body moves from one arena to another.

The Body Dressed

Tattoos stay, the buffed body softens slowly, body paint comes and goes quickly, and of all temporary embellishments, clothing is the most common, supplementing the body literally from head to toe, and ranging from hats to shoes, underwear to diamond necklaces. Unlike makeup, perfume, and body paint, the body is dressed with objects that can be placed on the body, then removed without change to their original form. Body paint is decoration; it leans on the body, vanishes without it. But a jacket or belt is a form that can be ornamented, and that can be used as an ornament: it exists independently as an entity. For this reason it is necessary, in one phase, to study items of clothing as objects, as artistic creations in themselves. Many excellent works have carefully analyzed the form and function of the clothing and ornaments that dress the human body—the body that can be divided into zones for purposes of analytic completeness. Starting at the top, we can note studies of headdresses in Africa, wigs in Papua New Guinea, hats and headscarves in America.[49] But the great emphasis has been upon the clothing that covers the torso, arms and legs.

The study of dress has benefited from scholars who employ different modes of analysis. Bogatyrev took a semiotic approach in his important early study of the rural clothing of Moravian Slovakia. Anne Hollander, Jane Ashelford, Lou Taylor, and Joanne Entwistle study European dress by examining artifacts in museum collections and by using both literary and visual sources such as paintings, drawings, photographs, and films to discover historical patterns.[50] In her beautiful book on Chinese dress, Verity Wilson analyzes cut, design, embroidery, and accessories of the eighteenth through twentieth centuries.[51] In it, and in the book she co-authored, *Dress in Detail from Around the World,* Wilson provides formal studies of dress that consider both the broad patterns of the garments and their variety in small elements, such as methods of closure, necklines, pockets, and embroidered motifs.[52]

In Wilson's example, Chinese court dress, what is important is not the shape of the human body but the refined surface and form of the stitched garment, both of which designate social status.[53] Showcasing the beauty of the natural human form is not inevitable in dress: men and women have widely employed undergarments of all kinds to shape their bodies, creating a smooth and voluptuous surface onto which richly brocaded and finely cut textiles can be spread. In her exploration of the corset, Valerie Steele provides a cultural history of the aesthetic, medical, and social aspects of the controversial undergarment and ends her discussion by showing how the idea of the corset has now become internalized in diet and exercise, which yield the contemporary manifestation of the "hard body."[54]

A full study of the dressed body would start at the head, noting hats and wigs, hair wraps and hairclips, and then move down through the genres of clothing, including undergarments and overcoats, to end with the shoes. Students of footwear have—like many students of dress—focused on extreme cases: Chinese footbinding, for example, or Western stiletto heels, including the "pleaser," a transparent plastic high-heel platform sandal that is often associated with sex workers in the United States.[55] In her study of shoes and feet in India, Jutta Jain-Neubauer surveys the historical and contemporary forms and functions of shoes, taking care to describe the materials and processes of their making, and her attention expands beyond shoes to consider the representation of feet in works of art, such as miniature paintings and sculptures.[56] She notes, for example, the recurrent icon of the bare feet or slippers of Vishnu, crafted in silver as amulets or brocaded on prayer shawls, and intended as a sign of the devotee.[57]

Next, the dressed body is ornamented with jewelry, which is often the most exquisite and expensive of the body's beauties. Many scholarly works, including catalogs that accompany exhibitions, treat pieces of jewelry as objects of art.[58] Fine materials and craftsmanship attract the eye, and sumptuous books full of sumptuous objects provide a useful resource of jewelry types, classified by historical period, region, or ethnicity, or by form and material, in the manner of Lois Dubin's comprehensive survey of Native American jewelry.[59] The authors of a few recent books on the jewelry of India have examined form and iconography and, admirably, have moved on to contextualize exquisite works from historical, religious, and social perspectives, in some cases even addressing creation and use.[60]

The distinction of permanent and temporary bodily modifications—the tattoo added once, the makeup added daily—is conventional in body art study.[61] The antinomy can be approached in another way. We have seen that women in India think of some items as permanent fixtures in their lives and others as temporary possessions. When they buy a sari or a piece of gold jewelry, women spend more time and energy, bringing friends along to help them and seeking their advice before a purchase. When they buy a cotton *salwar suit* or a piece of artificial jewelry, women act quickly on whim, follow fashion easily and purchase things casually. The length of time the piece will be owned—the number of months or years a woman will use it, and whether she will pass it on as an heirloom—deeply influences her attitude. (Her feelings are also affected by the cost that connects to craft and materials; the better the materials, the longer she will own and use it.) Decisions about what to wear are also affected by temporal considerations that lie along the permanent-temporary spectrum. How long, you ask yourself, will I be wearing this thing? You might choose to wear an uncomfortable pair of high heels if you know it will be a brief event, and you will spend most of the time sitting down. The permanent versus temporary distinction in adornment is often made solely on the medium of application—permanent tattoo, temporary makeup—but other factors are relevant, such as the duration (in hours or years) of wearing or ownership; frequency of use; the cost and materials; and the time expended (the craftsman's, buyer's, and wearer's)—all determining whether something is a (relatively) permanent or (relatively) temporary component of the body art repertoire.

Use and Assemblage

From the material and formal dimensions of an object in isolation, we turn to consider how it is used—how it is placed in an assemblage of adornment on the body. The conditioning variables of assembly are the limits of possession, of what exists in the collection; the desire to save certain things from wear and tear; the presence or absence of matching accessories; the fear of theft or the evil eye; the association with other people, with memories and gifts; the weather, the season, the day and its religious association with a deity. Also taken into account is the way in which the body is affected by the jewelry and how the body, in turn, affects the jewelry: some people have allergic reactions to certain metals; nose rings tarnish from prolonged contact with the body. Such considerations influence the use of jewelry, and some pieces of jewelry continue to function even when they are not in use. A heavy, pricey pair of earrings might communicate high social status even in its absence, through the elongated earlobes and stretched piercing holes such as one sees in portrayals of the Buddha, a wealthy prince in his youth before he became enlightened. Ornaments on the feet and shoes of extreme form can permanently affect the gait; Nigerian brass anklets and Western ballet pointe shoes both affect movement even when they are not being worn.[62]

When we observe objects in use, in their actual contexts of wear, we gain understandings that an inspection of the artifact could never bring. The long headscarves worn by Rajasthani women as part of their ensemble of bodice and full skirt are used in a multitude of ways, ornamental and practical. When at home with mature male relatives women cover their heads out of respect. Outdoors, they cover their heads with headscarves—just as men cover their heads with turbans—to protect them from the blazing desert sun. Worn partially over the head, the scarf acts as a visor, shielding the sun from the eyes. The diaphanous cloth can be pulled down to cover the entire face, serving the same purpose as sunglasses, since women can see through the cloth. Worn over the face, the scarf prevents the sun—glaring off the surface of the pale bright sand—from darkening the women's faces: the face is most important for beauty and should be kept as fair as possible. The scarf pulled over the face also protects the eyes, ears, nose, and mouth against the sand that whirls through the ubiquitous sandstorms common in this part of the country. The rural people of Rajasthan carry loads on their heads; men's turbans and women's scarves provide a bit of cushioning for the head and prevent the load from slipping; the hair beneath the scarf is rich with slippery coconut oil. Examples of these headscarves, which are found in many museum collections, might be studied for their formal qualities—the colors and patterns, embroidery and mirrorwork—but their functions (providing modesty, comfort in carrying,

403

and a means of portable shade) will only be learned when we see them in use, doing their job of beautifying and protecting the body in the harsh environment where the Rajasthani women live and labor.

Objects of adornment are put to use in combination with others—with a dress, a hairstyle, a tattoo. The categorical distinctions useful for study blend in life, merge when different ways of beautifying and protecting come together in assemblage. Indian women devote much attention to putting an outfit together. They keep artful combinations in mind, relegating some things to the background while highlighting others. And then Mohammad Sharib, the owner of a jewelry shop, expands the idea of assemblage beyond the materials to include the behavior and virtue of the wearer and the radiance of the whole, the presence of the body as a work of art that has melded disparate parts into a new unity—this is the final and most important goal in our study. Yet the final act, the completion of the whole process, with a few notable exceptions has rarely been the focus of studies of body art.[63]

One such exception is the fine exhibition by the Metropolitan Museum of Art's Costume Institute titled "Rara Avis." This path-breaking exhibit featured the haute couture clothing of one woman, Iris Barrel Apfel, and also the accessories, shoes, bags, and coats that went along with the outfits. Mrs. Apfel dressed the mannequins herself, showing us how she wore these clothes. The exhibit, as the Metropolitan claims, "is a fascinating examination of the power of dress and accessories to assert style above fashion, the individual above the collective."[64]

Contexts of Meaning and Function

All products of culture, material as well as verbal, exist only in some context, and they shift in significance as they shift from context to context. To this point, in unfolding the model, I have described production (the making of things), commerce (their sale), and assemblage (the adornment, from head to toe, of the body). All of these acts occur in contexts that align with the conventional master categories of material culture study: creation, communication, and consumption—conceived as a circle, for consumption carries from receiving to using, and using is part of an act that—certainly in the assembly of commodities into an adorned body—produces an object. Then this new assembled object is offered and consumed—when, let us say, an adorned woman enters a party where she is seen. This act of being seen occurs in some context, and we can amplify the contextual range by adding to production, commerce, and assemblage a series of social contexts in which the assemblage becomes meaningful.

But even before that, we must acknowledge that in every context there is a historical dimension. The goldsmith at work, the merchant and customer in interaction, the woman dressing herself in private and then coming out to be seen in different scenes—all of them are guided in their acts by past experiences and influenced in their lives by events rolling beyond memory behind them. History is a prime context, one realm in which creations take on significance and become accessible to interpretation.

History

Historical study entails examination of change and continuity in time and space, opening for us multiple directions of inquiry. From an etic standpoint, we could trace the long history of fashion, noting the changes in style that give a rhythmic pulse to time as it expands over a wide territory, transcribing through things a clear pattern of development. Adopting an emic perspective we could, through interviews, attempt to understand the changes that are thought to be important by the people of a particular community, whose idea of history would probably be shallower in time and certainly narrower in space, but possibly more complex in its formulation.

At work in India, I did not employ a classic historical approach that would have taken me into libraries, archives, and museums. I chose to spend my time in the streets, shops, ateliers, and homes, learning from life. Were I to have taken the historical turn, I would have built contexts around clothing by using ancient images of the gods in stone, Mughal miniature paintings, accounts written by early travelers to India and Banaras in particular, colonial photographs and records, images from old Bollywood films, advertisements from magazines and newspapers, and examples of jewelry and textiles from museum collections. I chose, instead, to focus on other types of historical accounts, narrower, tighter, but significant nonetheless. The goldsmiths Chaman Lal and B. D. Soni were interested in the splendors of the jewelry of the distant Mughal past, but most people, both merchants and customers, were more concerned with the fashion history of the last few years. Their knowledge enabled them to date things exactly, bringing them embarrassment if they were stuck with old stock to sell or old-fashioned, outdated things to wear.

405

Similarly, the sellers and makers of clothing and saris, Hemant Khanchandani and Hashim Ansari, were interested in historical designs, since reviving an old style was one way they could capture a new market; but, knowing their customers well, they were always careful to add contemporary detailing to historically based commodities. The far past interested them, but it was imperative for them to be well-versed in the latest departures in fashion.

Indian women are generally deeply knowledgeable about a short, immediate history of fashion, which they gather from magazines and Bollywood films. In addition, of course, they are interested in their own personal histories, particularly as they break into stages. This personal history is defined by more than the cultural patterning of rites of passage. It gathers the little events of life and the subtle, unceremonial patterns marked by losing or gaining weight or by shifts in personal taste—all of which, the cultural and public, the private and personal, become influences in every decision about what to wear today.

Understanding the historical contexts of clothing is essential to the study of body art, and a reach for such understanding is found in much of the best writing. In the body art literature, history seems to be employed in six ways, each one shedding its distinct light on the acts and consequences of bodily adornment. In the first category of historical study, artifacts—usually examples of jewelry, for clothing is more perishable—are used to reconstruct the cultures of the distant past. Beautiful pieces of ancient Egyptian and pre-Columbian jewelry have been used to gain an entrance to the mythologies of these ancient cultures, as well as to learn something about the social life of the people, both the nobility and commoners, who were regularly buried with their jewelry.[65]

A second common and conventional approach adopts a vertical perspective, measuring change over time by arranging costumes sequentially. Through a focus on origin and evolution, the goal is to find a pattern in a historical sequence, then to explain it meaningfully, usually in terms of some large force, such as economic or political change, or some evolution of style. Many books on the history of costume and jewelry, the history of fashion, and the art history of clothing operate in that manner. A third method, by contrast, is based on a horizontal procedure that locates changes in body art within a historical period, driving the examination not backward in time, but outward into society, the aim being to find explanations within the contemporaneous social context. This technique has been used effectively to analyze particular periods in the United States, by examining, say, the clothing of eighteenth-century Williamsburg, or the changes in the ready-to-wear clothing and makeup industries in the late nineteenth and early twentieth centuries.[66] Items of apparel are of clear importance for the study of economic or political developments, because the opulence or simplicity of the clothing depicted in portraits, or reflected in probate inventories, can be set into tension with the self-conscious public pronouncements of the people of the era.

Three additional historical approaches center on the contemporary. One seeks to understand an item in the present by tracing its historical development; the folklorist Linda Ballard used that method in her study of Irish dance costume.[67] Scholars also use the past to contextualize the present during studies of the revival of body art forms that had once been abandoned, usually under the horrific pressure of colonial rule. One such revival has seen the resurgence of tattoo traditions in Polynesia, most notably in the Marquesas Islands, Tahiti, Samoa, and among the Maori in New Zealand.[68] Finally, one last technique involves the methodical documentation of the present in order to capture completely one moment in time. That is certainly one of my goals in India—recording details that could seem trivial today but will, I am sure, seem amazing in a couple of decades. And we are fortunate that outside observers in the nineteenth century had such a goal or we would not have the invaluable records of Native Americans, made in the days when George Catlin made his paintings and Edward Curtis took his photographs. Today, such documentary efforts have been wittily and usefully devoted to recording street fashion in Tokyo and New York.[69]

The people of the past shared this documentary urge, especially with regard to the elite and royalty. After the death of the Ottoman Emperor Süleyman the Magnificent in 1565, all of his personal effects, including his splendid kaftans and his humble underclothing, were preserved and labeled to represent the great man—the warrior, the giver of laws, the emperor of a vast realm—as well as his era, the Ottoman zenith. The point to emphasize here is that in an effort to preserve the essence of a great leader, his clothes and ornaments were deemed just as important as his official documents. The purpose of this last historical approach is to create a record of the aesthetic sensibility, the patterns in choice, and the personal interpretations of a group of people in a certain place, at a certain time, as a contribution to history. And that, I repeat, is one reason for my study in Banaras, among women of a certain generation, religion, caste, and class, from the period when the twentieth century turned into the twenty-first.

The Individual

Personal history is realized through body art in a series of intimate contexts. In those contexts people exhibit their personalities, biographies, and psychologies. I have stressed this dimension in this book because, though it seems to me obvious, and obviously important, it has been underappreciated in studies of body art. Though individuals stand forth in folkloristic studies of material culture, they seem to vanish into the big schemes and theoretical rhetoric of most studies of adornment. By focusing on individual craftsmen and merchants, and especially by spending much time with real women, I was able to see how abstract principles—aesthetics, religions, or fashions—manifested themselves concretely in the contexts of the everyday. And my commitment to real people in real situations allowed me to extract general principles from specific instances, coming to an understanding of the importance of early childhood influences, the variables of joint family dynamics and spousal love, and the personal reactions to judgments, reprimands, and compliments from strangers and intimates. A close study of individuals also discloses the essential contexts of learning and influence, key conditions for understanding the creative urge of body art.

To emphasize the personal qualities of dress seems to be an unsurprising point. Clothes are considered by many to be the most personal of all possessions, and they are believed by many to carry the essence of the wearer. Hawaiians in the past, for example, believed that the ceremonial feather cloaks made specifically for individual chiefs embodied power. On the death of the chief his cloaks were given to Europeans, including the ill-fated Captain Cook, since wearing somebody else's garments could bring harm to the body.[70] People may be driven to used clothing by economic necessity, as many in developing nations are, or they might choose old clothes out of a stylish, "vintage" persuasion, but in many societies people do not favor the practice of buying and wearing second-hand clothes. In India, certainly, people prefer new clothes, clothes that belong to them alone.

Nina, Neelam, and Mukta, the heroines of my story, wear certain things at certain times, depending on their moods and expectations. Nina Khanchandani finds saris beautiful and owns many, but she does not wear them often, choosing instead the comfort of *salwar suits*. A systematic study of the contents of her wardrobe would not reveal her choice of comfort over aesthetics, or her adherence to softened familial rules over the social norms for married women. We would have to see her, meet her, talk to her. With Neelam Chaturvedi we saw how national history, in her case the partition of India and Pakistan, can have tremendous impact on families and individuals. Neelam's adult choices are directly shaped by her childhood, through the positive associations and negative impressions that were gathered and stored in a young girl's mind. Neelam, self-conscious of influences from her youth, is careful about the impressions she is creating on the children she teaches at school. From Mukta Tripathi's reflections we learned yet another reason to focus on individuals: a personal, in-depth interview becomes the venue through which the self and the significance of personal repertoire is articulated. Mukta judges herself, and hopes to be judged by others, not in relation to other women, but rather in relation to herself, to other ways she has appeared at other times, creating other versions of herself to fit the scene. The constant point of reference is a personal one, above those that are familial, social, or engulfed by major patterns of culture and history.

Most of the books on body art, following the norms of history, tend to generalize about societies, giving names and biographical reality only to those individuals who are peculiarly prominent in some way or other. Although such studies provide a reading of the general trends of dress and adornment for the group under consideration, individual nuances and variations within the larger picture get lost when specific personal repertoires go undocumented. Like the historical, the anthropological record, oddly, does not generally contain information about specific individuals. The tendency is to swallow them into an anonymous, amorphous mass or, as in the example of a few recent books, to treat them as fictionalized composites or give them pseudonyms (even though there are accompanying photographs which, ironically, would reveal their identities instantly to anyone for whom their identities mattered; this practice, said to protect the informant, seems, instead, to be designed to protect the authors).

As a member of the curatorial team that assembled the exhibition "Body Art: Marks of Identity" at the American Museum of Natural History in 1999,[71] I became aware of the limitations of the available documentary records the museum had on the artifacts of non-Western people. As a result, the exhibition was richly nuanced, revealing individual choices and opinions in the cases dedicated to Western tattoo and piercing traditions, but non-Western cultures came across as homogenous, with no dissenting views and no individual voices—strange, given the word "identity" in the subtitle of the exhibition. By not recognizing foreign people as individuals, books, documentary films, and museum exhibitions raise an unbreachable wall between us and them, reinforcing the assumption that members of ethnic or tribal groups are somehow uniform, socially oriented, and stuck in tradition, while the members of our own society are idiosyncratic, multi-dimensional, and individually creative.

Few surveys of body art have focused on individual practitioners or attended to the personal choices that are influenced by biography, lifestyle, and personality, a sense of aesthetics and personal motivations. Alan Govenar's important book and film on the tattoo artist Stoney St. Clair presents Stoney's life history and provides a crucial document within the study of tattoos in the United States. Govenar's "folk autobiography,"[72] written entirely in the first person, was constructed out of transcriptions of a series of oral narratives. Daniel Wojcik's interviews with pop singer Perry Farrell, about the creation of his personal look, show the self-consciousness with which he created his self-image, merging cultural influences with personal desires to achieve a heightened sense of individuality.[73] Millions of others are similarly self-conscious of their presentation of self through choices of hairstyle and clothing, but the scholarly record does not carry such information for very many for the world's people. In his memoirs on his own body art, Peter Trachtenberg locates each one of his seven tattoos within major events of his biography, situating them in personal significance and showing how the tattoos literally inscribe his momentary state of mind onto his body, making it a permanent site for the commemoration of his own history.[74]

The Individual in Temporal Contexts

All human beings progress through certain life stages, culturally defined and differently conceived for each gender. Successful transitions between stages are not only socially relevant but personally significant moments, visually marked by changes in body art. In India, as elsewhere, people position themselves in shared historical time, but men and women also ground themselves firmly in the realm of personal time, as demonstrated in the three chapters on the lifecycle. Women move through the stages of infant, child, pubescent girl, unmarried young lady, newly married woman, married with children, mother-in-law, and finally, elderly, widow, and deceased. These stages are clearly marked by the presence and absence of certain clothes and jewelry. Age and marital status are communicated by an intricate vocabulary of makeup, *bindi, sindur,* hairstyle, by the type of clothing and its fabric, print, and color, and also by the amount, variety, fashionability, and material of ornaments.

While official rites of passage are accompanied by these culturally shared visual markers, the unofficial consequences of age—such as weight gain, wrinkles, gray hair, the feeling that the beauty of youth is waning—also become factors women consider when deciding whether or not they should continue to attend to fashion and wear the clothing of youth: the jeans, the bright colors and bold prints. Men in India, as in many other places, visually express maturity by growing a mustache, or a beard if they are Muslim, offering a sign of manhood to the world. Age also affects hairstyle and the general maintenance of the body. In India, young adults are the ones who diet and work out, keeping their minds on their physiques. Children are not yet self-conscious about their bodies and older people resign themselves to being out of shape. Sometimes the discrepancy between the body of different generations is a consequence of fashion preference and not of a traditional mandate about developmental status: older people tend to feel that jeans should belong to the young, and that fully mature people of both genders should appear "dignified," dressed appropriately and more traditionally.

Body art's celebration of the lifecycle is well handled in the scholarly literature. Many volumes, such as *Wedding Dress Across Cultures* by Helen Bradley Foster and Donald Clay Johnson, focus on the most significant of these transitions—the wedding—and the beautiful and ornate clothing worn by the bride and groom.[75] Other religious rituals that require specialized clothes include baptisms, circumcision rites, communions, and—the currently fashionable practice among the Jewish elite of the United States—lavish bar mitzvahs and bat mitzvahs, for which parents spend thousands of dollars for a party and a designer outfit for the honored child. Many coming-of-age events are social in nature, and they contain elaborate customs of costume. High school proms are a good example, cotillions another, and both of them mark times when adolescents change into young adults.[76] In her study of African American cotillion and beautillion balls in Iowa, Annette Lynch describes the appropriation of the format of the debutante ball to showcase the young men

411

and women of the region. These events incorporate traditional styles of clothing that are meant to display the charm, and ultimately the marriageability, of the participants.[77]

As the data from India demonstrate, body art not only marks the rite of passage and the person undergoing the transition, it also signals a permanent transformation, a new state of being that will hold from that day forward. In diverse cultures in Africa, rites of passage were until recently literally inscribed onto the body through scarification in rituals where women were scarred either before they could get married, or at the onset of puberty and after the birth of a child.[78] Conversely, ritual isolation was marked by some people, such as the Nuba of southeastern Sudan, by a *lack* of desirable body art; non-participants who were isolated during initiation, funeral, and childbirth rituals would symbolically remove themselves by placing talc on their bodies, which radically differentiated them from the participants with their shiny oiled bodies.[79]

In many places, status within the life stages is displayed through a lexicon of clothing, as it is in India. Andrea Rugh, in her fine documentation of dress in contemporary Egypt, shows how women designate their status—asexual child, single, married, and finally older woman and widow—through their choices in color and fit of dress, the formality of the modesty overdress, and the fabric and tying style of the head covering.[80] Comparably, Liza Dalby explains that the kimono in Japan, historically and now perhaps only ceremonially, displays the distinct stages of a woman's life by certain discernible variables, such as the length and shape of the sleeve, the color and print of the fabric, and how it is worn: how high is the sash at the waist, the *obi*, tied, how close to the chin do the kimono sides overlap, and how much of the nape is visible?[81] Dalby also discusses the significance of yet another temporal dimension, the change of the seasons. Depending on the season, a particular kimono fabric (satin, gauze, crepe, or damask) will be selected, the kimono will be lined or not, and certain combinations of acceptable colors and motifs, which reflect the floral and faunal qualities of that time of year, will be chosen.[82] The example of the kimono must bring Hashim Ansari of Banaras to mind. He explained that in his workshop, saris are woven in particular colors ("English" pastel hues or bright "village" tones), certain fabrics (silk, cotton, georgette, or synthetic blends), and varying degrees of heaviness (amount of brocading)—depending on the season. In both cases, women celebrate seasonal change with a change of clothing.

The Individual in Spatial Contexts

While the world's people are moving through the stages in the lifecycle, they are also literally moving, passing from one physical context to another. Body art, unlike other forms of material culture, is employed as an ambulatory means by which the self is positioned in space. In their dress, people create and acknowledge spatial range and distinction, sharpening concepts of public, shared, and private space. In the city of Banaras, as we have seen, village women anchor themselves in the countryside by wearing the orange *sindur* and "gaudy" jewelry and saris that communicate to the urbanites their rural identity. Some women position themselves geographically in two spaces simultaneously by layering their body art, wearing, for example, the marital bangles of two regions at one time.

Neelam Chaturvedi showed us how one person can negotiate her way through different scenes within a geographic location. Neelam, like most people in India, does not divide space into the simple categories of public and private. She defines space by the people who occupy each arena and the potential relationship she might have with them. Neelam carefully chooses what to wear in each of these contexts: the truly private space of her bedroom; the semi-private places of social interaction within her joint-family home; her workplace, which is occupied by a stable core of non-familial persons; the familiar public area of the market; and the utterly public spaces outside of town, where she, anonymous, will encounter no acquaintances.

In her excellent study of dress in rural Gujarat, Emma Tarlo discusses how women, moving through shared space, choose to shift into privacy while they are in public by covering themselves with a veil and making themselves temporarily inaccessible.[83] Margaret Mills shows that in Afghanistan, women may use the veil as disguise, to smuggle arms or move anonymously through public space.[84] In fact, the use of the veil—a portable means of creating private space by women in many parts of Asia and Africa—is a fascinating topic, and one that has been studied by scholars, most notably by Fadwa El Guindi.[85]

In the expanse of space, we discover studies of the people who have been displaced from their homelands—either against their will, as in the case of Africans brought to America in captivity; as refugees, like the Hmong from Southeast Asia; or as willing immigrants, like the Indians, my people, who have settled into diasporic communities in England, South Africa, the West

Indies, Canada, and the United States.[86] Exploring dress in the diaspora deepens our understanding of the complexities of identity, and it widens the spatial conceptualization of body art. Ethnic people living abroad often prefer to wear a "timeless" version of their native dress, since, having lost close touch with the homeland, they cannot keep up with the nuanced and constant changes in fashion there. The development of new, global fashions that mix and match native and foreign elements to create "fusion" designs then circle back, returning to the homeland and influencing the local elite who, as a matter of fashion, adopt a version of their traditional dress that has been reinvented in London, Paris, or New York.[87]

The Individual in Social Occasions

It is obvious that people have occasions in mind when they buy or choose something to wear, but Mukta Tripathi has taught us just how complex that idea has to be. When Mukta gets ready for a party, pleasing herself and preparing for the judgments the beholders will pass, she takes her time, selecting her sari and jewelry in advance, sometimes even ordering floral jewelry well ahead of time to add fragrance to her display. Special occasions provide Mukta with a point of reference against which she contrasts her ordinary self in simple clothes. Fancy things are worn for fancy occasions, but wearing things too fancy around the house would be inappropriate, giving neighbors and friends, as Mukta explained, a cause for concern or gossip. Socially derived norms, in other words, are basic to decisions of appropriateness in contexts of viewing.

Historical studies of European costume are often, in fact, studies of dress for special occasions. They detail exquisite ball gowns for ladies and elegant suits for gentlemen. Most anthropological works on body art also highlight the special dress and ornamentation of rituals and celebrations; anthropologists, too, are drawn to the exceptional and extreme by the very beauty and power of the paint, ornaments, and special gear that goes with the heightened, celebratory occasion.[88] Scholars of costume are drawn to wedding gowns as well as ball gowns because, being rarely used, they survive, and because the wedding costume tends to mark an intense and exalted instance of a culture's idea of clothing. In India, the peculiar power of the wedding as the key event in a life expands, so that in addition to the clothing of the bride and groom—her gold, his turban—the clothing of all who are in attendance is also especially fine, probably, at least in the case of the women, purchased and worn specifically for this reception.

Studies of ethnic clothing frequently rely on the documentation of traditional dress that is worn exclusively for special occasions, such as dance performances. The powwows and stomp dance events held by Native Americans in the United States and Canada provide a good example. Powwow costume might hold to a specific tribal identity or widen to a pan-Indian look.[89] In her study of dance costumes of the land that was then Yugoslavia, Elsie Dunin discusses a phenomenon found in many parts of the world: the appropriation and revival of ethnic dress by local dance troops for folkloric performances presented to foreign and especially to native tourists.[90] Dunin notes that in the recent past, special costumes were displayed and danced to mark a ritual occasion, while now these performances are the occasion.[91] With the proliferation of folkloric performances at home or in international venues, like the annual Smithsonian Folklife Festival, ethnic clothes are self-consciously stylized and revitalized for the display occasions where ethnic or national identity is most stridently displayed through dress.[92] Scholarly documentation of festive dress in books, archives, and museums has provided an invaluable resource for people with a desire to revive their own traditions. In the Muzeul Țăranului Român, in Bucharest, Romania, there are two distinct sections devoted to costumes: one in which the regional clothing of Romania is displayed, and another where clothing from the neighboring cultures—Macedonian, Bulgarian, Hungarian, Turkish—is labeled and displayed. Though neither section contains much written contextual information, the exhibit of real clothes assembled into complete ensembles is richly comprehensive in its rendering of styles for both genders, with their beautiful embroidery and full panoply of accessories, such as scarves, shoes, jewelry, and even detailed hairstyles. Even though people in Romania wear ordinary European clothes on a daily basis, this permanent exhibition of regional special occasion dress is a reminder of heritage, and a source of inspiration for creators of reproductions or designers of new departures.

Though extraordinary dress, because of its survival and its inherent excellence, carries the scholarly attention away, the great need in body art studies is close, serious attention to everyday dress. We need to know what people think about their own clothes. Across the world, many people, men in particular, have abandoned their native dress in exchange for generic Western costume, for suits and slacks and shirts deemed, perhaps, to be professional or cosmopolitan. In India, almost all women wear traditional forms of clothing on a daily basis. Men who wear suits to work might relax at home in a *lungi-dhoti,* or *kurta-pyjama,*[93] and dress traditionally on special occasions. In many places women do as Indian men do: they wear modern Western clothes every day, but traditional clothes for special ritual occasions. On New Year's Day in 2002, at the Yasaka Shinto shrine in Kyoto, we witnessed hundreds of young Japanese women beautifully clad in kimonos, accompanied by young men in stylish Western shirts and pants.[94] Such a sight is not rare, and it is especially typical among ethnic people living in the diaspora. The men wear the suit that has become the international sign of the middle-class worker, but the women often come out in beautiful native costume for formal occasions. As it is in India, so it is often in the Indian diaspora. For women, traditional dress—the elegant sari—is part of a formal public display of identity; for men, native dress is a comfortable, casual alternative to wear at home.

Special occasion dress, like the celebrations of carnival, is not usually an aberration, an inversion of daily norms, but rather, an exaggeration, an extreme public version of what is always present. In appreciating the communicative powers of festive dress, we come into engagement with the cultural values that people seek to highlight during ritual occasions, making it imperative to study commemorative dress as well as daily attire, as Bogatyrev suggested as early as 1937. Another reason to study both special occasion and everyday dress is to note the interplay between the two. During my fieldwork in Bahia, Brazil, I was able to locate levels of communication in the displays of beads. Strung into necklaces for daily wear, the beads signaled religious affiliation, but worn for carnival and festive occasions, other messages were added and sent simultaneously to people who understood the codes of bead color and type, thickness and order, mode and context of display, and who could therefore read out complicated religious, political, and social messages.[95]

The Individual in Society

Dress functions to mark the various identities of individuals: social, religious, occupational, sexual, and ultimately, personal. In India bodily adornment signals gender, religion, caste, occupation, socioeconomic class, and village or city residence. The evident nature of clothing as a device of cultural expression and social communication has brought anthropologists and folklorists into the study of body art.

The patterns revealed in body art correlate with the patterns implicated in other mediums of collective expression, such as myth. This important point has been demonstrated in classic studies, such as the analysis of Northwest Coast tattoos and face painting by Franz Boas, of women's body painting in Brazil by Claude Lévi-Strauss, of Sudanese bodily designs by James Faris, of self-decoration in Papua New Guinea by Andrew and Marilyn Strathern, and of Polynesian tattoos by Alfred Gell.[96] Bogatyrev's landmark study of Moravian Slovakian costumes beautifully shows how multiple social messages—about wealth, age, marital status, social structure, outside influence, aesthetics, and magic—are layered one on top of another in a functional simultaneity.[97] His semiotic analysis takes into account the form and function of clothes; sometimes he views clothing practically—as something to cover and protect the body—and sometimes he sees clothing as a sign, a nonverbal communication of a complex bundle of social and personal messages.[98] And surely he was right; clothing is, at all times, both of those things: practical, and complexly significant.

In the Papua New Guinea Highlands, body paint, wigs, and aprons had (and still have) the power to unify a cluster of people into a coherent coalition, making them allies, while separating them from their competitors and enemies.[99] Body art expresses communal identity while gathering urban or rural associations,[100] marking factions within a group, and revealing the individual who stands at once in the society and in one or more of its internal groupings.[101] The communication of gender, affiliation, and rank in clothing continues even after death in portraits and in the remarkable tombstones of Ottoman Turkey that carry above the shoulders the headgear of status: the fez of the gentleman, the truncated cone of the Mevlevi dervish, the ponderous turban of the religious or political leader.

Body art, as the great anthropologists have demonstrated, reveals the structure of society, its coherence into a unit, its subdivision into complementary segments. In body art terms, the most important of society's subsets is gender, a biological and cultural division that is patently expressed in clothes and ornaments. As Ruth Barnes and Joanne Eicher state clearly in the introduction to *Dress and Gender,* dress both marks and makes gender.[102] Gender becomes explicit in the study of clothing, for example, in *Men and Women* by Claudia Kidwell and Valerie Steele, and gender is implicit in all studies of body art. The literature on this topic is rich. Most objects, practices, and styles of bodily adornment tend to be specific to one gender or another.

Studies of men's body art include face and body painting traditions, business suit fashion, "dandy" style dress associated with sophisticates, and also wigs, clothes, and shoes. This list can expand to armor and uniforms, to medals, guns, and swords as body art accessories, flaunted and carried by men to make them appear powerful, sophisticated, and beautiful. Studies of body art specific to women include clothes, makeup, henna, hair, and jewelry, and also corsets, high heels, and the slippers of Chinese footbinding. Some works have even looked at the fashions and rites of bodily decoration associated with pregnancy.[103]

In studies of gender-specific dress (which arguably includes most expressions of body art), the link between self-ornamentation and sexual attraction becomes conspicuous. Many forms of body art are created self-consciously to attract members of the opposite sex, or the same sex if that is the desire. Sexual attraction may not be the sole goal, but it is generally one in the bundle of aims when the body is prepared for viewing and evaluation, especially if we welcome into consideration communication through clothes by homosexuals and transsexuals as well as heterosexual people.[104] Examination of the witty play with norms by homosexuals, and of the various practices of cross-dressing, unveils much about the expected norms for people of different genders. Revealing studies have dealt with India's *hijras,* who are cross-dressed eunuchs, with the Native American "two-spirits" or *berdache,* with Samoan *fa'afafines,* and even with the gallant women who cross-dressed as men to fight in the American Civil War.[105] However different in cultural terms, all these people share some aspect of cross-dressing, and they help us refine our understanding of the way identity is transformed, created, and represented through clothing, ornaments, makeup, and behavior. And our understanding continues to complicate and sophisticate, in the context of sexual attraction, when we study courtesans, geishas, and sex workers, whose self-presentation can be read as an exaggerated version of beauty, femininity, and sexuality.[106]

Gender is basic, but the study of body art regularly shows how religious identity is expressed through clothes, hairstyle, and accessories—a *burqa,* side locks, or a *yarmulke*—and the absence or presence of certain ornaments, such as a pendant depicting Jesus on a cross, or a flash of red *sindur* on the hair part. Specialized apparel indicates differences of religion and culture to others, and also to the self. The Hasidic Jewish community distinguishes itself by specialized clothing for each gender: the men in large black hats, black kaftans, beards, and side locks (*peyes*), and the women in long-sleeved dresses, wearing either turbans or wigs (*sheitel*), since they are not supposed to show their hair in public.[107] Someone passing by will recognize these people as orthodox Jews, and members of their community will be able to tell, by specifics of dress alone, which of the six social classes of Hasidic Jews somebody belongs to; the people so dressed will be reminded by their clothing of their responsibilities in behavior.[108]

The Amish in the United States wear distinctive clothes in public—the men in trousers with flaps and buttons, wide-brimmed black hats and beards, the women in organdy caps and long hair parted in the middle, wearing plain, long dresses, bold in color but without patterns or stripes. The Amish wear these clothes to hedge themselves away from the world, keeping others out, reminding themselves of the obligation to behavioral plainness. Yet John Hostetler's excellent study of Amish culture shows how subtle communication is accomplished within the variables of the clothing, including color and fabric, and the style of the headgear that signals different congregations within the United States and the marital status of both genders.[109] Members of other religious groups, such as the Pentecostals, identify themselves with clothes that are plain and intentionally unfashionable, such as women's dresses with high necklines and long sleeves, worn with no makeup, no jewelry, and plain hairstyles. Elaine Lawless explains that while outsiders judge this look to be low in status and associate it with rural Midwesterners who cannot afford to follow fashion, the Pentecostals themselves see it as an aspect of their "holiness."[110]

Members of the Church of Latter-day Saints wear certain undergarments that are received during a private temple ceremony at marriage. These garments are not seen by others; they are worn for the private and personal communication of religious identity and spiritual protection.[111] Distinctive clothes of this kind act as visual (or tactile) signs to members of the Hasidic Jewish, Amish, Pentecostal, and Mormon communities, reminding them that they belong to a distinct religious group within the United States. They are unlike others, and, dressed distinctly, they know they should behave appropriately. Philosophical and political commitment often flows from religious conviction, and religious dress in context—the dress of Muslims or Jews in Jerusalem—implies a political stance. In Marjane Satrapi's recollections of post-revolution Iran, she tells how women (by allowing a few wisps of hair to show from the headscarf) and men (by sporting a mustache or tucking in their shirts) literally wore on their bodies their opposition to the new fundamentalist government.[112]

Clothing incarnates diverse aspects of the identity, and it is through dress that an individual's attributes and personality are indicated, whether of the Hindu gods, as we saw in the chapter on *darshan,* or of the characters in films and theatrical productions, in which evocative, distinguishing traits are communicated physically by the costume designer who shares a visual cultural vocabulary of body art with the members of the audience. Carl Köhler's *A History of Costume* is one of several books that include illustrations and measured patterns for the reproduction of apparel by theatre, dance, and movie companies.[113]

Clothing can also designate a temporary status in occupational dress, like the farmer's overalls, the theatrical costume of the opera singer, and the uniform of the soldier, pilot, or nurse.[114] While the function of a uniform is to create a visually stable look, literally a *uniform* attire, many people feel a need during affiliation to distinguish themselves as individuals, as both belonging and not belonging to a group. These seemingly conflicting agendas are often resolved effortlessly. At carnival time, in the city of Salvador da Bahia, Brazil, I have documented how the five thousand men of the group called Filhos de Gandhy (Sons of Gandhi) are able to express group and individual identities at the same time. While all of the men wear the trademark costume of a white terrycloth turban, a long tunic, and blue socks with white sandals, many strive to differentiate themselves and look more beautiful than the others by donning optional ornaments, such as beads, ribbons, baby pacifiers as pendants, cowry shells, sunglasses, and even tinted contact lenses.[115]

Professional uniforms visually designate the working status of people in the military, law enforcement, medical, technical, or service ranks.[116] Military uniforms serve to dissociate the recruits from their civilian identities by homogenizing clothing and hair to form a visually collective force. Still, ways remain of expressing personal identity within this framework, most obviously through the medals and decorations that visually communicate the valued traits of service and courage.[117] Like carnival costumes, uniforms allow for a subtle personalization that the careful eye can detect. Close study of the uniforms of the Confederate officers of the American Civil War has uncovered much about the individuals who wore them. It addition to the obvious differences of physical stature revealed by the size of the clothes and the rank blatantly displayed on all military uniforms, an analysis of the cut, collar, lining, button placement, and sleeve braids reveals regional identity—there was, for example, a distinct style of officer's frock coat made in Charleston, South Carolina. And within the general frame of rank, much room remained for personal as well as regional difference, exemplifying the Confederate ideology of states' rights and free expression and resulting in officer's uniforms of varying hues and degrees of ornamentation, in line with the personal taste and age of the officer as well as his region and rank.[118]

When body art is used to identify individuals as members of certain factions within the larger society, it can at the same time position people in stern opposition to another group, intentionally inverting or negating an opposed style. Not only does Confederate gray contrast with Union blue, but Confederate diversity of uniform contrasts with Union regularity. Accordingly, the study of the body decoration of one group of people must take into account the diversity of the population; it must note the coherence of one tradition and the way it transforms or opposes the tradition of another. Other than the ways in which gendered costume provides such an instance, the literature on body art tends not to treat such patterns of structural conflict. Scholars of fashion in the Western world focus on the small elite who follow haute couture, or the few youths who signal their belonging to their own group through displays of excessive piercings and tattoos. Both of these factions are marginal elements of mainstream society.

Punk style, Daniel Wojcik explains, was created as a reaction to the conservative mainstream practice, and as a departure from the hippie aesthetic. The natural, flowing, free and floral look of the hippie was subverted, upturned, and transformed into the hard and edgy, violent, and artificial look of the punk.[119] Reinterpreting Wojcik's data, I would say that, while the punks thought of themselves as aberrant and derisive, their language of communication aligned with the mainstream. Band names—The Sex Pistols, Suicidal Tendencies—painted on studded leather jackets and evoking the aesthetics of graffiti, urbanity, and toughness, were displays of consumer loyalty, advertisements taken out of the culture of high capitalism and placed on the self—a branding with a brand, an identification of the self with a recognizable label, much as the mainstream folks have the words Tommy Hilfiger or Ralph Lauren, The Gap or Old Navy written on their attire. Likewise, the practice by punk riot grrrls to write words (Slut, Bitch) on their bodies with lipstick might have inspired the current trend in the United States of cute, innocent T-shirts worn by mainstream young women bearing similarly ironic words on their chests (Princess, Angel). It could seem that the punk goal is an aesthetic negation. But it takes hours to dress in the punk style, and it has held tightly to its tradition for thirty years. It is a highly evolved distinct form of beauty, once outrageous to others, still appealing to the members of the groups for whom beauty is not shiny blond hair and pink lipstick, but black makeup and purple hair sculptured with great difficulty into a mohawk.

An apparently rebellious streak runs through many current fashions. From bohemians to beatniks to hippies to punks, rebellions through body art are quite conventional, a point my undergraduate students at Indiana University seem reluctant to accept. Annoyed at his parents, a boy rebel, aged eighteen, gets a tattoo in the United States. It is little surprise that an American boy would know a moment of rebellion; it is culturally expected. He chooses to put his rebellion into the form of a tattoo, located on the upper arm, in a design chosen from a standard flash sheet, or a word in Kanji, or a "neo-tribal" design, usually thought of as Celtic but actually from Borneo. But every aspect of his choice is conventional, because he is not only expressing his rebellion and his personal identity, he is expressing his generational and cultural identity, acting in a way that is broadly understandable and particularly acceptable, even admirable, to the group of peers who make up his relevant cohort of reference.

Communication in body art is often reactive. City people refine their look in contrast to country people. Groups—punks, preppies—coalesce in opposition to others in society. The young dress to separate themselves from those of the aging generation. The Tiv of Nigeria and the Nuba of Sudan created new designs peculiar to their age grades.[120] The American hippies of the sixties, with their luxuriant hair and freewheeling tie-dyed designs, separated themselves from the look of their parents, the crew cuts and modest plaids. Then the kids of hippie parents created the punk look to signal generational liberation. And the children of punk parents created the grunge look of the nineties that overturned the mannered style of the punks and reverted, in some measure, to hippie aesthetics. The reaction of the new generation is based not on the look of their parents in youth, but to what they can see in the appearance of their parents in middle age—attesting to the importance of visual stimuli in the creation of one's own look, and complicating simple patterns of historical succession. The crew cut of the fifties brings loose and flowing hair in the sixties, which brings the extravagantly mannered hairdos of the eighties, which bring us to the crew cuts and shaved heads of our day.

An analysis of different groups—hippies, punks, yuppies, grunge, neo-tribal, hip hop—within a single society, reveals that all factions work within one whole; different fashions are all part of one cultural system. Styles are created in reaction to the modes of dress of others, negating them or appropriating them, as we see in the fashion designer Giovanni Versace's version of punk style or the singer Madonna's borrowing of Puerto Rican fashion from the streets of New York City. In another complex example, a look common among urban lesbians—flannel shirts, men's white undershirts ("wife beaters"), baseball caps, and wallet chains—while originating with truck drivers, has now been appropriated by Hollywood stylists, making it a mainstream, heterosexual fashion statement.[121] Every group has its own standard of beauty; attention to tiny detail, and communication through dress, is similar among all groups, while the variables of beauty differ from subgroup to subgroup. A study of the aesthetics of rebellion will inevitably reveal—in contradiction and inversion—the aesthetic preferences of the mainstream. Diverse styles interlock in body art systems.

Our documentation of body art must account for the diversity of the population by noting what is worn by the people of the mainstream, what is worn by the youthful and fashionable fringe; and, most importantly, we must see all of a society's body art as linked in transformational and oppositional dialogue, as different parts of a cultural conversation that unfolds visually in the streets.

During my fieldwork in India, I did not concentrate on that important topic. I chose not to stress diversity among groups, for had I studied women of different religions, castes, and classes, women from the city and from the country, my results would have shown again that body art differentiates groups. Instead, I concentrated on the diversity *within* a group, among middle-class urban women, intending to discover the degree to which will operates with tradition to make the daily creation a personal expression. But that personal expression contained an oppositional quality.

While I worked, women told me repeatedly that what they normally wear is distinctly different from the "gaudy" style of the village women or the servants—who together make up the fringe elements of this society and its vast majority. They also told me that their dress was markedly different from the brazen look of the Bollywood stars. And clearly, these Hindu women did not dress like Muslims; as middle-aged women they did not dress like girls or widows. Their choices expressed systematically who they were and who they were not.

Contrasting styles clarify both identity and opposition, and they offer opportunities. The adoption of another's style can be a vehicle for upward mobility. In India, this can be accomplished by appropriating a higher caste's embroidery style (sanskritization), or by dressing in imitation of the "advanced" people of the cities if you live in the village, or, if you live in a city like Banaras, you can always move up in style by trying to look like the hipsters of Bombay or New Delhi.[122] In the past, British colonial officers and their wives attempted to elevate their status by mimicking an elite dressing tradition, partaking in a sort of sanskritization of their own by donning evening gowns and dinner jackets in the sweltering heat of India or Africa.[123] People are themselves in negative relation or in positive relation to others.

Assessment

My model for the study of body art ends in contexts of gaze. Here people assess the completed work of their own bodily assemblage and place themselves before others for evaluation. With *darshan* as the great instance in India, it can be asserted that the act of seeing is seldom neutral. Seeing leads to positive and negative evaluations, resulting in approval, praise, envy, or reprimand. In order to comprehend such judgments, it is necessary to determine the variables of beauty and acceptability, to understand as a created unit the factors spread through the model: history, the individual's personality, the contexts of time, space, age, occupation, gender, religion, and social order. In other words, through gaze, judgment is passed on both personal aesthetics and social propriety. The resultant visual (and moral) opinion is based on the relationship between the person and the beholder; it includes consideration of who the person is—gender, life stage, family, subsets of society—and of where the person is being seen, whether the setting is rural or urban, private or public, at home or abroad, and finally the nature of the social occasion: commonplace, festive, or ceremonial, secular or sacred.

After breaking down the complex act of bodily adornment in order to devise a systematic procedure for study, we put it all back together again in this final component of the model, in which the parts become the whole of creation, ready for assessment. When Mathuri Chaubey characterized self-adornment, she explained the importance of evaluating the self as an object of beauty that embodied an acceptable look, that avoided what she called the "excesses" and "mistakes" of adornment. Of interest to us now are the roles of self-assessment, of mirroring, and of the influence of the audience in the creation of body art.

Evaluation of body art rises conspicuously in moments of cross-cultural encounter—during Captain Cook's Pacific voyages of exploration in the eighteenth century, for instance, or the intrusion of soldiers, new rulers, and missionaries during the long era of violent colonialism. One outcome of fascination and revulsion was a deeper understanding of the way we clothe and treat our bodies, and how adornment defines who we are, and how the adornment of other people defines them as radically "other." Curiosity developed during exploration and colonial expansion. "Exotics" from beyond were put on display at world's fairs. "Exotics" from within were exhibited in traveling carnivals and circus sideshows. As we come to see the world as a commercialized "global village," a desire to see how differences survive, to see how others present themselves through their dress abides. The mood is more admiring than disparaging in ethnic arts festivals, museum exhibitions, and publications such as the *National Geographic* magazine, but curiosity about difference continues.

Although there is a fair amount of literature on how we have looked at others, less has been written on how people look at themselves. Chastened by anthropology in its early classic phase, we should be less interested in our assessments as outsiders than in learning how to understand the culturally relevant assessments made in terms of *native aesthetic systems.* Since items of dress act as signs, as Bogatyrev demonstrated, the informed local viewer knows what to look for and how to read the messages that are set before everyone's eyes. To complete interpretation in line with the model of body art presented here, we aim for an understanding of what the insider is seeing, to understand the choices Mathuri Chaubey makes when she dresses in front of a mirror. In India I was told that if you see a woman wearing a golden necklace, these are the thoughts you would have: If, during close visual scrutiny, she seemed to be a village woman or a servant, you would assume the necklace was "artificial gold," since she could not afford to wear real gold, or if it were really gold, you would assume she stole it from her employer. If, on the other hand, the woman looked rich, like a "smart lady," then even if she were wearing "artificial gold," you would assume that such a chic person would be wearing real gold. The golden necklace might be the same, but the assessments of beauty and worth (real or fake), and subsequent judgments of moral character (pretty and sophisticated or peasant and thief) are cultural, relying on nuances of communication accessible only to insiders.

One way to understand native aesthetics is to solicit assessments. Mari

Lyn Salvador asked Kuna Indians in Panama to rank a given set of *mola* blouses, discussing the design, motifs, sewing, color, and the success of overall execution.[124] In Papua New Guinea, Michael O'Hanlon sought appraisals of body art from the spectators at festival dances, gaining access to meanings and communicative intent through the evaluative commentary of the insiders.[125] This exercise reveals not only the aesthetics of body art, but also the moral and symbolic meanings the art holds in the culture.

Another approach has been to learn what is considered beautiful, as a way of understanding the physical and behavioral attributes that are favored in a given culture. One avenue is to study works of art, such as sculptural representations, as statements of idealized beauty. An analysis of (male and) female beauty contests offers another way to understand the shared standards of beauty that inspire people in their own acts of adornment.[126] Much of body art has as its primary goal the showcasing of natural or acquired beauty.[127] As James Faris makes clear in his documentation of body decoration among the Nuba of Sudan, individuals who did not look beautiful—for reasons of illness, injury, or old age—did not even bother to decorate, for decoration belonged exclusively within the domain of the beautiful.[128] We can generalize that the world over, a primary goal of body art is to display beauty, which is often defined by such variables as symmetry, gendered contrast, grace, youth, health, and prosperity.

The question of beauty is, of course, contextual, even within a culture. Many traditional societies have favored plump women as representing abundance, health, and the promise to be good workers and good breeders, but Western television shows have recently diffused a slim standard of beauty, also signaling wealth and health,[129] to many parts of the world. In India, some young women have come to abandon traditional clothes that are meant to augment hips, busts, and bellies, feeling such clothing belongs to a standard of beauty that is no longer relevant.[130]

Adornment accentuates at once the beautiful and the acceptable. How can one fit in and pass without being beautiful? This question leads into an investigation of social norms of appropriateness (which are not necessarily those of beauty), and we see that the answer will take into account the social variables of the model—age and gender, status and religion, location and occasion. As long as social taboos are avoided and grave mistakes are not made, people are allowed to pass; not everyone is expected to be spectacular in appearance. Acceptability is, of course, utterly contextual; it depends on who you are. It might or might not be acceptable to wear a miniskirt, a turban, or high heel go-go boots. Acceptability also depends, as examples from India consistently demonstrate, on the fitness of parts within the wholeness of a particular assemblage. While a certain pair of shoes would be suitable for one outfit, it might look outlandish with another.

The acceptable clarifies in contrast with the unacceptable. Nina, Neelam, and Mukta revealed a steady awareness of unacceptability in their dress. They knew that some things were wrong because of their age, marital status, and the position of their family in society. Women in India keep negative examples in their heads while they get dressed, trying consciously, perhaps, to look like a beautiful movie star, but at the same time, trying *not to* look like a "dancing girl" or *hijra*. (When I asked, they had no trouble in describing exactly what constitutes the attire of these two undesirable categories.) When trying on clothes and looking in the mirror, men and women ask themselves, "Does this flatter me?" "Does it make me look attractive?" And they ask, "Does it make me look fat?" "Does it make me look ugly?" "Is it right?" Their goal is to achieve a positive example while, at the same time, avoiding the images defined as negative in their societies.

We end with the central theme of this book. People, fluent in the complex language of body art, make educated choices. They might choose to strive toward a shared standard of beauty, hoping to be admired, to be envied and emulated. They might choose to repel, to shock, through a display of an alternative vision of what it is to be beautiful. They might choose to fit in, to pass without notice or reprimand, avoiding the expenditure of time, money, and energy it takes to get so lavishly adorned that admiration or revulsion ensues. Whatever they choose to communicate through their body art, people are acting willfully, with knowledge of what is beautiful, what is ugly, and what is acceptable. Small daily acts of self-adornment fill with volition and meaning. They employ the language of a shared culture and system of aesthetics to produce a self-conscious communication of the self.

Directions in Study

India provides good ground for a study of the lively and complex tradition of contemporary body art. This is the case partly because of the firm cultural pattern of making visual discriminations, reflecting the nature of a divided society, one interested in maintaining the distinctions among different religions and castes, ethnic and regional groups, as well as genders, occupations, and ranks in society. These discriminatory discriminations reveal an analytic mind that can easily read a type of a bangle or a style of draping a sari to know instantly the identity of the wearer. (Is this tendency to division culturally constructed in the Indian mind, a mind that once excelled in math and astronomy and now excels in computer programming?) Variables of dress and what they denote are known to everyone, just as people know which surnames indicate which castes. Add to this attention to distinction the visual nature of Indian culture, and you have a place where messages are sent and received visually through a grammar of bodily ornamentation.

The study of clothing in India reveals the tremendous importance of marriage, yet unlike other places in the world, such as Egypt or the United States, unmarried women do not flaunt a sexy beauty to entice men, nor is there a prolonged period of engagement as in many parts of Africa. Marriage is the most sharply marked rite of passage. On her wedding day a woman is the most decorated she will ever be, and after her marriage her new position will be celebrated in gaudy clothes and shiny ornaments. This explosion of ornamentation with marriage seems to suggest a general desire to protect the beautiful virgin, which is linked possibly to India's history of hostile invasions. In its richness, Indian body art also incorporates the pervasive supernatural aspect of culture: pendants for the gods, astrological rings, and amulets with Sanskrit mantras and Koranic inscriptions. India's history is literally built into its body art: Mughal *salwar* pants, Islamic motifs on saris, British wallpaper motifs on shawls, and globalizing Hollywood and Bollywood references in trendy clothes and jewelry.

It helped that I developed a model for body art in a place where distinctions and visual communication are so important, where weddings are so extravagant, where the culture's depths come into play in adornment; but distinctions, if subtle, and visual communication, if little acknowledged, are to be found everywhere. The model might be generally helpful, and it has certainly guided me toward completeness.

Though this study has been necessarily fragmentary—there are a billion people in India—the conceptual completeness of the model indicates key arenas for future inquiry. In India, as elsewhere, male adornment needs further study, and the topic of facial hair and hairstyles would make a good focus. The size and shape of the mustache among Hindus, particularly in Rajasthan, the beards of Muslims and Sikhs, and the new clean-shaven styles from the West would reveal much about personal and cultural identity, just as a historical tracing of facial hair from India, through England, to the America of the Civil War would yield an interesting story of countermoves in colonial history. Men's clothes also deserve study in modern India, where preferences indicate status—the post-colonial "safari suit" among urban workers, the business suit among the affluent, with its accessories: shoes, watch, glasses, briefcase, and the most coveted accessory nowadays, a scooter or a car with a hired driver, allowing the body to pass through the dust and smoke of the streets to emerge fresh and unscathed at its destination.

The village is the most important topic not covered in this book. The "gaudy" look of the village, though disparaged in the city, is a coherent cultural creation, conditioned by finances and available materials, as all creations are, but shaped by intention into a presentation of the self as rich with personal and social complexity as urban creations are. Muslim women in India, whether they live in cities or villages, similarly deserve a full-length study in which a model like the one I have outlined would reveal a range of choices that yield a total look. Muslim women's attire cannot be reduced to the contentious issue of the veil.

A major topic not explored in this book is the role of adornment in the Indian diaspora. The practice of painting the hands with henna has been appropriated in the West, changing its name, its color, and its designs, and then the Western trend has returned to India, where new asymmetrical designs are fashionable. Comparably, *kurta* tops worn with jeans became stylish in the West and then in India. Western standards of beauty—slim figures and auburn hair—as well as hip-hop fashions of baggy pants and shaved heads for men, bounce back from the diaspora and mix with diasporic fashions, such as *bhangra* music, to create the hybrid style of communities of Indian people throughout the world.

Away in England or America, in Trinidad or South Africa, and at home in India, north or south, in the village or the city, people—women and men, rich and poor, Hindu, Muslim, Sikh, Jain, and Christian—get dressed everyday. The model ends, and the day begins in assemblage. Its parts match, cohering into a transitory unit that is at once beautiful and useful, personally satisfying and socially appropriate. Rani rises. To the music of sliding glass bangles, she wraps her body in a sari and places on her forehead the *bindi* that will tell the world she is married, that will add to her presence the grace of four moons.

Glossary

Aarti: Formal Hindu worship of a particular deity, involving chanting, incense, and especially the circular motion of lights.

Akhara: A male place for exercise, especially for wrestling.

Almari: A wardrobe made of wood or metal.

Banarasi Sari: Silk brocaded sari, hand-woven in the city of Banaras.

Barat: A wedding procession consisting of the groom, his family and friends, and hired musicians, which goes from the groom's house to the bride's house, where the wedding is to take place.

Bichiya: Toe rings worn by women, usually on the second toe, as a symbol of marriage.

Bindi: A dot of color on the forehead, usually worn by women as a symbol of marriage.

Blouse: A midriff-length, tight fitting woman's blouse that is worn with a sari.

Burqa: A veiling garment in the form of a coat that often includes a hood to cover the head.

Choli: A midriff-length, tight fitting woman's blouse, often backless.

Chura: Marriage bangles, especially from the states of Rajasthan, Gujarat, and Punjab.

Churi: Thin bangles.

Churidar Pyjama: Tight-fitting trousers with folds of cloth below the knee.

Darshan: Eye to eye connection between a Hindu deity and a worshiper.

Dehati: As a noun, a villager; as an adjective, descriptive of village taste.

Desi: Native, local, Indian.

Dhobi: Hired launderer.

Dhoti: Men's draped lower garment.

Dupatta (also *Chunni*): Women's long scarf, part of an ensemble, usually a *salwar suit,* worn draped over the head or across the chest.

Durbar: A royal court, a hall of audience. It also refers to the ceremony in which kings made themselves available to an audience.

Gali: A narrow lane or alley in a city.

Ghat: Sets of steps where the city descends to the river.

Ghungru: Cluster of bells attached to items of jewelry.

Hathphul: A hand ornament that clasps at the wrist, with the central piece resting on the back of the hand, and chains extending to five finger rings.

Hijra: A male transvestite, sometimes but not always a eunuch.

Jaimal: Part of a Hindu wedding ceremony, during which the bride and groom ritually exchange garlands of flowers.

Jamdani Sari: Fine hand-woven sari, brocaded on cotton in the countryside, east of Dhaka, Bangladesh.

Jhumka: Bell-shaped ornament, also referred to as umbrella-shaped, often dangling from earrings, and sometimes from bangles.

Kameez: Tunic top, often part of a *salwar suit* ensemble. Also called a *kurta.*

Kangan: Thick fancy bangles, diverse in ornamentation.

Karas: Bangles with decorated ends, often depicting the stylized heads of animals.

Karkhana: Craft workshop.

Karigar: Craftsman.

Kumari: Unmarried woman.

Kundan: A technique of setting gemstones in gold that is often associated with the Mughal era.

Kurta: Tunic top, often part of a *salwar suit* ensemble. Also called a *kameez.*

Lehanga: Women's full skirt. Often used to describe the entire fancy clothing ensem-

431

ble consisting of three pieces: bodice, full skirt, and long scarf. Frequently worn by brides during the *jaimal* ceremony.

Linga: The iconic form of Lord Shiva.

Mandir: Hindu temple.

Mangalsutra: A sacred marriage necklace, usually made of tiny black beads and gold.

Mantikka: A gold or silver ornamental *bindi* for the forehead, suspended from a chain that attaches to the hair.

Maxi: Cotton, ankle-length dress worn around the house or to sleep in.

Mehendi: Henna.

Mina (Gulabi Mina): Polychrome enamel work on metal. *Gulabi mina,* pink enamel, consisting of pink designs painted on a white enamel background, often associated with the arts of Jaipur and Banaras.

Minawallah: Master of the art of enameled jewelry.

Murti: A representation of a Hindu deity in stone, metal, or clay.

Najar (Nazar): The evil eye.

Nauratan: A traditional arrangement of nine specific gemstones assembled in a single ornament.

Paan: A chewable quid composed of a wrapped betel leaf, lime paste, areca nut, and assorted spices.

Palloo: Elaborate end-piece of the sari, often worn hanging down the back to display the intricate design and craft of the sari.

Parampara: Tradition.

Patola Sari: Fine double-ikat silk saris, notably woven by the Salvi family in Patan, Gujarat.

Payal: Anklets, usually worn by women as a symbol of marriage.

Petticoat: Ankle-length drawstring skirt, worn under a sari, into which the sari is tucked.

Prashad: A blessing from the gods, usually in the form of sweets, which is given to the worshiper by the officiating priest.

Puja: Hindu worship ceremony.

Pujari: Officiating Hindu priest at a *puja,* a ceremony for worship.

Pundit: Hindu priest.

Purdah: Veiling practice.

Pyjama: Drawstring trousers.

Rukdraksh Beads: Seed beads sacred to Shiva, worn by his devotees, believed to have sacred and healing powers.

Rup: Form, shape, appearance, or aspect. Often used to describe a deity's incarnations.

Salwar Suit (also *Salwar Kameez* or *Punjabi*): Women's clothing ensemble consisting of three pieces: tunic top, drawstring trousers, and long scarf.

Sasural: Conjugal home. The ancestral home of the husband, in which the new bride lives with her new extended family.

Shauk: Interest, enthusiasm, passion.

Shringar: Decoration; the romantic essence of the arts; a decorated woman; a woman engaged in the act of self-adornment.

Shervani: Man's knee-length coat, often worn by grooms during the *jaimal* ceremony.

Shobha: Grace.

Sindur: Colored powder, usually red, worn on the part in the hair by women as a symbol of marriage.

Suhagin: A woman who is in the blissful stage of marriage; a married woman; a woman whose husband is alive.

Tarika: A mode, a method, a manner of being.

Tikka (also *Bindi*): A dot of color on the forehead, usually worn by women as a symbol of marriage.

Zari: Silver, gold, or brass brocading, often added to silk Banarasi saris.

Notes

1. Body Art in Banaras

1. See Agee and Evans, *Let Us Now Praise Famous Men*, pp. xx, 127–286.

2. There are many definitions of folklore, the most generally accepted one being Dan Ben-Amos's "artistic communication in small groups." "Toward a Definition of Folklore in Context"; p. 14.

3. The terms "body art," "dress," "ornamentation," and "adornment" are used interchangeably in this book to mean aesthetic and conscious alterations (weight loss, piercing, hair cut) and supplementations (clothes, jewelry, makeup, accessories) to the body. This broad understanding of the aesthetic decorations and changes to the body is supported by the framing definition used by the "Dress, Body, Culture" series edited by Joanne Eicher.

4. The definition of *rasa* appears in the Sanskrit glossary of Coomaraswamy's *The Transformation of Nature in Art*, p. 225. For a clear description of all nine *rasas* and their role in the appreciation of Indian art, see Dehejia's *Indian Art*, pp. 20–22.

5. Brijbhushan, in her book *Masterpieces of Indian Jewellery*, lists specific ornament types, each categorized by their shape and the part of the body they adorn. For north India, for example, she lists 70 distinct types of ornaments: 4 for the head, 9 for the forehead, 11 for the ears, 6 for the nose, 1 for the teeth, 17 for the neck, 6 for the arms, 12 for the wrists, 5 for the fingers, 4 for the toes, and 2 for the waist. See section titled "List of Ornaments of Ancient and Modern India," pp. 45–49.

6. The 2001 India Census lists the population of the city at 1,100,748, just above one million. In the 2002 *Road Guide to Varanasi*, p. 4, the permanent population is listed at 925,962 and the number of daily pilgrims estimated to be from 125,000 to 250,000.

7. In her book *Darśan*, Eck describes the sacredness of Kashi, Banaras, on pp. 73–75. In *Banaras: City of Light*, Eck expands on the notion of Kashi as the center of the cosmic world in chapter 7, pp. 283–303.

8. Cultural geographer Singh, in his book *Banaras Region*, devotes a section to Varanasi as "the mini India"; pp. 66–68.

9. This was approximately the breakdown of the city's population given by most of the people I spoke with, both Hindus and Muslims, in estimating their city's religious divide. Regardless of whether or not this statistic is actually accurate, it reveals that Hindus and Muslims each feel that they represent roughly half of the city's population, with Hindus having a slight majority. Local cultural geographer Singh, in his *Banaras Region* guidebook, p. 28, comes close to this estimate, stating that Muslims comprise a little more than a third of the population, just above 33% (66% Hindus). Sociologist Derné, however, citing the government of India's District Census Handbook, gives the religious breakdown as 75% Hindu to 25% Muslim; p. 3.

10. Glassie shows how different contexts can be grouped into three master categories—creation, consumption, and communication—in chapter 2, pp. 41–86, of *Material Culture*.

11. Bogatyrev, *The Functions of Folk Costume in Moravian Slovakia*.

12. Strathern and Strathern, *Self-Decora-*

tion in Mount Hagen, and Faris, *Nuba Personal Art.*

13. Dalby, *Kimono;* Rugh, *Reveal and Conceal;* Wilson, *Chinese Dress;* Baumgarten, *What Clothes Reveal;* and Steele, *The Corset.*

14. The "Dress, Body, Culture" series is published by Berg.

15. Some sources that handle these topics well are: Mines's *Public Faces, Private Voices;* essays in Mines and Lamb's *Everyday Life in South Asia;* Derné's *Culture in Action;* essays in Appadurai, Korom, and Mills's *Gender, Genre and Power in South Asian Expressive Traditions;* and Flueckinger's *Gender and Genre in the Folklore of Middle India.*

16. Raheja and Gold, *Listen to the Heron's Words.*

17. Nabar makes this point in *Caste as Woman,* 124–126. Deen, in *Broken Bangles,* uses the symbolism of bangles as shackles— "they dazzle, they distract—and they bind." Deen believes that once women are able to break free of tradition, by breaking the bangles, they are free from "customs that oppress and deaden"; p. xi. On p. 65, she continues her argument by stating that women are "immobilised" in traditional clothes while men get to wear Western pants and shirts. Another way to look at this would be to see men's outfits as a symbol of servitude to the West, an occupational attire forced upon Indian men by the British rulers (see Cohn's excellent article "Cloth, Clothes, and Colonialism: India in the Nineteenth Century," and Tarlo's *Clothing Matters*), while the women were able to retain a sense of identity, of a cultural mode of dress not tainted by the Raj. Symbolic rhetoric of this type does not quite work if one actually looks at the history of clothing choices during colonial times.

18. Liddle and Joshi, *Daughters of Independence.*

19. Tarlo's book, *Clothing Matters,* examines men's colonial clothing decisions, the role of clothes during India's independence, and the importance of clothing among members of different castes in village Gujarat. In *White Saris and Sweet Mangoes,* Lamb looks at elderly Bengali women and their adherence to or subversion of norms about old age and widowhood, including those of clothing. Jones's article, "The Eloquent Sari," provides a brief exploration of the sari as a political and personal liberator for women in mythology and literature.

20. Divakaruni, *Arranged Marriage,* pp. 17–33.

21. Ali, *Brick Lane,* p. 201.

22. Ali, *Brick Lane:* description of Razia, who, after acquiring a British passport, starts to regularly wear a Union Jack sweatshirt, p. 134; "Bombay Look" description on p. 194; men's fusion style worn by Karim described on p. 277.

23. Ali, *Brick Lane,* p. 278.

24. I use the definition of performance set forth by Bauman, in which an act of communication is artistically rendered, to be evaluated by the audience; *Story, Performance, and Event,* p. 3.

25. Entwistle, concluding chapter of *The Fashioned Body,* pp. 237–239.

26. See the preface of Hollander's *Seeing through Clothes,* especially p. xiv, where she, an art historian, describes the study of ethnic dress as one in which the garments should be studied for their formal qualities, since in these non-Western cases, "the individual human being does not seem able to animate the costume. He does not give it any extra dimension, nor does it in turn enhance his face and body personally." But Western dress, by contrast, serves "to contribute to the making of a self-conscious individual image, an image linked to all other imaginative and idealized visualizations of the human body."

3. Gaze, Sacred and Secular

1. Eck, *Darśan,* pp. 73–75. For a general discussion of *darshan,* see also Babb "Glancing: Visual Interaction in Hinduism."

2. Payne's novel about Banaras, *Sister India,* accurately describes a scene in which foreign tourists are taken to the Golden

Temple just to be told that they cannot enter, but that they may look through a peephole at the interior of the *mandir;* pp. 120–122. Dinesh Prince Chaubey, the owner of a sightseeing business, told me an interesting story involving the former prime minister Rajiv Gandhi's Italian-born wife Sonia, who was stopped from entering a Hindu temple in Kathmandu, because she was considered to be a foreigner. Gandhi himself refused to enter, as protest, and subsequently, the government of India stopped sending aid, including medicine, to Nepal. Many people, including Chaubey himself, have told me that the Vishvanath Temple, with similar restrictive policies, is owned by the government of India. This fact would reveal the hypocrisy of the government in its alleged reaction to the Gandhi incident. When I asked Chaubey where he took tourists in Banaras, he said that there are five places: The Shiva Temple at Banaras Hindu University, the Durga Temple, Sarnath, the *ghats,* and "silk shopping."

3. Glassie, in *Art and Life in Bangladesh,* describes a Saraswati Puja event in Dhaka, pp. 158–167. On p. 162, Glassie observes the large size of the head and eyes, allowing the goddess to hold the gaze of her worshipers.

4. Mitter, *Much Maligned Monsters,* p. viii.

5. Glassie, *Art and Life in Bangladesh,* p. 162.

6. Glassie, in *Art and Life in Bangladesh,* p. 154, notes how the graceful features of the statues echo perfections in nature: the eye like the eye of a deer or the petal of a lotus; the eyebrow like a bow; the thighs like the trunk of a young elephant; the calf like a spawning fish; the fingers like beans in a pod.

7. The emphasis on the face of Durga is due to the fact that during the Durga Puja festival, large statues of the goddess are widely commissioned for public display and worship.

8. Thakurta, in her article "Women as 'Calendar Art' Icons," notes that the faces of the goddesses Lakshmi and Saraswati are usually the faces of Bollywood actresses Hema Malini or Sridevi. Since the faces of the goddesses are interchangeable, Hema Malini can be the model for Lakshmi, Saraswati, or Durga; p. 96.

9. In "Feminine Identity and National Ethos in Indian Calendar Art," Uberoi observes a "symbiotic" relationship between the calendar art and film industries, one in which actors portray gods because they look like the calendar art images, yet calendar art images are produced to look like the popular actors of the time; p. 43. In Das Gupta's study of Indian cinema, *The Painted Face,* he talks of an audience's rejection of actors who were cast to play gods, because they did not resemble the popular calendar art images of these deities; p. 21.

10. For an analysis of Hanuman and his worship among the wrestlers of Banaras, see Alter's "Hanuman and the Moral Physique," pp. 127–144.

11. Kramrisch, *The Hindu Temple.*

12. Menon's wonderful new adaptation of the *Ramayana* contains rich descriptions of these and other episodes involving bodily adornment.

13. This beautiful necklace is illustrated in Jain and Aggarwala, *National Handicrafts and Handlooms Museum,* p. 63. For a detail of the necklace, see Untracht, *Traditional Jewelry of India,* p. 39.

14. The argument about worshipers and priests serving as ornaments to the gods is developed in Waghorne's excellent and succinct article "Dressing the Body of God." See Untracht, *Traditional Jewelry of India,* pp. 192–195, for a brief discussion of temple jewelry, and p. 195, for a description of *darshan* of a bejeweled god. For photographs depicting a statue of Shiva richly ornamented in flowers and jewelry, see Krishnan and Kumar's *Dance of the Peacock,* pp. 200–201.

15. The artist Raja Ravi Varma's (1848–1906) paintings of the Hindu pantheon and his establishment of one of the first printing presses in India (in 1891) led to the popu-

larization and iconographic standardization of calendar art images in India in the early twentieth century. There are many books written on Ravi Varma. For an overview of calendar art traditions and contemporary worship practices, see Del Bonta's "Calendar Prints and Indian Traditions" and "Calendar Art"; Smith's "Impact of 'God Posters' on Hindus and Their Devotional Traditions"; Inglis's "Suitable for Framing"; Larson's "A Postmodernist Perspective on India's Popular Religious Art"; and Pal's "The Printed Image."

16. Lutgendorf's article, "All in the (Raghu) Family," describes the ritualized watching of the *Ramayana* television serial, an activity perceived by many as a form of *darshan*. He carefully notes the extension of the retelling of the story through this medium, adding scenes and emphasizing certain episodes. Lutgendorf observes (p. 246) the homogeneity in the depiction of gods in the television series: they look like the drawings in the *Amar Chitra Katha* comic books, which in turn look like the paintings of the gods in calendar art. Lutgendorf cites J. S. Hawley as stating that the director of the *Ramayana* television serial hired the *Amar Chitra Katha* artists as set and costume designers, p. 251.

17. For description, history, and analyses of this important medium of religious education, see Pritchett's "The World of *Amar Chitra Katha*," Hawley's "The Saints Subdued: Domestic Virtue and National Integration in *Amar Chitra Katha*," and Sarin's "Comic Books, India."

18. Larson and Pal's exhibition catalog, *Changing Myths and Images,* reproduces posters and calendar art images, including those from the H. Daniel Smith Poster Archive at Syracuse University. The catalog contains some of the popular imagery of the most memorable scenes from the *Ramayana,* such as the marriage of Ram and Sita, p. 42; Bharat's worship of Ram's sandals, the abduction of Sita, and Lakshman's revival after ingesting Himalayan herbs brought by Ha-

numan, p. 43; and the battle between Ram and Ravan, the enthronement of Ram and Sita, and Sita's trial by fire, p. 44.

19. Glassie, "Mud and Mythic Vision," p. 205.

20. For a deep exploration of this, see Glassie's "Mud and Mythic Vision."

21. Glassie's interviews with Bangladeshi sculptor Haripada Pal reveal that the artist knows 108 different images of the goddess Kali. While most people might recognize Kali by her common stance, that of holding the sword on her left hand, Pal's deeper knowledge allows him to see the many aspects of the goddess, depicted slightly differently, including those that show Kali with the sword on the right hand; "Mud and Mythic Vision," p. 218.

22. Varma's calendar art images of women, representing the nation and ideal womanhood, have directly influenced the depiction of Hindu goddesses in this medium, and the appreciation of the beauty of women in general. Thakurta, in "Women as 'Calendar Art'," traces the historical genealogy of the mass-produced image of ideal women. She cites C. V. Raman Pillai's novel *Marthanda Varma,* in which a character is described to be as beautiful as a Ravi Varma painting, anticipating the influence of Varma's depictions on the standard of ideal beauty; p. 96. Contemporary artist Pushpamal N has photographs taken of herself as she poses in classic Ravi Varma calendar art images, portraying goddesses and ordinary women, who have, according to the exhibition curator Chaitanya Sambrani, "been raised to the status of canon through their oleographic reproductions"; "On the Double Edge of Desire," p. 23.

23. Ramaswami, in his book *Temples in South India,* also mentions the system of tickets and the long lines in order to take *darshan* of the statue, p. 13.

24. Ramaswami, in *Temples of South India,* describes the historical practice of giving the Balaji statue extravagant gifts of pre-

cious jewels, starting in the ninth century. Some of these include gold cups, bejeweled crowns, silver plates, swords encrusted with diamonds and other precious stones, and thirty thousand gold coins. He states that the temple is considered to be the richest in the country (pp. 11–12).

25. Jain and Aggarwala, *National Handicrafts and Handlooms Museum*, p. 55.

26. Waghorne, *The Raja's Magic Clothes.*

27. The kingly *dubars* were also self-consciously captured in paintings and photographs, as Waghorne's book illustrates. A great study of Indian photographs is Pinney's *Camera Indica*. Other studies that look at the photographic gaze include two articles by Mathur: "Wanted Native Views," on colonial postcards, and "Re-visualising the Missionary Subject," on artist Ayisha Abraham and her computer generated photographs.

28. For the history and illustrations of the famous diamond, see Untracht, *Traditional Jewelry of India,* pp. 315–316; Krishnan and Kumar, *Dance of the Peacock,* pp. 38–40; Keay, *The Crown Jewels,* pp. 24–25, 59–60.

29. See Dundes, "Wet and Dry, The Evil Eye."

30. Kapur, *Difficult Daughters,* pp. 205–206. This novel has a poignant scene that depicts the tension of the professor's communication to his first wife that he has now taken a second wife. Not knowing how to break it to his family, the second wife, Virmati, stands at the door in full bridal ornaments—*sindur,* Punjabi shell bangles, and sari. Her attire successfully communicates, non-verbally, that she has arrived married to the professor; p. 208.

31. A related belief is that the overall mood of a movie might affect the personality of an unborn baby. In Divakaruni's *Sister of My Heart,* a pregnant woman's mother-in-law encourages her to watch comedies or videos of the *Ramayana* in the hope that these will have a positive effect on her grandchild; p. 225.

32. Mukherjee, *Desirable Daughters,* p. 7.

33. The mirror is often used as a symbol of female vanity in syncretized African religions in the Caribbean and Latin America. The Haitian Vodou goddesses La Siren and Erzuli Freda, and the Brazilian Candomblé goddesses Yemanjá and Oxum, often hold mirrors into which they gaze, appreciating their immense beauty. Ritual gifts to these deities include mirrors, perfume, makeup, and soap—presents meant to indulge their vanity. For an exploration of mirrors in Western art, see Hollander's *Seeing Through Clothes,* chapter 6.

34. In dance performances, such as in Bharatnatyam, Radha gracefully adds bangles to her arms or lines her eyes with kohl in preparation for a meeting with her beloved Krishna.

35. See Tarlo's *Clothing Matters,* chapter 2, for a sample of written accounts by the British of what Indians were wearing. Hardgrave's book on Flemish artist Balthaza Solvyns reproduces the artist's late eighteenth- to early nineteenth-century etchings of Hindus into categories, including those of caste and occupation, and fakirs and religious mendicants. Albums of the East India Company c. 1830, a few pages of which are illustrated in Stronge, Smith, and Harle's *A Golden Treasury,* p. 39, show detailed paintings of couples from different caste and religious groups of India. This tendency is still present; recent Dover Publications children's coloring book, *Fashions from India,* and paper dolls, *Traditional Fashions from India,* both categorize the detailed drawings of costumes by ethnic, occupation, and religious groups.

36. See Cohn, "Cloth, Clothes, and Colonialism: India in the Nineteenth Century," and Tarlo, *Clothing Matters,* pp. 38–52, for a description of how the British and the Indians dressed in colonial India, and the orders the British received to explicitly dress apart from local Indians.

37. Lynton's *The Sari* contains detailed descriptions of sari types and wearing styles associated with many of the regions of India.

38. See Bhandari, *Costume, Textiles and Jewellery of India,* pp. 105–111 for descriptions and illustrations showing the specifics of the draping styles.

39. Bhandari, in *Costume, Textiles and Jewellery of India,* describes how the variables of the turban—style of tying, color, design, materials, measurements, and embellishments—can signal occupation, community, region, and socioeconomic identity; pp. 113–116.

40. The *bindi* is such a strong sign of Indian identity that white supremacists who engaged in hate crimes and harassment of Indians in New Jersey called themselves "dotbusters"; Prashad, *The Karma of Brown Folk,* pp. 87–92.

41. The narrator of Mukherjee's novel *Desirable Daughters,* claims to have once had the ability to distinguish, just by looking, where in north India somebody was from, including the "related religions and nationalities"; p. 195. Distinctions are also being made between urban and rural. For example, in a new *Spider-Man* comic book, written by Jeevan Kang and devised specifically for the Indian market by Marvel Comics, the main character is made fun of by his urban classmates, called "dhoti boy," while a sympathetic female friend says she is also from the village, and her mother tried to make her wear a *salwar kameez* suit. Traditional clothes are signs of backward generic "village identity" for these characters.

42. These ornaments reflect the women from the states of Tamil Nadu and Gujarat, Rajasthan and Maharastra, respectively.

43. Three articles—Frater's "Elements of Style" and "Rabari Dress" and Fisher's "Bajara"—give specific details of ethnic identification of textiles and embroideries. See also Bhandari's great book, *Costume, Textiles and Jewellery of India.*

44. *India Abroad,* "India News Special," September 17, 2004, p. A10.

45. Kumar, "Why Do Hindus and Muslims Fight?" p. 350.

46. Tarlo, pp. 101–127.

47. Leslie, in "The Significance of Dress for the Orthodox Hindu Woman," pp. 209–210, explains that a vertical mark of one or more lines on the forehead signals a follower of Vishnu, and that three horizontal lines mark a devotee of Shiva. She notes that the shape of a *tilak* mark on the forehead may communicate caste: a bamboo leaf for the priestly Brahmin, a big fish for the Kshatriya warrior, a smaller fish for the Vaishya merchant, and a half-moon for the lowly Shudra. For a brief description and illustrations of sectarian marks and stamps, see Untracht, *Traditional Jewelry of India,* pp. 23–26. See also Maheswarajah's "Caste Mark (Bindi, Bottu)," p. 100, for more examples of marks that specify particular ethnic and caste groups.

48. Leslie, "The Significance of Dress for the Orthodox Hindu Women," p. 201. See also Weinberger-Thomas, pp. 24–28, for a description of color associations and their communication about different moods and the castes of India.

49. See Jeffery, *Frogs in a Well,* section on *burqa,* pp. 150–159. One reason to wear a *burqa* is to demonstrate wealth and high social status. In Sidhwa's novel, *The Bride,* a character, Miriam, starts observing strict *purdah* as soon as her husband moves up in social status and importance; p. 51. Mills's study of veiled women in Afghanistan shows that women are able to move freely in the male public realm by wearing a *chador* covering, providing them with anonymity, mobility, and a sense of power; "Sex Role Reversals, Sex Changes, and Transvestite Disguise in the Oral Tradition of a Conservative Muslim Community in Afghanistan," p. 211.

50. In another Bollywood movie, *Veer-Zaara,* the Muslim heroine is transformed into a Hindu during a Punjabi festival merely by a costume change, reinforcing the central theme of the movie, that differences between Hindus and Muslims are mostly superficial. Mukherjee, in *Desirable Daughters,*

notes that Hindus and Muslims in Bengal, despite differences of appearance and dietary and caste restrictions, are fundamentally the same, p. 6.

51. An informant of Jeffery, in *Frogs in a Well,* complains about the wide *burqa* her mother would prefer she wear, a covering that conceals her figure, making her look like a water buffalo; p. 153.

52. My main tape-recorded interviews with Anjali Devi took place on June 22 and June 25, 2001, in her house in Banaras.

53. In *Culture in Action,* Derné's informants tell him that in order to keep honor—*izzat*—in the eyes of society, people should not engage in certain activities in front of others, such as drinking whiskey; one may do it in the privacy of the home, or even abroad, away from the watchful, and judgmental, eyes of elders; pp. 70–71.

54. Page 186.

55. Lahiri, "Hell-Heaven"; p. 73.

56. Handa, *Of Silk Saris and Mini-Skirts;* pp. 61–62.

57. The main tape-recorded interviews with Mathuri Chaubey took place on July 22, July 24, and September 8, 1996; on July 31, 2001; and on June 25, 2003.

4. Shopping for Clothes

1. The names of the *ghats* and other proper names in Banaras have many spellings; I have chosen to spell them as they are said, in an attempt to make them readable to an audience that is not familiar with the places. Parry's *Death in Banaras* details the cosmological and contemporary practices associated with the burning of dead bodies in the city. On pp. 24–26, he introduces the two main burning *ghats,* and recounts the famous story of Raja Harishchandra, after whom one of the *ghats* is named.

2. There are many versions of the story of the Ten Horse Sacrifice, all of which explain why the *ashwamedh* horse sacrifice was

multiplied by ten to appease the gods. Some written versions or references to the story can be found in: Lannoy, *Benares: A World Within a World,* pp. 211–212; Eck, *Banaras,* pp. 68, 152, 226; Singh and Rana, *Banaras Region,* p. 92.

3. Leslie, in "The Significance of Dress for the Orthodox Hindu Woman," discusses Sanskritic association between blouse wearing and class, including evidence from 1815 paintings which show women of high status depicted with bodices, those of middling status wearing no blouses but covering their breasts with their saris, and women of the lowest status leaving their breasts uncovered and exposed; p. 203. Lamb, in *White Saris and Sweet Mangoes,* talks about older women in Bengali villages who tie their saris around the waist, totally exposing their breasts, as they are not considered sexual anymore, and are allowed to subvert clothing and modesty norms that other women should follow; p. 204. Cohn, in "Cloth, Clothes and Colonialism," discusses a case in the early nineteenth century, in Tamil Nadu, of lower caste women not allowed to wear blouses or cover their chests in the company of Brahmins and other high status people; pp. 136–143. Mahmud, in "Methodology for the Study of Folk Costume of Bangladesh," says that sari blouses are new additions, coming to Bengal around the time the British arrived, and always associated with women of higher class.

4. Banerjee and Miller, *The Sari,* p. 24.

5. Lynton's book provides descriptions, illustrations, and photographs of most of these styles; further information can be found by looking at the descriptions of each region of India, or by looking at her index under "sari draping styles" on p. 207.

6. For a good treatment of the historical dimensions and contemporary variation within the *nivi* style, see Lynton, *The Sari,* including pp. 11 and 14, and the diagram on p. 15, which shows the stages of draping. Lynton, in her notes on p. 182, explains that Dongerkerry first used this term in the book

The Indian Sari, published in 1959. This style is becoming more popular, increasingly seen on politicians, television and movie actresses, and on models in product advertisements. Some village women still see it as a city style and find it pretentious, as stated by Banerjee and Miller, *The Sari,* pp. 102–103.

7. Lynton, *The Sari,* p. 14.

8. Another popular style I noticed worn by airline employees consisted of the sari tucked in below the belly button, a draping style seen on movie heroines. This was worn by women who were obviously unmarried (they wore no *sindur* or *bindi*). The very sexy attire seemed appropriate at the airport, as the audience of the body art consisted primarily of affluent people who can afford to travel by airplane.

9. This look, with the end of the sari tucked into the waist, implies a working status. The *hijra* character in Andrew Lloyd Webber and A. R. Rahman's musical, *Bombay Dreams,* wore her sari in this way throughout the performance to show her socioeconomic status.

10. The photographs in Banerjee and Miller, pp. 38–39, show some ways in which women use the *palloo* end of the sari.

11. Leslie, "The Significance of Dress for the Orthodox Hindu Woman," p. 204.

12. Tarlo, in *Clothing Matters,* explains that many village unmarried women opt to wear *salwar suits,* especially when attending university. She describes an incident where an unmarried girl, Leriben, has synthetic fabric *salwar suits* made for her, as her father wants her to look like an "educated girl." Other men in the village objected, believing that *salwar suits* are acceptable only on "Muslims or fancy city people"; pp. 185–186. Bhachu's book, *Dangerous Designs,* is devoted exclusively to the *salwar suit* fashion in India and especially abroad, including its appearance on Western elites such as the late Princess Diana and Cherie Booth, the wife of U.K. prime minister Tony Blair. On the theme of the diaspora, we see in Ali's *Brick Lane* that a *salwar suit* business becomes an economic salvation for immigrant Bangladeshi women in London, and Handa, in *Of Silk Saris and Mini-Skirts,* shows that the *salwar suit* is one of the ways in which young Indians in Canada visually express their heritage.

13. In their final chapter, titled "Modern Clothes," Banerjee and Miller discuss the importance of the *salwar suit;* pp. 238–253.

14. For a brief description of the construction of the *churidar pyjama,* see Bhandari, *Costume, Textiles and Jewellery of India,* pp. 109–110.

15. For a detailed description of the self-conscious clothing decisions made by Nehru, see Tarlo, *Clothing Matters,* chapter 4, especially pp. 108–125.

16. Jeffery, in *Frogs in a Well,* states that the Muslim women she studied consider the chiffon *dupatta* a vital part of the concealment of their bodies; without it, they feel naked; pp. 100–101. Rugh, in *Reveal and Conceal,* describes a form of outer wrap, called the *melaya liff,* which is made of slinky materials, provocatively clinging to the body, revealing more than it is concealing; p. 109. On pp. 146–147, Rugh talks about the inherent contradictions in the modesty garments, often tight and sexy, again, revealing an alluring body instead of concealing it from the male gaze.

17. For an exploration of both the advantages and disadvantages of the ready-to-wear clothes industry in the United States, see Joselit's *A Perfect Fit,* and Hollander's *Sex and Suits.*

18. While I visited Hemant and Parmanand often at their store and many times in their home, the main interviews took place on June 13 and June 23, 2001, and June 19 and June 28, 2003.

19. Magliocco's interview with neo-pagan henna artist Katya Madrid reveals a similar instinct to assess a customer's identity and lifecycle by reading what she is wearing and what she looks like; *Neo-Pagan Sacred Art and Altars,* p. 50.

20. Gillow and Barnard, in *Traditional Indian Textiles,* speculate that *chikan* embroidery from Lucknow is originally from Dhaka, Bangladesh, and so it might have been influenced by *jamdani* sari brocading; p. 119.

21. I have always heard this explanation, as *bandhana* is a common Hindi verb. Gillow and Barnard, in *Traditional Indian Textiles,* support this etymological claim, yet seem to stress the word's Sanskrit meaning, possibly implying to those who do not know, that *bandhana* is an ancient word rather than one common today as well; p. 92. Barnard, in his *Arts and Crafts of India* book, has a good description of the Rajasthani tie-dye method, pp. 128–129.

22. Bhachu, *Dangerous Designs.*

23. Lynton, in *The Sari,* gives an accessible, easy to follow explanation of each of these sari fabrics in her glossary, pp. 196–197.

24. Descriptions and photographs of many of these varieties of saris are found in sari survey books, such as Lynton's *The Sari* and Chishti's *Saris of India* and *Tradition and Beyond,* and in books about art and textiles of India, such as Gillow and Barnard's *Traditional Indian Textile,* Barnard's *Arts and Crafts of India,* Hacker and Turnbull's *Courtyard, Bazaar, Temple,* Askari and Arthur's *Uncut Cloth,* and Askari and Crill's *Colours of the Indus.* Folk art surveys of the different regions of India usually devote a section to the textile specialty of that place; examples are Krishna's *Arts and Crafts of Tamilnadu,* Nath and Wacziarg's *Arts and Crafts of Rajasthan,* and Sen's *Crafts of West Bengal.* In addition to traditional techniques, Banerjee and Miller look at computer-generated saris, p. 205.

25. This activity is well described in Bajwa's novel *The Sari Shop.*

26. Banerjee and Miller, *The Sari,* pp. 177–182.

27. The main tape-recorded interviews with Pinku Mookerjee took place at the Rinku Silk House on June 9 and June 21, 2001.

28. Glassie, *Turkish Traditional Art Today,* pp. 575–610, 647–683, 747–775.

5. Weaving Saris

1. The main tape-recorded interviews with Hashim Ansari took place on June 16, June 21, June 28, June 29, and July 28, 2001.

2. Mines and Lamb, in "Seven Prevalent Misconceptions about India's Caste System," p. 227, say that non-Hindus—Christians, Jains, Sikhs, Buddhists, and Muslims—all have some notion of a caste system.

3. Kumar, *The Artisans of Banaras.* See the section titled "The Identity of an Ansari," pp. 49–57.

4. A system that uses punch cards to select a pattern, the loom takes its name from J. M. Jacquard, who patented the device in 1804; Lynton, *The Sari,* p. 197.

5. See Barnard, *Arts and Crafts of India,* for a description and good photographs of Banarasi weavers; pp. 136–139.

6. These numbers correlate with Nita Kumar's speculation based on census reports between 1880 and 1980, which show a rise of weavers over the years. She says that only 15% of those involved in the sari trade are Hindus; *The Artisans of Banaras,* pp. 18–19.

7. For an elaboration on the importance of the skill, difficulty, and challenges of the dyeing process, see Barnard, *Arts and Crafts of India,* pp. 124–127, and Bhandari, *Costume, Textiles and Jewellery of India,* pp. 36–37.

8. For Kumar's version of what women of weaving families do, see *The Artisans of Banaras,* pp. 15–16.

9. To read more about the *rakhi,* or *raksha bandham,* celebration, see Freed and Freed, *Hindu Festivals in a North Indian Village,* pp. 250–256. A brief description of the practice, as well as photographs of *rakhi* ornaments, are found in Untracht, *Traditional Jewelry of India,* pp. 42–43.

10. See Grabar, "Patronage in Islamic Art."

11. To read more about the *jamdani* weaving process, see Glassie, *Art and Life in Bangladesh,* especially pp. 403–417. For further descriptions and photographs of *jamdani* saris, see Lynton's *The Sari,* pp. 45–47; Gillow and Barnard's *Traditional Indian Textiles,* pp. 119, 129, 140; Barnard's *Arts and Crafts of India,* pp. 138–139; Askari and Arthur's *Uncut Cloth,* pp. 30, 37; Sen's *Crafts of West Bengal,* pp. 65–81; and Jain and Aggarwala's *National Handicrafts and Handlooms Museum,* pp. 134–135.

12. Chishti, in her book *Tradition and Beyond,* illustrates *patola* saris by Chhotalal Salvi on pp. 45–49, and in the "Recollections" section, in which she interviews Martand Singh, there is information about the Salvi family and the saris they make; pp. 64–67.

13. De Bone's article "Patolu and Its Techniques," given to me by the Salvi brothers, succinctly explains the complicated process. The Salvi brothers have an excellent website (www.patanpatola.com) describing the history and process of their weaving and featuring photographs of their family and the awards they have won. For further descriptions and photographs of *patola* saris, see Lynton's *The Sari,* pp. 30–31; Chishti's *Tradition and Beyond,* pp. 40–50, 57–59; Gillow and Barnard's *Traditional Indian Textiles,* pp. 38–39, 88, 94–96, 99; Barnard's *Arts and Crafts of India,* pp. 133–134; Hacker and Turnbull's *Courtyard, Bazaar, Temple,* pp. 57–61; Askari and Arthur's *Uncut Cloth,* p. 27; and Jain and Aggarwala's *National Handicrafts and Handlooms Museum,* pp. 133, 143.

6. Making Jewelry

1. Untracht, *Traditional Jewelry of India,* p. 284.

2. My tape-recorded interview with Sandeep Singh took place on June 22, 1996.

3. For descriptions, and especially to see illustrations of ornaments with the beautiful Jaipur *mina* work, see Untracht, *Traditional Jewelry of India,* pp. 360–361; Stronge, Smith and Harle, *A Golden Treasury,* pp. 37–38; Keene, *Treasury of the World,* which illustrates enamel examples not specifically attributed to Jaipur, but some seem to be from there, pp. 62–85; and Nath and Wacziarg, *Arts and Crafts of Rajasthan,* pp. 92–97.

4. Some excellent folk art studies that handle the idea of craft workshops and the apprenticeship process include: Burrison's *Brothers in Clay,* especially the section on the Meaders Family; Hunt's *The Stonecarvers;* and Glassie's *The Spirit of Folk Art* and *Turkish Traditional Art Today.*

5. Untracht, *Traditional Jewelry of India;* Krishnan and Kumar, *Dance of the Peacock: Jewellery Traditions of India;* Stronge, Smith, and Harle, *A Golden Treasury: Jewellery from the Indian Subcontinent;* Barnard, *Arts and Crafts of India;* Jain and Aggarwala, *National Handicrafts and Handlooms Museum.*

6. For beautiful illustrations of this kind of bracelet, from both public and private collections, see Untracht, *Traditional Jewelry of India,* p. 270 (Rajastani bracelet in silver) and p. 363 (Banarasi enameled bracelet); Krishnan and Kumar's *Dance of the Peacock* has exquisite bracelets, some from Banaras and others from Rajasthan on pp. 128, 145, 245, and 246; Stronge, Smith, and Harle's *Golden Treasury* has a picture of a Rajasathani enameled bracelet on p. 90; Keene's *Treasury of the World* has illustrations of several bracelets on pp. 70 and 81; Brijbhushan, *Masterpieces of Indian Jewellery,* shows a close-up of the animal face, p. lxxxv; and Nath and Wacziarg's *Arts and Crafts of Rajasthan* shows a large illustration of one of these bracelets on p. 94.

7. The tape-recorded conversations with Chaman Lal and his family took place at their house on June 20, June 25, and July 26, 2001.

8. Krishnan and Kumar, *Dance of the Peacock,* p. 259. See also Untracht, *Traditional Jewelry of India,* p. 283, for a brief description of goldsmith guilds.

9. For more on the art of the goldsmith, including descriptions of different methods of crafting gold, see Untracht, *Traditional Jewelry of India,* pp. 282–303. Less informative descriptions can be found in Krishnan and Kumar, *Dance of the Peacock,* pp. 284–285; Barnard, *Arts and Crafts of India,* pp. 109–114; and Brijbhushan, *Masterpieces of Indian Jewellery,* pp. 31–39.

10. For additional references on the *kalam* tool in Bangladesh, India, Turkey, and Persia, see the note for pp. 399–402, which appear on p. 479 of Glassie's *Art and Life in Bangladesh.*

11. For examples of design catalogs similar to those owned by Chaman, see Krishnan and Kumar, *Dance of the Peacock,* pp. 266, 288, and 310. On p. 144 the authors illustrate a few pages from the album of J. B. Gentil, a Frenchman who was commissioned in the late eighteenth century to capture the popular jewelry types of that era. Gentil's paintings, held at the Victoria and Albert Museum, are also presented in Stronge, Smith, and Harle, *A Golden Treasury,* pp. 28–29. Photocopies of pages of sales and design catalogs, of private albums and those commissioned by the East India Company, circulate today to illustrate antique jewelry styles.

12. For a brief description and color photographs of stone setting, see Barnard, *Arts and Crafts of India,* pp. 112–113. A section titled "Varieties in Stone Settings," in Keene's *Treasury of the World,* reproduces jewelry with gemstones in the Al-Sabah collection in Kuwait; pp. 18–29.

13. Krishnan and Kumar, *Dance of the Peacock,* p. 270.

14. For further descriptions and photographs of the *kundan* process and individual pieces, see Untracht, *Traditional Jewelry of India,* pp. 364–367, and Krishnan and Kumar, *Dance of the Peacock,* pp. 274–276. This fine jewelry style has always been collected, and examples of *kundan* are found in some of the major collections of Indian jewelry, including the Victoria and Albert Museum

in London (illustrated in Stronge, Smith, and Harle's *A Golden Treasury*), Kuwait's Al-Sabah royal collection (in Keene's *Treasury of the World*), and New York's Metropolitan Museum of Art (a *kundan* necklace is illustrated in McConnell's *Metropolitan Jewelry,* p. 16).

15. For more on Tanjore paintings, see Krishna's *Arts and Crafts of Tamilnadu,* pp. 130–139, and especially Vyas and Daljeet's *Paintings of Tanjore and Mysore.*

16. For photographs and more description of Banarasi (pink) enamel, see Untracht, *Traditional Jewelry of India,* especially pp. 362–364. Krishnan and Kumar's *Dance of the Peacock,* has exquisite examples in color plates, on pp. 14, 182, 212, 214, and photos and description on pp. 276–278.

17. Krishnan and Kumar, *Dance of the Peacock,* p. 278.

18. Some people in Banaras told me about Babbu Singh. Chandramouli corroborates this in *Kashi* (although he calls the artist Babu Sinha), stating that *mina* work in the city today "appears to be in shambles"; p. 180. None of the jewelry books, including those by Untracht and by Krishnan and Kumar, state this particular fact.

19. Untracht, in *Traditional Jewelry of India,* supports the idea of a revival in the enameling craft of Banaras, p. 363.

20. For further descriptions of the *mina* process, see Untracht, *Traditional Jewelry of India,* pp. 357–366, and Krishnan and Kumar, *Dance of the Peacock,* pp. 276–280.

21. Although I met Gopal Prashad in 1996, the tape-recorded interviews that I use here took place on June 14, June 22, 2001, and June 24, 2003.

22. Untracht, in *Traditional Jewelry of India,* p. 362, addresses this paradox of *mina.* I will return to this topic, in an explicit exchange with local artisans and sellers, in chapter 7.

23. An interesting connection can be made between *paan* and jewelry. The cutters used to shave the areca nut and other betel

chewing paraphernalia, including spittoons, are often adorned, some even encrusted with precious gemstones, and displayed as ornaments in photographs and miniature paintings. See Brownrigg's *Betel Cutters* for a description of betel chewing, and for color plates showing the beauty of the cutters.

24. Many scholars writing about Banaras address the local philosophy of *masti,* of engaging in pleasurable activities. To read more about this, see Eck, *Banaras,* p. 304, Chandramouli, *Kashi,* pp. 201–213, and Kumar, *The Artisans of Banaras,* pp. 82, 99–100.

25. Although I met B. D. Soni in February 2001 and saw him again in June 2002, we spent about a week in Jaisalmer with him, during which the tape-recorded interviews that I use here took place, on July 6, July 7, July 8, July 10, and July 12, 2001.

26. To see examples of silver amulets from Rajasthan and Gujarat, see Untracht, *Traditional Jewelry of India,* pp. 97–102. For Rajasthani silver amulets, see Nath and Wacziarg, *Arts and Crafts of Rajasthan,* pp. 104–105.

7. Kanhaiya Lal

1. Although I spent much time at the Kanhaiya Lal store, and visited often, the main tape-recorded interviews with Shashi Shah took place at the store on April 17 and May 9, 1996. The interviews with Shantibhandra Shah quoted here took place at the store on June 28, 2001, and June 24, 2003.

2. In *Traditional Jewelry of India,* Untracht also describes the jewelry shops he has visited as having this same structure, p. 280.

3. To read more about the technique of making filigree jewelry, see Untracht, *Traditional Jewelry of India,* pp. 296–299.

4. Some items of jewelry suggest this use of reversing the necklace, or earring, and wearing it with the *mina* side out. A few illustrations in jewelry books also seem to support this notion, depicting the jewel with the *mina* side out. For examples of these, see Krishnan and Kumar's *Dance of the Peacock,*

pp. 270–271, and Keene's *Treasury of the World,* pp. 48, 51, and 52.

5. There is even the belief of ingesting gems, in powdered form, to cure health ailments. In Jain's book, *Occult Power of Gems,* there is a section titled "Gems and Diseases" that lists specific stones for specific health problems, pp. 82–87.

6. Rahu and Ketu were explained to me in Banaras as "imaginary planets," and so I use this term. Untracht, in *Traditional Jewelry of India,* refers to Rahu and Ketu as "ascending node" and "descending node" respectively. Although this sounds right, since I have never heard it articulated in this way, I am not sure if this is a regional understanding, or one commonly found throughout India. To read Untracht's descriptions of astrological rings, see pp. 304–311.

7. Untracht, *Traditional Jewelry of India,* p. 305.

8. To read more about this auspicious cluster of stones and to see illustrations of the stunning *nauratan* jewelry, see Untracht, *Traditional Jewelry of India,* pp. 304–311; Krishnan and Kumar, *Dance of the Peacock,* pp. 156, 221, 232, 250–254; Stronge, Smith, and Harle, *A Golden Treasury,* p. 89. For illustrations of two exquisite pieces in Kuwait's Al-Sabah collection, see Keene, *Treasury of the World,* pp. 41 and 85.

9. Sapphires are only unlucky for some people; many Hindu men and women wear sapphires. Outsiders to the tradition do not always understand the intricate system of gemology within Indian culture and generalize falsely about Indian attitudes toward gems. For instance, Klein, in his "novel thesis," *Jewelry Talks,* tells a fictional story while simultaneously telling the history of jewelry in the world, complete with footnotes. In a passage in which he describes a blue sapphire necklace made by Cartier for the Maharaja of Patna, Klein (incorrectly) points to the irony of it: it is considered Hindu, yet it has thirteen sapphires—"that would frighten any Hindu, taught to believe . . . [that] sapphires bring inexorable fortune"; p. 26.

10. The Freeds, in *Hindu Festivals in a North Indian Village,* say that the people of Shanti Nagar, where they did their fieldwork, buy new utensils and perhaps statues of Lakshmi and Krishna for the family *puja,* p. 95.

11. Untracht also states that among agricultural communities, the marriage season is linked to successful harvests; *Traditional Jewelry of India,* p. 280.

12. Roy, *Bengali Women,* p. 8.

13. To sample the immense aesthetic and regional varieties in bridal ornaments, see Untracht's comprehensive survey of Indian jewelry, especially the section titled "Marriage and Jewelry," pp. 156–191.

14. Lamb, in *White Saris and Sweet Mangoes,* describes the heartbreaking reality of one's daughter becoming part of another's family—although she emerges out of one's own womb, she will belong to another family and another lineage; pp. 84–87.

15. A recently divorced character in Kavita Daswani's novel, *The Village Bride of Beverly Hills,* announces to her mother: "They kept whatever jewelry you gave me . . . When I first got there, they got me a safe in the bank, but didn't let me put my name on it. I was stupid and agreed. When I left, they kept it all"; p. 247.

16. For a folkloristic analysis of "bigness" as an aesthetic criterion for songs, stories, and food, see Goldstein, "Notes toward a European-American Folk Aesthetic."

17. Gilbertson, in "To Ward Off Evil" writes about the Norwegian traditional practice of wearing metals—shiny things—to ward off evil spirits, particularly the *hundrefolk,* underground beings who abduct adults and babies. She states that infants during baptisms and brides during weddings are particularly susceptible since both are vulnerable to evil during this transition between two life stages. The beliefs that rites of passage are times when people should be protected, and that shiny things reflects evil away from the wearer, are also found in India.

18. Dubin, in her excellent book, *North American Indian Jewelry and Adornment,* says that the Navajo Indians would often pawn their silver and turquoise jewelry, and in the spring and fall, after shearing their sheep, would buy back their jewelry with the wool, and thus, like the village people of India, engage in a seasonal cycle, p. 517.

19. Underhill, *Why We Buy,* pp. 152–153.

20. In Untracht's description of jewelry store styles, he states that more sophisticated stores provide showroom displays of jewelry, and benches, so that the customers can sit away from the floor; p. 280.

8. Shopping along the Vishvanath Gali

1. Eck translates the Sanskrit "Vishvanath" in this way: *vishva* meaning "all" and *nath* meaning "lord," so Vishvanath is the Lord or Master of us all. The essence of both translations—Eck's and Yadav's—imply the same thing; *Banaras,* p. 120.

2. To read a brief sketch of this history, see Singh's *Banaras Region,* pp. 124–126, and Eck's *Banaras,* pp. 120, 127, 131–135.

3. For more on the painted wooden statues of Banaras, see Jain and Aggarwala, *National Handicrafts and Handlooms Museum,* pp. 192–196, 202; and Bussabarger and Robins' *The Everyday Art of India,* pp. 143, 144–145.

4. Untracht, in *Traditional Jewelry of India,* illustrates ornaments for Krishna, including his characteristic peacock feather headpiece; p. 46.

5. For illustrations and a description of these kinds of clothing and especially jewelry, see the section titled "Theatrical Jewelry" in Untracht's *Traditional Jewelry of India,* pp. 196–201.

6. For photographs of *rukdraksh* ornaments, both simple and ornate, see Untracht, *Traditional Jewelry of India,* pp. 24, 39, and 49; and Jain and Aggarwala, *National Handicrafts and Handlooms Museum,* p. 63.

7. For a beautiful photograph of a follower of Vishnu wearing ten *tulsi* beaded necklaces—one for each of Vishnu's avatars—see Untracht, *Traditional Jewelry of India,* p. 25. To read about the significance of *tulsi* and its link with Vishnu, see Narayan, "*Tulsi* (Basil)."

8. Underhill, in *Why We Buy,* says that shopping has always been the primary venue through which women engage in public life, often unaccompanied by their husbands; p. 114.

9. Urvashi Bandhu, in her *Beauty Tips for a Glowing Personality,* devotes one chapter to the *bindi.* She states that *bindis* should be chosen by careful consideration of the size of the forehead and the thickness of the eyebrows, and that they should match the woman's complexion. According to her expert opinion, red or maroon *bindi* looks good on a "wheatish complexion," a dark brown *bindi* on a "slightly dark complexion," while fair-skinned women may wear any color *bindi,* although, "of course, a dark colour would be exceptionally striking." She ends by giving her advice on suitable combinations of *bindi* and clothes, telling the reader which *bindi* colors "vibe well" with outfit colors; pp. 26–27.

10. The tape-recorded interview with Priya Upahar took place on August 8, 1996.

11. Divakaruni, *The Vine of Desire,* p. 184.

12. Underhill's extensive observation of shopping patterns in the United States confirms Priya's own observation. Underhill states, in *Why We Buy,* p. 102, that women spend more time shopping when they are with other women than they do when they are with their children or husbands. He says that women shopping by themselves spend less time than they do when they are with their children, but this discrepancy is probably a result of the nature of the shopping observed. Many of Underhill's observations take place in supermarkets, where the children's input is taken into account, as opposed to a jewelry store, where they are bored and nag their mothers to leave.

9. Assembling Bangle Sets

1. References to this small sculpture can be found in survey books about Indian art and books about Indian jewelry, such as Craven's *Indian Art,* p. 20, and Untracht's *Traditional Jewelry of India,* p. 172. To read a brief overview of bangles in prehistoric India, including a description of materials and varieties from 7000 BCE through the present, see Kenoyer's "Bangles."

2. My main interviews with the Gupta Brothers took place on June 24, June 27, and July 18, 1996.

3. Glassie's interviews with conch bangle makers in Bangladesh reveals that they are worn by Hindu married women because in mythic time Shiva gave the first pair of conch shell bangles to his wife Parvati; *Art and Life in Bangladesh,* p. 311. To read more about the bangles and the religious symbolism of the conch shell, see *Art and Life in Bangladesh,* pp. 308–313, and the notes for pp. 308–311, which appear on p. 475, in which additional sources for the bangles are listed, including the writings of James Hornell.

4. Non-Bengalis recognize a Bengali married woman by her red and white bangles. But inside the group, iron bangles are also of significance, and equally important. The presence of this would communicate auspicious marital bliss only to those on the inside, while the red and white ones signal Bengaliness to outsiders. To read more about the significance of iron bangles, see Fruzzetti, *The Gift of a Virgin,* pp. 92–93.

5. A website that provides Indian things (www.cooldesistuff.com) through the internet to international customers has bangles for sale from Bombay Fashions. Many of their bangles, including the monochrome ones, are sold in the 2.10 and bigger sizes, while others such as the "Devdas Jhumar"

varieties come in smaller sizes, presumably to fit the slender hands of the Indian women for whom these trendy bangles are available.

6. To read more about this, see the section titled "Colour Symbolism" in Bhandari's *Costume, Textiles and Jewellery of India,* pp. 42–43.

7. Although I had met the Manik brothers during my fieldtrip in 1996, the main interviews used here took place at their house on June 19 and June 28, 2001, and June 26, 2003.

8. To read more about bangles from the specific regions of India, see Untracht's *Traditional Jewelry of India*, the section titled "The Bangle," pp. 172–187.

9. Eck describes the common pilgrimage route, one in which the pilgrim walks the length of the old city through the *ghats,* stopping along the way for a dip in the Ganga and *darshan* of various deities, then the pilgrim takes his final bath in the Ganges, and as a climax, goes to take *darshan* at the Vishvanath Golden Temple; *Banaras,* pp. 220–232. Gomez ("Gol"), in his comic book style narrative titled *A Pilgrimage to Kashi,* illustrates a Bombay family's visit to the sacred city.

10. In Bajwa's novel, *The Sari Shop,* the main character's mother kept a fast for Shiva as an unmarried young woman, which insured her a good husband. Now, afraid of annoying Shiva, the mother continues the fast every Monday, taking sweets and flowers to a Shiva temple in Amristar; p. 43.

11. My main interviews with Anand Kumar all took place at the store, on June 11, June 19, June 27, 2001, and June 20, 2003.

12. For more on the making of glass bangles, see Untracht's *Traditional Jewelry of India,* pp. 182–186.

13. Katherine Forgacs observed and interviewed makeup artists at the Esteé Lauder makeup counter for a project for a graduate fieldwork class I taught in the spring of 2004. She learned that the makeup artists were taught to "translate" the "hottest" Hol-lywood looks into something their customers could wear. Their aim was to teach women not only how to apply the makeup, but also how to deal with "concerns": wrinkles, dark circles under the eyes, sun damage, or skin blemishes.

14. Audiocassettes and now CDs of the songs of the movie go on sale about two months before the release of the film. Montages of the scenes of the film are shown on television, giving women a chance to see the costumes and jewelry of the heroines and preview the upcoming fashion trends; Dywer and Patel, *Cinema India,* p. 32.

15. Dywer and Patel, in *Cinema India,* acknowledge Rekha's influence on styles of makeup and clothing—especially the low-cut "Rekha blouse," p. 97.

16. Dwyer and Patel's analysis of the costumes of Hindi films reveals the visual communication Bollywood stylists wish to convey with their careful selection of clothes and jewelry, meant to display the characters' attributes, lifestyles, and morality; *Cinema India,* pp. 81–100, especially p. 87.

10. Nina Khanchandani

1. The main tape-recorded interviews with Nina Khanchandani took place on June 18, July 27, and July 30, 2001, and on June 19 and June 28, 2003.

2. Leslie, in *The Perfect Wife,* her translation of Sanskrit religious law from the eighteenth century, states that a devoted wife, one who wishes her husband to live long, should wear, among other things: *sindur, bindi,* kohl eyeliner, and auspicious ornaments of marriage on the neck, ears, and hands; p. 96.

3. Fruzzetti, in *The Gift of a Virgin,* describes that the avoidance between a young wife and her male in-laws (and her mother-in-law) has do with a sense of shame associated with the fact that the woman has sexual relations with the son of the house, a necessity for procreation, but an embarrassing

activity nonetheless; p. 14. Tarlo observes the practice of veiling among Gujarati village women, showing nuanced contextual uses of the *ghunghat; Clothing Matters,* pp. 160–166.

4. Joshi, in his article "Continuity and Change in Hindu Women's Dress" describes the importance of garments as gifts, especially to married women; pp. 223–225.

5. The Teej and Karva Chauth festivals are practiced with much variation throughout north India. Generally speaking, the festivals are meant to demonstrate a wife's devotion to her husband through fasting, and they publicly celebrate the idea of marital bliss. In these festive occasions, women swing together, paint their hands with henna, and wear new clothes and bangles. To read more about these festivals, see Freed and Freed, *Hindu Festivals in a North Indian Village,* pp. 63–76 for Karva Chauth and pp. 241–250 for Teej.

6. Indian people of both genders and of all ages feel much pride in the fact that their women are recognized internationally for being beautiful. Some works that examine the largely positive attitudes toward the beauty pageant winners and their influence on feminine beauty are Anand's *The Beauty Game,* and two articles by Parameswaran: "Global Media Events in India" and "Global Queens, National Celebrities."

11. Neelam Chaturvedi

1. The tape-recorded interviews with Neelam Chaturvedi took place on April 8, July 13, July 20, and August 4, 1996, at her house in Banaras, and on July 4, 2003, in her new house in Jaipur, Rajasthan.

2. Wolpert, *A New History of India,* p. 348.

3. For example, Lynch's examination of African American debutante balls in the American Midwest shows a desire on the part of the women to appear proper and virtuous. Their mothers want to protect the virtue of the young women by not allowing them to be overly made up and therefore overly sexy. Lynch explains that this has been the case since slave times, when African American mothers tried to protect their vulnerable daughters from the master and his sons; *Dress, Gender and Cultural Change,* p. 94.

4. Many children grow up hearing war stories from their parents, some even experiencing these events firsthand. The horrific experiences are sometimes used to justify the restrictions on the child's behavior, including body presentation, as shown in Satrapi's memoir of the Iranian Revolution, *Persepolis.* The theme of innocent people carrying poison with them, allowing them to kill themselves before being captured, is not only part of the partition story of India and Pakistan, but also appears in holocaust narratives, an episode recounted in Spiegelman's *Maus,* p. 109. Some parents choose not to emphasize the events and memories of war, sparing the next generation the tragic details. Many children in Banaras today have no idea of the massacres and hate crimes that took place in 1947 against Muslims, Hindus, and Sikhs, as demonstrated by Kumar's interviews with young school children in Banaras; "Why Do Hindus and Muslims Fight? Children and History in India," p. 345.

5. Wedding ceremonies are associated with innocent fun for young children, especially girls, who do not yet experience the anxiety and fear that their own weddings might one day entail. Parvati, a small child in Kapur's novel, *Difficult Daughters,* has only positive associations with her sisters' weddings, for these include new clothes, good food, henna on her hands, and a house full of guests; p. 222. A children's book, English's *Nadia's Hands,* likewise, shows the delight of a young Pakistani-American girl participating in a marriage, and wearing henna on her hands.

6. This episode between the sari seller, Ramchand, and the professor, Mrs. Sachdeva, can be found on p. 28. Mrs. Sachdeva ap-

pears at the house of her rich pupil in professional attire, this time wearing a "muted rust and beige sari and a thin string of pearls." Although looking dignified, in the style of a teacher, the affluent woman whose house she has gone to views Mrs. Sachdeva as belonging to the "ordinary, professor-type, service-class women"; p. 91.

7. The Savannah College of Art and Design, in Savannah, Georgia, for example, posts on their online faculty handbook guidelines for "appearance and proper attire" in which they specify that no casual, dirty, revealing, or tight clothes are allowed for professors of either gender. Brigham Young University, in Provo, Utah, mandates that their student body adhere to an "educational system honor code" that is consistent with the principles of the Church of Jesus Christ of Latter-day Saints. Men should be clean-shaven, "avoiding extreme styles or colors," while women should stay away from clothing that is sleeveless, backless, or revealing, and from dresses and skirts with a hem above the knee.

8. Banerjee and Miller, *The Sari*, p. 67.

9. Appadurai, "How to Make a National Cuisine," p. 9.

12. Mukta Tripathi

1. The main tape-recorded conversations with Mukta Tripathi took place on May 8, May 10, and May 11, 1996, and on June 19 and June 28, 2003.

2. Facial scrubs made of chickpea flour are common in India, considered to be part of an indigenous Ayurvedic beauty system. Women learn the beauty recipes like the one Mukta uses from family members or from books such as Sachs's *Ayurvedic Beauty Care*, locally published by Motilal Banarsidass Publishers and readily available in Banaras' bookstores.

3. Wadley, "One Straw from a Broom Cannot Sweep," pp. 13–14.

4. Leslie, "The Significance of Dress for the Orthodox Hindu Woman," p. 207, and *The Perfect Wife*, p. 291.

5. For a brief discussion of flowers as personal adornment, including flowers strung together as garlands to be worn for weddings, or by deities and dignitaries, see Untracht, *Traditional Jewelry of India*, pp. 30–33.

6. The theme of food as a source of self-esteem and as a venue for expression of the self is found in a few works of contemporary Indian fiction. In Divakaruni's short story "Affair," the main character, Abha, an efficient cook, senses that her marriage is about to fall apart, and retreats "to the kitchen with its shiny rows of canisters, its racks of spices all carefully labeled, its gleaming tiles and faucets that usually made me feel sane and in control"; p. 233. In Malladi's *Serving Crazy with Curry*, the main character recuperates from a failed suicide attempt by not speaking, and cooking instead, communicating to her family through the food she makes. In Shamsie's novel, *Salt and Saffron*, a character, Miriam, does not speak either, but she communicates her emotions not through the cooking of elaborate dishes, like the previously mentioned women, but rather through the conception of wonderful combinations of dishes into artful meals, which are then prepared by the hired cook.

7. Glassie, in *The Spirit of Folk Art*, works toward a deep definition of art—defined by medium, process, or function—arriving at the conclusion that art is concentration, commitment, and passion; pp. 86–88. To read the argument in its entirety, see the section titled "Art," pp. 36–88.

8. Fruzzetti, in her ethnography, *The Gift of a Virgin*, describes a typical day in the life of a married Hindu woman, showing how little free time women have, especially those who live in joint-family households; pp. 100–101. By completing her household chores in the afternoon, a time when wives rest, Mukta is able to manipulate her free

time in order to spend time with her husband when he returns from work.

9. Radner and Lanser, "Strategies of Coding in Women's Cultures," p. 3.

10. Kapur, *Difficult Daughters*, p. 230. Tarlo, in *Clothing Matters*, notes how women communicate their wishes to the men of their households by taking control of their own bodies—by starving, by not speaking, or even by withdrawing sexual pleasures; p. 189.

11. Nair, *Ladies Coupé*, pp. 52–53. To read more about the *kolam* threshold designs, see Nagarajan's "Hosting the Divine" and Huyler's "Creating Sacred Spaces."

12. Radner and Lanser, "Strategies of Coding in Women's Cultures," pp. 11–13.

13. After the Wedding

1. Roy, in *Bengali Women*, explains the psychological dimension of older women's rationale for not being as decorated as they were when they were younger. Older women feel that there is no need to be ornamented anymore as they are beyond the desire and lust of their husbands, and people in their social circles will criticize and make fun of them for still paying attention to their appearances; pp. 131–132. In *White Saris and Sweet Mangoes*, Lamb describes the change in adornment for older, post-menopausal women, who stop wearing fancy saris and jewelry, perfume and hair ribbons. Her older informants told her that they feel they no longer need to display their physical attractiveness, so they relax into a plainer look comprised of white cotton saris and minimum jewelry; p. 201. Jeffery's fieldwork among Muslim women in New Delhi, presented in *Frogs in a Well*, shows that Muslim women also feel that they should stop wearing makeup, satin saris, and bright colors when their daughters reach puberty, when their daughters-in-law start arriving, and especially when they have become widows; p. 107.

2. To read an overview of the kinds of life cycle rituals celebrated in South Asia,

see Hanchett, "Life Cycle Rituals." She concludes her article with a useful bibliography. Indian objects depicting and celebrating rites of passages illustrate the catalog *Aditi: The Living Arts of India*, which accompanied the impressive exhibition "Aditi—A Celebration of Life" at the National Museum of Natural History, Smithsonian Institution, in 1985.

3. Basham, in *The Wonder That Was India*, explains in greater detail each of these stages, pp. 159–171.

4. Nabar, *Caste as Woman*, p. 41.

5. Parry, *Death in Banaras*, p. 157. Another example of the connection between marriage and death comes from Fruzzetti's account of the rituals a widow undergoes. With a bath, both widow and bride leave behind a stage in life. Likewise, the bride's father or brother gives her first set of marriage clothes, and her first set of widow's clothing. Fruzzetti explains that the two stages—marriage and widowhood—mark the beginning and end of the union between male and female; *The Gift of a Virgin*, p. 105.

6. Fruzzetti, *The Gift of a Virgin*, p. 117.

7. Nabar in *Caste as Woman*, and Deen in *Broken Bangles*; see endnote 17 in chapter 1.

8. Basham briefly explains that divorce has always been prohibited by Sanskrit religious law, but that custom allowed for certain classes of people to get divorced; *The Wonder That Was India*, pp. 173–174.

9. Mukherjee, "The Tenant," p. 108, in *The Middleman and Other Stories*. In Mukherjee's novel *Desirable Daughters*, the lead character, Tara Bhattacharjee, a divorced woman, explains that all Indian men, especially the married ones, find divorced women loose, available, and "extra attractive." Soon after her divorce, many of her husband's friends arrive, alone, at her house, hoping to sleep with her; pp. 188–189. The perception of divorced women as sexually available is not restricted to Indian culture, but found in other Asian and Middle Eastern places as well. Satrapi's memoir, *Persepolis 2*, tells of a recently divorced woman in

Iran, who "from the minute she had the title of divorced woman, the butcher, the pastry chef, the baker, the fruit and vegetable seller, the itinerant cigarette seller, even beggars in the street, all made it clear they'd like to sleep with her"; p. 178.

10. Leslie, *The Perfect Wife,* p. 303.

11. Nabar recounts her own father's wish, at the last stages of his fatal illness, that his wife die before him, so she would not know the "pain and unjust horror of Indian widowhood"; *Caste as Woman,* p. 144.

12. Indians are not the only ones who feel that jeans should be in the domain of young people. An article in the *New York Times* "Sunday Styles" section on Camilla Parker Bowles, just before her marriage to Prince Charles, reported the uproar among British style watchers, who were appalled that the 57-year-old would wear jeans in public. British newspapers carried such comments as "Jeans are a young person's garment," and "Wearing jeans past a certain age just isn't *done*" (April 3, 2005, p. 11, emphasis in original).

13. Friedan, *The Feminine Mystique,* chapter 1, pp. 15–32.

14. Wadley, in speaking about joint family households, explains that balance in the family is maintained by young people showing respect to the elders; sons should respect their parents, and more importantly, daughters-in-law, regardless of age and status, must obey the wishes of their mothers-in-law regarding household responsibilities, such as food preparation; "One Straw from a Broom Cannot Sweep," pp. 16–17. Mathur Jaffrey's new memoir, *Climbing the Mango Trees,* recounts in detail the pleasures and also the frustrations of living in a large joint-family household. She describes well the freedom that her nuclear family, and especially her parents, experienced when they lived in Kanpur, away from the family home in Delhi.

15. The main tape-recorded interviews with Mathuri Chaubey took place on July 22, July 24, and September 8, 1996; on July 31, 2001; and on June 25, 2003.

16. Kinsmen of the deceased shave their heads, armpits, and mustaches on the occasion of the ritual mourning of the dead, as Lamb demonstrates in *White Saris and Sweet Mangoes,* p. 171; for a detailed explanation of the ritual shaving of the head, especially of the chief mourner, see Parry's *Death in Banaras,* pp. 76, 94, 187, 197.

17. Wadley's "One Straw from a Broom Cannot Sweep," Tarlo's *Clothing Matters,* Lamb's *White Saris and Sweet Mangoes,* and Fruzzetti's *The Gift of the Virgin,* are all excellent studies that show the inherent tensions in the relationship between a mother-in-law and her daughter-in-law in different parts of India. The difficult relationship between these two categories of women is often used as a literary theme in the fiction of Indian authors, both male and female. For example, in Jha's *The Blue Bedspread,* four co-workers compare horror stories about their mothers-in-law, each hoping to show how terrible her own situation is; pp. 128–132.

18. According to a system of classification derived from Ayurvedic medicine, foods are either "hot" or "cold." The specifics of this system vary with region; certain items, such as wheat, lentils, and papayas, might be considered "hot" in one region and "cold" in another. To read more about this, see Sen, *Food Culture in India,* pp. 161, 175; Collingham, *Curry,* pp. 7–9; Ray, *The Migrant's Table,* pp. 22–29.

19. Leslie explains in *The Perfect Wife,* that these practices are prescribed by Sanskrit religious law; pp. 298–304. Lamb, in *White Saris and Sweet Mangoes,* shows that by restricting their appearances, diets, and behavior, certain women—those who have just given birth, those who have entered puberty, and widows—"cool" their bodies as a way of controlling their sexuality; p. 193. Weinberger-Thomas explains in *Ashes of Immortality* that long hair has sexual associations, so a widow should represent her post-sex stage by shaving her head; p. 143.

20. Parry, in his comprehensive study of death rituals, explains that there are gendered expressions of grief and mourning;

each gender plays a different role in the death and funerary rites of a deceased person (pp. 152–158). There are personal interpretations for these gendered behaviors. For example, Neelam Chaturvedi told me that women do not accompany the corpse to the funeral pyre because women are associated with life—by giving birth—and should not witness death.

21. Anthropological works that describe this ritual include Parry's *Death in Banaras,* Lamb's *White Saris and Sweet Mangoes,* and Fruzzetti's *The Gift of a Virgin.* The dramatic ritual is powerfully rendered in works of literature, such as Divakaruni's short story "Clothes" in *Arranged Marriage,* Lahiri's *The Namesake,* Mukherjee's story "The Management of Grief" in *The Middleman and Other Stories,* Kapur's *Difficult Daughters,* Nair's *Ladies Coupé,* Mehta's *Inside the Haveli,* and Kamdar's *Motila's Tattoos.*

22. Nair, *Ladies Coupé,* p. 4.

23. Lamb, *White Saris and Sweet Mangoes,* p. 204.

24. Lamb explains the belief that a widow, especially a young widow, is seen as a woman whose sexuality has been activated by a man, but who now has no outlet for that sexual energy, so she is seen as promiscuous. Lamb notes that the slang word *randi,* to mean "slut," is also used for both "widow" and "prostitute"; p. 221. See also Weinberger-Thomas, pp. 146–147.

25. Lamb, *White Saris and Sweet Mangoes;* pp. 220–229.

26. Fruzzetti, *The Gift of a Virgin,* p. 13.

27. To read more about the controversial sacrifice/murder of Roop Kanwar in Deorala, Rajasthan, see Hawley's edited volume *Sati,* containing many scholarly essays on this *sati* case, Bumiller's journalistic account, in *May You Be the Mother of a Hundred Sons,* pp. 62–74; and chapter 11, "The Agitation Against Sati," in Kumar's *The History of Doing.*

28. Leslie, in *The Perfect Wife,* says that according to Sanskrit religious duty, one way to avoid misbehavior as a widow is to end your life, keeping your virtue and your husband's honor intact; pp. 298–304. Nan-

dy explains in "Sati: A Nineteenth-Century Tale of Women, Violence and Protest," that, according to the pro-*sati* literature, widows were believed to "stray from the path of virtue" in the absence of their husbands' guiding presence, and so *sati* was "an enforced penance, a death penalty through which the widow expiated her responsibility for her husband's death"; pp. 9–10.

29. Hawley explains in the introduction to his anthology on *sati* that killing oneself before one's husband is cremated is one way to avoid becoming a widow; p. 13. For discussion of *sati* in colonial times, see Mani's "Contentious Traditions." Many of the essays in Chakravarti and Gill's *Shadow Lives* expand on the terrible position of widows in India. Deepa Mehta's new film, *Water,* is a fictional, historical account of widows in Banaras (the local government did not allow her to film it in Banaras; it was shot in Sri Lanka instead). While the movie depicts the terrible situation of a widow in India, it distorts the reality to an extent, reinforcing negative stereotypes about India, showing that the mistreatment of widows and the sexual assault on children are both sanctioned by ancient Sanskrit law and tradition. Mira Nair's film *Monsoon Wedding,* on the other hand, also deals with the topic of the sexual abuse of children but treats it as an aberration, a practice not condoned by Indian tradition or culture. To read a critical analysis of Mehta's *Water,* see Katrak's "Still Waters Run Deep."

30. Hawley, *Sati,* pp. 11–15.

31. Weinberger-Thomas, *Ashes of Immortality,* pp. 11–21, 119–133.

32. Parry argues, in *Death in Banaras,* that the high-caste widow, who is socially bound to her late husband, is "herself half dead"; p. 157. Leslie, in *The Perfect Wife,* translates Sanskrit religious law as stating that a widow should "willingly mortify her body, living on flowers, roots and fruits"; p. 299, and also Chakravarti and Gill, *Shadow Lives,* p. 41. Lamb, in *White Saris and Sweet Mangoes,* depicts on a chart a man and a woman as single,

married, and widowed. While each start out as a half circle, they are joined together as a full circle in marriage, and subsequently, the widower returns to the state where he was before marriage, while the widow remains forever attached to the missing half—her dead husband; p. 232. Fruzzetti explains, in *The Gift of a Virgin,* that when a woman marries a man, he gives her the symbols of marriage—bangles, *sindur*—which are taken away when he dies. The woman, in turn, gives her husband her sexuality, her reproductive power, her femaleness, which are not returned when her husband dies; these are lost forever, causing a part of her to be symbolically dead; p. 103.

33. Mrs. Gandhi's influence ranged from her political display of homespun cotton saris, as shown in Tarlo's *Clothing Matters,* pp. 109, 123, 125, 322, and her savvy fashion sense, as shown by Banerjee and Miller in *The Sari,* pp. 128–129, 198, 219–222. Banerjee and Miller point out in their book that Indira Gandhi, shortly after becoming a widow, wore a white sari for three years, from 1961–1964; p. 138. Mrs. Gandhi became India's first female prime minister in 1966. Bumiller, in *May You Be the Mother of a Hundred Sons,* reports that Indians viewed Indira Gandhi as "the epitome of style, an elegant, immaculately groomed woman whose silk saris were the envy of all the society matrons in town"; p. 150.

34. Red, yellow, and pink are associated with "happiness, prosperity, and passion"; see the section titled "Sexual Coloring" in Weinberger-Thomas' *Ashes of Immortality,* pp. 24–28.

35. Banerji, *Pather Panchali.*

36. Nabar recounts in *Caste as Woman* the common blessing that older women bestow upon younger women: "May you be a *sowbhagyavati*"; p. 151.

37. Bhandari explains the Rajasthani "ritual of the turban" on page 115; she describes turbans on pp. 113–116.

38. A woman whose husband has passed away but whose son is alive is considered "half a widow"; Weinberger-Thomas, pp. 132, 252.

14. Before the Wedding

1. Kamdar, *Motiba's Tattoos,* p. 28.

2. Jeffery, in the introduction to her book *Frogs in a Well,* explains the interpretations of *purdah* by Muslims and Hindus. She states, for example, that differences occur in the age and marital status of the girl to be veiled, in the rules about which males she should observe *purdah* around, and what garments she should use to conceal herself. There are similarities among Hindus and Muslims, as Jeffery points out, namely in the practice of restricting the girls' movements after puberty, prescriptions on some concealment of the female body, and keeping boys and girls separated; p. 3.

3. Ali, *Brick Lane,* p. 107.

4. Lahiri, *Interpreter of Maladies,* p. 159. Goffman, through his study of mental patients, observes that one way people recognize an "oncoming psychosis" is through a person's disregard of her or his appearance and hygiene, ceasing to adhere to societal norms about respectable "personal front"—the conscious management of one's appearance; *Behavior in Public Places,* pp. 25–27.

5. This tape-recorded interview took place on July 8, 2001.

6. In Jeffery's *Frogs in a Well,* Muslim women living in New Delhi explain their demure dress as a consequence of *sharam* and criticize the inappropriate and sexy dress of foreign women as representing *besharam,* shamelessness; pp. 107–110. Although clad in *burqas* while out on the public streets, these women are also targets of "eve teasing"; pp. 154–155.

7. This tape-recorded interview took place on August 7, 1996.

8. Rugh, *Reveal and Conceal,* p. 134.

9. The change in a woman is made more dramatic in certain traditions, in which the bride, just before the wedding day, is given

oil massages, her hair and body kept dirty. She is clothed in old things until the glorious moment of the wedding, when she has a ritual bath and changes into magnificent dress. Sidwa describes this transformation of a young bride, who is kept dirty for a whole week "the better to bloom, bathed and perfumed, swathed in red silks, hair, throat and arms aglow with jewels, on the day of the wedding"; *The Bride,* p. 90.

10. Anand, *The Beauty Game,* pp. 156–157.

11. For more on how Bollywood actresses embody an idealized female beauty, see Dwyer and Patel's *Cinema India,* pp. 20 and 32.

12. Anthropologist Lamb describes how the people of the village where she did fieldwork disapproved of her "open" hair, causing her to tie it up; *White Saris and Sweet Mangoes,* p. 193. Similarly, whenever I wore my hair loose, especially in Banaras, men on the streets could comment, saying "Bombay" to me, implying that Bollywood actresses are the ones that wear their hair "open," even though many of the images of Hindu goddesses show them with their hair loose, falling on their backs and shoulders.

13. Leslie, in *The Perfect Wife,* explains that, according to Sanskrit religious law, a married woman must line her eyes with kohl (collyrium) as a sign of *suhagin,* wifely ornamentation; p. 96. The text continues, stating that since eyes that are lined with kohl are attractive—the kohl makes the eyes look bigger and the woman more beautiful—this practice is forbidden for women who are menstruating, whose husbands are away, or who are widows; p. 97.

14. Anand, *The Beauty Game,* p. 122. Anand elaborates that dark-skinned women may model certain products, such as contact lenses, but never cosmetics, since cosmetic companies do not want to be endorsed by a dark-skinned person; p. 125.

15. For a discussion of whitening products, see Anand, *The Beauty Game,* pp. 125–129, and pp. 149 and 179 for testimonials by women who believe the cream gives

them lighter skin. A preoccupation with skin color is a theme in many Indian novels. In Jha's *The Blue Bedspread,* the narrator's dark-skinned sister uses Fair and Lovely cream without positive results until her husband suggests that they wait for a more effective product; p. 103. The protagonist, Anju, in Daswani's novel *For Matrimonial Purposes,* is single and desperate to get married. She is spotted at a family wedding, where it is observed that she "had nice features, but was a little on the dark side," prompting her aunt to immediately send over a jar of "Promise of Fairness" cream; p. 38. When Anju returns to Bombay after spending time in New York, she is determined to return to her hometown "at least two shades fairer" to impress her old friends. In the absence of a fairness cream in New York, she reverts to the traditional face cream made of chickpea flour and lemon juice; p. 154.

16. During an interview with reporter Bumiller, the Bollywood superstar Rekha recounted how she lost weight by exercising to Jane Fonda's workout videos, losing her voluptuous figure, which she referred to as "a round ball of flesh"; *May You Be the Mother of a Hundred Sons,* p. 187. In *Cinema India,* Dwyer and Patel describe how different body types are used to portray different roles: former models, toned and thin, are cast as Westernized, modern women, while curvaceous actresses with big hips and breasts are cast to play "traditional roles"; p. 84.

17. In an interview taped in India but broadcast on America's National Public Radio on April 8, 2004, Jaina Doctor, a teacher of "art of living" in Bombay, says that while Indian women wanted to "be voluptuous and to be curvaceous," today they want to look like Western models, "skinny and tall and long-legged."

18. Anand, *The Beauty Game,* p. 143.

19. Much of Anand's discussion of contemporary Indian beauty in her book *The Beauty Game,* focuses on the pageant winners and their influence.

20. To read about the protest, and the

threat of self-immolation by feminists during the pageant, see Russell's "Miss World Comes to India" and especially Parameswaran's "Global Media Events in India."

21. Gossip film magazines, launched in the 1970s, provided women with an arena to talk about female sexuality by discussing stars' off screen sexual exploits; Dwyer and Patel, *Cinema India*, p. 33.

22. Nagrath's review of India Fashion Week 2002 describes the prominent presence of "fusion" outfits, mixing Western and Indian elements to show a modern look, one that is in opposition, as Nagrath says, to notions of "traditional" and "ethnic"; pp. 366–367. The incorporation of ethnic or foreign elements into an Indian style (of dressing) is not new, and in fact, is a traditional practice.

23. For a description of gyms and fitness centers in the metropolis of India, see Anand, *The Beauty Game*, pp. 73–78.

24. Some articles in newspapers and magazines address the ancient, traditional regimens. Parameswaran, in "Global Queens, National Celebrities," for example, quotes a newspaper article that acknowledges that Indian beauty queens have a unique mix of "cosmic within the cosmetic West." The article further praises Mehta, the trainer for Miss World Lara Dutta, who put Dutta on a vegetarian diet, made her meditate, chant, recite mantras, and visualize in the early mornings.

25. The association of deities with days of the week (and the specifics of the fast) vary not only within the different regions and castes of India, but as Freed and Freed show in their study of one village, it can vary within a single group; *Hindu Festivals in a North Indian Village*, pp. 136–141, 176–179.

26. As Fruzzetti explains, virgins pray to Shiva to give them a husband like him, and once married, women pray to him for their husbands' health and well being; *The Gift of a Virgin;* p. 104.

27. Kumar, in *The Artisans of Banaras,* describes and analyzes the practice and phi-

losophy of the *akhara,* this favorite leisure activity of Banaras, pp. 111–124.

28. See Dwyer and Patel, *Cinema India,* p. 83, for a discussion of the changing physique of the male Bollywood star.

29. Anand, in the introduction to her book *The Beauty Game,* makes sweeping generalizations about India and its women, focusing on the late 1980s and early 1990s. She claims that the Indian population is moving forward, prospering economically and visiting foreign countries. Women about a decade ago were abandoning tailors for "fashionable jeans, shirts, skirts and blouses," entering the workforce, and "women took to driving like ducks to water." Anand concludes by stating that "Looking good was something these women could afford, and notions of style, fashion, what was in or out came to them from the media"; p. xii. These kinds of statements are made un-self-consciously by many (feminist) writers who generalize the entire population of India by looking at their own elite socioeconomic group: educated and affluent people living in Bombay or New Delhi. Obviously the majority of the population of India, male and female, was not visiting foreign countries or driving cars. Anand's argument would imply that most of the country, devoid of the pleasures of Western media and taste, was not interested in looking good and being stylish. Has the West introduced the notions of fashion and a healthy self-esteem to India? This kind of thinking reveals the deep-seated colonial attitude still present among the Indian elite.

30. There is a variety of books containing Ayurvedic home remedies and beauty products that are inspired by ancient herbal therapy; the best known of these are associated with Shahnaz Husain and her beauty empire. Urvashi Bandhu, a "health and beauty specialist" in Bombay, gives home remedies for beauty products in her book *Beauty Tips for a Growing Personality.* On p. 15, she declares, "The Romans, the Egyptians and the ancient Indians in particular, were very beauty conscious."

31. *Hindustan Times,* 7/7/2003.

32. Many older people partially blame Hindi films for their bad influence on young people, especially when it comes to love marriages, as documented by Fruzzetti in *The Gift of a Virgin,* p. 10.

15. The Wedding

1. To read more about the *shervani,* see Bhandari's *Costume, Textiles and Jewellery of India,* p. 102.

2. The main tape-recorded interviews with Shalini Shrivastava took place on May 24 and June 6, 1996.

3. *India Abroad,* September 17, 2004, pp. A37–39. In Mukherjee's short story "The Tenant," a character reads through the matrimonial ads in *India Abroad* noticing that "All over America, 'handsome, tall, fair' engineers, doctors, data processors—the new pioneers—cry their eerie love call"; *The Middleman and Other Stories,* p. 109.

4. The site contains matrimonial ads that can be sorted by "Community" (Bengali, Gujarati, Hindi), "Religion" (Hindu, Sikh, Muslim), and by "Country" (India, USA, UAE). Shaadi.com also provides information on wedding planning, marriage rituals, health and beauty, home and kitchen, astrology, and wedding fashion. Indians residing in the diaspora are able to meet each other through this internet site and also learn what the latest fashion in wedding *lehangas* is, and even download exciting recipes to spice up the new marriage.

5. Shamsie, *Salt and Saffron,* p. 129.

6. "Arranged Marriage," by Carol Equer-Hamy, Dominant 7, 2001.

7. In Daswani's book *For Matrimonial Purposes,* the main character scrutinizes the photos of prospective grooms: one sends a photograph of himself at an outdoor cafe in Barcelona, sitting in the sun with an espresso; p. 43. Another, less favorable, candidate sends a picture of himself at his clothing shop. The photograph captures him standing erect, proud, at a counter of shirts. "And slung around his neck, like a noose, was a measuring tape," a sartorial mistake that made a bad impression on the prospective bride and her aunt; p. 120.

8. See Fruzzetti, *The Gift of a Virgin,* p. 32, for more on the scrutiny of photographs.

9. Suri, *The Death of Vishnu,* pp. 100–103.

10. For a list and brief description of the variety of Indian wedding ornaments, see Untracht's *Traditional Jewelry of India,* the section titled "Marriage and Jewelry," pp. 156–191.

11. Johnson, "Pragmatism and Enigmas: The Panetar and Gharcholu Saris in Gujarati Weddings."

12. Fuzzetti, *The Gift of a Virgin,* p. 39.

13. This is the argument given to explain dowry, but as Nirmala Banerjee shows in her article "Sexual Division of Labour," the working of the dowry system is much more complicated than a mere economic compensation for the bride's lack of productivity in the groom's household.

14. A painting by Indian artist Bikash Bhattacharjee, titled "Thakur Mathura Das (Child Bride)" shows a little girl with bridal painting on her face, sitting next to an old man who could be her father or her new husband. The caption for this painting, in the catalog for the exhibition *Timeless Visions,* in which the painting was displayed, reads "Thakur is the honorific title of Mathura Das, the man in the picture; his relation to the child bride is unspecified"; p. 70.

15. The opening scene of Jagmohan Mundhra's 2001 film *Bawandar* ("Sandstorm") shows a mass wedding event in which dozens of little Rajasthani kids sit together as priests chant and unite them in matrimony.

16. In Mukherjee's new novel *The Tree Bride,* the young bride's father, right after learning of the sudden death of the young groom en route to the wedding ceremony, marries his daughter to a tree at the appoint-

ed auspicious hour of her marriage, saving her from widowhood. Girls were also symbolically married to rocks or crocodiles; p. 33.

17. In Mehta's novel *Inside the Haveli*, a character explains how the system of property division works—daughters receive none of the property of the deceased parents because they were given their share of the family's wealth in the form of gold during their weddings; p. 90.

18. To read more about bride burnings, see chapter 7, "The Campaign Against Dowry," in Kumar's *The History of Doing*, and Bumiller's *May You Be the Mother of a Hundred Sons*, pp. 44–62.

19. Divakaruni's short stories "The Disappearance," "The Ultrasound," and "Affair," in the collection of stories titled *Arranged Marriage*.

20. Mukherjee, *Wife*, p. 14.

21. For descriptions of specific items of dowry, see Fuzzetti's *The Gift of a Virgin*, Lewis's *Village Life in Northern India*, Dickey's "Anjali's Prospect: Class Mobility in Urban India," Elson's *Dowries from Kutch*, Frater's "Rabari Dress," Tarlo's *Clothing Matters*, and Tambiah's "Dowry and Bridewealth and the Property Rights of Women in South Asia." Many works of fiction by Indian authors detail the dowry items given and received, including Mukherjee's *Wife*, Bapsi's *The Bride*, Mehta's *Inside the Haveli*, Devi's *A Princess Remembers*, Kapur's *Difficult Daughters*, and Daswani's *For Matrimonial Purposes*.

22. Edwards, in describing Rabari wedding dress in the Kutch region of Gujarat, explains that the grooms are extravagantly dressed to express the celebratory tone of the event, while the brides are modestly attired in observance of veiling traditions; "Marriage and Dowry Customs of the Rabari of Kutch," pp. 72–73.

23. Mukherjee's novel, *Desirable Daughters*, describes how both locals and the groom's family scrutinize the bride's beauty and her dowry, noticing the quality of the materials of the gifts; p. 12.

24. Some brides may go to a beautician to get their makeup applied, usually at salons in five-star hotels such as the Oberoi, as described by Anand in *The Beauty Game*, p. 79.

25. The main tape-recorded interview with Ashok Kumar took place at his school on June 22, 1996.

26. Many beauticians believe that no matter how expensive your outfit is, if your face looks like "it was dipped in flour," the whole look is ruined; Hammer's *The Asian Bridal Look Book*, p. 14. The goal is to make the bride look beautiful, "like a vision of coordinated beauty," p. 15.

27. With some brides it is hard to tell if they are Muslim or Hindu, since they wear similar clothing, jewelry, and makeup. For example, in *Jatree*, the in-flight magazine of Biman—Bangladesh Airlines—the cover photograph and the accompanying article, "Brides in Bangladesh," show the adornment of a typical "Bengali bride in all her wedding finery"; p. 3. The article never indicates whether she is Hindu or Muslim, self-consciously uniting by ethnicity a country that is divided by religious difference. Likewise, the cover photograph of Foster and Johnson's *Wedding Dress Across Cultures* shows a Bangladeshi bride, Farhana Sultana, wearing the ornament associated with Muslim brides, the *jhumar* on the left side of the head, and tiny dots on her forehead, above the eyebrows—usually associated with Hindu brides.

28. In Bajwa's novel *The Sari Shop*, an affluent young bride in Punjab flies in a hired beautician from New Delhi, not trusting the skills of the local Amritsar beautician that her parents had hired. The bride is motivated to hire a professional from a five-star hotel because of the fear of looking ugly in her wedding photos; p. 127.

29. *Celebrating Dreams: Weddings in India*.

30. *The Asian Bridal Look Book*, by Hammer, Naveeda, and Haider, tells the reader to first choose the color of the outfit she intends to wear, and then, find the appropri-

ate makeup, jewelry and *bindi,* all selected to match the color of the outfit, and the style—traditional or modern. The latter half of the book presents a variety of elaborate hairstyles that one could, in theory, replicate at home (although they look very difficult to sculpt without the help of a professional hairstylist).

31. Characters in Suri's *The Death of Vishnu* rely on scenes from Bollywood films as instruction (or inspiration) during the first night after marriage. This is done by Vinod, p. 187, and Kavita, on p. 100.

32. To read more about henna in India, see Saksena's *Art of Rajasthan,* pp. 55–105 and Untracht's *Traditional Jewelry of India,* pp. 26–27. Susan Slymovic and Amanda Dargan's film *The Painted Bride* shows a henna party in New York City, and Annanda Rathi's film *Marriages in Heaven* documents henna application at a wedding party in San Francisco. For henna among Moroccan women, see Kapchan's "Morrocan Women's Body Signs," Messina's "Henna Party," and Genini Izza's film *For Eye's Delight.*

33. The art of henna in the United States differs from that of India in many ways. American henna can appear on parts of the body that are usually not painted in India, such as stomachs, backs, upper arms, and thighs. Also, henna designs in the West tend to replicate tattoo motifs such as Celtic, Borneon or "neo-tribal." The main difference between henna in India and the United States is in the cultural meanings and social contexts of display: American "henna parties" are secular gatherings, unlike weddings or other religious festivals in India. See Shukla, "Henna Art," for more details.

34. Some Gujarati and Rajasthani designs are asymmetrical, covering the hand in henna motifs while a diagonal strip of design flows from the base of the palm to the tip of the index finger. This uncommon painting style is more saturated than the sparse, trailing asymmetrical style that is popular now. Mode's book *Indian Folk Art* has a photograph that shows several painted hands,

some of them in this asymmetrically dense style; p. 173. Chapbooks of henna designs, particularly those with "Arabic" motifs, also show this asymmetrical design.

35. Celebrities such as Madonna made this design popular in the United States. The motif is featured in many henna "how-to" books such as Roome's *Mehndi,* on pp. 106, 111, 134, and the color plates between pp. 82 and 83; Fabius's *Mehndi,* page 101; and Batra's *The Art of Mehndi,* pp. 38, 39, 41, 80, 92, and 121.

36. These little chapbooks, sold on the streets, are published by Lakshmi Prakashan, 4734 Bally Maran, New Delhi, 110006. An article in the *Hindustan Times* Sunday Magazine on the dangers of "adulterated mehendi" and the skin rashes women were getting from it, shows a large hand with henna paste on it, trailing down from the index finger to the forearm; February 18, 2001, Part III.

37. April 25, 2004.

38. For descriptions and details of village weddings, see Lewis, *Village Life in Northern India,* chapter 5, "The Marriage Cycle," pp. 157–195. Other anthropological accounts include Dube's *Indian Village,* pp. 119–124; Viramma, Racine, and Racine's *Viramma: Life of a Dalit;* and Hobson's *Family Web,* pp. 137–158. Several of the articles in Marriott's edited volume *Village India* and Mines's and Lamb's *Everyday Life in South Asia* also include some discussion of marriage rites and rituals.

39. Although the groom wears an off-white or cream outfit, it is not seen as a bad omen, since the color white marks the woman, not the man, as someone who has lost a spouse to death.

40. Women customarily did not attend wedding processions and still do not attend funeral ones. On both occasions, men express, through their bodies and behaviors, the appropriate emotion. During certain funeral processions for people who have lived long lives, Parry says that distant male mourners "dance in a burlesque of female sexuality"; *Death in Banaras,* p. 155. The dancing of the

men during the *barat* is often feminine and exaggerated, as if they embody the gestures and dancing style that the women among them are not allowed to express.

41. *Bhangra* music and dance is popular in India, I believe, partly because of its immense popularity in England, and its involvement with the London underground club scene, where it mingles with Caribbean music. In Ali's novel about South Asians in London, *Brick Lane,* Karim, a young Bangladeshi male, says that to be cool, you have to be Punjabi and tap into the *bhangra* style. In England, many South Asian Muslims find a happy-go-lucky persona—on the caricatured model of the Punjabi—to be a protective cover, unintimidating to British people who, since September 11, 2001, and July 7, 2005, have become tensely suspicious of foreigners.

42. White is a color associated with purity and with maleness (Bhandari, p. 42). While white is the color of Hindu grooms, red is often the color of Hindu brides, and so it would follow that the combination of red and white symbolizes the marital state and appears as the colors of the wifely saris in Bengal and the bridal bangles in Bengal and Rajasthan.

43. Jeffery, *Frogs in a Well,* p. 104.

44. This is how Hosain refers to a bride in her short story "A Woman and a Child," p. 137, in the collection of stories titled *Phoenix Fled.*

45. To read about the origins of Mughal cuisine and its association with feasts, see Collingham's *Curry.* On p. 27 she notes the usual presence of these dishes, including the *biriyani,* in wedding banquets. Sen's *Food Culture in India* has a brief section on special occasion food, pp. 139–163. In Bajwa's novel *The Sari Shop,* a sari seller sneaks inside a fabulous wedding reception for one of his affluent customers and is mesmerized by the abundance of the dinner menu and the forty desserts, only three of which he tastes; pp. 130–133. In Daswani's novel *For Matrimonial Purposes,* women look forward to attending a fancy wedding reported to be organized by a Bollywood film producer featuring, among other delightful things, "a hundred stalls serving different foods"; p. 95.

46. To read more about the *gota* fringe, see Bhandari, pp. 59–60.

47. To read more about *galis*—insult songs—see Gold's "Sexuality, Fertility, and Erotic Imagination in Rajasthani Women's Songs," pp. 57–62, and Raheja's "On the Uses of Irony and Ambiguity," pp. 93–94. Flueckiger, in *Gender and Genre in the Folklore of Middle India,* also analyzes songs as a means of expressing the alienation of the daughter-in-law, and the tensions with her mother-in-law; pp. 86–94.

48. As Leslie explains in her article "The Significance of Dress for the Orthodox Hindu Woman," the wearing of *sindur* is an old custom, a description of it found in Khujuraho, dated AD 953. Leslie says that *sindur* is more common in North India, a rarity in Tamil Nadu today; pp. 206–207.

49. The *mangalsutra* is the auspicious necklace placed around the bride's neck by her groom and, ideally, worn by her every day of her life, until she becomes a widow. Although it is associated with Gujarat and parts of South India, many people from the other regions of India have appropriated the marriage necklace tradition. Descriptions of the necklace, albeit brief ones, can be found in Untracht's *Traditional Jewelry of India,* p. 167, and Krishnan and Kumar's *Dance of the Peacock,* pp. 142, 159, and 236.

50. Lamb explains in *White Saris and Sweet Mangoes* that when the groom places *sindur* on the part of his bride's hair, he symbolically sexually activates her; p. 214.

51. This account is slightly different from the one recorded by Lamb in her fieldwork. She reports that a woman takes her husband's half, but that he does not take her within him; it is not an exchange, as I heard, but an incorporation of the man within the woman. To read Lamb's account in Bengal, see *White Saris and Sweet Mangoes,* pp. 231–232.

52. The connection between *sindur* and

blood is an obvious one, resulting in a theme that emerges in works of art. For example, in Suri's novel *The Death of Vishnu,* a Muslim man wonders about the red on the hair part of Hindu women, that makes "their skulls look freshly cracked open in neat red lines"; p. 174. In Lahiri's short story "Mrs. Sen," both a little boy and a policeman wonder if she has hurt her head and if the vermilion on her hair part is a scab; *The Interpreter of Maladies,* pp. 117, 134. The relationship between *sindur* and a wound is portrayed in the recent remake of the Bollywood film *Devdas.* The hero accidentally hits the head of the heroine—his beloved—with a piece of jewelry which leaves a red scab in the place where the *sindur* would have been, had they been allowed to marry each other.

53. Cooper and Gillow's book *Arts and Crafts of India* includes a typical *sindur* box sold in the Vishvanath Gali in Banaras; p. 49. Older examples of beautiful *sindur* boxes in museum collections are illustrated in Sethi, Devi, and Kurin's *Aditi,* p. 76, and Jain and Aggarwala's *National Handicrafts and Handlooms Museum,* p. 93.

54. The practice of seeing the bride's face at the groom's house is found among Muslims as well, as described by Jeffery in *Frogs in a Well,* p. 105.

55. The main character in Mishra's *The Romantics,* a novel set in Banaras, acknowledges knowing nothing about love or relationships, only knowing that love is supposed to follow marriage; p. 132. The fact that there are "love" marriages versus "arranged" marriage implies that the latter does not involve love yet, but it will (hopefully) follow. Puri's collected narratives of women discussing love and arranged marriages show the ambiguity in young people's ideas of what love is, and when exactly it should develop; *Woman, Body, Desire in Post-Colonial India,* pp. 138–153.

56. See Rusva, *Umrao Jan Ada,* p. 22 for the kinds of seductive thoughts a young courtesan has about the glamorous clothes and jewelry she might one day wear.

57. To read more about the pollution of the menstrual cycle, see Fruzzetti's *The Gift of A Virgin,* pp. 96–97, and especially Leslie's *The Perfect Wife,* the section titled "The Religious Duties of the Menstruating Woman," pp. 283–287.

16. The Study of Body Art

1. Glassie, *Material Culture,* p. 41.

2. See Glassie's *Material Culture,* chapter 2, pp. 41–86.

3. John Burrison, *Brothers in Clay;* Henry Glassie, *Turkish Traditional Art Today,* Part 3; *Kütahya, Art and Life in Bangladesh,* and *The Potter's Art;* Charles Zug, *Turners and Burners.*

4. Glassie, *The Spirit of Folk Art,* p. 241.

5. Kitchener, *The Holiday Yards of Florencio Morales.* Jack Santino's writings on Halloween decorations also document public displays: "The Folk *Assemblage* of Autumn" and *All Around the Year.*

6. Turner, *Beautiful Necessities.* Magliocco's *Neo-Pagan Sacred Art and Altars* discusses both the construction of altars and personal style by men and women who identify themselves as Neo-Pagans.

7. Warren Roberts, *Log Buildings of Southern Indiana;* Henry Glassie, *Folk Housing in Middle Virginia* and *Vernacular Architecture;* Thomas Carter, *Images of an American Land* and *Invitation to Vernacular Architecture.*

8. Michael Owen Jones, *Craftsman of the Cumberlands,* John Vlach, *Charleston Blacksmith,* and Henry Glassie, *Art and Life in Bangladesh.* Other portraits of individual artists include Ralph Rinzler's of the potter Cheever Meaders in Rinzler and Sayers, *The Meaders Family;* John Burrison's of Cheever's son Lanier Meaders in *Brothers in Clay;* Rosemary Joyce's of the basket maker Dwight Stump in *A Bearer of Tradition;* and Barbara Babcock's of the figurative potter Helen Cordero in Babcock and Monthans, *The Pueblo Storyteller.* Most of the volumes

in the Folk Art and Artists Series, edited by Michael Owen Jones and published by the University Press of Mississippi, emphasize individual creators and their creations.

9. Bronner, *The Carver's Art.*

10. Babcock and Monthans, *The Pueblo Storyteller* and Fry, *Stitched from the Soul.* Other studies of female artists include Karen Duffy's *Carry It On for Me*, Mary Washington Clarke's *Kentucky Quilts and Their Makers*, and Linda Pershing's *Sew to Speak.*

11. Cosentino, *Vodou Things;* see also *Sacred Arts of Haitian Vodou.* Another great study of religion and art is found in the book that resulted from the collaboration between folklorist Robin Evanchuck and Santería priest Ysamur Flores-Peña; their book is titled *Santería Garments and Altars.*

12. Mardi Gras masks in Cajun Louisiana, as studied by Carl Lindahl and Carolyn Ware, provide an example of an overt marker of identity; *Cajun Mardi Gras Masks.* Gerald Pocius's studies of the landscape and textile arts of Newfoundland reveal the subtle cross-currents of identity that material culture contains; *A Place to Belong* and *Textile Traditions of Eastern Newfoundland.*

13. See Hall and Metcalf, Jr., *The Artist Outsider.*

14. Peterson "Translating Experience and the Reading of a Story Cloth," and "Plastic Strap Baskets: Containers for a Changing Context." Folklorists have also found the small unit of creation—the family or workshop—to be a key to identity. John Burrison's grand study of the folk pottery of Georgia and Charles Briggs's study of wood carving in New Mexico both stress the importance of the family in identity and creative action; Burrison, *Brothers in Clay,* and Briggs, *The Wood Carvers of Córdova, New Mexico.* Marjorie Hunt's beautiful book and film on Italian-American stone carvers in Washington, D.C., illuminates the social dynamics of the atelier, showing how artists teach and learn, developing an identity as members of a team, and reminding us that, in fact, nobody creates in pure isolation; Hunt, *The Stone Carvers.*

15. The scholarly works cited here exemplify parts of the model that I present, and do not represent an exhaustive survey of the available literature on the topic. See Roach-Higgins, Eicher, and Johnson's book *Dress and Identity,* for an annotated bibliography of works primarily on clothing; pp. 487–503, and Hansen's "The World in Dress" for another overview of the trends in dress, fashion, and culture.

16. Examples of survey books on folk arts that include nice illustrations and discussions of clothing and textiles are: Moes' *Mingei: Japanese Folk Art;* Kalter's *The Arts and Crafts of Turkestan;* Wulff's *The Traditional Crafts of Persia;* Baud-Bovy's *Peasant Art in Switzerland;* Schlee's *German Folk Art;* Nelson's *Norwegian Folk Art;* Hansen's *European Folk Art;* and Razina, Cherkasova, and Kantsedikas' *Folk Art in the Soviet Union.*

17. Some great books on Hungarian textile and costumes include: Hofer and Fél, *Hungarian Folk Art;* Gáborján, *Szürujjasok* (Felt Jackets); Gáborján, *Cifraszürök* (Overcoats); Kocsis, *Zoboralji Hímzések* (Folk Embroidery of Zobor Region); Varjú-Ember, *Úrihímzés* (Embroidery); Lengyel, *Népi Kézimunkák* (Folk Embroideries); Györffi and Viski, *Amagyarság Néprajza* (Hungarian Ethnography); and Balogh-Horváth, *Hungarian Folk Jewelry.* Attesting to the centrality of clothing in life, one book on a peasant woman from Hungary includes descriptions of her embroidery, weaving, spinning, and methods for making dresses, in addition to her recollections of childhood games, harvest, and marriage: Vankóné Dudás, *Falum Galgamácsa* (My Village Galgamácsa). My colleague, the great folklorist Linda Dégh, was the one who introduced me to the literature on Hungarian costumes, and to the book on village life.

18. Lynton, *The Sari;* and Chishti's *Tradition and Beyond, Saris of India: Bihar and West Bengal,* and *Saris of India: Madhya Pradesh;* and Banerjee and Miller's *The Sari.* Some scholars have focused on the structure of the loom and the technology of weaving,

to understand not only the aesthetics of the textile arts, but also the weaver's perceptions and communicative intentions. One such study is Doran Ross's splendid investigation of Ghanaian *kente* cloth in *Wrapped in Pride.*

19. Mari Lyn Salvador's *The Art of Being Kuna.*

20. Faris, *Nuba Personal Art;* Strathern and Strathern, *Self-Decoration in Mount Hagen;* and O'Hanlon, *Reading the Skin.*

21. St. Clair and Govenar, *Stoney Knows How.* See also Drewal's "Art or Accident," in which he talks about scarification in Nigeria, another form of permanently marking the skin of another. Drewal notes tools and techniques as well as aesthetics of design in this excellent article.

22. Good studies of these tattoo interactions include Sanders's *Customizing the Body* and Margo DeMello's *Bodies of Inscription.* See also Rubin's "The Tattoo Renaissance" and Govenar's "The Variable Context of Chicano Tattooing."

23. See Sanders's *Customizing the Body* for an exploration of the interaction of client and tattoo artist, and expectations and aesthetic evaluations.

24. Anthropological studies that look at acquisition, trade, and barter of tools and materials of self-decoration include: Lévi-Strauss's *Tristes Tropiques,* Strathern and Strathern's *Self-Decoration in Mount Hagen,* O'Hanlon's *Reading the Skin,* Faris's *Nuba Personal Art,* Schieffelin and Crittenden's *Like People You See in a Dream,* and Boas's studies of Northwest Coast Indians (see Boas, *Kwakiutl Ethnography,* and Jonaitis's compilation of Boas's essays, *A Wealth of Thought*).

25. See Hossain, *The Company Weavers of Bengal,* and Mitra, *The Cotton Weavers of Bengal.*

26. See Cohn, *Colonialism and Its Forms of Knowledge,* especially chapter 5, "Cloth, Clothes, and Colonialism: India in the Nineteenth Century"; Tarlo, *Clothing Matters;*

and Bean, "Gandhi and *Khadi,* The Fabric of Indian Independence."

27. Bhachu, *Dangerous Designs.* See also Raghuram's "Fashioning the South Asian Diaspora: Production and Consumption Tales."

28. Steiner, *African Art in Transit.* Essays in Kreamer and Fee's *Objects as Envoys* look at cloth circulating as gifts, and the varied communications and associations they carry.

29. Eicher and Roach-Higgins, "Definition and Classification of Dress: Implications for Analysis of Gender Roles," p. 18.

30. Rudofsky, *The Unfashionable Human Body.* On pp. 122–123, he has images of four plaster figures which show how the shape of the human body corresponds to the fashions of the time, such as: a 1870s figure conforms to the bustle shape, with her rear end sticking out; a "monobosom" figure of 1904; a hobble skirt, one legged figure from 1913; and a concave, flat body representing the flapper of 1920s. These figures are from Rudofsky's Museum of Modern Art exhibition "Are Clothes Modern?" A recent exhibition and catalog at the Metropolitan Museum of Art, titled *Extreme Beauty,* portrays the relationship between clothes and the human body in an equally provocative manner.

31. Boone, *Radiance from the Waters.* De Rachewiltz's *Black Eros,* while providing a general, sweeping look at African cultures, does contain some photographic examples of body art practices, especially in the chapter on dress and ornament.

32. Strathern and Strathern, *Self-Decoration in Mount Hagen,* p. 40.

33. To read more about the genre of stage western wear, see George-Warren and Freedman, *How the West Was Worn,* and Nudie and Cabrall, *Nudie: The Rodeo Tailor.*

34. To read about Noh theatre costumes—their history, categories, masks, and design patterns—and to see color illustrations of the costumes and the process of getting dressed up, see Yamaguchi's beautiful book *Sculpture in Silk.*

35. To read more about tattoo and piercing practices in India, see the following: Untracht, *Traditional Jewelry of India;* Mode, *Indian Folk Art;* Teilhet-Fisk, "The Spiritual Significance of Newar Tattoos"; Rubin, "Tattoo Trends in Gujarat"; and Danda and Danda, "Body Painting: An Age-Old Tradition."

36. To read more about the Mangbetu, see Schildkrout and Keim's *African Reflections.* For more on plastic surgery, see Gilman's *Making the Body Beautiful.*

37. Rubin's volume, *Marks of Civilization,* contains excellent articles on scarification, including: Roberts's "Tabwa Tegumentary Inscription," Berns's "Ga'anda Scarification: A Model for Art and Identity," Bohannan's "Beauty and Scarification Amongst the Tiv," Drewal's "Beauty and Being: Aesthetics and Ontology in Yoruba Body Art," and Vogel's "Baule Scarification: The Mark of Civilization."

38. There are many great sources for information and illustrations of the history of tattoos. For Polynesia, see Robley's *Maori Tattooing,* Blackburn's *Tattoos from Paradise,* and Gell's *Wrapping in Images.* For Japan, see photographer Fellman's beautiful *The Japanese Tattoo.* For the United States and Europe, see McCabe's *New York City Tattoo,* Hardy's *Pierced Hearts and True Love,* Caplan's *Written on the Body* and "Speaking Scars," and Dye's "The Tattoos of Early American Seafarers, 1796–1818." For a comprehensive overview of the literature on tattoos, see also Schildkrout's "Inscribing the Body."

39. The most famous of these is probably Vale and Juno's *Modern Primitives.* Other non-scholarly yet popular books are Polhemus and Randall's *The Customized Body,* Miller's *The Body Art Book,* and Polhemus' book for children, *Body Art.*

40. Most of the studies of these topics tend to be both ahistorical and non-contextual, with the exception of a few works. Good studies of contemporary phenomena include Posey's "Burning Messages" and "The Body Art of Brotherhood" and Winge's encyclopedia entries on these practices: neotribal, branding, implants, modern primitives, scarification, and tattoos.

41. Reischer and Koo do an excellent job of surveying the relevant literature on body image, particularly in relation to weight gain and loss; "The Body Beautiful."

42. Works on this topic include: Klein's *Little Big Men,* Haywood's *Bodymakers,* and Moore's *Building Bodies.* Fernando Orejuela, who has just completed an excellent dissertation at Indiana University on the topic of bodybuilding, suggested these readings to me. The subject of female bodybuilding has been explored in the New Museum of Contemporary Art's "Picturing the Modern Amazon," and the accompanying catalog is by Frueh, Fierstein, and Stein.

43. Interesting studies of facial hair include Peterkin's *One Thousand Beards,* and Robinson's "Fashions in Shaving and Trimming of the Beard."

44. Larson and Hoskyn's book *The Mullet* is not a scholarly study, yet it documents this popular hairstyle well through photographs and illustrations. Inness-Smith and Webb have compiled a book, *Bad Hair,* that reprints posters from barbershops and salons, showing atrocious hairstyles. This book is an invaluable record of hair fashions from the 1970s to 2000.

45. Rooks, *Hair Raising;* Hitelbeitel and Miller's *Hair: Its Power and Meaning in Asian Cultures;* Obeyesekere's *Medusa's Hair.* White and White's book, *Stylin',* looks at African American hairstyles in different historic periods. McClellans' *History of American Costume,* like other books of this kind, contains illustrations of the different ways in which men could wear their hair in the nineteenth century: natural, powdered, and in a queue; p. 560. McCracken's book *Big Hair* is not a scholarly exploration like the others, yet it documents cultural associations with certain hairstyles and colors, especially for women.

46. For henna in India, see Saksena's *Art*

of *Rajasthan*, pp. 55–105, and Untracht's *Traditional Jewelry of India*, pp. 26–27. For documentation of henna application among Pakistanis and Indians in the United States, see Susan Slymovic and Amanda Dargan's film *The Painted Bride* and Annanda Rathi's film *Marriages in Heaven*. For henna in Morocco, see Kapchan's "Morrocan Women's Body Signs," Messina's "Henna Party," and Genini Izza's film *For Eye's Delight*.

47. Strathern and Strathern, *Self-Decoration in Mount Hagen*; O'Hanlon, *Reading the Skin*; Faris, *Nuba Personal Art*; Beckwith and Van Offelen's *Nomads of Niger*; and Werner Herzog's fabulous film on the Wodaabe, "Herdsmen of the Sun."

48. Richard Gould, personal communication, New York City, 1999.

49. For a collection of hats and headdress from Africa, see Arnoldi and Kreamer's *Crowning Achievements* and Cunningham and Marberry's *Crowns*. For a brief exploration of the *yarmulke*, see Baizerman's "The Jewish *Kippa Sruga* and the Social Construction of Gender in Israel." The Stratherns and O'Hanlon describe the wearing and making of wigs in Papua New Guinea. For African American headwrap, see Foster's "New Raiments of Self," chapter 6. For American and European hats, see Wilcox's *The Mode in Hats and Headdress*, Byrde's *The Male Image*, chapter 10, and Joselit's *A Perfect Fit*, chapter 4. To read about women making their own hats and bonnets during the U.S. Civil War, see Tandberg, "Confederate Bonnets."

50. Bogatyrev, *The Functions of Folk Costume in Moravian Slovakia;* Hollander, *Seeing Through Clothes;* Ashelford, *The Art of Dress;* Taylor, *The Study of Dress History;* Entwistle, *The Fashioned Body.* Lurie's book, *The Language of Clothes,* though not as thorough as the ones just mentioned, provides a quick look at the ways in which clothing can communicate in society.

51. Wilson, *Chinese Dress.*

52. Wilson, Wearden, and Crill's *Dress in Detail from Around the World.*

53. Wilson, *Chinese Dress,* p. 9.

54. Steele, *The Corset.* Jennifer Ruby's book *Costume in Context: Underwear* provides a visually accessible overview of some of the undergarments worn to shape the body temporarily, such as women's stiffened bodices, bustles, and hoop skirts, and men's codpieces and the calf pads that made their ankles appear small. While the book is not scholarly, it provides a nice broad look at the varieties of underwear. See also Willett and Cunnington, *The History of Underclothes,* for descriptions and illustrations of undergarments from the fifteenth to the twentieth centuries. (It seems there was a pervasive aesthetic desire for tapering legs in eighteenth-century Europe, when men wore knee breeches with stockings and the legs of furniture descended to slim ankles.)

55. Historian Ko's writings on Chinese footbinding intelligently contexualize the controversial practice, talking both about the men and women who favored small, bound feet, and the shoes themselves. See Ko's "The Body as Attire: The Shifting Meanings of Footbinding in Seventeenth-Century China," *Every Step a Lotus: Shoes for Bound Feet* and *Cinderella's Sisters: A Revisionist History of Footbinding,* and Jackson's *Splendid Slippers.* Koda's *Extreme Beauty* devotes the last chapter to feet, discussing, among other shoes, the "pleaser." Joselit's *A Perfect Fit* has one chapter on shoes in America in the late nineteenth and early twentieth centuries. There is a new book edited by Riello and McNeil titled *Shoes: A History from Sandals to Sneakers.* This work is richly illustrated and nicely varied in scope, time, and geography in its examination of footwear. The Bata Shoe Museum in Toronto, Canada, has an excellent collection of shoes and exhibitions—some temporary, some semi-permanent, such as "All About Shoes," which traces the 4,500-year history of footwear.

56. Jain-Neubauer, *Feet and Footwear in Indian Culture.*

57. Wearing representations of Vishnu on

your body—on a shawl or pendant—signifies that the god is watching over you, but wearing god on your shoes would suggest that you are stepping on god. In 2000, a discount store in Manhattan sold shoes that had images of the Hindu gods on them—Shiva, Ganesh, and Gayatri—which sparked a full-blown internet campaign by Hindus in the United States and in India, demanding an apology from the manufacturer of the shoes, Fortune Dynamic. (The news item was even noted in the City section of the *New York Times* in August 2000.)

58. Books on jewelry may analyze the form or the culture or simply provide an illustration, yet all are useful for the study of jewelry. Some good books include: Borel's *The Splendor of Ethnic Jewelry;* Mack's *Ethnic Jewelry;* Boyer's *Mongol Jewelry;* Andrew's *Ancient Egyptian Jewelry;* McConnell's *Metropolitan Jewelry;* Fisher's *Africa Adorned;* Dubin's *The History of Beads;* Morris and Preston-Whyte's *Speaking with Beads;* Phillips' *Jewelry: From Antiquity to the Present;* Zapata's *The Jewelry and Enamels of Louis Comfort Tiffany;* Stronge, Smith, and Harle's *A Golden Treasury;* Manuel Keene's *Treasury of the World;* and Brijbhushan's *Masterpieces of Indian Jewellery.*

59. Dubin, *North American Indian Jewelry and Adornment.*

60. Untracht's *Traditional Jewelry of India,* and Krishnan and Kumar's *Dance of the Peacock.*

61. This is particularly true of the earlier works on body art that set the trend: Brain's *The Decorated Body* and Ebin's *The Body Decorated.*

62. Mack's *Ethnic Jewelry,* p. 10. See also Harris's "An Examination of the Pointe Shoe as Artifact through Ethnographic and Gender Analysis."

63. Analyses of the final act of adornment as a culmination of several choices can be found in the previously cited works by Strathern and Strathern, Faris, O'Hanlon, Drewal, and Bohannan, and in Michelman and Erekosima's "Kalabari Dress in Nigeria." Sophie Woodward's article "Looking Good: Feeling Right—Aesthetics of the Self" addresses specific decisions women make about their clothes, assessing ensembles that they have put together.

64. The exhibit, "Rara Avis: Selections from the Iris Barrel Apfel Collection," was organized by Stéphane Houy-Towner for the Metropolitan Museum of Art's Costume Institute. It ran from September 12, 2005, to January 22, 2006.

65. Andrews's *Ancient Egyptian Jewelry* and Alva and Donnan's *Royal Tombs of Sipán.*

66. Baumgarten's *What Clothes Reveal,* Joselit's *A Perfect Fit,* and Peiss's *Hope in a Jar.*

67. "Aspects of the History and Development of Irish Dance Costume." Mairead Dunley's excellent study of Irish clothing, *Dress in Ireland,* deserves special mention. She traces the history of Irish clothing, looking at the clothes worn by the rich and the poor, by men and women.

68. Photographer Neleman's book *Moko—Maori Tattoo* captures the diversity of the tattoo resurgence among the Maoris of New Zealand. See also Kjellegren and Ivory's *Adorning the World: Art of the Marquesas Islands,* the catalog to the first exhibit on Marquesas Islands art, at the Metropolitan Museum of Art, New York.

69. Photographer Aoki achieved this by methodical visual documentation of outrageously dressed youths in the Harajuku district of Tokyo, from about 1994 to 1999, and similarly photographer Bill Cunningham captures New York City styles in his regular feature "On the Street," which appears weekly in the *New York Times* "Sunday Styles" section. For a wonderful book on photography and fashion, see Joan Severa's *Dressed for the Photographer: Ordinary Americans and Fashion, 1840–1900.*

70. Kaeppler, "Ali'i and Maka'ainana," p. 459. Likewise, in Mughal India, the concept of *khilat* implied a cast-off garment given to a subject by a king, transferring along with

the item of clothing a bit of power and authority; F. W. Buckler, referenced by Cohn in "Cloth, Clothes, and Colonialism"; p. 114.

71. Enid Schidkrout, chair of the anthropology division, was the chief curator of the exhibition.

72. Yoder, in the foreword to St. Clair and Govenar's book *Stoney Knows How,* calls it a "folk autobiography"; p. vii.

73. Wojcik, *Punk and Neo-Tribal Body Art.*

74. Trachtenberg, *7 Tattoos.*

75. Foster and Johnson's *Wedding Dress Across Cultures.* Many of the articles in Eicher's *Dress and Ethnicity* and Welter's *Folk Dress in Europe and Anatolia* discuss wedding dress.

76. A good book on this topic is Haynes's excellent study of the San Antonio Coronation gowns, *Dressing Up Debutantes.*

77. Lynch, *Dress, Gender and Cultural Change.*

78. Most of these practices have been abandoned today due to missionary influences or colonial forces. See the studies by Faris and Berns for examples of scarification rites of this kind.

79. Faris, *Nuba Personal Art,* p. 55.

80. Rugh, *Reveal and Conceal.*

81. Dalby, *Kimono.* Norio Yamanaka, founder of the Sōdō Kimono Academy, explains in great detail the many rules for proper kimono wear and behavior; *The Book of Kimono.* To read about the various design and weaving techniques used to make a kimono and to see beautifully illustrated kimonos, including many detailed photographs, see Van Assche's *Fashioning Kimono.*

82. Dalby, *Kimono,* pp. 233–239.

83. Tarlo, *Clothing Matters,* p. 160.

84. Mills, "Sex Role Reversals, Sex Changes, and Transvestite Disguise in the Oral Tradition of a Conservative Muslim Community in Afghanistan," p. 192.

85. Some good works that discuss the veil in India include Jeffery's *Frogs in a Well,* and Tarlo's book. Studies of the veil in the Middle East include Rugh's *Reveal and Conceal,* and Guindi's book dedicated to the topic, *Veil.* There are many books on the tatted scarves that Turkish women wear on their heads, which are custom-made and usually part of women's dowries. Most of these are in Turkish (yet richly illustrated to give a sense of the artistry, color, and motif combinations). A recent article by Özlem Sandıkcı and Güliz Ger, "Aesthetics, Ethics and Politics of the Turkish Headscarf" addresses some contemporary concerns.

86. Discussion of African American clothing styles can be found in White and White, *Stylin',* and Foster's *"New Raiments of Self."* For Hmong immigrants and their dress, see Lynch, *Dress, Gender and Cultural Change.* Handa talks about ethnic dress preferences by Indian-Canadian young women in *Of Silk Saris and Mini-Skirts,* and Mani discusses clothing preferences among Indian-American college students in "Undressing the Diaspora."

87. For a general discussion of the nature of fusion and global fashions and for particular Asian case studies, see Niessen, Leshkowich, and Jones's *Re-Orienting Fashion.* Lynch, in *Dress, Gender and Cultural Change* gives a detailed example of fusion fashion among the Hmong in the Midwestern United States, pp. 64–65. For an aesthetic and economic exploration of Indian clothes in England, see Bhachu's previously cited *Dangerous Designs.* The analysis of global fashions, especially of trends that originated among diasporic populations, includes cultural expressions beyond clothing. For the case of globalized fashion in India, see Khan's "Asian Women's Dress." Two related artistic influences are also relevant: henna and *bhangra* music. For specific discussion of new henna motifs and designs, see Shukla's "Henna Art," and for *bhangra* among Canadian youths, see Handa's *Of Silk Saris and Mini-Skirts.*

88. For example, the studies of the Nuba, Mt. Hageners, and Wodaabe.

89. For distinct identities expressed through clothes, see Sturtevant's "Seminole Men's Clothing," Jackson's "Yuchi Ceremonial Clothing," and especially Roediger's *Ceremonial Costumes of the Pueblo Indians.* Several books document powwow dance costumes well, such as: Bernstein and Contreras's *We Dance Because We Can,* Harless's *Native Arts of the Columbia Plateau,* Heth's *Native American Dance,* MacDowell's *Contemporary Great Lakes Pow Wow Regalia,* and Johnson's *Spirit Capture.* Zsuzsanna Cselényi, who is writing her dissertation at Indiana University on powwow costumes, helped me identify these sources.

90. Dunin, *Dance Occasions and Festive Dress in Yugoslavia.* For another national example, see Ballard's "Aspects of the History and Development of Irish Dance Costumes."

91. Dunin, p. 37.

92. To read more about the Smithsonian Folklife Festival, see Kurin, *Reflections of a Culture Broker,* pp. 109–137, 141–168, and Kirshenblatt-Gimblett, *Destination Culture,* pp. 55–74.

93. Tarlo describes the dilemma of Indian men living under British rule and how they had two distinct clothing identities: outside of the home they wore Western clothes, and once inside, they changed into Indian clothes, partly to be comfortable and partly to avoid "polluting" the home with outside influences; *Clothing Matters,* pp. 52–56.

94. Reiko Brandon, in her essay "Kimono Memories," describes how today most women in Japan wear Western clothes on a daily basis, but on ceremonial occasions, including weddings, funerals, and New Year's Day, they wear kimonos. She describes a young couple at a Shinto shrine—the man in Western clothes, the woman in kimono—"Like yin and yang, Western clothing and traditional kimono coexist happily today in Japan." A photograph of this young couple appears on p. 47.

95. Shukla, "Beads of Identity in Salvador da Bahia, Brazil." To understand the broader context of Yoruba bead iconography and symbolism—in Nigeria, the United States, and Brazil—see the articles by Drewal and Mason in their excellent volume, *Beads, Body, and Soul.*

96. Boas, *Kwakiutl Ethnography,* and in Jonaitis's *A Wealth of Thought;* Lévi-Strauss, *Tristes Tropiques;* Faris, *Nuba Personal Art;* Strathern and Strathern, *Self-Decoration in Mount Hagen;* and Gell, *Wrapped in Images.*

97. Bogatyrev, *The Functions of Folk Costume in Moravian Slovakia.*

98. See Glassie's review of Bogatyrev's *The Functions of Folk Costume in Moravian Slovakia:* "Structure and Function, Folklore and the Artifact" in *Semiotica.*

99. The books by the Stratherns and by O'Hanlon show this well.

100. This point is demonstrated by Bogatyrev in Moravian Slovakia and Rugh in Egypt.

101. Dress can mark different factions within a group, as a reading of the patterns, motifs, and colors of knitted Turkish socks reveal the communal, village identity of the weaver and wearer; Özbel, *Knitted Stockings from Turkish Villages.* Another study of Turkish regional clothes is Sürür's *Female Costumes in the Aegean Region.*

102. Morphy, quoted in the introduction of Barnes and Eicher's *Dress and Gender,* p. 7.

103. See Bailey's "Clothes Encounters of the Gynecological Kind" and Genini Izza's film on Moroccan women, "For Eye's Delight," which shows the beauty treatments for pregnant women. An article in *New York Magazine* titled "The Perfect Little Bump" discusses how mothers-to-be in New York City do not want to gain too much weight, striving to achieve the perfect silhouette in maternity clothes.

104. Some studies of homosexual body art include: Cole's excellent study, *Don We Now Our Gay Apparel,* a book that looks at gay men's clothing, particularly in London and New York, and the various signifiers and com-

municative devices of apparel such as Oscar Wilde's green carnation, red neckties, suede shoes, and later various club looks. Rolley's "Love, Desire and the Pursuit of the Whole: Dress and the Lesbian Couple," Lawless's "Claiming Inversion," and the insightful section on nonverbal communication among gay men in Goodwin's *More Man Than You Will Ever Be;* pp. 25–28. Griggs's book, *S/he,* looks at the clothing choices made by transsexuals, on pp. 14–16, 42, 60–63. Her book expands on the practice of cross-dressing by showing how transsexuals cross-dress for secret fantasy and pleasure; prior to surgery, as mandated by therapists, to try out the new gender look; and after surgery, some may even dress as their previous gender to pass.

105. Nanda's *Neither Man Nor Woman* contains wonderful interviews with *hijras* in India, and her last chapter looks at other traditions of cross-dressing. The volume by Jacobs, Thomas, and Lang, *Two-Spirit People,* analyzes the complexity of Native American gender identities. Blanton and Cook's *They Fought Like Demons* looks at women who cross-dressed to pass as male soldiers in the American Civil War. Some movies, such as the excellent documentary *Paris Is Burning,* are also great sources to learn from.

106. Two great books on geishas that discuss the relationship between clothes, adornment and beauty are Dalby's *Geisha* and Iwasaki's *Geisha of Gion.*

107. To read more about the personal presentation of Hasidic Jewish men and women, see Poll's "The Hasidic Community" and Mintz's *Legends of the Hasidim.*

108. On p. 226 of his article, Poll offers a chart in which the markers of Hasidic identity are presented for each of the six classes, such as beards and side locks, large brim hats, and slipper-like shoes worn with white knee-socks.

109. Hostetler, *Amish Society,* section on dress on pp. 131–138. McLary's book looks at the material culture of the Amish of Northern Indiana. She shows not only that clothing styles are specific to broad regions of the Midwest, but that within the state of Indiana alone details of the cap, bonnets, and apron vary by county. She includes nice color photographs of the clothing of adults and children of both genders, displayed on mannequins, many of them wearing whole ensembles of clothing; pp. 15–37.

110. Lawless, *God's Peculiar People.* Lawless's film "Joy Unspeakable" contains wonderful interview segments in which women talk about their dress choices and parental prohibitions.

111. See McDannell's book *Material Christianity,* chapter 7, titled "Mormon Garments: Sacred Clothing and the Body," pp. 198–221.

112. Satrapi, *Persepolis,* p. 75.

113. Another such book is John Peacock's *Costume 1066–1990s,* which shows through detailed drawings the costume changes over the years, illustrating differences in the details of form, cut, print, and accessories.

114. See Buck's "The Countryman's Smock" for an example of a study of occupational clothing in England. The bib overall can be seen as a uniform of a worker, a garment worn by many involved in agricultural, industrial, and service jobs. To read about the design, marketing, and sales strategies of the overall, see Strawn, Farrell-Beck, and Hemken's "Bib Overalls."

115. Shukla, "Afro-Brazilian Avataras."

116. There are many books on the uniform, including Paul Fussel's *Uniforms.* See also Young's "Dress and Modes of Address: Structural Forms for Policewomen."

117. To read descriptions of uniforms, and especially to see color illustrations of some of the details, including medals, buttons, plumes, helmets, and swords, see Thompson, *The Uniforms of 1798–1803,* and Cassin-Scott and Fabb, *Ceremonial Uniforms of the World.*

118. Jensen, *A Catalog of Uniforms in the Collection of the Museum of the Confederacy,* p. 9.

119. Wojcik, *Punk and Neo-Tribal Body Art,* pp. 11–21.

120. For details, see Faris, *Nuba Personal Art,* and Bohannan, "Beauty and Scarification Amongst the Tiv."

121. I learned about this by reading an article that analyzed contemporary television fashion as a version of lesbian street looks. "The Subtle Power of Lesbian Style" in the *New York Times* "Sunday Styles," sec. 9, pp. 1, 6, June 27, 2004.

122. To read more about embroidery styles and identity, see Tarlo's *Clothing Matters,* chapter 7, and the three articles on embroidery in *Mud, Mirror and Thread,* especially Frater's "Elements of Style," pp. 106–107. Dressing like the "advanced" people is of course relative to who you are: women from the village often abandon their "folk" clothing for saris and *salwar suits,* as noted by Tarlo in her study of Gujarati village women. Women from less-sophisticated cities, like Banaras, try to emulate the look of people from New Delhi by wearing tight jeans, skirts, and dresses.

123. For more details, see Callaway's "Dressing for Dinner in the Bush: Rituals of Self-Definition and British Imperial Authority."

124. Salvador, *The Art of Being Kuna,* p. 177.

125. O'Hanlon, *Reading the Skin,* pp. 124, 138.

126. Cohen, Wilk, and Stoeltje; *Beauty Queens on the Global Stage.* See also Behrman's "The Fairest of Them All." In Werner Herzog's film on the Wodaabe, "Herdsmen of the Sun," women must select the most attractive men with specific cultural criteria in mind. In Salvador, Brazil, the parading group, Ilê Aiyê, chooses an Afro-Brazilian queen based not so much on beauty, but on how much "African-ness" she embodies in her look, gestures, dance, and costume.

127. See Bohannan's "Beauty and Scarification Amongst the Tiv" and Drewal's "Beauty and Being: Aesthetics and Ontology in Yoruba Body Art."

128. Faris, *Nuba Personal Art,* p. 54.

129. Reischer and Koo's useful review article "The Body Beautiful" examines the relevant literature on weight gain and loss, noting how, ironically, overweight people in the West are seen as undesirable, unfashionable, and poor. This conception is certainly true, as being fat is associated with poverty, eating cheap processed food or eating at fast food restaurants, and not being able to afford personal trainers, designer foods, or expensive gym memberships. See also Gremillion's "The Cultural Politics of Body Size."

130. Many Indian women I spoke with feel that the skirt of the *lehanga* outfit makes them look fat since the cut of the skirt augments the hips and the stomach. Lynch's interviews with Hmong women living in the United States reveals a similar sentiment: while traditional Hmong clothes make women appear bulkier—stronger and healthier—the young generation find that it makes them look fat; *Dress, Gender and Cultural Change,* p. 63.

Bibliography

Addonizio, Kim, and Cheryl Dumesnil, eds. *Dorothy Parker's Elbow: Tattoos on Writers, Writers on Tattoos.* New York: Warner Books, 2002.

Agee, James, and Walker Evans. *Let Us Now Praise Famous Men.* Boston: Houghton Mifflin Co., 1960 [1939].

Ahmed, Farida. "Brides of Bangladesh," in *Jatree:* In-flight magazine of Biman Bangladesh Airlines, July–September, 1988, pp. 4–8.

Ali, Monica. *Brick Lane.* New York: Scribner, 2003.

Alter, Joseph S. "Hanuman and the Moral Physique of the Banarasi Wrestler." In Bradley R. Hertel and Cynthia Ann Humes, *Living Banaras: Hindu Religion in Cultural Context,* pp. 127–144.

Altman, Patricia B., and Caroline D. West. *Threads of Identity: Maya Costume of the 1960s in Highland Guatemala.* Los Angeles: UCLA Fowler Museum of Cultural History, 1992.

Alva, Walter, and Christopher Donnan. *Royal Tombs of Sipán.* Los Angeles: UCLA Fowler Museum of Cultural History, 1993.

Andrews, Carol. *Ancient Egyptian Jewelry.* New York: Harry N. Abrams, 1990.

Aoki, Shoichi. *Fruits.* London: Phaidon, 2001.

Appadurai, Arjun. "How to Make a National Cuisine: Cookbooks in Contemporary India." *Comparative Studies in Society and History* 30, no. 1 (January 1988): 3–24.

Appadurai, Arjun, Frank J. Korom, and Margaret A. Mills, eds. *Gender, Genre, and Power in South Asian Expressive Traditions.* Philadelphia: University of Pennsylvania Press, 1991.

Arnoldi, Mary Jo, and Christine Mullen Kreamer. *Crowning Achievements: African Arts of Dressing the Head.* Los Angeles: UCLA Fowler Museum of Cultural History, 1995.

Arthur, Linda B., ed. *Religion, Dress and the Body.* Oxford: Berg, 1999.

Ash, Juliet, and Elizabeth Wilson, eds. *Chic Thrills: A Fashion Reader.* Berkeley: University of California Press, 1992.

Ashelford, Jane. *The Art of Dress: Clothes and Society 1500–1914.* London: The National Trust, 1996.

Askari, Nasreen, and Liz Arthur. *Uncut Cloth: Saris, Shawls and Sashes.* London: Merrell Holberton, 1999.

Askari, Nasreen, and Rosemary Crill. *Colours of the Indus: Costume and Textiles of Pakistan.* London: The Victoria and Albert Museum, 1997.

Atıl, Esin, ed. *Islamic Art and Patronage: Treasures from Kuwait.* New York: Rizzoli International, 1990.

Babb, Lawrence A. "Glancing: Visual Interaction in Hinduism." *Journal of Anthropological Research* 37, no. 4 (1981): 387–401.

Babb, Lawrence A., and Susan S. Wadley, eds. *Media and the Transformation of Religion in South Asia.* Philadelphia: University of Pennsylvania Press, 1995.

Babcock, Barbara A., Guy Monthan, and Doris Monthan. *The Pueblo Storyteller: Development of a Figurative Ceramic Tradition.* Tucson: University of Arizona Press, 1986.

Bagchi, Jasodrara, ed. *Indian Women: Myth and Reality.* Calcutta: Sangam Books, 1995.

Bailey, Rebecca. "Clothes Encounters of the

Gynecological Kind: Medical Mandates and Maternity Modes in the USA, 1850–1990." In Ruth Barnes and Joanne Eicher, eds., *Dress and Gender,* pp. 248–265.

Baizerman, Suzanne. "The Jewish *Kippa Sruga* and the Social Construction of Gender in Israel." In Ruth Barnes and Joanne Eicher, eds., *Dress and Gender,* pp. 92–105.

Bajwa, Rupa. *The Sari Shop.* New York: W. W. Norton and Co., 2004.

Ballard, Linda M. "Aspects of the History and Development of Irish Dance Costume." *Ulster Folklife* 40 (1994): 62–67.

Balogh-Horváth, Terézia. *Hungarian Folk Jewelry.* Budapest: Corvina Kiadó, 1983.

Bandhu, Urvashi. *Beauty Tips for a Glowing Personality.* Mumbai: Better Yourself Books, 2004.

Banerjee, Mukulika, and Daniel Miller. *The Sari.* Oxford: Berg, 2003.

Banerjee, Nirmala. "Sexual Division of Labour: Myths and Reality in the Indian Context." In Jasodrara Bagchi, ed., *Indian Women: Myth and Reality,* pp. 73–81.

Banerjee, Sumata. *Dangerous Outcast: The Prostitute in Nineteenth Century Bengal.* Calcutta: Seagull Books, 2000.

Banerji, Bibhutibhushan. *Pather Panchali: Song of the Road.* Trans. T. W. Clark and Tarapada Mukherji. Bloomington: Indiana University Press, 1968.

Barnard, Nicholas. *Arts and Crafts of India.* London: Conran Octopus, 1993.

Barnes, Ruth, and Joanne B. Eicher. *Dress and Gender: Making and Meaning.* Oxford: Berg, 1997.

Barnes, Sandra T., ed. *Africa's Ogun: Old World and New.* Bloomington: Indiana University Press, 1989.

Barthes, Roland. *The Language of Fashion.* Trans. Andy Stafford. Oxford: Berg, 2005.

Basham, A. L. *The Wonder That Was India.* Calcutta: Rupa and Co., 1967.

Batra, Sumita. *The Art of Mehndi.* New York: Penguin Studio, 1999.

Baud-Boyd, Daniel. *Peasant Art in Switzerland.* London: The Studio, 1924.

Bauman, Richard. *Story, Performance, and Event: Contextual Studies of Oral Narrative.* Cambridge: Cambridge University Press, 1986.

Baumgarten, Linda. *What Clothes Reveal: The Language of Clothing in Colonial and Federal America.* New Haven: Yale University Press, 2002.

Bean, Susan S. "Gandhi and *Khadi,* The Fabric of Indian Independence." In Annette Weiner and Jane Schneider, eds., *Cloth and the Human Experience,* pp. 356–376.

Beckwith, Carol, and Marion Van Offelen. *Nomads of Niger.* New York: Harry N. Abrams, 1993.

Behrman, Carolyn. "'The Fairest of Them All': Gender, Ethnicity and a Beauty Pageant in the Kingdom of Swaziland." In Joanne Eicher, ed., *Dress and Ethnicity,* pp. 195–206.

Ben-Amos, Dan. "Toward a Definition of Folklore in Context." In Américo Paredes and Richard Bauman, eds., *Toward New Perspectives in Folklore,* pp. 4–19.

Bergman, Ingrid. *Folk Costumes in Sweden.* Stockholm: The Swedish Institute, 2001.

Berns, Marla C. *The Essential Gourd: Art and History in Northeastern Nigeria.* Los Angeles: Museum of Cultural History, 1986.

———. "Ga'anda Scarification: A Model for Art and Identity." In Arnold Rubin, ed., *Marks of Civilization,* pp. 57–76.

Bernstein, Diane, and Don Contreras. *We Dance Because We Can: People of the Powwow.* Marietta, Ga.: Longstreet, 1996.

Berry, Burton Y. *Old Turkish Towels.* Chicago: College Art Association of America, University of Chicago, 1938 [1932].

Bhachu, Parminder. *Dangerous Designs: Asian Women Fashion the Diaspora Economies.* New York: Routledge, 2004.

Bhandari, Vandana. *Costume, Textiles and Jewellery of India: Traditions in Rajasthan.* London: Mercury Books, 2005.

Bhandari, Vandana, and Ruby Kashyap.

Celebrating Dreams: Weddings in India. National Institute of Fashion Technology Publication Division. New Delhi: Prakash Book Depot, 1999.

Blackburn, Mark. *Tattoos from Paradise: Traditional Polynesian Patterns.* Atglen, Pa.: Schiffer, 1999.

Blanton, DeAnne, and Lauren M. Cook. *They Fought Like Demons: Women Soldiers in the American Civil War.* Baton Rouge: Louisiana State University Press, 2002.

Boas, Franz. *Kwakiutl Ethnography.* Helen Cordere, ed. Chicago: University of Chicago Press, 1966.

Bogatyrev, Petr. *The Functions of Folk Costume in Moravian Slovakia.* The Hague: Mouton, 1971 [1937].

Bohannan, Paul. "Beauty and Scarification Amongst the Tiv." In Arnold Rubin, ed., *Marks of Civilization,* pp. 77–82.

Boone, Sylvia Ardyn. *Radiance from the Waters: Ideals of Feminine Beauty in Mende Art.* New Haven: Yale University Press, 1986.

Borel, France. *The Splendor of Ethnic Jewelry.* New York: Harry N. Abrams, 1994.

Boyer, Martha. *Mongol Jewelry.* London: Thames and Hudson, 1995.

Brain, Robert. *The Decorated Body.* New York: Harper and Row, 1979.

Brandon, Reiko M. "Kimono Memories: Personal Notes." In Annie Van Assche, ed., *Fashioning Kimono,* pp. 45–47.

Briggs, Charles L. *The Wood Carvers of Córdova, New Mexico: Social Dimensions of an Artistic "Revival."* Knoxville: University of Tennessee Press, 1980.

Brijbhushan, Jamila. *Masterpieces of Indian Jewellery.* Bombay: Taraporevala, 1979.

Bronner, Simon J. *The Carver's Art: Crafting Meaning from Wood.* Lexington: University Press of Kentucky, 1985.

Brown, Tamara, Gregory Parks, and Clarenda Phillips, eds. *African American Fraternities and Sororities: The Legacy and the Vision.* Lexington: University Press of Kentucky, 2005.

Brownrigg, Henry. *Betel Cutters: From the Samuel Eilenberg Collection.* Stuttgart: Edition Hansjörg Mayer, 1991.

Buck, Anne. "The Countryman's Smock." *Folklife: Journal of the Society for Folk Life Studies* 1 (1963): 16–34.

Bumiller, Elisabeth. *May You Be the Mother of a Hundred Sons: A Journey Among the Women of India.* New Delhi: Penguin Books India, 1990.

Burgess, Fred. *Antique Jewellery and Trinkets.* London: George Routledge and Sons, 1919.

Burman, Barbara, ed. *The Culture of Sewing: Gender, Consumption and Home Dressmaking.* Oxford: Berg, 1999.

Burrison, John A. *Brothers in Clay: The Story of Georgia Folk Pottery.* Athens: University of Georgia Press, 1983.

———. *Handed On: Folk Crafts in Southern Life.* Atlanta: Atlanta Historical Society, 1994.

———. *Shaping Traditions: Folk Arts in a Changing South.* Atlanta: Atlanta Historical Society, 2000.

Burroughs, Catherine, and Jeffery David Ehrenreich, eds. *Reading the Social Body.* Iowa City: University of Iowa Press, 1993.

Burton, Antoinette, ed. *Gender, Sexuality and Colonial Modernities.* London: Routledge, 1999.

Bussabarger, Robert F., and Betty Dashew Robins. *The Everyday Art of India.* New York: Dover, 1968.

Byrde, Penelope. *The Male Image: Men's Fashion in Britain 1300–1970.* London: B. T. Batsford, 1979.

Callaway, Helen. "Dressing for Dinner in the Bush: Rituals of Self-Definition and British Imperial Authority." In Ruth Barnes and Joanne B. Eicher, eds., *Dress and Gender,* pp. 232–247.

Caplan, Jane. "'Speaking Scars': The Tattoo in Popular Practice and Medico-Legal Debate in Nineteenth-Century Europe." *History Workshop Journal* 44 (1997): 107–142.

———. *Written on the Body: The Tattoo in European and American History.* Princeton: Princeton University Press, 2000.

Carter, Thomas, ed. *Images of an American Land.* Albuquerque: University of New Mexico Press, 1997.

Carter, Thomas, and Elizabeth Cromley. *Invitation to Vernacular Architecture: A Guide to the Study of Ordinary Buildings and Landscapes.* Knoxville: University of Tennessee Press, 2005.

Cassin-Scott, Jack, and John Fabb. *Ceremonial Uniforms of the World.* Edinburgh: John Bartholomew and Son, 1977 [1973].

Cerny, Charlene, and Suzanne Seriff, eds. *Recycled Re-Seen: Folk Art from the Global Scrap Heap.* New York: Museum of International Folk Art and Harry N. Abrams, 1996.

Chakravarti, Uma, and Preeti Gill, eds. *Shadow Lives: Writings on Widowhood.* New Delhi: Kali for Women, 2001.

Chandramouli, K. *Kashi: The City Luminous.* Calcutta: Rupa and Co., 1995.

Chaturvedi, Mahendra, and Dr. Bhola Nath Tiwar, eds. *A Practical Hindi-English Dictionary.* New Delhi: National Publishing House, 1992.

Chishti, Rta Kapur. *Saris of India: Bihar and West Bengal.* New Delhi: Vastra Kosh, 1995.

———. *Tradition and Beyond: Handcrafted Indian Textiles.* New Delhi: Roli Books, 2000.

Clarke, Mary Washington. *Kentucky Quilts and Their Makers.* Lexington: University Press of Kentucky, 1976.

Cohen, Colleen, Richard Wilk, and Beverly Stoeltje, eds. *Beauty Queens on the Global Stage: Gender, Contests, and Power.* New York: Routledge, 1996.

Cohn, Bernard S. "Cloth, Clothes, and Colonialism: India in the Nineteenth Century." In Bernard Cohn, *Colonialism and Its Forms of Knowledge,* pp. 106–162.

———. *Colonialism and Its Forms of Knowledge: The British in India.* Princeton: Princeton University Press, 1996.

Cole, Shaun. *'Don We Now Our Gay Apparel': Gay Men's Dress in the Twentieth Century.* Oxford: Berg, 2000.

Collazzo, Charles. *The Foot and Shoes: A Bibliography.* Toronto: Bata Shoe Museum Foundation, 1988.

Collingham, Lizzie. *Curry: A Tale of Cooks and Conquerors.* Oxford: Oxford University Press, 2006.

Coomaraswamy, Ananda K. *The Transformation of Nature in Art.* Cambridge: Harvard University Press, 1935.

Cosentino, Donald J., ed. *Sacred Arts of Haitian Vodou.* Los Angeles: UCLA Fowler Museum of Cultural History, 1995.

Cosentino, Donald J. "Madonna's Earrings: Catholic Icons as Ethnic Chic." In Charlene Cerny and Suzanne Seriff, *Recycled Re-Seen,* pp. 152–165.

———. *Vodou Things: The Art of Pierrot Barra and Marie Cassaise.* Jackson: University Press of Mississippi, 1998.

Craven, Roy C. *Indian Art.* New York: Thames and Hudson, 1976.

Cunningham, Michael, and Craig Marberry. *Crowns: Portraits of Black Women in Church Hats.* New York: Doubleday, 2000.

Dalby, Liza. *Geisha.* Berkeley: University of California Press, 1998 [1983].

———. *Kimono: Fashioning Culture.* London: Vintage, 2001.

Dallapiccola, Anna Libera. *Shastric Traditions in Indian Arts.* Stuttgart: Steiner Verlag Wiesbaden GMBH, 1989.

Danda, Ajit K., and Deepanjana Danda. "Body Painting: An Age-Old Tradition." *Indian Folklife* 3, no. 1 (December 2003): 11–14.

Das Gupta, Chidananda. *The Painted Face: Studies in India's Popular Cinema.* New Delhi: Roli Books Pvt., 1991.

Dasgupta, Shamita, ed. *A Patchwork Shawl: Chronicles of South Asian Women in America.* New Brunswick: Rutgers University Press, 1998.

Daswani, Kavita. *For Matrimonial Purposes.* New York: G. P. Putnam's Sons, 2003.

———. *The Village Bride of Beverly Hills.* New York: G. P. Putnam's Sons, 2004.

De Bone, Mary Golden. "Patolu and Its Techniques." *The Textile Museum Journal* 4, no. 3 (1976).

de Rachewiltz, Boris. *Black Eros: The Sexual Customs of Africa from Prehistoric Times to the Present Day.* London: George Allen and Unwin, 1964.

Deen, Hanifa. *Broken Bangles.* New Delhi: Penguin Books India, 1998.

Dehejia, Vidya. *Indian Art.* London: Phaidon, 1997.

Del Bonta, Robert J. "Calendar Prints and Indian Traditions." In Anna Libera Dallapiccola, *Shastric Traditions in Indian Arts,* pp. 453–455.

———. "Calendar Art." In Margaret Mills, Peter Claus, and Sarah Diamond, eds., *South Asian Folklore: An Encyclopedia,* pp. 89–90.

DeMello, Margo. *Bodies of Inscription: A Cultural History of the Modern Tattoo Community.* Durham: Duke University Press, 2000.

Derné, Steve. *Culture in Action: Family Life, Emotion, and Male Dominance in Banaras, India.* Albany: State University of New York Press, 1995.

Desai, Mathuri. "Mosques, Temples, and Orientalists: Hegemonic Imaginations in Banaras." *Traditional Dwellings and Settlements Review* 15, no. 1 (Fall 2003): 23–37.

Devi, Gayatri, and Santha Rama Rau. *A Princess Remembers: The Memoirs of the Maharani of Jaipur.* New Delhi: Vikas, 1994.

Devi, Mahasweta. *Breast Stories.* Trans. Gayatri Spivak. Calcutta: Seagull Books, 2002.

Dickey, Sara. "Anjali's Prospect: Class Mobility in Urban India." In Diane Mines and Sarah Lamb, *Everyday Life in South Asia,* pp. 214–226.

Divakaruni, Chitra Banerjee. *Arranged Marriage.* New York: Anchor Books, 1995.

———. *Sister of My Heart.* New York: Anchor Books, 2000.

———. *The Vine of Desire.* New York: Anchor Books, 2003.

Drewal, Henry John. "Beauty and Being: Aesthetics and Ontology in Yoruba Body Art." In Arnold Rubin, ed., *Marks of Civilization,* pp. 83–96.

———. "Art or Accident: Yoruba Body Artists and Their Deity Ogun." In Sandra Barnes, ed., *Africa's Ogun,* pp. 235–260.

Drewal, Henry John, and John Mason. *Beads, Body, and Soul: Art and Light in the Yorùbá Universe.* Los Angeles: UCLA Fowler Museum of Cultural History, 1998.

Dube, S. C. *Indian Village.* Ithaca: Cornell University Press, 1955.

Dubin, Lois Sherr. *The History of Beads: From 30,000 B.C. to the Present.* New York: Harry N. Abrams, 1987.

———. *North American Indian Jewelry and Adornment: From Prehistory to the Present.* New York: Harry N. Abrams, 1999.

Duffy, Karen M. *Carry It On for Me: Tradition and Familial Bonds in the Art of Acoma Pottery.* Ph.D. dissertation, Bloomington, Indiana University, 2002.

Dundes, Alan. "Wet and Dry, The Evil Eye: An Essay in Indo-European and Semitic Worldview." In Alan Dundes, *Interpreting Folklore,* pp. 93–133.

———. *Interpreting Folklore.* Bloomington: Indiana University Press, 1980.

Dunin, Elsie Evancich. *Dance Occasions and Festive Dress in Yugoslavia.* Los Angeles: Museum of Cultural History, 1984.

Dunley, Mairead. *Dress in Ireland: A History.* Cork: Collins, 1999.

Dye, Ira. "The Tattoos of Early American Seafarers, 1796–1818." *Proceedings of the American Philosophical Society* 133, no. 4 (December 1989): 520–554.

Dyer, Rachel, and Divia Patel. *Cinema India: The Visual Culture of Hindi Film.* London: Reaktion Books, 2002.

Ebin, Victoria. *The Body Decorated.* London: Thames and Hudson, 1979.

Eck, Diana. *Darśan: Seeing the Divine Image in India.* Chambersburg, Pa.: Anima Books, 1981.

————. *Banaras: City of Light*. Princeton: Princeton University Press, 1982.

Edwards, Eiluned. "Marriage and Dowry Customs of the Rabari of Kutch: Evolving Traditions." In Helen Bradley Foster and Donald Clay Johnson, *Wedding Dress Across Cultures*, pp. 67–84.

Eicher, Joanne B., ed. *Dress and Ethnicity*. Oxford: Berg, 1995.

Eicher, Joanne B. "The Anthropology of Dress." *Dress* 27 (2000): 59–70.

Eicher, Joanne B., and Mary Ellen Roach-Higgins. "Definition and Classification of Dress: Implications for Analysis of Gender Roles." In Ruth Barnes and Joanne B. Eicher, eds., *Dress and Gender*, pp. 8–28.

El Guindi, Fadwa. *Veil: Modesty, Privacy and Resistance*. Oxford: Berg, 1999.

Elson, Vickie G. *Dowries from Kutch: A Women's Folk Art Tradition in India*. Los Angeles: Museum of Cultural History, 1979.

English, Helen W. Drutt, and Peter Dormer. *Jewelry of Our Time: Art, Ornaments and Obsession*. New York: Rizzoli, 1995.

English, Karen. *Nadia's Hands*. Honesdale, Pa.: Boyds Mills, 1999.

Entwistle, Joanne. *The Fashioned Body: Fashion, Dress and Modern Social Theory*. Cambridge: Polity, 2000.

Eraly, Abraham. *The Mughal Throne: The Sage of India's Great Emperors*. London: Phoenix, 2004.

Fabius, Carine. *Mehndi: The Art of Henna Body Painting*. New York: Three Rivers, 1998.

Faris, James C. *Nuba Personal Art*. London: Duckworth, 1972.

————. "Significance of Difference in the Male and Female Personal Art of the Southeast Nuba." In Arnold Rubin, ed., *Marks of Civilization*, pp. 29–40.

Fellman, Sandi. *The Japanese Tattoo*. New York: Abbeville, 1986.

Ferris, William. *Local Color: A Sense of Place in Folk Art*. New York: McGraw-Hill, 1982.

Fisher, Angela. *Africa Adorned*. New York: Harry N. Abrams, 1984.

Fisher, Nora. "Bajara: Adornment of a People of All India." In Nora Fisher, ed., *Mud, Mirror and Thread: Folk Traditions of Rural India*, pp. 136–171.

Fisher, Nora, ed. *Mud, Mirror and Thread: Folk Traditions of Rural India*. Ahmedabad: Mapin, 1993.

Flores-Peña, Ysamur, and Roberta J. Evanchuk. *Santería Garments and Altars: Speaking Without a Voice*. Jackson: University Press of Mississippi, 1994.

Flueckiger, Joyce Burkhalter. *Gender and Genre in the Folklore of Middle India*. Ithaca: Cornell University Press, 1996.

Foster, Helen Bradley. *"New Raiments of Self": African American Clothing in the Antebellum South*. Oxford: Berg, 1997.

Foster, Helen Bradley, and Donald Clay Johnson, eds. *Wedding Dress Across Cultures*. Oxford: Berg, 2003.

Frater, Judy. "Elements of Style: The Artisan Reflected in Embroideries of Western India." In Nora Fisher, ed., *Mud, Mirror and Thread: Folk Traditions of Rural India*, pp. 66–109.

————. "Rabari Dress: Adornment that Tells of Tradition." In Nora Fisher, ed., *Mud, Mirror and Thread: Folk Traditions of Rural India*, pp. 110–135.

Freed, Stanley A., and Ruth S. *Hindu Festivals in a North Indian Village*. New York: American Museum of Natural History, 1998.

Friedan, Betty. *The Feminine Mystique*. New York: W. W. Norton & Co., 2001.

Friedman, Sara L. "Embodying Civility: Civilizing Processes and Symbolic Citizenship in Southeastern China." *The Journal of Asian Studies* 63, no. 3 (August 2004): 687–718.

Frueh, Joanna, Laurie Fierstein, and Judith Stein. *Picturing the Modern Amazon*. New York: New Museum Books and Rizzoli, 1999.

Fruzzetti, Lina M. *The Gift of a Virgin:*

Women, Marriage, and Ritual in a Bengali Society. Delhi: Oxford University Press, 1990.

Fry, Gladys-Marie. *Stitched from the Soul: Slave Quilts from the Ante-Bellum South.* New York: Dutton Studio Books, 1990.

Fussell, Paul. *Uniforms: Why We Are What We Wear.* Boston: Houghton Mifflin Co., 2002.

Gáborján, Alice. *Szürujjasok.* [Felt Jackets]. Budapest: Néprajzi Múzeum, 1993.

———. *Cifraszürök.* [Overcoats]. Budapest: Néprajzi Múzeum, 1994.

Garduño, Blanca, and José Antonio Rodríguez, eds. *Pasion Por Frida.* Museu Estudio Diego Rivera. Mexico City: De Grazia Art and Cultural Foundation, 1991.

Gell, Alfred. *Wrapping in Images: Tattooing in Polynesia.* Oxford: Clarendon, 1993.

Gentles, Margaret. *Turkish and Greek Island Embroideries from the Burton Yost Berry Collection in the Art Institute of Chicago.* Chicago: The Art Institute of Chicago, 1964.

George-Warren, Holly, and Michelle Freedman. *How the West Was Worn.* New York: Autry Museum of Western Heritage and Harry N. Abrams, 2001.

Gilbertson, Laurann. "To Ward Off Evil: Metal on Norwegian Folk Dress." In Linda Welters, ed., *Folk Dress in Europe and Anatolia,* pp. 199–210.

Gillow, John, and Nicholas Barnard. *Traditional Indian Textiles.* London: Thames and Hudson, 1991.

Gilman, Sander L. *Making the Body Beautiful: A Cultural History of Aesthetic Surgery.* Princeton: Princeton University Press, 1999.

Glassie, Henry. *Pattern in the Material Folk Culture of the Eastern United States.* Philadelphia: University of Pennsylvania Press, 1968.

———. "Structure and Function, Folklore and the Artifact." *Semiotica* 7, no. 4 (1973): 313–351.

———. *Folk Housing in Middle Virginia: A Structural Analysis of Historic Artifacts.* Knoxville: University of Tennessee Press, 1996 [1975].

———. *The Spirit of Folk Art.* New York: Harry N. Abrams, 1989.

———. *Turkish Traditional Art Today.* Bloomington: Indiana University Press, 1993.

———. *Art and Life in Bangladesh.* Bloomington: Indiana University Press, 1997.

———. *Material Culture.* Bloomington: Indiana University Press, 1999.

———. *Vernacular Architecture.* Bloomington: Indiana University Press, 2000.

———. "Mud and Mythic Vision: Hindu Sculpture in Modern Bangladesh." In Gregory Schrempp and William Hansen, eds., *Myth: A New Symposium,* pp. 203–222.

Goffman, Erving. *Behavior in Public Places: Notes on the Social Organization of Gatherings.* New York: The Free Press, 1963.

Gold, Ann Grodzins. "Sexuality, Fertility, and Erotic Imagination in Rajasthani Women's Songs." In Gloria Goodwin Raheja and Ann Grodzins Gold, *Listen to the Heron's Words,* pp. 30–72.

Golden, Arthur. *Memoirs of a Geisha.* New York: Vintage Books, 1999.

Golding, Paul R., with Virendra Singh, trans. *Tales of Banaras: The Flowing Ganges.* New Delhi: Book Faith India, 1997.

Goldstein, Kenneth S. "Notes toward a European-American Folk Aesthetic: Lessons Learned and Singers and Storytellers I Have Known." *Journal of American Folklore* 104, no. 412 (Spring 1991): 164–178.

Gómez, Miguel Andrea "Gol." *A Pilgrimage to Kashi: Banaras, Varanasi, Kashi: History, Mythology and Culture of the Strangest and Most Fascinating City in India.* Varanasi: Indica Books, 1999.

Goodwin, Joseph P. *More Man Than You'll Ever Be: Gay Folklore and Acculturation in Middle America.* Bloomington: Indiana University Press, 1989.

477

Goody, Jack, and T. J. Tambiah. *Bridewealth and Dowry.* Cambridge: Cambridge University Press, 1973.

Govenar, Alan. "The Variable Context of Chicano Tattoo." In Arnold Rubin, ed., *Marks of Civilization,* pp. 209–218.

Grabar, Oleg. "Patronage in Islamic Art." In Esin Atıl, ed., *Islamic Art and Patronage,* pp. 27–39.

Gremillion, Helen. "The Cultural Politics of Body Size." *Annual Review of Anthropology* 34 (2005): 13–32.

Griggs, Claudine. *S/he: Changing Sex and Changing Clothes.* Oxford: Berg, 1998.

Gröning, Karl. *Body Decoration: A World Survey of Body Art.* New York: Vendome, 1998.

Guy, Ali, Eileen Green, and Maura Banim, eds. *Through the Wardrobe: Women's Relationships with Their Clothes.* Oxford: Berg, 2001.

Györffy, István, and Károly Viski. *A magyarság néprajza.* [Hungarian Ethnography]. Third edition, Vol. 2. Budapest: Királyi Magyar Egyetemi Nyomda, circa 1937.

Hacker, Katherine F., and Krista Jensen Turnbull. *Courtyard, Bazaar, Temple: Traditions of Textile Expression in India.* Seattle: University of Washington Press, 1982.

Hall, Cally. *Gemstones.* London: Dorling Kindersley, 1994.

Hall, Michael D., and Eugene W. Metcalf, Jr., eds. *The Artist Outsider: Creativity and the Boundaries of Culture.* Washington, D.C.: Smithsonian Institution Press, 1994.

Hamilton, Roy W., ed. *Gift of the Cotton Maiden: Textiles of Flores and the Solor Islands.* Los Angeles: UCLA Fowler Museum of Cultural History, 1994.

Hammer, Ruby, Naveeda, and Nina Haider. *The Asian Bridal Look Book.* South Wales, UK: Sweet Lyall, 2005.

Hanchett, Suzanne. "Life Cycle Rituals." In Margaret Mills, Peter Claus, and Sarah Diamond, eds., *South Asian Folklore: An Encyclopedia,* pp. 354–358.

Handa, Amita. *Of Silk Saris and Mini-Skirts: South Asian Girls Walk the Tightrope of Culture.* Toronto: Women's Press, 2003.

Hansen, H. J., ed. *European Folk Art.* New York: McGraw-Hill, 1968.

Hansen, Karen Tranberg. "The World in Dress: Anthropological Perspectives on Clothing, Fashion, and Culture." *Annual Review of Anthropology* 33 (2004): 369–392.

Haque, Zulekha. *Gahana: Jewellery of Bangladesh.* Dhaka: Bangladesh Small and Cottage Industries Corp., 1984.

Hardgrave, Robert L., Jr. *A Portrait of the Hindus: Balthazar Solvyns & the European Image of India, 1760–1824.* New York: Oxford University Press, 2004.

Hardin, James, and Alan Jabbour, eds. *Folklife Annual 88–89.* Washington, D.C.: Library of Congress, 1989.

Hardy, Don Ed. *Pierced Hearts and True Love: A Century of Drawings for Tattoos.* Honolulu: The Drawing Center and Hardy Marks Productions, 1995.

Harless, Susan, ed. *Native Arts of the Columbia Plateau: The Doris Swayze Bounds Collection.* Seattle: University of Washington Press, 1998.

Harris, Kristin M. "An Examination of the Pointe Shoe as Artifact through Ethnographic and Gender Analysis." *Material History Review* 58 (Fall 2003): 4–12.

Hawley, John Stratton, ed. *Sati: The Blessing and the Curse: The Burning of Wives in India.* Oxford: Oxford University Press, 1994.

———. "The Saints Subdued: Domestic Virtue and National Integration in *Amar Chitra Katha.*" In Lawrence Babb and Susan Wadley, *Media and the Transformation of Religion in South Asia,* pp. 107–134.

Haynes, Michaele Thurgood. *Dressing Up Debutantes: Pageantry and Glitz in Texas.* Oxford: Berg, 1998.

Hertel, Bradley R., and Cynthia Ann Humes.

Living Banaras: Hindu Religion in Cultural Context. New Delhi: Manohar, 1998.

Heth, Charlotte, ed. *Native American Dance: Ceremonial and Social Traditions.* Washington, D.C.: National Museum of the American Indian and Smithsonian Institution Press, 1992.

Heywood, Leslie. *Bodymakers: A Cultural Anatomy of Women's Body Building.* New Brunswick: Rutgers University Press, 1998.

Hiltebeitel, Alf, and Barbara D. Miller, eds. *Hair: Its Power and Meaning in Asian Cultures.* Albany: State University of New York Press, 1998.

Hobson, Sarah. *Family Web: A Story of India.* Chicago: Academy Chicago, 1982 [1978].

Hofer, Tamás, and Edit Fél. *Hungarian Folk Art.* Oxford: Oxford University Press, 1979.

Hollander, Anne. *Seeing Through Clothes.* New York: Avon Books, 1975.

———. *Sex and Suits: The Evolution of Modern Dress.* New York: Kodansha American, 1994.

Horton, Laurel, and Paul Jordan-Smith. "Deciphering Folk Costume: Dress Codes among Contra Dancers." *Journal of American Folklore* 117, 466 (Fall 2004): 415–440.

Horwitz, Tony. *Confederates in the Attic: Dispatches from the Unfinished Civil War.* New York: Vintage Books, 1999.

Hosain, Attia. *Phoenix Fled.* New York: Penguin Books, 1988.

Hossain, Hameeda. *The Company Weavers of Bengal: The East India Company and the Organization of Textile Production in Bengal 1750–1813.* New Delhi: Oxford University Press, 1988.

Hostetler, John A. *Amish Society.* Baltimore: John Hopkins Press, 1963.

Hunt, Marjorie. *The Stone Carvers: Master Craftsmen of Washington National Cathedral.* Washington, D.C.: Smithsonian Institution Press, 1999.

Huyler, Stephen. "Creating Sacred Spaces: Women's Wall and Floor Decorations in Indian Homes." In Nora Fisher, *Mud, Mirror and Thread,* pp. 172–191.

Inglis, Stephen R. "Suitable for Framing: The Work of a Modern Master." In Lawrence Babb and Susan Wadley, *Media and the Transformation of Religion in South Asia,* pp. 51–75.

Innes-Smith, James, and Henrietta Webb. *Bad Hair.* New York: Bloomsbury, 2002.

Iwasaki, Mineko. *Geisha of Gion.* With Rande Brown. London: Pocket Books, 2002.

Jackson, Beverly. *Splendid Slippers: A Thousand Years of an Erotic Tradition.* Berkeley: Ten Speed Press, 1997.

Jackson, Jason. "Yuchi Ceremonial Clothing: Dressing for the Dance." *American Indian Art Magazine* 23, no. 3 (Summer 1998): 32–41.

Jacobs, Sue-Ellen, Wesley Thomas, and Sabine Lang, eds. *Two-Spirit People: Native American Gender Identity, Sexuality, and Spirituality.* Urbana: University of Illinois Press, 1997.

Jaffrey, Madhur. *Climbing the Mango Trees: A Memoir of a Childhood in India.* New York: Alfred A. Knopf, 2006.

Jain, Jyotindra, and Aarti Aggarwala. *National Handicrafts and Handlooms Museum.* Ahmedabad: Mapin, 1989.

Jain, Manik Chand. *Occult Power of Gems.* New Delhi: Ranjan, 1998.

Jain-Neubauer, Jutta. *Feet and Footwear in Indian Culture.* Ahmedabad: The Bata Shoe Museum and Mapin, 2000.

Jayapal, Pramila. *Pilgrimage: One Woman's Return to a Changing India.* New Delhi: Penguin Books India, 2000.

Jeffery, Patricia. *Frogs in a Well: Indian Women in Purdah.* London: Zed Books, 1979.

Jensen, Les. *A Catalogue of Uniforms in the Collection of the Museum of the Confederacy.* Richmond, Va.: The Museum of the Confederacy, 2000.

Jha, Raj Kamal. *The Blue Bedspread.* New York: Random House, 1999.

Johnson, Donald Clay. "Pragmatism and Enigmas: The Panetar and Gharcholu Saris in Gujarati Weddings." In Helen Bradley Foster and Donald Clay Johnson, *Wedding Dress Across Cultures*, pp. 85–92.

Johnson, Tim, ed. *Spirit Capture: Photography from the National Museum of the American Indian.* Washington, D.C.: Smithsonian Institution Press, 1998.

Jonaitis, Aldona, ed. *A Wealth of Thought: Franz Boas on Native American Art.* Seattle: University of Washington Press, 1995.

Jones, Dorothy. "The Eloquent Sari." *Textile: The Journal of Cloth and Culture* 2, no. 1 (Spring 2004): 52–63.

Jones, Michael Owen. *The Hand Made Object and Its Maker.* Berkeley: University of California Press, 1975.

———. *Exploring Folk Art: Twenty Years of Thought on Craft, Work, and Aesthetics.* Logan: Utah State University Press, 1987.

———. *Craftsman of the Cumberlands: Tradition and Creativity.* Lexington: University Press of Kentucky, 1989.

Jordan, Rosan A., and Susan J. Kalčik, eds. *Women's Folklore, Women's Culture.* Philadelphia: University of Pennsylvania Press, 1985.

Joselit, Jenna Weissman. *A Perfect Fit: Clothes, Character, and the Promise of America.* New York: Henry Holt and Co., 2001.

Joseph-Witham, Heather R. *Star Trek Fans and Costume Art.* Jackson: University Press of Mississippi, 1996.

Joshi, O. P. "Continuity and Change in Hindu Women's Dress." In Ruth Barnes and Joanne Eicher, eds., *Dress and Gender*, pp. 214–231.

Joyce, Rosemary O. *A Bearer of Tradition: Dwight Stump, Basketmaker.* Athens: University of Georgia Press, 1989.

Justice, Christopher. *Dying the Good Death: The Pilgrimage to Die in India's Holy City.* Albany: State University of New York Press, 1997.

Kaeppler, Adrienne L. "Ali'i and Maka'ainana: The Representation of Hawaiians in Museums at Home and Abroad." In Ivan Karp, Christine Mullen Kreamer, and Steven Lavine, *Museums and Communities*, pp. 458–475.

Kalter, Johannes. *The Arts and Crafts of Turkestan.* London: Thames and Hudson, 1983.

Kamdar, Mira. *Motiba's Tattoos: A Granddaughter's Journey into Her Indian Family's Past.* New York: Public Affairs, 2000.

Kang, Jeevan. *Spider-Man India.* New York: Marvel Comics, 2005.

Kapchan, Deborah. "Moroccan Women's Body Signs." In Katherine Young, ed., *Bodylore*, pp. 3–34.

Kapur, Manju. *Difficult Daughters.* London: Faber and Faber, 1998.

Karp, Ivan, Christine Mullen Kreamer, and Steven D. Lavine. *Museums and Communities: The Politics of Public Culture.* Washington, D.C.: Smithsonian Institution Press, 1992.

Katrak, Ketu. "Still Waters Run Deep." *India Currents* 20, no. 4 (July 2006): 10–12.

Keay, Anna. *The Crown Jewels.* Surrey: Historic Royal Palaces, 2002.

Keene, Manuel. *Treasury of the World: Jewelled Arts of India in the Age of the Mughals.* New York: Thames and Hudson, 2001.

Kendall, Laurel. *Getting Married in Korea: Of Gender, Morality, and Modernity.* Berkeley: University of California Press, 1996.

Kenoyer, Jonathan Mark. "Bangles." In Margaret Mills, Peter Claus, and Sarah Diamond, eds., *South Asian Folklore: An Encyclopedia*, pp. 51–52.

———. "Jewelry and Adornment." In Margaret Mills, Peter Claus, and Sarah Diamond, eds., *South Asian Folklore: An Encyclopedia*, pp. 308–309.

———. "Metal and Metalworking." In Margaret Mills, Peter Claus, and Sarah Diamond, eds., *South Asian Folklore: An Encyclopedia*, pp. 398–402.

Khan, Naseem. "Asian Women's Dress: From Burqah to Bloggs—Changing Clothes for Changing Times." In Juliet Ash and

480

Elizabeth Wilson, eds., *Chic Thrills,* pp. 61–74.

Khan, Shamsuzzaman, ed. *Folklore of Bangladesh.* Dhaka: Bangla Academy, 1992.

Kidwell, Claudia Brush, and Valerie Steele. *Men and Women: Dressing the Part.* Washington, D.C.: Smithsonian Institution Press, 1989.

Kirshenblatt-Gimblett, Barbara. *Destination Culture: Tourism, Museums, and Heritage.* Berkeley: University of California Press, 1998.

Kitchener, Amy V. *The Holiday Yards of Florencio Morales: "El Hombre de las Banderas."* Jackson: University Press of Mississippi, 1994.

Kjellegren, Eric, and Carol S. Ivory. *Adorning the World: Art of the Marquesas Islands.* Metropolitan Museum of Art. New Haven: Yale University Press, 2005.

Klein, Alan. *Little Big Men: Bodybuilding Subculture and Gender Construction.* Albany: State University of New York Press, 1993.

Klein, Richard. *Jewelry Talks.* New York: Pantheon Books, 2001.

Ko, Dorothy. "The Body as Attire: The Shifting Meanings of Footbinding in Seventeenth-Century China." *Journal of Women's History* 8, no. 4 (Winter 1997): 8–27.

———. *Every Step a Lotus: Shoes for Bound Feet.* Los Angeles: University of California Press, 2001.

———. *Cinderella's Sisters: A Revisionist History of Footbinding.* Berkeley: University of California Press, 2005.

Kocsis, Aranka. *Zoboralji Hímzések.* [Folk Embroidery of the Zobor Region]. Budapest: Néprajzi Múzeum, 1994.

Koda, Harold. *Extreme Beauty: The Body Transformed.* New Haven: Metropolitan Museum of Art and Yale University Press, 2001.

Köhler, Carl. *A History of Costume.* New York: Dover, 1963 [1928].

Kramrisch, Stella. *The Hindu Temple.* Calcutta: University of Calcutta, 1946.

Kreamer, Christine Mullen, and Sarah Fee. *Objects as Envoys: Cloth, Imagery, and Diplomacy in Madagascar.* Washington, D.C.: Smithsonian Institution, 2002.

Krishna, Nandita. *Arts and Crafts of Tamilnadu.* Ahmedabad: Mapin, 1992.

Krishnan, Usha R. Bala, and Meera Sushil Kumar. *Dance of the Peacock: Jewellery Traditions of India.* Mumbai: India Book House, 1999.

Krody, Sumru Belger. *Flowers of Silk and Gold: Four Centuries of Ottoman Embroidery.* London: Merell Holberton, 2000.

Kroeber, A. L. "On the Principle of Order and Civilization as Exemplified by Changes in Fashion." *American Anthropologist,* New Series 21, 3 (1919): 235–263.

Küchler, Susanne, and Daniel Miller, eds. *Clothing as Material Culture.* Oxford: Berg, 2005.

Kumar, Nita. *The Artisans of Banaras: Popular Culture and Identity, 1880–1986.* Princeton: Princeton University Press, 1988.

———. *Friends, Brothers, and Informants: Fieldwork Memoirs of Banaras.* Berkeley: University of California Press, 1992.

———. "Why Do Hindus and Muslims Fight? Children and History in India." In Diane Mines and Sarah Lamb, eds., *Everyday Life in South Asia,* pp. 337–356.

Kumar, Radha. *The History of Doing: An Illustrated Account of Movements for Women's Rights and Feminism in India, 1800–1990.* London: Verso, 1993.

Kurin, Richard. *Reflections of a Culture Broker: A View from the Smithsonian.* Washington, D.C.: Smithsonian Institution Press, 1997.

Lahiri, Jhumpa. *Interpreter of Maladies.* New York: Houghton Mifflin Co., 1999.

———. *The Namesake.* New York: Houghton Mifflin Co., 2003.

———. "Hell-Heaven." *The New Yorker,* May 24, 2004, pp. 73–81.

Lamb, Sarah. *White Saris and Sweet Mangoes: Aging, Gender, and Body in North India.* Berkeley: University of California Press, 2000.

Lane, Kenneth Jay. *Faking It.* New York: Harry N. Abrams, 1996.

Lannoy, Richard. *Benares: A World Within a World: The Microcosm of Kashi Yesterday and Today.* Varanasi: Indica Books, 2002.

Larson, Gerald James. "A Postmodernist Perspective on India's Popular Religious Art." In Gerald Larson and Pratapaditya Pal, *Changing Myths and Images,* pp. 24–28.

Larson, Gerald James, and Pratapaditya Pal. *Changing Myths and Images: Twentieth-Century Popular Art in India.* Bloomington: Indiana University India Studies Program and Indiana University Art Museum, 1997.

Larson, Mark, and Barney Hoskyns. *The Mullet: Hairstyle of the Gods.* New York: Bloomsbury, 1999.

Lawless, Elaine J. *God's Peculiar People: Women's Voices and Folk Tradition in a Pentecostal Church.* Lexington: University of Kentucky Press, 1988.

———. "Claiming Inversion: Lesbian Constructions of Female Identity as Claims for Authority." *Journal of American Folklore* 111, no. 439 (Winter 1998): 3–22.

Lehri, Roxana. *Folk Designs from India.* Amsterdam: Pepin Press, 1999.

Lengyel, Györgyi. *Népi Kézimunkák.* [Folk Embroideries]. Budapest: Kossuth Könyvkiadó, 1978.

Lenius, Oscar. *A Well-Dressed Gentleman's Pocket Guide.* London: Prion, 1998.

Leslie, Julia I. *The Perfect Wife: The Orthodox Hindu Woman according to the Strīdharmapaddhati of Tryambakayajvan.* Delhi: Oxford University Press, 1989.

———. "The Significance of Dress for the Orthodox Hindu Woman." In Ruth Barnes and Joanne Eicher, eds., *Dress and Gender: Making and Meaning,* pp. 198–213.

Lévi-Strauss, Claude. *Tristes Tropiques.* New York: Atheneum, 1975 [1955].

Lewis, Oscar. *Village Life in Northern India: Studies in a Delhi Village.* New York: Vintage Books, 1958.

Lindahl, Carl, and Carolyn Ware. *Cajun Mardi Gras Masks.* Jackson: University Press of Mississippi, 1997.

Locke, Liz, and Theresa A. Vaughan, eds. *Women's Folklore and Folklife: An Encyclopedia of Beliefs, Customs, Tales, Music, and Art.* Santa Barbara, Calif.: ABC-CIO, forthcoming.

Lurie, Alison. *The Language of Clothes.* New York: Random House, 1981.

Lutgendorf, Phillip. "All in the (Raghu) Family: A Video Epic in Cultural Context." In Lawrence Babb and Susan Wadley, *Media and the Transformation of Religion in South Asia,* pp. 217–253.

Lynch, Annette. *Dress, Gender and Cultural Change: Asian American and African American Rites of Passage.* Oxford: Berg, 1999.

Lynton, Linda. *The Sari: Styles, Patterns, History, Techniques.* New York: Thames and Hudson, 1995.

MacDowell, Marsha, ed. *Contemporary Great Lakes Pow Wow Regalia: "Nda Maamawigaami (Together We Dance)."* East Lansing: Michigan State University Museum, 1997.

Mack, John, ed. *Ethnic Jewelry.* New York: Harry N. Abrams, 1988.

Mackrell, Alice. *An Illustrated History of Fashion: 500 Years of Fashion Illustration.* New York: Costume and Fashion Press, 1997.

Magliocco, Sabina. *Neo-Pagan Sacred Art and Altars: Making Things Whole.* Jackson: University Press of Mississippi, 2001.

Maheswarajah, H. M. "Caste Mark (Bindi, Bottu)." In Margaret Mills, Peter Claus, and Sarah Diamond, eds., *South Asian Folklore: An Encyclopedia,* pp. 99–100.

Mahmud, Firoz. "Methodology for the Study of Folk Costume of Bangladesh." In Shamsuzzaman Khan, *Folklore of Bangladesh,* pp. 16–21.

Malladi, Amulya. *Serving Crazy with Curry.* New York: Ballantine, 2004.

Mani, Bakirathi. "Undressing the Diaspora." In Nirmal Puwar and Parvati Raghuram,

South Asian Women in the Diaspora, pp. 117–135.

Mani, Lata. "Contentious Traditions: The Debate on Sati in Colonial India." In Kumkum Sangari and Sudesh Vaid, eds., *Recasting Women: Essays in Colonial History,* pp. 88–126.

Marriott, McKim. *Village India: Studies in the Little Community.* The American Anthropological Association Memoir no. 83: University of Chicago Press, 1955.

Mathur, Saloni. "Re-visualising the Missionary Subject: History, Modernity and Indian Women," in *Third Text* 37, Winter 1996–1997, pp. 53–61.

———. "Wanted Native Views: Collecting Colonial Postcards of India." In A. Burton, ed., *Gender, Sexuality and Colonial Modernities,* pp. 95–115.

McCabe, Michael. *New York City Tattoo: The Oral History of an Urban Art.* Honolulu: Hardy Marks Productions, 1997.

McClellan, Elizabeth. *History of American Costume.* Book 1: 1607–1800. New York: Tudor, 1937.

McConnell, Sophie. *Metropolitan Jewelry.* New York: The Metropolitan Museum of Art, 1991.

McCourt, Malachy. *The Claddagh Ring.* Philadelphia: Running Press, 2003.

McCracken, Grant. *Big Hair: A Journey into the Transformation of Self.* Woodstock: Overlook, 1996.

McDannell, Colleen. *Material Christianity: Religion and Popular Culture in America.* New Haven: Yale University Press, 1995.

McLary, Kathleen. *Amish Style: Clothing, Home Furnishings, Toys, Dolls, and Quilts.* Bloomington: Indiana University Press, 1993.

Mehta, Rama. *Inside the Haveli.* New Delhi: Penguin Books India, 1996.

Menon, Ramesh. *The Ramayana.* New York: North Point, 2001.

Messina, Maria. "Henna Party," in *Natural History Magazine* 97, no. 9 (1988): 40–47.

Michelman, Susan O., and Tonye Erekosima.

"Kalabari Dress in Nigeria: Visual Analysis and Gender Implications." In Ruth Barnes and Joanne Eicher, eds., *Dress and Gender,* pp. 164–182.

Miller, Jean-Chris. *The Body Art Book: A Complete, Illustrated Guide to Tattoos, Piercings, and Other Body Modifications.* New York: Berkley Books, 1997.

Mills, Margaret. "Sex Role Reversals, Sex Changes, and Transvestite Disguise in the Oral Tradition of a Conservative Muslim Community in Afghanistan." In Rosan Jordan and Susan Kalčik, eds., *Women's Folklore, Women's Culture,* pp. 187–213.

Mills, Margaret, Peter J. Claus, and Sarah Diamond, eds., *South Asian Folklore: An Encyclopedia.* New York: Routledge, 2003.

———. "Dowry and Bridewealth." In Margaret Mills, Peter Claus, and Sarah Diamond, eds., pp. 164–165.

Mines, Diane, and Sarah Lamb. "Seven Prevalent Misconceptions about India's Caste System." In Diane Mines and Sarah Lamb, eds., *Everyday Life in South Asia,* pp. 227–228.

Mines, Diane, and Sarah Lamb, eds. *Everyday Life in South Asia.* Bloomington: Indiana University Press, 2002.

Mines, Mattison. *Public Faces, Private Voices: Community and Individuality in South India.* Berkeley: University of California Press, 1994.

Mintz, Jerome R. *Legends of the Hasidim.* Chicago: University of Chicago Press, 1968.

Mishra, Pankaj. *The Romantics.* New York: Anchor Books, 2001.

Mitra, Debendra Bijoy. *The Cotton Weavers of Bengal 1757–1833.* Calcutta: Firma KLM, 1978.

Mitter, Partha. *Much Maligned Monsters: History of European Reactions to Indian Art.* Oxford: Clarendon, 1977.

Mode, Heinz. *Indian Folk Art.* Trans. Peter Ross and Betty Ross. New York: Alpine Fine Arts Collection, 1985.

Moes, Robert. *Mingei: Japanese Folk Art from the Montgomery Collection.* Alexandria, Va.: Art Services International, 1995.

Moore, Pamela, ed. *Building Bodies.* New Brunswick: Rutgers University Press, 1997.

Morris, Jean, and Eleanor Preston-Whyte. *Speaking with Beads: Zulu Arts from Southern Africa.* London: Thames and Hudson, 1994.

Muggleton, David, and Rupert Weinzierl, eds. *The Post-Subcultures Reader.* Oxford: Berg, 2003.

Mukherjee, Bharati. *Wife.* New York: Penguin Books, 1975.

———. *The Middleman and Other Stories.* New York: Grove, 1988.

———. *Desirable Daughters.* New York: Hyperion, 2002.

———. *The Tree Bride.* New York: Hyperion, 2004.

Nabar, Vrinda. *Caste as Woman.* New Delhi: Penguin Books India, 1995.

Nagarajan, Vijaya. "Hosting the Divine: The *Kolam* in Tamilnadu." In Nora Fisher, ed., *Mud, Mirror and Thread,* pp. 192–203.

Nagrath, Sumati. "(En)countering Orientalism in High Fashion: A Review of India Fashion Week 2002." *Fashion Theory: The Journal of Dress, Body & Culture* 7, no. 3–4 (September/December 2003): 361–376.

Nair, Anita. *Ladies Coupé.* New York: St. Martin's Griffin, 2001.

Nanda, Serena. *Neither Man Nor Woman: The Hijras of India.* Belmont, Calif.: Wadsworth, 1999.

Nandy, Ashis. "Sati: A Nineteenth-Century Tale of Women, Violence and Protest." In Ashis Nandy, *At the Edge of Psychology,* pp. 1–31.

———. *At the Edge of Psychology.* Delhi: Oxford University Press, 1980.

Narayan, Kirin. "*Tulsi* (Basil)." In Margaret Mills, Peter Claus, and Sarah Diamond, eds., *South Asian Folklore: An Encyclopedia,* p. 619.

———. "Wedding Songs." In Margaret Mills, Peter Claus, and Sarah Diamond,

eds., *South Asian Folklore: An Encyclopedia,* pp. 634–635.

Nath, Aman, and Francis Wacziarg. *Arts and Crafts of Rajasthan.* Ahmedabad: Mapin, 1994.

Neleman, Hans. *Moko—Maori Tattoo.* Zurich: Edition Stemmle, 1999.

Nelson, Marion, ed. *Norwegian Folk Art: The Migration of a Tradition.* New York: Abbeville, 1995.

Newman, Harold. *An Illustrated Dictionary of Jewelry.* London: Thames and Hudson, 1981.

Niessen, Sandra, Ann Marie Leshkowich, and Carla Jones. *Re-Orienting Fashion: The Globalization of Asian Dress.* Oxford: Berg, 2003.

Nudie, Jamie Lee, and Mary Lynn Cabrall. *Nudie: The Rodeo Tailor.* Salt Lake City: Gibbs Smith, 2004.

Nylén, Anna-Maja. *Swedish Peasant Costumes.* Trans. William Cameron. Stockholm: Nordiska Museet, 1949.

Obeyesekere, Gananath. *Medusa's Hair: An Essay on Personal Symbols and Religious Experience.* Chicago: University of Chicago Press, 1981.

O'Hanlon, Michael. *Reading the Skin: Adornment, Display and Society among the Wahgi.* London: British Museum, 1989.

Orejuela, Fernando. *The Body as Cultural Artifact: Performing the Body in Bodybuilding Culture.* Ph.D. dissertation, Bloomington, Indiana University, 2005.

Özbel, Kenan. *Knitted Stockings from Turkish Villages.* Ankara: Türkiye İş Bankası Cultural Publications, 1981.

Pal, M. K. *Jewellery and Ornaments in India—A Historical Outline.* Census of India, Series no. 1, Paper no. 1. New Delhi: Office of the Registrar General, India, Ministry of Home Affairs, 1970.

Pal, Pratapaditya. "The Printed Image: An Iconographic Excursus." In Gerald Larson and Pratapaditya Pal, *Changing Myths and Images,* pp. 29–38.

Parameswaran, Radhika. "Global Queens,

National Celebrities: Tales of Feminine Triumph in Post-Liberalization India." *Critical Studies in Media Communication* 21, no. 4 (1994): 346–370.

———. "Global Media Events in India: Contests over Beauty, Gender and Nation." *Journalism Communication Monographs* 3, no. 2 (Summer 2001).

Paredes, Américo, and Richard Bauman, eds. *Toward New Perspectives in Folklore.* Bloomington, Ind.: Trickster, 2000 [1972].

Parry, Jonathan P. *Death in Banaras.* Cambridge: Cambridge University Press, 1994.

Paterek, Josephine. *Encyclopedia of American Indian Costume.* Santa Barbara, Calif.: ABC-CIO, 1994.

Payne, Peggy. *Sister India.* New York: Riverhead Books, 2001.

Peacock, John. *Costume 1066–1990s.* London: Thames and Hudson, 2003 [1986].

Peiss, Kathy. *Hope in a Jar: The Making of America's Beauty Culture.* New York: Henry Holt and Co., 1998.

Pershing, Linda. *Sew to Speak: The Fabric Art of Mary Milne.* Jackson: University Press of Mississippi, 1995.

Peterkin, Allan. *One Thousand Beards: A Cultural History of Facial Hair.* Vancouver: Arsenal Pulp Press, 2001.

Peterson, Sally. "Translating Experience and the Reading of a Story Cloth." *Journal of American Folklore* 101, no. 99 (1988): 6–22.

———. "Plastic Strap Baskets: Containers for a Changing Context." In James Hardin and Alan Jabbour, eds., *Folklife Annual 88–89,* pp. 138–147.

Phillips, Clare. *Jewelry: From Antiquity to the Present.* London: Thames and Hudson, 1996.

Phoenix and Arabeth. *Henna (Mehndi) Body Art Handbook: Complete How-to Guide.* Ukiah, Calif.: (self-published), 1997.

Pinney, Christopher. *Camera Indica: The Social Life of Indian Photographs.* Chicago: University of Chicago Press, 1997.

Pocius, Gerald L. *Textile Traditions of Eastern Newfoundland.* Ottawa: National Museum of Canada, 1979.

———. *A Place to Belong: Community Order and Everyday Space in Calvert, Newfoundland.* Athens: University of Georgia Press, 1991.

———, ed. *Living in a Material World: Canadian and American Approaches to Material Culture.* St. Johns', Newfoundland: Institute of Social and Economic Research, Memorial University of Newfoundland, 1991.

Polhemus, Ted, and Housk Randall. *The Customized Body.* London: Serpent's Tail, 1996.

———. *Body Art: The Total Guide to Body Decoration.* Boston: Element Children's Book, 1998.

Poll, Solomon. "The Hasidic Community." In Mary Ellen Roach-Higgins, Joanne Eicher, and Kim Johnson, *Dress and Identity,* pp. 224–235.

Posey, Sandra Mizumoto. "Burning Messages: Interpreting African American Fraternity Brands and Their Bearers." *Voices: The Journal of the New York Folklore Society,* Fall 2004, pp. 42–45.

———. "The Body Art of Brotherhood." In Tamara Brown, Gregory Parks, and Clarenda Phillips, eds., *African American Fraternities and Sororities,* pp. 269–293.

Prashad, Vijay. *The Karma of Brown Folk.* Minneapolis: University of Minnesota Press, 2000.

Pritchett, Frances W. "The World of *Amar Chitra Katha.*" In Lawrence Babb and Susan Wadley, *Media and the Transformation of Religion in South Asia,* pp. 76–106.

Puri, Jyoti. *Woman, Body, Desire in Post-colonial India: Narratives of Gender and Sexuality.* New York: Routledge, 1999.

Puwar, Nirmal, and Parvati Raghuram. *South Asian Women in the Diaspora.* Oxford: Berg, 2003.

Radner, Joan. *Feminist Messages: Coding in Women's Folk Culture.* Chicago: University of Illinois Press, 1993.

Radner, Joan N., and Susan S. Lanser, "Strategies of Coding in Women's Cultures." In Joan Radner, *Feminist Messages,* pp. 1–29.

Raghuram, Parvati. "Fashioning the South Asian Diaspora: Production and Consumption Tales." In Nirmal Puwar and Parvati Raghuram, *South Asian Women in the Diaspora,* pp. 67–85.

Rahbari, Reza. "Unveiling Muslim Women: A Trajectory of Post-Colonial Culture." *Dialectical Anthropology* 25 (2000): 321–332.

Raheja, Gloria Goodwin, and Ann Grodzins Gold. *Listen to the Heron's Words: Reimagining Gender and Kinship in North India.* Berkeley: University of California Press, 1994.

———. "On the Uses of Irony and Ambiguity: Shifting Perspectives on Patriliny and Women's Ties to Natal Kin." In Gloria Goodwin Raheja and Ann Grodzins Gold, *Listen to the Heron's Words,* pp. 73–120.

Ramaswami, N. S. *Temples of South India.* Bangalore: Vasan Publications, 1998.

Ramusack, Barbara N., and Sharon Sievers. *Women in Asia: Restoring Women to History.* Bloomington: Indiana University Press, 1999.

Ray, Sangeeta. *En-Gendering India: Woman and Nation in Colonial and Postcolonial Narratives.* Durham: Duke University Press, 2000.

Razina, Tatyana, Natalia Cherkasova, and Alexander Kantsedikas. *Folk Art in the Soviet Union.* New York: Harry N. Abrams, 1990.

Reddy, Gayatri. *With Respect to Sex: Negotiating Hijra Identity in South India.* Chicago: University of Chicago Press, 2005.

Reischer, Erica, and Kathryn S. Koo. "The Body Beautiful: Symbolism and Agency in the Social World." *Annual Review of Anthropology* 33 (2004): 297–317.

Riello, Giorgio, and Peter McNeil, eds. *Shoes: A History from Sandals to Sneakers.* Oxford: Berg, 2006.

Rinzler, Ralph, and Robert Sayers. *The Meaders Family: North Georgia Potters.* Washington, D.C.: Smithsonian Institution Press, 1980.

Roach, Mary Ellen, and Joanne Eicher. *Dress, Adornment, and the Social Order.* New York: John Wiley and Sons, 1965.

Roach-Higgins, Mary Ellen, Joanne B. Eicher, and Kim K. P. Johnson, eds. *Dress and Identity.* New York: Fairchild, 1995.

Roberts, Allen F. "Tabwa Tegumentary Inscription." In Arnold Rubin, ed., *Marks of Civilization,* pp. 41–56.

Roberts, Mary Nooter, and Allison Saar. *Body Politics: The Female Image in Luba Art and the Sculpture of Alison Saar.* Los Angeles: UCLA Fowler Museum of Cultural History, 2000.

Roberts, Warren. *Log Buildings of Southern Indiana.* Bloomington, Ind.: Trickster, 1996 [1984].

Robinson, Dwight E. "Fashions in Shaving and Trimming of the Beard: The Men of the Illustrated London News, 1842–1972." *The American Journal of Sociology* 81, no. 5 (March 1976): 1133–1141.

Robley, H. G. *Maori Tattooing.* New York: Dover, 2003 [1896].

Roediger, Virginia More. *Ceremonial Costumes of the Pueblo Indians.* Berkeley: University of California Press, 1961.

Rolley, Katrina. "Love, Desire and the Pursuit of the Whole: Dress and the Lesbian Couple." In Juliet Ash and Elizabeth Wilson, eds., *Chic Thrills,* pp. 30–39.

Rooks, Noliwe M. *Hair Raising: Beauty, Culture, and African American Women.* New Brunswick: Rutgers University Press, 1996.

Roome, Loretta. *Mehndi: The Timeless Art of Henna Painting.* New York: St. Martin's Griffin, 1998.

Ross, Doran H. *Wrapped in Pride: Ghanaian Kente and African American Identity.* Los Angeles: UCLA Fowler Museum of Cultural History, 1998.

Roy, Manish. *Bengali Women.* Chicago: University of Chicago Press, 1992.

Rubin, Arnold. "The Tattoo Renaissance." In Arnold Rubin, ed., *Marks of Civilization,* pp. 233–262.

———. "Tattoo Trends in Gujarat." In Arnold Rubin, ed., *Marks of Civilization,* pp. 141–153.

———, ed. *Marks of Civilization: Artistic Transformations of the Human Body.* Los Angeles: Museum of Cultural History, 1988.

Ruby, Jennifer. *Costume in Context: Underwear.* London: B. T. Batsford, 1996.

Rudofsky, Bernard. *The Unfashionable Human Body.* New York: Van Nostrand Reinhold, 1984 (1971).

Rugh, Andrea B. *Reveal and Conceal: Dress in Contemporary Egypt.* Syracuse: Syracuse University Press, 1986.

Rushdie, Salman. *Midnight's Children.* New York: Avon Books, 1980.

Russell, Andrew. "Miss World Comes to India." *Anthropology Today* 13, no. 4 (August 1997): 12–14.

Rusva, Mirza Muhammad Hadi. *Umrao Jan Ada.* Trans. David Matthews. Calcutta: Rupa and Co., 1996.

Sachs, Melanie. *Ayurvedic Beauty Care: Ageless Techniques to Invoke Natural Beauty.* Delhi: Motilal Banarasidass, 1998.

Saksena, Jogendra. *Art of Rajasthan: Henna and Floor Decorations.* Delhi: Sundeep Prakashan, 1979.

Salvador, Mari Lyn. *The Art of Being Kuna: Layers of Meaning Among the Kuna of Panama.* Los Angeles: UCLA Fowler Museum of Cultural History, 1997.

Sambrani, Chaitanya. *Edge of Desire: Recent Art in India.* New York: Asia Society and Art Gallery of Western Australia, 2005.

———. "On the Double Edge of Desire." In Chaitanya Sambrani, *Edge of Desire,* pp. 12–33.

Sanders, Clinton R. *Customizing the Body: The Art and Culture of Tattooing.* Philadelphia: Temple University Press, 1989.

Sandıkcı, Özlem, and Güliz Ger. "Aesthetics, Ethics and Politics of the Turkish Headscarf." In Susanne Küchler and Daniel Miller, *Clothing as Material Culture,* pp. 61–82.

Sangari, Kumkum, and Sudesh Vaid. *Recasting Women: Essays in Colonial History.* New Delhi: Kali for Women, 1999.

Santino, Jack. "The Folk *Assemblage* of Autumn: Tradition and Creativity in Halloween Folk Art." In John Vlach and Simon Bronner, eds., *Folk Art and Art Worlds,* pp. 151–170.

———. *All Around the Year: Holidays and Celebrations in American Life.* Urbana: University of Illinois Press, 1994.

Sarin, Amita Vohra. "Comic Books, India." In Margaret Mills, Peter Claus, and Sarah Diamond, eds., *South Asian Folklore: An Encyclopedia,* pp. 117–118.

Sarkar, Tanika. *Hindu Wife, Hindu Nation: Community, Religion, and Cultural Nationalism.* Bloomington: Indiana University Press, 2001.

Satrapi, Marjane. *Persepolis: The Story of a Childhood.* New York: Pantheon Books, 2003.

———. *Persepolis 2: The Story of a Return.* New York: Pantheon Books, 2004.

Schieffelin, Edward L., and Robert Crittenden. *Like People You See in a Dream: First Contact in Six Papuan Societies.* Stanford: Stanford University Press, 1991.

Schildkrout, Enid, and Curtis A. Keim. *African Reflections: Art from Northeastern Zaire.* Seattle: American Museum of Natural History and University of Washington Press, 1990.

———. "Inscribing the Body." *Annual Review of Anthropology* 33 (2004): 319–344.

Schildkrout, Enid, and Donna K. Pido. "Serendipity, Practicality, and Aesthetics: The Art of Recycling in Personal Adornment." In Charlene Cerny and Suzanne Seriff, *Recycled Re-Seen,* pp. 152–165.

Schlee, Ernst. *German Folk Art.* Tokyo: Kodansha International, 1980.

Schrempp, Gregory, and William Hansen, eds. *Myth: A New Symposium.* Bloomington: Indiana University Press, 2002.

Sciama, Lidi D., and Joanne B. Eicher, eds. *Beads and Bead Makers: Gender, Material Culture and Meaning*. Oxford: Berg, 1998.

Sen, Colleen Taylor. *Food Culture in India*. Westport, Conn.: Greenwood, 2004.

Sen, Prabhas. *Crafts of West Bengal*. Ahmedabad: Mapin, 1994.

Seth, Vikram. *A Suitable Boy*. New York: Perennial, 1994.

Sethi, Rajeev, Pria Devi, and Richard Kurin. *Aditi: The Living Arts of India*. Washington, D.C.: Smithsonian Institution Press, 1986.

Severa, Joan. *Dressed for the Photographer: Ordinary Americans and Fashion, 1840–1900*. Kent: Kent State University Press, 1995.

Shamsie, Kamila. *Salt and Saffron*. New York: Bloomsbury, 2000.

Shankar, Lavina Dhingra, and Rajini Srikanth. *A Part, Yet Apart: South Asians in Asian America*. Philadelphia: Temple University Press, 1998.

Shukla, Pravina. "Beads of Identity in the Carnival of Salvador da Bahia, Brazil." In Henry Drewal and John Mason, *Beads, Body, and Soul*, pp. 187–197.

———. "Beautiful Brides in India." *Voices: The Journal of New York Folklore* 26 (Fall/Winter 2000): 28–33.

———. "Afro-Brazilian Avatars: Gandhi's Sons Samba in South America." *Indian Folklore Research Journal* 1, no. 1 (May 2001): 35–45.

———. "The Study of Dress and Adornment as Social Positioning." *Material History Review* 61: Spring 2005: 4–16.

———. "Dowry." In Liz Locke and Theresa A. Vaughan, eds., *Women's Folklore and Folklife: An Encyclopedia of Beliefs, Customs, Tales, Music, and Art*. Santa Barbara, Calif.: ABC-CIO, forthcoming.

———. "Henna Art." In Liz Locke and Theresa A. Vaughan, eds., *Women's Folklore and Folklife: An Encyclopedia of Beliefs, Customs, Tales, Music, and Art*. Santa Barbara, Calif.: ABC-CIO, forthcoming.

Sidwa, Bapsi. *The Bride*. New York: St. Martin's, 1983.

———. *Cracking India*. Minneapolis: Milkweed Editions, 1991.

Simpson, Hilary. "Shawls Off for the Lancers!" *Ulster Folklife* 40 (1994): 49–55.

Singh, Khushwant. *Train to Pakistan*. Delhi: Ravi Dayal, 1988.

Singh, Martand, Rta Kapur Chishti, and Amba Sanyal. *Saris of India: Madhya Pradesh*. Seattle: University of Washington Press, 1991.

Singh, Rana P. B. *Where Cultural Symbols Meet: Literary Images of Varanasi*. Varanasi: Tara Book Agency, 1989.

———, ed. *Banaras (Varanasi): Cosmic Order, Sacred City, Hindu Traditions*. Varanasi: Tara Book Agency, 1993.

Singh, Rana P. B., and Pravin S. Rana. *Banaras Region: A Spiritual and Cultural Guide*. Varanasi: Indica Books, 2002.

Smith, Daniel H. "Impact of 'God Posters' on Hindus and Their Devotional Traditions." In Lawrence Babb and Susan Wadley, ed., *Media and the Transformation of Religion in South Asia*, pp. 24–50.

Snowden, James. *The Folk Dress of Europe*. New York: Mayflower Books, 1979.

Spiegelman, Art. *Maus: A Survivor's Tale I: My Father Bleeds History*. New York: Pantheon Books, 1986.

St. Clair, Leonard L., and Alan B. Govenar. *Stoney Knows How: Life as a Tattoo Artist*. Lexington: University Press of Kentucky, 1981.

Steele, Valerie. *The Corset: A Cultural History*. New Haven: Yale University Press, 2001.

———. *The Fan: Fashion and Femininity Unfolded*. New York: Rizzoli, 2002.

———, ed. *Encyclopedia of Clothing and Fashion*. New York: Charles Scribner's Sons, 2004.

Steiner, Christopher B. *African Art in Transit*. Cambridge: Cambridge University Press, 1994.

Strathern, Andrew, and Marilyn Strathern. *Self-Decoration in Mount Hagen*. Toronto: University of Toronto Press, 1971.

Strawn, Susan, Jane Farell-Beck, and Ann R. Hemken. "Bib Overalls: Function and Fashion." *Dress* 32 (2005): 43–55.

Stronge, Susan, Nima Smith, and J. C. Harle. *A Golden Treasury: Jewellery from the Indian Subcontinent.* London: Victoria and Albert Museum, 1988.

Sturtevant, William. "Seminole Men's Clothing." *Essays on the Verbal and Visual Arts,* Proceedings of the 1966 Annual Spring Meeting of the American Ethnological Society. Seattle: University of Washington Press, 1967.

Sun, Ming-Ju. *Traditional Fashions from India: Paper Dolls.* Mineola: Dover, 2001.

Suri, Manil. *The Death of Vishnu.* New York: W. W. Norton & Co., 2001.

Sürür, Ayten. *Ege Bölgesi Kadın Kıyafetleri* [Female Costumes in the Aegean Region]. İstanbul: Akbank, 1983.

Tambiah, S. J. "Dowry and Bridewealth and the Property Rights of Women in South Asia." In Jack Goody and T. J. Tambiah, *Bridewealth and Dowry,* pp. 59–166.

Tandberg, Gerilyn. "Confederate Bonnets: Imagination and Ingenuity." *Dress* 32 (2005): 14–26.

Tarlo, Emma. *Clothing Matters: Dress and Identity in India.* London: Hurst & Co., 1996.

Taylor, Lou. *The Study of Dress History.* Manchester: Manchester University Press, 2002.

Teilhet-Fisk, Jehanne. "The Spiritual Significance of Newar Tattoos." In Arnold Rubin, ed., *Marks of Civilization,* pp. 135–139.

Thakurta, Tapati Guha. "Women as 'Calendar Art' Icons: Emergence of Pictorial Stereotype in Colonial India." *Economic and Political Weekly* 26, no. 43 (October 26, 1991): 91–99.

Thompson, F. Glenn. *The Uniforms of 1798–1803.* Dublin: Four Courts, 1998.

Tierney, Tom. *Fashions from India.* (Coloring Book.) Mineola: Dover, 2003.

Trachtenberg, Peter. *7 Tattoos: A Memoir in the Flesh.* New York: Penguin Books, 1997.

Turner, Kay. *Beautiful Necessities: The Art and Meaning of Women's Altars.* New York: Thames and Hudson, 1999.

Turner, Terence S. "The Social Skin." In Catherine Burroughs and Jeffery David Ehrenreich, eds., *Reading the Social Body,* pp. 15–37.

Uberoi, Patricia. "Feminine Identity and National Ethos in Indian Calendar Art." *Economic and Political Weekly* 25, no. 17 (April 28, 1990): 41–48.

Underhill, Paco. *Why We Buy: The Science of Shopping.* New York: Simon and Schuster, 1999.

Untracht, Oppi. *Traditional Jewelry of India.* New York: Harry N. Abrams, 1997.

Vale, V., and Andrea Juno. *Modern Primitives.* San Francisco: V/Search, 1989.

Van Assche, Annie, ed. *Fashioning Kimono: Dress and Modernity in Early Twentieth Century Japan.* Milan: 5 Continents, 2005.

Vankóné Dudás, Juli. *Falum Galgamácsa* [My Village Galgamácsa]. Szentendre: Studia Comita Pensia 4, 1976.

Varjú-Ember, Mária. *Úrihímzés* [Embroidery]. Budapest: Akadémiai Kiadó, 1981.

Venables, D. R., and R. E. Clifford. *Academic Dress of the University of Oxford.* Oxford: John and Peter Venables, 1998 [1957].

Vidyarthi, L. P. *The Sacred Complex of Kashi: A Microcosm of Indian Civilization.* New Delhi: Concept Publishing Co., 1979.

Viramma, Josiane Racine, and Jean-Luc Racine. *Viramma: Life of a Dalit.* Trans. Will Hobson. New Delhi: Social Science, 2000.

Vlach, John Michael. *Charleston Blacksmith: The Work of Philip Simmons.* Athens: University of Georgia Press, 1981.

Vlach, John Michael, and Simon J. Bronner, eds. *Folk Art and Art Worlds.* Ann Arbor: UMI Research Press, 1986.

Vogel, Susan. "Baule Scarification: The Mark of Civilization." In Arnold Rubin, ed., *Marks of Civilization,* pp. 97–105.

von Solodkoff, Alexander. *Masterpieces from*

the House of Fabergé. New York: Harry N. Abrams, 1984.

Vyas, Chintamani, and Dr. Daljeet. *Paintings of Tanjore and Mysore.* Jhansi: Geeta Publishers, 1988.

Wadley, Susan S. "One Straw from a Broom Cannot Sweep: The Ideology and Practice of the Joint Family in Rural North India." In Diane P. Mines and Sarah Lamb, *Everyday Life in South Asia,* pp. 11–22.

Waghorne, Joanne Punzo. "Dressing the Body of God: South Indian Bronze Sculpture in Its Temple Setting." *Asian Art* 3 (Summer 1992): 9–33.

———. *The Raja's Magic Clothes: Re-visioning Kingship and Divinity in England's India.* University Park: Pennsylvania State University Press, 1994.

Weinberger-Thomas, Catherine. *Ashes of Immortality: Widow-Burning in India.* Trans. Jeffrey Mehlman and David Gordon White. Chicago: University of Chicago Press, 1999.

Weiner, Annette B., and Jane Schneider. *Cloth and Human Experience.* Washington: Smithsonian Institution Press, 1989.

Welters, Linda, ed. *Folk Dress in Europe and Anatolia: Beliefs about Protection and Fertility.* Oxford: Berg, 1999.

White, Shane, and Graham White. *Stylin': African American Expressive Culture from Its Beginnings to the Zoot Suit.* Ithaca: Cornell University Press, 1998.

Wilcox, R. Turner. *The Mode in Hats and Headdress: Including Hair Styles, Cosmetics and Jewelry.* New York: Charles Scribner's Sons, 1945.

Willett, C., and Phillis Cunnington. *The History of Underclothes.* New York: Dover, 1992.

Wilson, Verity. *Chinese Dress.* London: Victoria and Albert Museum, 1986.

Wilson, Verity, Jennifer Wearden, and Rosemary Crill. *Dress in Detail from Around the World.* London: Victoria and Albert Museum, 2004.

Winge, Theresa. "Constructing 'Neo-Tribal' Identities Through Dress: Modern Primitives Body Modifications." In David Muggleton and Rupert Weinzierl, eds., *The Post-Subcultures Reader.*

———. "Branding." In Valerie Steele, ed., *Encyclopedia of Clothing and Fashion.*

———. "Implants." In Valerie Steele, ed., *Encyclopedia of Clothing and Fashion.*

———. "Modern Primitive Subculture." In Valerie Steele, ed., *Encyclopedia of Clothing and Fashion.*

———. "Scarification." In Valerie Steele, ed., *Encyclopedia of Clothing and Fashion.*

———. "Tattoos." In Valerie Steele, ed., *Encyclopedia of Clothing and Fashion.*

Wojcik, Daniel. *Punk and Neo-Tribal Body Art.* Jackson: University of Mississippi Press, 1995.

Wolpert, Stanley. *A New History of India.* Oxford: Oxford University Press, 1982.

Woodward, Christine, and Roger Harding. *Gemstones.* New York: Sterling Publishing Co., 1988.

Woodward, Sophie. "Looking Good: Feeling Right—Aesthetics of the Self." In Susanne Küchler and Daniel Miller, *Clothing as Material Culture,* pp. 21–39.

Wulff, Hans E. *The Traditional Crafts of Persia.* Cambridge: MIT Press, 1966.

Yamaguchi, Akira. *Sculpture in Silk: Costumes from Japan's Noh Theatre.* New York: Art Capital Group, 2003.

Yamanaka, Norio. *The Book of Kimono: The Complete Guide to Style and Wear.* Tokyo: Kodansha International, 1982.

Young, Katherine, ed. *Bodylore.* Knoxville: University of Tennessee Press, 1993.

Young, Malcolm. "Dress and Modes of Address: Structural Forms for Policewomen." In Ruth Barnes and Joanne Eicher, eds., *Dress and Gender,* pp. 266–285.

Zapata, Janet. *The Jewelry and Enamels of Louis Comfort Tiffany.* New York: Harry N. Abrams, 1993.

Zug, Charles G., III. *Turners and Burners: The Folk Potters of North Carolina.* Chapel Hill: University of North Carolina Press, 1986.

Index

aarti, 29, 59

Aas Art Centre, 331, 358

adornment. *See bindi;* creativity through personal adornment; henna; makeup; *shringar; sindur*

Aggarwala, Aarti, 39, 115

Agrawal, Piyush, 138, 139, 140, 151, 164

Akbar, 98

akhara, 340–341

Ali, Asif, 189, 190

Ali, Monica, 14, 328

Anand, Anita, 334, 336

Ansari, Hashim, 94, 95–104, 106, 131, 133, 188, 204, 217, 383, 406, 412

Ansari, Shameem, 9, 93, 94, 97, 98

Apfel, Iris Barrel, 404

Ashelford, Jane, 400

assemblage, 216–217, 387, 389, 402–404

astrological rings, 140–143, 173, 175–176, 180

Aurangzeb, 168

Azam Ghar, 278, 352, 370, 372, 373

Babcock, Barbara, 388

Bagga, Interjit Singh, 128, 129, 144

Bajwa, Rupa, 254

Ballard, Linda, 407

Banaras, 8; communities, 9, 45, 78, 80; *darshan,* 27; *ghats,* 59, 93; *masti,* 128; *mina,* 114, 120; temples, 8, 29. *See also* pilgrimage

Banaras Hindu University, 9, 78, 116, 332, 333, 335, 345

Banarasi saris, 9, 14, 24, 65, 83, 85–90, 92–112, 115, 126, 133, 249, 353, 375. *See also* standards of excellence; *zari*

Banerjee, Mukulika, 65, 84, 255

Bangladesh, 14, 15, 31, 53, 84, 110, 165

bangles, 22, 24, 25, 48, 116–117, 119, 184–218, 245–247, 251, 254, 257, 258,

276, 279, 281, 316, 321, 351, 363, 378–379

Barnard, Nicholas, 115

Barnes, Ruth, 417

Baumgarten, Linda, 12

beauticians, 331, 357–359, 361–364, 374, 376

beauty, 33, 40, 50, 336–337, 348, 349, 361; divine, 30, 31–32, 34, 39, 48; facial, 266, 271, 322, 359, 376–377; feminine ideals, 31, 35, 38, 47, 48, 134, 135, 148, 150, 157, 166, 178, 179, 181, 183, 189, 263, 265–272, 283, 297, 333–334, 336–341, 358–359, 361, 426–427, 429

beauty pageant winners, 31, 38, 238, 338–339

Bengal, 22, 31, 53, 128, 139, 166

Berns, Marla, 398

Bhachu, Parminder, 395

Bharat Kala Bhavan, 116

bindi, 14, 20, 21, 22, 41, 165, 167, 168, 176, 177–178, 179, 181, 189, 213, 242, 266, 271, 276, 277, 289, 311, 316, 322, 323, 325, 326, 327, 332, 334, 336, 339, 346, 351, 359, 361, 374, 395

Boas, Franz, 417

body: dressed, 400–402; modified, 397–400; in motion, 396–397; static, 395–396

body art definition, 3

body shaping, 398–399

Bogatyrev, Petr, 12, 400, 416, 417, 425

Bohannan, Paul, 398

Bollywood: fashion influence, 31, 65, 71, 131, 180, 192, 199, 210–202, 203, 208, 211–214, 267–270, 293, 336, 337–341, 362, 364, 398, 406, 423, 427; movies, 31, 32, 46, 71, 199–201, 203, 211, 212, 242, 243, 249, 268–269, 337–342, 362, 366, 377, 405, 406

Bombay (Mumbai), 14, 17, 72, 78, 81, 82, 85, 86, 111, 130, 131, 139, 159, 192, 216, 221–223, 233, 236, 251, 336, 340, 398, 424

Boone, Sylvia, 396

Brazil, 6–8, 416, 420

brides, 40, 41, 43, 320, 346–347, 352, 378

British Raj, 41, 44, 45, 394, 424

Bronner, Simon, 388

burqa, 46, 47, 48, 189, 328, 418

Burrison, John A., 387

Calcutta (Kolkata), 45, 53, 84, 114, 139, 184, 192

caste, 94, 224, 227, 273–275, 298, 348

Catlin, George, 407

celebrations, 143, 170, 236–238

Chadha, Gurinder, 68

Chakravarti, Uma, 321

Chaturvedi, Neelam, 43, 106, 108, 109, 239–262, 263, 267, 286, 298–301, 308, 311, 370, 371, 379, 384, 395, 396, 408, 409, 413, 427

Chaturvedi, Vidhu, 4, 239, 260

Chaubey, Mathuri, 54–56, 311–323, 330, 372, 378, 379, 424–425

Chauk, 60, 137, 170

children's adornment, 141, 168, 223, 241, 247, 305, 327–328, 329

Chishti, Rta, 392

choice, 5, 24, 225, 230, 231–232, 235–238, 245, 252, 273, 298–301, 384, 386, 389, 395

Chourshia, Vishnu Shankar, 175

clothes, 19, 256, 278, 391–395, 400–404, 406–408, 417–429; jeans, 13, 14, 53, 64, 71, 212, 259, 305, 309, 323, 328, 332, 333, 339, 346, 398; in lifecycle, 305–379; men's, 44–46, 71, 87, 164, 171, 306, 325, 340, 345, 349, 356, 366, 403, 415, 416, 418, 429; Western, 45, 53, 212, 259, 324–325, 339, 349, 415. *See also* diaspora; dress as communication of identity; dress in social settings; *salwar suits;* sari

color symbolism, 171–172, 187–188, 296, 305, 315, 316, 318, 322, 324, 325, 374–375, 378

commerce: clothing, 59–91, 100, 104, 105, 108, 109, 111, 112, 235, 247–250, 252–254, 255, 258, 262, 265, 269, 270–271, 280, 350, 352, 393–395, 409, 427; interactions between merchant and customer, 138, 156–166, 175, 180–181, 183, 186, 187, 193–194, 197–198, 204, 206–208, 210–218; choice, 64–73, 82–84; jewelry, 83, 133, 134, 135, 136–218. *See also* merchants; pre-shopping

communal tensions, 9, 84, 86, 87, 89, 93, 97, 103, 108, 127–128, 165, 241–243

communication through dress, 4, 17, 225, 234, 235, 257, 262, 280, 292, 294–295, 296, 298–301, 325–326, 350. *See also* dress as communication of identity

competition, 231, 255, 261–262, 332, 370

compulsory jewelry, 6, 145, 177, 225, 227, 237, 250, 251, 252, 256, 263, 272–273, 311, 326, 333, 346, 351

Cook, Captain James, 408, 425

Cosentino, Donald, 388

costumes, 170, 397, 407, 415, 416, 420

craft apprenticeship: jewelry, 118, 121, 133; sari, 97, 98

craftsmen: jewelry, 114, 115–119, 123–135, 138, 139, 157–158; textile and clothing, 65, 86–90, 92–112

creativity, 10, 15, 131, 133, 386–388, 391–393, 404–405, 410, 424–427

creativity through personal adornment, 13, 15, 19–25, 190, 199, 201–202, 204, 206–207, 210, 212–215, 216–217, 232, 234, 238, 249, 262, 289–291, 293, 297–298, 300–301, 321–323, 340–341, 358, 395–404

cross-dressing, 418. *See also hijras*

Curtis, Edward, 407

Dada, Phallu, 31

Dalby, Liza, 12, 412

darshan, 4, 8, 23, 26–40, 43, 44, 48, 49, 50, 51, 55, 169, 171, 177, 189, 194, 278, 280, 342, 349, 368, 374, 376, 420, 424

Das, Tulsi, 35, 176

Dashaswamedh Ghat, 10, 47, 59–60, 237

Dashaswamedh Road, 60, 62, 63, 66, 67, 70–73, 78, 109, 167–168, 184

Dayaram Fashion Centre, 73–75, 77, 105, 128, 323, 393

death and adornment, 306, 309, 315–318, 320–321, 323. *See also* widows

Devi, Anjali, 50–51, 52, 54, 117, 118, 125, 134–135

Dhar, Nitu, 51, 309

diaspora, 8, 9, 14, 53, 69, 354, 413–414, 416, 429

Divakaruni, Chitra Banerjee, 14, 179, 315, 354

Divali, 143, 170

divorce, 308–309, 349

Dixit, Mathuri, 31

domestic routines, 19–20, 22, 23, 228, 275–276, 285–292, 294, 297, 300–301, 310, 377–379

dowry, 9, 147, 224, 230, 316, 336, 348–349, 352–357, 372–373

dress as communication of identity: age, 22, 46, 49, 53, 64, 74, 75, 141, 148, 149, 168, 187, 193, 194, 223, 241, 247, 272, 274–276, 305–306, 308, 309, 311, 313–316, 317, 322–323, 324–325, 327–333, 377–379, 410–411; caste, 45–46; ethnicity, 128; individual identity, 170, 172, 188, 193, 214, 217, 225, 231–232, 234, 237–238, 245, 257, 262, 265, 268, 288, 297, 300, 308, 408–410; marital status, 22, 197, 205, 227, 238, 245, 251, 252, 272–276, 306, 308–313, 334 (*see also* brides; *kumari;* widows); region, 9, 22, 44, 46, 68, 74, 81, 85, 86, 185, 189–190, 193, 204, 236, 245, 246, 361; religion, 45–47, 80, 103, 164–166, 172–173, 175–177, 418–419; rural residence, 68, 88, 102, 130, 145, 149, 151, 153–155, 193–194, 199, 205, 216, 237, 251, 254, 265, 372, 413, 423, 424, 429 (*see also* gaudy aesthetics); socioeconomic class, 5, 55, 139, 147–148, 149, 151, 153–155, 179, 193, 204, 232, 265, 267; urban residence, 102, 130, 131, 145, 149, 151, 153–155, 193–194, 199, 205, 216, 237, 251, 334, 346, 372

dress in social settings, 413–414; college, 69, 72, 74, 75, 185, 205, 259, 331–332, 347; home, 69, 147, 149, 167, 176–178, 205, 225–228, 237, 250–251, 256–258, 259, 261, 277–280, 286, 294, 333, 346, 378; inappropriate, 21, 51, 71, 72, 166, 256, 279–280, 294, 296–297, 309, 317–318, 323, 328, 331, 332, 338–339; special occasions, 23, 69, 82–84, 148, 187, 205, 227, 230–231, 234, 236, 249, 255, 277, 280, 282–284, 332–333, 371, 414–416; vacation, 51, 53, 258–259; work, 69, 249–255, 261, 322, 334, 336

Drewal, Henry, 398

Dubey, Nirmala, 38, 137

Dubin, Lois, 402

Dunin, Elsie, 415

durbar, 40, 280, 368

Durga, 31, 32, 84

Eck, Diana, 8, 27

economic functions, 23, 137, 146, 147, 153, 154–155, 180–181, 230, 234, 280, 353, 354–355

Eicher, Joanne, 12, 395, 417

El Guindi, Fadwa, 413

embroidery, 68, 74, 75, 83

ensemble creation, 23–25, 48, 54, 134–135, 149–150, 157, 166, 178, 179, 181, 183, 189, 190, 193, 198, 202, 204, 207–208, 214–217, 230, 234, 252, 266, 268, 282, 293–294, 297, 359, 361, 425–427

Entwistle, Joanne, 18, 400

eve-teasing, 233, 308, 331

fabrics, 24, 63, 65, 69, 74, 76, 77, 81, 83, 100–102, 254, 256, 412; cotton, 81, 106, 108, 110; *khadi,* 45; silk, 89, 102, 105, 106, 108, 110; synthetics, 81, 82

family. *See sasural*

Faris, James, 12, 392, 417, 426

Farrell, Perry, 410

fashion, 24, 211–217, 223, 224, 228, 231–233, 236, 241, 243, 249, 251, 257, 267–269, 293, 305, 312, 316, 317, 318, 324, 331–332, 337–340, 352, 378, 414,

429; jewelry, 128, 139, 165–166, 180, 183, 184–185, 188, 192, 208, 211–212; *salwar suits,* 69, 71, 75, 77; sari, 68, 83, 100, 106; tourist, 130; Western influence, 53, 139. *See also* Bollywood

flowers, 45, 283–284, 361, 366, 367

folklore as a discipline, 3, 12, 15–16, 17, 386–389, 393, 408

food: commercial, 159, 160, 161, 191, 258–259; domestic, 3, 20, 78, 86, 221, 222, 238, 285–291, 315, 339–340; special occasion, 144, 161, 237, 368

Foster, Helen Bradley, 411

Friedan, Betty, 310

Fruzzetti, Lina, 308, 320, 353

Fry, Gladys-Marie, 388

Gandhi, Indira, 321

Gandhi, Mohandas K. (Mahatma), 5, 26–27, 45, 394

Ganesh, 17, 131, 144, 228, 340

Ganges (Ganga), 8, 27, 47, 59, 60, 167, 237

gaudy aesthetics, 25, 153–154, 155, 185, 190, 205, 275, 318, 377, 413, 423, 429

Gell, Alfred, 417

gemstones, 118–120, 125, 126, 139, 140–143, 355, 359. *See also* astrological rings

Gill, Preeti, 321

Gilman, Sander, 398

Glassie, Henry, 387, 388

Godaulia, 60, 64, 71, 82, 137, 151, 162, 164, 168

Gold, Ann Grodzins, 13

Gour, Rajesh Kumar, 31, 38, 49

Govenar, Alan, 392, 410

Gujarat, 45

Gupta, Rabindranath, 188

Gupta, Rupali, 331–332, 358

hair, 11, 21, 327, 336, 337, 357–359, 361, 399; facial hair, 45, 87, 312, 399, 411, 419, 428–429; hairstyles, 21, 25, 150, 226, 253, 270, 282, 311–312, 320–322, 422, 428–429

Handa, Amita, 53

Hanuman, 32, 33, 36, 38, 171, 228, 340–341, 374

Harle, J. C., 115

Hasan, Parveen, 165–166

hathphul, 278, 281, 345, 356, 365, 367, 368

Hawley, John Stratton, 321

health, 141, 172–173, 175–176, 177

henna, 168, 180, 278, 281, 328, 331, 357–358, 361, 362–365, 367, 399, 429

hijras, 25, 293, 418, 427

Hiltebeiel, Alf, 399

Hinduism, 5, 30–35, 39, 48, 69, 168–171; *murti,* 5, 26, 27, 30, 31, 32, 34, 38, 39, 47, 60, 84, 169–171; ornamentation, 5, 29, 30, 32, 33, 39, 49, 131, 165, 168–171, 172, 173, 175–176, 372, 340–341, 374–375 (*see also rukdraksh* beads); temples, 8, 29, 30, 32. *See also darshan; puja; pundit*

history, 405–408

Hollander, Anne, 400

Hostetler, John, 419

imitation jewelry, 25, 55, 167, 168, 178–183, 185, 191, 230–231, 259, 280

Jacquard loom, 89, 93–94, 95, 96, 97, 98, 99, 100, 104, 108, 112, 405

Jahangir, 121

Jain, Jyotindra, 39, 115

Jain-Neubauer, Jutta, 401

Jeffery, Patricia, 46, 72, 367

jewelry, 11, 22–23, 113–166, 168, 173, 175–176, 180–181, 265, 266, 270, 274, 275, 278, 372. *See also* commerce; compulsory jewelry; imitation jewelry; marriage; production

jewelry's sound, 22, 245–247, 254, 258, 274–275, 312, 314, 333, 377, 396–397

Johnson, Donald Clay, 411

Jones, Michael Owen, 388

judgments: of others, 44, 252, 255, 259, 261–262, 272, 279–280, 292, 294, 295–297, 305–306, 312, 316–318, 320, 332, 370–371, 424–427; of the self, 25, 43, 51, 54, 248, 261–262, 268–272, 278, 282, 292, 294, 321–323, 294

Kajol, 269
Kamdar, Mira, 315, 328
Kandpaal, Sugyan, 309, 338
Kanhaiya Lal store, 114, 115, 135, 136–166, 175, 176, 178, 180, 181, 183, 186, 194, 199, 213, 217, 309, 354, 364, 393
Kapoor, Karishma, 364
Kapur, Manju, 41, 295, 315
Khan, Shah Rukh, 268, 342
Khanchandani, Hemant, 73–82, 85, 86, 105, 106, 128, 151, 156, 199, 213, 217, 221, 222, 223, 232, 235, 323, 324, 352, 364, 383, 406
Khanchandani, Jaya, 78, 222, 226, 227, 237
Khanchandani, Nina, 50, 78, 221–238, 239, 251, 262, 263, 267, 298–301, 308, 311, 323, 324, 352, 370, 379, 384, 386, 408–409, 427
Khanchandani, Parmanand, 73, 76, 77, 78, 80, 82, 221, 223, 224, 235
Khanchandani, Priya, 78, 233
Khanchandani, Puspa Devi, 222, 229, 323
Kidwell, Claudia, 417
Kitchener, Amy, 387
Koh-i-Nur, 41
Köhler, Carl, 420
Koralia, Manisha, 342
Krishna (Gopal), 43, 120, 169–170, 171, 188, 228, 327
Krishnan, Usha, 115
Kumar, Anand, 196, 197–211, 214, 215–217, 249, 394
Kumar, Ashok, 358–359, 361–362, 363, 364, 374
Kumar, Meera, 115
Kumar, Mintu, 196, 198
Kumar, Nita, 45, 94
Kumar, Raj, 189, 190, 211
Kumar, Rajesh, 170–171
Kumar, Ravish, 116–117, 118, 119, 120
kumari (maidens), 313, 330–336, 340, 346, 349, 351, 370, 374
kundan, 120, 125, 130, 134, 202, 356, 359

Lahiri, Jhumpa, 53, 315, 328
Lakshmi, 31, 32, 143–144, 228, 274

Lal, Chaman, 48, 116–120, 133, 134–135, 151, 217, 391, 405
Lamb, Sarah, 14, 317, 320
Lanka, 33
Lanser, Susan, 295
Lawless, Elaine, 419
Leslie, Julia, 279
Lévi-Strauss, Claude, 417
Lewis, Oscar, 364
love, 299, 312, 320, 341–343, 374, 377
love marriages, 239, 242, 257, 299, 312, 320, 341–343, 346, 348, 374, 377
Lucknow, 74, 121, 345, 378
Luxa Road, 60, 64, 74, 77
Lynch, Annette, 411
Lynton, Linda, 68, 392

Ma, Yo-Yo, 110
Madanpura, 60, 64, 82, 84, 86, 105
Madonna, 423
Mahabharata, 34, 171
makeup, 42, 48, 208, 248, 250–251, 254, 270–271, 275, 277, 278, 285, 305, 327, 337, 339, 341, 347, 351, 357–359, 361–362, 378, 397
Malini, Hema, 31
mangalsutra, 25, 45, 165, 181, 273, 299, 323, 336, 374
Manik, Ashok Kumar, 191, 192, 196, 323–324
Manik, Daya, 176, 194, 197
Manik, Preetam Kumar, 191, 192, 194, 212, 349, 350
Manik, Prempati, 194, 323
Manik, Priya Kumar, 191, 193–194, 197
Manik, Sant Kumar, 191, 192, 194, 196, 205, 208, 210, 214, 217
marriage: *barat,* 306, 366–367, 371; *bidai,* 145, 358, 368, 375–376; bridal jewelry, 22, 53, 144, 145–146, 187, 193, 205, 275–276, 355–361, 363, 366, 368, 369, 372, 373, 375 (see also *hathphul; mangalsutra*); ceremony, 40, 344, 345, 348–350, 353–355, 357–379; child marriages, 144–145, 353–354; engagement party, 345, 360–351; food, 144, 161, 368, 371; *jaimal,* 187, 241, 361,

363, 366, 367, 371; ladies' *sangeet,* 358, 362–364; *lehanga,* 68, 72, 193, 241, 332, 345, 351, 361, 368, 371; sari, 82, 84, 112; seasons, 144, 364; trousseau, 82, 84, 112, 351–352, 353, 355; village, 144; wedding dress, 414–415. *See also* brides; dowry; love marriages; *sasural*
material culture, method and theory, 16, 386–388, 408
Meenekar, Gopal Prashad, 9, 116, 117, 118, 119, 120–122, 124, 133, 134, 138, 139, 140
Mehta, Rama, 315
merchants: jewelry, 115, 133, 136, 137, 148, 151–153, 156–166, 178–183, 184, 185, 190, 193–194, 196, 197–218; textile, 63, 72, 73–91, 104, 105, 108, 109, 112, 211–218, 394
Metropolitan Museum of Art, 404
Miller, Barbara, 399
Miller, Daniel, 65, 84, 255
Mills, Margaret, 413
mina, 9, 22, 105, 116, 119, 122, 125, 134; Banaras, 114, 120; functions, 125–126, 139–140; Jaipur, 114, 115, 120; making, 121–122, 125; pink, 9, 115, 120, 121, 122, 125
miniature paintings, 125
Mishra, Laxmi, 331, 358
moo-dikhai, 275, 376
Mookerjee, Pinku, 84–91, 97, 100, 102, 105, 106, 128, 151
Mughal aesthetics, 86–87, 116, 120, 121, 122, 126, 127, 165, 170, 368, 405
Mukherjee, Bharati, 43, 309, 315, 355

Nabar, Vrinda, 306
Nagar, Gopal Ram, 116, 119–120
Nair, Anita, 53, 295, 315, 316
Nair, Mira, 84, 363
National Handicrafts and Handlooms Museum, 33
nauratan, 142
*nazar / naja*r (evil eye), 17, 41, 50, 141, 154, 363
Nehru, Jawarhalal, 71
New Delhi, 33, 46, 69, 72, 111, 115, 116, 159, 192, 251, 259, 310, 334, 339, 340, 398, 424
Nishad, Salik, 14, 177–178, 181, 189, 395

Obeyesekere, Gananath, 399
O'Hanlon, Michael, 392, 426

paan, 94, 126–127, 159, 192, 216, 336
Pakistan, 78, 224, 239, 241, 242, 243, 244, 409
Pandey, Ramesh, 115, 138
Partition, 241–242, 243, 244, 409
Parvati, 37, 43, 176, 375
performance theory, 16, 388
permanent and temporary body art, 402
photography, 40, 43, 76–77, 187, 199, 202, 349, 359, 361, 367–368, 372, 407
pilgrimage, 8, 27, 59, 60, 167, 168–169, 184, 185, 186, 188–189, 193, 194
Powell, Colin, 110
prashad, 27, 60, 168, 176, 184, 185
pre-shopping, 158–159, 210
Priya Bangles, 188, 190–217, 249
production, 391–393; custom-made jewelry, 115, 119, 138, 180; custom-tailored clothes, 6, 103, 214; jewelry, 48, 113–135, 138, 139, 157, 158, 180; *salwar suit,* 76–77, 80–81; sari, 9, 86–90, 92–112, 133, 154, 155 (*see also* Jacquard loom). *See also* craftsmen; tailors
puja, 21, 26, 27, 29, 30, 34, 59, 143, 169–171, 197, 366, 372, 375
pundit, 29, 30, 33, 59, 140, 141–142, 143, 168, 172, 175, 176, 194, 233, 345, 366, 372
Punjab, 22, 41, 69, 71, 115, 128, 139, 239, 241, 242, 246, 247, 250, 257, 258, 366, 368
purdah, 46, 72, 223–224, 225–226, 227, 328, 330, 367, 396, 413. See also *burqa*

Qayoom, Abdul, 99, 100, 133

Radha, 32, 169–170
Radner, Joan, 295
Raheja, Gloria, 13
Rai, Aishwarya, 31, 201, 238

Rajasthan, 15, 45, 74, 103, 114, 115, 120, 128, 130, 171, 184, 325, 403
Ram, 8, 17, 32, 33, 36, 143, 170–171, 188, 374
Ram *lila,* 35, 170
Rama Bangles, 188–189
Ramayana, 33–35, 171, 176
rangoli (*kolam*), 169, 295–296
Ravan, 33
Ray, Satyajit, 376
Rinku Silk House, 84, 85, 86, 97, 105, 128
Roach-Higgins, Mary Ellen, 395
Roberts, Allen, 398
Rooks, Noliwe, 399
Rudofsky, Bernard, 396
Rugh, Andrea, 12, 72, 333, 412
rukdraksh beads, 33, 172–173, 175
Rushdie, Salman, 241, 364

sadhu, 172–174
Salvador, Mari Lyn, 392, 425–426
Salvi, Bharat, 110, 111
Salvi, Rohit, 110, 111
Salvi, Vinayak, 110, 111
salwar suits, 21, 46, 49, 53, 69, 70, 71–86, 103, 225, 226, 227, 234, 235, 238, 241, 250, 256, 273, 305–306, 309, 323, 328, 330, 332, 333, 334–335, 339, 346, 347, 349, 364, 393, 395, 409; *churidar pyjama,* 71, 76, 77; *dupatta,* 69, 71, 72, 75, 76, 225–226, 254, 345, 367, 376, 396–397, 403–404; ensemble, 69, 75, 76, 77; fashion, 69, 71, 75, 77; *kurta,* 69, 71, 74, 75, 76, 77
Sankat Mochen Hanuman Temple, 175, 372, 374
Saraswati, 31
sari, 9, 19, 20, 21, 24, 25, 64–69, 70, 82–91, 225, 227, 234, 241, 247–249, 252–254, 256, 273, 345, 349, 351, 352–353, 378, 384, 396–397, 409, 412, 416; colors, 20–21, 24, 102, 103, 106, 108, 109; design, 89, 94, 97, 98, 99, 100, 102, 103, 105–106, 108, 109–112; creativity, 68, 69, 83, 88–90, 99, 102, 103, 105–106, 108–112; *jamdani,* 109–112; *nivi* style, 65, 68; *palloo,* 68,

69, 99, 105, 227, 248; *patola,* 109, 110–112; regional styles, 68, 83. *See also* Banarasi saris; commerce; production
sasural (conjugal home), 274–276, 377–379; daughter-in-law's ornamentation, 312–314, 333, 379; relations with male in-laws, 224, 226, 227, 228, 235, 274–275, 346; relations with mother-in-law, 222, 224, 228, 230, 232, 256, 273–274, 276, 299, 305, 310, 311–314, 324, 379
sati, 321
Satrapi, Marjane, 419
scarification, 398
sensory appreciation, 43–44, 104, 106, 108, 284. *See also* jewelry's sound
Shah, Shantibhandra, 138, 139–140, 145, 151, 156–164, 181, 194, 199, 213, 217
Shah, Shashi, 138, 140, 143, 144–145, 147–156, 309, 364
Shamsie, Kamila, 348–349
Sharib, Mohammad, 164–166, 396, 404
shauk, 156, 158, 193, 198, 205, 228, 275–276, 288–290, 309, 347, 377–378
Shiva (Vishvanath), 8, 27, 32, 37, 40, 59, 81, 165, 167, 171–173, 176, 184, 189, 197, 228, 340, 374–375
shobha (grace), 17, 150, 171, 173, 178
Shreebarshira, Somnia, 332–335, 379
Shri Chand & Bros. Bangle Shop, 184–189, 212, 213
Shridevi, 31, 293
shringar, 4, 169–172, 176, 194, 251
Shrivastava, Shalini, 344–347, 350, 351–352, 354, 357–358, 360, 362, 379
Shukla, Bobby, 8
Shukla, Divya, 6
Shukla, Neeru, 43, 83, 245
Sidwa, Bapsi, 241
Sindh, 76, 77, 78, 80, 128, 221–222, 224, 227–228, 230, 236, 237
sindur, 21, 22, 153–154, 165–166, 167, 168, 176, 228, 266, 276, 277, 278, 308, 315, 316, 321, 322, 323, 326, 334, 339, 346, 351, 359, 363, 372, 374–376, 413
Singh, Babbu, 121
Singh, Khushwant, 341

Singh, Sandeep, 114, 115, 126, 138, 155
Singh, Vijay Bhadu, 141, 143
Sita, 32, 33, 36, 171, 374
skin color, 25, 47, 178, 265, 266, 270, 336–337, 348, 349, 361, 395–396, 403
Smith, Nima, 115
Smithsonian Folklife Festival, 110, 415
social functions, 3, 4, 5, 6, 40–41, 383–384, 386, 404–427
Sonarpura, 84, 92, 93, 96, 99
Soni, Bhagwan Das (B.D.), 48, 128, 130–135, 156, 212, 217, 321, 324–325, 330, 355–357, 392, 405
Soni, Govind Lal, 130, 131, 325, 355
Soni, Ram Chandra (R.C.), 130, 131, 356
Soni, Ram Pyari, 330–331, 355–357
Soni, Salik Ram, 115, 123
Soni, Sati Devi, 324–325
St. Clair, Leonard "Stoney," 392–393, 410
standards of excellence: Banarasi sari, 87–90, 98, 99, 102, 109, 112; jewelry, 127, 133, 140, 156, 179
Steele, Valerie, 12, 399, 401, 417
Steiner, Christopher, 395
Strathern, Andrew and Marilyn, 12, 392, 397, 417
Stronge, Susan, 115
studying bodily arts, 15–16, 383–429
Süleyman the Magnificent, 407
Suri, Manil, 349, 377

tailors, 63, 65, 68, 71, 75, 76, 77, 80, 81, 83, 103, 214
Taj Mahal, 40
Tanjore painting, 120
Tarlo, Emma, 14, 45, 413
tattoos, 41, 46, 364, 392–393, 397, 398, 410, 422
Taylor, Lou, 400
television, 337–339

Trachtenberg, Peter, 410
Tripathi, Mukta, 50, 106, 190, 263–301, 305–308, 311, 370, 379, 383, 384, 395, 397, 408–409, 414, 427
turbans, 171
Turner, Kay, 387

uniforms, 41, 69, 287, 306, 334, 336, 420–421
Untracht, Oppi, 115
Upahar, Priya, 178–183, 217

Varma, Ravi, 38
Versace, Giovanni, 423
Victoria and Albert Museum, 111, 115
Vishnu, 38–39, 49, 173, 340, 401
Vishvanath (Golden) Temple, 8, 23, 27, 29, 40, 60, 78, 81, 141, 167–168, 176, 177, 189, 194, 197
Vishvanath Gali, 29, 141, 167–183, 184–185, 186, 188, 189, 190, 191, 194, 195, 197, 198, 211, 257, 358
vision and communication, 27, 41, 44, 56, 349, 424. See also darshan
Vlach, John Michael, 388
Vogel, Susan, 398

Wadley, Susan, 274
Waghorne, 34, 40
Weinberger-Thomas, Catherine, 321
widows, 21, 194, 296, 309, 315–318, 320–325, 349, 354, 366, 379
Wilson, Verity, 12, 401
Wojcik, Daniel, 410, 421

zari, 88–89, 90, 95, 97, 100, 102, 103, 105, 106, 154, 155
zenana, 117
Zug, Charles G., 387

PRAVINA SHUKLA is Associate Professor in the Department of Folklore and Ethnomusicology at Indiana University, where she teaches courses on dress and body art, food, museums, and material culture. Her museum experience includes exhibitions at the UCLA Fowler Museum of Cultural History and at the American Museum of Natural History in New York City. Her two major interests—carnival in Brazil and women's culture in India—have resulted in extensive fieldwork, exhibitions, and publications. Shukla has lectured on material culture, dress, and adornment in the United States, and also in India, Bangladesh, Canada, and Israel.